TURBO C++ PROFESSIONAL HANDBOOK

TURBO C++ PROFESSIONAL HANDBOOK

Chris H. Pappas
William H. Murray

BORLAND·OSBORNE/McGRAW·HILL
PROGRAMMING SERIES

Osborne **McGraw-Hill**
2600 Tenth Street
Berkeley, California 94710
U.S.A.

For information on translations and book distributors outside of the U.S.A.,
write to Osborne **McGraw-Hill** at the above address.

A complete list of trademarks appears on page 751.

TURBO C++ PROFESSIONAL HANDBOOK

  34567890 DOC 99876543210

ISBN 0-07-881598-3

To my Aunt Edna and cousin Paul

—Chris H. Pappas

To my son, Paul

—William H. Murray

CONTENTS AT A GLANCE

CONTENTS

ACKNOWLEDGMENTS

We would like to thank the people at Borland International that have been so positive toward this project. In particular, Nan Borreson helped greatly with pre-release copies of software and technical literature. Thanks must also go to Spencer Kimball for helping us with two programming problems we just couldn't seem to solve on our own. Thanks to the programmers at Borland who built such a fine compiler. Programmers will praise you for the easy-to-use integrated programming environment and mouse support. Special recognition must go to those unsung technical writers at Borland responsible for preparing the documentation for the package components — you have done an outstanding job.

INTRODUCTION

ABOUT THIS BOOK

This book highlights Borland's C++ Professional package, which includes the C++ compiler, Turbo Assembler, Turbo Debugger, and Turbo Profiler. You will find the book effective whether you are using the entire package or have purchased the components mentioned above separately. You don't have to be a professional programmer to use this book. This book teaches you C, C++, and assembly language from the ground up and was designed for either the novice or professional who owns Borland's sophisticated programming environment as well as for those interested in learning more about procedure-oriented and object-oriented programming (OOP). The *Turbo C++ Professional Handbook* is a multifaceted book designed with you, the programmer, in mind. We will guide you through many traps and potential pitfalls encountered by program developers. By the time you reach the end of this book, you will be able to efficiently use your Professional C++ package and write and debug sophisticated C, C++, and assembly language code. We have made every effort to make this book "readable" and to help form a foundation for future study.

HOW THIS BOOK IS ORGANIZED

This book can be used in a variety of ways depending on your background and programming needs. The book itself is divided into five major sections.

Chapters 1, 2, 3, and 4 introduce you to the programming tools contained in the Borland C++ Professional package.

Chapters 5, 6, 7, 8, 9, 10, 11, and 12 teach the foundational programming concepts need by the C and C++ languages. These are procedure-oriented chapters teaching traditional programming concepts.

Chapters 14 and 15 show you how to utilize the various C and C++ libraries provided by Borland. Here you will learn of many features that will allow you to control your computer's hardware and also use extensive graphics routines.

Chapters 16, 17, 18, 19, and 20 teach assembly language programming foundations and fundamentals. You will learn to use high-speed assembly language code to control your computer's keyboard and screen options. You will also learn how to combine C code with assembly language routines and pass arguments, and even interface with external hardware circuits.

Chapters 13 and 21 build upon the ideas introduced in earlier chapters to teach you the concepts and definitions of object-oriented programming (OOP). Here you will learn how procedure-oriented and object-oriented programs differ and how to write a simple object-oriented program. The object-oriented program developed in Chapter 21 is similar to earlier programs using the procedure-oriented approach.

Chapter 1 will help you select specific sections of this book if you are interested in a selected study of C, C++, or assembly language. For the novice programmer, we of course recommend starting with Chapter 1 and ending with Chapter 21. The ability to write advanced C, C++, and assembly language code is the reward for diligent work and an honest programming effort.

CONVENTIONS USED IN THIS BOOK

- The following conventions have been used throughout this book:
- When referring to something that applies equally to C and C++, the reference will be to C.

- Function names and other reserved words appear in boldface type.

- Keywords, variables, and constants appear in italic type.

- Program listings are shown in typewriter-style text.

- Text for you to enter from the keyboard is printed in boldface.

- The first time a technical term is mentioned, it is printed in italic type.

ADDITIONAL HELP FROM OSBORNE/McGRAW-HILL

Osborne/McGraw-Hill provides top-quality books for computer users at every level of computing experience. To help you build your skills, we suggest that you look for the books in the following Osborne/M-H series that best address your needs.

The "Teach Yourself" Series is perfect for beginners who have never used a computer before or who want to gain confidence in using program basics. These books provide a simple, slow-paced introduction to the fundamental usage of popular software packages and programming languages. The "Mastery Learning" format ensures that concepts are learned thoroughly before progressing to new material. Plenty of exercises and examples (with answers at the back of the book) are used throughout the text.

The "Made Easy" Series is also for beginners or users who may need a refresher on the new features of an upgraded product. These in-depth introductions guide users step-by-step from the program basics to intermediate-level usage. Plenty of "hands-on" exercises and examples are used in every chapter.

The "Using" Series presents fast-paced guides that quickly cover beginning concepts and move on to intermediate-level techniques, and even some advanced topics. These books are written for users who are already familiar with computers and software, and who want to get up to speed fast with a certain product.

The "Advanced" Series assumes that the reader is already an experienced user who has reached at least an intermediate skill level, and is ready to learn more sophisticated techniques and refinements.

The "Complete Reference" is a series of handy desktop references for popular software and programming languages that list every command, feature, and function of the product, along with brief, detailed descriptions of how they are used. Books are fully indexed and often include tear-out command cards. "The Complete Reference" Series is ideal for all users, beginners and pros.

The "Pocket Reference" is a pocket-sized, shorter version of "The Complete Reference" Series, and provides only the essential commands, features, and functions of software and programming languages for users who need a quick reminder of the most important commands. This series is also written for all users and every level of computing ability.

The "Secrets, Solutions, Shortcuts" Series is written for beginning users who are already somewhat familiar with the software, and for experienced users at intermediate and advanced levels. This series gives clever tips and points out shortcuts for using the software to greater advantage. Traps to avoid are also mentioned.

Osborne/McGraw-Hill also publishes many fine books that are not included in the series described above. If you have questions about which Osborne book is right for you, ask the salesperson at your local book or computer store, or call us toll-free at (800) 262-4729.

OTHER OSBORNE/MCGRAW-HILL BOOKS OF INTEREST TO YOU

We hope that *Turbo C++ Professional Handbook* will assist you in using Borland's compiler and will also pique your interest in learning more about other ways to better use your computer.

If you're interested in expanding your skills so you can be even more "computer efficient," be sure to take advantage of Osborne/McGraw-Hill's large selection of top-quality computer books that cover all varieties of popular hardware, software, programming languages, and operating systems. While we cannot list every title here that may relate to Turbo C++ and to your special computing needs, here are just a few related books that complement *Turbo C++ Professional Handbook*.

Using Turbo Pascal 5, by Steve Wood, is a fast-paced guide that quickly takes you from Turbo Pascal 5.0 fundamentals to intermediate-level programming techniques and even some advanced topics. Learn about the system's integrated source-level debugger, 8087 floating-point emulation support for procedural parameters, and more.

Turbo Pascal DiskTutor, by Werner Feibel, is a book/disk package that features a streamlined version of the Turbo Pascal 5.5 compiler along with a disk of examples and a book that thoroughly covers Turbo Pascal 5.0 and 5.5 and object-oriented programming step-by-step. Just load the compiler and the examples disk and follow the instructions in the book. It's perfect for beginning programmers as well as experienced programmers who want a quick introduction to Turbo Pascal.

Turbo Pascal 5.5: The Complete Reference, by Stephen K. O'Brien, is a comprehensive encyclopedia that lists every Turbo Pascal 5.0 and 5.5 command, feature, and programming technique. Conveniently organized for quick and easy reference and filled with clear examples and time-saving details, this lasting reference is great for programmers at all skill levels.

Turbo Pascal Advanced Programmer's Guide, also by Stephen K. O'Brien, provides a wealth of clever ways to extend Turbo Pascal 5, beginning with power tools that include programming pointers and tricks for designing the user interface. You'll learn how to write safe memory resident programs, use the program segment prefix, and master the mouse.

A Special Diskette Offer:

A diskette is available containing all of the program listings in this book. To use the diskette, you will need a computer with the Turbo C++ compiler properly installed and running. Send a bank check, money order, or personal check in U.S. currency for $29.95 for the 5-1/4" or 3-1/2" diskette to the address below. Please allow three weeks for personal checks to clear. No purchase orders, please. All foreign orders outside North America must have a check drawn on a U.S. bank (U.S. currency) for $35.00 for the 5-1/4" or 3-1/2" diskette. Foreign orders will be sent air mail.

Please send me the program listings included in the *Turbo C++ Professional Handbook* by Pappas and Murray. Enclosed is a money order, bank check or personal check for $29.95 ($35.00 - foreign orders) in U.S. funds, which covers the cost of the diskette and all handling and postage. Sorry, no purchase orders can be accepted! This coupon may be copied.

Check One: 5-1/4"   360K format: _____

             3-1/2"   1.44 M format: _____

Name: _____

Address: _____

City: _____ State: _____ Zip: _____

Country: _____

Mail to: Nineveh National Research
              Turbo C++ Diskette Offer
              P.O. Box 2943
              Binghamton, N.Y. 13902

This is solely the offering of the authors. Osborne/McGraw-Hill takes no responsibility for the fulfillment of this offer. Please allow four to six weeks for delivery.

WHY THIS BOOK IS FOR YOU

This book was written with two main goals: to help people become more familiar with the Borland C++ Professional package and to help people with different programming backgrounds become proficient in C, C++, and assembly language programming. This is quite a task, even for a book containing 773 and some pages, but it was written with you in mind. We believe in teaching by example. We have made every effort to make each example simple, complete, and bug-free. These are examples which you can study, alter, and expand into programs tailored to fit your needs.

Our two major goals are divided into several tasks: First, we introduce you to the powerful programming tools provided in your Borland package. These include the C++ editor, C++ compiler, Turbo Assembler, Turbo Debugger, and Turbo Profiler. This book will compliment your Borland reference manuals and help you get a quick start with each of these components.

Second, programmers need a thorough understanding of each programming language they intend to use. You will find that this book covers all the important programming concepts in the C, C++, and assembly languages. If you are a novice programmer, these chapters will form the solid

1

foundation you need to write more sophisticated programs. For the advanced programmer, these chapters will serve as a reference source while also introducing you to exciting C++ concepts.

Third, you will learn how to debug program code and write programs that are free of syntax problems and logical programming errors.

Finally, you will gain an understanding of how procedural programming differs from object-oriented programming and how to develop simple OOP programs.

This book will serve as a lasting reference and teaching guide to the Borland C++ Professional package and also to the languages it supports.

LEARN MORE ABOUT TURBO C++

Here is an excellent selection of other Osborne/McGraw-Hill books on Turbo C++ that will help you build your skills and maximize the power of the Borland compiler you have selected.

Using Turbo C++, by Herbert Schildt, is a fast-paced guide that quickly takes you from Turbo C++ fundamentals to intermediate-level programming techniques using C++.

Turbo C++ DiskTutor, by Paul Chui and Greg Voss, is a book/disk package that features a streamlined version of the Turbo C++ compiler along with a disk of examples and a book that thoroughly covers Turbo C++ and object-oriented programming step-by-step. Just load the compiler and the examples disk and follow the instructions in the book. It's perfect for programmers who want a detailed introduction to Turbo C++.

Turbo C++: The Complete Reference, by Herbert Schildt, is a comprehensive encyclopedia that lists every Turbo C and Turbo C++ command, feature, function, and programming technique. This lasting reference is great for programmers at all skill levels.

1

THE SUM OF THE PARTS
MAKES THE WHOLE

Have you ever found yourself in a hardware store, ready to make a purchase, and been faced with a decision between two possible tools? One tool is marked *general purpose* and the other is marked *professional.* Our experience has been that general-purpose tools are great for occasional use, but in the long run, they don't hold up under extended use. On the other hand, professional quality tools are usually built better, contain additional features, and will weather the storm of constant heavy duty use. Which tool do you buy? Your decision is usually based on price, features, quality, and intended use.

When you purchased the Turbo C++ package, you were probably looking for a programming tool, or set of tools, that offers flexibility and performance and that will hold up under heavy duty use. This package of tools should not become outdated as your programming skills increase. You made the right decision. You don't have to be a professional programmer in order to use the Turbo C++ package.

This book attempts to do three basic things. First, it helps you explore and understand the definitions and uses for the individual components in your Professional C++ package. Second, it is a complete C, C++, and assembly language text. It teaches you the definitions and skills for writing programs in C, C++ , and assembly language. By the end of this book, you should have learned the skills that can move you from a beginning to an intermediate level of programming in each of these languages. Third, this book will show you how to integrate the components of the Professional package so that you can blend C, C++, and assembly language into the best possible finished program.

In this chapter you'll be introduced to the Turbo C++ Professional package with all of its components, and you'll find out how to install and run the package on your computer.

THE LAYOUT OF THE PROFESSIONAL PACKAGE

The Turbo C++ Professional package can be overwhelming when you first take it out of the box. Don't be intimidated, however. Just separate manuals, disks, and literature into different piles. Set the disks and literature aside for now and examine the stack of manuals. You can separate this stack into two categories: user's guides and reference guides. The user's guides contain the installation instructions for each component in the package. (Installation is covered a little later in this chapter.) They also contain detailed information for all of the features of each component. The reference guides, on the other hand, contain reference information for each language. They include detailed information on function calls and other mnemonics. Never lose these manuals.

Now separate the manuals into three categories: C++, assembly language, and the debugger. The following sections explain what these three products are, what they do, and how they are used.

The C and C++ Compiler

You use the components of the C++ package to write stand-alone programs in C or C++. The C language provides a general-purpose programming environment that is structured, modular, and compiled. C is quickly becoming a required language for systems programmers and beginners alike. When you install your C++ software, you will have the option of working in a fully integrated development environment or using the compiler in a command-line mode.

The C++ compiler converts program code into object code. When you write C or C++ programs, your source code name will usually end with a *.c* or *.cpp* extension. Here are some sample source code names:

myfirst.c
mysecond.cpp
counter.c
multiplier.cpp

After successful compiling, your disk will also contain object files, such as:

myfirst.c
mysecond.cpp
counter.c
multiplier.cpp
myfirst.obj
mysecond.obj
counter.obj
multiplier.obj

Object files contain a translation of the original source code that the computer can read directly. To get the final executable file, the object code is linked with the linker. The linker sets the memory addresses where the executable code will be located when the program is executed. The linker usually produces files with the *.exe* extension. When the object files are linked, your disk will contain the following:

myfirst.c
mysecond.cpp
counter.c
multiplier.cpp
myfirst.obj
mysecond.obj
counter.obj
multiplier.obj
myfirst.exe
mysecond.exe
counter.exe
multiplier.exe

You can run the executable files just by typing their name at the command-line prompt. You will learn how to enter and execute simple C and C++ code in Chapter 2.

The Assembler

You use the components of the assembler package to write stand-alone programs in assembly language. Assembly language is machine specific (microprocessor) and, as a result, is not nearly as portable as C code. The Borland assembler will allow you to develop code for the Intel family of microprocessor chips. These currently include the 8086, 8088, 80186, 80286, 80386, and 80486.

Assembly language is a cryptic programming language that permits you to write code closely associated with the actual machine code of the computer. While many programmers judge it harder to learn and program with, assembly language offers the skillful programmer the advantages of speed and complete hardware control. You can write stand-alone assembly language programs with the Borland editor, and then assemble and link them.

The assembler converts program code into object code. When you write assembly language programs, your source code name will usually end with the *.asm* extension. Here are some assembly language source code names:

scrclear.asm
timer.asm

After successful assembly, your disk will also contain object files, such as:

scrclear.asm
timer.asm
scrclear.obj
timer.obj

Object files from assembly language also contain a translation of the original source code that the computer can read directly. To get the final executable file, the object code is linked with the linker. When the object files from the assembly language programs are linked, your disk will contain the following:

scrclear.asm
timer.asm
scrclear.obj
timer.obj
scrclear.exe
timer.exe

You can run the executable files just by typing their name at the command-line prompt. You will learn how to enter and execute simple assembly language code in Chapter 3.

The Debugger and the Profiler

When you write C, C++, or assembly language programs, you will eventually make mistakes. The errors you make can be divided into two broad categories: syntax errors and programming errors. Syntax errors are reported to you when you compile or assemble program code. If the errors are serious enough, the compiler or assembler will abort the process and no executable file will be produced. To repair this type of error, enter the editor and fix the code at the designated line. The Borland reference guides will be invaluable for this. Syntax errors are often the easiest errors to fix. (Editing and code correction will be discussed in detail in Chapter 2.)

Your program may compile or assemble correctly—with no errors reported—and still not work as you intended. If so, it is usually a programming error—a bug in your programming logic. Programming errors are harder to track down than syntax errors. Borland's debugger is designed to help you locate programming errors as quickly as possible. To use the debugger, you must have an executable program, even if it doesn't execute correctly. You will learn how to write programs that integrate into the debugger environment in Chapter 4.

Finally, the Profiler is a tool that will help you write more efficient code. By using the Profiler, you will learn where your program is spending time during execution. This can help you write more efficient C and C++ code and may suggest an assembly language routine to speed up that operation. You will learn how to use the Profiler in Chapter 4.

INSTALLATION WITH YOUR SYSTEM

The success and ease of use of your Turbo C++ Professional package depends a great deal on the computer system it is installed on and the installation options that you choose. The following sections suggest how to optimize your programming environment.

Your Computer

Borland's Turbo C++ Professional package will operate on a wide range of IBM and IBM-compatible computers. The *Turbo C++ User's Guide* discusses the minimum system requirements, but this book suggests the following system profile:

PC XT/AT or PS/2 computer
DOS 3.2 or later
640K RAM memory
Color Monitor (graphics)
Coprocessor Chip
20 MB Hard Disk
Mouse

If your computer doesn't currently have a hard disk, make the purchase of a hard disk your number one priority. As you develop your programming skills, switching floppy disks in and out of the computer will very· quickly become boring and time-consuming. A hard disk will greatly improve your programming efficiency. If you have an older PC, consider adding a hard-disk card.

If your system contains the components suggested in the preceding profile, you will be able to move quickly and efficiently between the various components of the Turbo C++ Professional package.

Setting Up Your System

You must install each of the products in your Turbo C++ Professional package separately. The order of the installation is not critical, but you should install the C and C++ compiler first, the assembler next, and the debugger and profiler last. Start installation by placing the first disk in your disk drive and typing **install**.

As you step through the installation process, accept the suggested defaults unless you know that another option will be required. You can change these defaults, including the path names, later if you want. When you install the C++ compiler, you will have to decide which memory models to include in your environment. The various memory models will be discussed in Chapter 5, but only the small memory model will be used in the programs in this book. If you install only the small memory model, you can free a large amount of disk space. You can add other memory models later if you need them.

Once you have installed each of the products, return to the subdirectory that contains the C++ compiler. You can enter the integrated environment by typing **tc**.

THE LAYOUT OF THIS BOOK

Chapters 1 to 4 provide the information for setting up and testing your programming environment. The next three chapters are designed to get you programming in C, C++, and assembly language as quickly as possible. They explain how to use the most important features of your compiler, assembler, debugger, and profiler.

Chapters 5 to 15 discuss all of the C and C++ concepts important to beginning and intermediate programmers. These chapters contain programs that have been fully debugged and tested.

Chapters 16 to 19 discuss the fundamentals of assembly language programming. Here you will learn how to develop and write stand-alone assembly language programs that will bring speed and hardware control to your system.

Chapters 20 and 21 are devoted to advanced programming features and techniques. In Chapter 20, you will learn how to link C or C++ object code to assembly language code. There are examples for interfacing simple hardware circuits to your computer. Chapter 21 continues C++ programming by introducing you to the terms, definitions, and programs associated with object-oriented programming. You will learn about the latest programming concept integrated with many Borland languages. OOP promises to be the foundation for many professional programs that will be developed in this decade.

The professional programming tools are in place, the manuals are safely stored and ready for use, the book is open—you're ready to start. If you want to learn the details of each product and the language it supports, start with Chapter 2 and continue through to Chapter 21.

If your programming goals are a little more selective, here are some suggestions about chapters to read:

Fast start on each product: Chapters 2-4

Assembly language only: Chapters 3-4, 16-19

C and C++ only: Chapters 2, 4-15, 21

If you want to start developing C and C++ programs as quickly as possible, turn to Chapter 2 now. If you're interested in assembly language, go to Chapter 3. Once you have finished one of these chapters, you can turn to the section of the book that is of immediate interest to you and continue to build your programming skills.

2

GETTING STARTED WITH THE TURBO C++ COMPILER

In this chapter you will learn

- The basic commands necessary to enter, edit, save, compile, debug, and run a program
- How to get context-sensitive help on any editor command, programming environment option, or C and C++ language feature
- How to manage all of the programming environment's windows
- How to use the Project utility to manage multiple source files
- How to block and either move, copy, or delete sections of text
- How to find or find and replace selected text
- How to undo an editing change
- How to print selected text
- How to save a file when your disk is full

The Borland C++ compiler you have just purchased is a robust software development environment. It enables you to do anything from examine the contents of a single variable or the values passed to a function on the call stack, to single-stepping through your program or just jumping to a particular subroutine.

In this chapter, you will learn how to use many of the development time-saving features incorporated in the programming environment along with some of those features unique to the C language. You will also learn about many additional compiler operating details that you can refer back to later as needed.

The chapter will use simple program segments to explain the features and utilities that are absolutely necessary for managing the majority of programming problems.

THE MAIN WINDOW

Welcome to the new world of windows. Depending on the compilers you have used in the past, just bringing up the Borland C++ compiler's integrated environment can be exciting. The compiler has windows, controls, scroll bars, function keys, and many menus (see Figure 2-1).

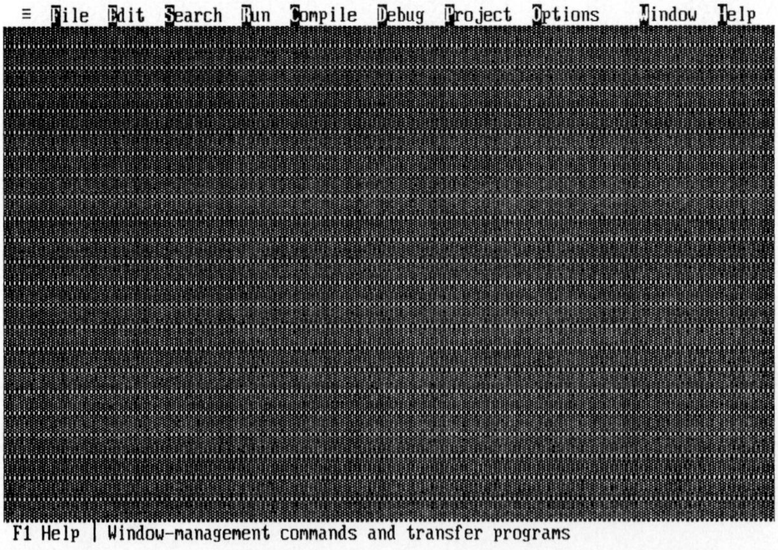

Figure 2-1.   The Main window

Across the top of the window are the main menu options: " ≡ " (System menu), "File," "Edit," "Search," "Run," "Compile," "Debug," "Project," "Options," "Window," and "Help." The bottom of the window highlights the uses for various function keys: F1 - Help (currently active), F2 - Save, F3 - Open, ALT-F9 - Compile, F9 - Make, and F10 - Menu.

Knowing a few basics will help this seem less overwhelming. You can access any main menu option in one of three ways: You can click on the option with the mouse, press F10, and then use the left or right arrow key to highlight the option and press ENTER. You can also press the ALT (as in ALTernate) key with the color-coded letter in the menu option you would like to activate. For example, you can select the "File" option by pressing ALT-F. (ALT-space selects the ≡ system menu.)

HELP

When all else fails, press F1. Getting context-sensitive help anywhere within the programming environment is as simple as selecting the desired menu option and then pressing the F1 key. You will see a detailed explanation of the feature. To back out of a Help window, simply press the ESC key (under most circumstances, the ESC key will undo many different operations).

Depending on the help topic invoked, you may be prompted to go to an additional Help window. To back up to the previous Help window, press ALT-F1. By the way, suppose you are using the editor and have nested yourself with several layers of Help windows and then pressed ESC to leave the Help utility. By pressing ALT-F1 instead of just F1, you will return to the last Help window that was displayed. The Help utility is so complete that you may, under many circumstances, not need to refer to Borland's C++ User's Guide.

Moreover, if you are in the Edit window, you can use the Help utility to get immediate assistance with key language features. Place the cursor on a C keyword and press CTRL-F1 to get a brief explanation of the syntax and usage for the selected item.

If you find yourself totally lost, press F1 twice to see a help screen on the Help utility. Figure 2-2 shows the second page of this Help window, which lists the help categories available.

You can also invoke help by selecting the "Help" option from the main menu. Figure 2-3 displays the menu listing the various options along with

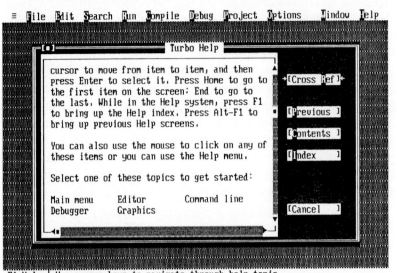

Figure 2-2.   Help window listing help topics

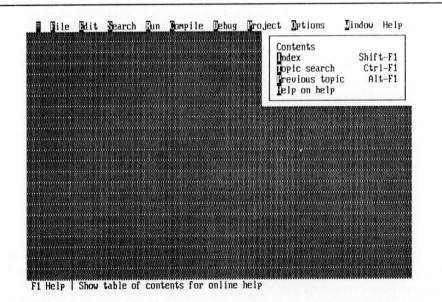

Figure 2-3.   The Help main menu

their equivalent hotkeys. The "Contents" option (Figure 2-4) shows all of the major help categories, while the "Index" option (Figure 2-5) gives you access to a 23-window indexed help file. For this last option, simply highlight the desired feature or command and press ENTER, or double click the left mouse button to obtain the requested help information.

Notice that you can press ALT-F1 to bring the previously selected help screen to the foreground. You can employ this key combination to backtrack through an entire editing session's worth of help requests.

YOUR FIRST PROGRAM

This section is designed to give you the basics necessary to enter, edit, compile, run, debug, save, and reload a simple program. But before you enter your first program, you will need to make a few necessary setup decisions.

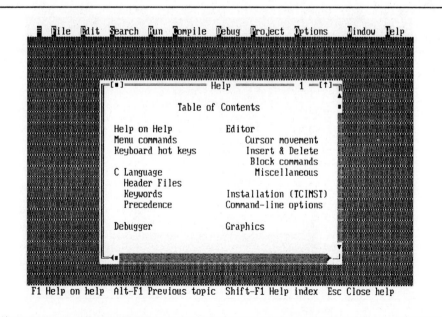

Figure 2-4.   The Help table of contents

Minimal Setup

You can install Borland's C++ compiler quickly on one 1.44 MB 3 1/2-inch floppy disk or in a hard disk subdirectory. The question becomes where to put your files. If you have a hard disk, you may want to place your files on it (maybe in the same subdirectory as the compiler, maybe elsewhere). You may also want to put your program files on a floppy so that you can transport them from office to home.

An easy approach to defining output file locations is to use the ALT-O option from the main menu and then type **D** for "Directories." Either click on the box marked "Output Directory," or tab to it and enter the location for your output files. For example, if you were developing a payroll program, you might want it saved in drive A on the PAYROLL directory (see Figure 2-6).

If, for the time being, you want all of your files to go to drive A and the PAYROLL subdirectory, make certain that you save the definition when you press ESC to leave the Directories submenu. You accomplish this by typing **S** for "Save."

```
  ▤  File  Edit  Search  Run  Compile  Debug  Project  Options    Window  Help
 ┌─[■]═══════════════════ Help ═════════════ 1 ═[↑]╖
 │ Turbo Help Index                                  ▲
 │                                                   ■
 │   #define          #elif            #else
 │   #error           #if              #ifdef
 │   #include         #line            #pragma
 │   $cap             $col             $config
 │   $drive           $edname          $errcol
 │   $errname         $exename         $ext
 │   $mem             $name            $noswap
 │   $prompt          $save            _8087
 │   _AL              _argc            _argv
 │   _BH              _BL              _BP
 │   _CH              _chmod           _CL
 │   _close           _control87       _creat    ▼
 │ ◄■─────────────────────────────────────────►
 F1 Help on help  Alt-F1 Previous topic  Shift-F1 Help index  Esc Close help
```

Figure 2-5.   The Help index

Of course, each time you create a file, you can specify where it is to be saved when you select the "Save" (F2) option. You could accomplish the same single file storage location by pressing F2 and then naming the file A:\PAYROLL\PAYROLL1.C.

Creating

If you are using the Borland compiler for the first time, you will see a screen similar to the one in Figure 2-1 when you start the compiler by typing **tc**. The largest portion of your display will show a pale blocked pattern. This is your work area and it is currently empty.

Whether this is your first program or you have been experimenting with several of the supplied programs, starting a new file is as simple as clicking the mouse on the word "File," and then clicking on the word "New." Notice that the work area now changes to a solid background with a bright border (see Figure 2-7).

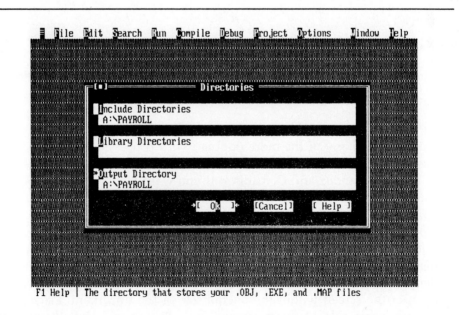

Figure 2-6.   The Directories window

To gain experience with the editor, enter the following C program exactly as is, *including* any mistakes:

```c
/* A simple demonstration program */
#include <stdio.h>
#define SIZE 5
void print_them(int index,char continu,int int_aray[SIZE]);
main()
{
  int index;
  int int_aray[SIZE];
  char continue=0;

  print_them(index,continue,int_aray);

  Printf("\n\nWelcome to a trace demonstration!");
  printf(\nWould you like to continue (Y/N) ");
  scanf("%c",continue);

  if(continue == 'Y')
    for(index=0; index < SIZE; index++) {
      printf("\nPlease enter an integer: ");
      scanf("%d",&int_aray[index]);
    }

  print_them(index,continue,int_aray);

  return(0);
}
void print_them(int index, char continue, int int_aray[SIZE])
{
  printf("\n\n%d",index);
  printf("\n\n%d",continue);
  for(index=0; index < SIZE, index++)
    printf("\n%d",int_aray[index]);
}
```

If you have used any of the more popular word processing packages, most of the editing keys (BACKSPACE, INS, DEL, PGUP, PGDN, and so on) work exactly the same in the Borland C and C++ editor. If you want to move to the first line in your program, press CTRL along with PGUP. To move to the last line in your program, use the CTRL key in conjunction with PGDN.

You can also use the scroll bars along the right-hand side of the window. Clicking the mouse on the up arrow symbol ▲ will move the display contents down. Clicking on the down arrow symbol ▼ will move the display contents up. The ■ symbol on the scroll bar (not [■]) indicates the relative position of the screen within the overall size of the document. Placing the mouse on either side of the ■ symbol and clicking will shift the display either up or down one whole screen's worth, like the PGUP and PGDN keys. Placing the mouse over the ■ symbol, holding the left mouse button down, and dragging it to a new location on the scroll bar rapidly advances the display through the file.

If you want a particular window to occupy the entire screen, click the mouse on the [↑] arrow, or press F5. Repeatedly pressing F5 will toggle between original size and full-screen. Clicking the mouse on the [■] symbol closes the associated window.

The editor comes equipped with many advanced features that you can easily review by pressing F1 and then PGDN while in the editor. Two features in particular that are worth experimenting with are Find (CTRL-QF), Find & Replace (CTRL-QA), and the block commands (CTRL-KB, begin; CTRL-KK, end).

You use the block commands to highlight a section of code to be either moved (CTRL-KV), copied (CTRL-KC), deleted (CTRL-KY), or written to disk (CTRL-KW). This last option can be very useful when you are working on a large project where only a portion of a program needs to be shared with other individuals. Reading a block saved to disk is as easy as placing the cursor within your source code where you want the code inserted and pressing CTRL-KR for

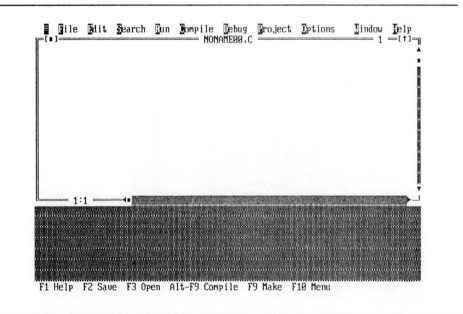

Figure 2-7.   Starting a new file

read from disk. The editor will then prompt you for the name of the file to import. Don't forget the drive and subdirectory when specifying the file name for any file not in the default directory.

Saving

There is absolutely no excuse for losing a file when in the compiler. To save a file, either press F2 or click the mouse on "Save." You should *always* save after each screen's worth of data entry.

Compiling

To compile a program, press ALT-F9 or click on the Compile main menu and then the Compile command. When you pressed ALT-F9, you should have seen a compile window indicating the number of lines compiled along with any associated warning and error messages. The example program has 2 warnings and 22 errors. Press any key to get back to the edit process (see Figure 2-8). Figure 2-9 shows the error messages you should have encountered if you entered and compiled the preceding program.

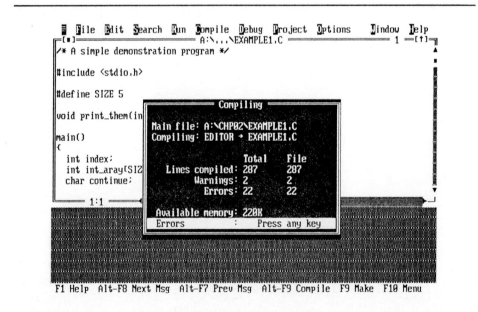

Figure 2-8.   Compiler Warnings and Errors window

Syntax Errors

The Message window at the bottom of the display (press F5, if you don't see a Message window) lists the possible error conditions encountered in your program. The first error encountered is highlighted in the Message window. By pressing the F6 key, you can switch between the Message window and the Edit window. When you switch to the Edit window, the cursor will automatically be placed on the line of the error. This allows you to make any necessary corrections quickly.

The first error was caused because a C language reserved word, **continue**, was used for a variable name—something that can happen when you use a new language for the first time. Using whatever method you feel comfortable with (hopefully the Find & Replace command), change all **continue**s to *continu* and recompile the program. Notice how the number of warnings dropped to 0 and the number of errors went down to 10. By the way, when you changed the **continue**s, did you make sure to save the changes?

```
  ≣  File  Edit  Search  Run  Compile  Debug  Project  Options    Window  Help
                         A:\CHP02\EXAMPLE1.C                   1
/* A simple demonstration program */

#include <stdio.h>

#define SIZE 5

void print_them(int index,char continu,int int_aray[SIZE]);

main()
{
  int index;
  int int_aray[SIZE];
█ char continue;
       13:9
[■]                            Message              2 [↑]
 Compiling A:\CHP02\EXAMPLE1.C:                                        ▲
 Error A:\CHP02\EXAMPLE1.C 13: Declaration does not specify a tag or an identi■
 Error A:\CHP02\EXAMPLE1.C 13: Declaration missing ; in function main
 Error A:\CHP02\EXAMPLE1.C 13: Misplaced continue in function main
 Warning A:\CHP02\EXAMPLE1.C 15: Unreachable code in function main          ▼
 ◄■                                                                    ►
 F1 Help  Alt-F8 Next Msg  Alt-F7 Prev Msg  Alt-F9 Compile  F9 Make  F10 Menu
```

Figure 2-9.   *example.c* program error messages

Figure 2-10 shows the updated Message window. Notice that the error says there is an illegal symbol on line 18. The actual error is on line 17. There is a missing opening quotation mark before the \nWould. To date, there is no compiler that is entirely accurate with error messages. At best, error messages are flags indicating that a rule wasn't followed somewhere within the syntax of your source code. Sometimes the error message is right, and other times the error occurs one line above the flagged line. Worse yet, the error may be at the beginning of an entire function (this occurs most often with mismatched braces).

If you correct the quotation mark error and recompile the program, you should be down to one error. Figure 2-11 highlights the problem. The *for* loop repetition test hasn't been followed by a semicolon; in this case, the error message was correct. If you fix this problem, you should be able to compile your program without any errors.

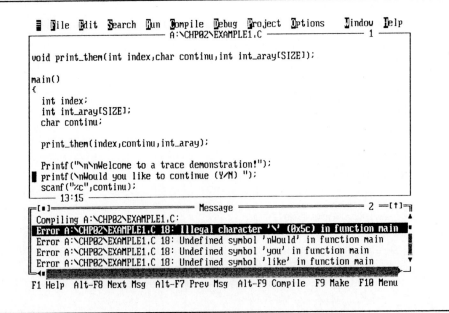

Figure 2-10.   Updated *example.c* program error messages

Running

With an error- and warning-free compile, you are now ready to run your program. Pressing CTRL-F9 executes a program. You could also have clicked the mouse on the "Run" option and then used the Run command. Pressing CTRL-F9 will also perform a compile and then execute the program (assuming no errors) if the program has not been previously compiled.

What happened when you ran the program? You got an error message. Even though you no longer have syntax errors according to the compiler, you may still have linker or run-time errors. Figure 2-12 highlights the problem. The message says that the symbol **_Printf** is undefined. Pressing F6 will take you back to the Edit window but does *not* correctly position the cursor. In this case, it takes some experience with the language to realize that the error message is accurate. Since C and C + + are case sensitive, the **printf** function is not the same as the **Printf** function. Line 17 of the program has incorrectly referenced the **printf** function with an uppercase letter P. If you correct this error, you will have an executable program.

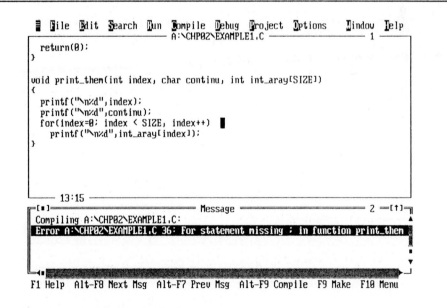

Figure 2-11.   *for* statement error message

Viewing the Output Window

What happened when you ran the corrected program? First, you were asked to type a **Y** or **N** to continue (if your output statement said "continu," you used the global Find & Replace and didn't check all uses of the word). Next, you were prompted for five integer values; then, the next thing you knew, you were back in the editor. To view your output screen, simply press ALT-F5. Any key combination after this will place you back into the editor.

Debugging Made Easy

Just when you thought you had gotten rid of all of the syntax and linker errors, you encountered a run-time error. Fortunately, the Borland C and C++ environment has incorporated many powerful tracing capabilities.

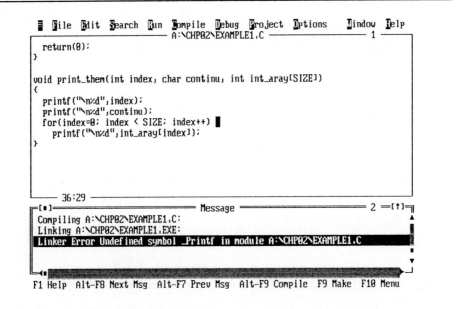

Figure 2-12.   Linker error message

Logical Errors

You can often correct logical errors by doing a single trace through your program. You accomplish this in one of several ways.

How to Single-Step Through a Program

If you press F7, you instruct the environment to run your program line by line, or in *single-step mode.* (This assumes that you have turned source debugging on. To turn source debugging on, select the main menu "Option," and then type **B** for debugger. Click "Source debugging" on.) However, under many circumstances this will not be enough. What good will it do you to single-step through your program if you can't see what is happening to your data? By adding watches in conjunction with single-step mode, you can trace each line of code as it affects selected variables.

How to Use the Watch Window

To trace a variable, put it into the Watch window by placing the cursor on the selected identifier and pressing CTRL-F7. If you press ALT-W, and then type **W** again, the lower portion of your screen will display the Watch window. (Depending on the options you have selected and in which order, the lower portion of your display may show the Message window. If you close the Message window, you can split the display between the Edit and the Watch windows.) Now, when you use F7 to single-step through your program, you can actually see the contents of the selected variables change.

How to Skip Debugged Subroutines

The F8 key is slightly different than F7. When you use F8 to single-step through a program and the statement about to be executed is a call to a function, F8 will execute the function completely and continue single-stepping from the line of code below the function call. In contrast, F7 would have traced into the invoked function line by line.

Add *index, array int_aray,* and *continu* to the Watch window by placing the cursor on the definition of each variable (*int index, int int_aray[SIZE],* and *char continu*) and pressing CTRL-F7 once for each variable. The Watch window should appear at the bottom of your display. If it doesn't, you have probably zoomed the Edit window. Press F5 to restore the split screen appearance. Try single-stepping through your program by using the F7 key.

How to Restart the Program

You can reset your program for another run by pressing CTRL-F2 after you have made one complete or partial pass through the source code. Try restarting the example program and single-step through it using the F8 key. Notice how this last trace option skipped over tracing into function **print_them**.

Depending on the run options you selected, you may or may not have noticed some things going wrong as you single-stepped through the example program. For instance, did the Watch window show you that the variable *continu* ever contained a 'Y'? Did your program perform the single-step process, but execute with strange results when you ran the executable version from outside the environment? Maybe you saw an error message that said "Null pointer assignment."

The problem is small and subtle. Look closely at the following line from the source code:

```
scanf("%c",continu);
```

Here is the correction:

```
scanf("%c",&continu);
```

The difference is both subtle and disastrous. Make the correction in your program and watch what happens to *continu*'s value in the Watch window.

To move on to the next debugging example, you need to unclutter your screen. Remove the Watch window altogether by pressing ALT-D, then type **W** and **R** to "Remove all watches."

How to Set a Breakpoint

To skip major portions of already debugged code, you can set a breakpoint. Place your cursor on the if(continu == 'Y') statement in the example file you have been working with. Now press CTRL-F8. The entire line should become highlighted; you have just set a breakpoint. To run your program up to this breakpoint, press CTRL-F9. Notice how the program executes up to the *if* statement and then stops. At this point, you can go into single-step mode with either F7 or F8.

You can set multiple breakpoints throughout your program. Each time you press CTRL-F9, you will execute up to the next breakpoint. To remove a single breakpoint, simply place the cursor on the line with the breakpoint set and press CTRL-F8 again. CTRL-F8 is a toggle: The first time you press it, the breakpoint is set; the second time you press it, the breakpoint is removed. You can delete all breakpoints by pressing ALT-D, then **B** for "Breakpoints," and **D** for "Delete."

How to Evaluate and Change a Variable's Contents

The Borland C++ compiler allows you not only to view but to change the contents of variables while the program is executing. Reload the example program and set a watch on the variable *continu*. Single-step through the program with either F7 or F8 until the Watch window displays *continu*'s contents of a 'Y'.

You are now going to try the "Evaluate/Modify..." option by pressing ALT-D for "Debug," followed by **E** for "Evaluate/Modify...". In the Expression field, type the variable name **continu**. You should see 'Y' in the Result field. Either tab down to the New Value field, or click on the field with the mouse and enter '**N**'. Notice how the Result field now shows 'N' too (see Figure 2-13).

Press the ESC key or click on the [■] symbol to close the Evaluate and Modify window. Notice how the Watch window changes *continu*'s contents from 'Y' to 'N' also (see Figure 2-14). Now when you single-step through your program, it will react as if the user had entered a No instead of a Yes.

Reloading a Program

Each time you start the editing environment, your last program is automatically loaded into memory. In addition, the last list of files you edited is automatically saved. You can retrieve it by pressing ALT-F (for "File"), typing **O** (for "Open)", and using the cursor or mouse to select one of the files listed.

MANAGING WINDOWS

The new Borland programming environment allows you to simultaneously view multiple files, a Watch window, a Message window, a Project window, and more. The programming environment has a window management feature.

Figure 2-15 shows the list of options available when you select the "Window" main menu item. The first option, CTRL-F5, allows you to resize or relocate the active window. By using the cursor keys after pressing CTRL-F5, you can shift the active window left or right and up or down. By holding down the SHIFT key and using the arrow keys, you can resize the active window.

The "Zoom" option forces the active window to occupy the entire display. When you select the "Tile" option, the programming environment will resize all windows and place them next to each other much like a tiled floor. By pressing F6, you can cycle through all open windows, making each one the active window. You can close any active window with the ALT-F3 hotkey.

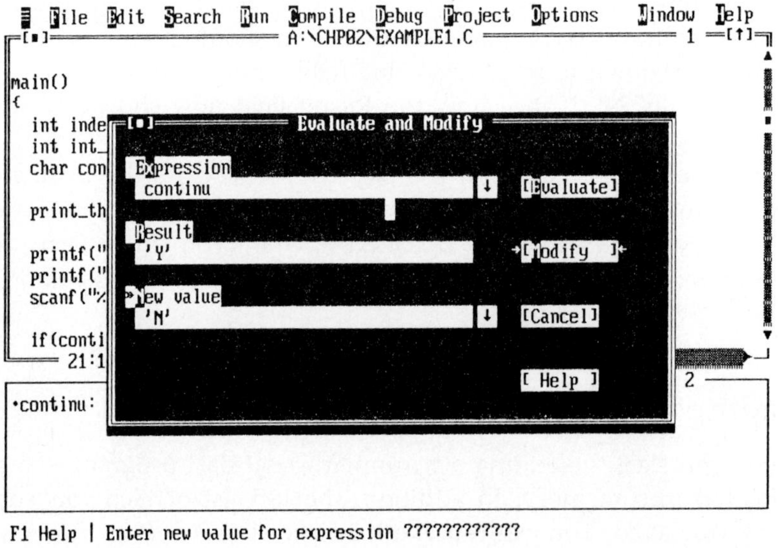

Figure 2-13. Evaluate and Modify window

You can also activate a window by selecting the Window menu and choosing any one of the viewable window categories ("Message," "Output," and "Watch"). As you've already seen, pressing CTRL-F5 will switch you to the User Screen window.

When you must know the current contents of the microprocessor registers, just select the "Window Register" option. Figure 2-16 shows an example CPU window.

The last two options in this menu section allow you to view the Project window and the Project Notes window. You can use the Project Notes window to save critical comments regarding the current status of a project's development.

You can use the "List" option, or the ALT-0 hotkey (the number 0, not the letter O), to display a list of open windows. You can quickly switch to any of the open windows by highlighting the desired window and pressing ENTER.

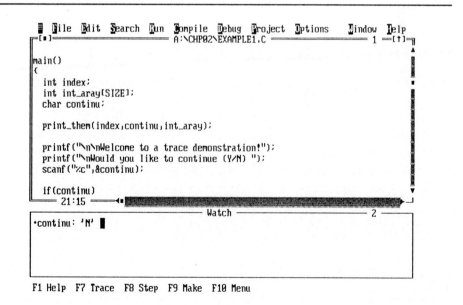

Figure 2-14.   Watch window showing changed contents of the variable *continu*

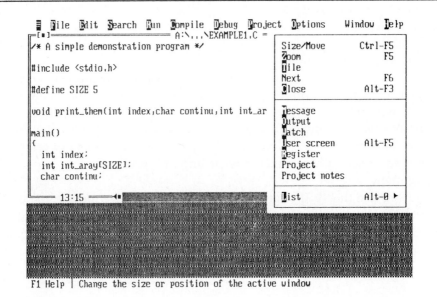

Figure 2-15.   Window main menu options

MULTIPLE SOURCE FILE MANAGEMENT

Many times a single C or C++ listing will contain multiple files. When you are ready to edit, compile, and link the individual files it will be necessary to use the editor to separate each from the composite listing.

In this section, you will use the editor's block commands as you break down the example program into separate files. You will break down the listing into the following three files. File one will be called *myinclud.h:*

```
/****************** MYINCLUD.H FILE ******************/

#include <stdio.h>
#define SIZE 5
```

File two will be called *mymain.c:*

```
/****************** MYMAIN.C FILE ******************/

void print_them(int index,char continu,int int_aray[SIZE]);
```

```
main()
{
  int index;
  int int_aray[SIZE];
  char continue=0;

  print_them(index,continue,int_aray);

  Printf("\n\nWelcome to a trace demonstration!");
  printf(\nWould you like to continue (Y/N) ");
  scanf("%c",continue);

  if(continue == 'Y')
    for(index=0; index < SIZE; index++) {
      printf("\nPlease enter an integer: ");
      scanf("%d",&int_aray[index]);
    }
  print_them(index,continue,int_aray);

  return(0);
}
```

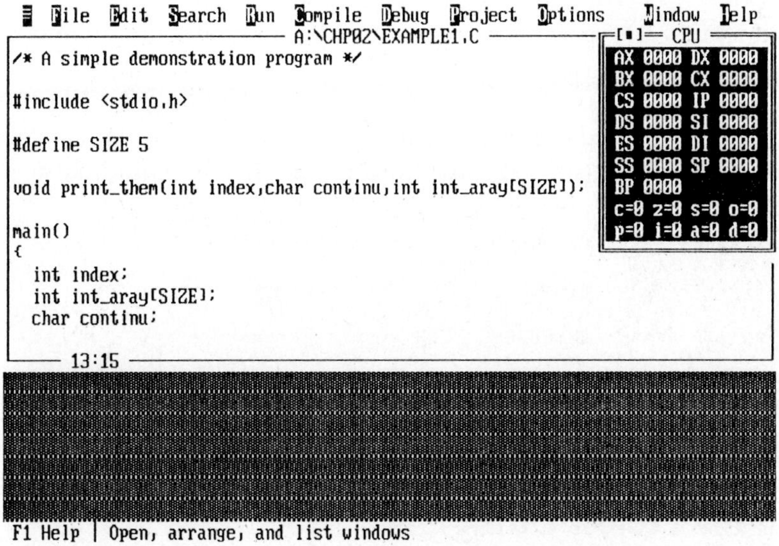

```
 ▤ File  Edit  Search  Run  Compile  Debug  Project  Options     Window  Help
                  ┌─── A:\CHP02\EXAMPLE1.C ──────┐┌─[■]═ CPU ═══┐
/* A simple demonstration program */              │AX 0000 DX 0000│
                                                  │BX 0000 CX 0000│
#include <stdio.h>                                │CS 0000 IP 0000│
                                                  │DS 0000 SI 0000│
#define SIZE 5                                     │ES 0000 DI 0000│
                                                  │SS 0000 SP 0000│
void print_them(int index,char continu,int int_aray[SIZE]);│BP 0000│
                                                  │c=0 z=0 s=0 o=0│
main()                                            │p=0 i=0 a=0 d=0│
{                                                 └───────────────┘
  int index;
  int int_aray[SIZE];
  char continu;

└─ 13:15 ─
```

```
F1 Help │ Open, arrange, and list windows
```

Figure 2-16.   Using the CPU window to display registers and flags contents

and file three will be called *onefunc.c:*

```
/******************* ONEFUNC.C FILE *******************/

void print_them(int index, char continue, int int_aray[SIZE])
{
  printf("\n\n%d",index);
  printf("\n\n%d",continue);
  for(index=0; index < SIZE, index++)
    printf("\n%d",int_aray[index]);
}
```

Block Commands

Reload the example program into memory if you have been experimenting with additional environment options. Marking a block of code is a simple process. Place the cursor in the row and column you wish to designate as the beginning of the code block, and then press CTRL-KB (for begin). Next, move the cursor to the row and column you wish to designate as the end of the defined block and press CTRL-KK. The entire code block will be highlighted.

Beginning at the top of your program, block off the code shown for *myinclud.h.* Once the block is highlighted, save it to the disk by pressing CTRL-KW (for write). The editor will ask you for the name of the file. Remember to include any paths if necessary. Make certain you name the file *myinclud.h.*

Repeat this process of defining the block and writing the block to disk until you have created the last two files: *mymain.c* and *onefunc.c.* If you like, you can edit each file so that it includes the file header comments:

```
/******************* MYINCLUD.H FILE *******************/

/******************* MYMAIN.C FILE *******************/

/******************* ONEFUNC.C FILE *******************/
```

Comments like these help other programmers know which file they are viewing.

Using the Project Utility

Whenever you create a C or C++ program using multiple source files, you need to tell the compiler which files are necessary for creating the executable version of the program. You do this by defining a project file. The project file simply contains the names of all source or object files needed to create the program.

Creating a Project File

To define a project file, press ALT-P for "Project," and type O for "Open." A window will open at the bottom of the screen (Figure 2-17). By pressing the INS (Insert) key, you can enter the names of the files needed to create the program. At this time, enter the names of the files *mymain* (*myinclud.h*) and *onefunc* (*myinclud.h*). Make certain you precede the file names with any needed paths.

Debugging with Multiple Source Files

With this accomplished, press F10 to return to the main menu and then press F9 to compile the program. The Message window informs you that *SIZE* is undefined in *mymain.c*. Because the #include "myinclud.h" statement has

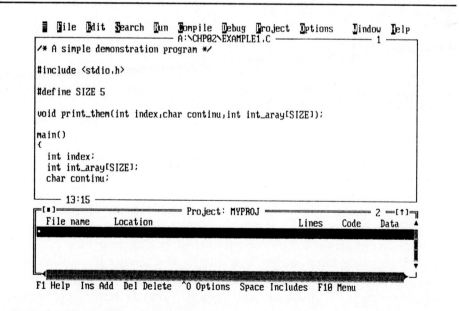

Figure 2-17.   Example project window

not been added to *mymain.c, SIZE* is undefined. Edit the file so that the statement

```
#include "myinclud.h"
```

appears at the top of *mymain.c.* You may need to precede *myinclud.h* with a path if you are using subdirectories. For example:

```
#include "a:\johnproj\myinclud.h"
```

Save the change and press F9 again. Unfortunately, you still have the same problem with *onefunc.c.* Even though *mymain.c* knows about *myinclud.h,* since *onefunc.c* is a separate file, it needs its own **#include** statement, exactly like the one you just entered in *mymain.c.* When you have made and saved this second change, your program should compile without any errors. Press CTRL-F9 to run it.

To ensure that you will be able to view the source code associated with each message window error automatically, perform the following check. Press ALT-O for "Options," then type **E** for "Environment," then **P** for "Preferences." If the "New Window" option is checked within the "Source Tracking" section, you're all set. If not, just click the mouse on the option or tab over to it to make the necessary switch.

The *make* **Utility**

You use the *make* utility to create the executable version of your program (**.exe*). When invoked with the F9 key, the *make* utility will display the name of the file it is about to create—for example, *example.exe.*

The name for the file is determined in one of two ways. If you have defined a project file, the name of the project will be used as the file name. If you have not previously defined a project file, the name used for the executable version of your program will match the name of the file that is currently in the active Edit window.

The *make* utility checks that the executable version of your program reflects all updates made to any support files. For example, suppose that *example.exe* were generated by compiling and linking four files: *a.h, a.c, b.c,* and *c.c.* Two weeks later you go back into *b.c* and rewrite the sort algorithm to make it more efficient. The problem is that *example.exe* does not include this improvement. By invoking *make,* you can update *example.exe* so that it incorporates the new sort.

OTHER MENU OPTIONS

The compiler's menu options may seem overwhelming to the novice, challenging to the moderately experienced programmer, and obvious to an expert. The beginning of this chapter tried to provide you with an overview of the most immediately needed and useful options. The rest of the chapter will highlight supplemental environment features.

Restoring a Line

Suppose you're on a deadline and you delete a line of code so complex that you could never re-create it as quickly as you would need to. Just restore it! If you deleted the entire line by pressing CTRL-QY, you can restore the entire line with CTRL-QL. You can also use the "Edit Restore line" option to undo any editing change made to a line as long as you have not moved the cursor off the modified line.

Find, Find and Replace

When writing an algorithm, you often need to search for every occurrence of a particular variable or constant. While you are in the Edit window, you can begin a "find" by pressing CTRL-QF. Figure 2-18 shows the Find window. You enter the text you want to find and then check off the options to be used for the search. These options include whether the search should be case sensitive, whether the search should look for whole words only, whether it should be a global or restricted search, a forward or backward search from the current cursor location, or a search of the entire file. Once you have selected the find criteria, click the mouse on the Ok box, or tab over to the Ok box and press ENTER. You can continue a find with the same search criteria by pressing CTRL-L.

To execute a standard search and replace operation while in the Edit window, press CTRL-QA. Figure 2-19 displays the Replace window. This window is almost identical to the Find window. After you enter the text you want to find, you need to define the replacement text in the New Text field. You also have the one additional option "Prompt on replace." If you check this box, each found occurrence of the searched for text will cause the editor to stop and ask you for permission to make the requested substitution.

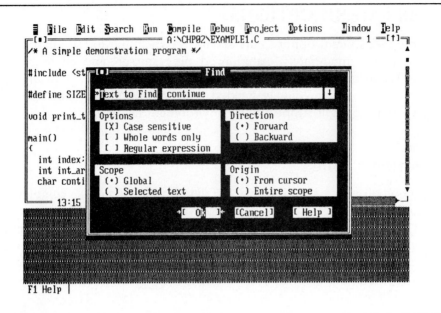

Figure 2-18.   Using the "Find" option

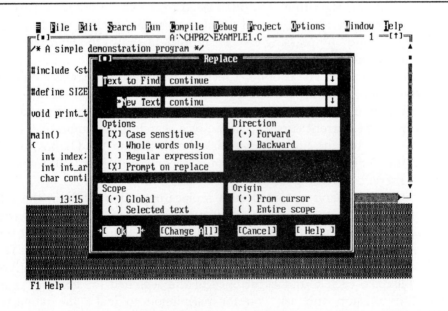

Figure 2-19.   Using the "Replace" option

Locate Function

A useful feature of the Search menu is the "Locate function. . ." option. This option works very differently than Find. If your application had a function called **calculate_payrate** that was called from four different locations in your source code, executing a Find for **calculate_payrate** would display all of the function calls, the function prototype, and the function header. "Locate function. . ." zips immediately to the definition of the function. In addition, when you select this option, a Locate function window opens that allows you to enter the name of the function to search for, or allows you to select any one of the functions you have searched for previously from a history list.

Cut and Paste

The Borland compiler incorporates a clipboard that you can use for cutting and pasting text. Figure 2-20 displays the Edit menu highlighting these options. Some of the options have hotkeys. Others you need to select by

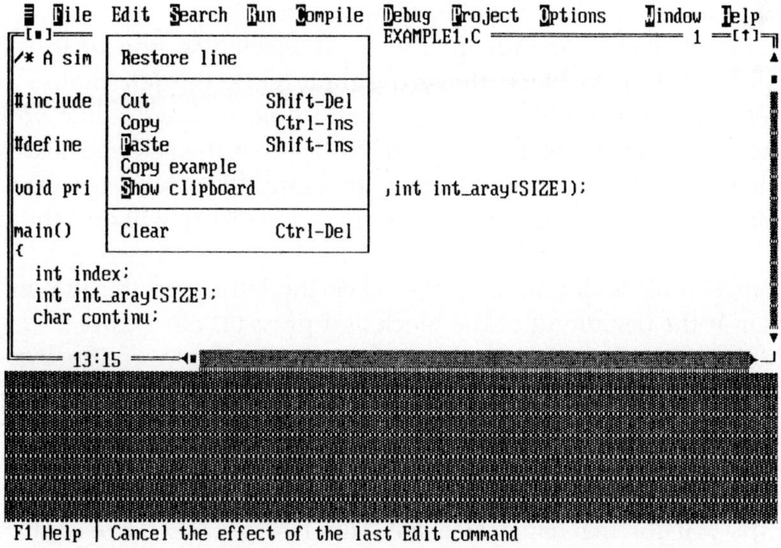

Figure 2-20.   The Edit main menu

pressing ALT-E (or clicking with the mouse) to select the Edit menu, and then highlighting the selected option and pressing ENTER (or clicking on the option with the mouse).

Since the editor allows you to have several files open at once, you can use the clipboard cut and paste option to make copies of, or transfer code from, one file to another. For these options to be activated, you must have previously defined a block of text (CTRL-KB to begin the block, CTRL-KK to end the block definition).

You can copy blocked text by pressing CTRL-INS. You cut blocked text by pressing SHIFT-DEL. To paste copied text from the clipboard to the selected file, first switch the Edit window emphasis to the destination file, place the cursor where you want the copied text, and press SHIFT-INS.

As a precautionary measure, you may choose to verify that the block of text you copied is correct. Do this by selecting the Edit menu and selecting the "Show clipboard" option. By selecting the "Clear" option instead, or by pressing CTRL-DEL, you can erase the contents of the clipboard.

Block Commands

At this point, you probably realize that there are many ways to perform the same editing operation. This holds true with the block commands, which in some ways resemble certain clipboard operations.

All of the block commands involve a preselected section of text. If you are using a mouse, to block the text simply click the left mouse button wherever you want the block to begin, and hold it down while you drag the cursor to where the block is to end. Notice that the selected text will be highlighted. If you don't have a mouse, pressing CTRL-KB will begin the block definition at the current cursor location. Pressing CTRL-KK will end the definition.

To cancel a block definition, either click the left mouse button, or place the cursor at the beginning of the block and press CTRL-KK. Figure 2-21 shows the Edit help window for the block commands. Some of the more frequently used block commands include CTRL-KC to copy a block, CTRL-KV to move a block, and CTRL-KY to delete a block.

In a large program, you may need to incorporate code or data created by someone else. By using the CTRL-KR command, you can instruct the editor to prompt you for the name of a file (don't forget the drive and path if necessary) to pull into the editor.

If you are creating a code segment that needs to be shared, first block the segment and then press CTRL-KW. The editor will now prompt you for a' file name to be used for saving the segment. A team member could then use CTRL-KR to read the segment.

When you need a hard copy of a portion of your program or data file, just block the needed segment, turn the printer on, and press CTRL-KP. The blocked text will automatically be sent to the printer.

Change Directory

When working on several projects at once, you may forget the name of a particular file. If the file is one you haven't worked on for several days, it may no longer be in the files list. For these and similar circumstances, you may need to change the editor's default directory. Figure 2-22 shows the File menu with the "Change Directory" option highlighted. If you select this option, you will see a window that displays the current path and allows you to change it (Figure 2-23). Simply type the desired drive and directory, (include the path when necessary). By changing the default directory, you redefine where the editor and compiler will save and look for files.

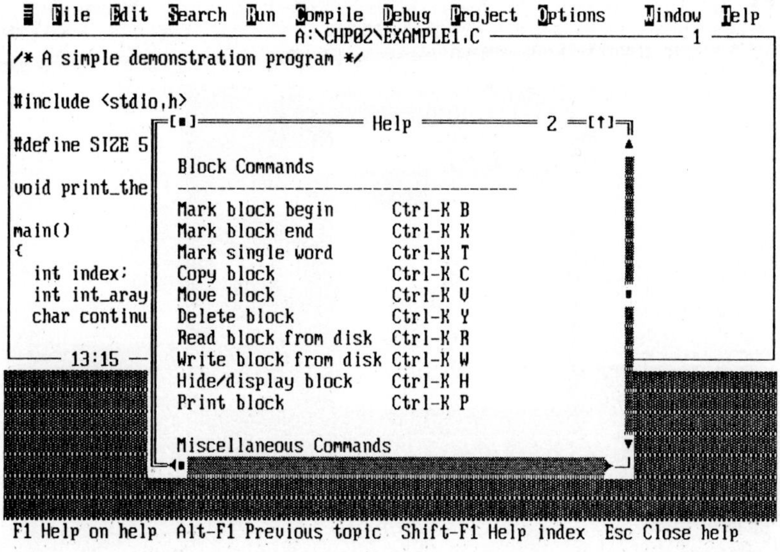

Figure 2-21.   Help for block commands

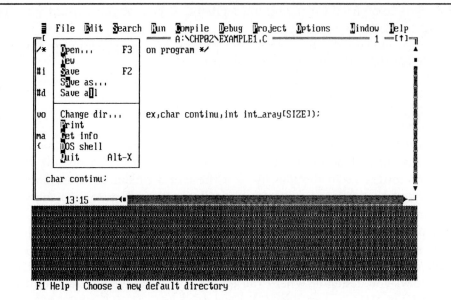

Figure 2-22.   Selecting the "Change dir. . ." option from the File main menu

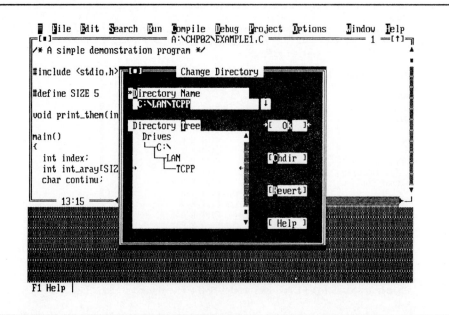

Figure 2-23.   The Change Directory window

DOS Shell

The "DOS Shell" option allows you to keep the editor running while you temporarily return to the operating system. This can be extremely useful under certain circumstances. Suppose that you go to save your file and, as a result of the last editing changes, the file is now too big to fit on the disk. If you quit the editor, you lose your editing changes. This is because the editor keeps everything in memory.

With the "DOS Shell" option, you can keep your file in the editor, go back to the operating system, format your disk, and then instantly pop back into the editor by typing **EXIT**. At this point, you would just need to press F2 to complete the save.

Printing

When you want a hard copy of the text in the active Edit window, you can press ALT-F for file, and type **P** for print. This approach would be much quicker than defining and then printing a block. In contrast, you can print any portion of a file by defining a block and then using CTRL-KP.

PUTTING YOUR KNOWLEDGE TO WORK

1. List two ways you can access a main menu item.

2. How do you save a program?

3. How do you compile a program?

4. How do you run a program?

5. Once you have compiled a program, pressed any key to return to the editor, and are viewing the Message window, how do you get the cursor to move to the line of code relating to each error message?

6. What are the steps required to put a variable into the Watch window?

7. How do you single-step through a program?

8. Explain the difference between single-stepping through a program using the F7 key and using the F8 key.

9. Describe how to define a block using a mouse and using keyboard commands.

10. What function key can you use to get context-sensitive help?

3

GETTING STARTED WITH
THE TURBO ASSEMBLER

In this chapter you will learn

- What assembly language is and why it is important

- How to use the Turbo Assembler (TASM)

- How to use the Turbo Linker (TLINK)

- How to use the various Assembler and Linker command-line switches

- How to create *.map* and *.lst* files

- How to use the powerful *make* utility with assembly language code

- What *masm* and ideal modes mean

- How to build simple mixed mode applications with C and assembly language

- How to track down errors

You probably want to try your new Turbo Assembler as soon as possible. This chapter is designed to help you get that quick start with the Turbo Assembler. For this reason, it describes how to use the Turbo Assembler, rather than how to write assembly language code. If you know how the Turbo Assembler operates, you might want to start with Chapter 16, which discusses how to develop your assembly language programming skills.

Borland's Turbo Assembler is a fast, one-pass assembler. Assembly language programs utilize mnemonics that represent machine instructions. For example, **add** is a mnemonic that will be converted to machine code upon assembly. A *one-pass assembler* resolves all references and generates all machine code on a single pass through your source code file. Assembly language is very machine dependent. *Machine dependence* means that programs written for computers using Intel's family of microprocessors will not run on Apple computers using Motorola microprocessors. The Turbo Assembler provides support for Intel microprocessors 8088 to 80486 and math coprocessors 8087 to 80387. Assembly code, for the Intel microprocessor series, is upward compatible. *Upward compatibility* means that programs written for the 8088 microprocessor will execute correctly on an 80486 microprocessor. Each new microprocessor actually contains a superset of the previous chip's machine instruction set. During the assembly process, ASCII files containing source code (*.asm*) are converted to machine code in object files (*.obj*) and then linked to produce executable files (*.exe*).

Assembly language has two major advantages over many higher level languages. First, it enables you to program the computer at the microprocessor (hardware) level. This is an advantage because if the task can be done on a computer, it can be done at the hardware level. With compilers, you are at the mercy of the design team as to which features you can and cannot address. Second, you can write the fastest possible executable code. Ultimately, compilers must translate instructions into machine code. Thus, a **printf** function in C might translate into 30 to 60 lines (or more) of machine code. This machine code might not be optimized for fastest performance. With assembly language, you write the code directly and can thus test programs for optimum performance.

SETTING UP THE ASSEMBLER

You can install the Turbo Assembler on floppy disks or a hard disk. To begin the installation process, insert the Turbo Assembler disk in the default drive and type

```
A>install
```

The installation program will provide default options and ask several questions during the process. You should select the default options unless you are an experienced user.

Once the installation process has been completed, your hard disk or floppies will contain numerous files. The most important files are *tasm.exe*, the Turbo Assembler; *tlink.exe*, the Turbo Linker; *make.exe*, the Turbo Command Line *make* utility; *tlib.exe*, the Turbo Librarian; and *tcref.exe*, the Turbo Cross-Reference utility. Borland includes additional utility and example programs to aid in the assembly language environment.

Borland's Turbo Assembler is highly compatible with other assemblers such as IBM's or Microsoft's MASM. In fact, the assembler you are about to use is even more powerful. Borland's TASM contains many enhancements to assembly language, including

- An extended command-line syntax

- Global directives

- Local symbols

- Extended range conditional jumps

- Ideal mode

- Union and structure nesting

- Emulated or non-emulated coprocessor operation

- Explicit segment overrides

- Constant segments

- Extended loop instructions for the 80386/80486

- Extended listing controls

- Alternate directives

- Predefined variables

- Improved operation of **shl** and **shr** mnemonics

- Enhancements to the MASM environment

You will learn about a number of these features now and in future assembly language chapters (Chapters 16, 17, 18, and 19). Don't panic if the terms are foreign to you. They are explained in more detail later.

THE ASSEMBLY PROCESS: THE FIRST EXAMPLE

The assembly process involves three steps. First, you enter the program with an editor and save it as an ASCII file. You can use any editor that saves the file in ASCII format. For example, you could use Borland's Sprint word processor (in ASCII mode) or the Turbo C++ editor. We recommend the Turbo C++ editor supplied with your professional package. Assembly language does not have a self-contained editing environment like other Borland products. You create all assembly language programs by issuing command-line statements. Additionally, all assembly language programs should have the *.asm* file extension. For example, you might type

```
tc myfirst.asm
```

This will take you into the Turbo C++ editor and name your assembly language file *myfirst.asm*. The file *myfirst.asm* will be located on the default drive and current subdirectory. If you are using this editor to write your assembly language code, you should set the tab size to 8. You can do this by selecting "Options/Environment/Tab size." Once the program is complete, you must save the file (use the F2 function key) and exit the editor.

The second step, after you have successfully entered and saved the source code, is to run the Turbo Assembler. The syntax can be as simple as

```
tasm myfirst
```

The Turbo Assembler will look on the current drive and subdirectory for a file named *myfirst.asm* and attempt to assemble the code. If successful, Turbo Assembler will create an additional file named *myfirst.obj*. The object file (*.obj*) contains the binary equivalents to your source code. You can combine object files for one program with object files for other programs, linking several files. If the assembly process occurs without any errors, your screen might receive a report something like this:

```
Turbo Assembler Copyright (c) 1988, 1990 Borland International

Assembling file:   MYFIRST.ASM
Error messages:    None
Warning messages:  None
Remaining memory:  332k
```

The third step, the linking process, is the job of the Turbo Linker. The Turbo Linker searches for a file with an *.obj* extension and converts it into an executable file with an *.exe* extension. To use the Turbo Linker, type

```
tlink myfirst
```

If the Turbo Linker is successful, you will see the following on your screen:

```
Turbo Link Copyright (c) 1987, 1990 Borland International
```

The assembler will report syntax warnings and errors to you. Sometimes you can ignore warning messages, but you can never ignore errors. If syntax errors occur in your code, you must bring the source code back into the editor and correct the mistakes.

In review, the three steps for creating an assembly language program are as follows:

1. Enter the source code with an editor, such as the Turbo C++ editor.

2. Assemble the source code with TASM.

3. Link the object file with TLINK.

Entering Your First Program with the Turbo C++ Editor

Assembly language programs, unlike most high-level compiler programs, require a certain amount of *overhead* in each program. This overhead tells the Turbo Assembler how to assemble your source code. You use directives to control the assembler and specify just how the code is to be assembled. More importantly, you use them to indicate the type of microprocessor on which you expect to run the program.

What follows is a simple program, used primarily to illustrate the overhead that you will use frequently throughout the assembly language programming chapters. Later chapters will cover the details of each assembly directive. Fortunately, the overhead will remain the same for most programs and is thus a good candidate for a batch file.

Using the editor provided with Turbo C++, enter the program shown in the listing. Name the program *myfirst.asm*.

```
        DOSSEG                      ;use Intel segment-ordering
        .MODEL  small               ;set model size

        .STACK  300h                ;set up 768 byte stack

        .DATA                       ;set up data location
SendIt  db      'Assembly Language is easy!','$'

        .CODE
Turbo   PROC    FAR                 ;main procedure declaration
        mov     ax,DGROUP           ;point ds toward .DATA
        mov     ds,ax

;*********************************************************

        lea     dx,SendIt           ;point to the message
        mov     ah,9                ;interrupt parameter
        int     21h                 ;call DOS print interrupt

;*********************************************************

        mov     ah,4Ch              ;return control to DOS
        int     21h
Turbo   ENDP                        ;end main procedure
        END                         ;end whole program
```

Once you have entered the program, save and exit the editor (by using function key F2). Figure 3-1 shows an editor screen with a partial listing of this program.

The actual program code is highlighted between the asterisks (*). The other material consists of assembler directives and code for correctly entering and leaving the DOS programming environment. When it executes correctly, this program will print a text message on the screen at the current cursor position.

Assembling the Program with TASM

To assemble this program, type

```
tasm myfirst
```

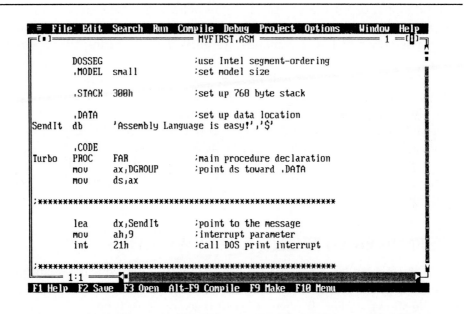

```
 =  File  Edit  Search  Run  Compile  Debug  Project  Options    Window  Help
[■]════════════════════════ MYFIRST.ASM ═══════════════════ 1 ═[ ]

           DOSSEG                      ;use Intel segment-ordering
           .MODEL   small              ;set model size

           .STACK   300h               ;set up 768 byte stack

           .DATA                       ;set up data location
SendIt  db       'Assembly Language is easy!','$'

           .CODE
Turbo   PROC     FAR                   ;main procedure declaration
           mov      ax,DGROUP          ;point ds toward .DATA
           mov      ds,ax

;*****************************************************************

           lea      dx,SendIt          ;point to the message
           mov      ah,9               ;interrupt parameter
           int      21h                ;call DOS print interrupt

;*****************************************************************
═══ 1:1 ═══
 F1 Help   F2 Save   F3 Open   Alt-F9 Compile   F9 Make   F10 Menu
```

Figure 3-1.   Using the Turbo C++ editor to write assembly language code

If you receive error messages, return to the editor and make sure that your source code matches the listing.

Linking the Program with TLINK

To link this program, type

```
tlink myfirst
```

If successful, do a listing of your default directory. You should have four files starting with the name *myfirst*. The file *myfirst.asm* is the original source code. The file *myfirst.obj* is the object code produced by the assembler. The file *myfirst.exe* is the executable code produced by the linker. TLINK will also produce a map file named *myfirst.map*. Map files are discussed later in this chapter.

To execute the program, type

```
myfirst
```

What do you see on the screen? Do you believe the message? For a large percentage of the stand-alone assembly language programs in this book, these assembly and link commands are all you need during the assembly process.

At times, however, you will need to use other link features. For example, you might want to combine several additional object modules to produce one executable file. You may also want to include the power of an external library. The Turbo Assembler and Linker provide assembly flexibility via command-line options and switches.

ASSEMBLER OPTIONS AND SWITCHES

The Turbo Assembler is a powerful program with numerous command-line options. It gives you greater flexibility during assembly than the simple example shown earlier. To view a list of these options, type

```
tasm
```

You should see a list similar to Table 3-1. For example, a useful command-line syntax might look like this:

```
tasm /zi myfirst,,,myfirst
```

If executed, the command-line syntax would assemble *myfirst.asm* to an object file named *myfirst.obj* (default name). Additionally, it would generate a listing file named *myfirst.lst* (default name) and a cross-reference file named *myfirst.xrf* (discussed later in this chapter). The *.obj* file would contain additional information for the Turbo Debugger as a result of the /zi option.

The Turbo Assembler also lets you include a configuration file. This configuration file, named *tasm.cfg*, allows a number of frequently used command-line syntax statements to be included each time *tasm* is executed. For example, you could use the Turbo C++ editor to create a file named *tasm.cfg*. The contents of that file might be

```
/c /la /zi
```

Table 3-1.   TASM's Command-Line Options

Option	Function
/a, /s	Alphabetic or source-code segment ordering
/c	Generate cross-reference in listing
/dSYM[= VAL]	Define symbol SYM = 0, or = value VAL
/e, /r	Emulated or real floating-point instructions
/h, /?	Display this help screen
/iPATH	Search PATH for include files
/jCMD	Jam in an assembler directive CMD (for example, /jIDEAL)
/kh#, /ks#	Hash table capacity #, string space capacity #
/l, /la	Generate listing: l = normal listing, la = expanded listing
/ml, /mx, /mu	Case sensitivity on symbols: ml = all, mx = globals, mu = none
/mv#	Set maximum valid length for symbols
/m#	Allow # multiple passes to resolve forward references
/n	Suppress symbol tables in listing
/o	Generate overlay code
/p	Check for code segment overrides in protected mode
/q	Suppress OBJ records not needed for linking
/t	Suppress messages if successful assembly
/w0, /w1, /w2	Set warning level: w0 = none, w1 = w2 = warnings on
/w −xxx, /w + xxx	Disable (−) or enable (+) warning xxx
/x	Include false conditionals in listing
/z	Display source line with error message
/zi, /zd	Debug info: zi = full, zd = line numbers only

If you then assembled the previous assembly language example, by typing

```
tasm myfirst
```

the Turbo Assembler would read *tasm.cfg* and insert the command-line syntax in the assembly statement immediately after the letters "tasm." In effect, the assembler would behave as if you had typed

```
tasm /c /la /zi myfirst
```

This syntax would produce *myfirst.obj* and *myfirst.lst*. The listing file would contain cross-reference information at the end of the file. The *.obj* file would contain full debug information. The next example shows what several of these options provide.

LINKER OPTIONS AND SWITCHES

The Turbo Linker is fast and compact. As mentioned, linkers are responsible for linking one or more object modules to form final executable code. The Linker reads one or more *.obj* files and produces a final executable file with an *.exe* extension.

The Turbo Linker also provides for several command-line options. To view the current options, type

```
tlink
```

Table 3-2. TLINK's Command-Line Options

Syntax:
TLINK objfiles, exefile, mapfile, libfiles
@xxxx indicates use response file xxxx

Option	Function
/m	Map file with publics
/x	No map file
/i	Initialize all segments
/l	Include source line numbers
/s	Detailed map of segments
/n	No default libraries
/d	Warn if duplicate symbols in libraries
/c	Lowercase significant in symbols
/3	Enable 32-bit processing
/v	Include full symbolic debug information
/e	Ignore Extended Dictionary
/t	Create COM file
/o	Overlay switch

TLINK will then list the current options on the screen, as shown in Table 3-2. If you are using linker options, you might use the following syntax:

```
tlink /m /s /l /v myfirst,,,
```

In this situation, TLINK will produce a map file with public symbols and will include source code line numbers along with a detailed map of program segments. (Map files are discussed later in this chapter.) The execut able file will be named *myfirst.exe* (by default). The map file will be named *myfirst.map* (by default). No library files are used in this link. You will see what these options provide in the next example.

IMPORTANT UTILITY PROGRAMS AND FILES

You will combine several command-line options when you assemble and link the first example again and explore the results.

For this case, assemble the program *myfirst.asm* by typing

```
tasm /zi myfirst,,,
```

Then link the resulting *.obj* file by typing

```
tlink /m /s /l /v myfirst,,,
```

When the process has been completed without errors, do a directory listing to view the files that start with *myfirst.* Type

```
dir myfirst.*
```

You should see a list of files on the screen, somewhat like this:

```
Volume in drive C is DOS
Directory of  C:\TASM

MYFIRST  OBJ      474   1-04-90   9:30a
MYFIRST  ASM      616   1-03-90   5:06a
MYFIRST  LST     2904   1-04-90   9:30a
MYFIRST  MAP      486   1-04-90   9:30a
MYFIRST  EXE      557   1-04-90   9:30a
         6 File(s)   15699968 bytes free
```

The next two sections explore the importance of the *.map* and *.lst* files and an important utility program named *make*. Later examples will illustrate further the power and usefulness of these tools. As you develop your assembly language programming skills, you can pick and choose which tools to use.

The Map File (.*map*)

Map files are created, by default, by the linker TLINK. The default map is a bare-bones map that lists the program's segments, starting address, and error messages generated upon link. You can gain additional detail by adding the /m and /s options to the linker command line. The /m option adds a list of sorted public symbols (if your program uses them). The /s option adds a detailed segment map.

To view the .*map* file created in the previous section, type

```
type myfirst.map
```

The .*map* file should include a listing somewhat like the following:

```
Start  Stop   Length Name           Class
00000H 00010H 00011H _TEXT          CODE
00012H 0002CH 0001BH _DATA          DATA
00030H 0032FH 00300H STACK          STACK

Detailed map of segments

0000:0000 0011 C=CODE  S=_TEXT G=(none) M=MYFIRST.ASM ACBP=48
0001:0002 001B C=DATA  S=_DATA G=DGROUP M=MYFIRST.ASM ACBP=48
0003:0000 0300 C=STACK S=STACK G=DGROUP M=MYFIRST.ASM ACBP=74

Address          Publics by Name

Address          Publics by Value

Line numbers for myfirst.obj(myfirst.asm) segment _TEXT

11 0000:0000  12 0000:0003  14 0000:0005  15 0000:0009
16 0000:000B  18 0000:000D  19 0000:000F

Program entry point at 0000:0000
```

This .*map* file, for the first example, does not contain any public symbols. You will learn more about map files in future assembly language chapters. This section just teaches you how to use the various tools to obtain the information.

The Listing File (.*lst*)

Listing (.*lst*) files are generated at assembly time by TASM. Listing files are not created by default; you must specifically request them. In the TASM command-line sequence, you make the request with the following syntax:

```
tasm [options]source[,object][,listing][,xref]
```

Typing

```
tasm myfirst,,,
```

creates a listing with the default name *myfirst.lst*. The first example creates a listing file. When you enter

```
type myfirst.lst
```

you can view the listing file:

```
Turbo Assembler                          01/04/90 09:30:04
Page 1
MYFIRST.ASM

 1                                       DOSSEG
 2 0000                                  .MODEL   small
 3
 4 0000                                  .STACK   300h
 5
 6 0000                                  .DATA
 7 0000   41 73 73 65 6D 62 6C + SendIt  db   'Assembly Language
                                               is easy!','$'
 8        79 20 4C 61 6E 67 75 +
 9        61 67 65 20 69 73 20 +
10        65 61 73 79 21 24
11
12 001B                                  .CODE
13 0000                         Turbo    PROC     FAR
14 0000   B8 0000s                       mov      ax,DGROUP
15 0003   8E D8                          mov      ds,ax
16
17 0005   8D 16 0000r                    lea      dx,SendIt
18 0009   B4 09                          mov      ah,9
19 000B   CD 21                          int      21h
20
21 000D   B4 4C                          mov      ah,4Ch
22 000F   CD 21                          int      21h
23 0011                         Turbo    ENDP
24                                       END
Turbo Assembler                          01/04/90 09:30:04
Page 2
Symbol Table


Symbol Name               Type    Value        Cref defined at #

??DATE                    Text    "01/04/90"
??FILENAME                Text    "MYFIRST "
??TIME                    Text    "09:30:04"
??VERSION                 Number  0101
@CODE                     Text    _TEXT              #2  #12
@CODESIZE                 Text    0                  #2
```

```
@CPU                      Text    0101H
@CURSEG                   Text    _TEXT                            #6   #12
@DATA                     Text    DGROUP                           #2
@DATASIZE                 Text    0                                #2
@FILENAME                 Text    MYFIRST
@WORDSIZE                 Text    2                                #6   #12
SENDIT                    Byte    DGROUP:0000                      #7   17
TURBO                     Far     _TEXT:0000                       #13
Groups & Segments         Bit Size Align  Combine Class
                                               Cref defined at #

DGROUP                    Group                                    #2   2   14
   STACK                  16  0300 Para    Stack    STACK #4
   _DATA                  16  001B Word    Public   DATA  #2   #6
   _TEXT                  16  0011 Word    Public   CODE  #2   2   #12
                                                                   12
```

Notice that the comments in this file have been omitted. This is a very wide listing. If you had shrunk the text size so the listing fit on a book page, you wouldn't have been able to read it. All *.lst* files normally contain the full comments originally placed in the program. Also notice that this file replicates your source code along with the equivalent machine code for each mnemonic. For example, line 18 contains the sequence

```
mov    ah,9
```

To the left of this statement is the machine code equivalent

```
B4   09
```

The B4 value is the machine code equivalent of moving a piece of immediate data into the **ah** register. These values are always specified in hexadecimal notation.

You might have noticed some additional symbols in this listing (+, r, and s). Table 3-3 contains the special listing file symbols. Most of these symbols are necessary in listings because the assembly process (TASM) that generates the listing file has no idea where the linker (TLINK) will place such things as code segments.

Listing files also contain symbol table information. The type and value of symbols are listed. Types include text, number, byte, far, and so on. Values can be numbers, variable names, and so on. While you now know names and types, you need a cross-reference table to know where these values are defined and used. For example, *SendIt* is defined on line 7 and used on line 17. This information can help you debug programs.

Table 3-3.   Special Listing File Symbols

Symbol	Function
r	Offset fixup type for symbols in the current module
s	Segment fixup type for symbols in the current module
sr	Both r and s
e	Offset fixup type for external symbol
se	Pointer fixup on an external symbol
so	Segment-only fixup
+	Object code truncated to next line

The *make* Utility

make is a Borland utility program that can facilitate your assembly and compiling process. The *make* utility is extremely powerful; only the features that fit your immediate needs are explained here.

You can use the *make* utility in large programs that require the assembly or compilation of a number of files to produce a final executable version. As you alter code, your only choice to this point has been to recompile or assemble everything each time you make a change. This is confusing and inefficient.

The *make* utility can free you from this routine for even the simplest programs. Here is a typical file that the *make* utility can use in the assembly process:

```
myfirst.exe: myfirst.obj
  tlink /m /l myfirst,,,

myfirst.obj: myfirst.asm
  tasm /zi myfirst,,,
```

The *make* utility works on the basis of dates and times. When you run *make*, it checks and compares the dates and times when, in this case, the *.exe*, *.obj*, and *.asm* files were created. If the *myfirst.asm* file has a later date and/or time than the *myfirst.obj* or *myfirst.exe* file, the *make* utility performs the specified assembly and link process to update that file. If no change has occurred in the *.obj* or *.exe* file, *make* skips the assembly and link steps.

In this fashion, a program's *make* file serves as an intelligent batch file, capable of providing all necessary information for assembly and linking. This book uses *make* files and the *make* utility frequently for C++ and assembly language programs.

To run the *make* utility, you have to create a file similar to the one in the previous listing. You can do this with the Turbo C++ editor. Name the file *myfirst*, without an extension. Once the file is created and saved, simply type

```
make -fmyfirst.mak
```

Notice the *-f* immediately in front of the file name; not even a single space is permitted. You need this option to tell *make* not to search for the default *make* file, named *makefile*. It is best to give the *make* file the same name as the program. The *-f* is a command-line option for the *make* utility. Table 3-4 shows other command-line options for *make*.

THE ASSEMBLY PROCESS: THE SECOND EXAMPLE

One of the major advantages of assembly language is its ability to control the hardware of the computer. The second example involves an assembly

Table 3-4.   Command-Line Options for *make*

Option	Function
-a	Creates an autodependency check
-D*identifier*	Defines an identifier
-D*iden = string*	Defines the identifier to the string
-I*directory*	*make* will search directory names for include files
-s	No commands are printed before execution
-n	Prints but doesn't execute commands (useful in debugging the *make* file)
-f*filename*	Uses the *make* file identified by *filename*
-? or -h	Prints the help message

language program that produces a chirping sound from the speaker. Sound can enhance your work on the computer by serving as a warning signal or an emphasis for a particular action.

The discussion concentrates on how to use the various assembler tools rather than on the actual assembly language program. You will learn how to control other hardware items in Chapter 20.

Entering Your Second Program

Use the Turbo C++ editor to enter the following assembly language program. Remember to name the program *mysecond.asm*. On the command line, type

```
tc mysecond.asm
```

The command-line argument you have just typed will assemble the following program:

```
;TURBO Assembly Language Programming Application
;Copyright (c) Chris H. Pappas and William H. Murray, 1990

;Program will generate a sound from the computer's speaker

        DOSSEG                  ;use Intel segment-ordering
        .MODEL  small           ;set model size
        .8086                   ;8086 instructions

        .STACK  300h            ;set up 768-byte stack

        .DATA                   ;set up data location
temp    dw      0               ;storage

        .CODE
Turbo   PROC    FAR             ;main procedure declaration
        mov     ax,DGROUP       ;point ds toward .DATA
        mov     ds,ax
        mov     dx,0            ;initialize dx to zero
        in      al,61h          ;get port info from speaker to al

        and     al,0FCh         ;mask info.  Keep lower two bits
more:   mov     temp,00h        ;initialize variable to zero
        inc     dx              ;increment dx register
        cmp     dx,15           ;have we done it 15 times?
        je      finish          ;if yes, end the program
go:     xor     al,02h          ;xor two bits of al register
        mov     cx,temp         ;get current frequency
        cmp     cx,258          ;has it reached 600 hertz?
        je      more            ;if yes, repeat sequence
        inc     temp            ;if no, increase frequency
        out     61h,al          ;send it to the speaker port
```

```
delay:  loop    delay           ;a small time delay
        jmp     go              ;continue
finish:

        mov     ah,4Ch          ;return control to DOS
        int     21h
Turbo   ENDP                    ;end main procedure
        END                     ;end whole program
```

This program uses **in** and **out** mnemonics to receive and send information to the specified hardware device.

Creating the *make* File

For this example, a *make* file will handle the assembly and linking process. You can also write the *make* file in the Turbo C++ editor by typing

```
tc mysecond.mak
```

Recall that the *make* file itself doesn't use an extension.

```
mysecond.exe: mysecond.obj
  tlink /m /s /l mysecond,,,

mysecond.obj: mysecond.asm
  tasm /zi mysecond,,,
```

Assembling and Linking the Program

With the two previous files (*mysecond* and *mysecond.asm*) residing in the default directory, you are now ready to use the *make* utility. Type

```
make -fmysecond
```

If no errors are encountered, your directory should now contain the following *mysecond* files:

```
Volume in drive C is DOS
Directory of  C:\TMASM

MYSECOND ASM    1417    1-06-90   8:45p
MYSECOND         112    1-06-90   8:44p
MYSECOND OBJ     598    1-08-90   9:11a
MYSECOND LST    4704    1-08-90   9:11a
MYSECOND MAP     906    1-08-90   9:11a
```

```
MYSECOND EXE       564    1-08-90   9:11a
        7 File(s)   15656960 bytes free
```

If the *make* utility encountered an error in your source code or *make* file, you will have to go back to the editor to correct the problem. You can then run the *make* utility again.

Considering All the Pieces

In the directory of *mysecond* files there are four ASCII files. The first two are the source code and *make* files that you originally created. The second two were created during the assembly and link process. Those files have the *.map* and *.lst* extensions.

The *.map* File (*mysecond.map*)

The *.map* file is created by the Linker and contains information on public symbols, source code line numbers, and a detailed map of program segments. You can view the *.map* file with the Turbo editor, or you can just type

```
type mysecond.map
```

You will then see

```
Start   Stop    Length  Name                Class

00000H  00031H  00032H  _TEXT               CODE
00032H  00033H  00002H  _DATA               DATA
00040H  0033FH  00300H  STACK               STACK

Detailed map of segments

0000:0000 0032 C=CODE  S=_TEXT G=(none) M=MYSECOND.ASM ACBP=48
0003:0002 0002 C=DATA  S=_DATA G=DGROUP M=MYSECOND.ASM ACBP=48
0004:0000 0300 C=STACK S=STACK  G=DGROUP M=MYSECOND.ASM ACBP=74

  Address           Publics by Name


  Address           Publics by Value


Line numbers for mysecond.obj(MYSECOND.ASM) segment _TEXT

18 0000:0000     19 0000:0003     21 0000:0005     22 0000:0008
23 0000:000A     24 0000:000C     25 0000:0012     26 0000:0013
```

```
27 0000:0016    28 0000:0018    29 0000:001A    30 0000:001E
31 0000:0022    32 0000:0024    33 0000:0028    34 0000:002A
35 0000:002C    38 0000:002E    39 0000:0030
Program entry point at 0000:0000
```

The *.lst* File (*mysecond.lst*)

This is your second look at a listing file. What can you tell about the machine code values next to the mnemonics? You can also view this file with the editor or by typing

```
type mysecond.lst
```

which will generate the following output:

```
Turbo Assembler        01/06/90 20:45:23        Page 1
MYSECOND.ASM
1                               ;TURBO Assembly Language
Programming                              Application
2                               ;Copyright (c) Chris H. Pappas and
                                William H. Murray, 1990
3
4                               ;Program will generate a sound
from                                    the computer's speaker
5
6                                       DOSSEG
7 0000                                  .MODEL   small
8                                       .8086
9
10 0000                                 .STACK   300h
11
12 0000                                 .DATA
13 0000   0000             temp         dw       0
14
15
16 0002                                 .CODE
17 0000                         Turbo    PROC     FAR
18 0000   B8 0000s                      mov      ax,DGROUP
19 0003   8E D8                         mov      ds,ax
20
21 0005   BA 0000                       mov      dx,0
22 0008   E4 61                         in       al,61h
23 000A   24 FC                         and      al,0FCh
24 000C   C7 06 0000r 0000   more:      mov      temp,00h
25 0012   42                            inc      dx
26 0013   83 FA 0F                      cmp      dx,15
27 0016   74 16                         je       finish
28 0018   34 02            go:          xor      al,02h
29 001A   8B 0E 0000r                   mov      cx,temp
30 001E   81 F9 0102                    cmp      cx,258
31 0022   74 E8                         je       more
```

```
32 0024  FF 06 0000r                        inc     temp
33 0028  E6 61                              out     61h,al
34 002A  E2 FE              delay:          loop    delay
35 002C  EB EA                              jmp     go
36 002E                     finish:
37
38 002E  B4 4C                              mov     ah,4Ch
39 0030  CD 21                              int     21h
40 0032                     Turbo   ENDP
41                                  END
```

```
Turbo Assembler            01/06/90 20:45:23          Page 2
Symbol Table


Symbol Name                Type   Value         Cref  defined at #
??DATE                     Text   "09/06/89"
??FILENAME                 Text   "MYSECOND"
??TIME                     Text   "20:45:22"
??VERSION                  Number 0101
@CODE                      Text   _TEXT         #7   #16
@CODESIZE                  Text   0             #7
@CPU                       Text   0101H         #8
@CURSEG                    Text   _TEXT         #12  #16
@DATA                      Text   DGROUP        #7
@DATASIZE                  Text   0             #7
@FILENAME                  Text   MYSECOND
@WORDSIZE                  Text   2             #8   #12  #16
DELAY                      Near   _TEXT:002A    #34  34
FINISH                     Near   _TEXT:002E    27   #36
GO                         Near   _TEXT:0018    #28  35
MORE                       Near   _TEXT:000C    #24  31
TEMP                       Word   DGROUP:000    #13  24   29   32
TURBO                      Far    _TEXT:0000    #17


Groups & Segments  Bit Size Align Combine Class
                                              Cref  defined at #


DGROUP             Group                       #7  7  18
  STACK            16  0300 Para  Stack  STACK  #10
  _DATA            16  0002 Word  Public DATA   #7  #12
  _TEXT            16  0032 Word  Public CODE   #7  7  #16  16
```

ASSEMBLER MODES: MASM AND IDEAL

If you have worked with Intel assembly language code, you are probably familiar with IBM's or Microsoft's Macro Assembler. The Turbo Assembler perfectly emulates both the IBM and Microsoft assemblers by using the same directives and syntax. Thus, a program written for MASM will assemble correctly with TASM and vice versa.

Borland's assembler actually contains a superset of MASM directives and abilities. In plain language, this means that TASM is a more powerful product that offers extended capabilities.

For example, normal assembly language programming syntax is handled the same way by all three assemblers. TASM also offers an *ideal* mode of operation. TASM's ideal mode allows you to write clear, concise code whose operation you can easily understand. Ideal mode uses MASM's keywords, operators, and statement syntax in a reorganized and easy to understand structure. You enter ideal mode in a program by using the directive **ideal**. You can return to the default *masm* mode by using the *masm* directive. One advantage to ideal mode directives, in addition to clarity, is that ideal mode programs assemble faster than conventional code.

Let's compare one line of code written in the default *masm* syntax and another written in ideal mode.

```
masm mode:      mov bx,es:[bp+10][si+4]
ideal mode:     mov bx,[es:bp+si+14]
```

This piece of code loads the value at offset **bp + si + 14** in segment **es** into the **bx** register. Which is easier to understand?

```
masm mode:      mov cx,10[bx]
ideal mode:     mov cx,[bx+10]
```

This piece of code loads the value given by the address **bx** with an offset of 10 bytes, not ten times the address at **bx**. Ideal mode can help you avoid confusion.

MIXED MODES: THE THIRD AND FOURTH EXAMPLES

The Professional package gives you great programming flexibility. From this environment, you can develop stand-alone C++ programs, stand-alone assembly language programs, or mixed mode programs. *Mixed mode* programs are programs that combine the best features of C++ and assembly language in one executable file. Mixed mode programs can take advantage of the speed and hardware control abilities of assembly language and combine them with the high-level programming power of C. The mixed mode environment is also used in Chapter 20.

The C Code for the Third Example

This section describes a small C program that will be combined with assembly code at link time. The C program will send two integers to the assembly code module. The assembly code module will add the numbers and return the sum to the C program. The C program will then print the sum to the screen. You could accomplish this whole program with one line of C code; however, the program shows you how you can splice two pieces of code in the Turbo C Professional environment. Study the following listing, named *mythird.c:*

```
/*
 *    A simple C program that is combined with assembly
 *    language code.
 *    Copyright (c) Chris H. Pappas and William H. Murray, 1990
 */

#include <stdio.h>

int Summer(int,int);

int Num1,Num2;

main()
{
    Num1=792;
    Num2=564;
    printf("The sum of the two numbers is: %d\n", Summer(Num1,Num2));
    return(0);
}
```

This C program uses an external function called **Summer**. Actually, **Summer** is the name of the assembly language module. This function will pass two variables, *Num1* and *Num2*, to the assembly language program. The assembly language program will in turn return the sum to the **printf** function.

The Assembly Code for the Third Example

The assembly language program is named *summer.asm.* It looks similar to the previous examples. The first difference is in the data declaration. Most

C compilers, including Turbo C++ Professional, expect all external labels to begin with an underscore character. This fixup is handled automatically by the new assembly language directives.

```
;TURBO Assembly Language & C Programming Application
;Copyright (c) Chris H. Pappas and William H. Murray, 1990

;This program will be interfaced to a C program named MYTHIRD.C
;It will not run in stand-alone mode.

        DOSSEG                      ;use Intel segment-ordering
        .MODEL  small               ;set model size
        .8086                       ;8086 instructions

        .CODE
        PUBLIC  C Summer
Summer  PROC    C NEAR Num1:WORD,Num2:WORD    ;main procedure declaration
        mov     ax,Num1             ;get first number
        add     ax,Num2             ;add second number

        ret                         ;return
Summer  ENDP                        ;end main procedure
        END                         ;end whole program
```

You might have noticed that the code for returning the operator to the DOS environment is missing. Only a **ret** mnemonic is used. This is because this code is not a stand-alone program, but a function called from a C program. Thus, when the assembly language program has completed its task, it must return to the calling program, not to DOS.

Splicing the C and Assembly Code for the Third Example

Before you can combine the two pieces of code, you have to enter each one with the editor. Again, name the C code *mythird.c* and the assembly language code *summer.asm*. From the command line, type

```
tcc mythird summer.asm
```

In one step, the C code is compiled into an *.obj* file named *mythird.obj*, the assembly language code is assembled into an *.obj* file named *summer.obj*, and the two *.obj* files are linked to form an *.exe* file named *mythird.exe*.

To execute the resulting code, type

```
mythird
```

The following message should be returned to your screen:

```
The sum of the two numbers is: 1356
```

The C Code for the Fourth Example

In the fourth example, you learn how to use a C program to report the contents of an assembly language program's **ax** registers. In assembly language, all numeric screen I/O (input and output) is done by routines that you must write yourself. By using mixed mode programming, you can tap C's powerful **printf** function and get the job done with much less effort. If used wisely, this program lets you experiment with assembly language code, investigate various mnemonic operations, and report the result to the screen without using a debugger.

The C program named *myfourth.c* is not much longer than the one in the previous example, as you can see from the listing.

```
/*
 *    A C program that is combined with assembly language
 *    code.  Reports ax register contents to screen.
 *    Copyright (c) Chris H. Pappas and William H. Murray, 1990
 */

#include <stdio.h>

int Report(void);

main()
{
  printf("The register contains: %X (hexadecimal)\n", Report());
  return(0);
}
```

The power in this program module is in the **printf** function. The **printf** function allows you to print numeric information to the screen. The last example printed the sum of two decimal numbers. This example will print the contents of the **ax** register, in hexadecimal. You'll learn more about **printf** in Chapter 5. An external assembly module named **Report** is used to pass the integer from the assembly language module to the C program.

The Assembly Code for the Fourth Example

This program uses an assembly module named *report.asm*. This module does not receive any values from the C program and only returns one—the contents of the **ax** register.

```
;TURBO Assembly Language & C Programming Application
;Copyright (c) Chris H. Pappas and William H. Murray, 1990

;This program will be interfaced to a C program named MYFOURTH.C

;It will not run in stand-alone mode.

        DOSSEG                  ;use Intel segment-ordering
        .MODEL   small          ;set model size
        .8086                   ;8086 instructions

        .CODE
        PUBLIC   C Report
Report  PROC                    ;main procedure declaration

        mov      ax,0AAh        ;move value into ax
        mov      cl,2           ;get multiplier
        shl      ax,cl          ;multiply by 4

        ret                     ;return
Report  ENDP                    ;end main procedure
        END                     ;end whole program
```

Splicing the C and Assembly Code for the Fourth Example

Before you can combine the two pieces of code, you have to enter each one with the Turbo C++ editor. Name the C code *myfourth.c* and the assembly language code *report.asm*. From the command line, type

```
tcc myfourth report.asm
```

The C code is compiled into an *.obj* file named *myfourth.obj*, the assembly language code is assembled into an *.obj* file named *report.obj* and the two *.obj* files are combined by the linker to form an *.exe* file named *myfourth.exe*.

In this program, a hexadecimal number, AAh, is moved into the **ax** register. Then a 2 is moved into the **cl** register. Finally, the shift-left mnemonic, **shl**, is called. This will shift the information in the **ax** register two places to the left, which has the effect of multiplying the number in **ax** by 4.

In binary, 0AAh would be   0000 0000 1010 1010.

One shift to the left   0000 0001 0101 0100 (154h).

One additional shift   0000 0010 1010 1000 (2A8h).

It should therefore be no surprise that when the program is executed, this result is reported to the screen:

```
The register contains 2A8 (hexadecimal)
```

To see the results for yourself, once you have obtained an *.exe* file, type

```
myfourth
```

TRACKING DOWN ASSEMBLY LANGUAGE ERRORS: THE FIFTH EXAMPLE

Some people believe that they never make mistakes. These people don't make good programmers. Whether you program in a high-level language or in assembly language, you will make a mistake sooner or later.

   In assembly language, syntax errors and bugs are bound to creep into the best of code. Catching syntax errors is the job of the assembler, and finding bugs is the job of the Turbo Debugger. This section concentrates on what the assembler can and can't do in terms of eliminating syntax errors. In Chapter 4, you will learn how to operate the Turbo Debugger for C, C++, and assembly language programs.

Catching Hidden Errors

To illustrate what the assembler can and cannot do, errors have been added to the first example in this chapter. However, if you look at the code, it seems innocent enough. This program is named *myerrors.asm.*

```
        DOSSEG                          ;use Intel segment-ordering
        .MODEL  small                   ;set model size

        .STACK  300h                    ;set up 768-byte stack

        .DATA                           ;set up data location
SendIt  db      'Assembly Language is easy!','$'

        .CODE
Turbo   PROC    FAR                     ;main procedure declaration
        mov     ax,DGROUP               ;point ds toward .DATA
        mov     ds,ax

        lea     dl,SendIt               ;point to the message
        mov     ah,901                  ;interrupt parameter
        int     bx,cx                   ;call DOS print interrupt

        mov     ah,4Dh                  ;return control to DOS
        int     25h
Turbo   ENDP                            ;end main procedure
        END                             ;end whole program
```

This program can be assembled and linked with the following *make* file.

```
myerrors.exe: myerrors.obj
  tlink /m /s /l myerrors,,,

myerrors.obj: myerrors.asm
  tasm /zi myerrors,,,
```

The Assembler's Error Report

The *make* utility reports the assembly and link process of *myerrors.asm* to the screen as follows:

```
MAKE    Copyright (c) 1987, 1990 Borland International

Available memory 451477 bytes

        tasm /zi myerrors,,,
Turbo Assembler   Copyright (c) 1988, 1990 Borland International

Assembling file:   MYERRORS.ASM
**Error** MYERRORS.ASM(14) Argument to operation or instruction
                            has illegal size
**Error** MYERRORS.ASM(15) Constant too large
**Error** MYERRORS.ASM(16) Illegal use of register
Error messages:     3
Warning messages:  None
Remaining memory:  306k

** error 1 ** deleting myerrors.obj
```

First, notice that there are two classes of errors: error messages and warning messages. Of the two, error messages are worse. Error messages will block the completion of the assembly process. You will not get an executable file (*.exe*) if one error is detected. In contrast, warning messages let you know that something unexpected happened during assembly or that the assembler had to make an assumption about something you were doing. Warning messages will allow the assembly process to complete. Be careful, however; the executable file might not execute.

The assembler has detected three major errors in the *myerrors* source code. You should make note of the three line numbers and the associated error messages before returning to the editor.

The first error reported is associated with line 14:

```
**Error** MYERRORS.ASM(14) Argument to operation or instruction
                          has illegal size
```

If you look up the **lea** mnemonic, you will see that the address of *SendIt* must be returned to a 16-bit register. The **dl** register is an 8-bit register.

```
lea     dl,SendIt       ;point to the message
```

The second error occurs on line 15:

```
**Error** MYERRORS.ASM(15) Constant too large
```

The **ah** register is an 8-bit register capable of holding integers up to 0FFh (hexadecimal) or 255 (decimal). Obviously, 901 (decimal) is too large for this register. The **ax** register might be the proper choice.

```
mov     ah,901          ;interrupt parameter
```

Finally, the last error reported occurs on line 16:

```
**Error** MYERRORS.ASM(16) Illegal use of register
```

The **int** instruction uses an immediate piece of data. In this case, the line should have contained a 21h, instead of the two registers.

```
int     bx,cx          ;call DOS print interrupt
```

If you are using illegal syntax, the assembler will catch the error. Until you become more familiar with assembly language, the error and warning messages will seem curt and not too helpful. However, as your programming experience increases, these brief messages will be all you need to get the program up and running as fast as possible.

You might not have noticed that two errors went completely undetected. Look at the following two lines of code, which are wrong:

```
mov     ah,4Dh         ;return control to DOS
int     25h
```

The value to be moved into the **ah** register should be 4Ch and the interrupt number for a return to DOS should be 21h. Why did the assembler catch the first three errors and bypass the last two? The assembler missed the last two errors because they are bugs, not syntax mistakes. The two lines of code are syntactically correct.

In other words, to master assembly language programming, you must learn the proper use of assembly language syntax and the various mnemonics. The assembler will help you with syntax, and the debugger will help you with proper use of the various instructions.

Remember, a program that does not report any error or warning messages can still crash the system.

THERE'S MORE TO COME

If you have made it this far, congratulations. If you are new to assembly language, don't be discouraged if you still don't understand how all of the pieces interlock. Remember, this chapter introduced you to the various tools for the assembly language environment. Later assembly language chapters (Chapters 16, 17, 18, 19, and 20) will concentrate on language features and less on the tools. If you forget how to use the assembler, how to link a program, or how to create a *.map* or *.lst* file, return to this chapter.

PUTTING YOUR KNOWLEDGE TO WORK

1. What are the advantages of assembly language?

2. What is a mnemonic?

3. Describe the process of creating, assembling, and linking a program.

4. Describe how a *.map* file might be useful.

5. Describe why you might want to generate a *.lst* file.

6. What does the *make* utility do? Why is it an important tool?

7. What does *masm* mode mean? What does ideal mode mean? How do you insert ideal mode code into a program?

8. What is the advantage of splicing C and assembly language code?

9. How do you compile, assemble, and link a mixed mode program?

10. Describe and give two examples of syntax errors. What will help you discover syntax errors?

4

GETTING STARTED WITH THE TURBO DEBUGGER AND PROFILER

In this chapter you will learn

- The purpose of a debugger

- How to start the Turbo Debugger

- How to use the Debugger with C, C++, and assembly language code

- How to repair simple logical errors and how to examine registers and data with the Debugger

- The purpose of a profiler

- How to start the Turbo Profiler

- How to use the Profiler with a graphics program

- How to interpret program performance with the Profiler's statistical summary

TOOLS OF THE TRADE

A carpenter goes to work with a tool box containing saws, hammers, screw drivers, tape measures, and so on. Carpenters even carry claw hammers to remove incorrectly placed nails. Programmers also go to work with a tool box. Typically, programmers use editors, compilers, linkers, and assemblers. However, just as the carpenter carries a claw hammer to fix mistakes, the programmer also has a variety of tools for correcting programming errors and streamlining code. Borland provides two such tools: the Turbo Debugger and the Turbo Profiler. The Debugger will help you correct logical errors in program development, while the Profiler will help make your finished routines run as fast as possible.

This chapter will get you started quickly with the Turbo Debugger and Turbo Profiler. It does not contain detailed discussions of either product or their options. Instead, it includes several short examples that illustrate important properties and choices for each product. You can always obtain help via the F1 key in either the Debugger or Profiler. For additional information, consult the user's guides.

The Debugger—Searching Out

Programming errors can be divided into two major groups: syntax errors and logical errors. *Syntax errors* are errors in language implementation. For example, missing semicolons, brackets, or undeclared variables are syntax errors. *Logical errors* are generated when the programmer makes an incorrect assumption in implementing code. For example, not extending the range of a control loop to include the correct boundary conditions and testing the wrong variable in a decision-making process are logical errors.

Both types of errors are common in programming—no programmer writes error-free code for a program of any consequence. Syntax errors are flagged by the compiler or assembler and must be corrected before an executable file (.exe) can be created. A program with no syntax errors still might not run correctly due to logical errors. You can locate logical errors with the Turbo Debugger, but you must first have an executable program to use the Debugger. In other words, you must correct all syntax errors before you can fix logical errors.

The Profiler—an Efficiency Expert

When developing professional programs, speed is a primary factor in program execution. The Turbo Profiler shows where your programs are spending time. Control loops, for example, use lots of execution time. The Profiler can indicate these areas and allow you to redesign portions of your code. The Profiler is usually used after syntax and logical errors have been removed from your program.

GETTING STARTED WITH THE TURBO DEBUGGER

The job of the Turbo Debugger is to search out and help you eliminate logical errors. For example, consider this simple program, which the developer thought would print the numbers from 1 to 5 on the screen:

```
/*
*       C program to print the numbers 1 to 5 to
*       the screen.
*       Copyright (c) Chris H. Pappas and William H. Murray, 1990
*/

#include <stdio.h>

main()
{
  int i;

  for (i=0;i<5;i++)
    printf("%d\n",i);

  return(0);
}
```

Perhaps you already recognize the logical error. The *for* loop should be initialized to start at 1 and end at a value less than 6. In the original form, the program prints the numbers 0, 1, 2, 3, and 4 to the screen. The Turbo Debugger will help find this type of error.

A Look at the Debugger

You can enter the Turbo Debugger by typing one of the following from the Debugger's subdirectory:

```
TD
TD386                (if you have an 80386/80486 computer)
TD MYFILE
TD386 MYFILE
```

If the TD or TD386 command is followed by an executable file name, that file will automatically be loaded when the Debugger starts. Figure 4-1 is a Debugger screen obtained by using the program shown earlier in this chapter and by typing

```
TD TEST.EXE
```

As you can see, the Debugger screen contains a menu bar at the top and a function-key bar at the bottom. This is Borland's typical user interface. The menu bar at the top lists *global menus,* menus that are always available and always visible at the top of the screen. They are accessible from the keyboard or the mouse. You can access global menu features by pressing F10

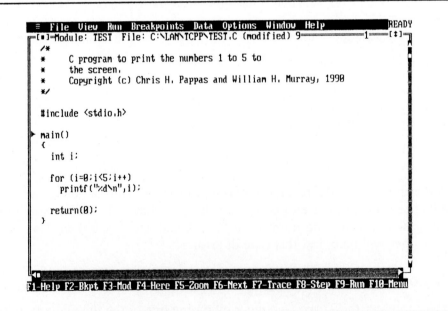

Figure 4-1. The initial Turbo Debugger screen

and using the arrow key or by pressing the highlighted letter of the global menu name. Options chosen from a global menu often produce a local menu with additional user choices. You select options in a local menu by pressing the ALT-F10, CTRL-F10 key combinations or by clicking the right mouse button on the desired option.

What follows is a quick overview of the important global menu items on the Turbo Debugger screen. You can get additional information for each option from Borland's online help or the Turbo Debugger user's guide. The various function keys are also covered later in this section.

The Desktop Manager Menu

The Desktop Manager menu is shown in Figure 4-2. The "Repaint desktop" option allows you to clean up your screen if it has been overwritten. The "Restore standard" option restores your screen to the layout it had when you started the Debugger.

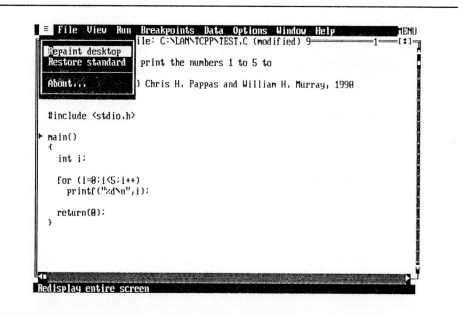

Figure 4-2.   Selecting the Debugger's Desktop menu

The File Menu

The most important File menu selections allow you to open a file for debugging, change the directory, return to the DOS shell, and quit the Debugger (Figure 4-3). Note that the bottom of the figure contains a brief explanation of the currently selected menu item.

The View Menu

The View menu contains options for some of the Debugger's most important features (Figure 4-4). You use the "Breakpoints" option to set breakpoints in your program. The program can then operate at full speed until it encounters the breakpoint. This is useful for examining memory locations without having to single-step through the entire program. The "Watches" option allows you to track values in specified variables as your program executes. The "Variables" option shows you the currently accessible variable names for your program. The "CPU," "Dump," "Registers," and "Numeric processor" options are most useful for assembly language debugging

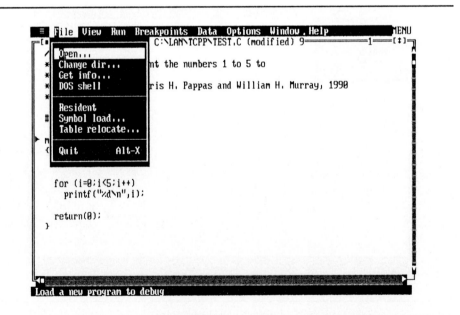

Figure 4-3.   Selecting the Debugger's File menu

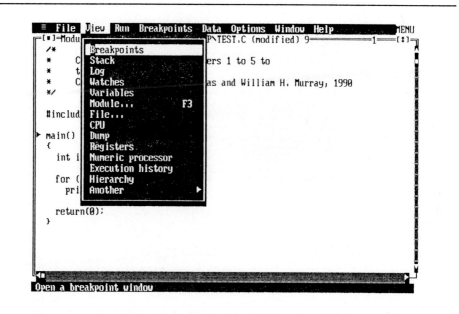

Figure 4-4.   Selecting the Debugger's View menu

and allow you to examine the contents of the CPU, memory, register values, and stack values on the numeric coprocessor if one is installed in your computer.

The Run Menu

Figure 4-5 shows the Run menu options. "Run" executes your program at full CPU speed. "Go to Cursor" executes your program down to the cursor. "Trace into" executes a single line of source code and stops. Procedures and function calls are not skipped. "Step over" executes a single line of source code and stops. It will skip procedure and function calls. "Execute to..." executes the program until the address specified in the dialog box is reached. "Program reset" reloads the specified file from disk for debugging.

The Breakpoints Menu

Figure 4-6 shows the Breakpoints menu. "Toggle" sets or clears breakpoints at the specified address in the module or CPU window. "Delete all" allows you to remove all breakpoints.

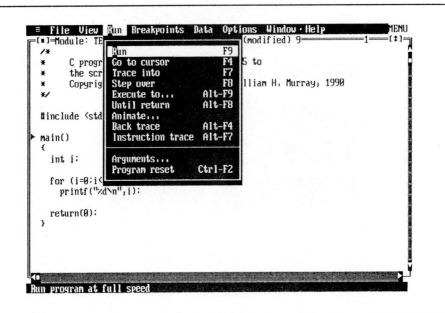

Figure 4-5.   Selecting the Debugger's Run menu

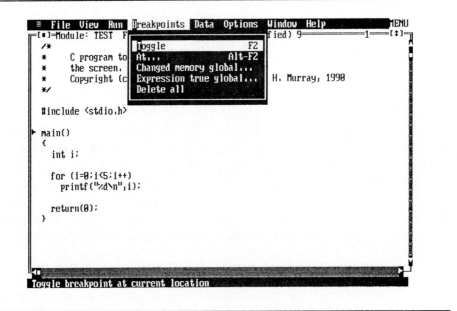

Figure 4-6.   Selecting the Debugger's Breakpoints menu

The Data Menu

The Data Menu allows you to examine and change program data (Figure 4-7). "Inspect..." is a dialog box that prompts for a variable name that contains the data you want to inspect. "Evaluate/modify..." opens another dialog box that prompts for an expression to evaluate.

The Options Menu

The Options menu enables you to set values that affect the overall operation and appearance of the Debugger (Figure 4-8). Most of the choices in this menu produce dialog boxes for changing the stated options. If you alter default settings for the debugger, use the "Save options..." dialog box to save your new configuration. Remember, help is as close as the F1 key.

The Window Menu

The Window menu allows you to alter the window currently in the Debugger (Figure 4-9). For example, "Zoom" allows you to enlarge or shrink the

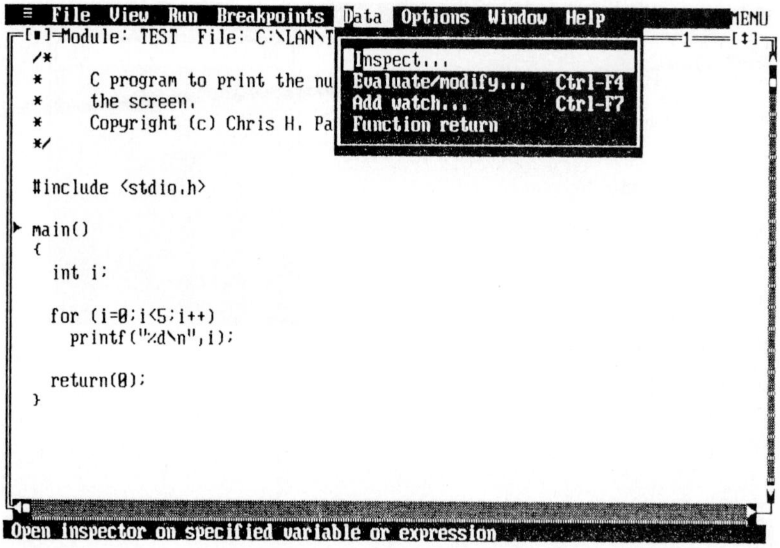

Figure 4-7.   Selecting the Debugger's Data menu

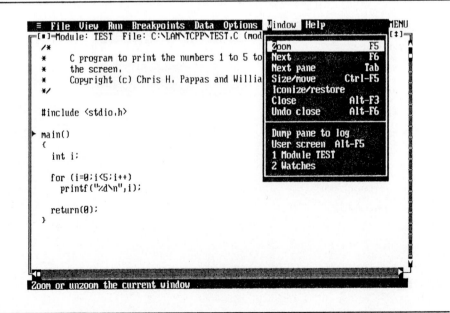

≡ File View Run Breakpoints Data Options Window Help   MENU
┌[■]═Module: TEST File: C:\LAN\TCPP\TE┌─────────────────────┐═1═══[↕]═┐
│ /*   │ Language... Source │
│ *   C program to print the numbers │ Macros   ► │
│ *   the screen.   │ Display options...   │
│ *   Copyright (c) Chris H. Pappas a│ Path for source...   │
│ */   │ Save options...   │
│   │ Restore options...   │
│ #include <stdio.h>   └─────────────────────┘
│
│► main()
│ {
│   int i;
│
│   for (i=0;i<5;i++)
│   printf("%d\n",i);
│
│   return(0);
│ }
│
Set the expression language

Figure 4-8. Selecting the Debugger's Options menu

≡ File View Run Breakpoints Data Options Window Help   MENU
┌[■]═Module: TEST File: C:\LAN\TCPP\TEST.C (mod┌──────────────────┐[↕]═┐
│ /*   │ Zoom   F5 │
│ *   C program to print the numbers 1 to 5 to│ Next   F6 │
│ *   the screen.   │ Next pane   Tab │
│ *   Copyright (c) Chris H. Pappas and Willia│ Size/move Ctrl-F5│
│ */   │ Iconize/restore │
│   │ Close   Alt-F3 │
│ #include <stdio.h>   │ Undo close Alt-F6│
│   ├──────────────────┤
│► main()   │ Dump pane to log │
│ {   │ User screen Alt-F5│
│   int i;   │ 1 Module TEST   │
│   │ 2 Watches   │
│   for (i=0;i<5;i++)   └──────────────────┘
│   printf("%d\n",i);
│
│   return(0);
│ }
│
Zoom or unzoom the current window

Figure 4-9. Selecting the Debugger's Window menu

current window. "Next" lets you switch or activate alternate windows on the screen. "Size/move" enables you to size the window. "User screen" permits you to view any output from your program that is sent to the screen. You can also implement many of these options with various function-key combinations, as you can see in the figure.

The Help Menu

The Help menu, shown in Figure 4-10, allows you to examine an index of items or specify a previous topic. If you select the "Index" option, the Debugger will list a group of items for which help is available. You can select these items with the arrow keys or with the mouse. Press PGDN for additional lists of items.

Function Keys

The function-key options listed at the bottom of your Debugger screen offer shortcuts to many of the global menu options. The function-key options

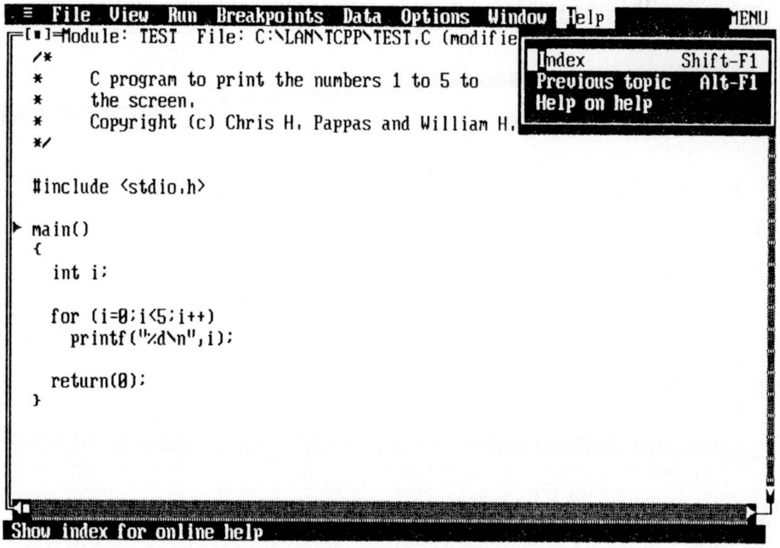

Figure 4-10.   Selecting the Debugger's Help menu

will change as you switch from menu to menu. Usually, they represent a shortcut to the menu items of the currently selected global menu. Remember, you can obtain help by pressing F1. F8 will single-step you through program code while F9 will run your whole program at full CPU speed. F5 is always a quick means of zooming windows.

Debugging a Simple C Program

The first example uses the Debugger to find the error in the example program shown earlier. First, use the Debugger to enter and compile the program. The Debugger requires an *.exe* file for operation, so all syntax errors will have to be eliminated. Now, switch to the Debugger's subdirectory and start the Debugger by typing **TD TEST.EXE**.

You should now see a screen similar to Figure 4-11. Notice that two windows are displayed by default—the Module window and the Watch window. The double border around the Module window indicates that it is

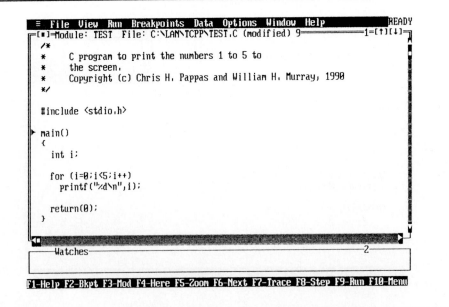

Figure 4-11.   Initial Module and Watch windows for C debugging example

the active window. Also notice that a small arrow on the extreme left of the screen points to **main( )**. This arrow indicates the starting point for program execution.

Recall that this program is expected to print the numbers from 1 to 5 on the screen, but actually prints the digits 0, 1, 2, 3, and 4. Since there is only one variable, *i*, set that in a Watch window to keep an eye on it during program execution.

Figure 4-12 shows the path required to add the variable to the Watch window. Select the Data menu and then the "Add watch..." dialog box. Figure 4-13 shows the dialog box.

Figure 4-14 shows that *i* has been added to the Watch window. Figure 4-14 shows a screen after the first pass through the *for* loop. If you use the F8 function key, you can execute the program one line at a time. Alternately, you can set breakpoints at important locations. The 0 value of *i* is the first indication of a logical error. Since the value in *i* is printed to the screen, *i* will have to be initialized to 1 instead of 0 if the first number is to be a 1.

```
 ≡  File  View  Run  Breakpoints  Data  Options  Window  Help        MENU
┌─[■]=Module: TEST   File: C:\LAN\T                              ═══1=[↑][↓]═┐
│  /*                              ┌─Inspect...                            │
│  *      C program to print the nu│ Evaluate/modify...   Ctrl-F4          │
│  *      the screen.              │ Add watch...         Ctrl-F7          │
│  *      Copyright (c) Chris H. Pa│ Function return                       │
│  */                              └───────────────────────────────        │
│                                                                          │
│  #include <stdio.h>                                                      │
│                                                                          │
│▶ main()                                                                  │
│  {                                                                       │
│      int i;                                                              │
│                                                                          │
│      for (i=0;i<5;i++)                                                   │
│        printf("%d\n",i);                                                 │
│                                                                          │
│      return(0);                                                          │
│  }                                                                       │
└─■────────────────────────────────────────────────────────────────────▼─┘
  ┌──Watches───────────────────────────────────────────2──────────────┐
  │                                                                    │
  └────────────────────────────────────────────────────────────────────┘
  Open inspector on specified variable or expression
```

Figure 4-12.   Preparing to add a variable to the Watch window

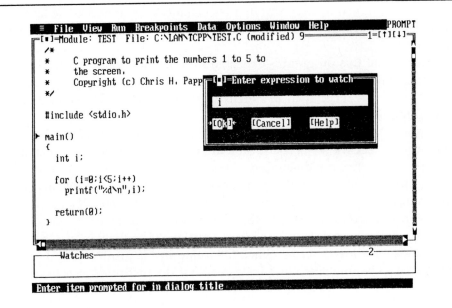

Figure 4-13.   Entering the variable to watch

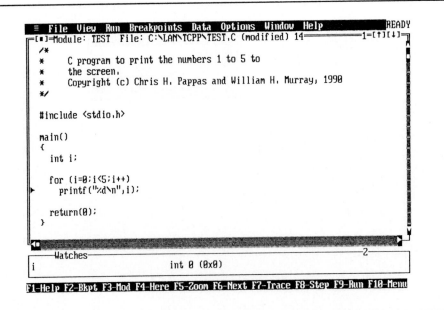

Figure 4-14.   Observe the variable after one pass through the *for* loop

Figure 4-15 shows the program after the control loop has been exited. Notice that the arrow is now pointing to **return (0)**. The last value for *i* is 5. Recall that the numbers printed to the screen were 0, 1, 2, 3, and 4. What happened to the 5? The increment operator incremented *i* to 5 after the print statement, but the last value printed was 4.

To repair this program, alter the *for* loop to read (you will have to return to the editor to make this change):

```
for (i=1;i<6;i++)
```

You can exit the Debugger by using ALT-X or selecting the "Quit" option from the File menu.

Debugging a Simple Assembly Language Program

The assembly language debugging example uses the *mysecond.asm* program from the previous chapter.

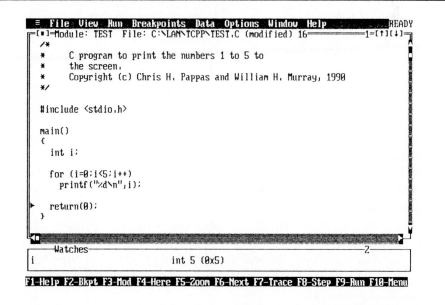

Figure 4-15.   Observe the variable after the final pass through the *for* loop

```
;TURBO Assembly Language Programming Application
;Copyright (c) Chris H. Pappas and William H. Murray, 1990

;Program will generate a sound from the computer's speaker

        DOSSEG                  ;use Intel segment-ordering
        .MODEL  small           ;set model size
        .8086                   ;8086 instructions

        .STACK  300h            ;set up 768-byte stack

        .DATA                   ;set up data location
temp    dw      0               ;storage

        .CODE
Turbo   PROC    FAR             ;main procedure declaration
        mov     ax,DGROUP       ;point ds toward .DATA
        mov     ds,ax

        mov     dx,0            ;initialize dx to zero
        in      al,61h          ;get port info from speaker to al

        and     al,0FCh         ;mask info.  Keep lower two bits
more:   mov     temp,00h        ;initialize variable to zero
        inc     dx              ;increment dx register
        cmp     dx,15           ;have we done it 15 times?
        je      finish          ;if yes, end the program
go:     xor     al,02h          ;xor two bits of al register
        mov     cx,temp         ;get current frequency
        cmp     cx,258          ;has it reached 600 hertz?
        je      more            ;if yes, repeat sequence
        inc     temp            ;if no, increase frequency
        out     61h,al          ;send it to the speaker port
delay:  loop    delay           ;a small time delay
        jmp     go              ;continue
finish:

        mov     ah,4Ch          ;return control to DOS
        int     21h
Turbo   ENDP                    ;end main procedure
        END                     ;end whole program
```

There are no logical errors in the preceding program, but you will use the Turbo Debugger to examine variables and registers during program execution. This alone makes the Debugger a very useful tool to assembly language programmers.

Recall that you must enter the assembly language program with an editor, such as the one supplied with Turbo C++, and then assemble and link it. The following *make* file will prepare this program for the Debugger:

```
mysecond.exe: mysecond.obj
    tlink /v mysecond;
```

```
mysecond.obj: mysecond.asm
  tasm /zi mysecond;
```

You might want to review Chapter 3 to understand the assembler and linker options shown in the *make* file. You enter the Debugger with the line of code TD MYSECOND.EXE. Figure 4-16 shows the initial Debugger screen. Notice that the arrow is pointing to the first executable line of code.

```
mov        ax,DGROUP              ;point ds toward .DATA
```

Figure 4-17 shows a breakpoint set on the **out** mnemonic. The program can be executed at full speed until this point is reached. Also notice that the *temp* variable was placed in the Watch window and that the register window has been opened.

With the Turbo Debugger, you can now debug assembly language programs at the source code level while watching variables, registers, and so on.

```
 ≡  File  View  Run  Breakpoints  Data  Options  Window  Help            READY
┌─[■]─Module: mysecond  File: C:\LAN\TA\mysecond.asm 18═══════════════1=[↑][↓]─┐
│                                                                              ░│
│              .CODE                                                           ░│
│    Turbo     PROC    FAR                ;main procedure declaration          ░│
│  ►           mov     ax,DGROUP          ;point ds toward .DATA               ░│
│              mov     ds,ax                                                    │
│                                                                              ░│
│              mov     dx,0               ;initialize dx to zero               ░│
│              in      al,61h             ;get port info from speaker to al    ░│
│              and     al,0FCh            ;mask info. Keep lower two bits       ░│
│    more:     mov     temp,00h           ;initialize variable to zero          │
│              inc     dx                 ;increment dx register                │
│              cmp     dx,15              ;have we done it 15 times?            ░│
│              je      finish             ;if yes, end the program             ░│
│    go:       xor     al,02h             ;xor lower two bits of al register   ░│
│              mov     cx,temp            ;get current frequency               ░│
│              cmp     cx,258             ;has it reached 600 hertz?           ░│
│              je      more               ;if yes, repeat sequence             ░│
│              inc     temp               ;if no, increase frequency           ░│
│◄░░░░░░░░░░░░░░░░░░░░░░░░░░░░░░░░░░░░░░░░░░░░░░░░░░░░░░░░░░░░░░░░░░░░░░░░░░░░░░►  │
│   ┌─Watches──────────────────────────────────────────────2─┐                 │
│   │                                                         │                 │
│   └─────────────────────────────────────────────────────────┘                │
└──────────────────────────────────────────────────────────────────────────────┘
 F1-Help F2-Bkpt F3-Mod F4-Here F5-Zoom F6-Next F7-Trace F8-Step F9-Run F10-Menu
```

Figure 4-16.   Initial Module and Watch windows for assembly language debugging example

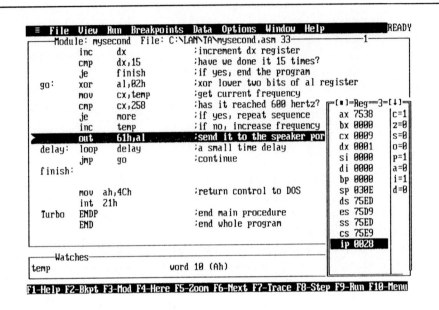

```
≡  File  View  Run  Breakpoints  Data  Options  Window  Help        READY
┌──Module: mysecond  File: C:\LAN\TA\mysecond.asm 33─────────1─────┐
│           inc    dx              ;increment dx register          │
│           cmp    dx,15           ;have we done it 15 times?       │
│           je     finish          ;if yes, end the program        │
│    go:    xor    al,02h          ;xor lower two bits of al register│
│           mov    cx,temp         ;get current frequency          │
│           cmp    cx,258          ;has it reached 600 hertz? ┌─[■]=Reg═3=[↓]┐
│           je     more            ;if yes, repeat sequence  │ax 7538│c=1│
│           inc    temp            ;if no, increase frequency│bx 0000│z=0│
│           out    61h,al          ;send it to the speaker por│cx 0009│s=0│
│    delay: loop   delay           ;a small time delay       │dx 0001│o=0│
│           jmp    go              ;continue                 │si 0000│p=1│
│    finish:                                                 │di 0000│a=0│
│                                                            │bp 0000│i=1│
│           mov    ah,4Ch          ;return control to DOS    │sp 030E│d=0│
│           int    21h                                       │ds 75ED│   │
│    Turbo  ENDP                   ;end main procedure       │es 75D9│   │
│           END                    ;end whole program        │ss 75ED│   │
│                                                            │cs 75E9│   │
│                                                            ├─ip 0028─┤
└──Watches─────────────────────────────────────────────────┘
│ temp                        word 10 (Ah)                         │
└──────────────────────────────────────────────────────────────────┘
F1-Help F2-Bkpt F3-Mod F4-Here F5-Zoom F6-Next F7-Trace F8-Step F9-Run F10-Menu
```

Figure 4-17.   A breakpoint set at the **out** mnemonic

Debugging a Simple C++ Program

You have already seen how the Debugger can help locate errors in C source code and display important register information for assembly language programs. The next Debugger example examines a C++ program that uses operator overloading. (Operator overloading is covered in more detail in Chapters 13 and 14.) In this example, operator overloading allows the program to add, subtract, multiply, and divide complex numbers.

This program is also free of logical errors and shows the use of the Watch window, the CPU window, the Variable window, and the Class Hierarchy window. The program, named *complex.cpp*, is shown in the following listing:

```
//
//   A C++ program that demonstrates how to use complex
//   arithmetic with overloaded operators.  Here complex
//   numbers are directly added, subtracted, multiplied, and
//   divided.
```

```
//    Copyright (c) Chris H. Pappas and William H. Murray, 1990
//

#include <iostream.h>
#include <complex.h>

main()
{
  double x1=5.6, y1=7.2;
  double x2=-3.1, y2=4.8;

  complex z1=complex(x1,y1);
  complex z2=complex(x2,y2);

  cout << "The value of z1 + z2 is: " << z1+z2 << "\n";
  cout << "The value of z1 * z2 is: " << z1*z2 << "\n";
  cout << "The value of z1 - z2 is: " << z1-z2 << "\n";
  cout << "The value of z1 / z2 is: " << z1/z2 << "\n";
  return (0);
}
```

Details of this program's operation will not be explained until Chapters 13 and 14 but let's look at the information the Debugger can provide. First, Figure 4-18 shows a typical Watch window with two variables, *z1* and *z2*.

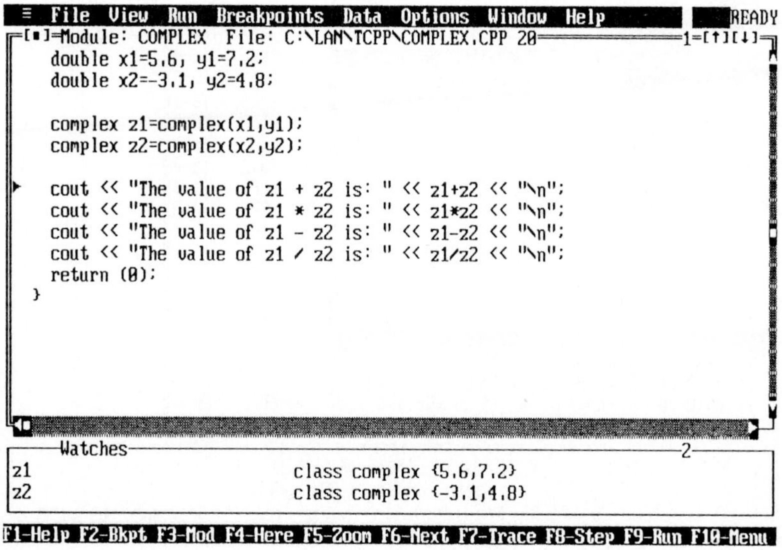

Figure 4-18.   The Module and Watch windows for a C++ program

The variables belong to the **complex** class. Notice that this is the only place you actually see the values for these variables — the program does not print them to the screen. These could also be observed in the Variable window.

If you are interested in how the CPU is processing this information, you can open the CPU window. Figure 4-19 shows the CPU window when the program is about to execute the first **cout** command. The figure shows the C++ code converted to equivalent assembly language code in the upper-left corner. Register values and a small portion of the program's data dump are also shown. Previous examples have shown you how to place program variables in a Watch window for observation. As mentioned, you can also examine variable values in the variable window. Figure 4-20 is a Variable window for this example. Can you find all of the values used in this example? Finally, Figure 4-21 shows a Class Hierarchy window.

The program uses two other classes in addition to the **complex** class: **ostream** and **streambuf**. The Class Hierarchy window will help you as you study C++ classes in Chapter 13.

```
≡ File  View  Run  Breakpoints  Data  Options  Window  Help          READY
┌[■]=CPU 80386══════════════════════════════════════╤═3=[↑][↓]═╤──1──┐
│#COMPLEX#20:  cout << "The value of z1 + z2 i▲│ ax FFB6  │c=0 │     │
│  cs:02A8▶68E200      push    00E2            ●│ bx 0012  │z=0 │     │
│  cs:02AB 8D46C0      lea     ax,[bp-40]       │ cx 0924  │s=1 │     │
│  cs:02AE 50          push    ax               │ dx 0012  │o=0 │     │
│  cs:02AF 8D46D0      lea     ax,[bp-30]       │ si 0000  │p=0 │     │
│  cs:02B2 50          push    ax               │ di 0012  │a=0 │     │
│  cs:02B3 1E          push    ds               │ bp FFF6  │i=1 │     │
│  cs:02B4 8D46B0      lea     ax,[bp-50]       │ sp FF76  │d=0 │     │
│  cs:02B7 50          push    ax               │ ds 01C1  │    │     │
│  cs:02B8 E8F200      call    #COMPLEX#oper▓│ es 01BF  │    │     │
│  cs:02BB 83C408      add     sp,0008          │ ss 01C1  │    │     │
│  cs:02BE 8D46B0      lea     ax,[bp-50]       │ cs 7969  │    │     │
│  cs:02C1 50          push    ax            ▼│ ip 02A8  │    │     │
│◄▶                                              ►│          │    │     │
│  ds:0000 00 00 00 00 54 75 72 62     Turb      │          │    │     │
│  ds:0008 6F 20 43 20 2D 20 43 6F  o C - Co     │          │    │     │
│  ds:0010 70 79 72 69 67 68 74 20  pyright      │ ss:FF78 9F0A │   │
│  ds:0018 31 39 38 39 20 42 6F 72  1989 Bor     │ ss:FF76▶A150 │   │
│                                                │          ╘═2═╛     │
│z1                          class complex {5,6,7,2}                  │
│z2                          class complex {-3,1,4,8}                 │
└────────────────────────────────────────────────────────────────────┘
 F1-Help F2-Bkpt F3-Mod F4-Here F5-Zoom F6-Next F7-Trace F8-Step F9-Run F10-Menu
```

Figure 4-19.   Opening the CPU window

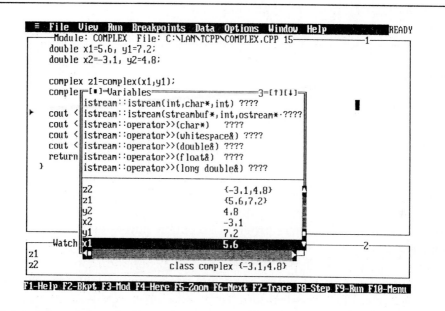

Figure 4-20.   The Variable window

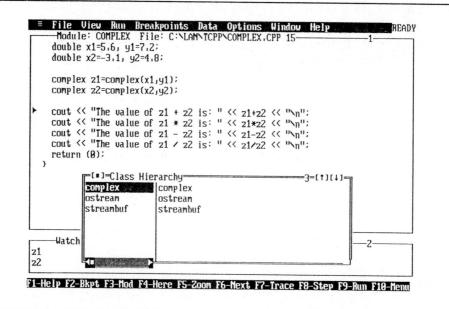

Figure 4-21.   The Class Hierarchy window

From now on, each programming chapter in this book will contain at least two programs that use the Turbo Debugger to help you view program parameters.

GETTING STARTED WITH THE TURBO PROFILER

The Profiler, or performance analyzer, is similar to an efficiency expert: It analyzes your program's performance in terms of hot spots and bottlenecks. Hot spots are places where your program spends a lot of time, while bottlenecks are places where program execution slows due to poorly developed algorithms, and so on. By pointing out these problem areas, the Turbo Profiler helps you develop code that operates faster and more efficiently.

The Profiler operates with almost any programming language that also produces a *.map* file. This includes Turbo Assembler, BASIC, C, Pascal, and even programs compiled with Microsoft products.

To get you started with the Turbo Profiler, this section uses a program that is developed and explained in Chapter 15. This program is an interactive graphics program that draws a presentation quality pie chart on the EGA or VGA screen. Again, details of the program's operation are not necessary for our purposes.

```
/*
 *    A C++ program that demonstrates how to produce a
 *    presentation quality pie chart for EGAHI or VGAHI screens.
 *    Copyright (c) Chris H. Pappas and William H. Murray, 1990
 */

#include <graphics.h>
#include <conio.h>
#include <stdlib.h>

#define MAXWEDGE 10

main()
{
  char s1[10];
  char leg[10][50];
  char label1[50],label2[50];
```

```
int gdriver=DETECT,gmode,errorcode;
int nwedges,midx,midy,i;
double totalwedge,temp;
double startangle,endangle;
double wedgesize[MAXWEDGE],wedgeangle[MAXWEDGE];

printf("THIS PROGRAM WILL DRAW A PIE CHART.\n\n");
printf("Chart titles are optional.\n");
printf("Enter top of chart label.\n");
gets(label1);
printf("Enter bottom of chart label.\n");
gets(label2);
printf("\n\n");

printf("Enter up to 10 values for the pie wedges.\n");
printf("Value are followed by a carriage return.\n");
printf("No value and carriage return ends input.\n");

nwedges=0;
for (i=0;i<MAXWEDGE;i++) {
  printf("wedge value #%d ",i+1);
  gets(s1);
  if (strlen(s1) == 0) break;
  wedgesize[i]=atof(s1);
  nwedges++;
  printf("legion label: ");
  gets(leg[i]);
}

totalwedge=0.0;
for (i=0;i<nwedges;i++)
  totalwedge+=wedgesize[i];

for (i=0;i<nwedges;i++)
  wedgeangle[i]=(wedgesize[i]*360.0)/totalwedge;

initgraph(&gdriver,&gmode,"");

errorcode=graphresult();
if (errorcode != grOk) {
  printf("Graphics Function Error: %s\n",
          grapherrormsg(errorcode));
  printf("Hit key to stop:");
  getch();
  exit(1);
}

/* get maximum x & y coordinate values for mode */
midx=getmaxx()/2;
midy=getmaxy()/2;

startangle=0.0;
endangle=wedgeangle[0];
for (i=0;i<nwedges;i++) {
  setcolor(BLACK);
```

```
    setfillstyle(SOLID_FILL,BLUE+i);
    pieslice(midx/2,midy,(int)startangle,(int)endangle,midy/2);

    startangle+=wedgeangle[i];
    endangle+=wedgeangle[i+1];
  }

  /* print legend names and colors */
  setcolor(WHITE);
  moveto(midx+100,midy-80);
  outtext("Legend");
  for (i=0;i<nwedges;i++) {
    setfillstyle(SOLID_FILL,BLUE+i);
    bar(midx+100,(midy-50)+10*i,midx+110,(midy-40)+10*i);
    moveto(midx+120,(midy-48)+10*i);
    outtext(leg[i]);
  }

  /* print optional pie chart labels */
  setcolor(WHITE);
  settextjustify(CENTER_TEXT,CENTER_TEXT);
  moveto(midx/2,midy+150);
  outtext(label2);
  settextstyle(0,0,2);
  moveto(midx,midy-150);
  outtext(label1);
  getch();
  closegraph();
  return (0);
}
```

A Look at the Profiler

You must enter, compile, and link the preceding program with the Turbo C++ compiler. You can then enter the Turbo Profiler by typing either of the following two lines from the Turbo Profiler subdirectory:

TPROF
TPROF *program _ name*

For this example, enter

TPROF PIE

Figure 4-22 shows the initial Profiler screen with the source code in the Module window. Notice that the Profiler also has a global menu bar at the

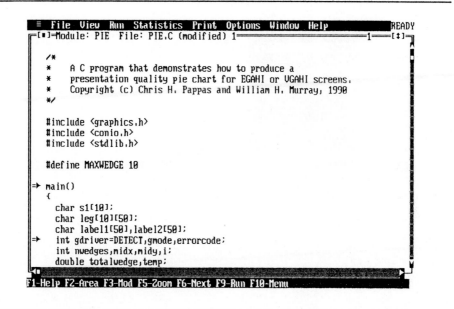

```
≡ File View Run Statistics Print Options Window Help        READY
╔[▪]═Module: PIE  File: PIE.C (modified) 1══════════════════1══[↕]═╗
║                                                                  ║
║    /*                                                            ║
║     *    A C program that demonstrates how to produce a          ║
║     *    presentation quality pie chart for EGAHI or VGAHI screens. ║
║     *    Copyright (c) Chris H. Pappas and William H. Murray, 1990 ║
║     */                                                           ║
║                                                                  ║
║    #include <graphics.h>                                         ║
║    #include <conio.h>                                            ║
║    #include <stdlib.h>                                           ║
║                                                                  ║
║    #define MAXWEDGE 10                                           ║
║                                                                  ║
║ ⇒► main()                                                        ║
║    {                                                             ║
║      char s1[10];                                                ║
║      char leg[10][50];                                           ║
║      char label1[50],label2[50];                                 ║
║ ⇒►   int gdriver=DETECT,gmode,errorcode;                         ║
║      int nwedges,midx,midy,i;                                    ║
║      double totalwedge,temp;                                     ║
║ ◄▒▒▒▒▒▒▒▒▒▒▒▒▒▒▒▒▒▒▒▒▒▒▒▒▒▒▒▒▒▒▒▒▒▒▒▒▒▒▒▒▒▒▒▒▒▒▒▒▒▒▒▒▒▒▒▒▒►      ║
╚══════════════════════════════════════════════════════════════════╝
 F1-Help F2-Area F3-Mod F5-Zoom F6-Next F9-Run F10-Menu
```

Figure 4-22. Initial Module window for the Turbo Profiler

top of the screen and a function-key bar at the bottom—like the Turbo Debugger. The View, Run, and Statistics global menus are the most important for getting started.

View

The View menu is shown in Figure 4-23. The "Module" option shows the source code for the program. The "Execution Profile" option provides the statistical information for the program after execution. The "Callers" option provides information on how many times a routine is called. "Overlays" gives information on language overlays used. "Interrupts" provides information on system interrupts used by the program. "Files" show file activity during program execution. "Areas" gives information concerning data collection in your program, at marked locations. "Routines" lists routines that can be used by area markers. "Disassembly" converts the current profile area into assembly language code.

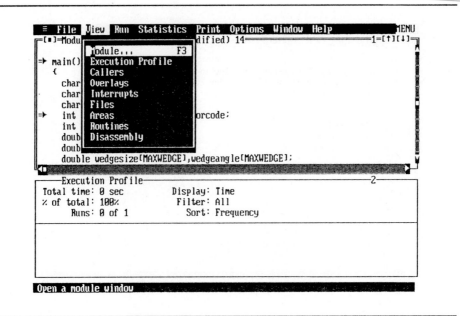

Figure 4-23.   The Profiler's View menu

Run

The Run menu is shown in Figure 4-24. The most important option in this menu is the "Run" option, which will execute your program code and collect the statistical information for the profiler. You can also execute the program with the F9 function key.

Statistics

The Statistics menu, shown in Figure 4-25, allows you to specify which statistical information will be gathered. You can enable the following options: "Callers," "Files," "Interrupts," and "Overlays." You can obtain additional information from the Help menu or by selecting help with the F1 function key.

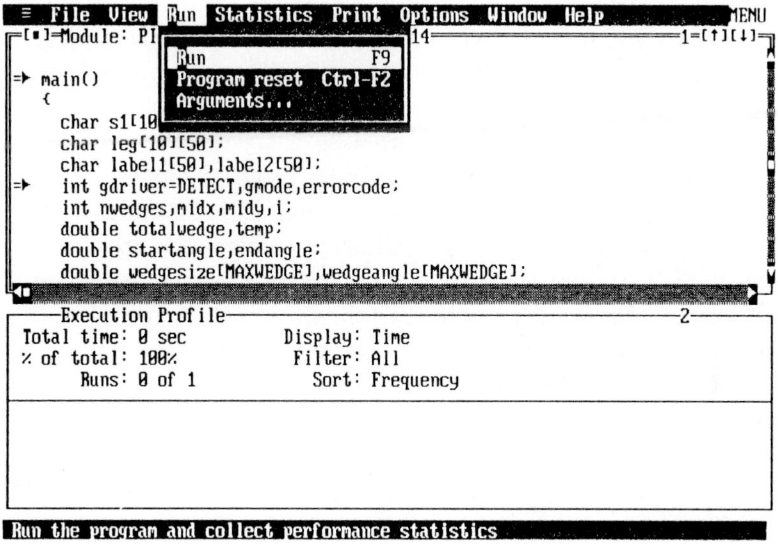

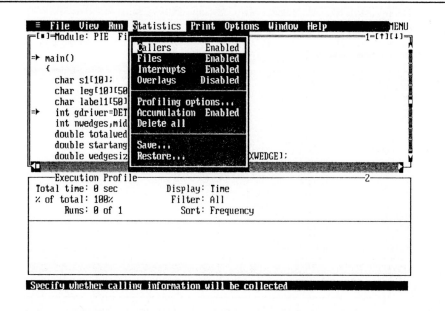

Figure 4-24.   The Profiler's Run menu

Figure 4-25.   The Profiler's Statistics menu

Profiling a Program

You can execute *pie*, the graphics program shown earlier in this section, by selecting the Run menu and then the "Run" option. The information retrieved is returned to the Execution Profile window, which has been sized to full screen, as shown in Figure 4-26.

The execution times for various lines of program code are listed from greatest to least. If you examine the original listings, note that, for this example, the greatest time is spent gathering information from the user.

Figure 4-27 is a composite collection of the Routine, Areas, and Interrupts windows. The Routines window shows which C routines are called. The Areas window shows locations marked in the source code for data collection. Finally, the Interrupts window shows which system interrupts are called and how often.

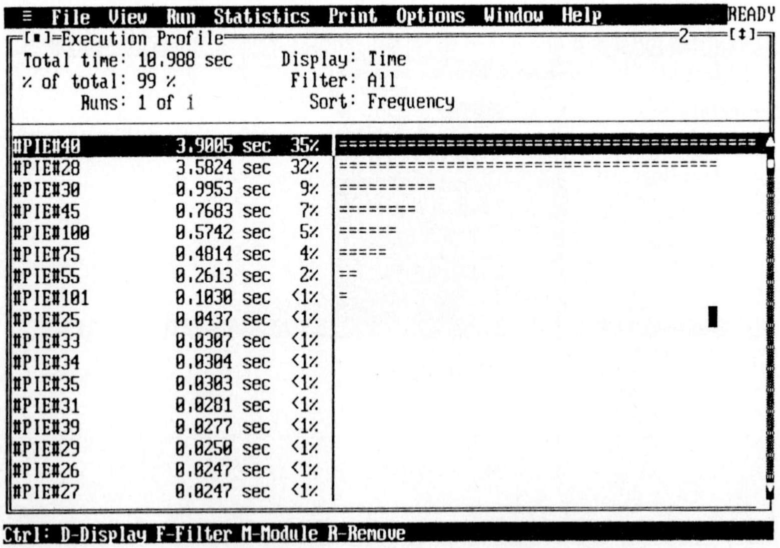

```
 ≡ File  View  Run  Statistics  Print  Options  Window  Help        READY
┌[■]=Execution Profile════════════════════════════════════2═══[↑]═
│ Total time: 10.988 sec     Display: Time
│ % of total: 99 %           Filter: All
│        Runs: 1 of 1          Sort: Frequency
│
│ #PIE#40      3.9005 sec  35%  ║=======================================
│ #PIE#28      3.5824 sec  32%  ║====================================
│ #PIE#30      0.9953 sec   9%  ║==========
│ #PIE#45      0.7683 sec   7%  ║========
│ #PIE#100     0.5742 sec   5%  ║======
│ #PIE#75      0.4814 sec   4%  ║=====
│ #PIE#55      0.2613 sec   2%  ║==
│ #PIE#101     0.1030 sec  <1%  ║=
│ #PIE#25      0.0437 sec  <1%  ║                        █
│ #PIE#33      0.0307 sec  <1%  ║
│ #PIE#34      0.0304 sec  <1%  ║
│ #PIE#35      0.0303 sec  <1%  ║
│ #PIE#31      0.0281 sec  <1%  ║
│ #PIE#39      0.0277 sec  <1%  ║
│ #PIE#29      0.0250 sec  <1%  ║
│ #PIE#26      0.0247 sec  <1%  ║
│ #PIE#27      0.0247 sec  <1%  ║
└Ctrl: D-Display F-Filter M-Module R-Remove════════════════════
```

Figure 4-26.   An Execution Profile window for the sample program

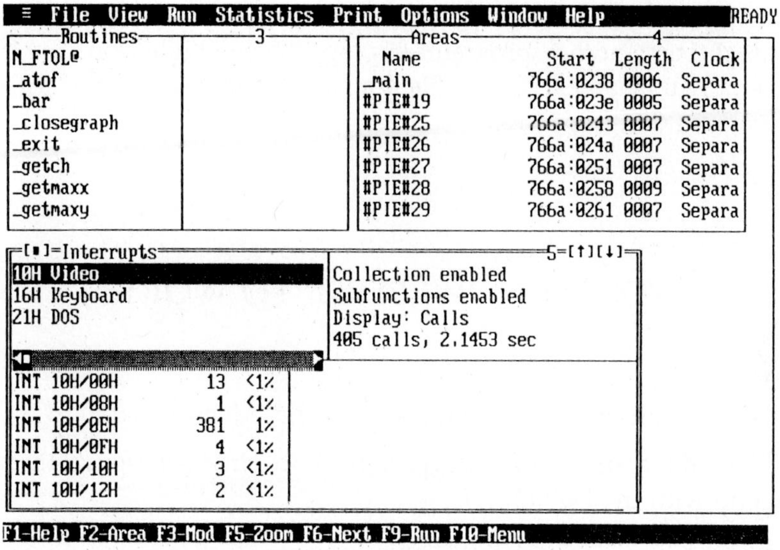

```
 ≡ File  View  Run  Statistics  Print  Options  Window  Help          READY
┌─Routines──────────────3─────┐┌─Areas──────────────────────4──────────┐
│M_FTOL@                      ││   Name        Start  Length  Clock    │
│_atof                        ││ _main       766a:0238 0006  Separa    │
│_bar                         ││ #PIE#19     766a:023e 0005  Separa    │
│_closegraph                  ││ #PIE#25     766a:0243 0007  Separa    │
│_exit                        ││ #PIE#26     766a:024a 0007  Separa    │
│_getch                       ││ #PIE#27     766a:0251 0007  Separa    │
│_getmaxx                     ││ #PIE#28     766a:0258 0009  Separa    │
│_getmaxy                     ││ #PIE#29     766a:0261 0007  Separa    │
└─────────────────────────────┘└───────────────────────────────────────┘
┌─[■]=Interrupts══════════════┐═════════════════════5=[↑][↓]═┐
│10H Video                    │Collection enabled            │
│16H Keyboard                 │Subfunctions enabled          │
│21H DOS                      │Display: Calls                │
│                             │405 calls, 2.1453 sec         │
│◄▒▒▒▒▒▒▒▒▒▒▒▒▒▒▒▒▒▒▒▒▒▒▒►    │                              │
│INT 10H/00H      13  <1%     │                              │
│INT 10H/08H       1  <1%     │                              │
│INT 10H/0EH     381   1%     │                              │
│INT 10H/0FH       4  <1%     │                              │
│INT 10H/10H       3  <1%     │                              │
│INT 10H/12H       2  <1%     │                              │
└─────────────────────────────┴──────────────────────────────┘
 F1-Help F2-Area F3-Mod F5-Zoom F6-Next F9-Run F10-Menu
```

Figure 4-27.   A composite Profiler window of Routines, Areas, and Interrupts windows

PLANNING PROGRAM DEVELOPMENT

As you can see, writing the original C, C++, or assembly language program is only the first step in producing the best, fastest, and perhaps smallest executable program. For a C program, for example, you would usually use the Borland C++ Professional tools in the following manner:

- Use the Turbo C++ integrated programming environment to write, compile, and link your C program. The compiler identifies any syntax errors that occur.

- Use the Turbo Debugger to eliminate stubborn bugs in programming logic. To use the Debugger, you must eliminate all syntax errors for the compiler and linker to produce an executable file.

- Use the Turbo Profiler to streamline program operation. The Profiler shows you where your program is spending time and suggests where you might try another programming approach. While you can use the Profiler any time an executable file is available, it is usually the last step in the program design process.

PUTTING YOUR KNOWLEDGE TO WORK

1. What is a debugger? What is a profiler?

2. Explain the difference between a syntax and a logical error.

3. Why would a breakpoint be preferred to single-stepping through a program with the Debugger?

4. How can you view the coprocessor stack when debugging an assembly language program?

5. Name two windows in which you can view variable values.

6. What is the Profiler's execution profile window used for?

7. How can the Profiler help eliminate programming bottlenecks?

8. Explain where in the program development cycle you might use the Debugger.

5

C AND C++ FOUNDATIONS

In this chapter you will learn

- The history of the C language

- The relationship between C and other popular programming languages

- The strengths and weaknesses of C

- What ANSI C is and what it means to you

- The history of the C++ language

- What object-oriented programming is

- The basic elements of a C program

- Some of the similarities and differences between C and C++

By now, you should be thoroughly familiar with the Borland C++ environment. You have installed the professional package, configured it to your personal requirements, and practiced using the C compiler, the Assembler, and the Debugger.

   Starting with this chapter, you will explore the origins, syntax, and usage of the C and C++ languages. A study of C's history is a worthy endeavor. For example, you may fully appreciate the architectural beauty of a brand new house that you have just seen completed. However, it is the underlying structure of the edifice that will determine whether or not the building will still be standing in fifty years. Likewise, to recognize the valid popularity of the C language you need to understand its fundamental strengths.

HISTORY OF C

A history of the C language begins with a discussion of the UNIX operating system, since both the system and most of the programs that run on it are written in C. However, C is not tied to UNIX or any other operating system or machine. This codevelopment environment has given C a reputation for being a *system programming language* because it is useful for writing compilers and operating systems. It can also write major programs in many different domains.

UNIX was originally developed in 1969, on what would now be considered a small DEC PDP-7 at Bell Laboratories in New Jersey. UNIX was written entirely in PDP-7 assembly language. By design, this operating system was intended to be "programmer-friendly," providing useful development tools, lean commands, and a relatively open environment. Soon after the development of UNIX, Ken Thompson implemented a compiler for a new language called B.

At this point we need to digress to the origins and history behind Ken Thompson's B language. A true C ancestry would look like this:

Algol 60	Designed by an international committee in early 1960
CPL	(Combined Programming Language) developed at both Cambridge and the University of London in 1963
BCPL	(Basic Combined Programming Language) developed at Cambridge, by Martin Richards, in 1967
B	Developed by Ken Thompson, Bell Labs, in 1970
C	Developed by Dennis Ritchie, Bell Labs, in 1972

ANSI C   The American National Standards Institute committee is
                          formed for the purpose of standardizing the C lan-
                          guage, in 1983

Algol appeared only a few years after FORTRAN was introduced. This new
language was more sophisticated and greatly influenced the design of
future programming languages. Its authors paid careful attention to the
regularity of syntax, modular structure, and other features associated with
high-level structured languages. Unfortunately, Algol never really caught
on in the United States, perhaps because of its abstractness and generality.

The inventors of CPL intended to bring Algol's lofty intent down to the
realities of an actual computer. But like Algol, CPL was big. This made the
language hard to learn and difficult to implement and explains its eventual
downfall. Still clinging to the best of what CPL had to offer, BCPL's creators
wanted to boil CPL down to its basic good features.

Bringing the discussion back to the origins of B, when Ken Thompson
designed the B language for an early implementation of UNIX, he was
trying to further simplify CPL. He succeeded in creating a very sparse
language that was well suited for use on the hardware available to him.
However, both BCPL and B may have carried their streamlining attempts a
bit too far. They became limited languages, useful only for certain kinds of
problems.

For example, shortly after Ken Thompson implemented the B language,
a new machine was introduced, the PDP-11. UNIX and the B compiler were
immediately transferred to this machine. While the PDP-11 was larger than
its PDP-7 predecessor, it was still quite small by today's standards. It had
only 24K of memory, of which the system used 16K, and one 512K fixed
disk. Some considered rewriting UNIX in B, but the B language was slow
due to its interpretive design. There was another problem: B was word-
oriented while the PDP-11 was byte-oriented. For these reasons, work
began in 1971 on a successor to B, appropriately named C.

Dennis Ritchie is credited with creating C, which restored some of the
generality lost in BCPL and B. He accomplished this with his shrewd use of
data types, while maintaining the simplicity and computer contact that
were the original design goals of CPL.

Many languages that have been developed by a single individual (C,
PASCAL, LISP, and APL) have a cohesiveness missing from languages developed by large programming teams (Ada, PL/I, and Algol 68). In addition, a
language written by one person typically reflects the author's field of

expertise. Dennis Ritchie was noted for his work in systems software—computer languages, operating systems, and program generators. With C having a genetic link to its creator, one can quickly understand why C is a language of choice for systems software design. C is a relatively low-level language that lets you specify every detail in an algorithm's logic to achieve maximum computer efficiency. But C is also a high-level language that can hide the details of the computer's architecture, thereby increasing programming efficiency.

Relationship to Other Languages

You may be wondering about C's relationship to other languages. Here is a possible continuum:

Direct Neural Path Communication

.

.

.

Artificial Intelligence
Operating System Command Languages
Problem-Oriented Languages
Machine-Oriented Languages
Assembly Language

.

.

.

Actual Hardware

Starting at the bottom of the continuum and moving upward, the languages go from the tangible and empirical to the elusive and theoretical. The dots represent major advancements, with many steps left out. Early ancestors of the computer, like the Jacquard loom (1805) or Charles Babbage's "analytical engine" (1834), were programmed in hardware. The day may well come when you will program a machine by plugging a neural path communicator into a socket implanted into the temporal lobe (language memory) or Broca's area (language motor area) of the brain's cortex.

Assembly languages provide a fairly painless way for programmers to work directly with a computer's built-in instruction set and go back to the first days of electronic computers. Assembly languages forced you to think in terms of the hardware; you had to specify every operation in the machine's terms. You were always moving bits in or out of registers, adding them, shifting register contents from one register to another, and finally storing the results in memory. This was a tedious and error-prone endeavor.

The first high-level languages, such as FORTRAN, were created as alternatives to assembly languages. High-level languages were by design much more general and abstract, and they allowed the programmer to think in terms of the problem at hand rather than in terms of the computer's hardware.

Unfortunately, the creators of high-level languages made the fallacious assumption that everyone who had been driving a standard would always prefer driving an automatic! Excited about providing ease in programming, they left out some necessary options. FORTRAN and Algol are too abstract for systems-level work; they are *problem-oriented languages*, the kind used for solving problems in engineering, science, or business. Programmers who wanted to write systems software still had to rely on their machine's assembler.

Out of this frustration, a few systems software developers took a step backwards or lower in terms of the continuum and created the category of *machine-oriented languages*. As you saw in C's genealogy, BCPL and B fit into this class of very low-level software tools. These languages were excellent for a specific machine, but not much use for anything else — they were too closely related to a particular architecture. The C language is one step above machine-oriented languages yet is still a step below most problem-oriented languages. It is close enough to the computer to give you great control over the details of an application's implementation, yet far enough away to ignore the details of the hardware. This is why the C language is both a high- and low-level language.

Strengths of C

All computer languages have a particular look. APL has its hieroglyphic appearance, assembly language has its columns of mnemonics, Pascal has its easily read syntax, and then there's C. Many programmers new to C will find its syntax cryptic and perhaps intimidating. C contains few of the familiar and friendly English-like syntax structures found in many other programming languages. Instead, C has unusual-looking operators and a plethora of pointers. You will quickly grow used to C's syntax. New C programmers will soon discover a variety of language characteristics whose roots stem back to its original hardware/software progenitor. The following sections highlight the strengths of the C language.

Small Size

There are fewer syntax rules in C than in many other languages, and you can write a top-quality C compiler that will operate in only 256K of total memory. There are actually more operators and combinations of operators in C than there are keywords.

Language Command Set

As you would therefore expect, C is an extremely small language. In fact, the original C language contained a mere 27 keywords. The ANSI C standard (discussed later in the chapter) has an additional five reserved words. Turbo C++ added 11 more keywords. This brings the total keyword count to 43.

C does not include many of the functions commonly defined as part of other programming languages. For example, C does not contain any built-in input and output capabilities, nor does it contain any arithmetic operations (beyond those of basic addition or subtraction) or string-handling functions. Since language lacking these capabilities is of little use, C provides a rich set of library functions for input/output, arithmetic operations, and string manipulation. This agreed-upon library set is so common that it is practically part of the language. One of the strengths of C, however, is its loose structure, which enables you to recode these functions easily.

Speed

The C code produced by most compilers tends to be very efficient. The combination of a small language, a small run-time system, and a language close to the hardware makes many C programs run at speeds close to their assembly language equivalents.

Not Strongly Typed

Unlike Pascal, which is a strongly typed language, C treats data types somewhat more loosely. This is a carryover from B, which was also an untyped language. This flexibility allows you to view data in different ways. For example, at one point in a program the application may need to see a variable as a character and yet for purposes of upcasing (by subtracting 32) may want to see the same memory cell as the ASCII equivalent of the character.

A Structured Language

C includes all of the control structures you would expect of a modern language. This is impressive when considering that C predated formal structured programming. C incorporates *for* loops, if and if-else constructs, case (switch) statements, and *while* loops. C also enables you to compartmentalize code and data by managing their scope. For example, C provides local variables for this purpose and call by value for subroutine data privacy.

Support of Modular Programming

C supports the concept of separate compilation and linking, which allows you to recompile only the parts of a program that have been changed during development. This feature can be extremely important when you are developing large programs, or even medium-sized programs on slow systems. Without support for modular programming, the amount of time required to compile a complete program can make the change, compile, test, and modify cycle prohibitively slow.

Easy Interface to Assembly Language Routines

There is a well-defined method of calling assembly language routines from most C compilers. Combined with the separation of compilation and linking, this makes C a strong contender in applications that require a mix of high-level and assembler routines. You can also integrate C routines into assembly language programs on most systems.

Bit Manipulation

In systems programming, you often need to manipulate objects at the bit level. Because C's origins are so closely tied to the UNIX operating system, the language provides a rich set of bit manipulation operators.

Pointer Variables

An operating system must be able to address specific areas of memory. This capability also enhances the execution speed of a program. The C language meets these design requirements by using pointers. While other languages implement pointers, C is noted for its ability to perform pointer arithmetic. For example, if the variable *index* points to the first element of an array *student_records*, *index+1* will be the address of the second element of *student_records*.

Flexible Structures

In C all arrays are one-dimensional. Multidimensional arrangements are built from combinations of these one-dimensional arrays. You can join arrays and structures (records) in any manner, creating database organizations that are limited only by your ability.

Memory Efficiency

C programs tend to be very memory efficient for many of the reasons that they tend to be fast. The lack of built-in functions saves programs from having to include support for functions that are not needed by a particular application.

Portability

Portability is a measure of how easy it is to convert a program that runs on one computer or operating system to run on another computer or operating system. Programs written in C are currently among the most portable in the computer world. This is especially true for mini- and microcomputers.

Special Function Libraries

There are many commercial function libraries available for all popular C compilers. There are libraries for graphics, file handling, database support, screen windowing, data entry, communications, and general support functions. By using these libraries, you can save a great deal of development time.

Weaknesses of C

There are no perfect programming languages. Different programming problems require different solutions. It is the software engineer's task to choose the best language for a project. On any project, this is one of the first decisions that you need to make, and it is nearly irrevocable once you start coding. The choice of a programming language can also make the difference between a project's success or failure. This section covers some of the weaknesses of the C language so that you will have a better idea of when and when *not* to use C for a particular application.

Not Strongly Typed

The fact that it is not strongly typed is one of C's strengths but is also one of its weaknesses. Technically, typing is a measure of how closely a language enforces the use of variable types (for example, integer and floating point are two different types of numbers). In some languages, you cannot assign one data type to another without invoking a conversion function. This protects the data from being compromised by unexpected roundoffs.

As mentioned, C will allow an integer to be assigned to a character variable or vice versa. This means that you have to manage your variables properly. For experienced programmers, this task presents no problem. However, novice program developers may want to remind themselves that mismatched data type assignments can be the source of side effects.

A side effect in a language is an unexpected change to a variable or other item. Because C is a weakly typed language, it gives you great flexibility to manipulate data. For example, the assignment operator, =, can appear more than once in the same expression. This feature, which you can use to your advantage, means that you can write expressions that have no definite value. If C had restricted the use of the assignment and similar operators, or had eliminated all side effects and unpredictable results, C would have lost much of its power and appeal as a high-level assembly language.

Lack of Run-Time Checking

C's lack of checking in the run-time system can cause many mysterious and transient problems to go undetected. The run-time system could have easily detected the fact, for example, that you just overran an array. This is one of the costs of streamlining a compiler for the sake of speed and efficiency.

Why C?

C's tremendous range of features—from bit-manipulation to high-level for-matted I/O—and its relative consistency from machine to machine have led to its acceptance in science, engineering, and business applications. It has directly contributed to the wide availability of the UNIX™ operating system on computers of all types and sizes.

Like any other powerful tool, however, C imposes a heavy responsibility on its users. C programmers quickly adopt various rules and conventions in order to make their programs understandable both to themselves and to others. In C, programming discipline is essential. The good news is that it comes almost automatically with practice.

THE ANSI C STANDARD

The ANSI (American National Standards Institute) committee has developed standards for the C language. This section describes some of the significant changes suggested by the committee. A number of these changes are intended to increase the flexibility of the language while others attempt to standardize features previously left to the discretion of the compiler implementor.

Previously, the only standard was *The C Programming Language* by B. Kernighan and D. Ritchie (Bell Telephone Labs Inc., 1988). This book was not specific on some language details, which led to a divergence among compilers. The ANSI standard strives to remove these ambiguities. Although a few of the proposed changes could cause problems for some previously written programs, they should not affect most existing code.

The ANSI C standard provides an even better opportunity to write portable C code. The standard has not corrected all areas of confusion in the language, however, and because C interfaces efficiently with machine hardware, many programs will always require some revision when you move them to a different environment. The ANSI committee adopted as guidelines several phrases that collectively have been called the "spirit of C." Some of those phrases are

- Trust the programmer.

- Don't prevent the programmer from doing what needs to be done.

- Keep the language small and simple.

Additionally, the international community was consulted to ensure that ANSI (American) standard C would be identical to the ISO (International Standards Organization) standard version. Because of these efforts, C is the only language that effectively deals with alternate collating sequences, enormous character sets, and multiuser cultures.

The following list highlights just some of the areas that the ANSI committee addressed:

Feature	Standardized
Data types	Character, integer, floating point, and enumeration
Comments	/* means opening, */ means closing, // means that anything to symbol's right is ignored by the compiler
Identifier length	31 characters to distinguish uniqueness
Standard identifiers and header files	An agreed-upon minimum set of identifiers and header files necessary to perform basic operations such as I/O

Preprocessor statements	The **#** in preprocessor directives can have leading white space (any combination of spaces and tabs), permitting indented preprocessor directives for clarity. Some earlier compilers insisted that all preprocessor directives begin in column one

New preprocessor directives	Two new preprocessor directives have been added
	    #if defined (*expression*)
	    #elif (*expression*)

Adjacent strings	Adjacent literal strings should be concatenated. For example, this would allow a **#define** directive to extend beyond a single line
Standard libraries	The ANSI standard specifies a basic set of system-level and external routines, such as **read** and **write**
Output control	An agreed-upon set of escape codes representing formatting control codes such as newline, new page, and tabs
Keywords	An agreed-upon minimum set of verbs used to construct valid C statements
sizeof	The committee agreed that the **sizeof** function should return the type *size_t*, instead of a variable of size integer, which would possibly be system limiting
Prototyping	All C compilers should handle programs that do/don't employ prototyping
Command-line arguments	For the C compiler to handle command-line arguments properly, an agreed-upon syntax was defined
void pointer type	The *void* keyword can be applied to functions that do not return a value. A function that does return a value can have its return value cast to *void* to indicate to the compiler that the value is being deliberately ignored

Structure handling	Structure handling has been greatly improved. The member names in structure and union definitions need not be unique. Structures can be passed as arguments to functions, returned by functions, and assigned to structures of the same type
Function declarations	Function declarations can include argument-type lists (function prototyping) to notify the compiler of the number and types of arguments
Hexadecimal character constants	Hexadecimal character constants can be expressed by using an introductory \x followed by from one to three hexadecimal digits (0-9, a-f, A-F). For example, 16 decimal = \x10, which can be written as 0x10 using the current notation
Trigraphs	Trigraphs define standard symbol sequences that represent characters that may not be readily available on all keyboards. For example, you can substitute ??< for the more elaborate { } symbol

EVOLUTION OF C++ AND OBJECT-ORIENTED PROGRAMMING

Simply stated, C++ is a superset of the C language. C++ retains C's power and flexibility in dealing with the hardware/software interface, its low-level system programming, and its efficiency, economy, and powerful expressions. More exciting, C++ brings the C language into the dynamic world of object-oriented programming and makes it a platform for high-level problem abstraction, going beyond even Ada in this respect. C++ accomplishes all this with a simplicity and support for modularity similar to Modula-2, while maintaining the compactness and execution efficiency of C.

This new hybrid language combines the standard procedural language constructs, familiar to so many programmers, and the object-oriented model, which you can exploit fully to produce a purely object-oriented solution to a problem. In practice, a C++ application can incorporate both the procedural programming model and the newer object-oriented model. For the beginning C++ programmer, not only is there a new language to learn but there is also a new way of thinking and problem solving.

HISTORY OF C++

Not surprisingly, C++ has an origin similar to C. While C++ is somewhat like BCPL and Algol 68, it also contains components of Simula67. C++ can overload operators and include declarations close to their first point of application, features that are found in Algol 68. The concept of subclasses (or derived classes) and virtual functions is taken from Simula67. Like so many other popular programming languages, C++ represents an evolution and refinement of some of the best features of previous languages. Of course, it is closest to C.

Bjarne Stroustrup of Bell Labs is credited with developing the C++ language in the early 1980s. C++ was originally developed to solve some very rigorous event-driven simulations for which considerations of efficiency precluded the use of other languages. C++ was first used outside Dr. Stroustrup's language development group in 1983, and by the summer of 1987, the language was still going through a natural refinement and evolution. To date, there is no equivalent ANSI C++ organization involved in standardizing the language. However, the ANSI C standard does contain some of the key features of C++, such as function prototyping.

One key design goal of C++ was to maintain compatibility with C. The idea was to preserve the integrity of millions of lines of previously written and debugged C code, the integrity of many existing C libraries, and the usefulness of previously developed C tools. Because of the high degree of success in achieving this goal, many programmers find the transition to C++ much simpler than the transition from some other language (Pascal, for example) to C.

C++ supports large-scale software development. Because it includes increased type checking, many of the side effects experienced with loosely typed C applications are no longer possible.

The most significant enhancement of the C++ language is its support for object-oriented programming (abbreviated OOP). You will have to modify your approach to problem solving to derive all of the benefits of C++.

For example, objects and their associated operations must be identified and all necessary classes and subclasses must be constructed.

What follows is an example of how an abstract data object in C++ can improve upon an older language's limited built-in constructs and features. For example, a Fortran software engineer may want to keep records on employees. You could accomplish this with multiple arrays of scalar data that represent each set of data. All of the arrays are necessarily tied together by a common index. Should there be ten fields of information on each employee, ten array accesses would have to be made using the same index location in order to represent the array of records.

In C++, the solution involves the declaration of a simple object, *employee_records*, that can receive messages to insert, delete, access, or display information contained within the object. The manipulation of the *employee_records* object can then be performed in a natural manner. Inserting a new record into the *employee_records* object becomes as simple as

```
employee_records.insert(new_employee)
```

The *employee_records* object has been appropriately declared, the **insert** function is a method suitably defined in the class that supports *employee_records* objects, and the *new_employee* parameter is the specific information that is to be added. Note that the class of objects called *employee_records* is not a part of the underlying language itself. Instead, you extend the language to suit the problem. By defining a new class of objects or by modifying existing classes (creating a subclass), you achieve a more natural mapping from the problem space to the program space (or solution space). The biggest challenge is mastering this powerful enhancement.

Small Enhancements to C

The following sections detail minor (non-object-oriented) enhancements to the C language.

Comments   C++ introduces the comment to end-of-line delimiter, //. However, you can still use the comment brackets, /* and */.

Enumeration Names   The name of an enumeration is a type name. This feature streamlines the notation by not requiring you to place the qualifier **enum** in front of the enumeration type name.

struct or class Names   The name of a **struct** or **class** is a type name. This class construct does not exist in C. In C++, you don't need to use the qualifier **struct** or **class** in front of a **struct** or **class** name.

Block Declarations   C++ permits declarations within blocks and after code statements. This feature allows you to declare an identifier closer to its first point of application. It even permits you to declare the index for a loop within the loop.

```
for(int index=0;index<10;index++)
```

Scope Qualifier Operator   The scope qualifier operator : : is a new operator used to resolve name conflicts. For example, if a function has a local declaration for a variable *vector_location* and there exists a global variable *vector_location*, the qualifier : :*vector_location* allows the global variable to be accessed within the scope of the local function. The reverse is not possible.

The const Specifier   You can use the **const** specifier to lock the value of an entity within its scope. You can also use it to lock the data pointed to by a pointer variable, the value of the pointer address, or the values of both the pointer address and the data pointed to.

Anonymous Unions   You can define unions without a name anywhere that you can define a variable or field. You can use this feature for the economy of memory storage by allowing two or more fields of a structure to share memory.

Explicit Type Conversions   You can use the name of a predefined type or programmer-defined type as a function to convert data from one type to another. Under certain circumstances, you can use such an explicit type conversion as an alternative to a cast conversion.

Function Prototyping   C++ will make many Pascal, Modula-2, and Ada programmers happy, since it permits the specification by name and type for each function parameter inside the parentheses next to the function name. For example,

```
float income_average(float incomes[], int size)
{
  .
  .
  .
```

The equivalent C interface, under the ANSI standard, would look exactly the same. In this case, C++ influenced the ANSI standards committee.

The C++ translator will perform type checking to ensure that the number and type of values sent into a function when it is invoked match the number and type of the formal arguments defined for the function. The translator also checks that the function's return type matches the variable used in the expression invoking the function. This type of parameter checking is missing in most C systems.

Function Overloading   In C++, functions can use the same function names and each of the overloaded functions can be distinguished on the basis of the number and type of its parameters.

Default Function Parameter Values   You can assign default values to trailing sets of C++ function parameters. In this case, you can invoke the function using fewer than the total number of parameters. Any missing trailing parameters assume their default values.

Functions with an Unspecified Number of Parameters   By employing the ellipsis, ..., you can define C++ functions with an unknown number and type of parameters. When you use this feature, parameter type checking is suppressed to allow flexibility in the interface to the function.

Reference Parameters in a Function   By using the ampersand operator, &, you can declare a formal function parameter as a reference parameter. For example,

```
void increment(int& value_address)
{
  value++;
}

int i;
increment(i);
  .
  .
  .
```

Because &*value_address* is defined as a reference parameter, its address is assigned to the address of *i* when **increment** is invoked. The value of *i* that is sent in is incremented within function **increment** and returned to variable *i* outside of function **increment**. The address of *i* need not be explicitly passed into function **increment**, as in C.

inline Specifier   You can use the **inline** specifier to instruct the compiler to perform inline substitution of a given function at the location where the function is invoked.

The new and delete Operators   The **new** and **delete** operators that are introduced in C++ allow for programmer-controlled allocation and deallocation of heap storage.

Void Pointers and Functions That Return Void   In C++, the type *void* is used to indicate that a function returns nothing. You can declare pointer variables to point to *void*. You can then assign such pointers to any other pointer that points to an arbitrary base type.

Major Enhancements to C

The major enhancement to C involves the concept of object-oriented programming. The following sections briefly explain the C++ enhancements that make object-oriented programming possible.

Class Constructs and Data Encapsulation   The class construct is the fundamental vehicle for object-oriented programming. A class definition can encapsulate all of the data declarations, the initial values, and the set of operations (called methods) for data abstraction. Objects can be declared to be of a given class and messages can be sent to objects. Additionally, each object of a specified class can contain its own private and public set of data representative of that class.

Struct Class   A struct in C++ is a subset of a class definition and has no private or protected sections. This subclass can contain both data (as is expected in ANSI C) and functions.

Constructors and Destructors   Constructor and destructor methods are used to guarantee the initialization of the data defined within an object of a specified class. When you declare an object, the specified initialization constructor is activated. Destructors automatically deallocate storage for the associated object when the scope in which the object is declared is exited.

Messages   As you have seen, the object is the basic fabric of object-oriented programming. You manipulate objects by sending them messages. You send messages to objects (variables declared to be of a given class) by using a mechanism similar to invoking a function. The set of possible messages that you can send to an object is specified in the class description for the object. Each object responds to a message by determining an appropriate action to take based on the nature of the message. For example, if *my_obj* represents an object, and *my_method* represents a method with a single integer parameter, you could send a message to the object by using the following statement:

```
my_obj.my_method(5);
```

Friends   The concept of data hiding and data encapsulation implies a denied access to the inner structures that make up an object. The private section of a class is normally off limits to any function outside of the class. C++ allows you to declare other functions outside functions or classes to

   Single statements
   Conditional statements
   Loops
   Subroutines

- Programs must report the results of the data manipulation.

- A well-written application incorporates all of the fundamentals just listed,
  expressed using good modular design, self-documenting code (for instance, meaningful variable names), and a good indentation scheme.

Your First C Program

The following C program will illustrate the basic components of a C application. You should enter each example as you read about it.

```
/*
 *    Your first example C program.
 *    Copyright (c) Chris H. Pappas and William H. Murray, 1990
 */

#include <stdio.h>

main()
{
  printf(" HELLO World! ");
  return(0);
}
```

There is a lot happening in this short piece of code. First is the comment
block:

```
/*
 *    Your first example C program.
 *    Copyright (c) Chris H. Pappas and William H. Murray, 1990
 */
```

All well-written source code includes meaningful comments. A *meaningful*
comment respects the intelligence of the programmer while not assuming
too much. In C or C++, comments begin with the /* symbols and end with
*/. The compiler ignores anything between these unique symbol pairs. The
next statement

```
#include <stdio.h>
```

represents one of C's unique features known as a preprocessor statement. A *preprocessor statement* is like a precompile instruction. In this case, the statement instructs the compiler to retrieve the code stored in the predefined *stdio.h* file into the source code on the line requested. *stdio.h* is called a header file. *Header files* can include symbolic constants, identifiers, and function prototypes and have these declarations pulled out of the main program for purposes of modularity.

Following the **#include** statement is the **main** function declaration:

```
main()
{
    .
    .
    .
return(0);
}
```

All C programs are made up of function calls. Every C program must have one called **main**. The **main** function is usually where program execution begins and ends with a **return(0)** from **main**. A 0 return value indicates that the program terminated without any errors.

Following the **main** function header is the body of the function itself. Notice the { and } symbol pairs. These are called braces. Technically, braces are used to encapsulate multiple statements. These statements may define the body for a function, or they may bundle statements that are dependent on the same logic control statement, as is the case when several statements are executed based on the validity of an if statement. In this example, the braces define the body of the main program.

The line

```
printf(" HELLO World! ");
```

is the only statement in the body of the main program and is the simplest example of an output statement. The **printf** function has been previously prototyped in *stdio.h*. Because no other parameters are specified, the sentence will be printed to the display monitor.

Your First C++ Program

The next example performs the same function as the previous one, but it takes advantage of the features that are unique to C++.

```
//
//   Your first C++ example program.
//   Copyright (c) Chris H. Pappas and William H. Murray, 1990
//

#include <iostream.h>

main()
{
  cout << " HELLO World! ";

  return(0);
}
```

There are three major differences. First, the comment designator has been changed from the /* and */ pair to a //. Second, the **#include** file name has been changed to *iostream.h,* with the third change involving a different output call, **cout**. Many of the examples in the book will highlight the sometimes subtle and sometimes dazzling differences between C and C++.

Your Second C Program

At this point, you are probably waiting for a slightly more meaningful example. The following program not only outputs information but also prompts the user for input.

```
/*
 *    This C program prompts the user for a specified length,
 *    in yards, and then outputs the value converted to
 *    feet and inches.
 *    Copyright (c) Chris H. Pappas and William H. Murray, 1990
 */

#include <stdio.h>

main()
{
  int yard,feet,inch;

  printf("Please enter the length to be converted: ");
  scanf("%d",&yard);
  while(yard > 0 ) {
    inch=36*yard;
    feet=3*yard;
    printf("%d yard(s) = \n",yard);
    printf("%d feet \n",feet);
    printf("%d inches \n",inch);
    printf("Please enter another length to be \n");
    printf("converted (0 stops program): ");
    scanf("%d",&yard);
```

```
    }
    printf(">>> End of Program <<<");
    return(0);
}
```

Data Declarations   The first new thing in the program is the declaration of three variables:

```
int yard,feet,inch;
```

All C variables must be declared before they are used. The syntax for declaring variables in C requires the definition of the variable's type before the name of the variable. One of the standard data types supplied by the C language is integer. In this example, the integer type is represented by the keyword *int*, and the three variables *yard*, *feet*, and *inch* are defined.

User Input   The next unconventional statement is used to input information from the keyboard:

```
printf("Please enter the length to be converted: ");
scanf("%d",&yard);
```

The **scanf** function has a requirement that is called a format string. *Format strings* define how the input data is to be interpreted and represented internally. The *"%d"* function parameter instructs the compiler to interpret the input as integer data (in Turbo C and C++ an integer occupies 2 bytes). (Chapter 6 contains a detailed explanation of all of the C and C++ language data types.)

Address Operator   In the previous listing, the integer variable *yard* was preceded by an ampersand symbol, **&**. The **&** is known as an *address operator*. Whenever a variable is preceded by this symbol, the compiler uses the address of the specified variable instead of the value stored in the variable. The **scanf** function has been written to expect the address of the variable to be filled.

Loop Structure   One of the simplest loop structures to code in C is the *while* loop:

```
while(yard > 0) {
     .
     .
     .
}
```

This pretest loop starts with the reserved word *while* followed by a Boolean expression that evaluates to either TRUE or FALSE. The opening brace, {, and closing brace, }, are optional and are only needed when more than one executable statement is to be associated with the loop repetition. Braced statements are sometimes referred to as compound statements, compound blocks, or code blocks.

If you are using compound blocks, make certain that you use the agreed-upon brace style. While the compiler doesn't care where you place the braces (skipped spaces/lines), programmers reading your code will certainly appreciate the style and effort. You place opening loop braces at the end of the test condition, and the closing brace in the same column as the first character in the test condition.

Formatted Output   The second program contains more complex **printf** function calls:

```
printf("%d yard(s) = \n", yard);
printf("%d feet \n",feet);
printf("%d inches \n",inch);
printf("Please enter another length to be \n");
printf("converted (0 stops program):  ");
```

If you are familiar with the PL/I language developed by IBM, you will be at home with the concept of a control string. Whenever a **printf** function is invoked to print not only literal strings (any set of characters between double quotation marks) but also values, a format string is required. The format string represents two things: a picture of how the output string is to look, and the format interpretation for each of the values printed. Format strings are always between double quotation marks.

The following table breaks down the first **printf** format string

("%d yard(s) = \n", yard)

into its separate components:

Control	Action
%d	Takes the value of *yard*, interprets it as an integer, and prints it
yard(s)	After printing the integer *yard*, skips one blank space and then prints the literal 'yard(s) ='
\n	Once the line is complete, executes a newline feed
,	In this example, the comma separates the format string from the variable name(s) used to satisfy all format descriptors (in this case, only one %d)

The next two **printf** statements are similar in execution. Each statement prints a formatted integer value, followed by a literal string, and ending with a newline feed. If you ran the program, your output would look much like this:

```
Please enter the length to be converted: 4
4 yard(s) =
12 feet
144 inches
Please enter another length to be
converted (0 stops program): 0
```

Table 5-1 lists all of the output control symbols and describes how they can be used in format strings. Table 5-2 lists all of the C language value formatting controls. As you learn more about the various C data types, you can refer back to these two tables for a reminder of how the various controls affect input and output.

Using the Turbo Debugger   To examine the actual operation of this C code, you can use the Turbo Debugger. From the Integrated Environment, go to the Options menu, select the Debugger submenu, and change "Source Debugging" to ON. Now, start the Turbo Debugger and single step through the program. Use the Watch window to keep an eye on the variables *yard*, *feet*, and *inch*. Figure 5-1 shows a Turbo Debugger window.

Table 5-1.   C Output Controls

Control	Action Taken
'\a'	Printer sounds a beep
'\b'	Printer moves back one column
'\f'	Printer skips to column 1, line 1, or next page
'\n'	Printer skips to column 1 of next line
'\r'	Printer prints a carriage return
'\t'	Printer skips to next tab position
'\0'	Printer prints nothing (null character)
'\\'	Printer prints one backslash, \
'\''	Printer prints one single quote, '

Table 5-2.   C Value Formatting Controls

Control	Action Taken
%d	Prints a decimal integer
%6d	Prints a decimal integer, at least six characters wide
%f	Prints a floating point
%6f	Prints a floating point, at least six characters wide
%.2f	Prints a floating point, two characters after decimal point
%6.2f	Prints a floating point, at least six characters wide and two characters after decimal point
%o	Octal (letter "o")
%x	Hexadecimal (%X for uppercase letters)
%c	Character
%s	Character string
%%	Itself

d - integer values, f - floating point values, o - base eight values, x - hexadecimal values, c - characters, and s - strings

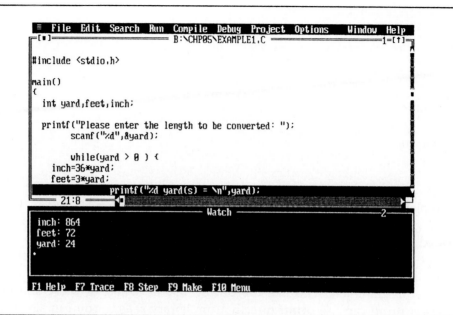

Figure 5-1.   Integrated Debugger converting 24 yards

Your Second C++ Program

The following C++ example is identical in function to the previous C example. However, there are some minor variations in the syntax.

```
//
//    This C++ program prompts the user for a specified length,
//    in yards, and then outputs the value converted to
//    feet and inches.
//    Copyright (c) Chris H. Pappas and William H. Murray, 1990
//

#include <iostream.h>

main()
{
  int yard,feet,inch;

  cout << "Please enter the length to be converted:  \n";
  cin >> yard;
```

```
  while(yard > 0 ) {
    inch=36*yard;
    feet=3*yard;
    cout << "yard(s) = " << yard << "\n";
    cout << "feet = " << feet << "\n";
    cout << "inches = " << inch << "\n";
    cout << "Please enter another length to be \n";
    cout << "converted (0 stops program): ";
    cin >> yard;
  }
  cout << ">>> End of Program <<<";
  return(0);
}
```

The **cout** and **cin** statements are the only major difference between the C++ example and its C counterpart. These statements use the < < (put to) and > > (get from) stream operators. These two operators have been overloaded to handle the output/input of all the predefined types. They can also be overloaded to handle the output/input of user-defined types such as rational numbers.

C++ programmers who like the power and flexibility of the C output function **printf** can use **printf** directly from library *stdio.h*. You can also use the **cout** form. The next two statements show the C and C++ function form equivalents:

```
printf("%d yard(s) = \n", yard);
cout << "yard(s) = " << yard << "\n";
```

Using the Turbo Debugger

Now, you will use the Turbo Debugger to examine the actual operation of this C++ code. From the Integrated Environment, go to the Options menu, select the Debugger submenu, and change "Source Debugging" to ON. Now, start the Turbo Debugger, and single step through the program. Use the Watch window to keep an eye on the variables *yard*, *feet*, and *inch*. Figure 5-2 shows a Turbo Debugger window.

Files

Of course, there will be times when an application wants either its input or output to deal directly with files rather than the keyboard and display

```
 ≡ File  Edit  Search  Run  Compile  Debug  Project  Options     Window  Help
╒[■]════════════════════ B:\CHP05\EXAMPLE2.CPP ═══════════════════════1=[↑]╕
│#include <iostream.h>                                                       ▓
│                                                                            ▓
│main()                                                                      ▓
│{                                                                           ·
│   int yard,feet,inch;                                                      ▓
│                                                                            ▓
│   cout << "Please enter the length to be converted:  \n";                  ▓
│   cin >> yard;                                                             ▓
│                                                                            ▓
│   while(yard >= 0 ) {                                                      ▓
│     inch=36*yard;                                                          ▓
│     feet=3*yard;                                                           ▓
│     cout << "yard(s) = " << yard << "\n";                                  ▓
╞═ 21:13 ═══╡▒▒▒▒▒▒▒▒▒▒▒▒▒▒▒▒▒▒▒▒▒▒▒▒▒▒▒▒▒▒▒▒▒▒▒▒▒▒▒▒▒▒▒▒▒▒▒▒▒▒▒▒▒▒▒▒▒▒▒▒█
╒══════════════════════════════ Watch ════════════════════════════════2═╕
│  inch: 1296                                                              │
│  feet: 108                                                              │
│  yard: 36                                                              │
│  ·                                                                      │
│                                                                         │
│                                                                         │
╘═════════════════════════════════════════════════════════════════════════╛
 F1 Help  F7 Trace  F8 Step  F9 Make  F10 Menu
```

Figure 5-2.   Integrated Debugger converting 36 yards

monitor. This brief introduction is an example of how to declare and use simple data files:

```
/*
 *     This C program demonstrates how to declare and use both
 *     input and output files.  The input file earnings.dat
 *     contains integer values that are taxed at a rate of
 *     20% for earnings less than $5000, and at 50% if greater
 *     than or equal to $5000.  The calculated tax value
 *     is written to the taxrate.dat file in integer form.
 *     Copyright (c) Chris H. Pappas and William H. Murray, 1990
 */

#include <stdio.h>

main()
{
  int earnings,tax;
  FILE *fin,*fout;

  fin=fopen("earnings.dat","r");
  fout=fopen("taxrate.dat","w");
```

```
while (!feof(fin)) {
  fscanf(fin,"%d",&earnings);
  fprintf(fout,"Earnings = %d greenbacks\n",earnings);
  if (earnings < 5000)
    tax=0.2*earnings;
    else
      tax=0.5*earnings;
  fprintf(fout,"Tax = %d greenbacks\n",tax);
 }

 return(0);
}
```

Each file in a C program must be associated with a *file pointer*. The file pointer points to information that defines various things about a file, including the path to the file, its name, and its status. A file pointer is a pointer variable of type **FILE** and is defined in *stdio.h*. The following statement from the example program declares two files *fin* and *fout*:

```
FILE *fin,*fout;
```

The next two statements in the program

```
fin=fopen("earnings.dat","r");
fout=fopen("taxrate.dat","w");
```

open two separate streams and associate each file with its respective stream. The statements also return the file pointer for each file. Since these are pointers to files, your application should never alter their values.

The second parameter to the **fopen** function is the file mode. Files may be opened in either text or binary mode. When in text mode, most C compilers translate carriage return-linefeed sequences into newline characters on input. During output, the opposite occurs. However, binary files do not go through such translations. Table 5-3 lists all of the valid file modes.

C performs its own file closing automatically whenever the application closes. However, at times you may want direct control over when a file is

Table 5-3.   C Valid File Modes

Mode	Usage
"r"	Opens a text file for reading
"w"	Opens a text file for writing
"r+"	Opens a text file for update reading or writing
"w+"	Creates a new file for update
"a"	Opens a file in append mode or creates a file for writing if the file does not exist
"a+"	Opens a file in append mode for updating at the end of the file or creates a file for writing if the file does not exist
"rb"	Opens a binary file for reading
"wb"	Opens a binary file for writing

closed. The following listing shows the same program modified to include the necessary closing function calls:

```
/*
 *    This C program demonstrates how to declare and use both
 *    input and output files.  The input file earnings.dat
 *    contains integer values that are taxed at a rate of
 *    20% for earnings less than $5000, and at 50% if greater
 *    than or equal to $5000.  The calculated tax value
 *    is written to the taxrate.dat file in integer form.
 *    Copyright (c) Chris H. Pappas and William H. Murray, 1990
 */

#include <stdio.h>

main()
{
  int earnings,tax;
  FILE *fin,*fout;

  fin=fopen("earnings.dat","r");
  fout=fopen("taxrate.dat","w");
```

```
while (!feof(fin)) {
   fscanf(fin,"%d",&earnings);
   fprintf(fout,"Earnings = %d dollars\n",earnings);
   if (earnings < 5000)
      tax=0.2*earnings;
      else
         tax=0.5*earnings;
   fprintf(fout,"Tax = %d dollars\n",tax);
   }
fclose(fin);
fclose(fout);

return(0);
}
```

The following program performs the same function as the previous one, but is coded in C++:

```
//
//    This C++ program demonstrates how to declare and use both
//    input and output files.  The input file earnings.dat
//    contains integer values that are taxed at a rate of
//    20% for earnings less than $5000, and at 50% if greater
//    than or equal to $5000.  The calculated tax value
//    is written to the taxrate.dat file in integer form.
//    Copyright (c) Chris H. Pappas and William H. Murray, 1990
//

#include <fstream.h>

main()
{
   int earnings,tax;
   ifstream f_in("a:\\earnings.dat");
   ofstream f_out("a:\\taxrate.dat");

   f_in >> earnings;
   while (!f_in.eof()) {
      f_out << "Earnings = " << earnings << " dollars\n";
      if (earnings < 5000)
         tax=0.2*earnings;
         else
            tax=0.5*earnings;
      f_out << "Tax = " << tax << " dollars\n";
      f_in >> earnings;
   }

   f_in.close();
   f_out.close();
   return(0);
}
```

Disk file input and output are slightly different in C++ than with C. Input and output facilities are not defined within the C++ language, but rather are implemented in C++ and provided as a component of a C++ standard library. This library is referred to as the **iostream** library. To perform file I/O the derived classes **ifstream** and **ofstream** must be used.

The short sample program above demonstrates how to declare an input file *f_in* and an output file *f_out* which are both opened in the default text mode. The program reads in integer values from *earnings.dat*, performs a simple calculation, and writes the results to *taxrate.dat*.

Some of you looking at the code may think that the file structure used looks slightly different from what you are normally used to. If so, you have probably been using the file structure for a C++ compiler using Release 1.2 specifications. The sample program was written using the new Release 2.0 standard. Chapter 11 will explain the new Release 2.0 file structure and discuss those changes necessary to upgrade a Release 1.2 program to the improved format.

PUTTING YOUR KNOWLEDGE TO WORK

1. Why is C called a middle-level language?

2. How large is the C language command set?

3. What is the advantage of a loosely typed language?

4. What is the disadvantage of a loosely typed language?

5. What is the ANSI committee trying to accomplish?

6. Give one example of a feature the ANSI committee had to detail.

7. Why is C++ called a hybrid language?

8. What is OOP?

9. What is a friend?

10. List the nine components of a program.

6

DATA

In this chapter you will learn

- What a valid identifier is

- How to declare and use the standard C data types: **char**, **int**, **float**, **double**, and **enum**

- How to use the **unsigned** modifier to change the range of values a variable can hold

- What a **const** and **volatile** identifier is used for

- Why the **pascal** and **cdecl** modifiers are so useful for programs called/calling other high-level language code

- About C's type conversions

- About the four storage classes: **auto**, **register**, **static**, and **extern**, and how they affect an identifier's scope

- How to use the various C operators, including bitwise, logical, relational, and others

- What operator precedence levels mean and how they apply to the C operators

- What a C library is and how it relates to header files

What you have learned so far of C and the C++ enhancements is only the tip of the iceberg. Starting with this chapter, you will explore the underlying structures of the C and C++ language. The great stability of C++ comes from the standard C and C++ data types and the modifiers and operations that you can perform on them.

WHAT ARE IDENTIFIERS?

Identifiers are the names that you use to represent variables, constants, types, functions, and labels in your program. You create an identifier by specifying it in the declaration of a variable, type, or function. You can then use the identifier in later program statements to refer to the associated item.

An identifier is a sequence of one or more letters, digits, or underscores that begins with a letter or underscore. Identifiers can contain any number of characters, but only the first 31 characters are significant to the compiler. (Other programs that read the compiler output, such as the linker, may recognize even fewer characters.)

C and C++ are case sensitive. This means that the compiler considers uppercase and lowercase letters to be distinct characters. For example, the compiler sees the variables *MAX* and *max* as two unique identifiers representing different memory cells. This feature enables you to create distinct identifiers that have the same spelling but different cases for one or more of the letters.

The selection of case can also help a programmer understand your code. For example, identifiers declared in *include* header files are often created with only uppercase letters. Because of this, whenever you encounter an uppercase identifier in the source file, you can assume that that identifier's definition is in an *include* header file.

Although it is syntactically legal, you should not use leading underscores in identifiers that you create. Often, identifiers beginning with an underscore can cause conflicts with the names of system routines or variables, and produce errors. As a result, programs that contain names beginning with leading underscores are not guaranteed to be portable.

Here are some sample identifiers:

```
k
count
temp1
reservations_plane1
fathom_6_ft
```

See if you can determine why the following identifiers are illegal:

```
1st_place
#lbs
action_taken!
```

The first identifier is illegal because it begins with a decimal number. The second identifier begins with a # symbol, and the last identifier ends with an illegal character.

Guess whether the following identifiers are legal or not:

```
O
OO
OOO
____
```

Actually, all four identifiers are legal. The first three use a different number of the uppercase letter "O." The fourth identifier consists of five underscore characters. These identifiers are not meaningful, but they are legal. However, while these identifiers meet the letter of the law, they greatly miss the spirit of the law, since all identifiers, function names, constants, and variables should use meaningful names.

Since uppercase and lowercase letters are considered distinct characters, each of the following identifiers is unique:

```
SIZE
size
Size
siZe
```

The C compiler's case-sensitivity can create tremendous headaches for the novice C programmer. For example, trying to reference the **printf** function, when it was typed **PRINTF**, will invoke unknown identifier complaints from the compiler. In Pascal, however, a **writeln** is a **WRITELN** is a **WriteLn**.

With experience, you would probably detect the preceding **printf** error, but can you see what's wrong with this next statement?

```
printf("%C",one_character);
```

Assuming that *one_character* was defined properly, you might think that nothing was wrong. Remember, however, that C is case sensitive—the "%C" print format has never been defined; only "%c" has.

For more advanced applications, some linkers may further restrict the number and type of characters for globally visible symbols. Also, the linker, unlike the compiler, may not distinguish between uppercase and lowercase letters. By default, the Turbo C++ Professional TLINK sees all public and external symbols, such as *MYVARIABLE, MyVariable,* and *myvariable,* as the same. However, you can make TLINK case sensitive by using the /c option. This would force TLINK to see the three example variables above as being unique. See your *Turbo C++ Programmer's Guide* for additional information on how to use this switch.

Finally, an identifier cannot have the same spelling and case as a keyword. The next section lists C and C++ keywords.

KEYWORDS

Keywords are predefined identifiers that have special meanings to the C compiler. You can use them only as defined. Remember, the name of a program identifier cannot have the same spelling and case as a C keyword. The C language keywords are listed in Table 6-1.

You cannot redefine keywords. However, you can specify text to be substituted for keywords before compilation by using C preprocessor directives (see Chapter 12).

STANDARD C AND C++ DATA TYPES

When you write a program, you are working with some kind of information that you can usually represent by using one of the seven basic C and C++ types: text or **char**, integer values or **int**, floating-point values or **float**, double floating-point values or **double**, enumerated or **enum**, valueless or **void**, and pointers.

Table 6-1.   Turbo C and C++ Keywords

C Keywords

asm	template	do	register
catch	this	double	return
class	virtual	else	short
delete	_ cs	enum	signed
_ export	_ ds	extern	sizeof
friend	_ es	far	static
inline	_ ss	float	struct
_ loadds	auto	for	switch
new	break	goto	typedef
operator	case	huge	union
private	catch	if	unsigned
protected	cdecl	int	void
public	char	interrupt	volatile
_ regparam	const	long	while
_ saveregs	continue	near	
_ seg	default	pascal	

C++ Keywords
not found in ANSI C

asm	friend	private	this
catch	inline	protected	virtual
class	new	public	
delete	operator	template	

Pseudoregister Variables

_ AH	_ BX	_ DL
_ AL	_ CH	_ DX
_ AX	_ CL	_ FLAGS
_ BH	_ CX	_ SI
_ BL	_ DH	_ SP
_ BP	_ DI	

- Text (data type **char**) is made up of single characters (a, Z, ?, 3) and strings ("He who has an ear to hear, let him hear"), usually 8 bits, or 1 byte, with the range of 0 to 255.

- Integer values are those numbers you learned to count with (1, 2, 7, −45, and 1345), usually, 16 bits wide, 2 bytes, or 1 word, with the range of −32,768 to 32,767.

- Floating-point values are numbers that have a fractional portion such as π (3.14159), and exponents (7.563×1021). These are also known as real numbers (usually, 32 bits, 4 bytes, or 2 words, with the range of 3.4E−38 to 3.4E+38).

- Double floating-point values have an extended range (usually, 64 bits, 8 bytes, or 4 words, with the range of 1.7E-308 to 1.7E+308).

- Enumerated data types allow for user-defined types.

- The type **void** signifies values that occupy 0 bits and have no value. You can also use this type to create generic pointers (see Chapter 10).

- The pointer data type doesn't hold information as do the other data types. Instead, each pointer contains the address of the memory location holding the actual data (see Chapter 10).

Characters

Every language uses a set of characters to construct meaningful statements. For instance, all books written in English use combinations of 26 letters of the alphabet, the 10 digits, and the punctuation marks. Similarly, C and C++ programs are written with a set of characters consisting of the 26 lowercase letters of the alphabet,

```
abcdefghijklmnopqrstuvwxyz
```

the 26 uppercase letters of the alphabet,

```
ABCDEFGHIJKLMNOPQRSTUVWXYZ
```

the 10 digits,

```
0 1 2 3 4 5 6 7 8 9
```

and the following symbols:

```
+ - * / =, . _ : ; ? \ " ' ~ | ! # % $ & ( ) [ ] { } ^ @
```

C and C++ also use the blank space, sometimes referred to as whitespace. Combinations of symbols, with no intervening blank space, are also valid C and C++ characters. In fact, the following code is a mixture of valid C and C++ symbols:

```
++ -- == && | | << >> >= <= += -= *= /= ?: :: /* */ //
```

The following C program illustrates how to declare and use **char** data types:

```c
/*
 *    A C program demonstrating the char data type and showing
 *    how a char variable can be interpreted as an integer.
 *    Copyright (c) Chris H. Pappas and William H. Murray, 1990
 *
 */

#include <stdio.h>

main()
{
  char uppercase_A='A', lowercase_a='a';

  printf("The character \'%c\' has a decimal ASCII"  \
         " value of %d\n",uppercase_A,uppercase_A);
  printf("The ASCII value represented in hexadecimal"\
         " is %X\n",uppercase_A);
  printf("If you add sixteen will you get \'%c\'\n",
          uppercase_A+16);
  printf("The calculated ASCII value in hexadecimal" \
         " is %X\n",(uppercase_A+16));
  printf("The character \'%c\' has a decimal ASCII"  \
         " value of %d\n",lowercase_a,lowercase_a);

  return(0);
}
```

The output from the program looks like this:

```
The character 'A' has a decimal ASCII value of 65
The ASCII value represented in hexadecimal is 41
If you add sixteen will you get 'Q'
The calculated ASCII value in hexadecimal is 51
The character 'a' has a decimal ASCII value of 97
```

The %X format control instructs the compiler to interpret the value as a hexadecimal number.

Three Integers

Turbo C++ Professional actually supports three types of integers. Along with the standard type **int**, the compiler supports **short int** and **long int**. These are most often abbreviated to **short** and **long**. Since the C language is so tied to the hardware, the actual sizes of **short**, **int**, and **long** depend upon the implementation. However, a variable of type **short** will not be larger than one of type **long**. Turbo C++ allocates 2 bytes for both types **short** and **int**. The type **long** occupies 4 bytes of storage.

Unsigned Modifier

Many C and C++ compilers also allow you to declare certain types as **unsigned**. Currently, you can apply the **unsigned** modifier to four types: **char**, **short int**, **int**, and **long int**. When one of these data types is modified to be **unsigned**, you can think of the range of values it holds as representing the numbers displayed on a car odometer. An automobile odometer starts at 000..., increases to a maximum of 999..., and then recycles back to 000..., it also only displays positive whole numbers. In a similar way, an unsigned data type can hold only positive values from 0 to the maximum number that can be represented.

For example, suppose that you are designing a new data type called **tiny**, and decide that **tiny** variables can hold only 3 bits. You also decide that the data type **tiny** is signed by default. Since a variable of type **tiny** can only contain the bit patterns 000 through 111 (or 0 to 7 decimal), and you want to represent both positive and negative values, you have a problem. You can't have both positive and negative numbers in the range 0 to 7 because you need one of the 3 bits to represent the sign of the number. Therefore, **tiny**'s range is a subset. When the most significant bit is 0, the value is positive. When the most significant bit is 1, the value is negative. This gives a **tiny** variable the range of −4 to +3, as shown in Table 6-2.

However, applying the unsigned data type modifier to a **tiny** variable would yield a range of 0 to 7, since the most significant bit can be combined with the lower 2 bits to represent a broader range of positive values instead of identifying the sign of the number (see Table 6-3).

This simple analogy holds true for any of the valid C data types defined to be of type **unsigned**. The storage and range for the fundamental C data types is summarized in Table 6-4. Table 6-5 lists the valid data type modifiers in all of the various legal and abbreviated combinations.

Table 6-2.   The Hypothetical Signed **tiny** Data Type

Unique Combinations of 0's and 1's	Decimal Equivalent
000	+0
001	+1
010	+2
011	+3
100	−1
101	−2
110	−3
111	−4

Floating Point

Turbo C++ uses the three floating-point types: **float, double,** and **long dou-ble.** While the ANSI C standard does not specifically define the values and storage to be allocated for each of these types, the standard does require each type to hold a minimum of any value in the range 1E−37 to 1E+37. As you see in Table 6-4, the Turbo C++ environment has greatly expanded upon this minimum requirement. Most C compilers have always had

Table 6-3.   The Hypothetical Unsigned **tiny** Data Type

Unique Combinations of 0's and 1's	Decimal Equivalent
000	+0
001	+1
010	+2
011	+3
100	+4
101	+5
110	+6
111	+7

Table 6-4.   Fundamental Type Storage and Range of Values

Type	Storage	Range of Values (Internal)
char	1 byte	−128 to 127
int	2 bytes	−32,768 to 32,767
short	2 bytes	−32,768 to 32,767
long	4 bytes	−2,147,483,648 to 2,147,483,647
unsigned char	1 byte	0 to 255
unsigned int	2 bytes	0 to 65,535
unsigned short	2 bytes	0 to 65,535
unsigned long	4 bytes	0 to 4,294,967,295
float	4 bytes	3.4E−38 to 3.4E+38
double	8 bytes	1.7E−308 to 1.7E+308
long double	10 bytes	3.4E−4932 to 1.1E+4932
pointer	2 bytes	(near, _cs, _ds, _es, _ss pointers)
pointer	4 bytes	(far,huge pointers)

Table 6-5.   Valid Data Type Modifier Abbreviations

Type Modifier	Abbreviations
signed char	char
signed int	signed, int
signed short int	short, signed short
signed long int	long, signed long
unsigned char	no abbrv.
unsigned int	unsigned
unsigned short int	unsigned short
unsigned long int	unsigned long

the types **float** and **double**. The ANSI C committee added the third type **long double**. Here are some examples of floating-point numbers:

```
float body_temp = 98.6;
double my_balance;
long double IRS_balance;
```

You can use **long double** on any computer, even one that has only two types of floating-point numbers. However, if the computer does not have a **long double** data type, the data item will have the same size and storage capacity as a **double**.

The following C++ program illustrates how to declare and use **float** variables:

```
//
//      A C++ program demonstrating use of the float data type.
//      Copyright (c) Chris H. Pappas and William H. Murray, 1990
//

#include <iostream.h>

main()
{

  long original_flags = cin.flags();
  float float1 = 3601.234, float2 = 0.0028, float3 = -142.1;

  cout << "\t\t" << float1 << "\t";
  cout.setf(ios::scientific);
  cout << float1 << "\n\n";

  cout.setf(ios::fixed);
  cout << "\t\t" << float2 << "\t\t";
  cout.flags(original_flags);
  cout.setf(ios::scientific);
  cout << float2 << "\n\n";

  cout.setf(ios::fixed);
  cout << "\t\t" << float3 << "\t";
  cout.flags(original_flags);
  cout.setf(ios::scientific);
  cout << float3 << "\n\n";

  cout.flags(original_flags);

  return(0);
}
```

The output looks like this:

```
3601.233887    3.601234e+03

0.0028         2.8e-03

-142.100006    -1.421e+02
```

Notice the different value printed depending on the print format specification **fixed** (default) or **scientific**.

Enumerated

When an enumerated variable is defined, it is associated with a set of named integer constants called the *enumeration set* (also see Chapter 12). The variable can contain any one of the constants at any time, and you can refer to the constants by name. For example, the definition

```
enum tank_pressure { OK,
                     LOW,
                     GULP=5 }  bills_tank;
```

creates the **enum** type of *tank_pressure,* the **enum** constants of *OK, LOW,* and *GULP,* and the **enum** variable of *bills_tank.* All the constants and variables are of type **int,** and each constant is automatically provided a default initial value unless another value is specified. In the preceding example, the constant name *OK* has the **int** value 0 by default since it is the first in the list and was not specifically overridden. The value of *LOW* is 1 since it occurs immediately after a constant with the value 0. The constant *GULP* was specifically initialized to the value 5. If another constant were included after *GULP,* it would have the **int** value of 6.

Having created *tank_pressure,* you can later define another variable, *chriss_tank,* as follows:

```
enum tank_pressure chriss_tank;
```

After this statement, it is legal to say

```
bills_tank  = OK;
chriss_tank = GULP;
```

which will place the value 0 into the variable *bills_tank,* and the value 5 into the variable *chriss_tank.*

One common mistake is to think that *tank_pressure* is a variable. It is a "type" of data that you can use later to create additional **enum** variables, such as *bills_tank.*

Since the name *bills_tank* is an enumeration variable of type *tank_pressure,* you can use *bills_tank* on the left of an assignment operator and it can receive a value. This occurred when the **enum** constant *OK* was explicitly assigned to it. The names *OK, LOW,* and *GULP* are names of constants; they are not variables and you cannot change their values.

You can perform tests on the variables in conjunction with the constants. The following C program shows a complete program that uses the preceding definitions:

```
/*
*       A C program demonstrating the use of enumeration variables
*       Copyright (c) Chris H. Pappas and William H. Murray, 1990
*/

#include <stdio.h>

main()
{
   enum tank_pressure { OK,
                        LOW,
                        GULP=5 }  bills_tank;
   enum tank_pressure chriss_tank;

   bills_tank = OK;
   chriss_tank = GULP;

   printf("The value of bills_tank is %d\n",bills_tank);

   if (chriss_tank == GULP)
     printf("The value of chriss_tank is %d\n",chriss_tank);

   if (bills_tank == chriss_tank)
     printf("bills_tank equals chriss_tank");
   else
     printf("bills_tank does not equal chriss_tank");

   return(0);
}
```

ACCESS MODIFIERS

The **const** and **volatile** modifiers are new to C and C++. They were added by the ANSI C standard to help identify variables that will never change (**const**) and variables that can change unexpectedly (**volatile**).

const Modifier

At times, you may need to use a value that does not change throughout the program. Such a quantity is called a *constant*. For example, if a program deals with the area and circumference of a circle, it will frequently use the constant value *pi=3.14159*. In a financial program, an interest rate might be a constant. In such cases, you can improve the readability of the program by giving the constant a descriptive name.

Using descriptive names can also help prevent errors. Suppose that you use a constant value (not a constant variable) at many points throughout the program. Suppose also that you type the wrong value at one or more of these points. If the constant has a name, a typographical error would then be detected by the compiler because you probably didn't declare the incorrect name.

Suppose that you are writing a program that repeatedly uses the value π. You might think that you should declare a variable called *pi* with an initial value of 3.14159. However, the program should not be able to change the value of a constant. For instance, if you inadvertently wrote *pi* to the left of an equal sign, the value of *pi* would be changed, causing all subsequent calculations to be in error. C and C++ provide mechanisms that prevent such errors from occurring—that is, you can establish constants whose values cannot be changed.

In C and C++, you declare a constant by writing **const** before the keyword (for instance, **int, float, double**) in the declaration. For example:

```
const int MAX=9,INTERVAL=15;
const float rate=0.7;
int index=0,count=10,object;
double distance=0.0,velocity;
```

Because a constant cannot be changed, it must be initialized in its declaration. The **int** constants *MAX* and *INTERVAL* are declared with values 9 and 15, respectively. The constant *rate* is of type **float** and has been initialized to 0.7. In addition, the **int** (nonconstant) variables *index, count,* and *object* have been declared. Initial values of 0 and 10 have been established for *index* and *count,* respectively. Finally, *distance* and *velocity* have been declared to be (nonconstant) variables of type **double**. An initial value of 0.0 has been established for *distance.*

You use constants and variables in the same way in a program. The only difference is that you cannot change the initial values assigned to the constants—that is, the constants are not *lvalues;* they cannot appear to the left of an equal sign.

Normally, the assignment operation assigns the value of the right-hand operand to the storage location named by the left-hand operand. Therefore, the left-hand operand of an assignment operation (or the single operand of a unary assignment expression) must be an expression that refers to a modifiable memory location.

Expressions that refer to memory locations are called *lvalue expressions*. Expressions referring to modifiable locations are modifiable *lvalues*. One example of a modifiable *lvalue* expression is a variable name declared without **const**.

#define Constants

C and C++ provide another method for establishing constants — the **#define** compiler directive. Suppose that you have the following statement at the beginning of a program:

```
#define VOLUME 10
```

The form of this statement is **#define** followed by two strings of characters separated by spaces. When the program is compiled, several passes are made through it. First, the compiler preprocessor carries out the **#include** and **#define** directives. When the preprocessor encounters the **#define** directive, it replaces every occurrence of *VOLUME* in the source files with the number 10.

In general, when the preprocessor encounters a **#define** directive, it replaces every occurrence of the first string of characters (*VOLUME*) in the program with the second string of characters (10). Additionally, no value can be assigned to *VOLUME* because it has never been declared as a variable. As a result of the syntax, *VOLUME* has all the attributes of a constant. Note that the **#define** statement is not terminated by a semicolon. If a semicolon followed the value 10, every occurrence of *VOLUME* would be replaced with 10;. The directive replaces the first string with *everything* in the second string.

The short programs that have been discussed so far would usually be stored in a single file. If a statement such as the **#define** for *VOLUME* appeared at the beginning of the file, the substitution of 10 for *VOLUME* would take place throughout the program. In Chapter 10, you will learn how to divide a program into many subprograms, with each subprogram being divided into separate files. Under these circumstances, the **#define** compiler directive would be effective only for the single file in which it is written.

You have just learned two methods for defining constants: the keyword **const** and the **#define** compiler directive. In many programs, the action of each of these two methods is essentially the same. On the other hand, the use of the modifier keyword **const** results in a "variable" whose value cannot be changed. Later you will see how you can declare variables in such a way that they exist only over certain regions of a program. The same can be said for constants declared with the keyword **const**. Thus, the **const** declaration is somewhat more versatile than the **#define** directive. Also, the **#define** directive is found in standard C and is therefore already familiar to C programmers.

volatile Modifier

The **volatile** keyword signifies that a variable can unexpectedly change because of events outside the control of the program. For example, the following definition indicates that the variable *timer* can have its value changed without the knowledge of the program:

```
volatile int timer;
```

You need a definition like this, for example, if *timer* is updated by hardware that maintains the current clock time. The program that contains the variable *timer* could be interrupted by the time-keeping hardware and the variable *timer* changed.

You should declare a data object **volatile** if it is a memory mapped device register or a data object shared by separate processes, as would be the case with a multitasking operating environment.

const and volatile

You can use the two modifiers **const** and **volatile** with any other data types—for example, **char** and **float**—as well as with each other. The following definition

```
const volatile constant_timer;
```

specifies that the program does not intend to change the value in the variable *constant_timer*. However, the compiler is also instructed, because of the **volatile** modifier, to make no assumptions about the variable's value from one moment to the next. Therefore, the compiler first issues an error message for any line of source code that attempts to change the value of the variable *constant_timer*. Second, the compiler will not remove the variable *constant_timer* from inside loops, since an external process can also be updating the variable while the program is executing.

pascal, cdecl, near, far, AND huge MODIFIERS

The modifiers **pascal** and **cdecl** are used most frequently in advanced applications. Turbo C++ allows you to write programs that can easily call other routines written in different languages. The opposite of this also holds true. For example, you can write a Pascal program that calls a C++ routine. When you mix languages in this way, you have to consider two very important issues: identifier names, and the way that parameters are passed.

When Turbo C++ compiles your program, it places all of the program's global identifiers (functions and variables) into the resulting object code file for linking purposes. By default, the compiler saves those identifiers using the case in which they were defined (upper, lower, or mixed). Additionally, the compiler appends an underscore to the front of the identifier (you can turn this feature off with the -u option). Since Borland's C++ integrated linking is case sensitive by default, any external identifiers that you declare in your program are also assumed to be in the same form, with a preceding underscore and the same spelling and case as defined.

pascal

The Pascal language uses a different calling sequence than C and C++. Pascal (along with FORTRAN) passes function arguments from left to right and does not allow variable-length argument lists. In Pascal, the called function removes the arguments from the stack. (In C and C++, the invoking function does so when control returns from the invoked function.)

A C or C++ program can generate this calling sequence in one of two ways: It can use the compile-time switch -p, which makes the Pascal calling sequence the default for all enclosed calls and function definitions; it can also override the default C calling sequence explicitly by using the **pascal** keyword in the function definition.

As mentioned, when C generates a function call, by default it precedes the function name with an underscore and declares the function as external. It also preserves the case of the name. However, with the **pascal** keyword, the underscore is not used and the identifier (function or variable) is converted to all uppercase

The following code segment demonstrates how to use the **pascal** keyword on a function (you can use the same keyword to ensure FORTRAN code compatibility):

```
int pascal myfunction(int value1, long value2, double value3)
{
     .
     .
     .
}
```

Of course, you can also give variables a Pascal convention, as shown here:

```
#define MAXELEMENTS 100

int pascal myfunction(int value1, long value2, double value3)
{
     .
     .
     .
}

int pascal mytable[MAXELEMENTS];

main()
{
   int a=5,result;
   long b=2.345;
   double c=7832.89901;

   result=myfunction(a,b,c);

   return(0);
}
```

In this example, **mytable** has been globally defined with the **pascal** modifier. Function **main** also shows how to make an external reference to a Pascal function type. Since both functions **main** and **myfunction** are in the same source file, the function **myfunction** is global to **main**.

cdecl

If the -p compile-time switch was used to compile your C or C++ program, all function and variable references were generated matching the Pascal calling convention. However, you will sometimes want to guarantee that certain identifiers in your program remain case sensitive and retain the initial underscore. This is most often the case for identifiers being used in another C file.

To maintain this C compatibility (preserving the case and the leading underscore), you can use the **cdecl** keyword. When you use the **cdecl** keyword in front of a function, it also affects how the parameters are passed.

Note: All C and C++ functions defined in the header files of Turbo C++, for example *stdio.h,* are of type **cdecl.** This ensures that you can link with the library routines, even when you are compiling by using the -p option. The following example was compiled by using the -p option and shows how you would rewrite the previous example to maintain C compatibility:

```
#define MAXELEMENTS 100

int cdecl myfunction(int value1, long value2, double value3)
{
     .
     .
     .
}

int cdecl mytable[MAXELEMENTS];

main()
{
   int a=5,result;
   long b=2.345;
   double c=7832.89901;
   extern int cdecl myfunction();

   result=myfunction(a,b,c);

   return(0);
}
```

near, far, and huge

The three modifiers **near, far,** and **huge** affect the action of the indirection operator *****. In other words, they modify pointer sizes to data objects. A **near** pointer is only 2 bytes long, a **far** pointer is 4 bytes long, and a **huge** pointer is also 4 bytes long. The difference between **far** and **huge** pointers deals with the form of the address (see Chapter 10).

DATA TYPE CONVERSIONS

In the programs so far, the variables and numbers used in any particular statement were all of the same type—for example, **int** or **float.** You can write statements that perform operations involving variables of different types. These operations are called *mixed mode* operations. Unlike some other programming languages, C and C++ perform automatic conversions from one type to another.

Data of different types are stored differently in memory. Suppose that the number 10 is being stored. Its representation will depend upon its type; that is, the pattern of 0's and 1's in memory will be different when 10 is stored as an **int** or when it is stored as a **float**.

Suppose that the following operation is executed

```
float_result = float_value2 * int_value;
```

where both *float_result* and *float_value2* are of type **float**, and the variable *int_value* is of type **int**. The statement is therefore a mixed mode operation. When the statement is executed, the value of *int_value* will be converted into a floating-point number before the multiplication takes place. The compiler recognizes that a mixed mode operation is taking place. Therefore, it generates code to perform the following operations. The integer value assigned to *int_value* is read from memory. This value is then converted to the corresponding **float** value, which is then multiplied by the real value assigned to *float_value2*, and the resulting **float** value is assigned to *float_result*. In other words, the compiler performs the conversion automatically. Note that the value assigned to *int_value* is unchanged by this process and remains of type **int**.

There is a *hierarchy of conversions*, in that the object of lower priority is temporarily converted to the type of higher priority for the performance of the calculation. Here is the hierarchy of conversions, from highest to lowest priority:

double
float
long
int
short

For example, the type **double** has a higher priority than type **int**. When a type is converted to one that has more significant digits, the value of the number and its accuracy are unchanged.

Look at what happens when a conversion from type **float** to type **int** takes place. Suppose that the variables *int_value1* and *int_value2* have been defined to be of type **int**, while *float_value* and *float_result* have been defined to be of type **float**. Consider the following sequence of statements:

```
int_value1 = 3;
int_value2 = 4;
float_value = 7.0;
float_result = float_value + int_value1/int_value2;
```

The division of *int_value1/int_value2* is not a mixed mode operation; instead, it represents the division of two integers, and its result is zero since the fractional part, 0.75 in this case, is discarded when integer division is performed. Therefore, the value stored in *float_result* is 7.0.

What if *int_value2* had been defined to be of type **float**? In this case, *float_result* would have been assigned the floating-point value 7.75, since the division of *int_value1/int_value2* was a mixed mode operation. Under these circumstances, the value of *int_value1* is temporarily converted to the floating-point value 3.0, and the result of the division is 0.75. When added to *float_value*, the result is 7.75.

The type of the value to the left of the equal sign determines the type of the result of the operation. For example, suppose that *float_x* and *float_y* were declared to be of type **float** and *int_result* was declared to be of type **int**. Consider the following statements:

```
float_x = 7.0;
float_y = 2.0;
int_result = 4.0 + float_x/float_y
```

The result of the division *float_x/float_y* is 3.5; when this is added to 4.0, the floating-point value generated is 7.5. However, this value cannot be assigned to *int_result* because *int_result* is of type **int**. The number 7.5 is therefore converted into an integer. When this is done, the fractional part is truncated. The resulting whole number is converted from a floating-point representation to an integer representation, and the value assigned to *int_result* is the integer number 7.

Explicit Type Conversions Using the Cast Operator

You have seen that the C and C++ compilers automatically change the format of a variable in mixed mode operations using different types. However, under certain circumstances, type conversions would be desirable although automatic conversion is not performed. For those occasions, you must specifically designate that a change of type is to be made. These explicit specifications also clarify to other programmers the statements involved. The C language provides several procedures that allow you to indicate that type conversion must occur.

One of these procedures is called the *cast operator*. Whenever you want to change the format of a variable temporarily, you simply precede the variable's identifier with the type (in parentheses) that you want it converted to. For example, if *int_value1* and *int_value2* were defined as type **int**, and *float_value* and *float_result* were defined as type **float**, the following three statements would perform the same operation:

```
float_result = float_value + (float)int_value1/int_value2;
float_result = float_value + int_value1/(float)int_value2;
float_result = float_value + (float)int_value1/(float)int_value2;
```

All three statements would perform a **float** conversion and division of the variables *int_value1* and *int_value2*. Due to the usual rules of mixed mode arithmetic, if either variable is cast to type **float**, a **float** division occurs. The third statement explicitly highlights the operation to be performed.

STORAGE CLASSES

Turbo C++ supports four storage class specifiers:

- **auto**

- **register**

- **static**

- **extern**

The storage class precedes the variable's declaration and instructs the compiler how the variable should be stored. Items declared with the **auto** or **register** specifier have local lifetimes. Items declared with the **static** or **extern** specifier have global lifetimes.

The four storage class specifiers affect the visibility of a variable or function, as well as its storage class. *Visibility* (sometimes defined as *scope*) refers to that portion of the source program in which the variable or function can be referenced by name. An item with a global lifetime exists throughout the execution of the source program.

The placement of a variable or a function declaration within a source file also affects storage class and visibility. Declarations outside all function definitions are said to appear at the *external* level. Declarations within function definitions appear at the *internal* level.

The exact meaning of each storage class specifier depends on whether the declaration appears at the external or internal level, and whether the item being declared is a variable or a function.

Variable Declarations at the External Level

Variable declarations at the external level may only use the **static** or **extern** storage classes. They are either definitions of variables or references to variables defined elsewhere. An external variable declaration that also initializes the variable (implicitly or explicitly) is a defining declaration:

```
static int int_value1 = 16;  // explicit

static int int_value1;       // implicit 0 by default

int int_value2 = 20;
```

Once a variable is defined at the external level, it is visible throughout the rest of the source file in which it appears. The variable is not visible prior to its definition in the same source file. Also, the variable is not visible in other source files of the program, unless a referencing declaration makes it visible.

You can define a variable at the external level only once within a source file. If you give the **static** storage class specifier, you can define another variable with the same name and the **static** storage class specifier in a different source file. Since each **static** definition is visible only within its own source file, no conflict occurs.

The **extern** storage class specifier declares a reference to a variable defined elsewhere. You can use an **extern** declaration to make visible a definition in another source file, or to make a variable visible above its definition in the same source file. The variable is visible throughout the remainder of the source file in which the declared reference occurs.

For an **extern** reference to be valid, the variable it refers to must be defined once, and only once, at the external level. The definition can be in any of the source files that form the program. The following C++ program demonstrates the use of the **extern** keyword:

```
//
//      Source File A
//

#include <iostream.h>

void function_a(void);
void function_b(void);

extern int int_value;                   // makes int_value visible
                                        // above its declaration

main()
{
   int_value++;                         // uses the above extern
                                        // reference
   cout << "\n" << int_value;           // prints 11
   function_a();

   return(0);
}

int int_value = 10;                     // actual definition of
                                        // int_value

void function_a(void)
{
   int_value++;                         // references int_value
   cout << "\n" << int_value;           // prints 12
   function_b();
}


//
//      Source File B
//

#include <iostream.h>

extern int int_value;                   // references int_value
                                        // declared in Source A

void function_b(void)
{
   int_value++;
   cout << "\n" << int_value;           // prints 13
}
```

Variable Declarations at the Internal Level

You can use any of the four storage class specifiers for variable declarations at the internal level (the default is **auto**). The **auto** storage class specifier declares a variable with a local lifetime. It is visible only in the block in which it is declared and can include initializers.

The **register** storage-class specifier tells the compiler to give the variable storage in a **register**, if possible. It speeds access time and reduces code size. It has the same visibility as the **auto** variable. If no registers are available when the compiler encounters a **register** declaration, the variable is given **auto** storage class and stored in memory.

A variable declared at the internal level with the **static** storage class specifier has a global lifetime but is visible only within the block in which it is declared. Unlike **auto** variables, **static** variables keep their values when the block is exited. You can initialize a **static** variable with a constant expression. It is initialized to 0 by default.

A variable declared with the **extern** storage class specifier is a reference to a variable with the same name defined at the external level in any of the source files of the program. The internal **extern** declaration is used to make the external level variable definition visible within the block. The next program segment demonstrates these concepts:

```
//
//      A simple C++ program illustrating the differences
//      between variables declared at the internal and
//      external levels.
//      Copyright (c) Chris H. Pappas and William H. Murray, 1990
//

#include <iostream.h>

void function_a(void);

int int_value1=1;

main()
{
  // references the int_value1 defined above
  extern int int_value1;

  // default initialization of 0, int_value2 only visible
  // in main()
  static int int_value2;

  // stored in a register (if available), initialized
  // to 0
  register int register_value = 0;
```

```
  // default auto storage class, int_value3 initialized
  // to 0
  int int_value3 = 0;

  // values printed are 1, 0, 0, 0:
  cout << int_value1 << "\n" << register_value << "\n";
  cout << int_value2 << "\n" << int_value3 << "\n";
  function_a();

  return(0);
}

void function_a(void)
{
  // stores the address of the global variable int_value1
  static int *pointer_to_int_value1= &int_value1;

  // creates a new local variable int_value1 making the
  // global int_value1 unreachable
  int int_value1 = 32;

  // new local variable int_value2
  // only visible within function_a
  static int int_value2 = 2;

  int_value2 += 2;

  // the values printed are 32, 4, and 1:
  cout << int_value1 << "\n" << int_value2 << "\n";
  cout << *pointer_to_int_value1;
}
```

Since *int_value1* is redefined in **function_a**, access to the global *int_value1* is denied. However, using a data pointer (see Chapter 10), the address of the global *int_value1* was used to print the value stored there.

Variable Scope Review

To review, there are four rules for variable visibility, also called *scope rules.* The four scopes for a variable are block, function, file, and program. A variable declared within a block or function is known only within the block or function. A variable declared external to a function is known within the file in which it appears, from the point of its appearance to the end of the file. A variable declared as **extern** in one source file and declared as **extern** in other files has program scope.

Function Declarations at the External and Internal Levels

When declaring a function at the external or internal level, you can use either the **static** or the **extern** storage class specifier. Unlike variables, functions always have a global lifetime. The visibility rules for functions are slightly different from the rules for variables.

Functions declared to be **static** are visible only within the source file in which they are defined. Functions in the same source file can call the **static** function, but functions in other source files cannot. Also, you can declare another **static** function with the same name in a different source file without conflict.

Functions declared as **extern** are visible throughout all source files that make up the program (unless you later redeclare such a function as **static**). Any function can call an **extern** function. Function declarations that omit the storage class specifier are **extern** by default.

OPERATORS

C has many operators not found in other languages. These include bitwise operators, increment and decrement operators, conditional operators, the comma operator, and assignment and compound assignment operators.

Bitwise Operators

Bitwise operators treat variables as combinations of bits rather than as numbers. They are useful for accessing the individual bits in memory, such as the screen memory for a graphics display. Bitwise operators can only operate on integral data types, not on floating-point numbers. Three bitwise operators act just like the logical operators, but they act on each bit in an integer. These are the AND &, OR |, and XOR ^. An additional operator is the one's complement ~, which simply inverts each bit.

AND

The logical AND operation compares two bits. If both bits are a 1, the result is a 1. Note that this is different from binary addition, where the comparison of two 1 bits results in a sum flag set to 0 and the carry flag set to 1.

Logical AND

Bit 0	Bit 1	Result
0	0	0
0	1	0
1	0	0
1	1	1

Very often, the AND operation is used to select out, or *mask,* certain bit positions.

OR

The logical OR operation compares two bits and generates a 1 result if either or both bits are a 1. The OR operation is useful for setting specified bit positions.

Logical OR

Bit 0	Bit 1	Result
0	0	0
0	1	1
1	0	1
1	1	1

XOR

The exclusive OR operation (XOR) compares two bits and returns a result of 1 only when the two bits are complementary. This logical operation can be useful when you need to complement specified bit positions, as with computer graphics applications.

Exclusive OR (XOR)

Bit 0	Bit 1	Result
0	0	0
0	1	1
1	0	1
1	1	0

The following example uses these operators with the hexadecimal and octal representation of constants. The bit values are shown for comparison.

```
0xF1     &   0x35        yields 0x31      (hexadecimal)
0361     &   0065        yields 061       (octal)
11110011 &   00110101    yields 00110011  (bitwise)
```

```
0xF1      |   0x35      yields 0xF5       (hexadecimal)
0361      |   0065      yields 0365       (octal)
11110011  |   00110101  yields 11110111   (bitwise)

0xF1      ^   0x35      yields 0xC4       (hexadecimal)
0361      ^   0065      yields 0304       (octal)
11110011  ^   00110101  yields 00000000 11000110 (bitwise)

~0xF1                   yields 0xFF0E     (hexadecimal)
~0361                   yields 0177416    (octal)
~11110011               yields 11111111 00001100 (bitwise)
```

Left Shift and Right Shift

C incorporates two shift operators: the left shift, < <, and the right shift, > >. The left shift moves the bits to the left and sets the rightmost bit (least significant bit) to 0. The leftmost bit (most significant bit) shifted out is discarded.

With unsigned **int** numbers, shifting the number one position to the left and filling the LSB with a 0 will double the number's value. The following C++ code demonstrates how you would code this:

```
unsigned int value1 = 65;
value1 <<= 1;
cout << value1;
```

In memory, examining the lower byte, you would see the following bit changes performed:

```
< < 0100 0001 (65 decimal)
    ─────────────────────
    1000 0010 (130 decimal)
```

The right shift operator, > >, moves bits to the right. The lower order bits shifted out are discarded. Halving an unsigned **int** number is as simple as shifting the bits one position to the right, filling the MSB position with a 0. A C-coded example would look similar to the preceding example, except for the compound operator assignment statement (discussed later in the chapter) and the output statement:

```
unsigned int value1 = 10;
value1 >>= 1;
printf("%d",value1);
```

Examining just the lower byte of the variable *value1* would reveal the following bit changes:

> \> > 0000 1010 (10 decimal)

— — — — — — — — — — — — —

> 0000 0101 (5 decimal)

Increment and Decrement

Adding one to or subtracting one from a number is so common in programs that C has a special set of operators to do this. They are the *increment* **+ +** and *decrement* **— —** operators. You must place the two characters next to each other without any whitespace. You can only apply them to variables, not to constants. Instead of coding

```
value1 = value1 + 1;
```

you can write

```
value1++;
```

or

```
++value1;
```

When these two operators are the sole operators in an expression, you don't have to worry about the different syntax. A *for* loop very often uses this type of increment for the loop control variable:

```
total = 0;
for(i = 1; i <= 10; i++)
   total = total + i;
```

A decrement loop would be coded as:

```
total = 0;
for(i = 10; i >= 1; i--)
  total = sum + i;
```

If you use these operators in complex expressions, you have to consider when the increment or decrement actually takes place. The postfix increment, for example i++, uses the value of the variable in the expression first, and then increments its value. However, the prefix increment, for example ++i, increments the value of the variable first, and then uses the value in the expression. Assume the following data declarations:

```
int i=3,j,k=0;
```

See if you can determine what happens in each of the following statements. For simplicity, assume the original initialized values of the variables for each statement:

```
k = ++i;          // i = 4, k = 4
k = i++;          // i = 4, k = 3
k = --i;          // i = 2, k = 2
k = i--;          // i = 2, k = 3
i = j = k--;      // i = 0, j = 0, k = -1
```

While the subtleties of these two operations may currently elude you, they are included in the C language because of definite situations that could not be eloquently handled in any other way. In Chapter 10 you will look at a program that uses array indices that need to be manipulated using the initially confusing prefix syntax.

Arithmetic Operators

The C language incorporates the standard set of arithmetic operators for addition +, subtraction −, multiplication *, division /, and modulus %. The first four operators need no explanation. However, the following example will help you understand the modulus operator:

```
int a=3,b=8,c=0,d;

d = b % a;          // returns 2
d = a % b;          // returns 3

d = b % c;          // returns an error message
```

The modulus operator returns the remainder of integer division. The last assignment statement attempts to divide 8 by 0, resulting in an error message.

Assignment Operator

The assignment operator in C is unlike the assignment statement in other languages. It is performed by an assignment operator, rather than an assignment statement. As with other C operators, the result of an assignment operator is a value that is assigned. An expression with an assignment operator can be used in a large expression such as:

```
value1 = 8 * (value2 = 5);
```

Here, *value2* is first assigned the value 5. This is multiplied by 8, with *value1* receiving a final value of 40.

If you overuse this feature, you can wind up with unmanageable expressions. There are two places in which this feature is normally applied. First, you can use it to set several variables to a particular value, as in:

```
value1 = value2 = value3 = 0;
```

The second use is most often seen in the condition of a *while* loop, such as:

```
while ((c = getchar()) != EOF) {
    .
    .
    .
}
```

This assigns the value that **getchar** returned to *c* and then tests the value against **EOF**. If it is **EOF**, the loop is not executed. The parentheses are necessary because the assignment operator has a lower precedence than the nonequality operator. Otherwise, the line would be interpreted as:

```
c = (getchar() != EOF)
```

The variable *c* would be assigned a value of 1 (TRUE) each time **getchar** returned **EOF**.

Compound Assignment Operators

The C language also incorporates an enhancement to the assignment statement used by other languages. This additional set of assignment operators allows for a more concise way of expressing certain computations. The following code segment shows the standard assignment syntax applicable in many high-level languages:

```
result = result + increment;
depth = depth - one_fathom;
cost = cost * 1.07;
square_feet = square_feet / 9;
```

The C language compound assignment statements would look like this:

```
result += increment;
depth -= one_fathom;
cost *= 1.07;
square_feet /= 9;
```

Looking closely at these two code segments, you will quickly see the required syntax. If you use a C compound assignment operator, you must remove the redundant variable reference from the right-hand side of the assignment operator and place the operation to be performed immediately before the =.

Table 6-6.   C and C++ Relational Operators

Operator	Meaning
= =	Equal (not assignment)
!=	Not equal
>	Greater than
<	Less than
> =	Greater than or equal
< =	Less than or equal

Table 6-7.   C and C++ Logical Operators

&&	AND
||	OR (SHIFT-\)
!	NOT

Relational and Logical Operators

All relational operators are used to establish a relationship between the values of the operands. They always produce a value of 1 if the relationship evaluates to TRUE or a value of 0 if the relationship evaluates to FALSE. Table 6-6 lists the C and C++ relational operators.

The logical operators AND &&, OR ||, and NOT ! produce a TRUE (1) or FALSE (0) based on the logical relationship of their arguments. The simplest way to remember how the logical AND && works is to say that an ANDed expression will only return a TRUE (1) when both arguments are TRUE (1). The logical OR || operation in turn will only return a FALSE (0) when both arguments are FALSE (0). The logical NOT ! simply inverts the value. Table 6-7 lists the C and C++ logical operators.

Have some fun with the following C program as you test the various combinations of relational and logical operators. See if you can predict the results.

```
/*
 *    A C program demonstrating some of the subtleties of logical
 *    and relational operators.
 *    Copyright (c) Chris H. Pappas and William H. Murray, 1990
 */

#include <stdio.h>

main()
{
  float value1, value2;

  printf("\nPlease enter a value1: " );
  scanf("%f",&value1);
  printf("Please enter a value2: ");
```

```
    scanf("%f",&value2);
    printf("\n");
    printf("  value1  > value2 is %d\n", (value1 > value2));
    printf("  value1  < value2 is %d\n", (value1 < value2));
    printf("  value1 >= value2 is %d\n",(value1 >= value2));
    printf("  value1 <= value2 is %d\n",(value1 <= value2));
    printf("  value1 == value2 is %d\n",(value1 == value2));
    printf("  value1 != value2 is %d\n",(value1 != value2));
    printf("  value1 && value1 is %d\n",(value1 && value2));
    printf("  value1 || value2 is %d\n",(value1 || value2));

    return(0);
}
```

You may be surprised at the results obtained for some of the logical comparisons. Remember, however, a strict comparison occurs for both data types **float** and **double** when values of these types are compared with zero—a number that is very slightly different from another number is still not equal. Also, a number that is just slightly above or below zero is still TRUE (1).

Here is the C++ equivalent of the preceding program:

```
//
//    A C++ program demonstrating some of the subtleties of logical
//    and relational operators.
//    Copyright (c) Chris H. Pappas and William H. Murray, 1990
//

#include <iostream.h>

main()
{
  float value1, value2;

  cout << "\nPlease enter a value1: ";
  cin >> value1;
  cout << "Please enter a value2: ";
  cin >> value2;
  cout << "\n";
  cout << "  value1  > value2 is " << (value1  > value2) << "\n";
  cout << "  value1  < value2 is " << (value1  < value2) << "\n";
  cout << "  value1 >= value2 is " << (value1 >= value2) << "\n";
  cout << "  value1 <= value2 is " << (value1 <= value2) << "\n";
  cout << "  value1 == value2 is " << (value1 == value2) << "\n";
  cout << "  value1 != value2 is " << (value1 != value2) << "\n";
  cout << "  value1 && value1 is " << (value1 && value2) << "\n";
  cout << "  value1 || value2 is " << (value1 || value2) << "\n";

  return(0);
}
```

Conditional Operator

You can use the *conditional operator* in normal coding, but its main use is creating macros (see Chapter 14). The operator has the syntax:

condition ? *true-expression* : *false-expression*

If the condition is TRUE, the value of the conditional expression is *true-expression*. Otherwise, it is the value of *false-expression*. For example, you could rewrite the following statement

```
if('A' <= c && c <= 'Z')
  printf("%c",'a' + c - 'A');
else
  printf("%c",c);
```

using the conditional operator:

```
printf("%c",('A' <= c && c <= 'Z') ? ('a' + c - 'A') : c );
```

Both statements will make certain that the character printed, *c*, is always lowercase.

Comma Operator

The *comma operator* evaluates two expressions where the syntax allows only one. The value of the comma operator is the value of the right-hand expression. The format for the expression is

left-expression, right-expression

The comma operator commonly appears in a *for* loop, where more than one variable is being iterated. For example:

```
for(min=0,max=length-1; min < max; min++,max--) {
  .
  .
  .
}
```

UNDERSTANDING OPERATOR PRECEDENCE LEVELS

The order of evaluation of an expression in C is determined by the compiler. This normally does not alter the value of the expression, unless you have written one with side effects. *Side effects* are those operations that change the value of a variable while yielding a value that is used in the expression, as seen with the increment and decrement operators. The other operators that have side effects are the assignment and compound assignment. Calls to functions that change values of external variables also are subject to side effects. For example:

```
value1 = 3;
result = (value1 = 4) + value1;
```

This could be evaluated in one of two ways: *value1* is assigned 4, and *result* is assigned 8 (4+4); value of 3 is retrieved from *value1*, and 4 is then assigned to *value1*, with *result* being assigned a 7.

There are, however, four operators for which the order of evaluation is guaranteed to be left-to-right: logical AND (&&), logical OR (||), the comma operator, and the conditional operator. Because of this default order of evaluation, you can specify a typical test as

```
while((c=getchar() != EOF) && (C!='\n'))
```

and know that the second part of the logical AND (&&) is performed after the character value is assigned to *c*.

Table 6-8 lists all of the C and C++ operators from highest to lowest precedence and describes how each operator is associated (left-to-right or right-to-left). All operators between lines have the same precedence level.

STANDARD C AND C++ LIBRARIES

Certain calculations are routinely performed in many programs and are written by almost all programmers. Taking the square root of a number is such a calculation. Mathematical procedures for calculating square roots use

Table 6-8.   Operator Precedence Levels

Description	Operator	Associates from	Precedence
Function expr	( )	left	Highest
Array expr	[]	left	
Struct indirection	->	left	
Struct member	.	left	
Incr/decr	+ + - -	right	
One's complement	~	right	
Unary NOT	!	right	
Address	&	right	
Dereference	*	right	
Cast	(type)	right	
Unary minus	-	right	
Size in bytes	sizeof	right	
Multiplication	*	left	
Division	/	left	
Remainder	%	left	
Addition	+	left	
Subtraction	-	left	
Shift left	<<	left	
Shift right	>>	left	
Less than	<	left	
Less than or equal	<=	left	
Greater than	>	left	
Greater than or equal	>=	left	
Equal	==	left	
Not equal	!=	left	
Bitwise AND	&	left	
Bitwise XOR	^	left	
Bitwise OR	|	left	
Logical AND	&&	left	
Logical OR	||	left	
Conditional	? :	right	
Assignment	= %= += -= *= /= >>= <<= &= ^= |=	right	
Comma	,	left	Lowest

combinations of the basic arithmetic operations of addition, subtraction, multiplication, and division.

It would be a waste of effort if every programmer had to design and code a routine to calculate the square root and then to incorporate that routine into the program. C and C++ resolve these difficulties by providing the programmer with *libraries of functions* that perform particular common calculations. With the libraries, you need only a single statement to invoke such a function.

This section will discuss functions that are commonly provided with the C and C++ compiler. These library functions are usually not provided in source form but in compiled form. When linking is performed, the code for the library functions is combined with the compiled programmer's code to form the complete program.

Library functions not only perform mathematical operations, but also handle many other common operations. For example, there are library functions that deal with reading and writing disk files, managing memory, input/output, and a variety of other operations. Library functions are not part of standard C or C++, but virtually every system provides certain library functions.

Most library functions are designed to use information contained in particular files that are supplied with the system. These files, therefore, must be included when the library functions are used. These files are also provided with the C++ compiler. They usually have the extension *.h* and are called header files. Table 6-9 lists the header files supplied with Turbo C++ Professional.

In general, different header files are required by different library functions. The required header files for a function will be listed in the description for that function. For example, the **sqrt** function needs the declarations found in the *math.h* header file. Your Turbo C++ reference manual lists all of the library functions and their associated header files.

The following list highlights the library categories provided by the Turbo C++ Professional compiler:

- Classification routines
- Conversion routines
- Directory control routines
- Diagnostic routines
- Graphics routines

- Input/output routines

- Interface routines (DOS, 8086, BIOS)

- Manipulation routines

- Math routines

- Memory allocation routines

- Process control routines

- Standard routines

- Text window display routines

- Time and date routines

Check your reference manual for a detailed explanation of the individual functions provided by each library.

PUTTING YOUR KNOWLEDGE TO WORK

1. Are the following identifiers valid?

   ```
   $Dollars
   tax_rate
   ERROR!
   ```

2. Write the data declarations for a program that needs to read in a **char** control code, an **int** count for all items sold, a **float** cost per item, and an **enum** type specifying the items sold.

3. What is the one factor you need to remember when assigning a value to an **unsigned** data type?

4. Explain how a variable can be a **const** and **volatile** at the same time.

5. Why were the **pascal** and **cdecl** modifiers necessary?

6. Where will C's automatic data type conversion capabilities get you in trouble?

Table 6-9.   Turbo C++ Include Files

Header File Name	Brief Description
alloc.h	Memory management functions
assert.h	Defines the assert debugging macro
bios.h	Declares ROM BIOS function calls
conio.h	Declares DOS console I/O routines
ctype.h	Character conversion macros
dir.h	Declares directory/path macros/functions
dos.h	Constant declarations for 8086-specific calls
errno.h	Defines constant mnemonics for error codes
fcntl.h	Symbolic constant declarations used with open
float.h	Contains parameters for floating-point routines
io.h	Low-level I/O routines and structure declarations
limits.h	Compile-time limitations, environmental params
math.h	Declares prototypes for math functions
mem.h	Declares memory-manipulation functions
process.h	Structures/declarations for spawn. . . and exec. . .
setjmp.h	Defines type jmp_buf used by long/setjmp
share.h	File-sharing function declarations
signal.h	Constants SIG_IGN and SIG_DFL defined for ssignal
stdarg.h	Defines macrosf used by vprintf, vscanf, etc.
stddef.h	Defines common data types and macros
stdio.h	Standard I/O declarations
stdlib.h	Commonly used conversion, search, sort, routines
string.h	Declares string manipulation functions
sys\ stat.h	Defines symbolic constants used for file open/close
time.h	Defines time-conversion routines
values.h	Defines important constants for UNIX Sys.V compat.

7. Can all externally defined variables (outside of any function block) have the storage classes **auto** and **register**?

8. Evaluate the following expressions using your understanding of operator precedence levels:

```
        assuming:    x = 11,     y = 6,     z = 1,     c = 'k'

                                                        Value

x > 9 && y != 3
x == 5 || y != 3
!(x > 14)
!(x > 9 && y != 23)
x <= 1 && y == 6 || z < 4
c >= 'a' && c <= 'z'
c >= 'A' || c <= 'Z'
c != 'd' && c != '\n'
z && y != 8 || 0
```

The answers, from top to bottom, are 1, 1, 1, 0, 1, 1, 1, 1, 1.

7

CONTROL

In this chapter you will learn

- How to declare and use the basic conditional C statements *if*, nested *if*, *if-else-if*, *switch*, and nested *switch*

- How to use the unique C **?** conditional to replace *if-else-if* statements

- How to declare and use the basic loop statements *for*, *while*, and *do-while*

- What the **break**, **continue**, and **exit** statements are and how you can use them to solve unique programming problems

- What an **atexit** function is, and how to declare and use one

To begin writing simple C programs, you need a few more tools. This chapter will discuss C's control statements. Many of these control statements are similar to other high-level language controls, such as *if*, *if-else*, and *switch* statements and *for*, *while*, and *do-while* loops. However, there are several new control statements unique to C, such as the **?** conditional, **break**, and **continue** statements.

CONDITIONAL STATEMENTS

The C language supports four basic conditional statements: the *if,* the *if-else,* the conditional *?,* and the *switch.* Most of the conditional statements can be used to selectively execute either a single line of code or multiple lines of related code (called a *block*). Whenever a conditional statement is associated with only one line of executable code, braces { } are *not* required around the executable statement. However, if the conditional statement is associated with multiple executable statements, braces are required to connect the block of executable statements with the conditional test.

if Statements

The *if* statement is used to execute a segment of code conditionally. The simplest form of the *if* statement is

if (*expression*)

    action;

Notice that the expression must be enclosed in parentheses. To execute an *if* statement, the expression must be evaluated to either TRUE (!0) or FALSE (0). If *expression* is TRUE, the *action* will be performed and execution will continue on to the next statement following the *action.* However, if *expression* evaluates to FALSE, the *action* will *not* be executed, and the statement following *action* will be executed. For example, the following code segment will print the message "Enjoy your health!" whenever the variable *body _ temp* equals 98.6:

```
if(body_temp == 98.6)
  printf("Enjoy your health!");
```

The syntax for an *if* statement associated with a block of executable statements looks like this:

if (*expression*) {

    action;

action;

action;

action;

};

The syntax requires that all of the associated statements be enclosed in a pair of braces **{}** and that each statement within the block end with a semicolon *;*. Here is an example compound *if* statement:

```
/*
 *     A C program demonstrating a compound if statement.
 *     Copyright (c) Chris H. Pappas and William H. Murray, 1990
 */

#include <stdio.h>

main()
{
  float trade_in_worth,new_car_cost,bank_loan,
        grandma_good_for,sons_motor_bike_worth,
        wifes_wedding_ring;

  printf("Ok, enter your dream car's cost: ");
  scanf("%f",&new_car_cost);

  trade_in_worth = 3000;
  bank_loan = new_car_cost - trade_in_worth;
  if(new_car_cost > 15000) {
    grandma_good_for = 2000;
    sons_motor_bike_worth = 1500;
    wifes_wedding_ring = 2500;
    bank_loan = new_car_cost - (trade_in_worth +
                                grandma_good_for +
                                sons_motor_bike_worth +
                                wifes_wedding_ring);
  }

  printf("Help, I need $%8.2f dollars!",bank_loan);

  return(0);
}
```

In this example, if the *new_car_cost* is more than $15,000, the new car buyer will have to beg, borrow, and hock everything that he or she can to purchase that new vehicle. Regardless of whether the *if* block was entered, the loan amount needed is printed.

if-else Statements

The *if-else* statement allows a program to take two separate actions based on the validity of a particular expression. The simplest syntax for an *if-else* statement looks like this:

if (*expression*)

   action1;

else

   action2;

In this case, if *expression* evaluates to TRUE, *action1* will be taken. Otherwise, when *expression* evaluates to FALSE, *action2* will be executed. A coded example looks like this:

```
if(mouse_move == LEFT)
  xposition = xposition - a_pixel;
else
  xposition = xposition + a_pixel;
```

This example increments or decrements the mouse's horizontal coordinate location based on the current contents of the variable *mouse_move*.

   Of course, either *action1, action2,* or both could be compound statements, or blocks, requiring braces. The syntax for these three combinations is straightforward:

if (*expression*) {

   action1a;

   action1b;

   action1c;

}

else

   action2;

if (*expression*)

   action1;

else {

   action2a;

```
      action2b;

      action2c;

}


if (expression) {

    action1a;

    action1b;

    action1c;

}
else {

    action2a;

    action2b;

    action2c;

}
```

Remember, whenever a block *action* is being taken, you don't follow the closing brace with a semicolon.

The following C program uses an *if-else* statement; the *if* part is a compound block:

```
/*
 *      A C program demonstrating the use of an if-else statement.
 *      Copyright (c) Chris H. Pappas and William H. Murray, 1990
 */

#include <stdio.h>

main()
{
  char c;
  int how_many,i,more_input;

  more_input=1;

  while(more_input == 1) {
    printf("Please enter the product name: ");
    if(scanf("%c",&c) != EOF) {
      while(c != '\n') {
        printf("%c",c);
        scanf("%c",&c);
```

```
     }
       printf("s purchased? ");
       scanf("%d",&how_many);
       scanf("%c",&c);

       for(i = 1;i <= how_many; i++)
          printf("*");
       printf("\n");
     }
     else
       more_input=0;
   }
   return(0);
}
```

The program prompts the user for a product name. While the user hasn't entered a ^Z (EOF), the program inputs the product name character by character, echoing the information to the next line. The "s purchased" string is appended to the product, requesting the number of items sold. Finally, a *for* loop prints the appropriate number of *s. Had the user entered a ^Z, the *if* portion of the *if-else* statement would have been ignored and program execution would have picked up with the *else* setting the *more_input* flag to 0, thereby terminating the program.

Nested *if-else*s

When nesting *if* statements, make sure that you know which *else action* will be matched up with which *if*. See if you can determine what will happen in this example:

```
if(out_side_temp < 50)
if(out_side_temp < 30) printf("Wear the down jacket!");
else printf("Parka will do.");
```

The listing is purposely misaligned so you have no visual clues about which statement goes with which *if*. If *out_side_temp* is 55, does the "Parka will do." message get printed? The answer is no. In this example, the *else action* is associated with the second *if expression*.

To simplify debugging under such circumstances, the C++ compiler has been written to associate each *else* with the closest *if* that does not already have an associated *else*.

Of course, proper indentation will always help clarify the situation:

```
if(out_side_temp < 50)
  if(out_side_temp < 30) printf("Wear the down jacket!");
  else printf("Parka will do.");
```

The same logic can also be represented by this listing:

```
if(out_side_temp < 50)
  if(out_side_temp < 30)
    printf("Wear the down jacket!");
  else
    printf("Parka will do.");
```

Each application you write will benefit most by one of the preceding two styles, as long as you are consistent throughout the source code.

See if you can figure out this example:

```
if(test1_expression)
  if(test2_expression)
    test2_action;
else
  test1_false_action;
```

This looks like just another example of what has been discussed. However, what if you wanted *test1_false_action* to be associated with *test1* rather than *test2?* The examples so far have all associated the *else action* with the second or closest *if.* They're indented to work the way you are logically thinking (as was the previous example); unfortunately, the compiler disregards indentation.

To correct this situation, you need to use braces:

```
if(test1_expression) {
  if(test2_expression)
    test2_action;
  }
else
  test1_false_action;
```

You solve the problem by making *test2_expression* and its associated *test2_action* a block associated with a TRUE evaluation of the *test1_expression.* This makes it clear that *test1_false_action* will be associated with the *else* clause of *test1_expression.*

if-else-if Statements

The *if-else-if* statement is often used to perform multiple successive comparisons. Its general form looks like this:

if(*expression1*)

   action1;

else if(*expression2*)

   action2;

else if(*expression3*)

   action3;

Of course, each *action* could be a compound block requiring its own set of braces (with the closing brace not followed by a semicolon). This type of logical control flow evaluates each expression until it finds one that is TRUE. When this occurs, all remaining test conditions are bypassed. In the previous example, no action would be taken if none of the expressions evaluated to TRUE.

   See if you can guess the result of this next example.

if (*expression1*)

   action1;

else if(*expression2*)

   action2;

else if(*expression3*)

   action3;

else

   default _ action;

Unlike the previous example, this *if-else-if* statement will always perform some *action*. If none of the *if(expression)*s evaluates to TRUE, the *else default _ action* will be executed. For example, the following program checks the value assigned to *conversion* to decide which type of conversion to perform. If the requested conversion is not one of the ones provided, the code segment prints an appropriate message.

```
if(conversion == YARDS)
  measurement = length / 3;
else if(conversion == INCHES)
  measurement = length * 12;
else if(conversion == CENTIMETERS)
  measurement = length * 12 * 2.54;
else if(conversion == METERS)
  measurement = (length * 12 * 2.54)/100;
else
  printf("No conversion required");
```

The ? Conditional Statement

The conditional statement ? provides a quick way to write a test condition. Associated *actions* are performed depending on whether the *expression* evaluates to TRUE or FALSE. You can use the ? operator to replace an equivalent *if-else* statement. The syntax for a conditional statement looks like this:

expression ? action1 : action2;

The ? operator is also sometimes referred to as the *ternary operator* because it requires three operands. The next two listings demonstrate how to rewrite an *if-else* statement using the conditional operator:

```
if(test)
  x = y;
else
  x = y * y;
```

Here is the same statement rewritten with the conditional operator:

```
x = test ? y : y * y;
```

The following C++ program uses the ? operator to calculate the sum or the difference of two integer values:

```
//
//    A C++ program demonstrating the use of the conditional?.
//    Copyright (c) Chris H. Pappas and William H. Murray, 1990
//

#include <iostream.h>

main()
```

```
{
  char ch;
  int answer,value1,value2;

  cout << "Please enter two integer values.\n";
  cin >> value1 >> value2;
  cout << "\nEnter '+' to get the sum, anything else " \
    "for subtraction: ";
  cin >> ch;
  answer = (ch == '+') ? value1 + value2 : value1 - value2;
  cout << "\n\nThe result is: " << answer;

  return(0);
}
```

The program uses the conditional assignment. The user enters two integers and a character. If the character is a +, the *answer* is assigned the sum of *value1* and *value2*. However, if the character is not a +, *value2* is subtracted from *value1*.

switch Statements

You will often want to test a variable or an expression against several values. You could use nested *if-else-if* statements to do this, or you could use a *switch* statement. Be very careful. Unlike many other high-level language selection statements, the C *switch* statement has a few peculiarities. The syntax for a *switch* statement looks like this:

switch (*integral expression*) {

    case *constant1*:

        statements1;

        break;

    case *constant2*:

        statements2;

        break;

        .

        .

        .

    case *constantn*:

statementsn;

break;

  default: *statements;*

}

Pay particular attention to the **break** statement. If this example had been coded in Pascal and *constant1* equaled the *integral expression, statements1* would have been executed, with program execution picking up with the next statement at the end of the *case* statement (below the closing brace, **}**).

In C, the situation is quite different. If the **break** statement had been removed from *constant1*'s code segment, a similar match used in the previous paragraph would have left *statements2* the next statement to be executed. The **break** statement causes the remaining portion of the *switch* statements to be skipped.

The following *if-else-if* code segment

```
if(x == 4)
  y = 7;
else if(x == 5)
  y = 9;
else if(x == 9)
  y = 14;
else
  y = 22;
```

can be rewritten using a *switch* statement:

```
switch(x) {
  case  4:
    y = 7;
    break;
  case  5:
    y = 9;
    break;
  case  9:
    y = 14;
    break;
  default:
    y = 22;
}
```

In this example, the value of x is consecutively compared to each *case* value looking for a match. When one is found, y is assigned the appropriate value and then the **break** statement is executed, skipping over the remainder of the *switch* statements. However, if no match is found, the *default* assignment is performed (y = 22). Since this is the last option in the *switch* statement, there is no need to include a **break**. A *switch default* is optional.

Proper placement of the **break** statement within a *switch* statement can be very useful. Look at the following example:

```
/*
*       A C program demonstrating the drop-through capabilities
*       of the switch statement.
*       Copyright (c) Chris H. Pappas and William H. Murray, 1990
*/

main()
{
  char letter='z';
  int vowel_count=0,constant_count=0;

  switch(letter) {
    case 'a':
    case 'A':
    case 'e':
    case 'E':
    case 'i':
    case 'I':
    case 'o':
    case 'O':
    case 'u':
    case 'U': vowel_count++;
              break;
    default : constant_count++;
  }
  return(0);
}
```

The preceding program illustrates two characteristics of the *switch* statement: how to enumerate several test values that all execute the same code section, and the drop-through characteristic.

Some other high-level languages have their own form of selection that allows for several test values, all producing the same result, to be included on the same selection line. In contrast, C requires a separate *case* for each. In the preceding example, the same effect has been created by not inserting a **break** statement until all possible vowels have been checked. Should *letter* contain a consonant, all of the vowel *case* tests will be checked and skipped until the *default* statement is reached.

The next C program uses a *switch* statement to invoke the appropriate function:

```
/*
*       A C program demonstrating the switch statement
*       Copyright (c) Chris H. Pappas and William H. Murray, 1990
```

```c
*/

#include <stdio.h>

#define QUIT 0
#define BLANK ' '

double fadd(float x,float y);
double fsub(float x,float y);
double fmul(float x,float y);
double fdiv(float x,float y);

main()
{
  float x,y;
  char blank,operator = BLANK;

  while (operator != QUIT) {
    printf("\nPlease enter an expression (a (operator) b): ");
    scanf("%f%c%c%f", &x, &blank, &operator, &y);

    switch (operator) {
      case '+': printf("answer = %4.2f\n", fadd(x,y));
              break;
      case '-': printf("answer = %4.2f\n", fsub(x,y));
              break;
      case '*': printf("answer = %4.2f\n", fmul(x,y));
              break;
      case '/': printf("answer = %4.2f\n", fdiv(x,y));
              break;
      case 'x': operator = QUIT;
              break;
      default : printf("\nOperator not implemented");
    }
  }
  return(0);
}

double fadd(float x,float y)
{
  return(x + y);
}

double fsub(float x,float y)
{
  return(x - y);
}

double fmul(float x,float y)
{
  return(x * y);
}

double fdiv(float x,float y)
{
  return(x / y);
}
```

```
  }
  return(0);
}
```

The program first asks the user to enter an integer code representing the day of the week that January begins on (0 for Monday, 1 for Tuesday, and so on). The second prompt asks for the year for the calendar, and then prints the year entered. The year entered is also used to generate a *leap_year_flag*. Using the modulus operator (**%**) with a value of 4 generates a remainder of 0 whenever it is leap year, and a nonzero value whenever it is not leap year.

Next, a 12 iteration loop is entered, printing the current month's name, and assigning *num_days_per_month* the correct number of days for that particular month. You accomplish all of this by using a *switch* statement to test the current *month* integer value.

Outside the *switch* statement, after the month's name has been printed, day-of-the-week headings are printed, and an appropriate number of blank columns are skipped depending on when the first day of the month was.

The last *for* loop actually generates and prints the dates for each month. The last statement in the program prepares the *day_code* for the next month to be printed.

if-else-if and *switch* Statements Combined

The following example program uses an enumerated type (**enum**) to perform the specified length conversions:

```
/*
 *    A C program demonstrating the if-else-if statement
 *    used in a meaningful way with several switch statements.
 *    Copyright (c) Chris H. Pappas and William H. Murray, 1990
 */

typedef enum conversion_type {YARDS, INCHES, CENTIMETERS, \
                          METERS} C_TYPE;
#include <stdio.h>

main()
{
  int user_response;
  C_TYPE conversion;
  int length=30;
  float measurement;

  printf("\nPlease enter the measurement to be converted : ");
  scanf("%f",&measurement);
```

```
    printf("\nPlease enter :          \
            \n\t\t 0 for YARDS         \
            \n\t\t 1 for INCHES        \
            \n\t\t 2 for CENTIMETERS \
            \n\t\t 3 for METERS        \
            \n\n\t\tYour response -->> ");

    scanf("%d",&user_response);

    switch(user_response) {
      case 0  :   conversion=YARDS;
                  break;
      case 1  :   conversion=INCHES;
                  break;
      case 2  :   conversion=CENTIMETERS;
                  break;
      default :   conversion=METERS;
    }

    if(conversion == YARDS)
      measurement = length / 3;
    else if(conversion == INCHES)
      measurement = length * 12;
    else if(conversion == CENTIMETERS)
      measurement = length * 12 * 2.54;
    else if(conversion == METERS)
      measurement = (length * 12 * 2.54)/100;
    else
      printf("No conversion required");

    switch(conversion) {
      case YARDS       : printf("\n\t\t  %4.2f yards",measurement);
                         break;
      case INCHES      : printf("\n\t\t  %4.2f inches",measurement);
                         break;
      case CENTIMETERS : printf("\n\t\t  %4.2f centimeters",
                                   measurement);
                         break;
      default          : printf("\n\t\t  %4.2f meters",measurement);
    }

    return(0);
}
```

In standard C, enumerated types only exist within the code itself, and cannot be input or output directly except as integers. The program uses the first *switch* statement to convert the input code to its appropriate conversion type. The nested *if-else-if* statements perform the proper conversion. The last *switch* statement prints the converted value with its appropriate literal type. Of course, the nested *if-else-if* statements could have been implemented by using a *switch* statement. (See Chapter 12 for more on enumerated types.)

LOOP STATEMENTS

The C language includes the standard set of repetition control statements: *for* loops, *while* loops, and *do-while* loops (called *repeat-until* loops in several other high-level languages). However, C provides four methods for altering the repetitions in a loop. All repetition loops can naturally terminate based on the expressed Boolean test condition. In C, however, a repetition loop can also terminate because of an anticipated error condition using either a **break** or **exit** statement. Repetition loops can also have their logic control flow altered by **break** or **continue** statements.

The basic difference between a *for* loop and a *while* or *do-while* loop has to do with the known number of repetitions. Typically, *for* loops are used whenever there is a definite predefined required number of repetitions. In contrast, *while* and *do-while* loops are reserved for an unknown number of repetitions.

for Loops

The syntax for a *for* loop looks like this:

for(*initialization _ exp; test _ exp; increment _ exp*)

   statement;

When the *for* loop statement is encountered, the *initialization _ exp* is executed first, at the start of the loop, and is never executed again. Usually, this statement involves the initialization of the loop control variable. Following this, the *test _ exp*, which is called the loop terminating condition, is tested. Whenever the *test _ exp* evaluates to TRUE, the statement or statements within the loop are executed. If the loop was entered, the *increment _ exp* is executed after all of the statements within the loop are executed. However, if *test _ exp* evaluates to FALSE, the statements within the loop are ignored, along with the *increment _ exp,* and execution continues with the statement following the end of the loop. The indentation scheme for *for* loops with several statements to be repeated looks like this:

for(*initialization _ exp; test _ exp; increment _ exp*) {

   statement _ a;

```
    statement b;

    statement _ c;

    statement _ n;
}
```

When several statements need to be executed, a pair of braces, {}, is required to tie their execution to the loop control structure.

The following example sums up the first ten integers. It assumes that *int_sum* and *int_value* have been predefined as integers.

```
int_sum = 0;
for(int_value=1; int_value <= 10; int_value++)
   int_sum += int_value;
```

After *int_sum* has been initialized to 0, the *for* loop is encountered. First, *int_value* is initialized to 1 (this is done only once). Then *int_value*'s value is checked against the loop terminating condition, < = 10. Since this is TRUE, a 1 is added to *int_sum*. Once the statement is executed, the loop control variable (*int_value*) is incremented by 1. This process continues nine more times until *int_value* is incremented to 11 and the loop terminates.

In C++, the same code segment could be written as follows (see if you can detect the subtle difference):

```
int_sum = 0;
for(int int_value=1; int_value <= 10; int_value++)
   int_sum += int_value;
```

C++ allows the loop control variable to be declared and initialized within the *for* loop. This brings up the issue of the proper placement of variable declarations. In C++, you can declare variables right before the statement that actually uses them. In the previous example, the local declaration for *int_value* is harmless, since *int_value* is only used to generate an *int_sum*, with *int_sum* having a larger scope than *int_value*. However, the following code segment

```
int int_sum = 0;
for(int int_value=1; int_value <= 10; int_value++)
   int_sum = int_sum + int_value;
```

would obscure the visual "desk check" of the variable *int_sum*, because it was not declared below the function head. For the sake of structured design and debugging, it is best to localize all variable declarations. You can rarely justify moving a variable declaration to a nonstandard place, sacrificing easily read, easily checked, and easily modified code.

The value used to increment *for* loop control variables does not have to be 1 or + +. The following example sums the even numbers up to 20:

```
even_sum = 0;
for(even_value=2; even_value <= 20; even_value+2);
  even_sum += even_value;
```

In this example, the loop control variable *even_value* is initialized to 2 and is incremented by 2. Of course, *for* loops don't always have to go from a smaller value to a larger one. The next example uses a *for* loop to read into an array of characters and then print the character string backwards:

```
//
//    A C++ program that accesses a for loop to read
//    characters into an array and then to print it backwards.
//    Copyright (c) Chris H. Pappas and William H. Murray, 1990
//

#include <stdio.h>

#define MAXLETTERS 10

main()
{
  char char_array[MAXLETTERS];
  int index;

  for(index = 0; index < MAXLETTERS; index++)
    char_array[index]=getchar();
  for(index = MAXLETTERS-1; index >= 0; index--)
    putchar(char_array[index]);

  return(0);
}
```

In this example, the first *for* loop initializes *index* to 0 (necessary since all array indexes are offsets from the starting address of the first array element) and reads characters in one at a time while there is room in the *char_array*. The second *for* loop initializes the loop control variable *index* to the offset of the last element in the array, and prints the characters in reverse order while *index* contains a valid offset. You could use this process to parse an infix expression that was being converted to prefix notation.

When you combine *for* loops, as in this next example, take care to include the appropriate braces { }, to make certain the statements execute properly:

```
/*
 *      A C program demonstrating the need for caution when
 *      nesting for loops.
 *      Copyright (c) Chris H. Pappas and William H. Murray, 1990
 */

#include <stdio.h>

main()
{
  int outer_value, inner_value;

  for(outer_value = 1; outer_value <= 4; outer_value++) {
    printf("\n%3d  --",outer_value);
    for(inner_value = 1; inner_value <= 5; inner_value++ )
      printf("%3d",outer_value * inner_value);
  }

  return(0);
}
```

The output produced by this program looks like this:

```
1  --   1   2   3   4   5
2  --   2   4   6   8  10
3  --   3   6   9  12  15
4  --   4   8  12  16  20
```

while LOOPS

Just like the *for* loop, the C *while* loop is a *pretest* loop. This means that *test-exp* is evaluated before the statements within the body of the loop are entered. Because of this, pretest loops may be executed from zero to many times. The syntax for a C *while* loop looks like this:

while(*test _ exp*)

　　statement;

For *while* loops with several statements, braces are needed:

while(*test _ exp*) {

　　statement _ a;

　　statement _ b;

　　statement _ c;

　　statement _ n;

}

Usually *while* loop control structures are used whenever an indefinite number of repetitions is expected. The following C program uses a *while* loop to average a user-defined list of numbers:

```
/*
 *      A C program using a simple while loop with a BOOLEAN flag.
 *      Copyright (c) Chris H. Pappas and William H. Murray, 1990
 */

#include <stdio.h>

#define TRUE 1
#define FALSE 0

main()
{
  int how_many=0, done=FALSE;
  float sum=0.0,input_value=0.0;
  double average=0.0;

  while(!done) {
    printf("\n Input a number to average (0 to quit): ");
    scanf("%d",&input_value);
    if(input_value != 0.0) {
      sum = sum + input_value;
```

```
        how_many++;
      }
      else
        done = TRUE;
  }

  how_many > 0 ? (average = sum/how_many) : (average = 0);

  printf("\n The sum of %d numbers is %d",how_many,sum);
  printf("\n The average of these numbers is %f",average);

  return(0);
}
```

The program begins by defining two **int** constants TRUE and FALSE that will be used as a flag to determine when the *while* loop will terminate. The *done* flag is initialized to FALSE, with the *while* loop repeating until the user enters a 0 value, which sets the *done* flag to TRUE. Since *while* loops only repeat while the test condition evaluates to TRUE, *!done* or *!TRUE* stops the repetitions.

The next C program prompts the user for input and output file names. The program then uses a *while* loop to read in and echo the input file of unknown size.

```
/*
*       A C program demonstrating how a while loop can be used
*       to process an input file of undetermined length.
*       Copyright (c) Chris H. Pappas and William H. Murray, 1990
*/

#include <stdio.h>
#include <process.h>

#define NAMELENGTH 30
#define NULLCHAR 1

main()
{
  FILE *fopen();
  int fclose();
  FILE *in_file;
  FILE *out_file;
  char in_file_name[NAMELENGTH+NULLCHAR],
  out_file_name[NAMELENGTH+NULLCHAR];
  int c,file_name_length;

  fputs("Please enter input file name: ",stdout);
  gets(in_file_name);

  fputs("Please enter output file name: ",stdout);
  gets(out_file_name);
```

```
if(( in_file=fopen(in_file_name,"r")) == NULL){
  printf("Input file cannot be opened");
} exit(1);
if(( out_file=fopen(out_file_name,"w")) == NULL){
  printf("Output file cannot be opened");
  exit(2);
  }

while(!feof(in_file)) {
  c=fgetc(in_file);
  fputc(c,out_file);
}

fclose(in_file);
fclose(out_file);

return(0);
}
```

In this example, the *while* loop contains two executable statements, so the brace pair is required. The program also illustrates the use of several file I/O statements such as **fgets**, **fgetc**, **fputc**, and **feof** (discussed in Chapter 11).

do-while Loops

The *do-while* loop differs from both the *for* and *while* loops in that it is a *post-test* loop. In other words, the loop is always entered at least once, and the loop condition is tested at the end of the first iteration. In contrast, *for* and *while* loops may execute from zero to many times, depending on the loop control variable. Since *do-while* loops always execute at least one time, they are best used whenever you are certain that you want the particular loop entered. For example, your program may need to present a menu to the user even if they just want to immediately quit the program. They will need to see the menu to know which key terminates the application.

The syntax for a *do-while* loop looks like this:

do

   action;

while(*test_condition*);

Braces are required for *do-while* statements that have compound actions:

do {

   action1;

action2;

action3;

actionn;

} while(*test_condition*);

The following C++ program uses a *do-while* loop to print a menu and obtain a valid user response:

```
//
//      A C++ program using a do-while loop to print a menu
//      and obtain a valid user response.
//      Copyright (c) Chris H. Pappas and William H. Murray, 1990
//

#include <iostream.h>
#include <conio.h>

main()
{
  int user_response,X,Y;

  clrscr();
  do {
    cout << "\t\t\t>>> Welcome to MenuIt <<<\n\n";

    cout << "\t\t\t    Instructions:    1\n";
    cout << "\t\t\t    Amortization:    2\n";
    cout << "\t\t\t    Loan Payoff:     3\n";
    cout << "\t\t\t    Principle:       4\n";
    cout << "\t\t\t    Interest Rate:   5\n";
    cout << "\t\t\t    Quit:            6\n";
    cout << "\n\t\t\tPlease enter your selection: ";

    X=wherex();
    Y=wherey();

    do {
      gotoxy(X,Y);
      cout << "    ";
      gotoxy(X,Y);
      cin >> user_response;
    } while ((user_response < 1) || (user_response > 6));

  } while(user_response != 6 );

  return(0);
}
```

To add interest to the program, the Turbo C++ *conio.h* header file has been included. The header file contains many useful function prototypes for controlling the monitor. The program uses three of these functions: **wherex**, **wherey**, and **gotoxy**. The two functions **wherex** and **wherey** return the current screen coordinates of the cursor. The **gotoxy** function moves the cursor to any preselected screen coordinate. All three functions either return or expect **int** arguments.

The program uses an outer *do-while* loop to print menu items, and continues to reprint the menu items until the user selects option 6 to quit.

Notice that the program also has a nested inner *do-while* loop. This loop makes certain that the user has entered an acceptable response (a number from 1 through 6). Since you don't want the user's incorrect guesses to be newlined all the way down the display screen, the inner loop uses the **gotoxy** statements to keep the cursor on the same line as the first response. This is accomplished by obtaining the cursor's original position after the input prompt "Please enter your selection: " is printed. Functions **wherex** and **wherey** were designed for this purpose.

Once the user has typed a response, the cursor's x and y coordinates change, which requires their original values to be stored in the variables *x* and *y* for repeated reference. Once inside the inner *do-while* loop, the first **gotoxy** statement blanks out any previously entered values (superfluous for the first user response entered), and then obtains the next number entered. This process continues until an acceptable *user_response* is obtained. When the inner *do-while* loop is exited, control returns to the outer *do-while* loop, which repeats the menu until the user enters a **6** to quit. See if you can rewrite the program using **gotoxy** so that the entire menu doesn't need to be reprinted with each valid *user_response*.

break Statement

The C **break** statement can be used to exit a loop before the test condition becomes FALSE. The **break** statement is similar in many ways to a **goto** statement, only the point jumped to is not known directly. When breaking out of a loop, program execution continues with the next statement following the loop itself.

```
/*
 *    A C program demonstrating the use of the break statement.
 *    Copyright (c) Chris H. Pappas and William H. Murray, 1990
```

```
*/

main()
{
  int i=1,sum=0;

  while(i < 10){
    sum = sum + i;
    if(sum > 20)
      break;
    i++;
  }

  return(0);
}
```

Use the Turbo Debugger to trace through the program. Trace the variables *sum* and *i*. Pay particular attention to which statements are executed after *sum* reaches the value 21.

Notice that when *sum* reaches the value 21, the **break** statement is executed. This causes the increment of *i* to be jumped over, *i++*, with program execution continuing on the line of code below the loop. In this example, the next statement executed was the **return**.

continue Statement

There is a subtle difference between the C **break** statement and the C **continue** statement. As you have seen, **break** causes the loop to terminate execution altogether. In contrast, **continue** causes all of the statements following it to be ignored but does not circumvent incrementing the loop control variable or the loop control test condition. In other words, if the loop control variable still satisfies the loop test condition, the loop will continue to iterate.

The following program demonstrates this concept using a number guessing game:

```
/*
 *    A C program demonstrating the use of the continue statement.
 *    Copyright (c) Chris H. Pappas and William H. Murray, 1990
 */

#include <stdio.h>

#define TRUE 1
#define FALSE 0
```

```
main()
{
  int lucky_number=77,
      input_value,
      number_of_tries=0,
      lucky=FALSE;

  while(!lucky){
    printf("Please enter your lucky guess: ");
    scanf("%d",&input_value);
    number_of_tries++;
    if(input_value == lucky_number)
      lucky=TRUE;
    else
      continue;
    printf("It only took you %d tries to get lucky!",
      number_of_tries);
  }

  return(0);
}
```

Enter the preceding program and trace the variables *input_value, number_of_tries,* and *lucky.* Pay particular attention to which statements are executed after *input_value* is compared to the *lucky_number.*

The program uses a *while* loop to prompt the user for a value, increments the *number_of_tries* for each guess entered, and then determines the appropriate action to take based on the success of the match. If no match was found, the *else* statement is executed. This is the **continue** statement. Whenever the **continue** statement is executed, the **printf** statement is ignored. Note, however, that the loop continues to execute. When the *input_value* matches the *lucky_number,* the *lucky* flag is set to TRUE and the **continue** statement is ignored, allowing the **printf** statement to execute.

Using break and continue Together

Both the **break** and **continue** statements can be combined to solve some interesting program problems. Consider the following C++ example:

```
//
//    A C++ program demonstrating the usefulness of combining
//    the break and continue statements.
//    Copyright (c) Chris H. Pappas and William H. Murray, 1990
//

#include <stdio.h>
```

```c
#include <ctype.h>

#define NEWLINE '\n'

main()
{
  int c;

  while((c=getchar()) != EOF)
  {
    if(isascii(c) == 0) {
      cout << "Not an ASCII character; ";
      cout << "not going to continue/n";
      break;
    }

    if(ispunct(c) || isspace(c)) {
      putchar(NEWLINE);
      continue;
    }

    if(isprint(c) == 0) {
      c = getchar();
      continue;
    }

    putchar(c);
  }

  return(0);
}
```

If the program receives the input

```
word control B  exclamation! apostrophe' period.
^Z
```

it produces this output:

```
word
control
B
exclamation

apostrophe

period
```

The program continues to read character input until the EOF character ^Z is typed. It then examines the input, removing any nonprintable characters, and places each "word" on its own line. It accomplishes this via some interesting functions defined in the *ctype.h,* including **isascii, ispunct, is-space**, and **isprint**. Each function is passed a character parameter and returns either a 0 or some other value indicating the result of the comparison.

The function **isascii** indicates whether the character passed falls into the acceptable ASCII value range; **ispunct** indicates whether the character is a punctuation mark; **isspace** indicates if the character is a space; and **isprint** reports whether the character parameter is a printable character.

Using these functions, the program determines whether to continue the program and what to do with the characters input if it continues.

The first test within the *while* loop evaluates whether the file is in readable form. For example, the input data could have been saved in binary format, rendering the program useless. If so, the associated *if* statements execute, printing a warning message and breaking out of the *while* loop permanently.

If all is well, the second *if* statement checks whether the character input is a punctuation mark or a blank space. If either of these conditions is TRUE, the associated *if* statements are executed, causing a blank line to be skipped in the output and executing the **continue** statement. The **continue** statement efficiently jumps over the remaining test condition and output statement but does not terminate the loop. It merely indicates that the character's form has been diagnosed properly and that it is time to obtain a new character.

If the file format is acceptable and the character input is not punctuation or a blank, the third *if* statement asks whether the character is printable. This test takes care of any control codes. Notice that the example input to the program included a ^B. Since ^B is not printable, this *if* statement immediately obtains a new character and then executes a **continue** statement. Similarly, this **continue** statement indicates that the character in question has been diagnosed, the proper action has been taken, and it is time to get another character. The **continue** statement also causes the **putchar** statement to be ignored while not terminating the *while* loop.

Finally, if all other tests have proved invalid, the input character is printed by the **putchar** statement and the loop is iterated again until a ^Z is entered. As you can see, the combination of the **break** and **continue** statements can lead to some interesting problem solutions.

exit Statement

Under certain circumstances, it is proper for a program to terminate long before all of its statements have been examined and/or executed. For these circumstances, C incorporates the **exit** library function. The **exit** function expects one integer argument called a *status value*. The UNIX and MS-DOS operating systems interpret a status value of 0 as a normal program termination and any nonzero status values as different kinds of errors.

The process that invoked the program can use the particular status value passed to **exit** to take some action. For example, if the program were invoked from the command line and the status value indicated some type of error, the operating system might display a message. In addition to terminating the program, **exit** writes all output waiting to be written and closes all open files.

The following C++ program averages a list of up to 30 grades. The program will exit if the user requests to average more than *SIZE* number of integers:

```
//
//      A C++ program demonstrating the use of the exit function
//      Copyright (c) Chris H. Pappas and William H. Murray, 1990
//

#include <iostream.h>
#include <process.h>

#define SIZE 30

main()
{
  int index,how_many,grades[SIZE];
  float sum=0.0,max_grade=0.0,min_grade=100.00,average;

  cout << "\nEnter the number of grades to be averaged: ";
  cin >>  how_many;
  if(how_many > SIZE) {
    cout << "\nYou can only enter up to " << SIZE << " grades" \
            << " to be averaged.\n";
    cout << "\n        >>> Program was exited. <<<\n";
    exit(0);
  }

  for(index = 0; index < how_many; index++) {
```

```
      cout << "\nPlease enter a grade " << index+1 << ":   ";
      cin >> grades[index];
   }

   for(index = 0; index < how_many; index++)
     sum = sum + grades[index];

   average = sum/(float)how_many;

   for(index = 0; index < how_many; index++) {
     if(grades[index] > max_grade)
       max_grade = grades[index];
     if(grades[index] < min_grade)
       min_grade = grades[index];
   }

   cout << "\nThe maximum grade is " << max_grade;
   cout << "\nThe minimum grade is " << min_grade;
   cout << "\nThe average grade is " << average;

   return(0);
}
```

The program begins by including the *process.h* header file. Either *process.h* or *stdlib.h* can be included to prototype the function **exit**. The constant *SIZE* is declared to be 30 and is used to dimension the array of **ints**, *grades*. After the remaining variables are declared, the program prompts the user for the number of grades to be entered. For this program, the user's response is to be typed next to the prompt.

The program inputs the requested value into the variable *how_many* and uses this for the *if* comparison. When the user wants to average more numbers than will fit in *grades*, the two warning messages are printed and then the **exit** statement is executed, terminating the program.

See if you can detect the two subtle differences between this program and the one that follows:

```
//
//     A C++ program demonstrating the use of the exit function
//     in relation to the difference between the process.h
//     and stdlib.h header files.
//     Copyright (c) Chris H. Pappas and William H. Murray, 1990
//

#include <iostream.h>
#include <stdlib.h>
```

```
#define SIZE 30

main()
{
  int index,how_many,grades[SIZE];
  float sum=0.0,max_grade=0.0,min_grade=100.00,average;

  cout << "\nEnter the number of grades to be averaged: ";
  cin >>  how_many;
  if(how_many > SIZE) {
    cout << "\nYou can only enter up to " << SIZE << " grades" \
            << " to be averaged.\n";
    cout << "\n           >>> Program was exited. <<<\n";
    exit(EXIT_SUCCESS);
  }

  for(index = 0; index < how_many; index++) {
    cout << "\nPlease enter a grade " << index+1 << ":   ";
    cin >> grades[index];
  }

  for(index = 0; index < how_many; index++)
    sum = sum + grades[index];

  average = sum/(float)how_many;

  for(index = 0; index < how_many; index++) {
    if(grades[index] > max_grade)
      max_grade = grades[index];
    if(grades[index] < min_grade)
      min_grade = grades[index];
  }

  cout << "\nThe maximum grade is " << max_grade;
  cout << "\nThe minimum grade is " << min_grade;
  cout << "\nThe average grade is " << average;

  return(0);
}
```

Including the *stdlib.h* header file instead of *process.h* makes visible two additional definitions: **EXIT_SUCCESS** (returns a value of 0) and **EXIT_FAILURE** (returns an unsuccessful value). This program used the **EXIT_SUCCESS** definition for a more readable parameter to the **exit** function.

atexit Statement

Whenever a program invokes the **exit** function or performs a normal program termination, it can also call any registered **exit** functions posted with **atexit**, as shown in the following C program:

```
/*
*       A C program demonstrating the relationship between the
*       function atexit and the order in which the functions
*       declared are executed.
*       Copyright (c) Chris H. Pappas and William H. Murray, 1990
*/

#include <stdio.h>
#include <stdlib.h>

void atexit_function1(void);
void atexit_function2(void);
void atexit_function3(void);

main()
{

  atexit(atexit_function1);
  atexit(atexit_function2);
  atexit(atexit_function3);

  printf("Atexit program entered.\n");
  printf("Atexit program exited.\n\n");
  printf(">>>>>>>>>> <<<<<<<<<<\n\n");

  return(0);
}

void atexit_function1(void)
{
  printf("atexit_function1 entered.\n");
}

void atexit_function2(void)
{
  printf("atexit_function2 entered.\n");
}

void atexit_function3(void)
{
  printf("atexit_function3 entered.\n");
}
```

The program output looks like this:

```
Atexit program entered.
Atexit program exited.

>>>>>>>>>> <<<<<<<<<<

atexit_function3 entered.
atexit_function2 entered.
atexit_function1 entered.
```

The **atexit** function uses the name of a function as its only parameter and registers the specified function as an **exit** function. Whenever the program terminates normally (as in the previous example) or invokes the **exit** function, all **atexit** declared functions are executed.

Technically, each time the **atexit** statement is encountered in the source code, the specified function is added to a list of functions that execute when the program terminates. When the program terminates, any functions that have been passed to **atexit** are executed, and the last function added is the first one executed. This explains why the *atexit_function3* output statement was printed before the similar statement in *atexit_function1*.

PUTTING YOUR KNOWLEDGE TO WORK

1. Are braces **{ }**, always required after an *if* statement?

2. Write a C program that converts a student's average to its equivalent letter grade by using nested *if-else-if* statements. Use the following grading criteria:

    A > = 90

    B > = 80

    C > = 70

    D > = 60

    F < 60

3. Using the conditional **?** statement, write an output statement in either C or C++ that has the following two possible outcomes:

    ```
    The smallest of ten values entered is 50.
    The largest of ten values entered is 50.
    ```

4. Rewrite as a *switch* statement the nested *if-else-if* statements used in the example program earlier in this chapter to convert a length to different measures.

5. From the example programs, can you say that all *for* loops are initialized to 0? If so, why? If not, why not?

6. Are *for* and *while* loops pretest loops?

7. How does a *do-while* loop differ from a *while* loop? How does it differ from a *for* loop?

8. Explain in your own words the difference between the **break** statement and the **continue** statement.

9. From a structured programming point of view, are program exits acceptable?

10. To gain additional experience with C++, take one of the C programs in the chapter and try rewriting it as a C++ program.

8

FUNCTIONS

In this chapter you will learn

- What a function is and how it is prototyped

- The various types of functions

- Arguments that can be passed to functions

- How to use *argc* and *argv* with **main**

- How to tap special library functions

- Special C++ features, including inline, overloading, and ellipses

Functions form the cornerstone of C and C++ programming. As you expand your programming skills, your programs will take on a modular appearance when you begin programming with functions. You do all C and C++ programming within a function. This is because all programs must include **main**, which is itself a function. If you have programmed in other languages, you will find C functions similar to modules in other languages. Pascal uses procedures and functions, Fortran uses just functions, and assembly language uses just procedures. How functions work determines to a large degree the efficiency, readability, and portability of C program code.

This chapter includes numerous C and C++ examples that illustrate how to write simple functions to perform specific tasks. The functions are short to make the concepts easier to understand and to prevent you from being lost in reams of code. Many of these examples use functions contained in the standard C and C++ libraries. Some C++ examples also show features unique to the C++ language. If you learn to write good functions, you are well on your way to becoming a power C programmer.

FUNCTION STYLE AND PROTOTYPING

C functions changed greatly during the ANSI standardization process. This new C standard is largely based on the function prototype used in C++. As you read various articles, books, and magazines dealing with C, you will see many variations used to describe C functions, as programmers attempt (or don't attempt) to conform to the ANSI C standard. Turbo C++ recognizes the ANSI standard and also earlier forms of C. The programs in this book conform to the ANSI standard whenever possible. This book also applies ANSI C standards to C++ code where appropriate.

Function Prototyping

Function declarations begin with the C and C++ function prototype. The function prototype is simple and is included at the start of program code to notify the compiler of the type and number of arguments that a function will use. It also enforces a stronger type checking than was possible when C was not standardized.

Although other variations are legal, whenever possible you should use the function prototype form that is a replication of the function's declaration line. For example,

```
return_type function_name(argument_type(s) argument_name(s));
```

The function can be of type **void**, **int**, **float**, and so on. The *return_type* gives this specification. The *function_name* is any meaningful name you choose to describe the function. If any information is passed to the function, you should give an *argument_type* followed by an *argument_name*. Argument types may also be of type **void**, **int**, **float**, and so on. You can pass many values to a function by repeating the argument type and name separated by a comma. It is also correct to list just the argument type, but that protype form is not used as frequently.

The function itself is an encapsulated piece of code that usually follows the **main** function definition. The function can take on the following form:

```
return_type function_name(argument_types and names)
{
   .
   .
   (data declarations and body of function)
   .
   .
   return();
}
```

Notice that the first line of the function is identical to the prototype that is listed at the beginning of a program. An actual function prototype and function, used in a program, is shown in the following C example:

```
/*
 *    C program to illustrate function prototyping.
 *    Function subtracts two integers and returns an integer
 *    result.
 *    Copyright (c) Chris H. Pappas and William H. Murray, 1990
 */

#include <stdio.h>

int subtractor(int x,int y);        /* function prototype */

main()
{
  int a=5;
  int b=93;
  int c;

  c=subtractor(a,b);
  printf("The difference is: %d\n", c);
  return (0);
}

int subtractor(int x,int y)         /* function declaration */
{
  int z;

  z=y-x;
  return(z);                        /* function return type */
}
```

The function is called **subtractor**. The prototype states that the function will accept two **int** arguments and return an **int** type. Actually, the ANSI standard suggests that every function be prototyped in a separate header file. As you might guess, this is how header files are associated with their appropriate C libraries. For simple programs, you can include the function prototype within the body of the program.

The equivalent function written for C++ looks almost identical:

```
//
//      C++ program to illustrate function prototyping.
//      Function subtracts two integers and returns an integer
//      result.
//      Copyright (c) Chris H. Pappas and William H. Murray, 1990
//

#include <iostream.h>

int subtractor(int x,int y);          // function prototype

main()
{
  int a=5;
  int b=93;
  int c;

  c=subtractor(a,b);
  cout << "The difference is: " << c << "\n";
  return (0);
}

int subtractor(int x,int y)           // function declaration
{
  int z;

  z=y-x;
  return(z);                          // function return type
}
```

Call-By-Value / Call-By-Reference

In the previous two examples, arguments were passed by value to the functions. When variables are passed in this manner, a copy of the variable's value is actually passed to the function. Since a copy is passed, the variable in the calling program is not altered. Calling a function by *value* is a popular means of passing information to a function and is the default method in C and C++. The major limitation to the call-by-value technique is that typically only one value is returned by the function.

In a call-by-*reference*, the address of the argument, rather than its value, is passed to the function. This approach requires less program memory than a call-by-value. When you use a call-by-reference, the variables in the calling program can be altered. Additionally, more than one value can be returned by the function; but more on that later.

The next example uses the **subtractor** function from the previous section. The arguments are now passed as a call-by-reference. In C, you achieve a call-by-reference by using a pointer as an argument. You can use this same technique with C++.

```
/*
 *    C program to illustrate a call-by-reference.
 *    Copyright (c) Chris H. Pappas and William H. Murray, 1990
 */

#include <stdio.h>

int subtractor(int *x,int *y);

main()
{
  int a=5;
  int b=93;
  int c;

  c=subtractor(&a,&b);
  printf("The difference is: %d\n", c);
  return (0);
}

int subtractor(int *x, int *y)
{
  int z;

  z=*y-*x;
  return(z);
}
```

In C, you can use variables and pointers as arguments in function declarations. C++ accepts these and adds a third argument type called a **reference** type. The **reference** type refers to a location, but does not require a dereferencing operator. Examine the following syntax carefully:

```
//
//    C++ program to illustrate an equivalent
//    call-by-reference.  Using the C++ reference type.
//    Copyright (c) Chris H. Pappas and William H. Murray, 1990
//

#include <iostream.h>

int subtractor(int &x,int &y);

main()
```

```
{
  int a=5;
  int b=93;
  int c;

  c=subtractor(a,b);
  cout << "The difference is:"
       << c << endl;
  return (0);
}

int subtractor(int &x,int &y)
{
  int z;

  z=y-x;
  return(z);
}
```

Notice the lack of pointers in the C++ program. The **reference** types are x and y. References to references, references to bit fields, arrays of references, and pointers to references are not allowed. Regardless of the method, a call-by-reference or **reference** type always uses the address of the argument. A call-by-reference is a favorite method of passing array information to a function. More about this technique in the next chapter.

Storage Classes and Functions

Data types can have storage classes affixed to their declarations, as you saw in Chapter 6. For example, a variable might be declared as:

```
static  int    myvariable;
```

Functions can also use **extern** and **static** storage class types. A function is declared with an **extern** storage class when it has been defined in another file, external to the present program. In a somewhat related manner, a function can be declared **static** when external access, apart from the present program, is not permitted.

Scope

The scope rules for variables used with functions are similar in C and C++. Variables can have a *local, file,* or *class* scope. Class scopes are discussed in Chapter 6.

A local variable may be used completely within a function definition. Its scope is then limited to the function. The variable is said to be accessible or visible within the function and has a local scope.

Variables with a file scope are declared outside of individual functions or classes. They have visibility or accessibility throughout the whole file. Variables of this type are global in range.

The same variable may be used with a file scope and later within a function definition with a local scope. In this case, the local scope takes precedence. C++ offers a new feature called the *scope resolution operator*, : :. When you use the resolution operator, a variable with local scope is changed to one with file scope. In this situation, the variable would possess the value of the global variable. The syntax is

: :*myvariable*

There are programming problems involving scope rules near the end of this chapter.

Recursion

Recursion occurs when a function calls itself. Recursion is permitted in both C and C++. You can generate the factorial of a number with recursion. (The factorial of a number is defined as the number multiplied by all successively lower integers.) For example,

$$6! = 6 * 5 * 4 * 3 * 2 * 1$$
$$\quad = 720$$

Take care when choosing data types, since the product increases very rapidly. As an example, the factorial of 14 is 87178291200.

```
/*
 *      C program illustrates recursive function calls.
 *      Calculation of the factorial of a number.
 *      Example:  5! = 5 x 4 x 3 x 2 x 1 = 120
 *      Copyright (c) Chris H. Pappas and William H. Murray, 1990
 */

#include <stdio.h>

double factorial(double answer);

main()
{
```

```
  double number=20.0;
  double fact;

  fact=factorial(number);

  printf("The factorial is: %15.0lf \n",fact);
  return (0);
}

double factorial(double answer)
{
  if (answer <= 1.0)
    return(1.0);
  else
    return(answer*factorial(answer-1.0));
}
```

Notice that the function includes a call to itself. Also notice that the **printf** function uses a new format code for printing a **double** value, %. . .**lf**. Here, the **l** is a modifier to the **f** and specifies a **double** instead of a **float**.

Figures 8-1 and 8-2 show a view from the Turbo Debugger. Watch the variable answer in the recursive function.

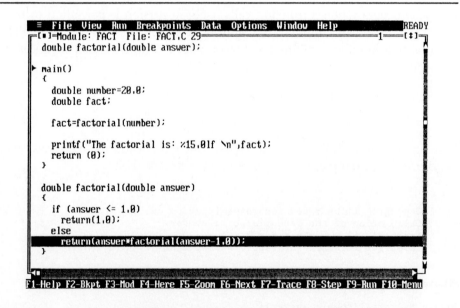

Figure 8-1.   Using the Debugger to examine a recursive function. Notice the breakpoint, which is set, in the figure

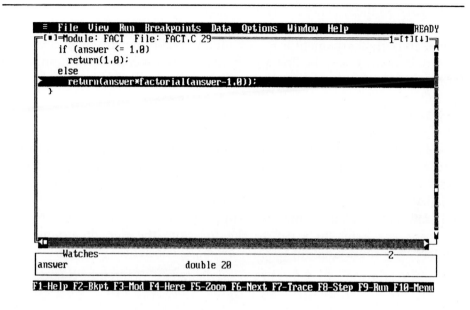

Figure 8-2.   The variable *answer* is set in the Watch window for the recursive function

FUNCTION ARGUMENTS

The following sections cover function arguments, which are arguments or parameters that are passed to the function. Function arguments are optional; some functions may receive no arguments while others may receive many. Function arguments can be mixed—that is, you can use any of the standard data types. Many of the following examples use functions from various C or C++ libraries. For additional details on these functions and their prototypes, consult your Borland C++ reference manuals.

Formal and Actual Function Arguments

The function definition contains an argument (or parameter) list called the *formal* argument list. The list may be empty or may contain any combination of types, such as integer, float, or character. When the function is actually called from within the body of the program, an argument list is also passed to the function. This list is called the *actual* argument list. When you write ANSI C code, there is usually a one-to-one match between the formal and actual argument lists, although in reality no strong enforcement is used. In many cases, the first argument supplied will provide information for any missing arguments in the list. In C, for example,

```
printf("This is decimal %d and octal %o",num);
```

passes only one argument to **printf**, although two are expected. The **printf** function replicates the *num* variable for the missing argument. In other cases, when fewer arguments are supplied, the missing arguments are initialized to meaningless values. C++ overcomes this problem, to a degree, by permitting a default value to be supplied with the argument. When an argument is missing in a call to the function, the default argument is automatically substituted. In C++, for example, consider

```
void myfunction(int x, int y=4, float z=4.78)
```

Here, if either *y* or *z* is not specified in the call to the function **myfunction**, the values shown (4 or 4.78) will be used.

Using void as an Argument

In ANSI C, you must use **void** to state explicitly the absence of function arguments. In C++, using **void** is wise but is not yet required. The following program has a simple function named **printer** that receives no arguments and does not return a value. The **main** function calls the function **printer**. When **printer** has completed its task, control is returned to the **main** function.

```
/*
*       C program will print a message with a function.
*       Function uses a type void argument and sqrt function
*       from the standard C library.
*       Copyright (c) Chris H. Pappas and William H. Murray, 1990
*/

#include <stdio.h>
#include <math.h>

void printer(void);
```

```
main()
{
  printf("This program will extract a square root. \n\n");
  printer();
  return (0);
}

void printer(void)
{
  double z=5678.0;
  double x;

  x=sqrt(z);
  printf("The square root of %lf is %lf  \n",z,x);
}
```

Notice that the **printer** function calls a C library function named **sqrt**. The prototype for this library function, contained in *math.h*, accepts a **double** and returns the square root as a **double** value.

Characters as Arguments

Characters can also be passed to a function. In the next example, a single character is intercepted from the keyboard in the function **main** and passed to the function **printer**. The **getch** function intercepts the character. In the standard C library, these other character functions are closely related to **getch**: **getc, getchar,** and **getche.** You can also use these functions in C++, but in many cases **cin** is probably a better choice. For more on **getch,** consult your Borland reference manuals. The function intercepts a character from the standard input device (keyboard) and returns a character value, without echo to the screen.

```
/*
 *    C program will accept a character from keyboard,
 *    pass it to a function and print a message using
 *    the character.
 *    Copyright (c) Chris H. Pappas and William H. Murray, 1990
*/

#include <stdio.h>

void printer(char ch);

main()
{
  char mychar;
```

```
    printf("Enter a single character from the keyboard. \n");
    mychar=getch();
    printer(mychar);
    return (0);
}

void printer(char ch)
{
    int i;
    for(i=0;i<10;i++)
      printf("The character is %c  \n",ch);
}
```

Note that a single character is passed to the function. The function then prints a message and the character ten times. The %c in the **printf** function specifies that a single character is to be printed.

Integers as Arguments

In the next example, a single **int** will be read from the keyboard with C's **scanf** function. That **int** will be passed to the function **radius**. The **radius** function uses the supplied radius to calculate and print the area of a circle, the volume of a sphere, and the surface area of a sphere.

```
/*
*     C program will calculate values given a radius.
*     Function uses a type int argument, accepts radius
*     from keyboard with scanf function.
*     Copyright (c) Chris H. Pappas and William H. Murray, 1990
*/

#include <stdio.h>

const float PI=3.14159;

void radius(int r);

main()
{
    int myradius;

    printf("Enter the radius, as an integer,\n");
    printf("from the keyboard. \n");
    scanf("%d",&myradius);
    radius(myradius);
    return (0);
}

void radius(int r)
{
```

```
    float area,volume,sarea;

    area=PI*(float) (r*r);
    volume=PI*4.0/3.0*(float) (r*r*r);
    sarea=PI*4.0*(float) (r*r);

    printf("The radius is %d  \n\n",r);
    printf("A circle would have an area of %f \n",area);
    printf("A sphere would have a volume of %f \n",volume);
    printf("The surface area of the sphere is %f \n",sarea);
}
```

While the value of **radius** is an **int** type, the calculations are cast to **float**.
Notice that *PI* was defined as a **const**.

Floats as Arguments

Floats are just as easy to pass as arguments as are integers. In the following
C example, two **float** values are passed to a function called **hypotenuse**.
Scanf intercepts both **float** values from the keyboard.

```
/*
 *      C program will find hypotenuse of a right triangle.
 *      Function uses a type float argument and accepts
 *      input from the keyboard with the scanf function.
 *      Copyright (c) Chris H. Pappas and William H. Murray, 1990
 */

#include <stdio.h>
#include <math.h>

void hypotenuse(float x,float y);

main()
{
  float ylength,xlength;

  printf("Enter the height of a right triangle. \n");
  scanf("%f",&ylength);
  printf("Enter the base of a right triangle. \n");
  scanf("%f",&xlength);
  hypotenuse(ylength,xlength);
  return (0);
}

void hypotenuse(float x,float y)
{
  double myhyp;

  myhyp=hypot((double) x,(double) y);
  printf("The hypotenuse of the triangle is %g \n",myhyp);
}
```

Table 8-1. Mathematical Functions Described in *math.h*

Function Name	Description
abs	Absolute value of a number
acos	Arc cosine
asin	Arc sine
atan	Arc tangent
atan2	Arc tangent of two numbers
atof	ASCII string to type **float**
cabs	Absolute value of complex number
ceil	Largest integer in list
cos	Cosine
cosh	Hyperbolic cosine
exp	Exponential value
fabs	Absolute value of float
floor	Smallest integer in list
fmod	Floating-point mod
hypot	Hypotenuse of right triangle
log	Natural logarithm
log10	Common logarithm
modf	Return mantissa and exponent
poly	Create polynomial
pow	Raise n to power x
pow10	Raise 10 to power x
sin	Sine
sinh	Hyperbolic sine
sqrt	Square root
srand	Random number initializer
tan	Tangent
tanh	Hyperbolic tangent

Notice that both arguments received by the **hypotenuse** are cast to **doubles** when used by the **hypot** function from *math.h*. All *math.h* functions accept and return **double** types. Table 8-1 shows other mathematical functions that your programs can use.

Doubles as Arguments

The **double** type is a very precise **float** value. As you have learned, all *math.h* functions accept and return **double** types. The following program will accept two **double** values from the keyboard. The function will raise the first number to the power specified by the second number. Now you can find out that $146.6^{3.2}$ is really equal to 8358270.07182.

```
/*
 *     C program will raise a number to a power.
 *     Function uses a type double argument and the pow function.
 *     Copyright (c) Chris H. Pappas and William H. Murray, 1990
 */

#include <stdio.h>
#include <math.h>

void power(double x,double y);

main()
{
  double xnum,ynum;

  printf("Enter the number to be raised to a power. \n");
  scanf("%lf",&xnum);
  printf("Enter the power. \n");
  scanf("%lf",&ynum);
  power(xnum,ynum);
  return (0);
}

void power(double x,double y)
{
  double result;

  result=pow(x,y);
  printf("The result is %lf \n",result);
}
```

This function uses the **pow** function prototyped in *math.h*.

Arrays as Arguments

In the following example, the contents of an array are passed to a function as a call-by-reference. Actually, the address of the first array element is passed via a pointer.

```
/*
 *    C program will call a function with an array.
 *    Function uses a pointer to pass array information.
 *    Copyright (c) Chris H. Pappas and William H. Murray, 1990
 */

#include <stdio.h>

void printer(int *data);

main()
{
   int myarray[5]={5,8,20,21,78};

   printf("Send information to function. \n");
   printer(myarray);
   return (0);
}

void printer(int *data)
{
   int i;

   for(i=0;i<5;i++)
     printf("The result is %d \n",data[i]);
}
```

Notice that when the function is called, only the name *array* is specified. In Chapter 9, you will learn more about arrays. In this case, by specifying the name of the array, you are providing the address of the first element in the array. Since *myarray* is an array of integers, you can pass an array by specifying a pointer of the element type.

You can also pass the address information by using an unsized array, as you can see in the C++ example. The information in *myarray* is transferred by passing the address of the first element.

```
//
//    C++ program will call a function with an array.
//    Function passes array information, and calculates
//    the average of the numbers.
//    Copyright (c) Chris H. Pappas and William H. Murray, 1990
//

#include <iostream.h>

void average(float data[]);

main()
{
   float myarray[10]={70.0,23.5,67.2,4.1,0.0,
                      1.25,8.0,3.14,1.0,78.234};
```

```
    cout << "Send information to averaging function. \n";
    average(myarray);
    return (0);
}

void average(float data[])
{
  int i;
  float total=0.0;
  float avg;

  for(i=0;i<10;i++) {
    total+=data[i];
    cout << "number " << i+1 << " is " << data[i] << "\n";
  }
  avg=total/i;
  cout << "\nThe average is " << avg << "\n";
}
```

The average is determined by summing each of the terms together and dividing by the total number of terms. The **cout** stream is used to format the output to the screen.

FUNCTION TYPES

This section will illustrate numerous function types. A *function type* is the type of value returned by the function. None of the previous examples have returned information from the function and thus were of type **void**.

Function Type void

You have already learned about **void** function types so the next example will be dressed up a bit. C and C++ permit numeric information to be formatted in hexadecimal, decimal, and octal, but not binary. Specifying data in a binary format is useful when you are doing binary arithmetic or developing bit masks. The function **binary** will convert a decimal number entered from the keyboard to a binary representation. The binary digits are not packed together as a single binary number but are stored individually in an array. To view the binary number, you must print the contents of the array.

```
/*
 *      C program illustrates the void function type.
 *      Program will print the binary equivalent of a number.
 *      Copyright (c) Chris H. Pappas and William H. Murray, 1990
 */

#include <stdio.h>

void binary(int number);

main()
{
  int number;

  printf("Enter a decimal number for conversion to binary.\n");
  scanf("%d",&number);
  binary(number);
  return (0);
}

void binary(int number)
{
  int i=0;
  int myarray[40];

  while (number !=0) {
    myarray[i]=(number % 2);
    number/=2;
    i++;
  }

  i--;
  for(;i>=0;i--)
    printf("%1d",myarray[i]);
  printf("\n");
}
```

You can convert base ten numbers to another base by dividing the number by the new base a successive number of times. In the case of conversion to a binary number, a two is repeatedly divided into a base ten number. The base ten number becomes the quotient from the previous division. The remainder, after each division, is either a one or a zero. The remainder becomes the binary digit. For example, to convert 10 to binary:

```
        quotient  remainder        --->1  0   1   0 (binary)
10/2      5           0  (lsb)     |   (msb)    (lsb)
5/2       2           1            |
2/2       1           0            |
1/2       0           1  (msb)     |
```

In the function, a *while* loop performs the arithmetic as long as *number* has not reached zero. The modulo operator determines the remainder and saves the bit in the array. Division is then performed on *number,* saving only the integer result. This process is repeated until the quotient (also *number* in this case) is reduced to zero.

The individual array bits, which form the binary result, must be unloaded from the array in reverse order, as you can see from the preceding numeric example. Study the *for* loop used in the function. Can you think of a way to perform this conversion and save the binary representation in a variable instead of an array?

Function Type char

Here is a minor expansion to an earlier example. The C function **uppercase** accepts a **char** argument and returns the same. For this example, a lowercase letter received from the keyboard is passed to the function. The function uses the **toupper** function (which is from the standard library and is prototyped in *ctype.h*) to convert the character to uppercase. Functions related to **toupper** include **toascii** and **tolower**.

```
/*
*    C program illustrates the character function type.
*    Function receives lowercase character and
*    converts it to uppercase.
*    Copyright (c) Chris H. Pappas and William H. Murray, 1990
*/

#include <stdio.h>
#include <ctype.h>

char uppercase(char letter);

main()
{
  char lowchar,hichar;

  printf("Enter a lowercase character.\n");
  lowchar=getchar();
  hichar=uppercase(lowchar);
  printf("%c\n",hichar);
  return (0);
}

char uppercase(char letter)
{
  return(toupper(letter));
}
```

Function Type int

The following function accepts and returns **int** types. The function **cube-number** accepts a number generated in **main** (0,2,4,6,8,10. . .), cubes the number, and returns the **int** value to **main**. The original number and the cube are printed to the screen.

```
/*
 *    C program illustrates the integer function type.
 *    Function receives integers, one at a time, and
 *    returns the cube of each, one at a time.
 *    Copyright (c) Chris H. Pappas and William H. Murray, 1990
 */

#include <stdio.h>

int cubenumber(int number);

main()
{
  int i,cube;

  for (i=0;i<20;i+=2) {
    cube=cubenumber(i);
    printf("The cube of %d is %d \n",i,cube);
  }
  return (0);
}

int cubenumber(int number)
{
  return (number*number*number);
}
```

Function Type long

The following C++ program accepts an **int** value as an argument and returns a **long**. The **long** type, used by Turbo C and other compilers, is not recognized as a standard ANSI type. The function will raise the number 2 to an integer power.

```
//
//    C++ program illustrates the long integer function type.
//    Function receives integers, one at a time, and
//    returns 2 raised to that integer power.
//    Copyright (c) Chris H. Pappas and William H. Murray, 1990
//

#include <iostream.h>
```

```
long twopower(int number);

main()
{
  int i;
  long weight;

  for (i=0;i<31;i++) {
    weight=twopower(i);
    cout << "2 raised to the " << i << " power is "
         << weight << endl;
  }
  return (0);
}

long twopower(int number)
{
  int t;
  long value=1;

  for (t=0;t<number;t++)
    value*=2;
  return (value);
}
```

The function simply multiplies the original number by the number of times it is to be raised to the power. For example, if you want to raise 2 to the fourth power (2^4), the program will perform the following multiplication:

$$2 * 2 * 2 * 2 = 16$$

Can you think of a function described in *math.h* that could achieve the same results?

Function Type float

The next C++ example will find the product of all the elements in an array. The array contains **float**s and will return a **float** product.

```
//
//      C++ program illustrates the float function type.
//      Function receives an array of floats and returns
//      their product as a float.
//      Copyright (c) Chris H. Pappas and William H. Murray, 1990
//

#include <iostream.h>
```

```
float times(float floatarray[]);

main()
{
  int i;
  float myarray[5]={1.2,4.5,7.05,6.14,0.09876};
  float product;

  product=times(myarray);
  cout << "The product of the array's numbers is: "
       << product << "\n";
  return (0);
}

float times(float floatarray[])
{
  int t;
  float temp;

  temp=floatarray[0];
  for (t=1;t<5;t++)
    temp*=floatarray[t];
  return (temp);
}
```

Since the elements are multiplied together, the first element of the array
must be loaded into *temp* before the *for* loop is entered.

Function Type double

The following C example accepts and returns a **double** type. The function
trigsine will convert an angle, expressed in degrees, to its sine value.

```
/*
 *     C program illustrates the double function type.
 *     Function receives integers from 0 to 90, one at a
 *     time, and returns the sine of each, one at a time.
 *     Copyright (c) Chris H. Pappas and William H. Murray, 1990
 */

#include <stdio.h>
#include <math.h>

const double PI=3.14159265359;

double trigsine(double angle);

main()
{
  int i;
  double sine;
```

```
  for (i=0;i<91;i++) {
    sine=trigsine((double) i);
    printf("The sine of %d degrees is %19.18lf \n",i,sine);
  }
  return (0);
}

double trigsine(double angle)
{
  double temp;
  temp=sin((PI/180.0)*angle);
  return (temp);
}
```

Notice that the **sin** function described in *math.h* is utilized by **trigsine** to obtain the answer. Angles must be converted from degrees to radians for all trigonometric functions. Recall that PI radians equals 180 degrees.

FUNCTION ARGUMENTS FOR MAIN

C and C++ can both accept command-line arguments. Command-line arguments are passed when the program is called from DOS. For example,

```
C>MYPROGRAM  Bill Chris Jeff Cindy Herb 10 20 30
```

In this example, eight values are passed from the command line to *myprogram*. Actually, it is **main** that is given specific information. One argument received by **main**, *argc,* is an **int** giving the number of command-line terms plus one. The program title is counted as the first term. The second argument is a pointer to the strings called *argv*. All arguments are strings of characters, so *argv* is of type **char** *[*argc*]. Since all programs have a name, *argc* is always one or greater. The following examples explain various techniques for retrieving information from the command line. The argument names *argc* and *argv* are required by the compiler and cannot be changed.

Strings

Since the arguments are passed as strings of characters, they are the easiest to work with. In the following example, the program anticipates that the user will enter several names on the command line. In fact, if *argc* isn't greater than two, the user will be returned to the command line with a reminder to try again and enter several names.

```
/*
*       C program illustrates how to read string data
*       into the program with a command-line argument.
*       Copyright (c) Chris H. Pappas and William H. Murray, 1990
*/

#include <stdio.h>

main(int argc, char *argv[])
{
  int i;
  double sine;

  if(argc<2) {
    printf("You must enter several names on the command\n");
    printf("line when executing this program!  Try again.\n");
    exit(0);
  }

  for (i=1; i<argc; i++)
    printf("Name #%d is %s\n",i,argv[i]);
  return (0);
}
```

The program is completely contained in **main**, with no additional functions. The names are received on the command line and printed to the screen in the same order. If numbers are entered on the command line, they will be interpreted as ASCII strings and must be printed as character data.

Integers

This C++ example will accept a single **int** number on the command line. Since the number is actually a character string, it must be converted to an integer via the **atoi** function. Then *number* is passed to the **binary** function. The function will convert the value in *number* to a string of binary digits and print them to the screen. When control is returned to **main**, *number* will be printed in octal and hexadecimal formats.

```
//
//      C++ program illustrates how to read an integer
//      into the program with a command-line argument.
//      Copyright (c) Chris H. Pappas and William H. Murray, 1990
//

#include <iostream.h>
#include <stdlib.h>

void binary(int digits);
```

```
main(int argc, char *argv[])
{
  void exit(char *c);

  int number;

  if(argc!=2) {
     cout << "Enter a decimal number on the command line.\n";
     cout << "It will be converted to binary, octal and\n";
     cout << "hexadecimal.\n";
     exit(0);
  }

  number=atoi(argv[1]);
  binary(number);
  cout << "The octal equivalent is: "
       << oct << number << endl;
  cout.setf(ios::uppercase);
  cout << "The hexadecimal equivalent is: "
       << hex << number << endl;
  return (0);
}

void binary(int digits)
{
  int i=0;
  int myarray[40];

  while (digits != 0) {
    myarray[i]=(digits % 2);
    digits/=2;
    i++;
  }

  i--;
  cout << "The binary equivalent is: ";
  for(;i>=0;i--)
    cout << dec << myarray[i];
    cout << "\n";
}
```

Of particular interest is the formatting of the various numbers. You learned earlier that the binary number is printed one digit at a time by unloading the array, *myarray,* in reverse order.

```
cout <<  dec << myarray[i]
```

When printing in octal format, the statement is

```
cout << "The octal equivalent is: "
     << oct << number
```

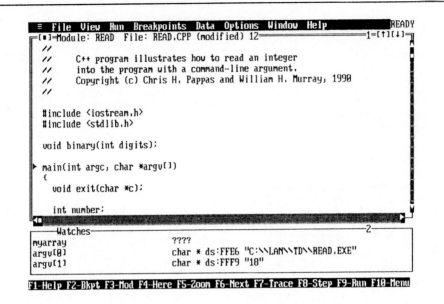

Figure 8-3.   Using the Debugger to examine a C++ numeric base converting program. argv[0] shows the title of the program while argv[1] is the number entered on the command line

You could also print the hexadecimal equivalent by substituting *hex* for *oct*. The problem is that the hexadecimal values a, b, c, d, e, and f are printed in lowercase. To print these values in uppercase, you need to use a different strategy:

```
cout, setf (ios::uppercase);
```

The formatter in **cout** permits formatting much like that permitted in C's **printf** function. See Chapter 11 for more details.

Figures 8-3 and 8-4 show a Turbo Debugger screen for this program. Examine the variables in each watch window.

Floats

As you can imagine, floats will not be any more difficult to intercept than integers. The following C example allows several angles to be entered on

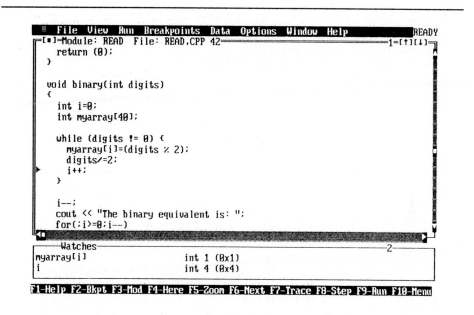

Figure 8-4.   The **binary** function of the base converting program is inspected

the command line. The sine of the angles will be extracted and printed to the screen. Since the angles are of type **float**, they can take on values such as 45.0, 76.32, or 0.02345.

```
/*
 *      C program illustrates how to read float data types
 *      into the program with a command-line argument.
 *      Copyright (c) Chris H. Pappas and William H. Murray, 1990
 */

#include <stdio.h>
#include <math.h>

const double PI=3.14159265359;

main(int argc, char *argv[])
{
  int i;
  double angle;

  if(argc<2) {
    printf("Enter several angles on the command line.\n");
    printf("Program will return the sine of the angles.\n");
    exit(0);
```

```
      }
      for (i=1; i<argc; i++) {
        angle=(double) atof(argv[i]);
        printf("The sine of %f is %15.141f\n",
               angle,sin((PI/180.0)*angle));
      }
      return (0);
    }
```

The **atof** function converts the command-line string argument to a **float** type. The program uses the **sin** function within the **printf** function to retrieve the sine information.

SPECIAL C++ FEATURES

C++ offers several special features for functions. The code for an *inline* function is replicated where the function is called in the program. By actually placing the code at the point of the function call, you save execution time in frequently called short functions. Inline functions are similar to assembly language macros, which are covered in Chapter 18. C++ also permits function *overloading*. Overloading permits you to give several function prototypes the same function name. Individual prototypes are then recognized by their type and argument list, not just by name. Overloading is useful where a function might have to work with different data types. C++ also lets you enter a variable number of arguments in the function's argument list. You can use ellipses where it is not possible, for whatever reason, to list all of a function's arguments. Since ellipses sidestep type checking, use them with caution.

Inline

The *inline* keyword is a directive, or rather a suggestion, to the C++ compiler to insert the function in a line. The compiler may ignore this suggestion for any of several reasons. For example, the function cannot contain a *for* loop or it might be too long. The *inline* keyword is used primarily to save time when short functions are called many times within a program.

```
//
//     C++ program illustrates the use of an inline function.
//     Inline functions work best on short functions that are
//     used repeatedly.  This example just prints a message
//     several times to the screen.
//     Copyright (c) Chris H. Pappas and William H. Murray, 1990
//

#include <iostream.h>

void printit(void);

main()
{
  int i;

  cout << "PRINT A MESSAGE SEVERAL TIMES: \n";

  for (i=0;i<11;i++)
    printit();
  return (0);
}

inline void printit(void)
{
  cout << "This is treated as an inline function! \n";
}
```

Overloading

The following example illustrates function overloading. Notice that two functions with the same name are prototyped within the same scope. The correct function will be selected based on the arguments provided. A function call to **times** will process **int** or **float** data correctly.

```
//
//     C++ program illustrates the function overloading.
//     Overloaded function receives an array of integers or
//     floats and returns either an integer or float product.
//     Copyright (c) Chris H. Pappas and William H. Murray, 1990
//

#include <iostream.h>

int times(int dataarray[]);
float times(float dataarray[]);
```

```
main()
{
  int i;
  int firstarray[5]={1,2,3,4,5};
  float secondarray[5]={1.2,4.5,7.05,6.14,0.09876};
  int product1;
  float product2;

  product1=times(firstarray);
  product2=times(secondarray);
  cout << "The product of the integer numbers is: "
       << product1 << "\n";
  cout << "The product of the float numbers is: "
       << product2 << "\n";
  return (0);
}

int times(int dataarray[])
{
  int t;
  int temp;

  temp=dataarray[0];
  for (t=1;t<5;t++)
    temp*=dataarray[t];
  return (temp);
}

float times(float dataarray[])
{
  int t;
  float temp;

  temp=dataarray[0];
  for (t=1;t<5;t++)
    temp*=dataarray[t];
  return (temp);
}
```

There are a few things to avoid when overloading a function. For example, if a function only differs in the function type (and not arguments), it cannot be overloaded. Also, a function cannot have the following argument list:

```
float  myfunction(int value)
float  myfunction(int &data)    //not allowed
```

This argument list is not allowed because each function would accept the same type of arguments. Overloading will also be discussed in Chapter 13.

Using a Variable Number of Arguments

You can use *ellipses* within the function's argument statement to indicate a variable number of arguments. For example,

```
void  myfunction(int x, float y, ...);
```

This syntax tells the C++ compiler that other arguments may follow. Naturally, type checking is suspended with ellipses.

PROGRAMMING PROBLEMS INVOLVING SCOPE

You may experience unexpected program results when using variables with different scope levels. For example, you can use a variable of the same name with both file and local scopes. The scope rules state that the variable with local scope (called a local variable) will take precedence over the variable with file scope (called a global variable). However, there are some problem areas that you might encounter in programming.

An Undefined Symbol in a C Program

In the following example, four variables are given a local scope within the function **main**. Copies of the variables *a* and *b* are passed to the function **multiplier**. This does not violate scope rules. However, when the **multiplier** function attempts to use the variable *c*, it cannot find the variable because the scope of the variable was to **main** only.

```
/*
 *    C program to illustrate problems with scope rules.
 *    Function is supposed to form a product of three numbers.
 *    Compiler signals problems since variable c isn't known
 *    to the function multiplier.
 *    Copyright (c) Chris H. Pappas and William H. Murray, 1990
 */

#include <stdio.h>

int multiplier(int x,int y);

main()
```

```
{
  int a=5;
  int b=9;
  int c=4;
  int d;

  d=multiplier(a,b);
  printf("The product is: %d\n", d);
  return (0);
}

int multiplier(int x,int y)
{
  int z;

  z=x*y*c;
  return(z);
}
```

The compiler issues a warning and an error message. It first warns you that the *c* variable is never used within the function and then issues the error message that *c* has never been declared in the function **multiplier**. One way around this problem is to give *c* a file scope.

Use a Variable with File Scope

In this example, the variable *c* is given a file scope. If you make *c* global to the whole file, both **main** and **multiplier** can use it. Also note that both **main** and **multiplier** can change the value of the variable. If you want functions to be truly portable, you should not allow them to change program variables.

```
/*
 *    C program to illustrate problems with scope rules.
 *    Function is supposed to form a product of three numbers.
 *    Previous problem is solved, c variable is given file scope.
 *    Copyright (c) Chris H. Pappas and William H. Murray, 1990
 */

#include <stdio.h>

int multiplier(int x,int y);

int c=4;

main()
{
  int a=5;
  int b=9;
```

```
   int d;

   d=multiplier(a,b);
   printf("The product is: %d\n", d);
   return (0);
}

int multiplier(int x,int y)
{
   int z;

   z=x*y*c;
   return(z);
}
```

This program will compile correctly and print the product 180 to the screen.

Overriding a Variable with File Scope by a Variable with Local Scope

The scope rules state that a variable with both file and local scope will use the local variable value over the global value.

```
/*
 *    C program to illustrate problems with scope rules.
 *    Function forms a product of three numbers, but which
 *    three?  Two are passed as function arguments.  The
 *    variable c has both a file and local scope.
 *    Copyright (c) Chris H. Pappas and William H. Murray, 1990
 */

#include <stdio.h>

int multiplier(int x,int y);

int c=4;

main()
{
   int a=5;
   int b=9;
   int d;

   d=multiplier(a,b);
   printf("The product is: %d\n", d);
   return (0);
}

int multiplier(int x,int y)
{
   int z;
```

```
      int c=2;

      z=x*y*c;
      return(z);
}
```

In this example, the variable *c* has both file and local scope. When *c* is used within the function **multiplier**, the local scope takes precedence and the product of 5 * 9 * 2 = 90 is returned.

A Scope Problem in C++

In the C++ example, everything proceeds smoothly until you print the information to the screen. The **cout** function prints the values for *a* and *b* correctly. When selecting the *c* value, it chooses the global variable with file scope. The program reports that the product of 5 * 9 * 4 = 90, clearly a mistake. You know that in this case, the **multiplier** function used the local value of *c*.

```
//
//    C++ program to illustrate problems with scope rules.
//    Function forms a product of three numbers.  The c
//    variable is of local scope and used by the function
//    multiplier.  However, main function reports that
//    the c value used is 4.  What's wrong here?
//    Copyright (c) Chris H. Pappas and William H. Murray, 1990
//

#include <iostream.h>

int multiplier(int x,int y);

int c=4;

main()
{
  int a=5;
  int b=9;
  int d;

  d=multiplier(a,b);
  cout << "The product of " << a << " * " << b
       << " * " << c << " is: " << d;
  return (0);
}

int multiplier(int x,int y)
{
  int z;
  int c=2;
```

```
  z=x*y*c;
  return(z);
}
```

If you actually want to form the product with a global value of *c,* how could you resolve this conflict? C++ would permit you to use the scope resolution operator mentioned earlier in the chapter.

Using the C++ Scope Resolution Operator

In this example, the scope resolution operator is used to avoid conflicts between a variable with both file and local scope. The last program reported an incorrect product since the local value was used in the calculation. Notice in the **multiplier** function the use of the scope resolution operator, : :.

```
//
//    C++ program to illustrate problems with scope rules,
//    and how to use the scope resolution operator.
//    Function multiplier uses resolution operator to
//    "override" local and utilize variable with file scope.
//    Copyright (c) Chris H. Pappas and William H. Murray, 1990
//

#include <iostream.h>

int multiplier(int x,int y);

int c=4;

main()
{
  int a=5;
  int b=9;
  int d;

  d=multiplier(a,b);
  cout << "The product of " << a << "  *  " << b
       << " * " << c << " is: " << d;
  return (0);
}

int multiplier(int x,int y)
{
  int z;
  int c=2;

  z=x*y*(::c);
```

```
   return(z);
}
```

The scope resolution operator, ::, need not be enclosed in parentheses—they are for emphasis. Now, the value of the global variable, with file scope, will be used in the calculation. When the results are printed to the screen, you will now see that 5 * 9 * 4 = 180.

PUTTING YOUR KNOWLEDGE TO WORK

1. What does a function type refer to? Give several examples.

2. What argument types are permitted in ANSI C? With the Borland C compiler?

3. What does function prototyping mean? Why is it needed? Is it required?

4. Write a simple program, using a function, that will divide two type **float** numbers. Use a call-by-value.

5. Write a simple program, using a function, that will divide two type **double** numbers. Use a call-by-reference.

6. In C++, what are the advantages of an *inline* function call?

7. In C++, explain what function overloading is and why it's important.

8. In C++, explain why you would use ellipses in function argument declarations.

9. Explain the purpose of the C++ scope resolution operator.

10. Write a C program that will convert a **float** type decimal number to binary. For example, 25.25 (decimal) would be 11001.01 (binary). Be careful; this is a tough program.

9

ARRAYS

In this chapter you will learn

- Why arrays are used
- The basic properties of an array
- How to define and initialize an array
- How to use array subscripts properly
- How to use **sizeof** with arrays
- What kind of array boundary checking the compiler performs
- How to declare and use character arrays
- How to define and use multidimensional arrays
- How to pass an array as an argument to a function
- How to use functions such as **gets**, **puts**, **fgets**, **fputs**, **sprintf**, and **stpcpy**, **strcat**, **strcmp**, and **strlen** with character arrays

Arrays, pointers, and strings are related topics in C. However, this chapter just covers arrays. In C and in C++, there are many uses for arrays that don't depend on a detailed understanding of pointers. In addition, since arrays are a large topic in themselves, it is best not to confuse the issue with a discussion of pointers. Pointers, however, allow you to understand how an array is processed. Chapter 10 will examine the topic of pointers and will complete this chapter's discussion of arrays.

WHAT ARE ARRAYS?

Arrays are indexed variables that contain many data items of the same type. Each array has one name, and you refer to the individual elements of the array by associating a subscript, or index, with the array name. In the C language, an array is not a basic type of data; instead, it is an aggregate type made up of other data types. In C, you can have an array of anything: characters, integers, floats, doubles, arrays, pointers, structures, and so on. The concept of arrays is more or less the same in both C and C++.

THE BASIC PROPERTIES OF AN ARRAY

An array has four basic properties:

- The individual data items in the array are called *elements*.
- All elements must be of the same data type.
- All elements are stored contiguously in the computer's memory, and the subscript (or index) of the first element is zero.
- The name of the array is a constant value that represents the address of the first element in the array.

Because all elements are assumed to be of the same size, you can not define arrays using mixed data types. If you did, it would be very difficult to determine where any given element was stored. The fact that all elements in an array are of the same size helps determine how to locate a given element. The elements are stored contiguously in the computer's memory (with the lowest address corresponding to the first element, and the highest address to the last element). In other words, there is no filler space between elements, and they are physically adjacent in the computer.

It is possible to have arrays within arrays — that is, multidimensional arrays. Actually, if an array element is a structure (covered in Chapter 12), other data types can exist in the array by existing inside the structure member.

Finally, the name of an array represents a constant value that cannot change during the execution of the program. For this reason, some forms of expressions that might appear to be valid are not allowed. You will eventually learn these subtleties.

DEFINING AN ARRAY

Here are two example array definitions:

```
char array_one[10];   /* an array of ten characters  */
int  array_two[12];   /* an array of twelve integers */
```

To define an array, write the array type, followed by a valid array name and a pair of square brackets enclosing a constant expression. The constant expression defines the size of the array. You cannot use a variable name inside the square brackets — in other words, you can't avoid specifying the array size until the program actually runs. The expression must reduce to a constant value, because the compiler has to know exactly how much storage space to reserve for the array. It is best to use defined constants to specify the size of the array, as in:

```
#define ARRAY_ONE_SIZE 10
#define ARRAY_TWO_SIZE 12

char array1[ARRAY_ONE_SIZE];
char array2[ARRAY_TWO_SIZE];
```

By using defined constants, you can ensure that subsequent references to the array will not exceed the defined array size. For instance, it is very common to use a defined constant as a terminating condition in a *for* loop that accesses array elements, as in this example:

```
#include <stdio.h>
#define ARRAY_ONE_SIZE 10
#define ARRAY_TWO_SIZE 12

char array1[ARRAY_ONE_SIZE];
char array2[ARRAY_TWO_SIZE];

main()
{
  int i;
  for(i = 0;i < ARRAY_ONE_SIZE; i++) {
    .
    .
    .
  }
  return(0);
}
```

INITIALIZING AN ARRAY

There are three methods for initializing arrays:

- By default when they are created. This only applies to global and static automatic arrays.

- Explicitly when they are created by supplying constant initializing data.

- During program execution by assigning or copying data into the array.

Only constant data can be used to initialize an array when it is created. If the array elements must receive their values from variables, you must initialize the array by writing explicit statements as part of the program code.

Initializing by Default

The ANSI C standard specifies that arrays are either *global* (defined outside of **main** and any other function) or *static automatic* (static, but defined after any opening brace) and will always be initialized to binary zero if no other initialization data is supplied. You can run the following program to make certain that your compiler meets this standard:

```
/*
 *     A C program to test default data initializations
 *     Copyright (c) Chris H. Pappas and William H. Murray, 1990
 */

#include <stdio.h>

#define ARRAY_ONE_SIZE 5
#define ARRAY_TWO_SIZE 5

int array_one[ARRAY_ONE_SIZE];              /* a global array */

main()
{
  static int array_two[ARRAY_TWO_SIZE]; /* a static array */
  printf("array_one[0]: %d\n",array_one[0]);
  printf("array_two[0]: %d\n",array_two[0]);
  return(0);
}
```

When you run the program, zeroes should verify that both array types are indeed automatically initialized. This program also shows that the first subscript for all arrays in C is zero. Unlike programs in other languages, a C program cannot think that the first subscript is 1. Remember, one of C's strengths was its close link to assembly language. In assembly language, the first element in a table is always at the zeroth offset.

Explicitly Initializing an Array

Just as you can define and initialize variables of type *int, char, float, double,* and so on, you can also initialize arrays. The ANSI C standard lets you supply initialization values for any array, global or otherwise, defined anywhere in a program. The following code segment illustrates how to define and initialize four arrays:

```
int numbers[3] = {1,2,3};
static float cost[5] =  {5.45,6.78,3.88,9.12,0.0};
static int more_numbers[3] = {1,2,3,4,5,6,7};
char vowels[] = {'a','e','i','o','u'};
```

The first example declares the *numbers* array to be 3 integers and provides the values of the elements in curly braces, separated by commas. As usual, a semicolon ends the statement. After the compiled program loads into the computer's memory, the reserved space for the *numbers* array will now contain the initial values, so they won't need assignments when the program executes. This is more than just a convenience — the actual initialization happens at a different time. If the program goes on to change the values of the *numbers* array, they stay changed. Many compilers permit you to initialize arrays only if they are global or static, as in the second example, where the initialization happens when the entire program loads.

The third example shows what happens if you put the wrong count in the array declaration. Many compilers consider this an error, while others reserve enough space to hold either the number of values you ask for or the number of values you provide, whichever is greater. This example will result in an error message indicating too many initializers. In contrast, when you ask for more space than you provide values for, the values go into the beginning of the array and the extra elements become zeroes. This also means that you don't need to count the values when you provide all of them. If the count is empty, as in the fourth example, the number of values determines the size of the array.

Unsized Array Initializations

Most compilers require either the size of the array or the list of actual values, but not both. For example, a program will frequently want to define its own set of error messages. You can do this in one of two ways. Here is one method:

```
char error1[31] = "File I/O ERROR - Notify SYSOP\n";
char error2[16] = "Disk not ready\n";
char error3[16] = "File not found\n";
```

This approach can become tedious — straining your eyes as you count the number of characters — and is very error prone. Here is an example of the second method:

```
char error1[] = "File I/O ERROR - Notify SYSOP\n";
char error2[] = "Disk not ready\n";
char error3[] = "File not found\n";
```

This method allows C to dimension the arrays automatically with unsized arrays. Whenever C encounters an array initialization statement and the array size is not specified, the compiler automatically creates an array large enough to hold all of the specified data.

An array with an empty size declaration and no list of values has a **NULL** length. If any declaration follows, the name of the **NULL** array refers to the same address, and storing values in the **NULL** array puts them in addresses allocated to *other* variables.

Also, unsized array initializations are not restricted to one-dimensional arrays. For multidimensional arrays, you must specify all but the leftmost dimension for C to index the array properly. With this approach, you can build tables of varying length and the compiler will automatically allocate enough storage.

USING ARRAY SUBSCRIPTS

A variable declaration usually reserves one or more cells in internal memory and through a lookup table associates a name with the cell or cells that you can use to access the cells. For example, the definition

```
int book;
```

reserves only one integer-sized cell in internal memory and associates the name *book* with that cell (see Figure 9-1). On the other hand, the definition

```
int books_in_stock[5];
```

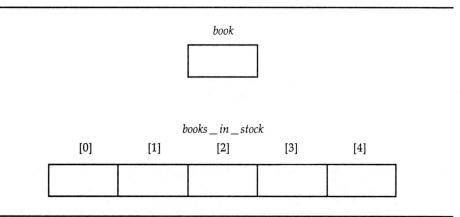

Figure 9-1.   How variables and arrays are stored in memory

reserves five contiguous cells in internal memory and associates the name *books _ in _ stock* with the five cells (see Figure 9-1). Since all array elements must be of the same data type, each of the five cells in the array *books _ in _ stock* can hold one *int.*

Consider the difference between accessing the single cell associated with the variable *book* and the five cells associated with the array *books _ in _ stock.* To access the cell associated with the variable *book,* you simply use the name *book.* For the array *books _ in _ stock,* you must specify an index to indicate exactly which cell among the five you wish to access. The statements

```
books_in_stock[0];
books_in_stock[1];
books_in_stock[2];
```

designate the first cell, the second cell, and the third cell of the array. When you access an array element, the integer enclosed in square brackets is the index, which indicates the *offset,* or the distance between the cell to be accessed and the first cell. Beginning programmers often make mistakes in the index value used to reference an array's first element. The first element is at index position [0] (not at index position [1]) since there is 0 distance between the first element and itself. As you can see, the third cell has an index value of 2 because its distance from the first cell is 2.

When dealing with arrays, you can use the square brackets in two quite different ways. When you are *defining* an array, you specify the number of cells in square brackets:

```
int books_in_stock[10];
```

But when you are *accessing* a specific array element, you use the array's name with an index enclosed in square brackets:

```
books_in_stock[5];
```

Assuming the previous declaration for the array *books _ in _ stock,* the following statement is illegal:

```
books_in_stock[10];
```

This statement attempts to reference a cell that is a distance of 10 from the first cell—that is, the eleventh cell. Because there are only ten cells in *books_in_stock*, the reference is an error. It is up to you to make sure that index expressions remain within the array's bounds.

Assume the following declarations:

```
#define NUMBER_OF_TITLES 10

int books_in_stock[NUMBER_OF_TITLES];
int index1 = 1;
int index2 = 2;
```

Now look what happens with the following set of executable statements:

```
books_in_stock[2];
books_in_stock[index2];
books_in_stock[index1 + index2];
books_in_stock[index2 - index1];
books_in_stock[index1 - index2];
```

The first two statements reference the third element of the array. The first statement uses a constant value expression, while the second statement uses a variable. The last three statements show that you can use expressions as subscripts as long as they evaluate to a valid integer index. Statement three has an index value of 3 and references the fourth element of the array. The fourth statement, with an index value of 1, accesses the second element of the array. The last statement is illegal because the index value −1 is invalid.

You can access any element in an array without knowing its size. For example, suppose that you want to access the third element in *books_in_stock*, an array of *ints*. Remember from Chapter 6 that different systems allocate different cell sizes to the same data type. On one computer system, an *int* might occupy 2 bytes of storage, whereas on another system, an *int* might occupy 4 bytes of storage. However, you can access the third element as *books_in_stock[2]* on *either* system. The index value indicates the number of elements to move, regardless of the number of bits allocated.

This offset addressing holds true for other array types. On one system, *int* variables might require twice as many bits of storage as *char* variables; on another system, *int* variables might require four times as many bits as *char* variables. Yet to access the fourth element in either an array of *ints* or an array of *chars*, you would use an index value of 3.

The following listing is the C++ equivalent of the program just discussed:

```
//
//   A C++ program to illustrate internal data storage.
//   Copyright (c) Chris H. Pappas and William H. Murray, 1990
//

#include <iostream.h>

#define SIZE 10

main()
{
  int array_index, int_array[SIZE];

  cout << "sizeof(int) is %d" << (int) sizeof(int) << "\n\n";

  for(array_index = 0; array_index < SIZE; array_index++) {
    cout << "&array[" << array_index << "] ";
    cout.setf(ios::uppercase);
    cout << hex << &int_array[array_index] << "\n";
    cout.setf(ios::dec);
  }

  return(0);
}
```

ARRAY BOUNDARY CHECKING

C array types offer faster executing code at the expense of zero boundary checking. Remember, since C was designed to replace assembly language code, error checking was left out of the compiler to keep the code concise. Without any compiler error checking, you must be very careful when dealing with array boundaries. For example, the following program incites no complaints from the compiler, and yet it can change the contents of other variables or even crash the program:

```
/*
 *   A C program you shouldn't run
 *   Copyright (c) Chris H. Pappas and William H. Murray, 1990
 */

#include <stdio.h>

#define LIMIT 10
#define TROUBLE 50

main()
```

```
{
  int collide[LIMIT], index;

  for(index=0; index < TROUBLE; index++)
    collide[index]=index;
  return(0);
}
```

ARRAYS AND STRINGS

While C supplies the data type *char,* it does not have a data type for
character strings. Instead, you must represent a string as an array of characters. The array uses one cell for each character in the string, with the final
cell holding the null character '\0';

The following program shows how you can represent the three states of
water as a character string. The array *water＿state1* is initialized character by
character with the assignment operator; the array *water＿state2* is initialized
by using the function **scanf**; and the array *water＿state3* is initialized in the
definition:

```
/*
 *    This C program will illustrate character strings
 *    Copyright (c) Chris H. Pappas and William H. Murray, 1990
 */

#include <stdio.h>

main()
{
  char        water_state1[4],            /* gas    */
              water_state2[6];            /* solid  */
  static char water_state3[7] = "liquid"; /* liquid */

  water_state1[0] = 'g';
  water_state1[1] = 'a';
  water_state1[2] = 's';
  water_state1[3] = '\0';

  printf("\n\n\tPlease enter the water state --> solid ");
  scanf("%s",water_state2);

  printf("%s\n",water_state1);
  printf("%s\n",water_state2);
  printf("%s\n",water_state3);
  return(0);
}
```

The definitions

```
char          water_state1[4],            /* gas    */
              water_state2[6];            /* solid  */
static char water_state3[7] = "liquid";   /* liquid */
```

show how C treats character strings as arrays of characters. Even though the state "gas" has three characters, the array *water_state1* has four cells—one cell for each letter in the state "gas" and one for the null character. Remember, '\0' counts as one character. Similarly, the state "solid" has five characters ("liquid" has six) but requires six storage cells (seven for *water_state3*), including the null character. Remember, you could also have initialized the *water_state3[7]* array of characters with braces:

```
static char water_state3[7] = {'l','i','q','u','i','d','\0'};
```

When you use double quotes to list the initial values of the character array, the system will automatically add the null terminator '\0'. You could also have written the same line as follows,

```
static char water_state3[] = "liquid";
```

using an unsized array. Of course, you could choose the tedious approach to initializing an array of characters, as was done with *water_state1*. A more common approach is to use the **scanf** function to read the string directly into the array, as was done with *water_state2*. The **scanf** function uses a '%s', conversion specification. This causes the function to skip whitespace (blanks, tabs, and carriage returns) and then to read into the character array *water_state2* all characters up to the next whitespace. The system will then automatically add a null terminator. Remember, the array's dimension must be large enough to hold the string along with a null terminator. Look at this statement one more time:

```
scanf("%s",water_state2);
```

Did you notice that *water_state2* was not preceded by the address operator **&**? While **scanf** was written to expect the address of a variable, an array's name, unlike simple variable names, is an *address expression*—the address of the first element in the array.

When you use the **printf** function with a '%s', the function is expecting the corresponding argument to be the address of some character string. The string is printed up to but not including the null character.

The following listing illustrates these principles using an equivalent C++ algorithm:

```
//
//    This C++ program will illustrate the use of character strings
//    Copyright (c) Chris H. Pappas and William H. Murray, 1990
//

#include <iostream.h>

main()
{
   char         water_state1[4],                 // gas
                water_state2[6];                 // solid
   static char water_state3[7] = "liquid";       // liquid

   water_state1[0] = 'g';
   water_state1[1] = 'a';
   water_state1[2] = 's';
   water_state1[3] = '\0';

   cout << "\n\n\tPlease enter the water state --> solid ";
   cin >> water_state2;

   cout << water_state1 << "\n";
   cout << water_state2 << "\n";
   cout << water_state3 << "\n";
   return(0);
}
```

The output from the program looks like this:

```
gas
solid
liquid
```

MULTIDIMENSIONAL ARRAYS

The term *dimension* represents the number of indexes used to reference a particular element in an array. All of the arrays discussed so far have been one-dimensional and require only one index to access an element. You can tell how many dimensions an array has by looking at its declaration. If there is only one set of brackets, the array is one-dimensional. Two sets of brackets indicate a two-dimensional array, and so on. Arrays of more than one dimension are called *multidimensional arrays*. The working maximum number of dimensions is usually three.

The following declarations set up a status array for disk sectors (although for a very small disk). The array is initialized while the program executes.

```
/*
 *    A C program using a two-dimensional array
 *    Copyright (c) Chris H. Pappas and William H. Murray, 1990
 */

#include <stdio.h>

#define TRACKS 5
#define SECTORS 4

main()
{
  int track;
  int sector;
  int status[TRACKS][SECTORS];
  int add;
  int multiple;

  for(track=0; track<TRACKS; track++)
    for(sector=0; sector<SECTORS; sector++) {
      add = SECTORS - sector;
      multiple = track;
      status[track][sector] = (track+1) *
      sector + add * multiple;
    }

  for(track=0; track<TRACKS; track++) {
    printf("ROW NUMBER: %d\n",track);
    printf("CELL OFFSETS\n");
    for(sector=0; sector<SECTORS; sector++)
      printf(" %d ",status[track][sector]);
    printf("\n\n");
  }
  return(0);
}
```

The program uses two *for* loops to calculate and initialize each of the array elements to their respective offset from the first element. The created array has five rows (TRACKS) and four columns (SECTORS) per row, for a total of 20 integer elements. Multidimensional arrays are stored in a linear fashion in the computer's memory. Elements in multidimensional arrays are grouped from the rightmost index inward. In the preceding example, *track* 1 *sector* 1 would be element five of the storage array. While the calculation of the offset appears to be a little tricky, note how easily each array element itself is referenced:

```
status[track][sector] = . . .
```

The output from the program looks like this:

```
ROW NUMBER: 0
CELL OFFSETS
  0   1   2   3

ROW NUMBER: 1
CELL OFFSETS
  4   5   6   7

ROW NUMBER: 2
CELL OFFSETS
  8   9  10  11

ROW NUMBER: 3
CELL OFFSETS
 12  13  14  15

ROW NUMBER: 4
CELL OFFSETS
 16  17  18  19
```

Multidimensional arrays can also be initialized in the same way as one-dimensional arrays. For example, the following program defines a two-dimensional array *powers* and initializes the array when it is defined. The function **pow** returns the value of x raised to the y power.

```
/*
 *    A C program that demonstrates how to initialize and access
 *    a two-dimensional array of double
 *    Copyright (c) Chris H. Pappas and William H. Murray, 1990
 */

#include <stdio.h>
#include <math.h>

#define ROWS 5
#define COLUMNS 3
#define BASE 0
#define RAISED_TO 1
#define RESULT 2
```

```
main()
{
  double powers[ROWS][COLUMNS]={
    2.3, 1, 0,
    2.9, 2, 0,
    2.1, 3, 0,
    2.2, 4, 0,
    2.4, 5, 0
  };

  int row_index, column_index;

  for(row_index=0; row_index < ROWS; row_index++)
    powers[row_index][RESULT] =
      pow(powers[row_index][BASE],powers[row_index][RAISED_TO]);

  for(row_index=0; row_index < ROWS; row_index++) {
    printf("    %d\n",(int)powers[row_index][RAISED_TO]);
    printf(" %2.1f = %.2f\n\n",powers[row_index][BASE],
      powers[row_index][RESULT]);
  }
  return(0);
}
```

The array *powers* was declared to be of type *double* because the function **pow** expects two *double* variables and returns a *double*. Of course, you must be careful when initializing two-dimensional arrays. Make certain that you know which dimension is increasing the fastest (always the rightmost dimension). The output from the program looks like this:

```
   1
2.3 = 2.30

   2
2.9 = 8.41

   3
2.1 = 9.26

   4
2.2 = 23.43

   5
2.4 = 79.63
```

ARRAYS AND FUNCTIONS

Just like other C variables, arrays can be passed from one function to another. Because you must understand pointers to understand arrays as function arguments, the topic is covered in more detail in Chapter 10.

Array Arguments in C

Consider a function **total** that computes the sum of the array elements *array_value[0], array_value[1],..., array_value[n].* Two parameters are required: an array parameter *array_value_received* to catch the array passed, and a parameter *current_index* to catch the index of the last item in the array to be totaled. Assuming that the array is an array of *ints* and that the index is also of type *int,* the parameters in **total** can be described as

```
int total(int array_value_received[], int current_index)
```

The parameter declaration for the array includes square brackets to tell the function **total** that *array_value_received* is an array name and not the name of an ordinary parameter. Note that the number of cells is *not* enclosed within the square brackets. Of course, the simple parameter *current_index* is declared as previously described. Invoking the function is as easy as

```
result = total(array_value,actual_index);
```

Passing the array *array_value* just involves entering its name as the argument. When passing an array's name to a function, you are actually passing the address of the array's first element. The expression

```
array_value
```

is really shorthand for

```
&array_value[0]
```

Technically, you can invoke the function **total** with either of the two following valid statements:

```
result = total(array_value,actual_index);
result = total(&array_value[0],actual_index);
```

In either case, within the function **total** you can access every cell in the array.

When a function is going to process an array, the calling function includes the name of the array in the function's argument list. This means that the function receives and carries out its processing on the actual elements of the array, not on a local copy as in single-value variables where functions pass only their values.

When a function is to receive an array name as an argument, there are two ways to declare the argument locally: as an array or as a pointer. Which method you use depends on how the function processes the set of values. If the function steps through the elements with an index, the declaration must be an array with square brackets following the name. The size can be empty since the declaration does not reserve space for the entire array, just for the address where it begins. Having seen the array declaration at the beginning of the function, the compiler permits brackets with an index to appear after the array name anywhere in the function.

The following program declares an array of five elements and, after printing its values, calls in a function to determine the largest value in the array. To do this, it passes the array name and size to the function **find_biggest**, which declares them as an array called *array[]*, and an integer called *size*. The function then passes through the array, comparing each element against the largest value it has seen so far. Every time it encounters a bigger value, it stores that new value in the variable *so_far_biggest*. At the end, it returns the largest value that it has detected for **main** to print.

```
/*
 *    A C program that demonstrates the passing of arrays
 *    Copyright (c) Chris H. Pappas and William H. Murray, 1990
 */

#include <stdio.h>

#define SIZE 5
int find_biggest(int array[],int size);

main()
{
  int numbers[SIZE] = {2,5,1,9,7};
  int i, is_big;

  printf("Here is the initial set of numbers -- ");
  for(i = 0; i < SIZE; i++)
    printf("%d ",numbers[i]);
  is_big = find_biggest(numbers,SIZE);
  printf("\nThe biggest number is %d: \n",is_big);
  return(0);
```

```
}

int find_biggest(int array[], int size)
{
  int k, so_far_biggest;

  so_far_biggest = 0;
  for(k = 0; k < size; k++)
    if (array[k] > so_far_biggest)
      so_far_biggest = array[k];
  return(so_far_biggest);
}
```

Array Arguments in C++

The following program has a format similar to the C programs examined so far. It demonstrates how to declare and pass an array argument.

```
//
//    A C++ program to demonstrate how to declare and pass arrays
//    Copyright (c) Chris H. Pappas and William H. Murray, 1990
//

#include <iostream.h>

#define MAXVALUES 10
void increment(int array[]);

main()
{
  int value_array[MAXVALUES]={1,2,3,4,5,6,7,8,9,10};
  int index;

  cout << "value_array before calling increment\n";
  for(index=0; index < MAXVALUES; index++)
    cout << "   " << value_array[index];

  increment(value_array);

  cout << "\n\nvalue_array after calling increment\n";
  for(index=0; index < MAXVALUES; index++)
    cout << "   " << value_array[index];
  return(0);
}

void increment(int array[])
{
  int local_index;

  for(local_index=0; local_index < MAXVALUES; local_index++)
    array[local_index] = array[local_index] + 1;
}
```

The output from the program looks like this:

```
value_array before calling increment
   1  2  3  4  5  6  7  8  9  10

value_array after calling increment
   2  3  4  5  6  7  8  9  10  11
```

What do the values in the output tell you about the array argument? Is the array passed call-by-value or call-by-reference? The function **increment** simply adds one to each array element. Since this incremented change is reflected back in **main**'s *value_array,* it seems that the parameter was passed call-by-reference. Remember, you know that this is true because you know that array names are addresses to the first array cell.

The following C++ program incorporates many of the array features discussed so far, including multidimensional array initialization, referencing, and arguments:

```
//
//    A C++ program that demonstrates how to define, pass,
//    and walk through the different dimensions of an array
//    Copyright (c) Chris H. Pappas and William H. Murray, 1990
//

#include <iostream.h>

void print_it(char char_array[][3][4]);

char array1[3][4][5]= {
              {
                {'T','h','i','s',' '},
                {'t','e','x','t',' '},
                {'i','s',' ','1','a'},
                {'y','e','r',' ','0'},
              },
              {
                {'A','B','C','D','E'}
              },
               };

int array2[4][3]={ {5},{6},{7},{8} };

main()
{
  int index_d1, index_d2, index_d3;
  char array3[2][3][4];

  cout << "sizeof array3        = " << sizeof(array3) << "\n";
  cout << "sizeof array3[0]     = " << sizeof(array3[0]) << "\n";
```

```
cout << "sizeof array3[0][0]    = " << sizeof(array3[0][0])
                                << "\n";
cout << "sizeof array3[0][0][0] = " << sizeof(array3[0][0][0])
                                << "\n";

print_it(array3);

cout << "array1[0][1][2] is    = " << array1[0][1][2] << "\n";
cout << "array1[1][0][2] is    = " << array1[1][0][2] << "\n";

cout << "print part of array1\n";
for(index_d2=0; index_d2 < 4; index_d2++)
  for(index_d3=0; index_d3 < 5; index_d3++)
    cout << array1[0][index_d2][index_d3];

cout << "\nprint all of array2\n";
for(index_d1=0; index_d1 < 4; index_d1++) {
  for(index_d2=0; index_d2 < 3; index_d2++)
    cout << array2[index_d1][index_d2];
  cout << "\n";
  }
}

void print_it(char array[][3][4])
{
  cout << "sizeof array       = " << sizeof(array) << "\n";
  cout << "sizeof array[0]    = " << sizeof(array[0]) << "\n";
  cout << "sizeof array1      = " << sizeof(array1) << "\n";
  cout << "sizeof array1[0]   = " << sizeof(array1[0]) << "\n";
}
```

Note how *array1* is defined and initialized. Braces group the characters so that they have a form similar to the dimensions of the array. This helps you to visualize the form of the array. The braces are not required in this case since you are not leaving any gaps in the array with the initializing data. If you were initializing just a portion of any dimension, various sets of the inner braces would be required to designate which initializing values should apply to which part of the array. The easiest way to visualize the three-dimensional array is to imagine three layers, each having a two-dimensional four-row-by-five-column array (see Figure 9-2).

The first four lines of the program output show the size of the array, various dimensions, and an individual element. The output illustrates how the total size of the multidimensional array is the product of all the dimensions times the size of the array data type—in this case, 2 * 3 * 4 * **sizeof**(*char*) or 24.

Notice how the array element *array1[0]* is in itself an array containing a two-dimensional array of [3][4], which gives *array1[0]* the size of 12. The size of *array1[0][0]* is 4, which is the number of elements in the final dimension since each element has a size of 1, as **sizeof(*array1[0][0][0]*)** shows.

To understand multidimensional arrays, you must realize that *array1[0]* is both an array name and a pointer constant. Because the program did not subscript the last dimension, the expression does not have the same type as the data type of each fundamental array element. Because *array1[0]* does not refer to an individual element, but rather to another array, it does not have the type of *char*! Since *array1[0]* has the type of pointer constant, it also cannot appear on the left of an assignment operator in an assignment expression.

Something very interesting happens when you use an array name in a function argument list, as was done when the function **print_it** was invoked with *array3*. While inside the function, if you perform a **sizeof** operation against the formal parameter that represents the array name, you do not correctly compute the actual size of the array. What the function

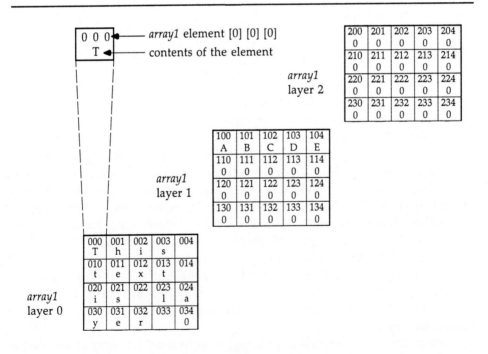

Figure 9-2.   A visual representation of *array1*

sees is only a copy of the address of the first element in the array. Therefore, the function **sizeof** will return the size of the address, not the item to which it refers.

The **sizeof** *array[0]* in function **print _ it** is 12 because it was declared in the function that the formal parameter was an array whose last two dimensions were [3] and [4]. You could not have used any other values when you declared the size of these last two dimensions, because the function prototype defined them to be [3] and [4]. Without a prototype, the compiler would not be able to detect the difference in the way the array was dimensioned. This would let you redefine the way you viewed the array's organization. The function **print _ it** also outputs the **sizeof** of the global *array1*. Interestingly, this shows that while a function may have access to global data directly, it only has access to the address of an array that is passed to a function as an argument.

Returning to the **main** function, the next two statements executed demonstrate how to reference specific elements in the *array1*. *array1[0][1][2]* references the zeroth layer, second row, third column, or 'x'. *array1[1][0][2]* references the second layer, row 0, third column, or 'C'.

The next block of code in **main** contains two nested *for* loops demonstrating that the arrays are stored in *row major order*. As you've already seen, the rightmost subscript (column) of the array varies the fastest when you view the array in a linear fashion. The first *for* loop pair hardwires the output to the zeroth layer and selects a row, with the inner loop traversing each column in *array1*.

The last nested *for* loop pair displays the elements of *array2* in the form of a rectangle, similar to the way that many people visualize a two-dimensional array. Look at the initialization of *array2*. Because each inner set of braces corresponds to one row of the array, and enough values were not supplied inside the inner braces, the system padded the remaining elements with zeroes!

The output from the program looks like this:

```
sizeof array3            = 24
sizeof array3[0]         = 12
sizeof array3[0][0]      = 4
sizeof array3[0][0][0]   = 1
sizeof array              = 2
sizeof array[0]           = 12
sizeof array1             = 60
sizeof array1[0]          = 20
```

```
array1[0][1][2] is      = x
array1[1][0][2] is      = C
print part of array1
This text is layer 0
print all of array2
500
600
700
800
```

STRING FUNCTIONS THAT USE ARRAYS

When standard input and output were discussed, functions that use character arrays as function arguments were not covered. Specifically, these functions are **gets**, **puts**, **fgets**, **fputs**, and **sprintf** (which are string I/O functions), and **stpcpy**, **strcat**, **strcmp**, and **strlen** (which are string manipulation functions).

gets, puts, fgets, fputs, and sprintf

```
/*
 *    A C program demonstrating string I/O functions
 *    Copyright (c) Chris H. Pappas and William H. Murray, 1990
 */

#include <stdio.h>

#define SIZE 20

main()
{
  char test_array[SIZE];

  fputs("Please enter the first string  : ",stdout);
  gets(test_array);
  fputs("The first string entered is    : ",stdout);
  puts(test_array);

  fputs("Please enter the second string : ",stdout);
  fgets(test_array,SIZE,stdin);
  fputs("The second string entered is   : ",stdout);
  fputs(test_array,stdout);

  sprintf(test_array,"This was %s a test","just");
  fputs("sprintf() created              : ",stdout);
  fputs(test_array,stdout);
  return(0);
}
```

Here is the output from the first run of the program:

```
Please enter the first string  : string one
The first string entered is    : string one
Please enter the second string : string two
The second string entered is   : string two
sprintf() created              : This was just a test
```

Because the strings that were entered were less than the size of *test_array,* the program works fine. However, when you enter a string that is longer than *test_array,* something like the following can occur when the program is run a second time:

```
Please enter the first string  : one two three four five
The first string entered is    : one two three four five
Please enter the second string : six seven eight nine ten
The second string entered is   : six seven eight ninsprintf() created
  : This was just a testPlease enter the first string : The first string entere
is    :e ten
The second string entered is   :
```

Take care when running the program. The **gets** function receives characters from standard input (**stdin**, the keyboard by default for most computers) and places them into the array whose name is passed to the function. When you press ENTER to terminate the string, a newline character is transmitted. When the **gets** function receives this newline character, it changes it into a null character, ensuring that the character array contains a string. No checking occurs to ensure that the array is large enough to hold all the characters entered.

The **puts** function echoes to the terminal just what was entered with **gets**. It also appends a newline character to the string where the null character appeared. Remember, the null character was automatically inserted into the string by the **gets** function. Therefore, strings that are properly entered with **gets** can be displayed with **puts**.

When you use the **fgets** function, you can guarantee a maximum number of input characters. This function stops reading the designated file stream when one fewer characters are read than the second argument specifies. Since the *test_array size* is 20, only 19 characters will be read by **fgets** from **stdin**. A null character is automatically placed into the string in the tenth position, and if you entered a newline character from the keyboard it would be retained in the string (it would appear before the null). The **fgets** function does not eliminate the newline character, as **gets** did, but merely appends the null character so that a valid string is stored. Much like **gets** and **puts**, **fgets** and **fputs** are symmetrical. **fgets** does not eliminate the newline character, nor does **fputs** add one.

To see how important the newline character is to these functions, look closely at the preceding output from the second run. Notice the phrase "sprintf( ) created" that follows immediately after the characters "six seven eight nin" that had just been entered. The second input string actually had five more characters than the **fgets** function read in (one less than SIZE of 19 characters). The others were left in the input buffer. The newline character that terminated the input from the keyboard was also dropped (it is left in the input stream because it occurs after the nineteenth character). Therefore, no newline character was stored in the string. Since **fputs** does not add one back, the next **fputs** output begins on the line where the previous output ended. You were relying on the newline character read by **fgets** and printed by **fputs** to help control the display formatting.

The function **sprintf**, which stands for "string **printf**," uses a control string with conversion characters, just like **printf**. However, **sprintf** places the resulting formatted data in a string rather than immediately sending the result to standard output. This can be beneficial if the exact same output must be created twice—for example, when the same string must be output to both the display monitor and the printer.

To review these functions:

- **gets** converts newline to a null.

- **puts** converts null to a newline.

- **fgets** retains newline and appends a null.

- **fputs** drops the null and does not add a newline; instead it uses the retained newline (if one was entered).

stpcpy, strcat, strcmp, and strlen

All of the functions discussed in this section are predefined in the *string.h* header file. Whenever you wish to use one of these functions, make certain that you include the header file in your program. The following program shows how to use the **strcpy** function:

```
/*
 *    A C program demonstrating how to use the strcpy function
 *    Copyright (c) Chris H. Pappas and William H. Murray, 1990
 */

#include <stdio.h>
#include <string.h>

#define LENGTH 17

main()
{
  char origin_string[LENGTH]="Here I go again!",
       destination_string[LENGTH];

  strcpy(destination_string,"String Constant");
  printf("%s\n",destination_string);

  strcpy(destination_string,origin_string);
  printf("%s\n",destination_string);
  return(0);
}
```

The **strcpy** function is used to copy the contents of one string, *origin_string,* into a second string, *destination_string.* The preceding program initializes *origin_string* with the message, "Here I go again!" The first **strcpy** function call actually copies the "String Constant" into *destination_string.* The second call to the **strcpy** function copies *origin_string* into the *destination_string* variable. The program outputs the following message:

```
String Constant
Here I go again!
```

The equivalent C++ program follows.

```
//
//    A C++ program demonstrating how to use the strcpy function
//    Copyright (c) Chris H. Pappas and William H. Murray, 1990
//

#include <iostream.h>
#include <string.h>

#define LENGTH 17

main()
{
  char origin_string[LENGTH]="Here I go again!",
       destination_string[LENGTH];
```

```
strcpy(destination_string,"String Constant");
cout << "\n" << destination_string;

strcpy(destination_string,origin_string);
cout << "\n" << destination_string;
return(0);
}
```

You can use the **strcat** function to append two separate strings. Both strings must be null terminated and the result itself is null terminated. The following program builds on your understanding of the **strcpy** function and introduces **strcat**:

```
/*
 *    A C program demonstrating how to use the strcat function
 *    Copyright (c) Chris H. Pappas and William H. Murray, 1990
 */

#include <stdio.h>
#include <string.h>

#define WORD_LENGTH 6
#define STRING_LENGTH 20

main()
{
   char part1[WORD_LENGTH]="In",
        part2[WORD_LENGTH]=" the ",
        prologue[STRING_LENGTH];

   strcpy(prologue,part1);
   strcat(prologue,part2);
   strcat(prologue,"beginning...");
   printf("%s\n",prologue);
   return(0);
}
```

In this example, both *part1* and *part2* are initialized, while *prologue* is not. First, the program **strcpy**s *part1* into *prologue*. Next, the **strcat** function is used to concatenate *part2* (" the ") to "In", which is stored in *prologue*. The last **strcat** function call demonstrates how a string constant can be concatenated to a string. Here, "beginning..." is concatenated to the now current contents of *prologue* ("In the "). The program outputs

```
In the beginning...
```

The following C program demonstrates how to use the **strcmp** function:

```
/*
 *    A C program that compares two strings using strcmp with
 *    the aid of the strlen function
 *    Copyright (c) Chris H. Pappas and William H. Murray, 1990
 */

#include <stdio.h>
#include <string.h>

main()
{
  char string1[]="one", string2[]="one";
  int shorter_one,result=0;

  shorter_one=strlen(string1);
  if (strlen(string2) >= strlen(string1))
    result = strncmp(string1,string2,shorter_one);
  printf("The string %s found", result == 0 ? "was" : "wasn't");
  return(0);
}
```

The **strlen** function returns the integer length of the string pointed to. In the preceding program, it is used in two different forms just to show what it can do. The first call to the function assigns the length of *string1* to the variable *shorter_one*. The second invocation of the function is actually encountered within the if condition. Remember, all test conditions must evaluate to a TRUE (1) or FALSE (0). The if test takes the results returned from the two calls to **strcmp** and then asks the relational question greater than or equal to ($> =$). If the length of *string2* is greater than or equal to that of *string1*, the **strcmp** function is invoked.

You might wonder why you use the greater than or equal to test instead of an equal to test. This method illustrates further how **strcmp** works. The **strcmp** function begins comparing two strings starting with the first character in each string. If both strings are identical, the function returns a value of 0. However, if the two strings aren't identical, **strcmp** returns a value less than 0 if *string1* is less than *string2*, or a value greater than 0 if *string1* is greater than *string2*. The relational test ($> =$) was used in case you would want to modify the code to include a report of equality, greater than, or less than for the compared strings.

The program terminates by using the value returned by *result*, along with the conditional operator (?:) to determine which message is printed. For this example, the program output is as follows:

```
The string was found
```

PUTTING YOUR KNOWLEDGE TO WORK

1. Name the four basic properties of an array.

2. How do you initialize a one-dimensional array of integers?

3. How do you initialize a two-dimensional array of characters?

4. When would you choose to use an unsized array?

5. What is the major difference between an array subscript in C and in other high-level languages?

6. Does the compiler do any array boundary checking?

7. Is an array of characters a string?

8. When passing an array to a function, do all dimensions need to be defined in the formal parameter list?

9. Does the function **fputs** automatically execute a newline at the end of the string printed?

10. Does the function **strlen** return a count of characters that does or does not include the null terminator?

10

POINTERS

In this chapter you will learn

- What a pointer variable is
- How to declare pointer variables
- How to use pointer variables
- What pointer arithmetic is
- How to use pointer arithmetic with arrays
- Pointer variable do's and don'ts
- How to use **sizeof** with pointer variables
- How to declare and use function pointers
- What dynamic memory allocation is and how to use it
- Why **void** pointers are so powerful

Most introductory programming courses use only static variables. *Static* variables, in this sense, are variables declared in the variable declaration block of the source code. While the program is executing, the application can neither obtain more of these variables nor deallocate storage for a variable. In addition, you have no way of knowing the address in memory for each individual variable or constant. To access an actual cell, you simply use the variable's name. For example, in C if you want to increment the **int** variable *century* by 100, you access *century* by name:

```
century += 100;
```

WHAT IS A POINTER VARIABLE?

An often more convenient and efficient way to access a variable is through a second variable that holds the address of the variable to be accessed. Chapter 8 introduced the concept of pointer variables, which are covered in more detail in this chapter. For example, suppose that you have an **int** variable called *contents_of_house* and another variable called *address_of_house* that can hold the address of a variable of type **int**. In C, preceding a variable with the address operator **&** returns the address of the variable instead of its contents. The syntax for assigning the address of a variable to a variable that holds addresses should look familiar:

```
address_of_house = &contents_of_house;
```

A variable that holds an address, such as *address_of_house*, is called a *pointer variable,* or simply a *pointer.* Figure 10-1 illustrates this relationship. The variable *contents_of_house* has been placed in memory at address 0318. After executing the preceding statement, the address of *contents_of_house* will be assigned to the pointer variable *address_of_house.* You express this relationship in English by saying that *address_of_house* points to *contents_of_house.* Figure 10-2 shows how this

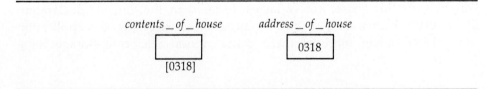

Figure 10-1.   A pointer variable

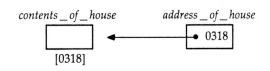

Figure 10-2.   The pointer variable *address_of_house* pointing to
contents_of_house

situation is often represented. The arrow is drawn from the cell that stores
the address to the cell whose address is stored.

To access the contents of the cell whose address is stored in
address_of_house, just precede the pointer variable with a *****,
(******address_of_house*). You have *dereferenced* the pointer *address_of_house*.
For example, if you execute the following two statements,

```
address_of_house = &contents_of_house;
*address_of_house = 10;
```

the value of the cell named *contents_of_house* will be 10 (see Figure 10-3).
You can think of the ***** as a directive to follow the arrow (Figure 10-3) to
find the cell referenced. Notice that if *address_of_house* holds the address
of *contents_of_house*, both statements that follow will have the same effect;
that is, both will store the value of 10 in *contents_of_house:*

```
contents_of_house = 10;
*address_of_house = 10;
```

Declaring Pointer Variables

As with any other language, C requires a definition for each variable.

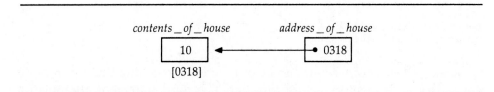

Figure 10-3.   Assignment using a pointer variable

The following statement defines a pointer variable *address_of_house* that can hold the address of an **int** variable:

```
int *address_of_house;
```

Actually, there are two separate parts to this declaration. The data type of *address_of_house* is

```
int *
```

and the identifier for the variable is

```
address_of_house
```

The asterisk following **int** means "pointer to"; that is, the data type

```
int *
```

is a pointer variable that can hold an address to an **int**.

This is a very important concept to remember. In C, unlike many other languages, a pointer variable holds the address of a particular data type. Here's an example:

```
char *address_to_a_char;
int *address_to_an_int;
```

The data type of *address_to_a_char* is different from the type of *address_to_an_int*. Run-time errors and compile-time warnings may occur in a program that defines a pointer to one data type and then uses it to point to some other data type. It is also poor programming practice to define a pointer in one way and then use it in another way. For example, look at the following code segment:

```
int *int_ptr;
float real_value = 23.45;
int_ptr = &real_value;
```

Here, *int_ptr* has been defined to be of type **int ***, meaning that it can hold the address of a memory cell of type **int**. The third statement attempts to assign *int_ptr* the address *&real_value* of a declared **float** variable.

Using Pointer Variables

The following code segment will exchange the contents of the variables *value1* and *value2* by using the address and dereferencing operators:

```
int value1 = 10, value2 = 20, temp;
int *int_ptr;

int_ptr = &value1;
temp = *int_ptr;
*int_ptr = value2;
value2 = temp;
```

The first line of the program contains standard definitions and initializations. The statement allocates three cells to hold a single **int**, gives each cell a name, and initializes two of them (Figure 10-4). It is assumed that the cell named *value1* is located at address 1395, that the cell named *value2* is located at address 3321, and that the cell named *temp* is located at address 0579.

The second statement in the program defines *int_ptr* as a pointer to an **int** data type. The statement allocates the cell and gives it a name (placed at address 1925). Remember, when the asterisk is combined with the data type (in this case **int**), the variable contains the address of a cell of the same data type. Because *int_ptr* has not been initialized, it does not point to any particular **int** variable. The fourth statement assigns *int_ptr* the address of *value1* (see Figure 10-5). The next statement in the program

```
temp = *int_ptr;
```

uses the expression *int_ptr* to access the contents of the cell to which *int_ptr* points: *value1*. Therefore, the integer value 10 is stored in the

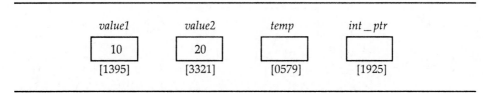

Figure 10-4.   Allocation and initialization of memory cells

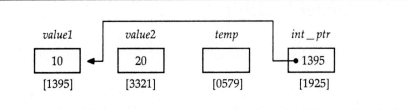

Figure 10-5.   Assignment to a pointer variable

variable *temp* (see Figure 10-6). If you had omitted the asterisk in front of *int_ptr*, the assignment statement would illegally store the contents of *int_ptr*, the address 1395, in the cell named *temp*, but *temp* is supposed to hold an **int**, not an address. The fifth statement in the program

```
*int_ptr = value2;
```

copies the contents of the variable *value2* into the cell pointed to by the address stored in *int_ptr* (see Figure 10-7). The last statement in the program simply copies the contents of one integer variable, *temp*, into another integer variable, *value2* (see Figure 10-8). Make certain that you understand the difference between what is being referenced when a pointer variable is preceded (*int_ptr*) and is not preceded (*int_ptr*) by an asterisk. For this example, the first syntax is a pointer to a cell that can contain an **int** value. The second syntax references the cell that holds the address to another cell that can hold an **int**.

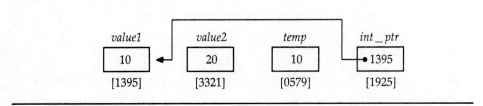

Figure 10-6.   Assignment using a pointer

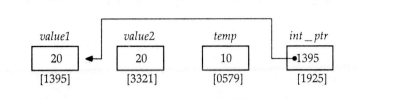

Figure 10-7.   Another assignment using a pointer

The following short program illustrates how you can manipulate the addresses in pointer variables:

```
char code1 = 'A', code2 = 'B';
char *char_ptr1, *char_ptr2, *temp;

char_ptr1 = &code1;
char_ptr2 = &code2;
temp = char_ptr1;
char_ptr1 = char_ptr2;
char_ptr2 = temp;
printf( "%c%c", *char_ptr1, *char_ptr2);
```

Figure 10-9 shows the cell configuration and values after the first four statements of the program have executed. When the fifth statement is executed, the contents of *char_ptr1* are copied into *temp* so that both *char_ptr1* and *temp* point to *code1* (see Figure 10-10). Executing the next statement

```
char_ptr1 = char_ptr2;
```

copies the contents of *char_ptr2* into *char_ptr1*, so that both pointers point to *code2* (see Figure 10-11). The next to last statement copies the address

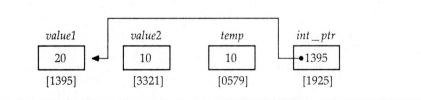

Figure 10-8.   An ordinary assignment

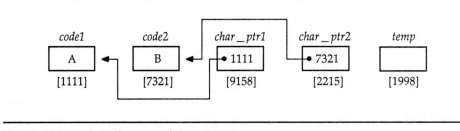

Figure 10-9.   Initial status of the program

stored in *temp* into *char_ptr2* (see Figure 10-12). When the **printf** statement is executed, you would see

BA

since the value of *char_ptr1* is "B", and the value of *char_ptr2* is "A". Notice how the actual values stored in the variables *code1* and *code2* haven't changed from their original initializations. However, since you have swapped the contents of their respective pointers, *char_ptr1* and *char_ptr2*, it appears that their order has been reversed. This is an important concept to grasp. Depending on the size of the data object, moving a pointer to the object can be much more efficient than copying the entire contents of the object.

Initializing Pointer Variables

Pointer variables, like many other variables in C, can be initialized in their definition. For example, the following two statements

```
int value1;
int *int_ptr = &value1;
```

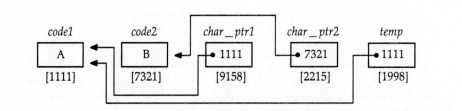

Figure 10-10.   After *temp* = *char_ptr1;*

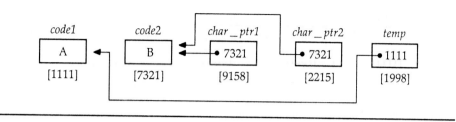

Figure 10-11.   After *char __ ptr1* = *char __ ptr2;*

allocate storage for the two cells *value1* and *int __ ptr*. The variable *value1* is an ordinary **int** variable and *int __ ptr* is a pointer to an **int**. Additionally, the code initializes the pointer variable *int __ ptr* to the address of *value1*. Be careful, however; the syntax is somewhat misleading. You are not initializing **int __ ptr* (which would have to be an **int** value) but *int __ ptr* (which must be an address to an **int**). The second statement in the previous listing can be translated into the equivalent two statements:

```
int *int_ptr;
int_ptr = &value1;
```

The following code segment shows how to declare and then initialize a string pointer:

```
/*
 *    A C program that initializes a string pointer and
 *    then prints out the string backwards then forwards
 *    Copyright (c) Chris H. Pappas and William H. Murray, 1990
 */

#include <stdio.h>
#include <string.h>

main()
{
  char *palindrome_ptr="Poor Dan is in a droop";
  int index;

  for (index=strlen(palindrome_ptr)-1; index >= 0; index--)
    printf("%c",palindrome_ptr[index]);
    printf(palindrome_ptr);

  return(0);
}
```

Pointers to Pointers

In C, you can define pointer variables that point to other pointer variables, which, in turn, point to the data, such as a **char**. Figure 10-13 represents this relationship visually; *char_ptr* is a pointer variable that points to another pointer variable whose contents can be used to point to 'A.'

You may wonder why this is necessary. The advent of OS/2 and the Windows programming environment signals the development of multitasking operating environments designed to maximize the use of memory. In order to compact the use of memory, the operating system has to be able to move objects in memory whenever necessary. If your program points directly to the physical memory cell where the object is stored, and the operating system moves it, disaster will strike. Instead, your application points to a memory cell address that will not change while your program is running (a *virtual_address*), and the *virtual_address* memory cell holds the *current_physical_address* of the data object. Now, whenever the operating environment wants to move the data object, the operating system just has to update the *current_physical_address* stored at the *virtual_address*. As far as your application is concerned, it still uses the unchanged address of the *virtual_address* to point to the updated address of the *current_physical_address*.

To define a pointer to a pointer in C, you simply increase the number of asterisks preceding the identifier:

```
char **char_ptr;
```

In this example, the variable *char_ptr* is defined to be a pointer to a pointer that points to a **char** data type. *char_ptr*'s data type is

```
char **
```

Each asterisk is read "pointer to." The number of pointers that must be followed to access the data item, or the number of asterisks that must be attached to the variable to reference the value to which it points, is called

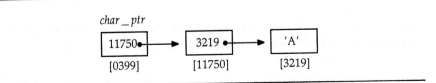

Figure 10-13.   A pointer to a pointer of type **char**

the *level of indirection* of the pointer variable. A pointer's level of indirection determines how much dereferencing must be done to access the data type given in the definition. Figure 10-14 illustrates several variables with different levels of indirection.

The first four lines of code in Figure 10-14 define three variables; the **int** variable *int_data,* the *int_ptr1* pointer variable that points to an **int** (one level of indirection), the *int_ptr2* variable that points to a pointer that points to an **int** (two levels of indirection), and *int_ptr3,* which illustrates that this process can be extended beyond two levels of indirection. The fifth line of code

```
int_ptr1 = &int_data;
```

is an assignment statement that uses the address operator. The expression assigns the address of *&int_data* to *int_ptr1.* Therefore, *int_ptr1*'s contents include 1112. Notice that there is only one arrow from *int_ptr1* to *int_data.* This indicates that *int_data,* or 5, can be accessed by dereferencing *int_ptr1* just once. The next statement,

```
int_ptr2 = &int_ptr1;
```

along with its accompanying picture, illustrates double indirection. Because *int_ptr2*'s data type is **int ****, to access an **int** you need to dereference the variable twice. After the preceding assignment statement, *int_ptr2* holds

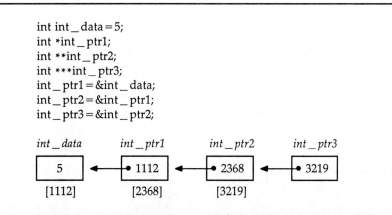

Figure 10-14.   Three variables using different levels of indirection: *int_ptr1,* *int_ptr2,* and *int_ptr3*

the address of *int_ptr1* (not the contents of *int_ptr1*); so *int_ptr2* points to *int_ptr1*, which in turn points to *int_data*. Notice that you must follow two arrows to get from *int_ptr2* to *int_data*.

The last statement demonstrates three levels of indirection

```
int_ptr3 = &int_ptr2;
```

and assigns the address of *int_ptr2* to *int_ptr3* (not the contents of *int_ptr2*). Note that the accompanying illustration shows that three arrows are now necessary to reference *int_data*.

To review, *int_ptr3* is assigned the address of a pointer variable that indirectly points to an **int**, as in the previous statement. However, ***int_ptr3** (the cell pointed to) can only be assigned an **int** value, not an address

```
***int_ptr3 = 10;
```

since ***int_ptr3* is an **int**.

C allows you to initialize pointers like any other variable. For example, you could have defined and initialized *int_ptr3* with the following single statement:

```
int ***int_ptr3=&int_ptr2;
```

Pointers to char and Arrays of Type char

A string constant such as "I/O Error" is actually stored as an array of characters with a null terminator added as the last character (see Figure 10-15). Because a **char** pointer can hold the address of a **char**, you can define and initialize it. For example,

```
char *char_ptr = "I/O Error";
```

defines the **char** pointer *char_ptr* and initializes it to the address of the first character in the string (see Figure 10-16). Additionally, the storage is allo-

'I'	'/'	'O'	' '	'E'	'r'	'r'	'o'	'r'	'\0'
[1100]	[1101]	[1102]	[1103]	[1104]	[1105]	[1106]	[1107]	[1108]	[1109]

Figure 10-15.   String constant stored as an array of characters

cated for the string itself. You could have written the same statement as:

```
char *char_ptr;
char_ptr = "I/O Error";
```

Once again, you must realize that *char_ptr* was assigned the address, not **char_ptr*, which points to the 'I.' The second example clarifies this by using two separate statements to define and initialize the pointer variable.

The following example highlights a common misconception about pointers to strings and pointers to arrays of characters:

```
char *string_ptr = "I/O Error";
static char char_array[0] = "Drive not ready";
```

The main difference between these two statements is that the value of *string_ptr* can be changed (since it is a pointer variable), but the value of *char_array* cannot be changed (since it is a pointer constant). Similarly, the following assignment statement is illegal:

```
/* NOT LEGAL */
char char_array[16];
char_array = "Drive not ready";
```

While the syntax looks similar to the correct code in the previous example, the assignment statement attempts to copy the address of the first cell of the storage for the string "Drive not ready" into *char_array*. Because *char_array* is a pointer constant, an error results.

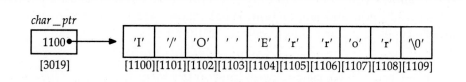

char_ptr

1100•	→	'I'	'/'	'O'	' '	'E'	'r'	'r'	'o'	'r'	'\0'
[3019]		[1100]	[1101]	[1102]	[1103]	[1104]	[1105]	[1106]	[1107]	[1108]	[1109]

Figure 10-16.   Initializing the pointer *char_ptr*

the storage for the string "Drive not ready" into *char_array*. Because *char_array* is a pointer constant, an error results.

The following input statement is incorrect because the pointer *string_ptr* has not been initialized:

```
/* NOT LEGAL */
char *string_ptr;
cin >> s;
```

To correct the problem, simply reserve storage for and initialize the pointer variable *string_ptr*:

```
char string[10];
char *string_ptr = string;
cin.get(string_ptr,10);
```

Since the value of *string* is the address of the first cell of the array, the second statement in the code not only allocates storage for the pointer variable, but initializes it to the address of the first cell of the array *string*. At this point, the **cin.get** statement is satisfied since it is passed the valid address of the character array storage.

Pointer Arithmetic

If you are familiar with assembly language programming, you have undoubtedly used actual physical addresses to reference information stored in tables. If you have only used subscript indexing into arrays, you have been effectively using the same assembly language equivalent. The only difference is that in the latter case, you allowed the compiler to manipulate the addresses for you.

Remember, one of C's strengths is its closeness to the hardware. In C, you can actually manipulate pointer variables. Many of the example programs have demonstrated how you can assign one pointer variable's address, or address contents, to another pointer variable of the same data type. C allows you to perform only two arithmetic operations on a pointer address—addition and subtraction. What follows are two different pointer variable types and some simple pointer arithmetic:

```
//
//    A C++ program demonstrating pointer arithmetic
//    Copyright (c) Chris H. Pappas and William H. Murray, 1990
//
```

```
#include <iostream.h>

#define MAXLETTERS 5

void main()
{
  int *int_ptr;
  float *float_ptr;

  int an_integer;
  float a_real;

  int_ptr = &an_integer;
  float_ptr = &a_real;

  int_ptr++;
  float_ptr++;

  return(0);
}
```

Assume that an **int** is 2 bytes and a **float** is 4 bytes. Also, *an_integer* is stored at memory cell address 2000, and *a_real* is stored at memory cell address 4000. When the last two lines of the program are executed, *int_ptr* will contain the address 2002 and *float_ptr* will contain the address 4004. You may have assumed that the increment operator **+ +** incremented by 1. However, this is not always true for pointer variables. Chapter 6 introduced the concept of operator overloading. Increment, **+ +**, and decrement, **− −**, are examples of this C++ construct. For the immediate example, *int_ptr* was defined to point to **int**s (which for your system are 2 bytes). For this reason, when the increment operation is invoked, it checks the variable's type and then chooses an appropriate increment value. For **int**s this value is 2 and for **float**s the value is 4 (on your system). This same principle holds true for whatever data type the pointer is pointing to. If the pointer variable pointed to a structure of 20 bytes, the increment or decrement operators would add or subtract 20 from the current pointer's address.

You can also modify a pointer's address by using integer addition and subtraction, not just the **+ +** and **− −** operators. For example, you can move four **float** values over from the one currently pointed to with the following statement:

```
float_ptr = float_ptr + 4;
```

Using the Turbo Debugger

Think about what this program does:

```
//
//     A C++ program to test your understanding of sizeof and
//     pointer arithmetic
//     Copyright (c) Chris H. Pappas and William H. Murray, 1990
//

#include <iostream.h>

main()
{
  float float_value = 23.45;
  float *float_ptr;
  size_t float_width;

  float_ptr = &float_value;

  float_width = sizeof(float);

  float_ptr = float_ptr + float_width;

  return(0);
}
```

From the Integrated Environment, go to the Options menu, select the Debugger submenu, and change "Source Debugging" to ON. Now start the Turbo Debugger and single step through the program. Use the Watch window to keep an eye on the variables *float _ ptr* and *float _ width*. Figure 10-17 shows a Turbo Debugger window.

The Debugger has assigned *float _ ptr* the address of *float _ value*, so *float _ ptr* contains an 46D2. The variable *float _ width* is assigned the **sizeof(float)**, which returns a 4. What happened when you executed the final statement in the program? The variable *float _ ptr* changed to 46E2 rather than 46D6. You forgot that pointer arithmetic considers the size of the object pointed to (4 × 4 byte **float**s = 16).

Actually, you were intentionally mislead by the name of the one variable *float _ width*. To make logical sense, the program should have been written in this way:

```
//
//     A C++ program using pointer arithmetic and variable
//     names not meant to trick the reader!
//     Copyright (c) Chris H. Pappas and William H. Murray, 1990
//
```

```
#include <iostream.h>

main()
{
  float float_value = 23.45;
  float *float_ptr;
  int number_of_elements_to_skip;
  float_ptr = &float_value;

  number_of_elements_to_skip = 4;

  float_ptr = float_ptr + number_of_elements_to_skip;

  return(0);
}
```

Pointer Arithmetic and Arrays

The following two programs index into a five-character array. Both programs read in five characters and then print the same five characters in reverse order. The first program uses the more conventional high-level

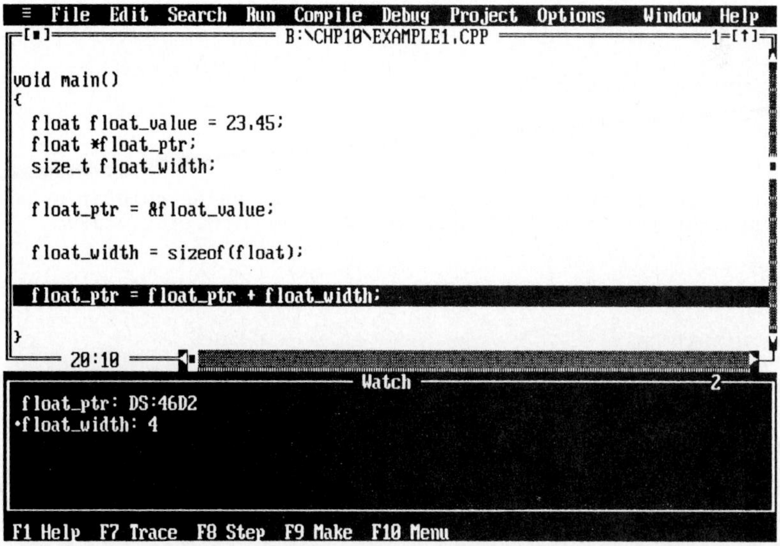

Figure 10-17.   Integrated Debugger showing current values for *float_ptr* and *float_width*

language approach of indexing with subscripts. The second program is identical except that the array elements are referenced by address using pointer arithmetic.

Here is the first example:

```
//
//    A C++ program that accesses array elements using array syntax
//    Copyright (c) Chris H. Pappas and William H. Murray, 1990
//

#include <iostream.h>

#define MAXLETTERS 5

main()
{
  char char_array[MAXLETTERS];
  int index;

  for(index = 0; index < MAXLETTERS; index++)
    char_array[index]=getchar();

  for(index = MAXLETTERS-1; index >= 0; index--)
    putchar(char_array[index]);

  return(0);
}
```

Here is the second example:

```
//
//    A C++ program that accesses array elements using pointer syntax
//    Copyright (c) Chris H. Pappas and William H. Murray, 1990
//

#include <iostream.h>

#define MAXLETTERS 5

main()
{
  char char_array[MAXLETTERS];
  char *char_ptr;

  int count;

  char_ptr=char_array;

  for(count = 0; count < MAXLETTERS; count++) {
    *char_ptr=getchar();
```

```
    char_ptr++;
}

  char_ptr=char_array + (MAXLETTERS - 1);

  for(count = 0; count < MAXLETTERS; count++) {
    putchar(*char_ptr);
    char_ptr--;
  }

  return(0);
}
```

Since the first example is straightforward, the discussion focuses on the second program. *char_ptr* has been defined to be of type **char ***, which means that it is a pointer to a **char**. Because each cell in the array *char_array* holds a **char**, *char_ptr* is suitable for pointing to each. The following statement

```
char_ptr=char_array;
```

stores the address of the first cell of *char_array* in the variable *char_ptr*.

The *for* loop reads MAXLETTERS and stores them in the array *char_array*. The statement

```
*char_ptr=getchar();
```

uses the dereference operator * to ensure that the target (that is, the left-hand side) of this assignment will be the cell to which *char_ptr* points, rather than *char_ptr* (which itself contains just an address). The idea is to store a character in each cell of *char_array*, not in *char_ptr*.

To start printing the array backwards, the program first initializes *char_ptr* to the last element in the array:

```
char_ptr = char_array + (MAXLETTERS - 1);
```

By adding 4 (MAXLETTERS - 1) to the initial address of *char_array*, *char_ptr* points to the fifth element. (Remember, these are offsets; the first element in the array is at offset 0.) Within the *for* loop, *char_ptr* is decremented to move backwards through the array elements. Make certain that you use the Debugger to trace through this example if you are unsure how *char_ptr* is modified.

Trouble with Increment and Decrement Operators

Just as a reminder, the following two statements do not perform the same cell reference:

```
*char_ptr++ = getchar();
*++char_ptr = getchar();
```

The first statement assigns the character returned by **getchar** to the current cell pointed to by *char_ptr* and then increments *char_ptr*. The second statement increments the address in *char_ptr* first and then assigns the character returned by the function to the cell pointed to by the updated address. Later in this chapter, you will use these two different types of pointer assignments to reference the elements of *argv*.

Pointer Comparisons

You have already seen the effect of incrementing and decrementing pointers using the + + and − − operators, and the effect of adding an integer to a pointer. Other operations may be performed on pointers. Some of these include

- Subtracting an integer from a pointer

- Subtracting two pointers (usually pointing to the same object)

- Comparing pointers using a relational operator such as < =, =, or > =

Since (pointer − integer) subtraction is so similar to (pointer + integer) addition, it should be no surprise that the resultant pointer value points to a storage location integer element before the original pointer.

Subtracting two pointers yields a constant value that is the number of array elements between the two pointers. This assumes that both pointers are of the same type and initially point into the same array. Subtracting pointers that are not of the same type or that initially point to different arrays will yield unpredictable results. No matter which pointer arithmetic operation you choose, however, there is no check to see if the pointer value calculated is outside the defined boundaries of the array.

Pointers of like type (that is, pointers that reference the same kind of data, like **int** and **float**) can also be compared to each other; the resulting TRUE (**int** 1) or FALSE (**int** 0) can either be tested or assigned to an integer, just like the result of any logical expression. Comparing two pointers tests whether they are equal, not equal, greater than, or less than each other. One pointer is less than another pointer if the first pointer refers to an array element with a lower number subscript (remember that pointers and subscripts are virtually identical). This operation also assumes that the pointers reference the same array.

Last of all, pointers can be compared to zero, the null value. In this case, only the test for equal or not equal is valid since testing for negative pointers makes no sense. The null value in a pointer means that the pointer has no value, or does not point to anything. Null, or zero, is the only numeric value that can be directly assigned into a pointer without a type cast.

Note that pointer conversions are performed on pointer operands. This means that any pointer may be compared to a constant expression evaluating to zero and any pointer can be compared to a pointer of type **void** * (in this last case, the pointer is first converted to **void** *).

Pointer Do's and Don'ts

The examples in this section have represented addresses as integers. This may suggest that a C pointer is of type **int**. However, a pointer holds the address of a particular type of variable but is not itself one of the primitive data types **int, float,** and so on. A particular system may allow a pointer to be copied into an **int** variable and an **int** variable to be copied into a pointer. However, C does not guarantee that pointers can be stored in **int** variables. To guarantee code portability, you should avoid the practice.

Also, not all arithmetic operations on pointers are allowed. For example, it is illegal to add two pointers, to multiply two pointers, or to divide one pointer by another.

sizeof Pointers

The actual size of a pointer variable depends on one of two things; the size of the memory model you have chosen for the application, or the use of the nonportable, implementation-specific *near, far,* and *huge* keywords.

The 80486 to 8088 microprocessors use a *segmented addressing* scheme that breaks an address into two pieces: a *segment* and an *offset*. Many local post offices have several walls of post office boxes, each with its own unique number. Segment:offset addressing is similar. To get to your post office box, you first need to know which bank of boxes, or wall, yours is on (the segment). You also need to know the actual box number (the offset).

When you know that all of your application's code and data will fit within one single 64K block of memory, you choose the small memory model. Applying this to the post office box metaphor, this means that all of your code and data will be in the same location (segment) or "wall," with the application's code and data having a unique box number (offset).

For applications that would occupy more than 64K, you would choose a large memory model. This could mean that all of your application's code would be located on one "wall," while all of the data would be on a completely separate "wall."

When an application shares the same memory segment for code and data, calculating an object's memory location simply involves finding out the object's offset within the segment—a simple calculation.

When an application has separate segments for code and data, calculating an object's location is a bit more complicated. First, you must calculate the code or data's segment, and then its offset within the respective segment. Naturally, this requires more processor time.

C++ also allows you to override the default pointer size for a specific variable by using the keywords **near, far,** and **huge.** Note however, that by including these in your application, you make your code less portable, since the keywords produce different results on different compilers. The **near** keyword forces an offset-only pointer when the pointers would normally default to segment:offset. The **far** keyword forces a segment:offset pointer when the pointers would normally default to offset-only. The **huge** keyword also forces a segment:offset pointer that has been normalized (check your user's guide for additional information on normalized pointers). The **near** keyword is generally used to increase execution speed, while the **far** keyword forces a pointer to do the right thing regardless of the memory model chosen.

For many applications, you can simply ignore this problem and allow the compiler to choose a default memory model. Eventually, however, you will run into problems with this approach, such as when you try to address an absolute location (some piece of hardware, perhaps, or a special area in memory) outside your program's segment area.

You may wonder why you can't just use the largest available memory model for your application. You can, but there is an efficiency price to pay. If all of your data is in one segment, the pointer is the size of the offset. However, if your data and code range all over memory, your pointer is the size of the segment and the offset, and both must be calculated every time you change the pointer. The next program uses the **sizeof** function to print the smallest pointer size and largest pointer size available.

The following C program prints the default pointer sizes, their *far* sizes, and their **near** sizes. The program also uses the *stringize* preprocessor directive, **#**, with the CURRENT_POINTER argument, so the name as well as the size of the pointer will be printed.

```
/*
 *   A C program illustrating the sizeof(pointers)
 *   Copyright (c) Chris H. Pappas and William H. Murray, 1990
 */

#include <stdio.h>

#define PRINT_SIZEOF(CURRENT_POINTER) \
   printf("sizeof\t("#CURRENT_POINTER")\t= %d\n", \
   sizeof(CURRENT_POINTER))

void main()
{
   char *reg_char_ptr;
   long double *reg_ldbl_ptr;
   char far *far_char_ptr;
   long double far *far_ldbl_ptr;
   char near *near_char_ptr;
   long double near *near_ldbl_ptr;

   PRINT_SIZEOF(reg_char_ptr);
   PRINT_SIZEOF(reg_ldbl_ptr);
   PRINT_SIZEOF(far_char_ptr);
   PRINT_SIZEOF(far_ldbl_ptr);
   PRINT_SIZEOF(near_char_ptr);
   PRINT_SIZEOF(near_ldbl_ptr);

   return(0);
}
```

The output from the program looks like this:

```
sizeof    (reg_char_ptr)    = 2
sizeof    (reg_ldbl_ptr)    = 2
sizeof    (far_char_ptr)    = 4
sizeof    (far_ldbl_ptr)    = 4
```

```
sizeof   (near_char_ptr)   = 2
sizeof   (near_ldbl_ptr)   = 2
```

FUNCTION POINTERS

So far, you have seen how various data items can be referenced by a pointer. As it turns out, you can also use pointers to access portions of code by using a pointer to a function. Pointers to functions serve the same purpose as pointers to data—they allow the function to be referenced indirectly, just as a pointer to a data item allows the data item to be referenced indirectly.

Pointers to functions have a number of important uses. For example, consider the **qsort** function, which has as one of its parameters a pointer to a function. The referenced function contains the necessary comparison that is to be performed between the array elements being sorted. **qsort** has been written to require a function pointer because the comparison process between two elements can be a complex process beyond the scope of a single control flag. You cannot pass a function by value—that is, pass the code itself. However, Č does support passing a pointer to the code, or a pointer to the function.

Many C and C++ books use the **qsort** function supplied with the compiler to illustrate function pointers. Unfortunately, they usually declare the function pointer to be of a type that points to other built-in functions. The following C and C++ programs demonstrate how to define a pointer to a function and how to create your own function to be passed to the *stdlib.h* function **qsort**:

```
/*
/    A C program showing how to declare and use a
/    function pointer with qsort()
/    Copyright (c) Chris H. Pappas and William H. Murray, 1990
*/

#include <stdio.h>
#include <stdlib.h>

#define MAX 10

int my_compare(const void *value1, const void *value2);
int (*function_ptr)(const void *, const void *);
```

```
main()
{
   int index;
   int int_array[MAX]={2,5,9,3,1,7,4,6,0,8};

   function_ptr=my_compare;
   qsort(int_array,MAX,sizeof(int),function_ptr);
   for(index = 0; index < MAX; index++)
     printf("%d ",int_array[index]);

   return(0);
}

int my_compare(const void *value1, const void *value2)
{
   return((*(int *)value1) - (*(int *) value2));
}
```

The function *my__compare* (the reference function) was prototyped to match the requirements for the fourth parameter to the function **qsort** (the invoking function).

   The fourth parameter to the function **qsort** must be a function pointer. This reference function must be passed two **const void *** parameters and must return a type **int**. This is because **qsort** uses the reference function for the sort comparison algorithm. Now that you understand the reference function **my__compare**'s prototype, take a minute to study the body of the reference function.

   If the reference function returns a value less than zero, the reference function's first parameter value is less than the second parameter's value. A return value of zero indicates parameter value equality, and a return value greater than zero indicates that the value of the first parameter was greater than that of the second. All of this is accomplished by the single statement in **my__compare**:

```
return((*(int *)value1) - (*(int *) value2));
```

Since both of the pointers were passed as type **void ***, they were cast to their appropriate pointer type **int *** and were then dereferenced, *****. The subtraction of the two values pointed to returns an appropriate value to satisfy **qsort**'s comparison criterion.

   While the prototype requirements for **my__compare** were interesting, the heart of the program begins with the pointer function declaration below the **my__compare** function prototype:

```
int my_compare(const void *value1, const void *value2);
int (*function_ptr)(const void *, const void *);
```

A function's type is determined by its return value and argument list signature. A pointer to **my‿compare** must specify the same signature and return type. You might think that the following statement would accomplish this:

```
int *function_ptr(const void *, const void *);
```

Unfortunately, the compiler interprets the statement as the definition of a function *function‿ptr* taking two arguments and returning a pointer of type **int ***. The dereference operator is associated with the type specifier, and not *function‿ptr*. Parentheses are necessary to associate the dereference operator with *function‿ptr*.

The corrected statement declares *function‿ptr* to be a pointer to a function taking two arguments and with a return type **int**—that is, a pointer of the same type required by the fourth parameter to **qsort**.

In the body of **main**, the only thing left to do is to initialize *function‿ptr* to the address of the function **my‿compare**. The parameters to **qsort** are the address to the base or zeroth element of the table to be sorted (*int‿array*), the number of entries in the table (*MAX*), the size of each table element (*sizeof(int)*), and a function pointer to the comparison function (*function‿ptr*). The C++ equivalent follows:

```
//
//   A C++ program showing how to declare and use a
//   function pointer with qsort()
//   Copyright (c) Chris H. Pappas and William H. Murray, 1990
//

#include <iostream.h>
#include <stdlib.h>

#define MAX 10

int my_compare(const void *value1, const void *value2);
int (*function_ptr)(const void *,const void *);

main()
{
    int index;
    int int_array[MAX]={2,5,9,3,1,7,4,6,0,8};
    function_ptr=my_compare;
    qsort(int_array,MAX,sizeof(int),function_ptr);
```

```
   for(index = 0; index < MAX; index++)
     cout << " " << int_array[index];

   return(0);
}

int my_compare(const void *value1, const void *value2)
{
   return((*(int *)value1) - (*(int *)value2));
}
```

Learning the syntax of a function pointer can be challenging. Here are a few examples:

```
int *(*(*ifunction_ptr)(int))[5];
float (*(*ffunction_ptr)(int,int))(float);
typedef double (*(*(*dfunction_ptr)())[5])();
   dfunction_ptr A_dfunction_ptr;
(*(*function_ary_ptrs())[5])();
```

The first statement defines *ifunction _ ptr* as a function pointer to a function that is passed an **int** argument and returns a pointer to an array of five **int** pointers.

The second statement defines *ffunction _ ptr* as a function pointer to a function that takes two **int** arguments and returns a pointer to a function taking a **float** argument and returning a **float.**

By using the **typedef** declaration, you can avoid the unnecessary repetition of complicated declarations. The **typedef** declaration (see Chapter 12) is read as *"dfunction _ ptr* is defined as a pointer to a function that is passed nothing and returns a pointer to an array of five pointers that point to functions that are passed nothing and return a **double."**

The last statement is a function declaration, not a variable declaration. The statement defines **function _ ary _ ptrs** to be a function taking no arguments and returning a pointer to an array of five pointers that point to functions taking no arguments and returning **int**s. The outer functions return the default C and C++ type **int**.

Luckily, you will rarely encounter complicated declarations and definitions like these. However, if you understand these declarations, you will be able to confidently parse the everyday variety.

DYNAMIC MEMORY ALLOCATION

When a C program is compiled, the computer's memory is broken down into four zones that contain the program's code, all global data, the stack, and the heap. The *heap* is an area of free memory (sometimes referred to as the *free store*) that is manipulated with the dynamic allocation functions **malloc** and **free**.

When **malloc** is invoked, it allocates a contiguous block of storage for the object specified and then returns a pointer to the start of the block. The function **free** returns previously allocated memory to the heap, permitting that portion of memory to be reallocated.

The argument passed to **malloc** is an unsigned integer that represents the needed number of bytes of storage. If the storage is available, **malloc** will return a **void** * that can be cast into the desired type pointer. The concept of **void** pointers was introduced in the ANSI C standard and means a pointer of unknown type, or a generic pointer. A **void** pointer cannot itself be used to reference anything (since it doesn't point to any specific type of data), but it can contain a pointer of any other type. Therefore, you can convert any pointer into a **void** pointer and back without any loss of information.

The following code segment allocates enough storage for 200 **float** values:

```
float *float_ptr;
int num_floats = 200;

float_ptr = (float *) malloc(num_floats * sizeof(float));
```

The **malloc** function has been instructed to obtain enough storage for 200 * the current size of a float. The cast operator (**float** *) is used to return a **float** pointer type. Each block of storage requested is entirely separate and distinct from all other blocks of storage. You can make no assumptions about where the blocks are located. Blocks are typically "tagged" with some sort of information that allows the operating system to manage their location and size. When the block is no longer needed, you can return it to the operating system by using the following statement:

```
free((void *) float_ptr);
```

Like C, C++ allocates available memory in two ways. When variables are declared, C++ creates them on the stack by pushing down the stack pointer. When these variables go out of scope automatically (for instance, when a local variable is no longer needed), C++ frees the space for that variable by moving up the stack pointer. The size of stack allocated memory must always be known at compilation.

Your application may also have to use variables with an unknown size at compilation. Under these circumstances, you must allocate the memory yourself, on the heap. You can think of the heap as occupying the bottom of the program's memory space and growing upward, while the stack occupies the top and grows downward.

Your C and C++ programs can allocate and release heap memory at any point. Unlike other variables, heap-allocated memory variables are not subject to scoping rules. These variables never go out of scope, so once you allocate memory on the heap, you are responsible for freeing it. If you continue to allocate heap space without freeing it, your program could eventually crash.

Most C compilers use the library functions **malloc** and **free** to provide dynamic memory allocation. In C++, however, these capabilities were considered so important that they were made a part of the core language. C++ uses **new** and **delete** to allocate and free heap memory. The argument to **new** is an expression that returns the number of bytes allocated; the value returned is a pointer to the beginning of this memory block. The argument to **delete** is the starting address of the memory block to be freed. The following two programs illustrate the similarities and differences between C and C++ applications that use dynamic memory allocation. Here is the C example:

```
/*
 *    A simple C program demonstrating the functions:
 *    malloc(), free()
 *    Copyright (c) Chris H. Pappas and William H. Murray, 1990
 */

#include <stdio.h>
#include <stdlib.h>

#define MAX 256

main()
{
  int * memory_block;
  memory_block=malloc(MAX * sizeof(int));
  if(memory_block == NULL)
    printf("Insufficient memory\n");
  else
    printf("Memory allocated\n");
  free(memory_block);

  return(0);
}
```

Note the second **#include** statement that brings in the *stdlib.h* header file, containing the definitions for both functions **malloc** and **free**. After the program defines the **int *** pointer variable *memory_block,* the **malloc** function is invoked to return the address to a memory block that is *MAX * sizeof(int) big.* A robust algorithm will always check for the success or failure of the memory allocation and explains the purpose behind the *if else* statement. The function **malloc** returns a NULL whenever there is not enough memory to allocate the block. This simple program ends by returning the allocated memory back to the heap with the function **free** and passing it the beginning address of the allocated block.

The C++ program does not look very different:

```
//
//    A simple C++ program demonstrating the functions:
//    new and delete
//    Copyright (c) Chris H. Pappas and William H. Murray, 1990
//

#include <iostream.h>
// #include <stdlib.h> not needed for malloc(), free()

#define MAX 256
main()
{
  int *memory_block;

  memory_block=new int[MAX];
  if(memory_block == NULL)
    cout << "Insufficient memory\n";
  else
    cout << "Memory allocated\n";
  delete(memory_block);

  return(0);
}
```

The only major difference between the two programs is the syntax used with the functions **new** and **free**. Whereas the function **malloc** requires the **sizeof** function to ensure proper memory allocation, the function **new** has been written to perform the **sizeof** function automatically on the declared data type it is passed. Both programs will allocate 256 2-byte blocks of consecutive memory (on systems that allocate 2 bytes per **int**).

Why void Pointers Are So Powerful

Now that you have a detailed understanding of pointer variables, you may begin to appreciate the need for the pointer type **void**. To review, a pointer is a variable that contains the address of another variable. If you always knew how big the pointer was, you wouldn't have to determine the pointer type at compile time. You would, therefore, also be able to pass an address of any type to a function. The function could then cast the address to a pointer of the proper type (based on some other piece of information) and perform operations on the result. This process would enable you to create functions that operate on a number of different data types.

That is precisely why C++ invented the **void** pointer type. The term **void** applied to a pointer means something different from **void** applied to function argument lists and return values (meaning "nothing"). A **void** pointer means a pointer to any type of data. The following C++ program demonstrates this use of **void** pointers:

```
//
//    A C++ program demonstrating the use of void pointers
//    Copyright (c) Chris H. Pappas and William H. Murray, 1990
//

#include <iostream.h>

#define LENGTH 40

void print_it(void *object, char flag);

main()
{
  char *string_ptr;
  int *int_ptr;
  float *float_ptr;
  char user_response,newline;

  cout << "Please enter the dynamic data type\n";
  cout << "    you would like to create.\n\n";
  cout << " Use (s)tring, (i)nt, or (f)loat ";
  cin >> user_response;
  cin.get(newline);

  switch(user_response) {
    case 's':
      string_ptr=new char;
      cout << "\nPlease enter a string: ";
      cin.get(string_ptr,LENGTH);
      print_it(string_ptr,user_response);
```

```
     break;
   case 'i':
     int_ptr=new int;
     cout << "\nPlease enter an integer: ";
     cin >> *int_ptr;
     print_it(int_ptr,user_response);
     break;
   case 'f':
     float_ptr=new float;
     cout << "\nPlease enter a float: ";
     cin >> *float_ptr;
     print_it(float_ptr,user_response);
     break;
   default:
     cout << "\n\n  Object type not implemented!";
  }

  return(0);
}

void print_it(void *object, char flag)
{
  switch(flag) {
    case 's':
      cout << "\nThe string read in:   " << str((char *) object);
      delete object;
      break;
    case 'i':
      cout << "\nThe integer read in: " << *((int *) object);
      delete object;
      break;
    case 'f':
      cout << "\nThe float value read in: ";
      cout <<  *((float *) object);
      delete object;
      break;
  }
}
```

The first statement of interest in the program is the **print_it** function prototype. Notice that the function's first formal parameter *object* is of type **void ***, or a generic pointer. Moving down to the data declarations notice three pointer variable types: **char ***, **int ***, and **float ***. These will eventually be assigned valid pointer addresses to their respective memory cell types.

The action in the program begins with a prompt that asks you to enter the data type you would like to create dynamically. Two separate input statements are used to handle your response. The first **cin** statement reads in the single character response but leaves the \n linefeed. The second input statement, **cin.get**(newline), remedies this situation.

The switch statement takes the user's response and invokes the appropriate prompt and pointer initialization. The pointer initialization takes one of three forms:

```
string_ptr=new char;

int_ptr=new int;

float_ptr=new float;
```

The statement

```
cin.get(string_ptr,LENGTH);
```

is used to input the character string and in this example limits the length of the string to LENGTH (40) characters. Since the **cin.get** input statement expects a string pointer first parameter, there is no need to dereference the variable when the **print _ it** function is invoked:

```
print_it(string_ptr,user_response);
```

Things get quieter if you want to input an **int** or **float**. The last two **case** options are the same except for the prompt and the reference variable's type.

Notice how the three invocations of the function **print _ it** have different pointer types:

```
print_it(string_ptr,user_response);

print_it(int_ptr,user_response);

print_it(float_ptr,user_response);
```

Function **print _ it** only accepts these parameters because the matching formal parameter's type is **void** *. Remember, to use these pointers you must first cast them to their appropriate pointer type. When using a string pointer with **cout**, you must cast the pointer to type **char** *. When passing a string to **cout** in this form, you do not dereference the cast pointer.

Creating **int** and **float** dynamic variables was similar; printing their values is also similar. The only difference between the last two **case** statements is the output string and the cast operator used.

While all dynamic variables disappear whenever a program terminates, each of the **case** options explicitly deletes the pointer variable. When and where your program creates and deletes dynamic storage is application dependent.

POINTERS AND ARRAYS

The following section includes many example programs that illustrate arrays and how they relate to pointers.

Character Arrays

Many string operations in C are performed by using pointers and pointer arithmetic to reference character array elements. This is because character arrays or strings tend to be accessed in a strictly sequential manner. Remember, all strings in C are terminated by a null, \0, which is a FALSE value. The following C++ program is a modification of a program used earlier to print palindromes. It illustrates the use of pointers with character arrays:

```
//
//   A C++ program that initializes a char pointer and
//   then prints out the array of chars backwards using pointers
//   Copyright (c) Chris H. Pappas and William H. Murray, 1990
//

#include <iostream.h>
#include <string.h>

main()
{
  char char_aray[]="Madam I'm Adam";
  char *char_ptr;
  int count;

  char_ptr=char_aray+(strlen(char_aray)-1);
  do {
    cout << *char_ptr;
    char_ptr--;
  } while (char_ptr >= &char_aray[0]);

  return(0);
}
```

After the program declares and initializes the *char_aray* palindrome, it creates a *char_ptr* of type **char ***. Remember that the name of an array is in itself an address variable. The body of the program begins by setting the *char_ptr* to the address of the last character in the array. This requires a call to the function **strlen**, which calculates the length of the character array. (The **strlen** function counts just the number of characters; it does not include in the count the null terminator, \0.)

You probably thought that was the reason for subtracting 1 from the function's returned value. Actually, the program has to consider that the first array character's address is at offset 0. Therefore, you want to increment the pointer variable's offset address to one less than the number of valid characters.

Once the pointer for the last valid array character has been calculated, the *do while* loop is entered. The loop uses the pointer variable to point to the memory location of the character to be printed and then prints it. It subsequently calculates the next character's memory location and compares this value with the starting address of *char_array*. As long as the calculated value is greater than or equal to the starting address, the loop iterates.

Arrays of Pointers

In C and C++, you are not restricted to making simple arrays and simple pointers. You can combine the two into arrays of pointers. An array of pointers is an array whose elements are pointers to other objects. Those objects can themselves be pointers. This means that you can have an array of pointers that point to other pointers.

The concept of an array of pointers to pointers is used extensively in the *argc* and *argv* command-line arguments for **main** (see Chapter 8). The following program finds the largest or smallest value entered on the command line. Command-line arguments can include numbers only, or they may be prefaced by a command selecting a choice for the smallest value entered (-s,-S), or the largest value entered (-l,-L).

```
//
//    A C++ program that uses an array of pointers to process
//    the command-line arguments argc, argv
//    Copyright (c) Chris H. Pappas and William H. Murray, 1990
//

#include <iostream.h>
#include <process.h>      // exit()
#include <stdlib.h>       // atoi()

#define BIGGEST 1
#define SMALLEST 0

int main(int argc,char *argv[])
{
  char *string_ptr;
  int num_values;
  int size_flag=0;
```

```
     int chosen_extreme=32767;

  if(argc < 2) {
     cout << "\nYou need to enter an -S,-s,-L,-l"
        " and at least one integer value";
     exit(0);
  }

  while(--argc > 0 && (*++argv)[0] == '-') {
     for(string_ptr=argv[0]+1; *string_ptr != '\0'; string_ptr++)
{
        switch(*string_ptr) {
           case 's':
           case 'S':
             size_flag=SMALLEST;
             chosen_extreme=32767;
             break;
           case 'l':
           case 'L':
             size_flag=BIGGEST;
             chosen_extreme=0;
             break;
           default:
          cout << "unknown argument " << *string_ptr << "\n";
             exit(1);
        }
     }
  }

  if(argc==0) {
     cout << "Please enter at least one number\n";
     exit(1);
  }

  num_values=argc;

  while(argc--) {
     int present_value;
     present_value=atoi(*(argv++));
     if(size_flag==BIGGEST && present_value > chosen_extreme)
        chosen_extreme=present_value;
     if(size_flag==SMALLEST && present_value < chosen_extreme)
        chosen_extreme=present_value;
  }

  cout << "The " << (size_flag ? "largest" : "smallest");
  cout << " of the " << num_values;
  cout << " value(s) input is " << chosen_extreme<< "\n";

  return(0);
}
```

Before looking at the source code, familiarize yourself with the following possible command combinations for invoking the program:

```
analyze
analyze 87
analyze 87 34
analyze -s 87
analyze -S 87 34
analyze -1 23
analyze -L 23 52
```

Looking at the **main** program, you will see the formal parameters *argc* and *argv* (see Chapter 8). To review, *argc* is an integer value containing the number of separate items, or arguments, that appeared on the command line. The variable *argv* refers to an array of pointers to character strings. Note that *argv* is not a constant; it is a variable whose value can be altered. The first element of the array, *argv[0]*, is a pointer to a string of characters that contains the program name.

At the first *if* statement, you find a test to determine if the value of *argc* is less than 2. If this test evaluates to TRUE, the user has typed just the name of the program *analyze* without any switches. Since this action would indicate that the user does not know the switch and value options, the program will prompt the user at this point with the valid options and then **exit**.

The *while* loop test condition evaluates from left to right, beginning with the decrement of *argc*. If *argc* is still greater than 0, the right side of the logical expression will be examined.

The right side of the logical expression first increments the array pointer *argv* past the first pointer entry (+ +*argv*), skipping the program's name, so that it now points to the second array entry. Once the pointer has been incremented, it is used to point (*+ +*argv*) to the zeroth offset ((*+ +*argv*)[0]) of the first character of the string pointed to. Obtaining this character, if it is a "-" symbol, the program concludes that the second program command was a possible switch, for example *-s or -L*.

The *for* loop initialization begins by taking the current pointer address of *argv*, which was just incremented in the line above to point to the second pointer in the array. Since *argv*'s second element is a pointer to a character string, the pointer can be subscripted, *argv[0]*. The complete expression argv[0] + 1 points to the second character of the second string pointed to by the current address stored in *argv*. This second character is the one past the command switch symbol '-'. Once the program calculates this character's address, it stores it in the variable *string_ptr*. The *for* loop repeats as long as the character pointed to, *string_ptr*, is not the null terminator, \0.

The program continues by analyzing the switch to see if the user wants to obtain the smallest or largest of the values entered. Based on the switch, the appropriate constant is assigned to the *size_flag*. Each case statement also initializes the variable *chosen_extreme* to an appropriate value for the comparisons that follow. Should the user enter an unrecognized switch, for example, -d, the default case, will take care of printing an appropriate message.

The second *if* statement now checks to see if *argc* has been decremented to 0. An appropriate message is printed if the switches have been examined on the command line and there are no values left to process. If so, the program terminates with an exit code of decimal 1.

A successful skipping of this *if* test means that there are now values from the command line that need to be examined. Since the program will now decrement *argc,* the variable *num_values* is assigned *argc*'s current value.

The *while* loop continues while there are at least two values to compare. The *while* loop only needs to be entered if there is more than one value to be compared, since the **cout** statement following the *while* loop can handle the command line with a single value.

The function **atoi** converts each of the remaining arguments into an integer and stores the result in the variable *present_value*. Remember, *argv++* needed to be incremented first, so that it points to the first value to be compared. Also, the *while* loop test condition had already decremented the pointer to make certain that the loop wasn't entered with only a single command value.

The last two *if* statements update the variable *chosen_extreme* based on the user's desire to find either the smallest or largest of all values entered. Finally, the results of the program are printed using an interesting combination of string literals and the conditional operator. The parentheses are needed around the conditional statement to prevent **cout** from printing a 0 or 1 based on the validity of the expression.

Pointers to Pointers

This next program demonstrates the use of pointer variables that point to other pointers. It is included here because it uses dynamic memory allocation. You may want to refer back to the general discussion of pointers to pointers before looking at the following program:

```
/*
 *     A C program demonstrating the use of double indirection
 *     Copyright (c) Chris H. Pappas and William H. Murray, 1990
 */

#include <stdio.h>

#define MAXELEMENTS 3

void print_values(int **value1, int **value2, int **value3);

void assign(int *vir_mem_ptr_aray[],int *dyn_blk_ptr);

main()
{
  int **value1, **value2, **value3;
  int *vir_mem_ptr_aray[MAXELEMENTS];
  int *dyn_mem_blk_ptr, *old_mem_blk_ptr;

  value1=&vir_mem_ptr_aray[0];
  value2=&vir_mem_ptr_aray[1];
  value3=&vir_mem_ptr_aray[2];

  dyn_mem_blk_ptr=(int *)malloc(MAXELEMENTS * sizeof(int));
  old_mem_blk_ptr=dyn_mem_blk_ptr;

  assign(vir_mem_ptr_aray,dyn_mem_blk_ptr);

  **value1=1;
  **value2=2;
  **value3=3;

  print_values(value1,value2,value3);

  dyn_mem_blk_ptr=(int *)malloc(MAXELEMENTS * sizeof(int));

  *dyn_mem_blk_ptr=**value1;
  *(dyn_mem_blk_ptr+1)=**value2;
  *(dyn_mem_blk_ptr+2)=**value3;

  free(old_mem_blk_ptr);

  assign(vir_mem_ptr_aray,dyn_mem_blk_ptr);

  print_values(value1,value2,value3);

  return(0);
}

void assign(int *vir_mem_ptr_aray[],int *dyn_mem_blk_ptr)
{
  vir_mem_ptr_aray[0]=dyn_mem_blk_ptr;
  vir_mem_ptr_aray[1]=dyn_mem_blk_ptr+1;
  vir_mem_ptr_aray[2]=dyn_mem_blk_ptr+2;
}
```

```
void print_values(int **value1, int **value2, int **value3)
{
  printf("%d\n",**value1);
  printf("%d\n",**value2);
  printf("%d\n",**value3);
}
```

The program highlights the concept of a pointer variable *value1, value2,* and *value3* pointing to a constant address, *&vir_mem_ptr_aray[0], &vir_mem_ptr_aray[1],* and *&vir_mem_ptr_aray[2],* whose pointer address contents can dynamically change.

Look at the data declarations in **main**. *value1, value2,* and *value3* have been defined as pointers to pointers that point to integers. Look at the various syntax combinations:

```
value1
*value1
**value1
```

The first syntax references the address stored in the pointer variable *value1*. The second syntax references the pointer address pointed to by the address in *value1*. The last syntax references the integer that is pointed to by the pointer address pointed to by *value1*. Make certain that you do not proceed until you understand these three different references.

The three variables *value1, value2,* and *value3* have all been defined as pointers to pointers that point to integers (**int ****). The variable *vir_mem_ptr_aray* has been defined as an array of integer pointers (**int ***) of the size MAXELEMENTS. The last two variables, *dyn_mem_blk_ptr* and *old_mem_blk_ptr,* are also pointers to integers (**int ***). Figure 10-18 shows what these six variables look like after their storage has been allocated, and in particular, after *value1, value2,* and *value3* have been assigned the address of their respective elements in the *vir_mem_ptr_aray.*

This array will hold the addresses of the dynamically changing memory cell addresses. Something similar actually happens in a true multitasking environment. Your program thinks that it has the actual physical address of a variable stored in memory, when it really has a fixed address to an array of pointers that in turn points to the current physical address of the data item in memory. When the multitasking environment needs to conserve memory by moving your data objects, it simply moves their storage locations and updates the array of pointers. However, the variables in your

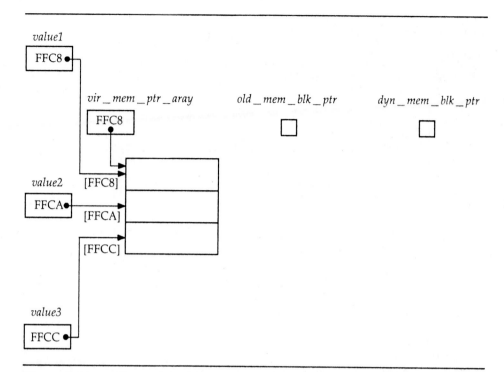

Figure 10-18.   How *value1, value2,* and *value3* get their initial addresses

program are still pointing to the same physical address, albeit not the physical address of the data, but of the array of pointers.

To understand how this operates, pay particular attention to the fact that the physical addresses stored in the pointer variables *value1, value2,* and *value3* never change once they are assigned.

Figure 10-19 illustrates what happens to the variables after the dynamic array *dyn_mem_blk_ptr* has been allocated, *old_mem_blk_ptr* has been initialized to the same address of the new array, and most importantly, how the physical addresses of *dyn_mem_blk_ptr*'s individual elements have been assigned to their respective counterparts in *vir_mem_ptr_aray.*

The pointer assignments were all accomplished by the **assign** function. **assign** was passed *vir_mem_ptr_aray* (call-by-value) and the address of the recently allocated dynamic memory block in the variable *dyn_mem_blk_ptr.* The function assigns the addresses of the dynamically allocated memory cells to each individual element of *vir_mem_ptr_aray.* Since the array was passed call-by-value, the changes are effective in the **main.**

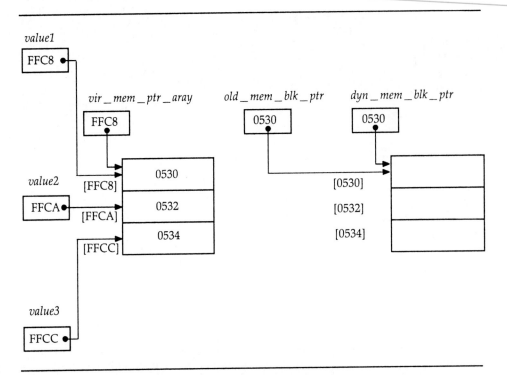

Figure 10-19.   The creation of the dynamic memory block

If you used the Turbo Debugger to print *value1* at this point, you would see FFC8 (the address of *vir_mem_ptr_aray*'s first element), and **value1* would print 0530 (or the contents of the address pointed to). You would encounter a similar dump for the other two pointer variables, *value2* and *value3*.

Figure 10-20 shows the assignment of three **int** values to the physical memory locations. Notice the syntax for accomplishing this:

```
**value1=1;
**value2=2;
**value3=3;
```

At this point, the program prints the values 1, 2, and 3, by calling the function **print_values**. Notice that the function has been defined as receiving three **int **** variables. Note also that the actual parameter list does not need to precede the variables with the double indirection operator, ******, since that is their type by declaration.

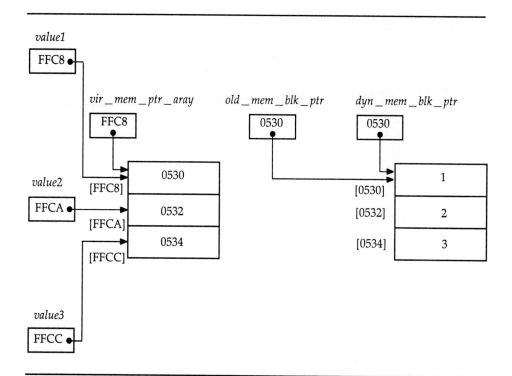

Figure 10-20.   Assigning the initial values 1, 2, and 3 to each memory cell

In Figure 10-21, the situation has become very interesting. A new block of dynamic memory has been allocated with the **malloc** function, with its new physical memory address stored in the pointer variable *dyn _ mem _ blk _ ptr*. *old _ mem _ blk _ ptr* still points to the previously allocated block of dynamic memory. Using the incomplete analogy to a multitasking environment, the figure would illustrate the operating system's desire to move the data objects' memory locations physically. Figure 10-21 also shows that the data objects themselves were copied into the new memory locations. The program accomplished this with the following three lines of code:

```
*dyn_mem_blk_ptr=**value1;
*(dyn_mem_blk_ptr+1)=**value2;
*(dyn_mem_blk_ptr+2)=**value3;
```

Since the pointer variable *dyn _ mem _ blk _ ptr* holds the address to the first element of the dynamic block, its address is dereferenced, pointing to the

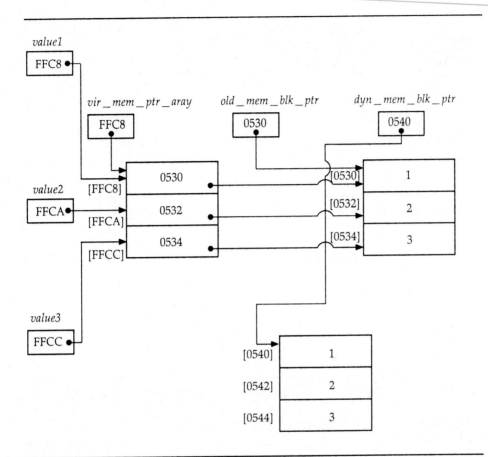

Figure 10-21. Creation and assignments of the second dynamic memory block

memory cell itself, and the 1 is stored there. Using a little pointer arithmetic, the other two memory cells are accessed by incrementing the pointer. The parentheses were necessary so that the pointer address was incremented before the dereference operator was applied.

Figure 10-22 shows what happens when the function **free** and the function **assign** are called to link the new physical address of the dynamically allocated memory block to the *vir_mem_ptr_aray* pointer address elements.

The most important fact to notice in this last figure is that the actual physical address of the three pointer variables *value1*, *value2*, and *value3* has

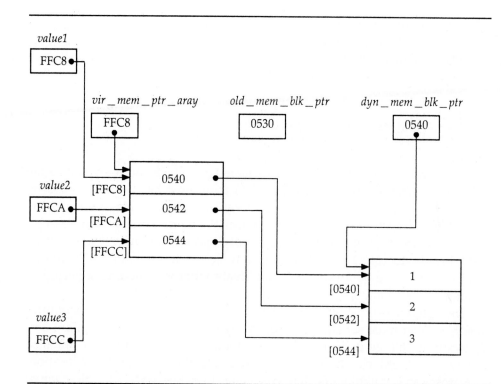

Figure 10-22.   Shows *vir_mem_ptr_aray* with its new physical memory
addresses

not changed. When the program prints the values pointed to, **value1*, and
so on, you still see the values 1, 2, and 3, even though their physical
location in memory has changed.

C++ REFERENCE TYPE

C++ provides a form of call-by-reference that is even easier to use than
pointers. First, let's examine the use of reference variables in C++. Like C,
C++ enables you to declare regular variables or pointer variables. In the first
case, memory is actually allocated for the data object; in the second case, a
memory location is set aside to hold an address for an object that

will be allocated at another time. C++ has a third kind of declaration—the *reference* type. Like a pointer variable, it refers to another variable location, but like a regular variable, it requires no special dereferencing operators. The syntax for a reference variable is

```
int value1=5;
int& ref_value1=value1;  // valid
int& value2;             // invalid: uninitialized
```

This example sets up the reference variable *ref_value1* and assigns it to the existing variable *value1*. The referenced location now has two names associated with it: *value1* and *ref_value1*. Because both variables point to the same location in memory, they are in fact the same variable. Any assignment made to *ref_value1* is reflected through *value1*; the inverse is also true, and changes to *value1* occur through any access to *ref_value1*. Therefore, with the reference data type, you can create what is sometimes referred to as an *alias* for a variable.

The reference type has a restriction that distinguishes it from pointer variables. You must set the value of the reference type at declaration, and you cannot change it during the run of the program. After you initialize this type in the declaration, it always refers to the same memory location. Therefore, any assignments that you make to a reference variable change only the data in memory, not the address of the variable itself. In other words, you can think of a reference variable as a pointer to a constant location. For example, using the preceding declarations, the following statement

```
ref_value1 *= 2;
```

doubles the contents of *value1* by multiplying 5 * 2. The next statement assigns *copy_value* (assuming that it is of type **int**) a copy of the value associated with *ref_value1*:

```
copy_value = ref_value1;
```

The next statement is also legal when you are using reference types:

```
int *value1_ptr = &ref_value1;
```

This statement assigns the address of *value1* to the **int** * variable *value1 _ ptr*.

The primary use of a reference type is as an argument (see Chapter 8 on functions) or as a return type of a function, especially when applied to user-defined class types (see Chapter 13).

Returning Addresses

When you return an address from a function using either a pointer variable or a reference type, you are giving the user a memory address. The user can read the value at the address, and if you haven't declared the pointer type to be **const**, the user can always write the value. By returning an address, you are giving the user permission to read and, for non-**const** pointer types, write to private data. This is a significant design decision. See if you can anticipate what will happen in this next program.

```
//
//    A C++ program demonstrating what NOT to do with
//    C++ reference variables
//    Copyright (c) Chris H. Pappas and William H. Murray, 1990
//

#include <iostream.h>

int *function_a(void);
int *function_b(void);

main()
{
  int *int_ptr=function_a();
  function_b();
  cout << "Correct value? " << *int_ptr;

  return(0);
}

int *function_a(void)
{
  int local_a=10;
  return &local_a;
}

int *function_b(void)
{
  int local_b=20;
  return &local_b;
}
```

Using the Turbo Debugger

To examine the actual operation of this code, you can use the Turbo Debugger. From the Integrated Environment, go to the Options menu, select the Debugger submenu, and change "Source Debugging" to ON. Now start the Turbo Debugger and single step through the program. Use the Watch window to keep an eye on the variable *int_ptr*. Figure 10-23 shows the Turbo Debugger window.

When **function_a** is called, local space is allocated on the stack for the variable *local_a*, and the value 10 is stored in it. At this point, **function_a** returns the address of this local variable (bad news). The second statement in the main program invokes **function_b**. **function_b** in turn allocates local space for *local_b* and assigns it a value of 20. So how does the **printf**

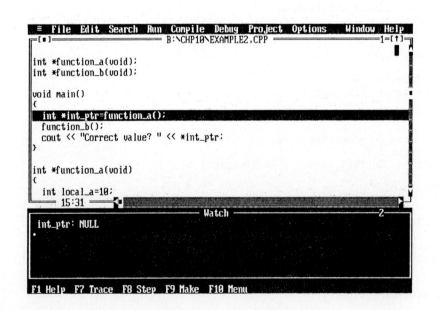

Figure 10-23.   The Integrated Debugger showing initial value of *int_ptr*

statement print a value of 20 when it was passed the address of *local_a* when **function_a** was invoked?

Actually, when the address of the temporary local variable *local_a* was assigned to *int_ptr* by **function_a**, the address to the temporary location was retained even after *local_a* went out of scope. When **function_b** was invoked, it also needed local storage. Since *local_a* was gone, *local_b* was given the same storage location as its predecessor. With *int_ptr* hanging on to this same busy memory cell, you can see why printing the value it now points to yields a 20. Take extreme care not to return the addresses of local variables.

When to Use Reference Types

To review, there are three main reasons for using C++ reference types (also see Chapter 13):

- Reference types lend themselves to more readable code by allowing you to ignore the details of how a parameter is passed.

- Reference types put the responsibility for argument passing on the programmer who writes the functions and not on the individual who uses them.

- Reference types are a necessary counterpart to operator overloading.

PUTTING YOUR KNOWLEDGE TO WORK

1. Which syntax is correct for declaring an **int** pointer variable?

```
int *int_ptr;
int * int_ptr;
int* int_ptr;
```

Answer: They all are.

2. Are the following two declarations equivalent?

```
int *int_ptrl, int_ptr2;
int *int_ptrl, *int_ptr2;
```

Answer: No. The first statement defines *int_ptr1* to be a pointer to an **int**, while *int_ptr2* is an **int** variable. The second statement defines two pointer variables.

3. Can a pointer variable be assigned the address of a constant?

4. Can a pointer variable be assigned the address of a register?

5. Using the following data declarations,

```
int int_aray[5];
int *int_ptr;
```

are the following two statements legal, although possibly redundant?

```
int_ptr=int_aray;
int_ptr=&int_aray[0];
```

6. Is the following **scanf** statement legal?

```
char *string_ptr;
scanf("%s",string_ptr);
```

7. Suppose that the pointer variable *int_ptr* points to an **int** and *float_ptr* points to a **float**. When both pointers are incremented using the increment operator, + +, do the pointer addresses increment by the same number of bytes?

8. Do all pointer variable types occupy the same number of bytes in memory?

9. Explain one reason for having a pointer to a function.

10. To make certain that you understand the concept of pointer variables, try writing a simple program that creates three different pointer variable types, all using from one to three levels of indirection. To gain experience with passing and returning these pointer types, write several functions that receive the pointer variables, manipulate them in some way, and then return the results to the invoking function. This exercise will make it easier to understand the more advanced C and C++ concepts to come.

11

INPUT AND OUTPUT IN C AND C++

In this chapter, you will learn

- What a stream is

- How to read and write characters

- How to read and write integers

- How to read and write floats and doubles

- How to read and write formatted I/O

- How to create files

- How to read and write to files

- How to control file access

- How to update Release 1.2 applications

Programmers are often frustrated by the inadequate input and output (I/O) facilities provided by many high-level languages. This is not the case with C, which has a very complete I/O function library. This chapter discusses the more than 20 different ways to perform I/O in C and C++.

INPUT AND OUTPUT IN C

The standard C library I/O routines allow you to read and write data to and from files and devices. The C language does not include any predefined file structures. Instead, all data is treated as a sequence of bytes. There are three basic types of I/O functions: stream, console and port, and low-level.

All of the stream I/O functions treat data files or data items as a stream of individual characters. If you select the appropriate stream function, your application can process data in any size or format required, from single characters to large, complicated data structures.

Technically, when a program uses the stream function to open a file for I/O, the opened file is associated with a structure of type **FILE** (predefined in *stdio.h*) that contains basic information about the file. Once the stream is opened, a pointer to the **FILE** structure is returned. This **FILE** pointer — sometimes called the *stream pointer* or *stream* — is used to refer to the file for all subsequent I/O.

All stream I/O functions provide buffered, formatted, or unformatted input and output. A buffered stream provides an intermediate storage location for all information that is input from the stream and output that is being sent to the stream. Disk I/O is time consuming, but stream buffering will streamline your application. Instead of inputting stream data one character or one structure at a time, stream I/O functions access data a block at a time. As the application needs to process the input, it merely accesses the buffer, a much faster process. When the buffer is empty, another disk block access is made.

The reverse is true for stream output. Instead of physically outputting all data as the output statement is executed, stream I/O functions place all output data into the buffer. When the buffer is full, the data is written to the disk.

Depending on the high-level language you use, there may be a problem with buffered I/O. For example, if your program has executed several output statements that do not fill the output buffer, causing it to dump to the disk, that information is lost when your program terminates. The solution usually involves making a call to an appropriate function to "flush" the buffer. Unlike other high-level languages, C solves this problem by automatically flushing the buffer's contents whenever the program terminates. Of course, a well written application should not rely on these automatic features but should always explicitly detail every action the program is to take. One additional note: If the application terminates abnormally when you are using stream I/O, the output buffers may not be flushed, resulting in loss of data.

The console and port I/O routines are similar in function and can be seen as an extension of the stream routines. They allow you to read or write to a terminal (console) or an input/output port (such as a printer port). The port I/O functions simply read and write data in bytes. Console I/O functions provide several additional options. For example, they enable you to detect whether a character has been typed at the console and whether the characters entered are echoed to the screen as they are read.

The last type of input and output is called low-level I/O. None of the low-level I/O functions perform buffering and formatting; instead, they invoke the operating system's I/O capabilities directly. These routines let you access files and peripheral devices at a more basic level than the stream functions. Files opened in this mode return a *file handle,* an integer value that is used to refer to the file in subsequent operations.

In general, it is bad programming practice to mix stream I/O functions with low-level routines. Since stream functions are buffered and low-level functions are not, attempting to access the same file or device by two different methods leads to confusion and eventual loss of data in the buffers. Therefore, you should use either stream or low-level functions exclusively on a given file. Table 11-1 lists the most commonly used C stream I/O functions.

Streams

To use the stream functions, your application must include the file *stdio.h.* This file contains definitions for constants, types, and structures used in the stream functions, as well as function declarations and macro definitions for the stream routines.

Many of the constants predefined in *stdio.h* can be useful in your application. For example, **EOF** is defined to be the value returned at end of file and **NULL** is the null pointer. Also, **FILE** defines the structure used to maintain information about a stream and **BUFSIZ** defines the default size, in bytes, of the stream buffers.

Table 11-1.   Common C Stream I/O Functions

Function	Definition
clearerr	Clears the error indicator for a stream and resets the end-of-file indicator to 0
fclose	Closes a stream
fcloseall	Closes all open streams
fdopen	Opens a stream using its handle obtained from **creat**, **dup**, **dup2**, or **open**
feof	Tests for end of file on a stream
ferror	Tests the stream for a read or write error
fflush	Flushes a stream
fgetc	Reads a character from a stream
fgetchar	Reads a character from **stdin**
fgetpos	Gets the current file pointer
fgets	Gets a string from a stream
filelength	Gets the stream size in bytes
fileno	Gets the file handle associated with a stream
flushall	Flushes all stream buffers
fopen	Opens a stream
fprintf	Writes formatted output to a stream
fputc	Writes a character to a stream
fputchar	Writes a character to **stdout**
fputs	Outputs a string to a stream
fread	Reads unformatted data from a stream
freopen	Reassigns a **FILE** pointer
fscanf	Reads formatted data from a stream
fseek	Repositions the **FILE** pointer to a given location
fsetpos	Positions the **FILE** pointer of a stream
fstat	Gets open file information
ftell	Returns current **FILE** pointer position
fwrite	Writes unformatted data items to a stream
getc	Reads a character from a stream (macro)
getchar	Reads a character from **stdin** (macro)
gets	Gets a string from **stdin**
getw	Reads an **int** item from the stream
perror	Prints a system error to **stderr**
printf	Writes formatted output to **stdout**
putc	Writes a character to a stream (macro)

Table 11-1.   Common C Stream I/O Functions (*continued*)

Function	Definition
putchar	Writes a character to **stdout** (macro)
puts	Writes a string to **stdout**
putw	Writes an **int** to a stream
remove	Removes a file
rename	Renames a file
rewind	Repositions the **FILE** pointer to the beginning of a stream
scanf	Scans and inputs formatted data from **stdin**
setbuf	Overrides automatic buffering, allowing the application to define its own stream buffer
setvbuf	Same as setbuf but also allows the size of the buffer to be defined
sprintf	Writes formatted data to a string
sscanf	Scans and inputs formatted data from a string
tmpnam	Generates a unique temporary file name in a given directory
ungetch	Pushes a character back to the keyboard buffer
vfprintf	Writes formatted output to a stream using a pointer to the format string
vfscanf	Scans and formats input from a stream using a pointer to the format string
vprintf	Writes formatted output to **stdout** using a pointer to the format string
vscanf	Scans and formats input from **stdin** using a pointer to the format string
vsprintf	Writes formatted output to a string using a pointer to the format string
vsscanf	Scans and formats input from a stream using a pointer to the format string

Opening Streams

You can use one of three functions to open a stream before input and output can be performed on it: **fopen**, **fdopen**, or **freopen**. The file mode and form are set at the time the stream is opened. The stream file may be opened for reading, writing, or both, and can be opened either in text or in binary mode.

All three functions—**fopen**, **fdopen**, and **freopen**—return a **FILE** pointer, which is used to refer to the stream. For example, if your program contains the line

```
infile = fopen("sample.dat","r");
```

you can use the **FILE** pointer variable *infile* to refer to the stream. (Table 5-3 listed the possible file modes.)

When your application begins execution, five streams are automatically opened. These streams are the standard input (**stdin**), standard output (**stdout**), standard error (**stderr**), standard printer (**stdprn**), and standard auxiliary (**stdaux**). By default, the standard input, standard output, and standard error refer to the user's console. This means that whenever a program expects input from the standard input, it receives that input from the console. Likewise, a program that writes to the standard output prints its data to the console. Any error messages generated by the library routines are sent to the standard error stream—that is, they appear on the user's console. The standard auxiliary and standard print streams usually refer to an auxiliary port and a printer.

You can use the five **FILE** pointers in any function that requires a stream pointer as an argument. Some functions, such as **getchar** and **putchar**, are designed to use **stdin** or **stdout** automatically. Since the pointers **stdin**, **stdout**, **stderr**, **stdprn**, and **stdaux** are constants rather than variables, don't try to reassign them to a new stream pointer value.

Redirecting Streams

Modern operating systems consider the keyboard and video display as files. This is reasonable, since the system can read from the keyboard as well as from a disk or tape file. Similarly, the system can write to the video display as well as to a disk or tape file. Suppose that your application reads from the keyboard and outputs to the video display. Now suppose that you want the input to come from a file called *test.dat*. You can use the same application if you tell the system to replace input from the keyboard, considered now as a file, with input from another file, namely *test.dat*. Changing the standard input or standard output is called *input redirection* or *output redirection*.

In MS-DOS, input or output redirection is effortless. You use < to redirect the input and > to redirect the output. Suppose that the executable version of your application is called *redirect*. The following system-level command will run the program *redirect* and use the file *test.dat* instead of the video display as input:

```
redirect < test.dat
```

The next statement will redirect both the input (*test.dat*) and the output (*out.dat*):

```
redirect < test.dat > out.dat
```

The last example will redirect the output (*out.dat*) only:

```
redirect > out.dat
```

Note, however, that you cannot redirect the standard error file **stderr**.

There are two techniques for managing the association between a standard file name and its connection to a physical file or device: redirection and piping. *Piping* involves directly connecting the standard output of one program to the standard input of another. Redirection and piping are normally controlled and invoked outside the program. In this way, the program need not concern itself with where the data is coming from or going to.

To connect the standard output from one program to the standard input of another program, you pipe them together by using the vertical bar symbol, I. Therefore, to connect the standard output of the program *stage1* to the standard input of the program *stage2*, you would type

```
stage1 | stage2
```

The operating system handles all the details of getting the output from *stage1* to the input of *stage2*.

Changing the Stream Buffer

All functions opened using the stream functions are buffered by default, except for the preopened streams **stdin, stdout, stderr, stdprn,** and **stdaux.** The two streams **stderr** and **stdaux** are unbuffered by default, unless they are used in one of the **printf** or **scanf** family of functions, in which case they are assigned a temporary buffer. These two streams can also be buffered with **setbuf** or **setvbuf.** The **stdin, stdout,** and **stdprn** streams are buffered; each buffer is flushed whenever it is full.

You can use the two functions **setbuf** and **setvbuf** to make a stream unbuffered, or you can use them to associate a buffer with an unbuffered stream. Note that buffers allocated by the system are not accessible to the user, but buffers allocated with the function **setbuf** or **setvbuf** are named by the user and can be manipulated as if they were variables. You can define a buffer to be of any size; if you use the function **setbuf,** the size is set by the constant **BUFSIZ** defined in *stdio.h.* If the application uses the function **setvbuf,** the program determines the size of the buffer.

Closing a Stream

The two functions **fclose** and **fcloseall** close a stream or streams. The **fclose** function closes a single file, while **fcloseall** closes all open streams except **stdin, stdout, stderr, stdprn,** and **stdaux.** However, if your program does not explicitly close a stream, the stream is automatically closed when the application terminates. Since the number of open streams is limited, it is good practice to close a stream when you finish with it.

Low-Level I/O

Table 11-2 lists the most commonly used low-level I/O functions. Low-level input and output calls do not buffer or format data. Files opened by low-level calls are referenced by a file handle. You use the **open** function to open files. You can use the **sopen** function to open a file with file-sharing attributes.

Low-level functions are different from their stream counterparts because they do not require the inclusion of the *stdio.h* header file. However, some common constants that are predefined in *stdio.h,* such as **EOF** and **NULL,** may be useful. Declarations for the low-level functions are given in the *io.h* header file.

Table 11-2.   Low-Level Input and Output Functions

Function	Definition
close	Closes a disk file
lseek	Seeks to the specified byte in a file
open	Opens a disk file
read	Reads a buffer of data
unlink	Removes a file from the directory
write	Writes a buffer of data

The low-level disk-file I/O system was originally created under the UNIX operating system. Because the ANSI standard committee has not standardized this low-level UNIX-like unbuffered I/O system, you should use the standardized buffered I/O system (described throughout this chapter) for all new projects.

Character Functions

Certain character input and output functions are defined in the ANSI standard and supplied by all C compilers. These functions access standard input and output and are considered high-level routines (as opposed to low-level routines, which access the machine hardware more directly). I/O in C is implemented through vendor-supplied functions rather than keywords defined as part of the language.

getc, putc, fgetc, and fputc

The most basic of all I/O functions are those that receive and send one character. The **getc** function receives one character from a specified file stream, like this:

```
int input_char;
input_char = getc(stdin);
```

The received character is passed back in the name of the function **getc** and then assigns the returned value to *input_char*. By the way, *input_char* isn't of type **char** because **getc** has been written to return an **int** type. Since the end-of-file marker size is system dependent, the marker might not fit in a single **char** byte size.

Function **getc** converts the integer into an unsigned character, guaranteeing that the ASCII values above 127 are not represented as negative values. Therefore, negative values can be used to represent unusual situations such as errors and the end of the input file. For example, the end of file has traditionally been represented by -1, although the ANSI standard states that the constant **EOF** represents some negative value.

Because **getc** returns an integer value, the data item that receives the value from **getc** must also be defined as an integer. While it may seem odd to use an integer in a character function, C actually makes little distinction between characters and integers. If a character is provided when an integer is needed, the character will be converted to an integer.

The complement to the **getc** function is **putc**. The **putc** function outputs one character to the file stream represented by the specified **FILE** pointer. To send the character that was just input to the standard output, use the following statement:

```
putc(input_char,stdout);
```

The **getc** function is normally buffered. In other words, when the application requests a character, control is not returned to the program until a carriage return is entered into the standard input file stream. All characters entered before the carriage return are held in a buffer and delivered to the program one at a time. The application invokes the **getc** function repeatedly until the buffer has been exhausted. After **getc** has sent the carriage return to the program, the next request for a character results in more characters accumulating in the buffer until a carriage return is entered again. This means that you cannot use the **getc** function for one-key input techniques that don't require pressing the carriage return.

Note that **getc** and **putc** are actually implemented as macros rather than as "true" functions. The functions **fgetc** and **fputc** are identical to their macro **getc** and **putc** counterparts.

getchar, putchar, fgetchar, and fputchar

The two macros **getchar** and **putchar** are actually specific implementations of the **getc** and **putc** macros. They are always associated with standard input (**stdin**) and standard output (**stdout**). The only way to use them on other file streams is to redirect either standard input or standard output from within the program.

The two examples used before could be rewritten using these two functions:

```
int input_char;
input_char = getchar();
```

and

```
putchar(input_char);
```

Like **getc** and **putc**, **getchar** and **putchar** are implemented as macros. The function **putchar** has been written to return an **EOF** value whenever an error condition occurs. You can use the following code to check for an output error condition. It's a bit confusing due to the check for **EOF** on output.

```
if(putchar(input_char) == EOF)
  printf("An error has occurred writing to stdout");
```

Both **fgetchar** and **fputchar** are the function equivalents of their macro **getchar** and **putchar** counterparts.

getch and putch

Both **getch** and **putch** are true functions. However, they do not fall under the ANSI C standard because they are low-level functions that interface closely with the hardware. For IBM-PC and compatible systems, these functions do not use buffering, which means that they immediately receive a character typed into the keyboard. They can be redirected, however, so they are not associated exclusively with the keyboard.

You can use the functions **getch** and **putch** exactly like **getchar** and **putchar**. Usually, a program running on the IBM-PC will use **getch** to trap keystrokes ignored by **getchar**—for example, PGUP, PGDN, HOME, and END. The function **getchar** sees a character entered from the keyboard as soon as the key is pressed; a carriage return is not needed to send the character to the program. This ability allows the **getch** function to provide a one-key technique that is not available with **getc** or **getchar**.

On an IBM-PC or true compatibles, the function **getch** operates very differently from **getc** and **getchar**. This is partly because the IBM-PC family can easily determine when an individual key on the keyboard has been pressed. Other systems, such as the DEC and VAX C, do not allow the hardware to trap individual keystrokes. These systems typically echo the input character and require that you press a carriage return (the carriage return character is not seen by the program unless no other characters have been entered). Under such circumstances, the carriage return returns a null character or a decimal zero. Additionally, the function keys are not available and produce unreliable results if they are pressed.

String Functions

In many applications, it is more natural to handle input and output in larger parcels than one character. For example, a file of car salespeople may contain one record per line, with each record consisting of four fields: salesperson's name, base pay, commission, and number of cars sold, with white space separating the fields. It would be tedious to use character I/O under these circumstances.

gets, puts, fgets, and fputs

Because of the organization of the file of salespeople, it's better to treat each record as a single character string and read or write it as a unit. The **fgets** function, which reads whole strings rather than single characters, is well suited to this task. In addition to the function **fgets** and its inverse **fputs**, there are the macro counterparts **gets** and **puts**.

The function **fgets** expects three arguments: the address of an array in which to store the character string, the maximum number of characters to store, and a pointer to a file to read. The function will read characters into the array until either the number of characters read in is one less than the size specified, all of the characters up to and including the next newline character have been read, or the end of file is reached, whichever comes first.

If **fgets** reads in a newline, the newline will be stored in the array. If at least one character was read, the function will automatically append the null string terminator \0. Suppose that the file *saleteam.dat* looks like this:

```
Harry Wilson 28000 0.10 10
Jane McMurphy 28000 0.10 10
Bob Anderson 35000 0.15 12
```

Assuming a maximum record length of 40 characters, including the newline, the following program will read the records from the file and write them to the standard output:

```c
/*
 *      A C program that demonstrates how to read in whole records
 *      using fgets and print them out to stdio using fputs.
 *      Copyright (c) Chris H. Pappas and William H. Murray, 1990
 */

#include <stdio.h>

#define MAX_REC_SIZE 40
#define NULL_CHAR 1

main()
{
  FILE *in_file;
  char record[MAX_REC_SIZE + NULL_CHAR];

  in_file=fopen("a:\\sales\\june\\saleteam.dat", "r");
  while(fgets(record,MAX_REC_SIZE + NULL_CHAR,in_file) != NULL)
    fputs(record,stdout);
  fclose(in_file);

  return(0);
}
```

Because the maximum record size is 40, you must reserve 41 cells in the array; the extra cell holds the null terminator \0. The program does not generate its own newline when it prints each record to the terminal; instead, it relies on the newline read into the array by **fgets**. The **fputs** function writes the contents of the array *record* to the file specified by the file pointer **stdout**.

If your program is accessing a file on a disk drive other than the one the compiler resides on, you may need to include a path in your file name. Notice this description in the preceding program; the double backslashes \\ are necessary to indicate a subdirectory. Remember that a single backslash \ usually indicates that a control or line continuation follows.

While the **gets** and **fgets** functions are similar in usage, the **puts** and **fputs** functions operate differently. The **fputs** function writes to a file and expects two arguments: the address of a null-terminated character string and a pointer to a file. **fputs** simply copies the string to the specified file; it does not add a newline to the end of the string.

The macro **puts**, however, does not require a pointer to a file, since the output automatically goes to **stdout**, and the function **puts** automatically adds a newline character to the end of the output string. See "String Functions That Use Arrays" in Chapter 9 for an excellent example of how these functions differ.

Integer Functions

For certain applications, you may need to read and write *stream* (or buffered) integer information. The C language incorporates two functions for this purpose: **getw** and **putw**.

getw and putw

The **getw** and **putw** functions are similar to **getc** and **putc**, but they input and output integer data instead of character data. You should use both **getw** and **putw** only on files that are opened in binary mode. The following program opens a binary file, writes ten integers to it, closes the file, and then reopens the file for input and echo:

```
/*
 *      A C program that uses the functions getw and putw on
 *      a file created in binary mode.
 *      Copyright (c) Chris H. Pappas and William H. Murray, 1990
 */

#include <stdio.h>

#define SIZE 10

main()
{
  FILE *integer_file;
  int a_value,values[SIZE],index;

  integer_file=fopen("a:\\integer.dat", "wb");
  if(integer_file == NULL) {
    printf("File could not be opened");
    exit(1);
  }

  for(index = 0;index < SIZE;index++) {
    values[index]=index+1;
    putw(values[index],integer_file);
  }
```

```
  fclose(integer_file);

  integer_file=fopen("a:\\integer.dat", "rb");
  if(integer_file == NULL) {
    printf("File could not be re-opened");
    exit(1);
  }

  while(!feof(integer_file)) {
    a_value=getw(integer_file);
    printf("%3d",a_value);
  }

    return(0);
  }
```

Review the output from this program and see if you can discover what went wrong:

```
1  2  3  4  5  6  7  8  9 10 -1
```

Because the integer value read in by the last loop may have a value equal to **EOF**, the program uses the function **feof** to check for the end-of-file marker. However, the function does not perform a look-ahead operation, as do some other high-level language end-of-file functions. In C, an actual read of the end-of-file value must be performed in order to flag the condition.

To correct this situation, you need to rewrite the program using a *priming read* statement:

```
/*
 *    A C program that uses the functions getw and putw on
 *    a file created in binary mode, correcting the EOF test.
 *    Copyright (c) Chris H. Pappas and William H. Murray, 1990
*/

#include <stdio.h>
#include <process.h>

#define SIZE 10

main()
{
  FILE *integer_file;
  int a_value,values[SIZE],index;

  integer_file=fopen("a:\\integer.dat", "wb");
  if(integer_file == NULL) {
```

```
      printf("File could not be opened");
      exit(1);
   }

   for(index = 0;index < SIZE;index++) {
      values[index]=index+1;
      putw(values[index],integer_file);
   }

   fclose(integer_file);

   integer_file=fopen("a:\\integer.dat", "rb");
   if(integer_file == NULL) {
      printf("File could not be opened");
      exit(1);
   }

   a_value=getw(integer_file);
   while(!feof(integer_file)) {
      printf("%3d",a_value);
      a_value=getw(integer_file);
   }

   return(0);
}
```

Before entering the final *while* loop, the priming read checks whether the file is empty. If it is not, a valid integer value is stored in *a_value*. If the file is empty, however, the function **feof** will prevent the *while* loop from executing.

Notice that the priming read necessitated a rearrangement of the statements within the *while* loop. If the loop is entered, *a_value* contains a valid integer. If the statements within the loop were the same as the original program, an immediate second **getw** function call would be performed, overwriting the first integer value. Because of the priming read, the first statement within the *while* loop must be an output statement. This is next followed by a call to **getw** to obtain another value.

Suppose that the *while* loop has been entered nine times. At the end of the ninth iteration, the integer numbers 1 through 8 have been echoed and *a_value* has been assigned a 9. The next iteration of the loop prints the 9 and inputs the 10. Since 10 is not **EOF**, the loop iterates, echoing the 10 and reading **EOF**. At this point, the *while* loop terminates because the **feof** function sees the end-of-file condition.

These two simple example programs highlight the need to proceed carefully when writing code based on the **feof** function. This programming task is peculiarly frustrating, since each high-level language tends to treat the end-of-file condition differently. Some languages read a piece of data and look ahead at the same time to see the end of file. Others, like C, do not.

Formatted Output

C's rich assortment of output formatting controls makes it easy to create a neatly printed graph, report, or table. The two main functions that produce this formatted output are **printf** and the file equivalent form **fprintf**.

printf and fprintf

The following example program defines four variable types—character, array-of-characters, integer, and real—and then demonstrates how to use the appropriate format controls on each variable. The source code contains many comments, and includes output line numbering to simplify associating the output generated with the statement that created it.

```
/*
 *      A C program demonstrating advanced conversions and formatting
 *      Copyright (c) Chris H. Pappas and William H. Murray, 1990
 */

#include <stdio.h>

main()
{
  char letter='A';
  static char string1[]="he who has an ear, ",
              string2[]="let him hear.";
  int int_value=4444;
  double pi=3.14159265;
  int ln=0;


  /*            conversions            */

  /*print the letter                   */
    printf("\n[%2d] %c",++ln,letter);

  /*print the ASCII code for letter    */
    printf("\n[%2d] %d",++ln,letter);

  /*print character with ASCII 90      */
    printf("\n[%2d] %c",++ln,90);
```

```
/* print int_value as octal value  */
printf("\n[%2d] %o",++ln,int_value);

/* print lower-case hexadecimal    */
printf("\n[%2d] %x",++ln,int_value);

/* print upper-case hexadecimal    */
printf("\n[%2d] %X",++ln,int_value);


/* conversions and format options  */

/* minimum width 1                 */
printf("\n[%2d] %c",++ln,letter);

/* minimum width 5, right-justify  */
printf("\n[%2d] %5c",++ln,letter);

/* minimum width 5, left-justify   */
printf("\n[%2d] %-5c",++ln,letter);

/* 19 non-null, automatically      */
printf("\n[%d] %s",++ln,string1);

/* 13 non-null, automatically      */
printf("\n[%d] %s",++ln,string2);

/* minimum 5 overridden, auto 19   */
printf("\n[%d] %5s",++ln,string1);

/* minimum width 25, right-justify */
printf("\n[%d] %25s",++ln,string1);

/* minimum width 25, left-justify  */
printf("\n[%d] %-25s",++ln,string2);

/* default int_value width, 4      */
printf("\n[%d] %d",++ln,int_value);

/* printf int_value with + sign    */
printf("\n[%d] %+d",++ln,int_value);

/* minimum 3 overridden, auto 4    */
printf("\n[%d] %3d",++ln,int_value);

/* minimum width 10, right-justify */
printf("\n[%d] %10d",++ln,int_value);

/* minimum width 10, left-justify  */
printf("\n[%d] %-d",++ln,int_value);

/* right justify with leading 0's  */
printf("\n[%d] %010d",++ln,int_value);

/* using default number of digits  */
printf("\n[%d] %f",++ln,pi);
```

```
/* minimum width 20, right-justify */
printf("\n[%d] %20f",++ln,pi);

/* right-justify with leading 0's  */
printf("\n[%d] %020f",++ln,pi);

/* minimum width 20, left-justify  */
printf("\n[%d] %-20f",++ln,pi);

/* left-justify with trailing 0's  */
printf("\n[%d] %-020f",++ln,pi);


/* additional formatting precision */

/* minimum width 19, print all 17  */
printf("\n[%d] %19.19s",++ln,string1);

/* prints first 2 chars            */
printf("\n[%d] %.2s",++ln,string1);

/* prints 2 chars, right-justify   */
printf("\n[%d] %19.2s",++ln,string1);

/* prints 2 chars, left-justify    */
printf("\n[%d] %-19.2s",++ln,string1);

/* using printf arguments          */
printf("\n[%d] %*.*s",++ln,19,6,string1);

/* width 10, 8 to right of '.'     */
printf("\n[%d] %10.8f",++ln,pi);

/* width 20, 2 to right/justify    */
printf("\n[%d] %20.2f",++ln,pi);

/* 4 decimal places, left-justify  */
printf("\n[%d] %-20.4f",++ln,pi);

/* 4 decimal places, right-justify */
printf("\n[%d] %20.4f",++ln,pi);

/* width 20, scientific notation   */
printf("\n[%d] %20.2e",++ln,pi);

return(0);
}
```

The output generated by the program looks like this:

```
[ 1] A
[ 2] 65
[ 3] Z
```

```
[ 4]  10534
[ 5]  115c
[ 6]  115C
[ 7]  A
[ 8]       A
[ 9]  A
[10]  he who has an ear,
[11]  let him hear.
[12]  he who has an ear,
[13]        he who has an ear,
[14]  let him hear.
[15]  4444
[16]  +4444
[17]  4444
[18]        4444
[19]  4444
[20]  0000004444
[21]  3.141593
[22]              3.141593
[23]  0000000000003.141593
[24]  3.141593
[25]  3.141593
[26]  he who has an ear,
[27]  he
[28]                    he
[29]  he
[30]              he who
[31]  3.14159265
[32]                 3.14
[33]  3.1416
[34]              3.1416
[35]              3.14e+00
```

You can neatly format your application's output by studying the previous example and selecting the combinations that apply to your program's data types.

fseek, ftell, and rewind

You can use the **fseek**, **ftell**, and **rewind** functions to determine or change the location of the file position marker. The function **fseek** resets the file position marker in the file pointed to by *file_pointer* to the number of *offset_bytes* from the beginning of the file (*from_where* = 0), from the current location of the file position marker (*from_where* = 1), or from the end of the file (*from_where* = 2). Borland C has predefined three constants that you can also use in place of the variable *from_where*: **SEEK_SET** (offset from the beginning of the file), **SEEK_CUR** (current file marker position), and **SEEK_END** (offset from end of file). The function **fseek** will return 0 if the seek is successful, and **EOF** otherwise. The general syntax for the function **fseek** looks like this:

fseek(*file__pointer,offset__bytes,from__where*);

The **ftell** function returns the current location of the file position marker in the file pointed to by *file__pointer*. This location is indicated by an offset, measured in bytes, from the beginning of the file. The syntax for the function **ftell** looks like this:

long__variable = **ftell**(*file__pointer*);

The value returned by **ftell** can be used in a subsequent call to **fseek**.

The function **rewind** simply resets to the beginning of the file the file-position marker in the file pointed to by *file__pointer*. The syntax for the function **rewind** looks like this:

rewind(*file__pointer*);

The following C program illustrates the functions **fseek**, **ftell**, and **rewind**:

```
/*
 *      A C program demonstrating the use of fseek, ftell, and rewind.
 *      Copyright (c) Chris H. Pappas and William H. Murray, 1990
 */

#include <stdio.h>

main()
{
  FILE *in_file;
  long location;
  char a_char;

  in_file=fopen("sample.dat","rt+");
  a_char=fgetc(in_file);
  putchar(a_char);
  a_char=fgetc(in_file);
  putchar(a_char);
  location=ftell(in_file);
  a_char=fgetc(in_file);
  putchar(a_char);
  fseek(in_file,location,0);
  a_char=fgetc(in_file);
  putchar(a_char);
  fseek(in_file,location,0);
  fputc('E',in_file);
  fseek(in_file,location,0);
  a_char=fgetc(in_file);
```

```
putchar(a_char);
rewind(in_file);
a_char=fgetc(in_file);
putchar(a_char);

    return(0);
}
```

The variable *location* has been defined to be of type **long**. This is because Turbo C++ supports files larger than 64K bytes. The input file *sample.dat* contains the string ABCD. After opening the file, the first call to **fgetc** gets the letter "A" and then prints it to the video display. The next statement pair inputs and prints the letter "B."

When the function **ftell** is invoked, *location* is set equal to the file-position marker's current location. This is measured as an offset, in bytes, from the beginning of the file. Since the letter "B" has already been processed, *location* contains a 2. This means that the file-position marker is pointing to the third character, which is 2 bytes over from the first letter "A."

Another I/O pair of statements now reads the letter "C" and prints it to the video display. After having executed this last statement pair, the file-position marker is 3 offset bytes from the beginning of the file, pointing to the fourth character "D."

At this point, the function **fseek** is invoked. It is instructed to move *location* offset bytes (or 2 offset bytes) from the beginning of the file (since the third parameter to the function **fseek** is a 0, as defined previously). This repositions the file-position marker to the third character in the file. The variable *a_char* is again assigned the letter "C" and is printed a second time.

The second time the **fseek** function is invoked, it uses the same parameters. The function **fseek** moves the pointer to the third character "C" (2 offset bytes into the file). However, the statement that follows doesn't input the "C" a third time, instead overwriting it with a new letter, "E." Since the file-position marker has now moved past this new "E," to verify that the letter was indeed placed in the file, the **fseek** function is invoked still another time.

The next statement pair inputs the new "E" and prints it to the video display. With this accomplished, the program invokes the **rewind** function, which moves the *file_pointer* back to the beginning of the file. When the **fgetc** function is then invoked, it returns the letter "A" and prints it to the file. The output from the program looks like this:

ABCCEA

You can use the same principles illustrated in this simple character example to create a random access file of records. Suppose that you have the following information for a file of individuals: social security number, name, and address. Suppose also that you are allowing 11 characters for the social security number, in the form *ddd-dd-dddd*, and that the name and address have an additional 60 characters (or bytes). So far, each record would be 11 + 60 bytes long, or 71 bytes.

All of the possible contiguous record locations on a random access disk file may not be full. The personnel record needs to contain a flag indicating whether or not that disk record location has been used or not, which will require adding 1 more byte to the personnel record. You'll also need 2 additional bytes to represent the record number, bringing the total for one person's record to 74 bytes. One record could look like this:

1 U123-45-6789Tina Tomassetti, 435 Main Street, Anywhere, USA

Record 1 in the file would occupy bytes 0 through 73, record two would occupy bytes 74 through 147, record three would occupy bytes 148 through 221, and so on. Using the record number in conjunction with the **fseek** function, you can locate any record location on the disk. For example, to find the beginning of record 2, you use the following statements:

```
offset_in_bytes=(record_number-1) * sizeof(ONE_PERSON)
fseek(in_file,offset_in_bytes,0);
```

Once the file-position marker has been moved to the beginning of the selected record, the information at that location can either be read or written using various I/O functions such as **fread** and **fwrite**.

With the exception of the comment block delimiter symbols, **/*** and ***/**, and the header file *stdio.h*, many C programs can be modified to work the same as C++. the program just discussed would work the same in C++. Just substitute the symbol **//** for both **/*** and ***/** (optional) and change *stdio.h* to *iostream.h.*

Using the Turbo Debugger

Try entering the next program and printing the value stored in the variable *current _ person.record _ number* after you have asked to search for record 25:

```
/*
 *      A C random access file program using fseek, fread, and fwrite.
 *      Copyright (c) Chris H. Pappas and William H. Murray, 1990
 */

#include <stdio.h>

#define START 1
#define FINISH 50
#define SS_LENGTH 11
#define DATA_LENGTH 60
#define VACANT 'V'
#define USED 'U'

typedef struct a_record {
  int record_number;
  char occupied;            /* V free, U used */
  char social_security[SS_LENGTH];
  char data[DATA_LENGTH];
} ONE_PERSON;

main()
{
  FILE *in_file;
  ONE_PERSON current_person;
  int index,record_choice;
  long int offset;

  in_file=fopen("A:\\random.dat","r+");

  for(index = START;index <= FINISH; index++) {
    current_person.occupied=VACANT;
    current_person.record_number=index;
    fwrite(&current_person,sizeof(ONE_PERSON),1,in_file);
  }

  printf("Please enter the record you would like to find.");
  printf("\nYour response must be between 1 and 50: ");
  scanf("%d",&record_choice);

  offset=(record_choice - 1) * sizeof(ONE_PERSON);
    fseek(in_file,offset,0);
    fread(&current_person,sizeof(ONE_PERSON),1,in_file);

  fclose(in_file);

  return(0);
}
```

The **typedef** has defined *ONE_PERSON* as a structure that has a 2-byte record number, a 1-byte occupied character code, an 11-byte character array to hold a social security number, and a 60-byte data field. This brings the total structure size to 2 + 1 + 11 + 60, or 74 bytes.

Once the program has opened the file in read-and-update text mode, it creates and stores 50 records, each with its own unique record number and all initialized to *VACANT*. The **fwrite** statement wants the address of the structure to output, the size in bytes of what it is outputting, how many objects to output, and which file to send it to. With this accomplished, the program asks the user which record they want to search for.

The program finds the record in two steps. First, an offset address from the beginning of the file must be calculated. For example, record 1 is stored in bytes 0 to 73, record 2 is stored in bytes 74 to 148, and so on. After subtracting 1 from the record number entered by the user, the program multiplies this value by the number of bytes occupied by each structure and calculates the offset. For example, record 2 is found with the following calculation: (2 - 1) x 74. This gives the second record a starting byte offset of 74. Using this calculated value, the **fseek** function is then invoked and moves the file-position marker *offset* bytes into the file.

If you ask to view records 1 through 10, all seems fine. However, when you ask to view record 11, you get garbage because the program opened the file in text mode. Records 1 through 9 are all exactly 74 bytes. Records 10 and up occupy 75 bytes. Therefore, the tenth record starts at the appropriate offset calculation but goes 1 byte further into the file. Record 11 is at the address calculated via the following modified calculation:

```
offset=((record_choice - 1) * sizeof(ONE_PERSON)) + 1;
```

This calculation won't work with the first nine records, however. The solution is to open the file in binary mode:

```
in_file=fopen("A:\\random.dat","r+b");
```

In text mode, the program tries to interpret any two-digit number as two single characters, increasing records with two-digit record numbers by 1 byte. In binary mode, the integer *record_number* is interpreted properly. Exercise care when deciding how to open a file for I/O.

Formatted Input

You can obtain formatted input for a C program by using the versatile **scanf** and **fscanf** functions. The **fscanf** function requires that you specifically designate the input file from which the data is to be obtained, while scanf does not. Table 11-3 lists all possible control string codes that you can use with **scanf**, **fscanf**, and **sscanf**.

scanf, fscanf, and sscanf

You can use all three input functions—**scanf**, **fscanf**, and **sscanf**—for extremely sophisticated data input. For example, consider the statement:

```
scanf("%2d%5s%4f",&int_value,a_string,&real_value);
```

The statement inputs only a two-digit integer, a five-character string, and a real number that occupies a maximum of four spaces (2.97, 12.5, and so on). See if you can begin to imagine what this next statement does:

```
scanf("%*[ \t\n]\"%[^A-Za-z]%[^\"]\"",s1,s2);
```

The statement begins by reading and not storing any white space. This is accomplished with the following format specification: *"%*[\t\n]"*. The * symbol instructs the function to obtain the specified data but not to save it in any variable. As long as only a space, tab, or new line are on the input line, **scanf** will keep reading until it encounters a double quote, ". This is accomplished by the \" format specification, which says that the input must match the designated symbol. However, the double quote is not input.

   Once **scanf** has found the double quote, it is instructed to input all characters that are digits into *s1*. The %[^A-Za-z] format specification accomplishes this with the caret modifier, ^, which says to input anything not an uppercase letter "A" through "Z" or lowercase letter "a" through "z." Had the caret been omitted, the string would have contained only alphabetic characters. The hyphen between *A* and *Z* and *a* and *z* indicates that the entire range is to be considered.

   The next format specification, %[^\"], instructs the input function to read into *s2* all remaining characters up to but not including a double quote. The last format specification, \", indicates that the string must match and end with a double quote. You can use the same types of input conversion control with the functions **fscanf** and **sscanf**. The only difference between these two functions is that **fscanf** requires that an input file be specified. The **sscanf** function is identical to **scanf** except that it reads the data from an array rather than a file.

Table 11-3.   Control Codes for **scanf, fscanf,** and **sscanf**

Code	Interpretation	Example Input	Receiving Address Parameter Type
c	a character	W	char
s	a string	William	char
d	**int**	23	int
hd	**short**	−99	short
ld	**long**	123456	long
o	octal	1727	int
ho	short octal	1727	short
lo	long octal	1727	long
x	hexadecimal	2b5	int
hx	short hexadecimal	2b5	short
lx	long hexadecimal	2b5	long
e	float as **float**	3.14159e + 03	float
f	same as e		
le	float as **double**	3.14159e + 03	double
lf	same as le		
[A-Za-z]	string with only chars	Test String	char
[0-9]	string with only digits	098231345	char

This next example shows how you can use **sscanf** to convert a string (of digits) to an **int**. If *int_value* is of type **int** and *a_string* is an array of **char** that holds a string of digits, the following statement

```
sscanf(a_string,"%d",&int_value);
```

will convert the string *a_string* into type **int** and store it in the variable *int_value*. Often the **gets** and **sscanf** functions are used in combination since **gets** reads in an entire line of input and **sscanf** interprets a string according to the specified format specifications.

A frequent problem with **scanf** occurs when students try to use it in conjunction with various other character input functions such as **getc, getch, getchar, gets,** and so on. For example, suppose **scanf** is used to input various data types that would otherwise require conversion from characters to something else. If the programmer tries to use a character input function such as **getch**, the function will not work as expected. The problem occurs because **scanf** sometimes doesn't read all of the data that is waiting to be read, and the waiting data can fool other functions (including **scanf**) into thinking that input has already been entered. To be safe, don't use other input functions in a program in which you use **scanf**.

INPUT AND OUTPUT IN C++

This section describes input and output in C++. Your Borland C compiler has been shipped with the latest C++ I/O Library. Starting with Release 2.0, certain I/O Library functions operate differently from their earlier Release 1.2 ancestor. This portion of the chapter begins by explaining those I/O operations that are most similar in the two releases. The last part of the chapter highlights the more dramatic library function changes.

The standard I/O library for C, described by the header file *stdio.h* is still available in C++. However, C++ introduces its own header files; for example, *iostream.h, fstream.h, strstream.h,* which implement their own collection of I/O functions.

The stream I/O is described as a set of classes in *iostream.h.* These classes overload the "put to" and "get from" operators < < and > >. To understand better why C++'s stream library is more convenient than its C counterpart, first review how C handles input and output. Recall that C has no built-in input or output statements; functions such as **printf** are part of the standard library, but not part of the language itself. Similarly, C++ has no built-in I/O facilities, giving you greater flexibility to produce the most efficient user interface.

In C, there is unfortunately little consistency among the I/O functions in terms of return values and parameter sequences. Because of this, programmers tend to rely on the formatted I/O functions **printf, scanf,** and so on—especially when the objects being manipulated are numbers or other noncharacter values. These formatted I/O functions are convenient and for the most part share a consistent interface. However, they are large and unwieldy because they must manipulate many kinds of values.

In C++, the class provides modular solutions to your data manipulation needs. The standard C++ library provides three I/O classes as an alternative to C's general-purpose I/O functions. These classes contain definitions for the same pair of operators, > > for input and < < for output, that are optimized for all kinds of data (see Chapter 13 for a discussion of classes).

cin, cout, and cerr

The C++ stream counterparts to **stdin**, **stdout**, and **stderr** are **cin**, **cout**, and **cerr**. These three streams are opened automatically when your program begins execution and become the interface between the program and the user. The **cin** stream is associated with the terminal keyboard. The **cout** and **cerr** streams are associated with the video display.

The > > and < < Operators

From the programmer's point of view, the key to the stream library is the output operator, which replaces the more familiar function call to **printf**. In C++, instead of writing

```
printf("%d\n",int_value);
```

to display a message on the video display, you use the more concise form:

```
cout << int_value << "\n";
```

This translates as: Output the value of *int_value* and then output a newline character. Notice that you didn't need to include a format specification since the < < output operator determines it for you.

The C equivalent requires first that *int_value* be converted to its character string form, since only string data can be displayed on a video monitor. As a general-purpose conversion function, **printf** contains all the code needed to handle the many possible combinations of value-to-output transformations. This extra code is linked into each program, whether or not it is needed. With the C++ stream library, only the code needed for a specific conversion is included. In other words, the C++ code for I/O operations is smaller and faster than the equivalent C code.

C++ also supplies a similar input operator, > >, that would convert the following C example

```
scanf("%d",&inv_value);
```

into

```
cin >> int_value;
```

Assuming that *int_value* has been defined to be of type **int**, the > > operator automatically performs the necessary conversion. The input operator replaces the standard **scanf** function. It is not a complete substitution, however, because the input operator only does the data conversions. The **scanf** function is a complete, formatted input facility that lets you describe the format of the input line. The stream input operator has the same advantages as the output function: the resulting code is smaller, more specific, and more efficient.

The following program demonstrates how to use the input operator > > to read different types of data:

```
//
//    A C++ program demonstrating how to use the << operator
//    to input a char, integer, float, double, and string.
//    Copyright (c) Chris H. Pappas and William H. Murray, 1990
//

#include <iostream.h>

#define LENGTH 30
#define NULL_CHAR 1

main()
{
  char response,carriage_return;
  int int_value;
  float float_value;
  double double_value;
  char your_name[LENGTH + NULL_CHAR];

  cout << "Would you like to enter some information?" << "\n";
  cout << "Please type a Y for yes and an N for no: ";

  cin  >> response;

  if(response == 'Y') {

    cout << "\n" << "Please enter an integer value: ";

    cin >> int_value;
    cout << "\n\n";

    cout << "Please enter a float value: ";
    cin >> float_value;
    cout << "\n\n";

    cout << "Please enter a double value: ";
    cin >> double_value;
    cout << "\n\n";

    cout << "Please enter your first name: ";
    cin >> your_name

    cout << "\n\n";

    return(0);
}
```

```
    return(0);

}
```

In this example, the output operator < < is used in its simplest form to output literal string prompts. Notice that although the program uses four different data types, each input statement looks identical except for the variable's name. If you are a fast typist but are tired of searching for **%**, **"**, and **&** symbols (required by **scanf**), the input operator makes code entry much simpler and less error-prone.

Actually, if you ran the preceding program using Release 1.2, you would have noticed a formatting inconsistency. When the program started, you would have seen something like this:

```
Would you like to enter some information?
Please type a Y for yes and an N for no: Y

Please enter an integer value:
                     5
```

This is because the Release 1.2 input stream is processing the carriage return you entered after typing the letter **Y**. The input operator > > reads up to but does not get rid of the carriage return. The following program demonstrates how to correct the problem. Fortunately, starting with Release 2.0, none of this is necessary.

```
//
//    A C++ program demonstrating how to use the << operator
//    to input a char, integer, float, double, and string.
//    Copyright (c) Chris H. Pappas and William H. Murray, 1990
//

#include <iostream.h>

#define LENGTH 30
#define NULL_CHAR 1

main()
{
    char response,carriage_return;
    int int_value;
    float float_value;
    double double_value;
    char your_name[LENGTH + NULL_CHAR];

    cout << "Would you like to enter some information?" << "\n";
    cout << "Please type a Y for yes and an N for no: ";
```

```
    cin  >> response;
    cin.get(carriage_return);

    if(response == 'Y') {

       cout << "\n" << "Please enter an integer value: ";
       cin >> int_value;
       cout << "\n\n";

       cout << "Please enter a float value: ";
       cin >> float_value;
       cout << "\n\n";

       cout << "Please enter a double value: ";
       cin >> double_value;
       cout << "\n\n";

       cout << "Please enter your first name: ";
       cin >> your_name;
       cout << "\n\n";
    }

    return(0);
}
```

Did you notice the change? After the user response is read in, this line executes

```
cin.get(carriage_return);
```

which processes the carriage return. When the program runs now, it looks like this:

```
Would you like to enter some information?
Please type a Y for yes and an N for no: Y

Please enter an integer value: 5
```

The following example demonstrates how to use the output operator < < in its various forms:

```
//
//     A C++ program demonstrating how to use the << operator
//     to output a char, integer, float, double, and string.
//     Copyright (c) Chris H. Pappas and William H. Murray, 1990
//

#include <iostream.h>
```

```
main()
{
  char c='A';
  int int_value=10;
  float float_value=45.67;
  double double_value=2.3e32;
  char fact[]="For all have...";

  cout << "Once upon a time there were ";
  cout << int_value << " people. \n";
  cout << "Some of them earned " << float_value;
  cout << " dollars per hour." << "\n";
  cout << "While others earned " << double_value << " per year!";
  cout << "\n\n" << "But you know what they say: \"";
  cout << fact << "\"" << "\n\n";
  cout << "So, none of them get an ";
  cout.put(c);
  cout << "!";

  return(0);
}
```

The output from the program looks like this:

```
Once upon a time there were 10 people.
Some of them earned 45.669998 dollars per hour.
While others earned 2.3e+32 per year!

But you know what they say: "For all have..."

So, none of them get an A!
```

Compare the C++ source code with the output from the program. Notice that the output operator < < does not automatically generate a newline character. You can still completely control when this occurs by including the newline symbol \n or **endl** when necessary. **endl** is very useful for outputting data in an interactive program because it not only inserts a newline into the stream but also flushes the output buffer. You can also use **flush**, however this does not insert a newline. Notice too that the newline symbol can be included after its own < < output operator, or as part of a literal string (look at the second and fourth < < statements in the program). In addition, note that the output operator isn't very helpful with doubles.

Had the following line of code

```
cout.put(c);
```

been written using Release 1.2

```
cout << c;
```

the last line of the program would have output:

```
So, none of them get an 65!
```

Under Release 1.2 the character is translated into its ASCII equivalent. This would have required you to use the **put** function to output character data.
Try running this next example:

```
//
//    A C++ program demonstrating what happens when you use
//    the input operator >> with string data.
//    Copyright (c) Chris H. Pappas and William H. Murray, 1990
//

#include <iostream.h>

#define LENGTH 30
#define NULL_CHARACTER 1

main()
{
   char name[LENGTH + NULL_CHARACTER];

   cout << "Please enter your first and last name: ";
   cin >> name;
   cout << "\n\nThank you, " << name;

   return(0);
}
```

A sample execution of the program looks like this:

```
Please enter your first and last name: Dave Deehan

Thank you, Dave
```

The input operator, < <, stops reading in information as soon as it encounters white space. White space can be a blank, tab, or newline. Therefore, when *name* is printed, only the first name entered is output.
You can solve this problem by rewriting the program and using the **cin.get** function:

```
//
//      A C++ program demonstrating what happens when you use
//      the input operator >> with cin.get to process an
//      entire string.
//      Copyright (c) Chris H. Pappas and William H. Murray, 1990
//

#include <iostream.h>

#define LENGTH 30
#define NULL_CHARACTER 1

main()
{
  char name[LENGTH + NULL_CHARACTER];

  cout << "Please enter your first and last name: ";
  cin.get(name,LENGTH);
  cout << "\n\nThank you, " << name;

  return(0);
}
```

The output from the program now looks like this:

```
Please enter your first and last name: Dave Deehan

Thank you, Dave Deehan
```

The **cin.get** function has two additional parameters. Only one of these, the number of characters to input, was used in the previous example. The function **cin.get** will read everything, including white space, until the maximum number of characters specified has been read in, up to the next newline. The optional third parameter, not shown, identifies a terminating symbol. For example,

```
cin.get(name,LENGTH,'*');
```

would read *LENGTH* characters into *name,* or all of the characters up to but not including a * symbol, or a newline, whichever comes first.

Formatted C++ Output (Release 1.2)

This section provides an explanation and example program demonstrating how to perform formatted output using the I/O Library Release 1.2. If you

have no need to perform any program conversions from Release 1.2, continue your reading with "Advanced C++ Input and Output" later in this
section.

You can view the output operator, < <, as a quick and dirty means for
outputting many common types of information. However, when you need
more precision, C++ provides the **form** function. The **form** function has two
properties that allow flexible use at a high level. First, you can print a list of
arguments of arbitrary length. Second, the printing is controlled by simple
formats. This is analogous to the **printf** function in *stdio.h*. For this reason,
the previous example program written with **printf** can be rewritten with
cout < < form:

```
//
// A C++ program demonstrating advanced conversions and
// formatting using the form function with <<.
// Copyright (c) Chris H. Pappas and William H. Murray, 1990
//

#include <stream.h>

main()
{
  char letter='A';
  static char string1[]="he who has an ear, ",
  string2[]="let him hear.";
  int int_value=4444;
  double pi=3.14159265;
  int ln=0;


  //conversions                      //

  // print the letter                //
  cout << form("\n[%2d] %c",++ln,letter);

  // print the ASCII code for letter //
  cout << form("\n[%2d] %d",++ln,letter);

  // print character with ASCII 132  //
  cout << form("\n[%2d] %c",++ln,90);

  // print int_value as octal value  //
  cout << form("\n[%2d] %o",++ln,int_value);

  // print lower-case hexadecimal     //
  cout << form("\n[%2d] %x",++ln,int_value);

  // print upper-case hexadecimal     //
  cout << form("\n[%2d] %X",++ln,int_value);


  // conversions and format options  //
```

```
// minimum width 1                     //
cout << form("\n[%2d] %c",++ln,letter);

// minimum width 5, right-justify  //
cout << form("\n[%2d] %5c",++ln,letter);

// minimum width 5, left-justify   //
cout << form("\n[%2d] %-5c",++ln,letter);

// 19 non-null, automatically       //
cout << form("\n[%d] %s",++ln,string1);

// 13 non-null, automatically       //
cout << form("\n[%d] %s",++ln,string2);

// minimum 5 overridden, auto 19    //
cout << form("\n[%d] %5s",++ln,string1);

// minimum width 25, right-justify //
cout << form("\n[%d] %25s",++ln,string1);

// minimum width 25, left-justify  //
cout << form("\n[%d] %-25s",++ln,string2);

// default int_value width, 4       //
cout << form("\n[%d] %d",++ln,int_value);

// printf int_value with + sign     //
cout << form("\n[%d] %+d",++ln,int_value);

// minimum 3 overridden, auto 4     //
cout << form("\n[%d] %3d",++ln,int_value);

// minimum width 10, right-justify //
cout << form("\n[%d] %10d",++ln,int_value);

// minimum width 10, left-justify   //
cout << form("\n[%d] %-d",++ln,int_value);

// right-justify with leading 0's   //
cout << form("\n[%d] %010d",++ln,int_value);

// using default number of digits   //
cout << form("\n[%d] %f",++ln,pi);

// minimum width 20, right-justify //
cout << form("\n[%d] %20f",++ln,pi);

// right-justify with leading 0's   //
cout << form("\n[%d] %020f",++ln,pi);

// minimum width 20, left-justify   //
cout << form("\n[%d] %-20f",++ln,pi);

// left-justify with trailing 0's   //
cout << form("\n[%d] %-020f",++ln,pi);
```

```
// additional formatting precision //

// minimum width 19, print all 17  //
cout << form("\n[%d] %19.19s",++ln,string1);

// prints first 2 chars              //
cout << form("\n[%d] %.2s",++ln,string1);

// prints 2 chars, right-justify   //
cout << form("\n[%d] %19.2s",++ln,string1);

// prints 2 chars, left-justify    //
cout << form("\n[%d] %-19.2s",++ln,string1);

// using printf arguments           //
cout << form("\n[%d] %*.*s",++ln,19,6,string1);

// width 10, 8 to right of '.'      //
cout << form("\n[%d] %10.8f",++ln,pi);

// width 20, 2 to right-justify     //
cout << form("\n[%d] %20.2f",++ln,pi);

// 4 decimal places, left-justify  //
cout << form("\n[%d] %-20.4f",++ln,pi);

// 4 decimal places, right-justify //
cout << form("\n[%d] %20.4f",++ln,pi);

// width 20, scientific notation    //
cout << form("\n[%d] %20.2e",++ln,pi);

   return(0);
}
```

You will find that the output from this program is identical to the output from its C counterpart.

ADVANCED C++ INPUT AND OUTPUT

One of the most exciting enhancements to the compiler is the new C++ I/O library, referred to as the *iostream* library. By not including input/output facilities within the C++ language itself, but rather implementing them in C++ and providing them as a component of a C++ standard library, I/O can evolve as needed. This new library replaces the earlier version of the

I/O library referred to as the *stream* library (described in Stroustrup's *The C++ Programming Language*) discussed in the previous section.

Undoubtedly, many of you will have encountered the earlier Release 1.2 *stream* library. This portion of the chapter is designed to both familiarize you with the newer release *iostream* library and to highlight the most frequently needed changes to upgrade to the new format.

At its lowest level, C++ interprets a file as a sequence, or *stream,* of bytes. At this level, the concept of a data type is missing. One component of the I/O library is involved in the transfer of these bytes. From the user's perspective however, a file is comprised of a series of intermixed alphanumerics, numeric values, or possibly, class objects. A second component to the I/O library takes care of the interface between these two viewpoints. The iostream library predefines a set of operations for handling reading and writing of the built-in data types. The library also provides for user-definable extensions to handle class types.

Basic input operations are supported by the **istream** class and basic output via the **ostream** class. Bi-directional I/O is supported via the **iostream** class, which is derived from both **istream** and **ostream**. There are four stream objects predefined for the user:

- **cin** An **istream** class object linked to standard input

- **cout** An **ostream** class object linked to standard output

- **cerr** An unbuffered output **ostream** class object linked to standard error

- **clog** A buffered output **ostream** class object linked to standard error.

Any program using the iostream library must include the header file *iostream.h*. Since *iostream.h* treats *stream.h* as an alias, programs written using *stream.h* may or may not need alterations depending on the particular structure used.

The new I/O library can also be used to perform input and output operations on files. A file can be tied to your program by defining an instance of one of the following three class types:

- **fstream** Derived from **iostream** and links a file to your application for both input and output

- **ifstream**   Derived from **istream** and links a file to your application for input only

- **ofstream**   Derived from **ostream** and links a file to your application for output only

The > > and < < Operators

The > > *extraction* operator and the < < *insertion* operator have been modified to accept arguments of any of the built-in data types including **char** *. They can also be extended to accept class argument types.

Probably the first upgrade incompatibility you will experience when converting a C++ program using the older I/O library will be the demised **cout** < < **form** extension. Under the new release each *iostream* library class object maintains a *format state* that controls the details of formatting operations, such as the conversion base for integral numeric notation or the precision of a floating-point value. A programmer can manipulate the format state flags using the **setf( )** and **unsetf( )** functions.

The **setf( )** member function sets a specified format state flag. There are two overloaded instances:

```
setf(long);
setf(long,long);
```

Table 11-4.   Format Flags

Flag	Meaning
ios::showbase	display numeric base
ios::showpoint	display decimal point
ios::dec	decimal numeric base
ios::hex	hexadecimal numeric base
ios::oct	octal numeric base
ios::fixed	decimal notation
ios::scientific	scientific notation

Table 11-5.   Format Bit Fields

Bit Field	Meaning	Flags
ios::basefield	integral base	ios::hex, ios::oct, ios::dec
ios::floatfield	floating point	ios::fixed ios::scientific

The first argument can be either a format bit *flag* or a format bit *field*. Table 11-4 lists the format flags you can use with the **setf(long)** instance (using just the format flag). Table 11-5 lists the format bit fields you can use with the **setf(long,long)** instance (using a format flag and format bit field).

There are certain predefined defaults. For example, integers are written and read in decimal notation. The programmer can change the base to octal, hexadecimal, or back to decimal. By default, a floating-point value is output with six digits of precision. This can be modified by using the **precision** member function. The following C++ program uses these new member functions to rewrite an earlier program that was written using I/O library Release 1.2. Each code section takes the original Release 1.2 statement and demonstrates how to convert to an equivalent for the new I/O library.

Undoubtedly, as you study other example C++ programs from magazine articles, trade journals, and the like, you will encounter the older Release 1.2 formatting. This program can be an invaluable reference tool for making the necessary conversions.

```
//
//      A C++ program demonstrating advanced conversions and
//      formatting member functions of Release 2.0.  The program
//      will illustrate how to convert each of the older
//      Release 1.2 form statements.
//      Copyright (c) Chris H. Pappas and William H. Murray, 1990
//

#include <string.h>
#include <strstream.h>
```

```
  cout.precision(4);
  cout << pi;

  // 4 decimal places, right-justify
  // R1.2  form("\n[%d] %20.4f",++ln,pi);
  row(); // [35]
  cout.width(20);
  cout << pi;

  // width 20, scientific notation
  // R1.2  form("\n[%d] %20.2e",++ln,pi);
  row(); // [36]
  cout.setf(ios::scientific);
  cout.width(20);
  cout << pi;
  cout.unsetf(ios::scientific);

  return(0);
}

void row (void)
{
  static int ln=0;
  cout << "\n[";
  cout.width(2);
  cout << ++ln << "] ";

}
```

The output from the program follows:

```
[ 1] A
[ 2] 65
[ 3] Z
[ 4] 10534
[ 5] 115c
[ 6] 115C
[ 7] A
[ 8]         A
[ 9] A
[10] he who has an ear,
[11] let him hear.
[12] he wh
[13] he who has an ear, let h

Corrected approach:

[14]          he who has an ear,
[15] let him hear.
[16] 4444
[17] +4444
[18] 4444
[19]         4444
[20] 4444
```

```
[21] 0000004444
[22] 3.141593
[23]                 3.141593
[24] 0000000000003.141593
[25] 3.141593
[26] 3.141593000000000000
[27] he who has an ear,
[28] he
[29]                        he
[30] he
[31]                he who
[32] 3.14159265
[33]                    3.14
[34] 3.1416
[35]                  3.1416
[36]              3.1416e+00
```

The following section highlights those output statements used in the program above that need special clarification. One point needs to be made, *iostream.h* is automatically included by *strstream.h*. The latter file is needed to perform string output formatting. If your application needs to output numeric data or simple character and string output you will only need to include *iostream.h*.

Character Output

In the new I/O library the insertion operator < < has been overloaded to handle character data. With the earlier release the following statement:

```
cout << letter;
```

would have output the ASCII value of *letter*. In the current I/O Library the letter itself is output. For those programs needing the ASCII value a cast is required:

```
cout << (int)letter;
```

Base Conversions

There are two approaches to outputting a value using a different base:

```
cout << hex << int_value;
```

```
// or
```

```
cout.setf(ios::hex,ios::basefield);
cout << int_value;
```

Both approaches cause the base to be *permanently* changed from the statement forward (not always the effect you want). Each value output will now be formatted as a hexadecimal value. Returning to some other base is accomplished with the **unsetf( )** function:

```
cout.unsetf(ios::hex,ios::basefield);
```

If you are interested in uppercase hexadecimal output use the following statement:

```
cout.setf(ios::uppercase);
```

When no longer needed you will have to turn this option off:

```
cout.unsetf(ios::uppercase);
```

String Formatting

Printing an entire string using the current I/O library is the same as with Release 1.2. However, string formatting has changed because the *cout < < form* method is no longer available. One approach to string formatting is to declare an array of characters and then select the desired output format, printing the string buffer:

```
padstring25[25+NULL_TERMINATOR];
    .
    .
    .
ostrstream(padstring25,sizeof(padstring25)) << "        "
  << string1;
```

The **ostrstream** member function is part of *strstream.h* and has three parameters; a pointer to an array of characters, the size of the array, and the information to be inserted. This statement appends leading blanks to right justify *string1*.

Portions of a string can be output using the **write** form of **cout**:

```
cout.write(string1,5);
```

This statement will output the first five characters of *string1*.

Numeric Formatting

Numeric data can be easily formatted with right or left justification, varying precisions, varying formats (floating point or scientific), leading or trailing fill patterns, and signs. There are certain defaults. For example, justification defaults to right, and to floating-point precision of six. The following code segment outputs *pi* left justified in a field width of 20, with trailing 0's:

```
cout.width(20);
cout.setf(ios::left);
cout.fill('0');
cout << pi;
```

Had the following statement been included, *pi* would have been printed with a precision of two:

```
cout.precision(d2);
```

With many of the output flags such as left justify, selecting uppercase hexadecimal output, base changes, and many others, it is necessary to unset these flags when no longer needed. The following statement turns left justification off:

```
cout.unsetf(ios::left);
```

Selecting scientific format is a matter of flipping the correct bit flag:

```
cout.setf(ios::scientific);
```

Values can be printed with a leading **+** sign by setting the **showpos** flag:

```
cout.setf(ios::showpos);
```

There are many minor details to the current I/O library functions that will initially cause some confusion. This has to do with the fact that certain operations once executed make a permanent change until turned off, while others only take effect for the next output statement. For example, an output width change, as in *cout.width(20);*, only affects the next value printed. That is why function **row( )** has to repeatedly change the width to get the output row numbers formatted within two spaces as in [1]. However, other formatting operations like base changes, uppercase, precision, and floating-point/scientific, remain active until specifically turned off.

File Input and Output

All of the examples so far have used the predefined streams **cin** and **cout**. It is possible that your program will need to create its own streams for I/O. If an application needs to create a file for input or output it must include the *fstream.h* header file (*fstream.h* **#includes** *iostream.h*). The classes **ifstream** and **ofstream** are derived from **istream** and **ostream** and inherit the extraction and insertion operations respectively. The following C++ program demonstrates how to declare a file for reading and writing using **ifstream** and **ofstream** respectively:

```
//
//      A C++ program demonstrating how to declare an
//      ifstream and ofstream for file input and output.
//      Copyright (c) Chris H. Pappas and William H. Murray, 1990
//

#include <fstream.h>

main()
{
  char ch;

  ifstream my_input("a:\my_input.in");
  if( !my_input )
    cerr << " Unable to open 'my_input' for input.";

  ofstream my_output("a:\myoutput.out");
  if( !my_output )
    cerr << " Unable to open 'my_output' for output.";

  while( my_output && my_input.get(ch) )
    my_output.put(ch);

  my_input.close();
  my_output.close();

  return(0);
}
```

The program declares *my_input* to be of class **ifstream** and is associated with the file *my_input.in* stored on the A: drive. It is always a good idea for any program dealing with files to verify the existence or creation of the specified file in the designated mode. By using the handle to the file *my_input* a simple *if* test can be generated to check the condition of the file. A similar process is applied to *my_output* with the exception that the file is derived from the **ostream** class.

The *while* loop continues inputting and outputting single characters while the *my_input* exists and the character read in is not **EOF**. The program terminates by closing the two files. Closing an output file can be essential to dumping all internally buffered data.

There may be circumstances when a program will want to delay a file specification or when an application may want to associate several file streams with the same file descriptor. The following code segment demonstrates this concept:

```
ifstream an_in_file;
     .
     .
     .
an_in_file.open("bobsales");
     .
     .
     .
an_in_file.close();
an_in_file.open("joesales");
     .
     .
     .
an_in_file.close();
```

Whenever an application wishes to modify the way in which a file is opened or used it can apply a second argument to the file stream constructors. For example:

```
ofstream my_output("my_output.out",ios::app|ios::noreplace);
```

declares *my_output* and attempts to append it to the file named *my_output.out*. Because **ios::noreplace** is specified, the file will not be created if *my_output.out* doesn't already exist. The **ios::app** parameter appends all writes to an existing file. Table 11-6 lists the second argument flags to the file stream constructors that can be logically ORed together.

Table 11-6.   Stream Operation Modes

Mode Bit	Action
ios::in	Open for reading
ios::out	Open for writing
ios::ate	Seek to EOF after file is created
ios::app	All writes added to end of file
ios::trunc	If file already exists truncate
ios::nocreate	Unsuccessful open if file does not exist
ios::noreplace	Unsuccessful open if file does exist
ios::binary	Opens file in binary mode (default text)

An **fstream** class object can also be used to open a file for *both* input and output. For example, the following definition opens file *update.dat* in both input and append mode:

```
fstream io("update.dat", ios::in|ios::app);
```

All **iostream** class types can be repositioned by using either the **seekg( )** or **seekp( )** member functions, which can move to an absolute address within the file or move a byte offset from a particular position. Both **seekg( )** (sets or reads the *get* pointer's position) and **seekp( )** (sets or reads the *put* pointer's position) can take one or two arguments. When used with one parameter, the **iostream** is repositioned to the specified pointer position. When used with two parameters, a relative position is calculated. The following listing highlights these differences assuming the declaration for *io* above:

```
streampos current_position = io.tellp();

io << my_object1 << my_object2 << my_object3;

io.seekp(current_position);
io.seekp( sizeof(MY_OBJECT), ios::cur );

io << new_object2;
```

The pointer *current_position* is first derived from **streampos** and initialized to the current position of the *put-file* pointer by the function **tellp( )**. With this information stored three objects are written to *io*. Using **seekp**, the *put-file* pointer is repositioned to the beginning of the file. The second **seekp** statement uses the **sizeof** function to calculate the number of bytes necessary to move one object's width into the file. This effectively skips over *my_object1*'s position permitting a *new_object2* to be written.

If a second argument is passed to **seekg** or **seekp**, it defines the direction to move: **ios::beg** (from the beginning), **ios::cur** (from the current position), and **ios::end** (from the end of file). For example:

```
io.seekg(5,ios::cur);
```

will move into the *get_file* pointer file five bytes from the current position, while:

```
io.seekg(-7,ios::end);
```

will move the *get_file* pointer seven bytes backward from the end of the file.

File Condition States

Associated with every stream is an error state. When an error occurs, bits are set in the state according to the general category of the error. By convention, inserters ignore attempts to insert things into an **ostream** with error bits set, and such attempts do not change the stream's state. The **iostream** library object contains a set of predefined condition flags, which monitor the ongoing state of the stream. Table 11-7 lists the seven member functions that can be invoked.

```
struct car {
  char make[15];
  char model[15];
  char title[20];
  int year;
  long int mileage;
  float price_new;
} hiscar,hercar,bankscar;
```

As with normal variable types, C and C++ allocate all necessary memory for the structure members.

You reference members of a structure by using the dot (.) operator. The syntax is

```
struct_name.member_name
```

where *struct_name* is the variable associated with the structure type and *member_name* is the name of any member of the structure.

In C, for example, you can place information in the *model* variable with a statement such as

```
gets(mycar.model);
```

Here, *mycar* is the name associated with the structure and *model* is a member of the structure. Likewise, you can use a **printf** function to print information for a structure member:

```
printf("%ld",mycar.mileage);
```

In C++, the syntax for accessing structure members is essentially the same:

```
cin >> mycar.make;
```

This statement will read the make of the car into the character array while

```
cout << mycar.price_new;
```

will display the purchase price of the car on the screen.

Structure members are treated like any other C or C++ variable, but you must always use the dot operator with them.

Creating a Simple Structure

The programming example in this section will use a structure similar to the **car** structure shown earlier. Study the listing that follows and see if you understand how the various structure elements are accessed.

```
/*
 *      C program illustrates how to create a structure.
 *      This example stores data about your car in
 *      the C structure.
 *      Copyright (c) Chris H. Pappas and William H. Murray, 1990
 */

#include <stdio.h>

struct car {
  char make[15];
  char model[15];
  char title[20];
  int year;
  long int mileage;
  float price_new;
} myauto;

main()
{
  printf("Enter the make of the car.\n");
  gets(myauto.make);
  printf("Enter the model of the car.\n");
  gets(myauto.model);
  printf("Enter the title number for the car.\n");
  gets(myauto.title);
  printf("Enter the model year for the car.\n");
  scanf("%d",&myauto.year);
  printf("Enter the current mileage for the car.\n");
  scanf("%ld",&myauto.mileage);
  printf("Enter the purchase price of the car.\n");
  scanf("%f",&myauto.price_new);
  getchar();      /* flush keyboard buffer */

  printf("\n\n\n");
  printf("A %d %s %s with title number #%s\n",myauto.year,
      myauto.make,myauto.model,myauto.title);
  printf("currently has %ld miles",myauto.mileage);
  printf(" and was purchased for $%5.2f\n",
      myauto.price_new);
  return (0);
}
```

The single **getchar** function call flushes the carriage return from the keyboard buffer. You may or may not need this function call in your program, depending on the type of computer you are using. A typical output from the preceding example illustrates how information can be manipulated with a structure:

```
A 1987 Ford LTD with title number #A143LFG3489FD
currently has 56732 miles and was purchased for $14879.54
```

Note that *myauto* has a global scope since it was declared outside of any function.

Passing a Structure to a Function

You will have many occasions to pass structure information to functions. When a structure is passed to a function, structure information is passed by value, thus the function will not alter the original structure. You can pass a structure to a function by using the following syntax:

```
function_name(variable associated with structure);
```

If *myauto* were local in scope to the **main** function, it could be passed to a function named **dataout** with the statement

```
dataout(myauto);
```

Naturally, the **dataout** prototype must declare the structure type it is about to receive.

```
void dataout(struct car autocompany);
```

Passing entire structures to functions is not always the most efficient way to reduce time and memory requirements. Where time is a factor, the use of pointers might be a better choice. The **malloc** function is often used for dynamically allocating structure memory when using linked lists. The last example in this chapter shows how that's done.

The following example shows how to pass a structure to a function. It is a simple modification of the last example. Observe how the *myauto* structure is passed to the **dataout** function.

```
/*
 *      C program illustrates how to pass a structure
 *      to a function.
 *      Copyright (c) Chris H. Pappas and William H. Murray, 1990
 */

#include <stdio.h>

struct car {
  char make[15];
  char model[15];
  char title[20];
  int year;
  long int mileage;
  float price_new;
};

void dataout(struct car autocompany);

main()
{
  struct car myauto;

  printf("Enter the make of the car.\n");
  gets(myauto.make);
  printf("Enter the model of the car.\n");
  gets(myauto.model);
  printf("Enter the title number for the car.\n");
  gets(myauto.title);
  printf("Enter the model year for the car.\n");
  scanf("%d",&myauto.year);
  printf("Enter the current mileage for the car.\n");
  scanf("%ld",&myauto.mileage);
  printf("Enter the purchase price of the car.\n");
  scanf("%f",&myauto.price_new);
  getchar();        /* flush keyboard buffer */
  dataout(myauto);
  return (0);
}

void dataout(struct car autocompany)
{
  printf("\n\n\n");
  printf("A %d %s %s with title number #%s\n",autocompany.year,
      autocompany.make,autocompany.model,autocompany.title);
  printf("currently has %ld miles",autocompany.mileage);
  printf(" and was purchased for $%5.2f\n",
      autocompany.price_new);
}
```

In this example, a whole structure was passed by value to the function. As you will see later in this chapter, you can also pass individual structure members to a function by value. The output from this program is similar to the output from the previous example.

Creating an Array of Structures

As you have seen, a structure is similar to a single card from a card file. You exploit the real power of structures when you use a collection of structures, called an *array of structures*. An array of structures is similar to the whole card file containing a great number of individual cards. By maintaining an array of structures, you can manipulate a database of information for a wide range of items. This array of structures might include information on all of the cars on a used car lot. This could enable a car dealer to use the database to determine, for example, all cars less than $3000 or all cars with automatic transmissions. Notice how the following code has been changed from earlier listings:

```
/*
 *      C program illustrates the use of an array of structures.
 *      This example creates a "used car inventory" for
 *      P and M Car Sales.
 *      Copyright (c) Chris H. Pappas and William H. Murray, 1990
 */

#include <stdio.h>

#define MAX_CARS 25

struct car {
   char make[15];
   char model[15];
   char title[20];
   char comment[80];
   int year;
   long int mileage;
   float retail;
   float wholesale;
};

main()
{
   int i,inven;
   struct car P_and_M[MAX_CARS];

   printf("How many cars in inventory?\n");
   scanf("%d",&inven);
   getchar();      /* flush keyboard buffer */
   for (i=0; i<inven; i++) {
```

```
        printf("Enter the make of the car.\n");
        gets(P_and_M[i].make);
        printf("Enter the model of the car.\n");
        gets(P_and_M[i].model);
        printf("Enter the title number for the car.\n");
        gets(P_and_M[i].title);
        printf("Enter a one line comment about the car.\n");
        gets(P_and_M[i].comment);
        printf("Enter the model year for the car.\n");
        scanf("%d",&P_and_M[i].year);
        printf("Enter the current mileage for the car.\n");
        scanf("%ld",&P_and_M[i].mileage);
        printf("Enter the retail price of the car.\n");
        scanf("%f",&P_and_M[i].retail);
        printf("Enter the wholesale price of the car.\n");
        scanf("%f",&P_and_M[i].wholesale);
        getchar();      /* flush keyboard buffer */
    }

    printf("\n\n\n");
    for (i=0; i<inven; i++) {
        printf("A %d %s %s cream-puff with %ld low miles.\n",
            P_and_M[i].year,P_and_M[i].make,P_and_M[i].model,
            P_and_M[i].mileage);
        printf("%s\n",P_and_M[i].comment);
        printf("Ask your P and M salesperson for bargain");
        printf(" #%s ONLY! $%5.2f.\n",P_and_M[i].title,
            P_and_M[i].retail);
        printf("\n\n");

    }

    return (0);

}
```

Here, P and M Auto Sales (not affiliated with Pappas and Murray) has an array of structures for holding information about the cars on their lot.

The variable, *P_and_M[MAX_CARS]*, associated with the structure is actually an array. In this case, *MAX_CARS* sets the maximum array size to 25. This means that data on 25 cars can be maintained in the array of structures. Now, however, you need to indicate which of the cars in the file you wish to view. The first array element is 0. Thus, you can access information on the first car in the array of structures with statements such as the following:

```
gets(P_and_M[0].title);
```

Notice that the array elements in the previous listing are actually accessed in a loop. Thus, element members are obtained with code such as

```
gets(P_and_M[i].title);
```

The following program output illustrates the small stock of cars on hand at P and M Auto Sales. It also shows how structure information can be rearranged in output statements.

```
A 1987 Lincoln Mark VII cream-puff with 89476 low miles.
A great riding car owned by a poor school teacher.
Ask your P and M salesperson for bargain #DS1543267BGDF ONLY!
$21567.00.

A 1967 Honda motorcycle cream-puff with 4564 low miles.
An economical means of transportation.  Owned by grandmother.
Ask your P and M salesperson for bargain #AG1543RED219 ONLY!
$1237.99.

A 1985 Buick Park Avenue cream-puff with 43500 low miles.
Runs great.  Owned by former dean of college.
Ask your P and M salesperson for bargain #156YUBA12ERR56 ONLY!
$10599.99.
```

```
≡ File View Run Breakpoints Data Options Window Help        READY
┌─Module: PM  File: PM.C 34───────────────────────────1─┐
│ scanf("%d",&inven);                                    │
│ getchar();       /* flush keyboard buffer */           │
│ for (i=0; i<inven; i++) {                              │
│▶    printf("Enter the make of the car.\n");            │
│     gets(P_and_M[i].make);                             │
│     printf("Enter the model of the car.\n");           │
│     gets(P_and_M[i].model);                            │
│     printf("Enter the title number for the car.\n");   │
│     gets(P_and_M[i].title);                            │
│     printf("Enter a one line comment about the car.\n");│
│     gets(P_and_M[i].comment);                          │
└────────────────────────────────────────────────────────┘
┌[■]Watches────────────────────────────────2=[↑][↓]┐
│P_and_M[0].retail        float 10567               │
│P_and_M[0].year          int 1987 (0x7C3)          │
│P_and_M[0].title         char [20] "AB142-AF-1345FG\0\x8F\xA9&\x8A"│
│P_and_M[0].model         char [15] "Park Avenue\0U\x8B\xEC"│
│P_and_M[0].make          char [15] "Buick\0\x02\x8E\x06\x07\xAA&\x8B4\x0B"│
│P_and_M struct car [50] {{"Buick\0\x02\x8E\x06\x07\xAA&\x8B4\x0B","Park Avenue│
└────────────────────────────────────────────────────┘
F1-Help F2-Bkpt F3-Mod F4-Here F5-Zoom F6-Next F7-Trace F8-Step F9-Run F10-Menu
```

Figure 12-1.   The Debugger is used to examine selected items in the program's **car** structure. Notice all six items that were added to the watch window

When you work with arrays of structures, be aware of the memory limitations of the memory model you are programming with—arrays of structures require large amounts of memory.

Examine the Turbo Debugger screen shown in Figure 12-1. What does it tell you about the memory locations of structure items?

Using Pointers with Structures

The following example establishes an array of structures similar to the last example. However, this example uses the arrow operator to access structure members. You can only use the arrow operator when a pointer to a structure has been established.

```
/*
 *     C program illustrates the use of pointers to an
 *     array of structures.  P and M used car inventory
 *     example is used again.
 *     Copyright (c) Chris H. Pappas and William H. Murray, 1990
 */

#include <stdio.h>

#define MAX_CARS 25

struct car {
  char make[15];
  char model[15];
  char title[20];
  char comment[80];
  int year;
  long int mileage;
  float retail;
  float wholesale;
};

main()
{
  int i,inven;
  struct car P_and_M[MAX_CARS],*P_and_Mptr;
  P_and_Mptr=&P_and_M[0];

  printf("How many cars in inventory?\n");
  scanf("%d",&inven);
  getchar();      /*  flush keyboard buffer */
```

```
for (i=0; i<inven; i++) {
  printf("Enter the make of the car.\n");
  gets(P_and_Mptr->make);
  printf("Enter the model of the car.\n");
  gets(P_and_Mptr->model);
  printf("Enter the title number for the car.\n");
  gets(P_and_Mptr->title);
  printf("Enter a one line comment about the car.\n");
  gets(P_and_Mptr->comment);
  printf("Enter the model year for the car.\n");
  scanf("%d",&P_and_Mptr->year);
  printf("Enter the current mileage for the car.\n");
  scanf("%ld",&P_and_Mptr->mileage);
  printf("Enter the retail price of the car.\n");
  scanf("%f",&P_and_Mptr->retail);
  printf("Enter the wholesale price of the car.\n");
  scanf("%f",&P_and_Mptr->wholesale);
  getchar();    /*  flush keyboard buffer */
  P_and_Mptr++;

}

P_and_Mptr=&P_and_M[0];
printf("\n\n\n");
for (i=0; i<inven; i++) {
  printf("A %d %s %s cream-puff with %ld low miles.\n",
        P_and_Mptr->year,P_and_Mptr->make,P_and_Mptr->model,
        P_and_Mptr->mileage);
  printf("%s\n",P_and_Mptr->comment);
  printf("Ask your P and M salesperson for bargain");
  printf(" #%s ONLY! $%5.2f.\n",P_and_Mptr->title,
        P_and_Mptr->retail);
  printf("\n\n");
  P_and_Mptr++;
}
return (0);
}
```

The array variable *P_and_M[MAX_CARS]* and the **P_and_Mptr* pointer are associated with the structure via the following statement:

```
struct car P_and_M[MAX_CARS],*P_and_Mptr;
```

The address of the array is then passed to the pointer with

```
P_and_Mptr=&P_and_M[0];
```

It is syntactically correct to refer to array members with this syntax:

```
gets((*P_and_Mptr).make);
```

However, the arrow operator makes the operation much cleaner:

```
gets(P_and_Mptr->make);
```

Passing an Array of Structures to a Function

Remember, using a pointer to a structure is faster than simply passing the whole structure to a function. This becomes evident when a program makes heavy use of structures. The following example shows how an array of structures can be accessed by a function with the use of a pointer:

```
/*
 *      C program illustrates how a function can access an array
 *      of structures with the use of a pointer.
 *      The P and M used car inventory is used again.
 *      Copyright (c) Chris H. Pappas and William H. Murray, 1990
*/

#include <stdio.h>

#define MAX_CARS 25

int inven;

struct car {
  char make[15];
  char model[15];
  char title[20];
  char comment[80];
  int year;
  long int mileage;
  float retail;
  float wholesale;
};

void dataout(struct car *autocompanyptr);

main()
{
  int i;
  struct car  P_and_M[MAX_CARS],*P_and_Mptr;
  P_and_Mptr=&P_and_M[0];

  printf("How many cars in inventory?\n");
  scanf("%d",&inven);
  getchar();      /*  flush keyboard buffer */
  for (i=0; i<inven; i++) {
    printf("Enter the make of the car.\n");
```

```
   gets(P_and_Mptr->make);
   printf("Enter the model of the car.\n");
   gets(P_and_Mptr->model);
   printf("Enter the title number for the car.\n");
   gets(P_and_Mptr->title);
   printf("Enter a one line comment about the car.\n");
   gets(P_and_Mptr->comment);
   printf("Enter the model year for the car.\n");
   scanf("%d",&P_and_Mptr->year);
   printf("Enter the current mileage for the car.\n");
   scanf("%ld",&P_and_Mptr->mileage);
   printf("Enter the retail price of the car.\n");
   scanf("%f",&P_and_Mptr->retail);
   printf("Enter the wholesale price of the car.\n");
   scanf("%f",&P_and_Mptr->wholesale);
   getchar();   /*  flush keyboard buffer */
   P_and_Mptr++;
   }
   P_and_Mptr=&P_and_M[0];
   dataout(P_and_Mptr);
   return (0);
}

void dataout(struct car *autocompanyptr)
{
  int i;
  printf("\n\n\n");
  for (i=0; i<inven; i++) {
    printf("A %d %s %s cream-puff with %ld low miles.\n",
           autocompanyptr->year,autocompanyptr->make,
           autocompanyptr->model,autocompanyptr->mileage);
    printf("%s\n",autocompanyptr->comment);
    printf("Ask your P and M salesperson for bargain");
    printf(" #%s ONLY! $%5.2f.\n",autocompanyptr->title,
           autocompanyptr->retail);
    printf("\n\n");
    autocompanyptr++;
  }
}
```

The first clue that this program will operate a little differently from the previous example comes from the **dataout** function prototype:

```
void dataout(struct car *autocompanyptr);
```

The function will expect to receive a pointer to the structure mentioned. In the **main** function, the array *P_and_M[MAX_CARS]* and the pointer *P_and_Mptr* are associated with the structure by

```
struct car  P_and_M[MAX_CARS],*P_and_Mptr;
```

After the information has been gathered for P and M Auto Sales, it is passed to **dataout** by passing the pointer.

```
dataout(P_and_Mptr);
```

The output from this example is similar to the output from the previous examples.

Using Structures in C++

The C++ example that follows is a modification of the previous C program. Syntactically, both of these languages handle structures in an identical manner.

```
//
//      C++ program illustrates the use of pointers when
//      accessing structure information from a function.
//      Note:  Comment line terminates with a period (.)
//      Copyright (c) Chris H. Pappas and William H. Murray, 1990
//

#include <iostream.h>

#define MAX_CARS 50

int inven;

struct car {
  char make[15];
  char model[15];
  char title[20];
  char comment[80];
  int year;
  long int mileage;
  float retail;
  float wholesale;
};

void dataout(struct car *autocompanyptr);

main()
{
  int i;
  char newline;
  struct car P_and_M[MAX_CARS],*P_and_Mptr;
  P_and_Mptr=&P_and_M[0];

  cout << "How many cars in inventory?" << endl;
  cin >> inven;
```

```
  for (i=0; i<inven; i++) {
    cout << "Enter the make of the car." << endl;
    cin >> P_and_Mptr->make;
    cout << "Enter the model of the car." << endl;
    cin >> P_and_Mptr->model;
    cout << "Enter the title number for the car." << endl;
    cin >> P_and_Mptr->title;
    cout << "Enter the model year for the car." << endl;
    cin >> P_and_Mptr->year;
    cout << "Enter the current mileage for the car." << endl;
    cin >> P_and_Mptr->mileage;
    cout << "Enter the retail price of the car." << endl;
    cin >> P_and_Mptr->retail;
    cout << "Enter the wholesale price of the car." << endl;
    cin >> P_and_Mptr->wholesale;
    cout << "Enter a one line comment about the car." << endl;
    cin.get(newline);   // process carriage return
    cin.get(P_and_Mptr->comment,80,'.');
    cin.get(newline);   // process carriage return
    cout << flush;
    P_and_Mptr++;
  }
  P_and_Mptr=&P_and_M[0];
  dataout(P_and_Mptr);
  return (0);
}

void dataout(struct car *autocompanyptr)
{
  int i;
  cout.setf(ios::fixed);   //format output for dollars and cents
  cout.precision(2);
  cout << "\n\n\n";
  for (i=0; i<inven; i++) {
    cout << "A " << autocompanyptr->year << " "
         << autocompanyptr->make  << " "
         << autocompanyptr->model << " with "
         << autocompanyptr->mileage << " low miles.\n";
    cout << autocompanyptr->comment << endl;
    cout << "Ask your P and M salesperson for bargain ";
    cout << "#" << autocompanyptr->title << " ONLY! $"
         << autocompanyptr->retail;
    cout << "\n\n";
    autocompanyptr++;
  }
}
```

The real difference between the two programs lies in how stream I/O is handled. Usually, you can use simple C++ **cout** and **cin** streams to replace the standard C **gets** and **printf** functions. For example:

```
cout << "Enter the wholesale price of the car.\n";
cin >> P_and_Mptr->wholesale;
```

However, when it comes to accepting a comment line, you use a different approach. Remember that **cin** will read character information until the first whitespace. In this case, a space between words in a line of comments serves as a whitespace. If **cin** were used, only the first word would be saved in the comment member of the structure. Instead, a variation of **cin** is used so that a whole line of text can be entered:

```
cout << "Enter a one line comment about the car.\n";
cin.get(newline);    // process carriage return
cin.get(P_and_Mptr->comment,length,'.');
cin.get(newline);    // process carriage return
```

First, **cin.get(***newline***)** is used much like the **getchar** function of earlier C programs. In a buffered keyboard system, you often need to strip the carriage return from the buffer. There are other ways to accomplish this, but they are less eloquent. The statement **cin.get(***newline***)** receives the carriage return character and saves it in *newline.* The variable *newline* is just a receptacle for the information, and is not actually used by the program. The comment line is accepted by

```
cin.get(P_and_Mptr->comment,length,'.');
```

Here, **cin.get** uses a pointer to the structure member, followed by the maximum length of the comment, *length,* followed by a termination character (.). In this case, the comment line will be terminated when 80 characters are entered or a period is typed. The period is not saved as part of the comment, so the period is added back when the comment is printed. Can you find where this is done?

More on Structures

There are a few things about structures that the previous examples have not touched upon. For example, you can pass individual structure members to a function. Furthermore, you can nest structures.

Passing Individual Members of a Structure to a Function

Passing individual structure members is an easy and efficient means of accessing limited structure information with a function. For example, you might use a function to print a list of wholesale prices of the cars available on the lot. In that case, just the wholesale price, which is a member of the structure, would be passed to the function. The call to the function might look like this

```
print_price(P_and_M.wholesale);
```

where **print _ price** is the function name and *P _ and _ M.wholesale* is the structure name and member.

Nesting Structures Within Structures

You can nest structures—that is, make one structure a part of a second structure. For example, you could include the following structure in another structure:

```
struct maintenance {
   long int oilchange;
   long int plugs;
   long int airfilter;
   long int tirerotation;
} carmain;
```

In the main structure, you could include the *carmain* structure as follows:

```
struct car {
   char make[15];
   char model[15];
   char title[20];
   char comment[80];
   struct maintenance carmain;
   int year;
   long int mileage;
   float retail;
   float wholesale;
} P_and_M[MAX_CARS];
```

If you want a particular member from *carmain,* you can reach it like this:

```
printf("%ld\n",P_and_M[0].carmain.oilchange);
```

Structures and Bit Fields

C, C++, and assembly language enable you to access individual bits within a larger data type, such as a byte. This feature is useful when you want to alter data masks used for system information and graphics. The ability to access individual data bits is built around the C and C++ structure.

For example, you may want to alter the keyboard status register in the computer. The register contains the following information:

	register bits
keyboard status: port (417h)	7 6 5 4 3 2 1 0

where bit 0 = Right SHIFT depressed (1)
      bit 1 = Left SHIFT depressed (1)
      bit 2 = CTRL depressed (1)
      bit 3 = ALT depressed (1)
      bit 4 = SCROLL LOCK active (1)
      bit 5 = NUMLOCK active (1)
      bit 6 = CAPS LOCK active (1)
      bit 7 = INS active (1)

To access and manipulate this information, you could create this structure:

```
struct keybits {
  unsigned char
              rshift   : 1,      /* lsb */
              lshift   : 1,
              ctrl     : 1,
              alt      : 1,
              scroll   : 1,
              numlock  : 1,
              caplock  : 1,
              insert   : 1;      /* msb */
} mykeys;
```

The bits are specified in the structure starting with the least significant bit (LSB) and progressing down to the most significant bit (MSB). You can specify more than one bit by typing the quantity (in place of the 1). Naturally, you can only use integer data types for bit fields.

The members of the bit field structure are accessed in the normal fashion.

UNIONS

A *union* is a data type that can be used in many different ways. For example, a particular union could be interpreted as an integer in one operation and a float or double in another. Although unions take on the appearance of a structure, they are quite different. A union can contain a group of many data types, all sharing the same location in memory. Nevertheless, a union can only contain information on one data type at a time.

The Syntax and Rules for Unions

You create a union by using the following syntax:

```
union type {
  type var1
  type var2
      .
      .
      .
  type varn
};
```

Use a semicolon for termination because the structure definition is actually a C and C++ statement.

The next example will use the following union:

```
union all_types {
  char c;
  int i;
  float f;
  double d;
} tdata;
```

The union is defined with the keyword *union* followed by the type or tag for the structure. In this example, **all_types** is the tag for the union. This union contains several members: a character, integer, float, and double. This union will allow **all_types** to save information on any one data type at a time.

The variable associated with the union is *tdata*. If this statement is contained in a function, the union is local in scope to that function. If the statement is contained outside of all functions, the structure will be global in scope. As with structures, you can associate several variables with the same union. In addition, you reference members of a union by using the dot operator with the following syntax

```
union_name.member_name
```

where *union_name* is the variable associated with the union type and *member_name* is the name of any member of the union.

Union members are treated like any other C or C++ variable, but you must always use the dot operator with them. However, unlike a structure, you cannot pass a union to a function. One way around this is to pass the value of the data type currently stored in the union. Almost all other operations that were valid for structures are also valid for unions.

Creating a Simple Union

The following C++ program creates a union of the type just discussed. This example shows that a union can contain the definitions for many types, but can only hold the value for one data type at a time.

```
//
//     C++ program illustrates the use of a union.
//     Creates a union containing several data types.
//     Copyright (c) Chris H. Pappas and William H. Murray, 1990
//

#include <iostream.h>

union all_types {
  char c;
  int i;
  float f;
  double d;
} tdata;
```

```
main()
{
  // valid I/O
  tdata.c='b';
  cout << tdata.c << "\n";
  tdata.i=1234;
  cout << tdata.i << "\n";
  tdata.f=12.34;
  cout << tdata.f << "\n";
  tdata.d=123456.78E+12;
  cout << tdata.d << "\n";

  // invalid I/O
  cout << tdata.c << "\n";
  cout << tdata.i << "\n";
  cout << tdata.f << "\n";
  cout << tdata.d << "\n";

  // union size
  cout << "The size of this union is: "
       << sizeof(all_types) << " bytes." << "\n";
  return (0);
}
```

The first part of this program simply loads and unloads information from the union. Everything works fine because the union is only called upon to store one type at a time. However, the second part of the program attempts to output each data type from the union. The only valid value is the double, since it was the last value loaded in the previous section of code.

```
98
1234
12.34
1.234568e+17
-128
14208
-5.382278e-24
1.234568e+17
The size of this union is: 8 bytes.
```

Unions set aside storage for the largest data type contained within the union. All other data types within the union share this memory.

You can use the Turbo Debugger to get an idea of what is happening with storage within a union. Examine Figure 12-2 and the Watch window.

MISCELLANEOUS ITEMS

There are two additional topics worth mentioning at this point: **typedef** and **enum**. Both **typedef** and **enum** can help clarify program code when used correctly.

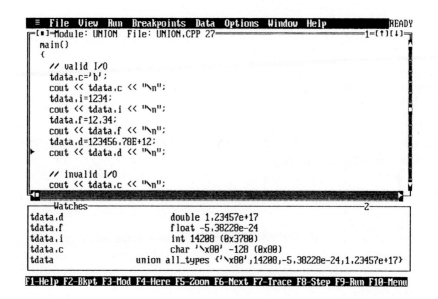

```
≡ File View Run Breakpoints Data Options Window Help       READY
┌[■]═Module: UNION  File: UNION.CPP 27══════════════════════1═[↑][↓]═┐
│ main()                                                              ▓
│ {                                                                   ▓
│   // valid I/O                                                      ▓
│   tdata.c='b';                                                      ▓
│   cout << tdata.c << "\n";                                         ▓
│   tdata.i=1234;                                                     ▓
│   cout << tdata.i << "\n";                                         ▓
│   tdata.f=12.34;                                                    ▓
│   cout << tdata.f << "\n";                                         ▓
│   tdata.d=123456.78E+12;                                           ▓
│ ► cout << tdata.d << "\n";                                         ▓
│                                                                    ▓
│   // invalid I/O                                                    ▓
│   cout << tdata.c << "\n";                                         ▓
│▓█▓▓▓▓▓▓▓▓▓▓▓▓▓▓▓▓▓▓▓▓▓▓▓▓▓▓▓▓▓▓▓▓▓▓▓▓▓▓▓▓▓▓▓▓▓▓▓▓▓▓▓▓▓▓▓▓▓▶
├─Watches────────────────────────────────────────────2─┐
│tdata.d                    double 1.23457e+17            │
│tdata.f                    float -5.38228e-24            │
│tdata.i                    int 14208 (0x3780)            │
│tdata.c                    char '\x80' -128 (0x80)       │
│tdata                      union all_types {'\x80',14208,-5.38228e-24,1.23457e+17} │
└───────────────────────────────────────────────────────┘
 F1-Help F2-Bkpt F3-Mod F4-Here F5-Zoom F6-Next F7-Trace F8-Step F9-Run F10-Menu
```

Figure 12-2.   The Watch window of the Debugger is used to examine various sized values being placed in the **union**

Typedef

You can associate new data types with existing data types by using **typedef**. For example, in a mathematically intensive program, you might want to use the data types **fixed**, **whole**, **real**, or **complex**. These new types can be associated with standard C types. The following example creates two new data types:

```
/*
 *      C program illustrates typedef.
 *      Creates two new types, "whole" and "real",
 *      which can be used in place of "int" and "float".
 *      Copyright (c) Chris H. Pappas and William H. Murray, 1990
 */

#include <stdio.h>

typedef int whole;
```

```
typedef float real;

main()
{
  whole i=567;
  real  myreal=3.14159;

  printf("The whole number is %d.\n",i);
  printf("The real number is %f.\n",myreal);
  return (0);
}
```

Employ **typedef** with care, since using too many newly created types can decrease program readability.

Enum

An **enum** data type allows you to create a data type with your choice in items. **enum** is useful when information can be best represented by a list of integer values such as the number of months in a year or the number of days in a week.

The following example contains a list of the number of months in a year. These are in an enumeration list with a tag name **months**. The variable associated with the list is *finish*. Enumerated lists will always start with 0 unless forced to a different integer value. In this case, January is the first month of the year.

```
/*
*       C program illustrates enum types.
*       Example calculates elapsed months in year, and
*       remaining months using enum type.
*       Copyright (c) Chris H. Pappas and William H. Murray, 1990
*/

#include <stdio.h>

enum months {
  January=1,
  February,
  March,
  April,
  May,
  June,
  July,
  August,
  September,
  October,
  November,
```

```
    December
} finish;

main()
{
  int current_month;
  int sum,diff;

  printf("Enter the current month (1 to 12).\n");
  scanf("%d",&current_month);
  getchar();

  finish=December;
  sum=(int)current_month;
  diff=(int)finish - (int)current_month;

  printf("\n%d month(s) down, %d to go this year.\n",sum,diff);
  return (0);
}
```

The enumerated list is actually a list of integer values, from 1 to 12 in this example. Since the names are equivalent to consecutive integer values, you can perform integer arithmetic with them. Thus, the integer variable *finish* is actually set to 12 when set equal to *December*.

This short program will perform some simple arithmetic and report the result to the screen:

```
Enter the current month (1 to 12).
3
3 month(s) down, 9 to go this year.
```

LINKED LIST

Linked lists form the gateway to advanced data structure techniques, and offer the advantage of dynamic allocation of structures. So far, every example program involving an array of structures has also included a definition for the total number of such structures. For example, MAX_CARS has been set to 25. This simply means that the program will accept data on 25 automobiles. If 60 or 70 cars are brought onto the car lot, the program itself will have to be altered to accommodate the increased number. This is because the structure allocation is *static*. You can immediately see the disadvantage of static allocation. One way around the problem is to set the number of structures higher than needed. If MAX_CARS is set to 5000, not even P and M Auto Sales could have an inventory that large. However, 5000 means that you are requiring the computer to set aside 100 times more memory than before. This is not a wise or efficient way to program. A better approach is to set aside memory *dynamically* as it is needed. With this approach, memory allocation for structures is requested as the inventory grows. Linked lists allow the use of dynamic memory allocation.

A *linked list* is a collection of structures. Each structure in the list contains an element or pointer that points to another structure in the list. This pointer serves as the link between structures. The concept is similar to an array but enables the list to grow dynamically. Figure 12-3 shows a simple linked list for the P and M Auto Sales program.

The linked list for this example includes a pointer to the next car in the inventory:

```
struct car {
  char make[15];
  char model[15];
  char title[20];
  char comment[80];
  int year;
  long int mileage;
  float retail;
  float wholesale;
  struct car *nextcar;
} P_and_M, *firstcar,*currentcar;
```

The pointer, *nextcar*, points to the address of the next related structure. Thus, the pointer in the first structure points to the address of the second structure, and so on. This is the concept of a linked list of structures.

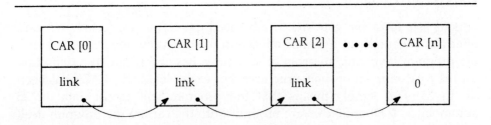

Figure 12-3.   The implementation of a traditional linked list

Components and Concerns in a Linked List

To make the linked list dynamic, you need a means for allocating memory as each new item is added to the list. In C, memory allocation is accomplished with the **malloc** function; in C++, **new** is used. In the complete program, in the section "A Simple Linked List," memory is allocated to the first structure with the code:

```
firstcar=(struct car *) new (struct car);
```

You can achieve subsequent memory allocation for each additional structure by placing a similar piece of code in a *while* loop:

```
while (datain(&P_and_M)==0) {
currentcar->nextcar=
  (struct car *) new (struct car);
if (currentcar->nextcar==NULL) exit(1);
currentcar=currentcar->nextcar;
*currentcar=P_and_M;
}
```

Thus, memory is allocated as needed. Note that the value returned by **new** was cast to an appropriate pointer type, using the structure's tag name **car**. The last structure in the list will have its pointer location set to **NULL**. Using **NULL** marks the end of a linked list. Can you see how that's done in the program code?

A Simple Linked List

The following program converts the P and M Auto Sales example to a linked list. Study the listing and see which items seem similar and which items have changed.

```
//
//     C++ program demonstrates a simple linked list.
//     P and M used car inventory example is used.
//     Copyright (c) Chris H. Pappas and William H. Murray, 1990
//

#include <stdlib.h>
#include <iostream.h>
```

```
struct car {
  char make[15];
  char model[15];
  char title[20];
  char comment[80];
  int year;
  long int mileage;
  float retail;
  float wholesale;
  struct car *nextcar;
} P_and_M, *firstcar,*currentcar;

void carlocation(struct car *node);
void dataout(struct car *carptr);
int datain(struct car *P_and_Mptr);

main()
{
  firstcar=(struct car *) new (struct car);
  if (firstcar==NULL) exit(1);
  if (datain(&P_and_M) != 0) exit(1);
  *firstcar=P_and_M;
  currentcar=firstcar;

  while (datain(&P_and_M)==0) {
  currentcar->nextcar=
    (struct car *) new (struct car);
  if (currentcar->nextcar==NULL) exit(1);
  currentcar=currentcar->nextcar;
  *currentcar=P_and_M;
  }
  currentcar->nextcar=NULL;
  carlocation(firstcar);
  return (0);
}

void carlocation(struct car *node)
{
  do {
    dataout(node);
  } while ((node=node->nextcar) != NULL);
}

void dataout(struct car *carptr)
{
  cout.setf(ios::fixed);   //set format for dollars and cents
  cout.precision(2);
  cout << "\n\n\n";
  cout << "A " << carptr->year << " " << carptr->make
       << " " << carptr->model << " cream-puff with "
       << carptr->mileage << " low miles." << endl;
  cout << carptr->comment << "." << endl;
  cout << "Ask your P and M salesperson for bargain ";
  cout << "#" << carptr->title << ", " << "ONLY! $"
       << carptr->retail << endl;
}
```

```
int datain(struct car *P_and_Mptr)
{
  char newline;

  cout << "\n(Enter new car information - a Q quits)\n\n";
  cout << "Enter the make of the car." << endl;
  cin >> P_and_Mptr->make;
  if (*(P_and_Mptr->make) == 'Q') return(1);
  cout << "Enter the model of the car." << endl;
  cin >> P_and_Mptr->model;
  cout << "Enter the title number for the car." << endl;
  cin >> P_and_Mptr->title;
  cout << "Enter the model year for the car." << endl;
  cin >> P_and_Mptr->year;
  cout << "Enter the current mileage for the car." << endl;
  cin >> P_and_Mptr->mileage;
  cout << "Enter the retail price of the car." << endl;
  cin >> P_and_Mptr->retail;
  cout << "Enter the wholesale price of the car." << endl;
  cin >> P_and_Mptr->wholesale;
  cout << "Enter a one line comment about the car." << endl;
  cin.get(newline);     // process carriage return
  cin.get(P_and_Mptr->comment,80,'.');
  cin.get(newline);     // process carriage return
  return(0);
}
```

First notice the three function prototypes:

```
void carlocation(struct car *node);
void dataout(struct car *carptr);
int datain(struct car *P_and_Mptr);
```

Note that all three functions are passed pointers. The first function, **carlocation**, checks the linked list for entries before calling the **dataout** function. The **dataout** function formats the output to each linked list structure, and is basically the same as in previous examples. For this program, input is done in a function called **datain**. This function returns an integer, 0 or 1. A 0 indicates successful data input, while a 1 indicates the user's wish to terminate input. The value returned by **datain** tells the code in the **main** function whether to allocate more memory and whether to set the *nextcar* pointer to a new linked item or **NULL**. If the user enters a **Q** when the make of the car is requested, the program will end data entry. With just those exceptions, the **datain** function is the same as in earlier examples.

Can you explain where the *nextcar* pointer will be pointing with each trip around the *while* loop? If you can, you have captured the essence of the linked list.

Linked lists in C++ are best implemented with object-oriented programming. The advantages of OOP will be shown in Chapter 21.

PUTTING YOUR KNOWLEDGE TO WORK

1. Sketch the composition of a structure, union, bit field, and enumeration type. Explain the syntax and members of each.

2. How can a structure be made local to a function, if the structure declaration is outside of all functions?

3. How are structure members typically passed to functions?

4. Why are pointers preferred when passing structure information to a function?

5. Design a structure that will hold a salesperson's information on a client. It should contain name, address, telephone, age, sex, most recent purchase, item purchased, and a date when the person should be contacted again.

6. Write a program, using an array of structures and the structure created in the last question, that will allow a salesperson to track 25 clients. Provide appropriate input and output routines in separate functions.

7. Name possible programming advantages for **union, typedef,** and **enum** types.

8. How is the concept of a linked list different from an array of structures?

9. Why is an array of structures considered *static?* Why are linked lists considered dynamic?

10. Revamp the program you created for question 6, but write it with a linked list instead.

13

CLASSES

In this chapter you will learn

- The components of a C++ class

- How to create and describe simple classes

- The concept of public, private, and protected class parts

- How to nest classes

- How to use constructors and destructors

- About overloading class member functions

- How to use friend functions

- Where to use the *this* pointer

- The importance of operator overloading

- How to define and use derived classes

- What virtual member functions are

The various data types, discussed in earlier chapters, give C and C++ the flexibility needed by programmers today. The *class* is a new C++ user-defined data type that gives you the advantages of a structure and the ability to limit access to specific data to functions that are also members of the class. As such, classes are one of C++'s greatest contributions to programming. The advanced features of the class include the ability to initialize and protect sensitive functions and data.

Think about this progression of power: One-dimensional arrays or vectors permit a collection of like data types to be held together. Next, structures permit related items of different data types to be combined in a group. Finally, C++ classes permit you to implement a data type and associate operators and member functions with it. Thus, you have the storage concept associated with a structure along with the member functions to operate on the storage variables. The *class* object forms the foundation for object-oriented programming in C and is discussed in more detail in Chapter 21.

FUNDAMENTAL CLASS CONCEPTS

In the following sections, you will learn how to create and manipulate the fundamental components of a C++ class. A class can have data and function members. Moreover, a class can include public, private, and protected parts. This concept allows parts, typically class variables, to be hidden from all functions except those that are members of the class.

The Syntax and Rules for Classes

The definition of a class begins with the keyword *class*. The class name or tag type immediately follows the keyword. The framework of the class is very similar to other type definitions that you have seen.

```
class type {
  type var1
  type var2
     .
     .
     .
public:
```

```
member function1
member function2
member function3
      .
      .
      .
} name associated with class type;
```

Member variables immediately follow the class declaration. These variables are by default *private* to the class and can only be accessed by the member functions that follow. Member functions usually follow a *public* declaration that allows access from functions external to the class. All class member functions have access to both public and private parts of a class.

What follows is a class definition that will be used in the second programming example in this chapter:

```
class angle {
  double value;

public:
  void set_value(double);
  double get_sine(void);
  double get_cosine(void);
  double get_tangent(void);
} deg;
```

This class has a type or tag name **angle**. A private variable, *value,* will share degree values among the various member functions. Four functions make up the function members of the class: **set_value**, **get_sine**, **get_cosine**, and **get_tangent**. The name that is associated with this class type is *deg.* Unlike this example, the association of a variable name with the class name or tag is most frequently made in the **main( )** function.

Structures as a Class

The last chapter developed numerous programs with the *struct* type, using the same format for both C and C++ structures. However, the keyword *struct* in C++ is more powerful than the equivalent keyword in C. In many respects, the structure in C++ is an elementary form of class. Examine the following code:

```
//
//      C++ program illustrates the simplest form of a class,
//      built on the C++ keyword "struct".  This program uses a
//      structure class to obtain the sine, cosine and tangent
//      of an angle.
//      Copyright (c) Chris H. Pappas and William H. Murray, 1990
//

#include <iostream.h>
#include <math.h>

const double ANG_TO_RAD=0.0174532925;

struct angle {
  double value;

  void set_value(double);
  double get_sine(void);
  double get_cosine(void);
  double get_tangent(void);
} deg;

void angle::set_value(double a)
{
  value=a;
}

double angle::get_sine(void)
{
  double temp;

  temp=sin(ANG_TO_RAD*value);
  return (temp);
}

double angle::get_cosine(void)
{
  double temp;

  temp=cos(ANG_TO_RAD*value);
  return (temp);
}

double angle::get_tangent(void)
{
  double temp;

  temp=tan(ANG_TO_RAD*value);
  return (temp);
}

main()
{
  // set angle to 60.0 degrees
  deg.set_value(60.0);
```

```
cout << "The sine of the angle is: "
    << deg.get_sine() << "\n";
cout << "The cosine of the angle is: "
    << deg.get_cosine() << "\n";
cout << "The tangent of the angle is: "
    << deg.get_tangent() << "\n";
return (0);
}
```

Notice that the structure definition contains member functions. These member functions can act upon the data contained in the class itself.

```
struct angle {
  double value;

  void set_value(double);
  double get_sine(void);
  double get_cosine(void);
  double get_tangent(void);
} deg;
```

Immediately under the *struct* definition, the various member functions are defined. The member functions are associated with the class via the scoping operator (::) and are usually defined immediately after the class or structure definition to which they belong. Other than that, they look like normal functions. The variable name associated with the *struct* (or *class*) is *deg*.

Examine the first part of the **main** function:

```
// set angle to 60 degrees
deg.set_value(60);
```

Here, the value 60.0 is being passed as an argument to the **set_value** function. Observe the syntax for this operation; **set_value** itself is very simple.

```
void angle::set_value(double a)
{
  value=a;
}
```

The function accepts the argument and assigns the value to the class variable *value*. This is one way of initializing class variables. From this point on in the class, each of the three remaining functions can access *value*. Their job is to calculate the sine, cosine, and tangent of the given angle. The respective values are printed to the screen from the **main** function with statements similar to this:

```
cout << "The sine of the angle is: "
    << deg.get_sine() << "\n";
```

You access the class member functions with the dot notation also used for structures. You can also assign pointer variables to a class, in which case you use the arrow operator. (You will see an example of this shortly.)

Structures in C++ can also contain a specification of public, private, or protected. Structure members are public by default. In this example, they are global in visibility with respect to the program. A private specification limits the visibility of the specified items to the members of the structure. You will learn more about the privacy specification in the next section.

A Simple Class

In a C++ class, the visibility of class members is private by default; that is, variables and functions are accessible only to members of the class. If the functions are to be visible beyond the class, you must specify this explicitly.

The conversion of the last example's structure to a true C++ class is straightforward. First, the *struct* keyword is replaced by the *class* keyword. Second, the members that are to have public visibility are separated from the private members of the class with the public declaration. Examine the complete program:

```
//
//      C++ program illustrates a simple but true class and
//      introduces the concept of private and public.
//      This program uses a class to obtain the sine,
//      cosine and tangent of an angle.
//      Copyright (c) Chris H. Pappas and William H. Murray, 1990
//

#include <iostream.h>
#include <math.h>

const double ANG_TO_RAD=0.0174532925;

class angle {
  double value;

public:
```

```
    void set_value(double);
    double get_sine(void);
    double get_cosine(void);
    double get_tangent(void);
} deg;

void angle::set_value(double a)
{
    value=a;
}

double angle::get_sine(void)
{
    double temp;

    temp=sin(ANG_TO_RAD*value);
    return (temp);
}

double angle::get_cosine(void)
{
    double temp;

    temp=cos(ANG_TO_RAD*value);
    return (temp);
}

double angle::get_tangent(void)
{
    double temp;

    temp=tan(ANG_TO_RAD*value);
    return (temp);
}

main()
{
    // set angle to 60.0 degrees
    deg.set_value(60.0);

    cout << "The sine of the angle is: "
        << deg.get_sine() << "\n";
    cout << "The cosine of the angle is: "
        << deg.get_cosine() << "\n";
    cout << "The tangent of the angle is: "
        << deg.get_tangent() << "\n";
    return (0);
}
```

In this simple example, the body of the program remains the same. The structure definition has been converted to a true class definition with private and public parts.

```
class angle {
    double value;
```

```
public:
  void set_value(double);
  double get_sine(void);
  double get_cosine(void);
  double get_tangent(void);
} deg;
```

The *value* variable is private to the class and is only accessible by the members of the class. The member functions have been declared public and are accessible from outside of the class. However, each class member, whether public or private, has access to all other class members, public or private.

Again, notice that class member functions are usually defined immediately after the class has been defined and before the **main( )** function. Non-member class functions are still defined after the function **main( )** and are prototyped in the normal fashion.

Nesting Structures and Classes

Recall from the previous chapter that you can nest structures in both C and C++. You can also nest C++ classes; however, be sure not to make the resulting declaration more confusing than necessary. The following example illustrates the concept of nesting:

```
//
//      C++ program illustrates the use of nesting classes.
//      This program calculates the wages for the employee named.
//      Copyright (c) Chris H. Pappas and William H. Murray, 1990
//

#include <iostream.h>

char newline;

class emp_class {
  struct emp_name {
    char first[20];
    char middle[20];
    char last[20];
  } name;
  struct emp_wage {
    double hours;
    double reg_sal;
    double ot_sal;
  } wage;
```

```
public:
  void info_in(void);
  void info_out(void);
};

void emp_class::info_in(void)
{
  cout << "Enter first name: ";
  cin >> name.first;
  cin.get(newline);      // flush carriage return
  cout << "Enter middle name or initial: ";
  cin >> name.middle;
  cin.get(newline);
  cout << "Enter last name:   ";
  cin >> name.last;
  cin.get(newline);

  cout << "Enter hours worked:   ";
  cin >> wage.hours;
  cout << "Enter hourly wage:    ";
  cin >> wage.reg_sal;
  cout << "Enter overtime wage: ";
  cin >> wage.ot_sal;
  cout << "\n\n";
}

void emp_class::info_out(void)
{
  cout.setf(ios::fixed);
  cout.precision(2);
  cout << name.first << " " << name.middle
       << " " << name.last << "\n";
  if (wage.hours <= 40)
    cout << "Regular Pay:   $"
         << wage.hours * wage.reg_sal << endl;
    else {
      cout << "Regular Pay:   $"
           << 40 * wage.reg_sal << endl;
      cout << "Overtime Pay: $"
           << (wage.hours-40) * wage.ot_sal << endl;
    }

}

main()
{
  emp_class widget;      // associate widget with class

  widget.info_in();
  widget.info_out();
  return (0);
}
```

In this example, two structures (simple classes) are nested within a class definition. The definition of a nested class can be quite straightforward.

```
class emp_class {
  struct emp_name {
    char first[20];
    char middle[20];
    char last[20];
  } name;
  struct emp_wage {
    double hours;
    double reg_sal;
    double ot_sal;
  } wage;

public:
  void info_in(void);
  void info_out(void);
};
```

The **emp _ class** class includes two nested class structs; **emp _ name** and **emp _ wage**. The nested classes, while part of the private section of the class, are actually available outside of the class. In other words, the visibility of the nested classes is the same as if they were defined outside of the **emp _ class** class. The individual member variables, for this example, are accessed through the public member functions: **info _ in** and **info _ out**.

These two member functions do not accept arguments and are of type **void**. **info _ in** prompts the user for data that will be passed to the nested structures. The information collected here includes the person's full name, the total hours worked during the week, the regular pay rate, and the overtime pay rate. When **info _ out** is called, the person's name, regular pay, and overtime pay will be printed to the screen.

```
Enter first name: John
Enter middle name or initial: James
Enter last name: Jones
Enter hours worked: 45
Enter hourly wage: 5.62
Enter overtime wage: 8.23

John James Jones
Regular Pay:  $224.80
Overtime Pay: $41.15
```

Examine the **main** function. The contents of this function are fairly short since most of the work is being done by the member functions of the class.

```
emp_class widget;    // associate widget with class
```

```
widget.info_in();
widget.info_out();
```

The variable *widget,* representing the Widget Manufacturing Company, is associated with **emp_class**. To request a member function, the dot operator is used. Next, *widget.info_in* is called to collect the employee information and then *widget.info_out* is called to calculate and print the payroll results.

Constructors and Destructors

A *constructor* is a class member function whose chief goal is to initialize class variables or allocate memory storage. The constructor has the same name as the class in which it is defined. Constructors can accept arguments and can be overloaded. The constructor is automatically executed when an object of the *class* type is created. Free store objects are allocated with the **new** operator and serve to allocate memory for the objects created. Constructors are generated by C++ if they are not explicitly defined.

A *destructor* is a class member function that is usually used to return memory allocated from free store memory. The destructor has the same name as the class in which it is defined, preceded by the tilde character ~. Destructors are typically the opposite of their constructor counterparts. The destructor is called automatically when a program passes beyond the scope of a class object or when the **delete** operator is applied to a class pointer. Unlike a constructor, a destructor cannot accept an argument and cannot be overloaded. Destructors can also be generated by C++ if not explicitly defined.

Creating a Simple Constructor and Destructor

The following program uses a constructor and destructor in the simplest form:

```
//
//      C++ program illustrates the use of constructors and
//      destructors in a simple program.
//      This program converts cents into appropriate coinage
//      (quarters, dimes, nickels and pennies).
//      Copyright (c) Chris H. Pappas and William H. Murray, 1990
//

#include <iostream.h>
```

```
const int QUARTER=25;
const int DIME=10;
const int NICKEL=5;

class coinage {                        // class name
  int i;

public:
  coinage() {cout << "Start!\n";}  // constructor
  ~coinage() {cout << "\nDone!";}  // destructor
  void get_pennies(int);
  int conv_to_quarters();
  int conv_to_dimes(int);
  int conv_to_nickels(int);
};

void coinage::get_pennies(int pen)
{
  i=pen;
  cout << i << " cents, converts to:\n";
}

int coinage::conv_to_quarters()
{
  cout << i/QUARTER << " quarter(s), ";
  return(i%QUARTER);
}

int coinage::conv_to_dimes(int d)
{
  cout << d/DIME << " dime(s), ";
  return(d%DIME);
}

int coinage::conv_to_nickels(int n)
{
  cout << n/NICKEL << " nickel(s), and ";
  return(n%NICKEL);
}

main()
{
  int c,d,n,p;

  cout << "Enter your cash in cents: ";
  cin >> c;

  // associate cash_in_cents with coinage class.
  coinage cash_in_cents;

  cash_in_cents.get_pennies(c);
  d=cash_in_cents.conv_to_quarters();
  n=cash_in_cents.conv_to_dimes(d);
  p=cash_in_cents.conv_to_nickels(n);
  cout << p << " penny(ies).";
```

```
   return (0);
}
```

This program uses four member functions. The first function passes the number of pennies to the private class variable i. The remaining three functions convert a quantity of pennies to the equivalent cash in quarters, dimes, and nickels. Examine the class and observe the placement of the constructor and destructor. The constructor and destructor function descriptions contain a simple message that will be displayed to prove that they were used automatically by the program.

```
class coinage {                    // class name
  int i;

public:
  coinage() {cout << "Start!\n";}  // constructor
  ~coinage() {cout << "\nDone!";}  // destructor
  void get_pennies(int);
  int conv_to_quarters();
  int conv_to_dimes(int);
  int conv_to_nickels(int);
};
```

The output from this program takes the form:

```
Enter your cash in cents: 69
Start!
69 cents, converts to:
2 quarter(s), 1 dime(s), 1 nickel(s), and 4 penny(ies).
Done!
```

When the function definition is included with member functions, it is said to be implicitly defined. Otherwise, member functions can be defined in the usual manner or declared inline explicitly.

Using a Constructor to Initialize a Member Variable

You can use constructors to initialize private class variables. In this case, the original class was modified slightly to eliminate the need for user input. However, with or without user input, the variable i will be initialized to 511 pennies.

```
class coinage {                      // class name
  int i;

public:
  coinage() {i=511;}                 // constructor
  ~coinage() {cout << "\nDone!";}    // destructor
  int conv_to_quarters();
  int conv_to_dimes(int);
  int conv_to_nickels(int);
};
```

Creating and Deleting Free Store Memory

The following example illustrates one of the most frequent uses for a constructor. A constructor is used to allocate memory for the *str* pointer with the **new** operator. The destructor is used to release the allocated memory back to the system when the object is destroyed, with the **delete** operator.

```
class string_data {
  char *str;
  int   max_len;

public:
  string_data(char *) {str=new char[max_len];}
  ~string_data() {delete str;}
  void get_info(char *);
  void send_info(char *);
};
```

The memory allocated by **new** to the pointer *str* can only be deallocated with a subsequent call to **delete**. For this reason, you will usually see memory allocated to pointers in constructors and deallocated in destructors. This also ensures that the allocated memory will be returned to the system if the variable assigned to the class passes out of its scope.

The memory used by ordinary data types, such as **integer** and **float**, is automatically restored to the system.

Overloading Class Member Functions

Class member functions, like ordinary functions, can be overloaded. The first example in this section illustrates the overloading of a class function named **ab**. This overloaded function will return the absolute value of an integer or double with the use of the math functions **abs**, which accepts and returns integer values, and **fabs**, which accepts and returns double values. With an overloaded function, the argument types determine which member function will actually be used.

```
//
//      C++ program illustrates overloading member functions
//      with a very simple class definition
//      Copyright (c) Chris H. Pappas and William H. Murray, 1990
//

#include <iostream.h>
#include <math.h>
#include <stdlib.h>

class absolute {
public:
   int ab(int);
   double ab(double);
};

int absolute::ab(int val1)
{
   int temp;

   temp=abs(val1);
   return (temp);
}

double absolute::ab(double val2)
{
   double temp;

   temp=fabs(val2);
   return (temp);
}

main()
{
   absolute number;

   cout << "the absolute value is "
        << number.ab(-123) << endl;
   cout << "the absolute value is "
        << number.ab(-123.45678) << endl;
   return (0);
}
```

Notice that the dot operator is used in conjunction with the member function name to pass a negative integer and negative double value. The value returned by each function is printed to the screen.

```
the absolute value is 123
the absolute value is 123.45678
```

Examine Figures 13-1 to 13-4 and notice the functions chosen as the various values are passed to the class.

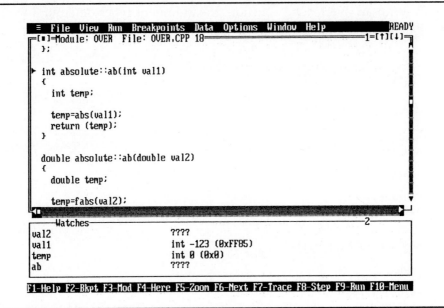

Figure 13-1.   Here, *absolute* can accept an **integer** or **double**. Note the position of the trace marker to the left of **int absolute**

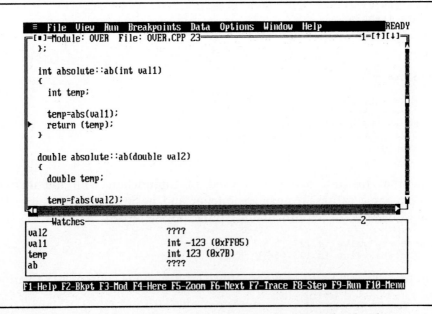

Figure 13-2.   The value of *val1* and *temp* after the absolute value has been determined

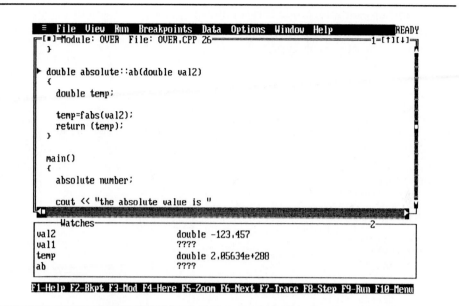

Figure 13-3.   The trace marker has been moved to a new position in this
Debugger screen. The absolute value of *val2* has not been
determined, so *temp* does not contain valid data

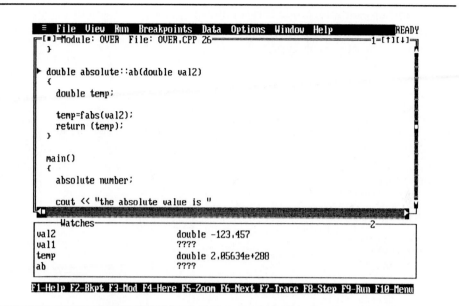

Figure 13-4.   The value of *val2* and *temp* after the absolute value has been
determined

In another example, angle information is passed to member functions in one of two formats—a double or a string. With member function overloading, you can process both types.

```
//
//      C++ program illustrates overloading member functions.
//      Allows angle to be entered in decimal or deg min sec
//      formats.
//      Copyright (c) Chris H. Pappas and William H. Murray, 1990
//

#include <iostream.h>
#include <math.h>
#include <string.h>

const double ANG_TO_RAD=0.0174532925;

class trig_angle {
  double angle;
  double ang_sine;

public:
  void mysine(double);
  void mysine(char *);
};

void trig_angle::mysine(double degrees)
{
  angle=degrees;
  ang_sine=sin(angle * ANG_TO_RAD);
  cout << "For an angle of " << angle << "\n";
  cout << "The sine is " << ang_sine << "\n";
}

void trig_angle::mysine(char *dat)
{
  char *deg,*min,*sec;

  deg=strtok(dat,"° ");
  min=strtok(0,"' ");
  sec=strtok(0,"\"");
  angle=atof(deg)+((atof(min))/60.0)+((atof(sec))/360.0);
  ang_sine=sin(angle * ANG_TO_RAD);
  cout << "For an angle of " << angle << "\n";
  cout << "The sine is " << ang_sine << "\n\n";
}

main()
{
  trig_angle value;

  value.mysine(45.0);
  value.mysine("45° 30' 15\"");   //make ° with alt-248
```

```
   value.mysine(60.45);
   value.mysine("30° 10' 00\"");
   return (0);
}
```

The **strtok** function prototyped in *string.h* is used three times in this program.

Here is the syntax for **strtok**:

```
char *strtok(str1, str2);    //Finds token in str1
char *str1;                  //String that has token(s)
const char *str2;            //String with delimiter chars
```

The **strtok** function will scan *str1*, looking for a series of character tokens. In this case, the tokens represent the angle reading in degrees, minutes, and seconds. The length of the tokens can vary. The string *str2* contains a set of delimiters, such as spaces, commas, or other special characters. The tokens in *str1* are separated by the delimiters in *str2*. Thus, all of the tokens in *str1* can be retrieved with a series of calls to the function. Function calls to **strtok** alter *str1* by inserting a null character after each token retrieved. With the first call to the function, the function returns a pointer to the first token. Subsequent calls return a pointer to the next token, and so on. When no more tokens exist, a null pointer is returned.

Since angle readings can include degrees, minutes, and seconds, **strtok** uses a degree symbol ° to find the first token. Next, a minute symbol ' will pull out the token containing the number of minutes. Finally, a \" is used for seconds (recall that the double quote, used by itself, is for terminating strings). Examine Figures 13-5 to 13-7, and see how the **strtok** function separates the string tokens.

You can see from the previous two examples that class member overloading gives you flexibility when dealing with different data formats.

Friend Functions

One of the advantages of classes is their ability to hide data. However, a class of functions called *friend functions* allows the sharing of private class information with nonmember functions. Friend functions, which are not

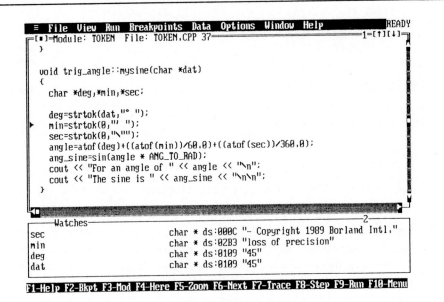

Figure 13-5.   The Debugger's Watch window will help show how the function **strtok** separates the angle information

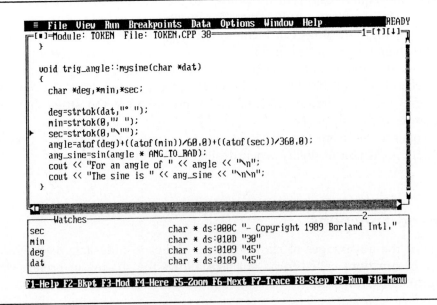

Figure 13-6.   The Watch window shows readings for *min, deg,* and *dat*

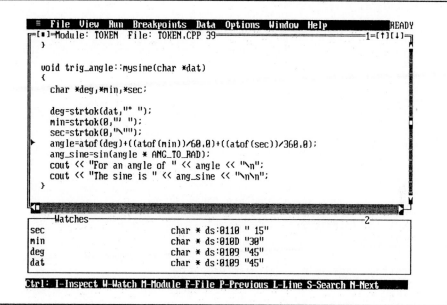

Figure 13-7. The Watch window now contains four valid values

defined in the class itself, can share the same class resources as member functions while remaining external to the class definition.

```
//
//      C++ program illustrates friend functions.
//      Program will collect a string of date and time
//      information from system.  Time information will
//      be processed and converted into seconds.
//      Copyright (c) Chris H. Pappas and William H. Murray, 1990
//

#include <iostream.h>
#include <string.h>   // for strtok function prototype
#include <stdlib.h>   // for atol & ltoa function prototype
#include <time.h>     // for time_t & tm structure

class main_time {
  long seconds;
  friend char * current_time(main_time);
public:
  main_time(char *);
};
```

```
main_time::main_time(char *tm)
{
    char *hrs,*mins,*secs;

    // info returned in string in format:
    // (day month date hours:minutes:seconds year)
    // move over three tokens, ie.
    // skip day, month and date!
    hrs=strtok(tm," ");
    hrs=strtok(0," ");
    hrs=strtok(0," ");

    // now begin to collect time info from string
    hrs=strtok(0,":");
    mins=strtok(0,":");
    secs=strtok(0," ");

    // convert to longs and accumulate total secs.
    seconds=atol(hrs)*3600;
    seconds+=atol(mins)*60;
    seconds+=atol(secs);
}

char * current_time(main_time);   // prototype

main()
{
    // get string of time & date information
    struct tm *ptr;
    time_t ltime;
    ltime=time(NULL);
    ptr=localtime(&ltime);

    main_time tz(asctime(ptr));

    cout << "Time string information: " << asctime(ptr)
         << "\n";
    cout << "Time in seconds: " << current_time(tz)
         << "\n";
    return (0);
}

char * current_time(main_time tz)
{
    char *ctbuf;
    ctbuf=new char[30];
    long int total_seconds;

    total_seconds=tz.seconds;
    ltoa(total_seconds,ctbuf,10);
        return (ctbuf);
}
```

In the class definition, notice the use of the keyword *friend* along with a description of the **current_time** function itself. Examine the listing and note that this function definition occurs after the **main( )** function.

In addition to illustrating the use of **friend** functions, this program has a number of other interesting features. In the function **main( )**, the system's time is retrieved with the use of *time_t* and its associated structure *tm*. In this program, *ltime* is the name of the variable associated with *time_t*. Local time is initialized and retrieved into the pointer, *ptr*, with the next two lines of code. By using *asctime(ptr)*, the pointer will point to an ASCII string of date and time information.

```
struct tm *ptr;
time_t ltime;
ltime=time(NULL);
ptr=localtime(&ltime);

main_time tz(asctime(ptr));
```

The date and time string is formatted in this manner:

day month date hours:minutes:seconds year \n \0

For example:

```
Wed Jan 24 15:26:35 1990
```

Chapter 15 contains a more detailed discussion of built-in functions, including those prototyped in *time.h*. For now, you need to follow these steps to retrieve the string information.

The string information is sent to the class by associating *tz* with the class **main_time**.

```
main_time tz(asctime(ptr));
```

The constructor **main_time(char *)** executes the code necessary to convert the string information to integer values. This is achieved with the **strtok** function.

Since we have a strange date/time format, **strtok** uses a space as the delimiter to skip over the day, month, and date. At this point, *hrs* collects unwanted tokens. The next delimiter is a colon, which will aid in collecting both hour and minute tokens from the string. Finally, the number of seconds can be found by reading the string until another space is encountered. The string information is then converted to a long and converted to

```
  void l_disp();
};
```

This derived class contains two functions: **loan_customer** and **l_disp**. The first function, **loan_customer**, uses the base class to obtain name, address, city, state, and zip code, and attaches the loan type and amount.

```
void loan::loan_customer()
{
  info_in();
  cout << "Enter Loan Type: ";
  cin.get(loan_type,19,'\n');
  cin.get(newline);
  cout << "Enter Loan Balance: ";
  cin >> l_bal;
  cin.get(newline);        //flush carriage return
}
```

The call to the **info_in** function is a call to a function that is part of the base class. The remainder of the preceding function obtains the loan type and amount.

The loan information is displayed in a similar manner. The base class function, **info_out**, prints the information gathered by the base class, while **l_disp** attaches the information from the derived class to the display. The process is repeated for the savings account customer. Thus, one base class serves as the data gathering base for two derived classes, each obtaining its own specific information.

The output from the program can take the form:

```
--Loan Customers--
Name: Iam Broke
Street: 401 Poor House Lane
City: Philadelphia
State: Pennsylvania
Zip: 19804
Loan Type: Auto Loan
Loan Balance: $ 9878.56

--Savings Customers--
Name: Igot Money
Street: 678 Snob Hill Parkway
City: Seattle
State: Washington
Zip: 23987
Savings Type: Money Market Saving
Savings Balance: $ 5643.11
```

PUTTING YOUR KNOWLEDGE TO WORK

1. How does the C++ class differ from the C++ structure? How are they similar?

2. Describe the terms public, private, and protected as they relate to classes.

3. Examine the section on nested classes and derived classes. In some respects, nested classes seem similar to derived classes. Why are they actually very different?

4. Describe the purpose of constructors and destructors. Why weren't they needed for structures in the previous chapter?

5. Describe a **friend** function. What is the danger in their use?

6. Why is operator overloading important and useful? Pick three operators from Table 13-1 and describe why, where, and how they could be overloaded.

7. Describe the concept of a derived class. Revisit the P and M Auto Sales Company of the previous chapter and describe how a derived class might be used. What components would you place in the base class?

8. Examine the material on base and derived classes in your *Turbo C++ Programmer's Guide*. Describe where the various access attributes—public, private, and protected—can and cannot be used with regard to derived classes.

9. Alter the programming example that converted a quantity of pennies to an equivalent amount of pocket change. Change it to include two additional coins—the half-dollar and the dollar.

10. Modify the last program in this chapter so that it will allow you to create a database of at least 20 savings and loan customers.

14

POWER PROGRAMMING – TAPPING IMPORTANT C AND C++ LIBRARIES

In this chapter you will learn

- How library functions are described in the various C and C++ header files

- Which header files contain the most often used library functions

- How to use and access the built-in library functions

- How to use the powerful character-manipulation routines

- How you can increase your programming skills with string functions

- How to perform data conversions with functions from the standard C library

- How to tap the power of arithmetic and trigonometric math functions and the new C++ complex number routines

- How to intercept date and time information from the system

C AND C++ LIBRARIES

In C and C++ programming, you rely heavily on functions built into compiler libraries. By using built-in functions, you are saved from having to "reinvent the wheel" each time you need a special routine. C and C++ offer extensive support for character, string, and math work. Most of these standard library functions are portable from one computer to another and from one operating system to another. Still, other functions are system or compiler dependent. Many of these special functions will be explained in the next chapter. Knowing where to locate the routines you need and how to call them properly will help you become a better programmer.

Many of the C and C++ functions have already been used heavily in earlier chapters. These include, for example, functions in *stdio.h* and *iostream.h*. Indeed, it is hard to do serious programming without these functions. However, this chapter will not review these routines. Instead, it focuses on the powerful built-in functions for character, string, and math work.

C AND C++ HEADER FILES

If you do a directory listing of your Turbo C++ *include* subdirectory, the following frequently used header files should be present. There will be others, but these are the header files that you will use most often. Since these files are in ASCII format, you should print a copy of their contents for a reference. These header files contain macros or function prototypes for the C library functions that you may wish to use in your programs.

bios.h	BIOS interrupts
complex.h *	Complex numbers for C++
conio.h	Console and port I/O
ctype.h *	Character functions
dos.h	DOS interrupts
graphics.h	Borland graphics routines
io.h	File handling and low-level I/O
iostream.h	Stream routines for C++
math.h *	Math functions
stdio.h	Stream routines for C

stdlib.h*	Standard library routines
string.h*	String functions
time.h*	Date and time utilities

Some header files are short while others are quite long. All contain function prototypes and many contain built-in macros.

This chapter will examine popular functions contained in the header files (marked with asterisks in the previous list). These files include *stdlib.h, complex.h, ctype.h, math.h, string.h,* and *time.h.* Additional system-dependent functions and functions unique to Turbo C++, contained in *bios.h, dos.h,* and *graphics.h,* will be discussed in the next chapter. Note that other functions, contained in *stdio.h, iostream.h,* and so on, have been covered throughout the book.

STANDARD LIBRARY FUNCTIONS

You can use the standard library functions (*stdlib.h*), listed next, for data conversion, memory allocation, and other miscellaneous operations:

_exit	Terminates program
_lrotl	Rotates an unsigned long to the left
_lrotr	Rotates an unsigned long to the right
_rotl	Rotates an unsigned integer to the left
_rotr	Rotates an unsigned integer to the right
abort	Aborts program — terminate abnormally
abs	Derives absolute value of an integer
atexit	Registers termination function
atof	Converts a string to a float
atoi	Converts a string to an integer
atol	Converts a string to a long
bsearch	Performs binary search of an array
calloc	Allocates main memory
div	Divides integers
ecvt	Converts a float to a string
exit	Terminates program
fcvt	Converts a float to a string

free	Frees memory
gcvt	Converts a float to a string
getenv	Gets a string from the environment
itoa	Converts an integer to a string
labs	Derives absolute value of a long
ldiv	Divides two long integers
lfind	Performs a linear search
lsearch	Performs a linear search
ltoa	Converts a long to a string
malloc	Allocates memory
putenv	Puts a string in the environment
qsort	Performs a quick sort
rand	Generates random numbers
realloc	Reallocates main memory
srand	Initializes random number generator
strtod	Converts a string to a double
strtol	Converts a string to a long
strtoul	Converts a string to an unsigned long
swab	Swaps bytes from *s1* to *s2*
system	Invokes DOS command.com file
ultoa	Converts an unsigned long to a string

Notice that almost half of the functions detailed in this header file perform data conversion from one format to another. Since the memory operations have already been used in several chapters, their operations will not be repeated in the following sections.

Data Conversions

The first important group of functions described in *stdlib.h* is the data converting functions. The principal job of these functions is to convert data from one format to another. For example, the **atof** function converts string information to a float.

The syntax of each function is shown in the following prototypes:

```
double atof(const char *s)
int atoi(const char *s)
long atol(const char *s)
char *ecvt(double value,int n,int *dec,int *sign)
```

```
char *fcvt(double value,int n,int *dec,int *sign)
char *gcvt(double value,int n,char *buf)
char *itoa(int value,char *s,int radix)
char *ltoa(long value,char *s,int radix)
double strtod(const char *s,char **endptr)
long strtol(const char *s,char **endptr,int radix)
unsigned long strtoul(const char *s,char **endptr,int radix)
char *ultoa(unsigned long value,char *s,int radix)
```

In these functions, *s points to a string, *value* is the number to be converted, *n* represents the number of digits in the string, and *dec* locates the decimal point relative to the start of the string. *sign* represents the sign of the number, *buf* is a character buffer, *radix* represents the number base for the converted value, and *endptr* is usually null. If not, the function sets it to the character that stops the scan.

Several of these functions will be illustrated in the following programs.

Converting a Float to a String

The **fcvt** function converts a float to a string. Information regarding the sign and location of the decimal point is also returned.

```
/*
 *     A C program that demonstrates how to use the fcvt
 *     function.
 *     Copyright (c) Chris H. Pappas and William H. Murray, 1990
 */

#include <stdlib.h>

main()
{
  int dec_pt,sign;
  char *ch_buffer;
  int num_char=7;

  ch_buffer = fcvt(-10.567845,num_char,&dec_pt,&sign);
  printf("The buffer holds: %s\n",ch_buffer);
  printf("The sign (+=0, -=1) is stored as a: %d\n",sign);
  printf("The decimal place is %d characters from left\n",
    dec_pt);
  return (0);
}
```

The output from this program is shown in the following listing. What potential uses might this function have?

```
The buffer holds: 105678450
The sign (+=0, -=1) is stored as a: 1
The decimal place is 2 characters from left
```

Converting a String to a Long Integer

The **strtol** function converts the supplied string, in the specified base, to its decimal equivalent. For example:

```
/*
 *    A C program that demonstrates how to use the strtol
 *    function.
 *    Copyright (c) Chris H. Pappas and William H. Murray, 1990
 */

#include <stdlib.h>
#include <stdio.h>

main()
{
  char *s="110011",*endptr;
  long long_number;

  long_number=strtol(s,&endptr,2);
  printf("The binary value %s is equal to %ld decimal.\n",
    s,long_number);
  return (0);
}
```

In this case, 110011 is contained in a string in binary format. The program produces the following results:

```
The binary value 110011 is equal to 51 decimal.
```

This is an interesting function since it allows a string of digits to be specified in one base and converted to another. You could use this function in a general base change program.

Searches and Sorts

The **bsearch** function performs a binary search of an array. The **qsort** function performs a quick sort. The **lfind** function performs a linear search for a key in an array of sequential records while the **lsearch** function performs a linear search on a sorted or unsorted table.

```
void *bsearch(const void *key,const void *base,
    size_t nelem,size_t width,int(*fcmp)(const void *,
    const void *)),

void qsort(void *base,size_t nelem,size_t width,
    int(*fcmp)(const void *,const void *)),

void *lfind(const void *key,const void *base,
    size_t *num,size_t width,int(*fcmp)
    (const void *,const void *)),

void *lsearch(const void *key, void *base,
    size_t *num,size_t width,int(*fcmp)
    (const void *,const void *)),
```

Note: Here, key represents the search key. *base* is the array to search. *nelem* contains the number of elements in the array. *width* is the number of bytes for each table entry. *fcmp* is the comparison routine used. *num* reports the number of records.

The next two programs illustrate the sort functions just described.

Sorting Integers with Quick Sort

Sorting data is important in any language. C and C++ provide the **qsort** function for sorting data, illustrated in the following example:

```
/*
 *    A C program that demonstrates how to use qsort.
 *    Copyright (c) Chris H. Pappas and William H. Murray, 1990
 */

#include <stdlib.h>

int int_comp(const void *i,const void *j);

int list[12]={96,54,72,87,12,29,35,54,11,12,75,-45};

main()
{
  int i;

  qsort(list,12,sizeof(int),int_comp);

  printf("The array after qsort:\n");
  for(i=0;i<12;i++)
    printf("%d ",list[i]);
    return (0);
```

```
}
int int_comp(const void *i,const void *j)
{
   return ((*(int *)i)-(*(int *)j));
}
```

The original list contains signed integers. The **qsort** function will arrange the original list in ascending order.

```
The array after qsort:
-45 11 12 12 29 35 54 54 72 75 87 96
```

Can you use **qsort** with floats? Why not alter the preceding program to see if you can.

Searching for an Integer in an Array

You can use the **bsearch** function to perform a search of an integer array. The value to be searched for, in the following example, is contained in *search __ number.*

```
/*
 *    A C program that demonstrates how to use the bsearch
 *    function.
 *    Copyright (c) Chris H. Pappas and William H. Murray, 1990
 */

#include <stdlib.h>
#include <stdio.h>

int int_comp(const void *i,const void *j);
int data_array[]={111,222,333,444,555,
                  666,777,888,999};

main()
{
   int *search_result;
   int search_number=444;

   printf("Is 444 in the data_array? ");
   search_result=bsearch(&search_number,data_array,9,
                         sizeof(int),int_comp);
   if (search_result) printf("Yes!\n");
     else printf("No!\n");
   return (0);
}

int int_comp(const void *i,const void *j)
{
```

```
    return ((*(int *)i)-(*(int *)j));
}
```

This program will print a simple message to the screen if the number is found in the array.

```
Is 444 in the data_array? Yes!
```

You can also use this function to search for a string of characters in an array.

Miscellaneous Operations

The functions described in this section perform a variety of operations, from calculating the absolute value of an integer to bit rotations. The bit rotation functions enable C to perform operations that were once exclusively in the realm of assembly language programs.

Abort or End

void abort(void)	Returns an exit code of 3
int atexit(atexit_t func)	Calls function prior to exit
void exit(int status)	Returns 0 for normal exit
int system(const char *command)	Command is a DOS command
void _exit(int status)	Terminates without action

Math

div_t div(int numer,int denom)	Divides and returns quotient and remainder in *div_t*
int abs(int x)	Determines absolute value of x
long labs(long x)	Determines absolute value of x
ldiv_t ldiv(long numer,long denom)	Similar to **div** with longs
int rand(void)	Calls random number generator
void srand(unsigned seed)	Seeds the random number generator

Rotate

unsigned long _lrotl(unsigned long val,int count)	Rotates the long *val* to the left
unsigned long _lrotr(unsigned long val,int count)	Rotates the long *val* to the right
unsigned _rotl(unsigned val, int count)	Rotates the integer *val* to the left
unsigned _rotr(unsigned val, int count)	Rotates the integer *val* to the right

Miscellaneous

char *getenv(const char *name)	Gets environment string
int putenv(const char *name)	Puts environment string
void swap(char *from,char *to,int nbytes)	Swaps the number of characters specified

Using the Random Number Function

C and C++ provide a random number generator. The generator can be initialized or seeded with a call to **srand**. The seed function accepts an integer argument and starts the random number generator.

```
/*
 *    A C program that demonstrates how to use the srand and
 *    rand, random number functions.
 *    Copyright (c) Chris H. Pappas and William H. Murray, 1990
 */

#include <stdlib.h>
#include <stdio.h>

main()
{
  int x;

  srand(3);

  for (x=0;x<10;x++)
    printf("Trial #%d, random number=%d\n",
           x,rand());
  return (0);
}
```

The following listing shows a sample of random numbers generated by **rand**:

```
Trial #0, random number=1038
Trial #1, random number=32467
Trial #2, random number=32686
Trial #3, random number=14075
Trial #4, random number=20
Trial #5, random number=30807
Trial #6, random number=5783
Trial #7, random number=16822
Trial #8, random number=23247
Trial #9, random number=14713
```

Random number generators are important in programming for statistical work and for applications that rely on generating random patterns.

Performing Bit Rotations on Data

C and C++ enable you to rotate the individual bits of integers and longs to the right and left. The next example performs two rotations in each direction:

```
/*
 *    A C program that demonstrates how to use the _rotl and
 *    _rotr bit rotate functions.
 *    Copyright (c) Chris H. Pappas and William H. Murray, 1990
 */

#include <stdlib.h>

main()
{
 unsigned int val = 0x1234;

 printf("rotate bits of %X to the left 2 bits and get %X\n",
        val,_rotl(val,2));
 printf("rotate bits of %X to the right 2 bits and get %X\n",
        val,_rotr(val,2));
}
```

The results of the rotations are shown next:

```
rotate bits of 1234 to the left 2 bits and get 48D0
rotate bits of 1234 to the right 2 bits and get 48D
```

With the bit rotation functions and the use of logical operators such as **and** and **or**, C enables you to manipulate data bit by bit.

CHARACTER FUNCTIONS

Characters are defined in most languages as single-byte values. The character macros and functions in C and C++, prototyped or contained in *ctype.h*, take integer arguments but only utilize the lower byte of the integer value. Automatic type conversion usually permits character arguments to be passed to the macros or functions. The following macros and functions are available:

isalnum	Checks for alpha-numeric character
isalpha	Checks for alpha character
isascii	Checks for ASCII character
iscntrl	Checks for control character
isdigit	Checks for decimal digit (0-9)
isgraph	Checks for printable character (no space)
islower	Checks for lowercase character
isprint	Checks for printable character
ispunct	Checks for punctuation character
isspace	Checks for whitespace character
isupper	Checks for uppercase character
isxdigit	Checks for hexadecimal digit
toascii	Translates character to ASCII equivalent
tolower	Translates character to lowercase if uppercase
toupper	Translates character to uppercase if lowercase

The character macros and functions allow characters to be tested for various conditions or to be converted between uppercase and lowercase characters.

Checking for Letters, Numbers, and ASCII Values

The following three macros allow ASCII-coded integer values to be checked via a lookup table. A zero is returned for false and a nonzero for true. A valid ASCII character set is assumed.

int isalnum(ch)	Checks for alphanumeric values A-Z, a-z, and 0-9. *ch* is integer
int isalpha(ch)	Checks for alpha values A-Z and a-z. *ch* is integer
int isascii(ch)	Checks for ASCII values 0-127 (0-7Fh). *ch* is integer

The following program checks the ASCII integer values from 0 to 127 and reports which of the preceding three functions produce a true condition for each case.

```
/*
 *    A C program that demonstrates how to use isalnum,
 *    isalpha, and isascii library functions.
 *    Copyright (c) Chris H. Pappas and William H. Murray, 1990
 */

#include <ctype.h>

main()
{
  int ch;
  for (ch=0;ch<=127;ch++) {
    printf("The ASCII digit %d is an:\n",ch);
    printf("%s",isalnum(ch) ? "   alpha-numeric char\n" : "");
    printf("%s",isalpha(ch) ? "   alpha char\n" : "");
    printf("%s",isascii(ch) ? "   ascii char\n" : "");
    printf("\n");
  }
  return (0);
}
```

A portion of the screen display is shown in the following listing:

```
The ASCII digit 56 is an:
  alpha-numeric char
  ascii char

The ASCII digit 64 is an:
  ascii char
```

```
The ASCII digit 65 is an:
  alpha-numeric char
  alpha char
  ascii char

The ASCII digit 90 is an:
  alpha-numeric char
  alpha char
  ascii char

The ASCII digit 127 is an:
  ascii char
```

These functions are useful in checking string data for correct data.

Checking for Control, Whitespace, Punctuation, and So On

The following nine macros allow ASCII-coded integer values to be checked via a lookup table. A zero is returned for false and a nonzero for true. A valid ASCII character set is assumed. The value *ch* is an integer.

int iscntrl(ch)	Checks for control character
int isdigit(ch)	Checks for digit 0-9
int isgraph(ch)	Checks for printable characters (no space)
int islower(ch)	Checks for lowercase a-z
int isprint(ch)	Checks for printable character
int ispunct(ch)	Checks for punctuation
int isspace(ch)	Checks for whitespace
int isupper(ch)	Checks for uppercase A-Z
int isxdigit(ch)	Checks for hexadecimal value 0-9, a-f, or A-F

The following program checks the ASCII integer values from 0 to 127 and reports which of the preceding nine functions give a true condition for each value:

```
/*
*    A C program that demonstrates several character
```

```
*       functions such as isprint, isupper, iscntrl, etc.
*       Copyright (c) Chris H. Pappas and William H. Murray, 1990
*/

#include <ctype.h>

main()
{
  int ch;
  for (ch=0;ch<=127;ch++) {
    printf("The ASCII digit %d is a(n):\n",ch);
    printf("%s",isprint(ch)  ? "   printable char\n" : "");
    printf("%s",islower(ch)  ? "   lower case char\n" : "");
    printf("%s",isupper(ch)  ? "   upper case char\n" : "");
    printf("%s",ispunct(ch)  ? "   punctuation char\n" : "");
    printf("%s",isspace(ch)  ? "   space char\n" : "");
    printf("%s",isdigit(ch)  ? "   char digit\n" : "");
    printf("%s",isgraph(ch)  ? "   graphics char\n" : "");
    printf("%s",iscntrl(ch)  ? "   control char\n" : "");
    printf("%s",isxdigit(ch) ? "   hexadecimal char\n" : "");
    printf("\n");
  }
  return (0);
}
```

A portion of the screen output is shown in the following listing:

```
The ASCII digit 29 is a(n):
  control char

The ASCII digit 38 is a(n):
  printable char
  punctuation char
  graphics char

The ASCII digit 52 is a(n):
  printable char
  char digit
  graphics char
  hexadecimal char

The ASCII digit 80 is a(n):
  printable char
  upper case char
  graphics char

The ASCII digit 96 is a(n):
  printable char
  punctuation char
  graphics char

The ASCII digit 127 is a(n):
  control char
```

Converting to ASCII, Lowercase, and Uppercase

The following three macros or functions allow ASCII-coded integer values to be translated. The macro **toascii** converts *ch* to ASCII by retaining only the lower 7 bits. The functions **tolower** and **toupper** convert the character value to the format specified. The macros **_tolower** and **_toupper** return identical results when supplied proper ASCII values. A valid ASCII character set is assumed. The value *ch* is an integer.

int toascii(ch)	Translates to ASCII character
int tolower(ch)	Translates *ch* to lowercase if uppercase
int _tolower(ch)	Translates *ch* to lowercase
int toupper(ch)	Translates *ch* to uppercase if lowercase
int _toupper(ch)	Translates *ch* to uppercase

The next example illustrates how the macro **toascii** translates integer information to correct ASCII values:

```
/*
 *    A C program that demonstrates how to use the
 *    toascii library function.
 *    Copyright (c) Chris H. Pappas and William H. Murray, 1990
 */

#include <ctype.h>

int ch;

main()
{
  for(ch=0;ch<=1024;ch++) {
    printf("The ASCII value for %d is %d\n",
         ch,toascii(ch));
  }
  return (0);
}
```

The following listing shows a portion of the output from this program:

```
The ASCII value for 0 is 0
The ASCII value for 1 is 1
The ASCII value for 2 is 2
The ASCII value for 3 is 3
The ASCII value for 4 is 4
The ASCII value for 5 is 5
          .
          .
The ASCII value for 128 is 0
```

```
The ASCII value for 129 is 1
The ASCII value for 130 is 2
The ASCII value for 131 is 3
The ASCII value for 132 is 4
The ASCII value for 133 is 5
                    .
                    .
                    .
The ASCII value for 256 is 0
The ASCII value for 257 is 1
The ASCII value for 258 is 2
The ASCII value for 259 is 3
The ASCII value for 260 is 4
The ASCII value for 261 is 5
                    .
                    .
                    .
The ASCII value for 384 is 0
The ASCII value for 385 is 1
The ASCII value for 386 is 2
The ASCII value for 387 is 3
The ASCII value for 388 is 4
The ASCII value for 389 is 5
```

MEMORY AND STRING FUNCTIONS

Strings in C and C++ are usually considered one-dimensional character arrays terminated with a null character. The string functions, prototyped in *string.h*, typically use pointer arguments and return pointer or integer values. You can study the syntax of each command in the next section, or in more detail in your Turbo C library reference. Buffer-manipulation functions such as **memccpy** through **memset** are also prototyped in *string.h*. The following functions are available:

memccpy	Copies from source to destination
memchr	Searches buffer for first *ch*
memcmp	Compares *n* characters in *buf1* and *buf2*
memcpy	Copies *n* characters from source to destination
memicmp	Same as **memcmp**, except case-insensitive
memset	Copies *ch* into *n* character positions in *buf*
strcat	Appends a string to another string
strchr	Locates first occurrence of a character in a string
strcmp	Compares two strings
strcmpi	Compares two strings (case-insensitive)
strcpy	Copies string to another string
strcspn	Locates first occurrence of a character in string from given character set
strdup	Replicates the string

```
   strcpy(buf1,"Well, are they similar or not?");
   strcpy(buf2,"Well, are they similiar or not?");
   /* 0 - identical strings except for case */
   /* x - any integer, means not identical */

   printf("%d\n",memicmp(buf1,buf2,40));
   /* returns a non-zero value */
   return (0);
}
```

If similar weren't spelled incorrectly in the second string, both strings would have been identical. A nonzero value is returned by **memicmp**.

Using memset to Load a Buffer

It is often necessary to load or clear a buffer with a predefined character. In those cases, you might consider using the **memset** function.

```
/*
 *     A C program that demonstrates how to use the memset
 *     library function to set the contents of a string buffer.
 *     Copyright (c) Chris H. Pappas and William H. Murray, 1990
 */

#include <string.h>

char buf[20];

main()
{
  printf("The contents of buf: %s",memset(buf,'%',15));
  buf[15] = '\0';
  return (0);
}
```

In this example, the buffer is loaded with 15 percent characters and a null character. The program will print 15 percent characters to the screen.

String Functions

Here are the syntax statements for the various string manipulating functions contained in *string.h*:

char *strerror(int errnum)	ANSI-supplied number
char *_strerror(char *s)	User-supplied message
size_t strlen(const char *s)	Null-terminated string
char *strlwr(char *s)	String to lowercase
char *strncat(char *s1,const char *s2,size_t n)	Append *n* char *s2* to *s1*
int strncmp(const char *s1,const char *s2,size_t n)	Compares first *n* characters of two strings
int strnicmp(const char *s1,const char *s2,size_t n)	Compares first *n* characters of two strings (case insensitive)
char *strncpy(char *s1,const char *s2,size_t n)	Copy *n* characters of *s2* to *s1*
char *strnset(char *s,int ch,size_t n)	Set first *n* characters of string to char setting
char *strpbrk(const char *s1,const char *s2)	Locate character from *s2* in *s1*
char *strrchr(const char *s,int ch)	Locate last occurrence of *ch* in string
char *strrev(char *s)	String to reverse
char *strset(char *s,int ch)	String to be set with *ch*
size_t strspn(const char *s1,const char *s2)	Search *s1* with char set in *s2*
char *strstr(const char *s1,const char *s2)	Search *s1* with *s2*
char *strtok(char *s1,const char *s2)	Finds token in *s1*. *s1* contains token(s), *s2* contains the delimiters
char *strupr(char *s)	String to uppercase

*s is a pointer to a string. *s1 and *s2 are pointers to two strings. Usually, *s1 points to the string to be manipulated and *s2 points to the string doing the manipulation. *ch* is a character value.

Comparing Two Strings

The following program uses the **strcmp** function and reports how one string compares to another:

```
/*
 *    A C program that demonstrates how to use the strcmp
 *    library function to compare two strings.
 *    Copyright (c) Chris H. Pappas and William H. Murray, 1990
 */

#include <string.h>
```

```
M_LOG10E          0.434294481903251827651
M_LN2             0.693147180559945309417
M_LN10            2.30258509299404568402
M_PI              3.14159265358979323846
M_PI_2            1.57079632679489661923
M_PI_4            0.785398163397448309616
M_1_PI            0.318309886183790671538
M_2_PI            0.636619772367581343076
M_1_SQRTPI        0.564189583547756286948
M_2_SQRTPI        1.12837916709551257390
M_SQRT2           1.41421356237309504880
M_SQRT_2          0.707106781186547524401
```

You might find that access to these constant values is handy, even if you don't utilize the functions described.

Mathematical Operations in C and C++

The math functions are relatively easy to use and understand if you are familiar with algebraic and trigonometric concepts. Many of these functions have been demonstrated in earlier chapters. Remember that all angle arguments are specified in radians.

double acos(double x)	Arc cosine
double asin(double x)	Arc sine
double atan(double x)	Arc tangent
double atan2(double y,double x)	Arc tan
double ceil(double x)	Greatest integer
double cos(double x)	Cosine
double cosh(double x)	Hyperbolic cosine
double exp(double x)	Exponential value
double fabs(double x)	Absolute value
double floor(double x)	Smallest integer
double fmod(double x,double y)	Modula operator
double frexp(double x,int *exponent)	Split to mantissa & exp
double hypot(double x,double y)	Hypotenuse
double ldexp(double x,int exponent)	x times 2 to exp power
double log(double x)	Natural log
double log10(double x)	Common log
double modf(double x,double *ipart)	Mantissa and exponent

double poly(double x,int degree,double co-effs[])	Polynomial
double pow(double x,double y)	x to y power
double pow10(int p)	10 raised to p
double sin(double x)	Sine
double sinh(double x)	Hyperbolic sine
double sqrt(double x)	Square root
double tan(double x)	Tangent
double tanh(double x)	Hyperbolic tangent

If you program in C and need to use complex number arithmetic, you must resort to using **struct complex** and the **cabs** function described in *math.h*. This is the only function available for complex arithmetic in C.

```
struct complex {double x,double y}
```

This structure is used by the **cabs** function. The **cabs** function returns the absolute value of a complex number.

Complex Arithmetic In C++

C++ programmers should use the C++ class **complex** described in *complex.h* for complex arithmetic. Operator overloading is provided for +, −, *, /, + =, − =, * =, / =, =, = =, and ! =. The stream operators, < < and > >, are also overloaded.

The following *math.h* functions, described in the previous section, are also overloaded:

```
friend double  abs(complex&)
friend complex acos(complex&)
friend complex asin(complex&)
friend complex atan(complex&)
friend complex cos(complex&)
friend complex cosh(complex&)
friend complex exp(complex&)
friend complex log(complex&)
friend complex log10(complex&)
friend complex pow(complex& base,double expon)
friend complex pow(double base,complex& expon)
friend complex pow(complex& base,complex& expon)
friend complex sin(complex&)
friend complex sinh(complex&)
```

```
friend complex sqrt(complex&)
friend complex tan(complex&)
friend complex tanh(complex&)
friend complex acos(complex&)
friend complex asin(complex&)
friend complex atan(complex&)
friend complex log10(complex&)
friend complex tan(complex&)
friend complex tanh(complex&)
```

Here are some additional complex mathematical operations described in *complex.h:*

friend double real(complex&)	The real part of a complex number
friend double imag(complex&)	The imaginary part of a complex number
friend complex conj(complex&)	The complex conjugate
friend double norm(complex&)	The square of the magnitude
friend double arg(complex&)	The angle in the plane
friend complex polar(double mag, double angle = 0)	Create a complex object given polar coordinates as arguments

Since the standard functions prototyped in *math.h* have been used extensively in earlier chapters, the next several examples are devoted to the new functions in *complex.h*.

Real and Imaginary Parts of a Complex Result

The following program shows how to use the complex functions **real** and **imaginary** to break apart a complex number:

```
//
//    A C++ program that demonstrates how to use the complex
//    function real and imaginary to break apart a complex number.
//    This program utilizes operator and function overloading.
//    Copyright (c) Chris H. Pappas and William H. Murray, 1990
//

#include <iostream.h>
#include <complex.h>
```

```
main()
{
  double x1=5.6, y1=7.2;
  double x2=-3.1, y2=4.8;

  complex z1=complex(x1,y1);
  complex z2=complex(x2,y2);
  complex zt;

  zt=z1+z2;

  cout << "The value of zt is: " << zt << "\n";
  cout << "The real part of the sum is: "
       << real(zt) << "\n";
  cout << "The imaginary part of the sum is: "
       << imag(zt) << "\n";
  return (0);
}
```

In this example, two complex numbers are added to form the complex sum, *zt*. Adding numbers in rectangular coordinates is fairly easy for humans, but look at the simplicity of the program and appreciate what C++ is accomplishing. Here are the results for this example:

```
The value of zt is: (2.5, 12)
The real part of the sum is: 2.5
The imaginary part of the sum is: 12
```

Overloaded Operators with Complex Numbers

The fundamental mathematical operators +, −, * and / are overloaded. This means that you can use them to perform complex arithmetic directly. Examine the following program code:

```
//
//   A C++ program that demonstrates how to use complex
//   arithmetic with overloaded operators.  Here complex
//   numbers are directly added, subtracted, multiplied and
//   divided.
//   Copyright (c) Chris H. Pappas and William H. Murray, 1990
//

#include <iostream.h>
#include <complex.h>

main()
{
  double x1=5.6, y1=7.2;
  double x2=-3.1, y2=4.8;
```

```
complex z1=complex(x1,y1);
complex z2=complex(x2,y2);

cout << "The value of z1 + z2 is: " << z1+z2 << "\n";
cout << "The value of z1 * z2 is: " << z1*z2 << "\n";
cout << "The value of z1 - z2 is: " << z1-z2 << "\n";
cout << "The value of z1 / z2 is: " << z1/z2 << "\n";
return (0);
}
```

This example shows how various operators can be overloaded. The program prints the sum, product, difference, and division of two complex numbers.

```
The value of z1 + z2 is: (2.5, 12)
The value of z1 * z2 is: (-51.92, 4.56)
The value of z1 - z2 is: (8.7, 2.4)
The value of z1 / z2 is: (0.5267994, -1.506891)
```

This opens new vistas for those inclined toward mathematics and engineering. Since **cout** can print the complex rectangular result, it must also be overloaded.

Rectangular to Polar Transformations

Complex numbers are often expressed in polar or rectangular forms. The following program adds two complex numbers, in polar format, and prints the result.

```
//
//    A C++ program that demonstrates how to use complex
//    arithmetic with overloaded operators.  Here rectangular
//    numbers are directly converted to their polar
//    equivalents.  Arithmetic is also done directly on polar
//    numbers.
//    Copyright (c) Chris H. Pappas and William H. Murray, 1990
//

#include <iostream.h>
#include <complex.h>

main()
{
  double m1=10.0,ang1=M_PI/6;     // 60 deg in radians
  double m2=20.0,ang2=M_PI_4;     // 45 deg in radians

  cout << "m1 and ang1 from polar to rectangular: "
```

```
            << polar(m1,ang1) << "\n";
    cout << "m2 and ang2 from polar to rectangular: "
            << polar(m2,ang2) << "\n";
    cout << "Add polar values then convert: "
            << polar(m1,ang1)+polar(m2,ang2) << "\n";
    return (0);
}
```

Use your calculator to check the results of these complex operations.

```
m1 and ang1 from polar to rectangular: (8.660254, 5)
m2 and ang2 from polar to rectangular: (14.14214, 14.14214)
Add polar values then convert: (22.80239, 19.14214)
```

If you work with complex numbers in mathematics or electrical engineering, these new features will be a big help. Don't forget that the functions require all angles to be radians.

Overloaded Functions and Complex Arithmetic

Many of the *math.h* functions are overloaded to let you use them with complex numbers. The following program illustrates several of these functions:

```
//
//    A C++ program that demonstrates how to use complex
//    arithmetic with overloaded math.h functions.  Here
//    the square root, cube, and absolute value of a number
//    in polar form is obtained.
//    Copyright (c) Chris H. Pappas and William H. Murray, 1990
//

#include <iostream.h>
#include <complex.h>

main()
{
  double m1=-10.4,ang1=M_PI/6;   // 30 deg in radians

  cout << "square root of polar m1 @ ang1: "
        << sqrt(polar(m1,ang1)) << "\n";
  cout << "cube of polar m1 @ ang1: "
        << pow(polar(m1,ang1),3) << "\n";
  cout << "absolute value of polar m1 @ ang1: "
        << abs(polar(m1,ang1)) << "\n";
  return (0);
}
```

Imagine being able to take the square root of a complex number with nothing more than a call to **sqrt**.

```
square root of polar ml @ angl: (0.8346663, -3.115017)
cube of polar ml @ angl: (3.443789e-13, -1124.864)
absolute value of polar ml @ angl: 10.4
```

TIME FUNCTIONS

The following section covers several time and date functions described in *time.h*. These functions offer a variety of ways to obtain different time and/or date formats for your program code.

asctime	Converts date and time to an ASCII string and uses the *tm* structure
clock	Determines the microprocessor's clock time for the current session
ctime	Converts date and time to a string
difftime	Calculates the difference between two times
gmtime	Converts date and time to GMT using *tm* structure
localtime	Converts date and time to *tm* structure
mktime	Converts time to calendar format. Uses *tm* structure
stime	Sets date and time for system
strftime	Allows formatting of date and time data for output
time	Obtains current time (system)
tzset	Sets time variables for environment variable *TZ*

For details of each function's syntax, see the next section.

Date and Time Variations

Many of the date and time functions described in the previous section use the *tm* structure defined in *time.h*.

```
struct tm  {
  int      tm_sec;
  int      tm_min;
  int      tm_hour;
  int      tm_mday;
  int      tm_mon;
  int      tm_year;
  int      tm_wday;
  int      tm_yday;
  int      tm_isdst;
};
```

The syntax for calling each date and time function differs according to the function's ability. The next listing shows the syntax for each:

char *asctime(const struct tm *tblock)	Converts the structure info to a 26-char string
clock _ t clock(void)	Determines the time in seconds. The returned value should be divided by the macro *CLK_TCK*
char *ctime(const time _ t *time)	Converts a time value, pointed to by **time,* into a 26-char string
double di(time _ t time2, time _ t time1)	Calculates the difference between *time2* and *time1* and returns a double
struct tm *gmtime(const time _ t *timer)	Accepts address of a value returned by the function **time** and returns a pointer to the structure with GMT information
struct tm *localtime(const time _ t *timer)	Accepts address of a value returned by the function **time** and returns a pointer to the structure with local time information
time _ t mktime(struct tm *tptr)	Converts time pointed to *tptr to a calendar time of same format as used by **time** function
int stime(time _ t *tp)	Sets the system time. *tp* points to the time in seconds as measured from GMT, January 1, 1970
size _ t strftime(char *s, size _ t maxsize, const char *fmt, const struct tm *t)	Formats date and time information for output

time _ t time(time _ t *timer)   Returns the time in seconds
                                                    since 00:00:00 GMT, January 1,
                                                    1970

void tzset(void)   Sets the global variables *daylight,*
                                                    timezone, and *tzname* based on
                                                    the environment string

For **size** and **strftime**, *s* points to the string information, *maxsize* is maximum string length, *fmt* represents the format, and *t* points to a structure of type *tm*. The formatting options include

%a	abbreviate weekday name
%A	full weekday name
%b	abbreviate month name
%B	full month name
%c	date and time information
%d	day of month (01 to 31)
%H	hour (00 to 23)
%I	hour (00 to 12)
%j	day of year (001 to 366)
%m	month (01 to 12)
%M	minutes (00 to 59)
%p	AM or PM
%S	seconds (0 to 59)
%U	week number (00 to 52), Sunday 1st day
%w	weekday (0 to 6)
%W	week number (00 to 52), Monday 1st day
%x	date
%X	time
%y	year, without century (00 to 99)
%Y	year, with century
%Z	time zone name
%%	character %a

For **tzset**, the *TZ* environment string uses the following syntax:

TZ = zzz[+/−]d[d]{lll}

Here, zzz represents a three-character string with the local time zone — for example, "EST" for Eastern Standard Time. The [+/−]d[d] argument contains an adjustment for the local time zones' difference from GMT (Greenwich Mean Time). Positive numbers are a westward adjustment while negative numbers are an eastward adjustment. For example, a five (5) would be used for EST. The last argument, {*lll*}, represents the local time zone daylight saving time—for example, EDT, for eastern daylight saving time.

Several of these functions will be used in example programs in the next section.

Using the localtime and asctime Functions

The following program will return date and time information by using the **localtime** and **asctime** functions:

```
/*
 *    A C program that demonstrates how to call the localtime and
 *    asctime functions.
 *    Copyright (c) Chris H. Pappas and William H. Murray, 1990
 */

#include <time.h>
#include <stdio.h>

struct tm *date_time;
time_t timer;

main()
{
  time(&timer);
  date_time=localtime(&timer);

  printf("The present date and time is: %s\n",
         asctime(date_time));
  return (0);
}
```

This program produces output similar to the following sample:

```
The present date and time is: Mon Jan 29 13:16:20 1990
```

Watch the *date_time* variable, shown in Figure 14-2, from the Turbo Debugger screen. The Debugger helps you get a feel for how data is being returned.

Using the gmtime and asctime Functions

This program is similar to the last example. Instead of using the **localtime** function, it uses the **gmtime** function. Do you notice what's different about the output?

```
/*
*    A C program that demonstrates how to call the gmtime and
*    asctime functions.
*    Copyright (c) Chris H. Pappas and William H. Murray, 1990
*/

#include <time.h>
#include <stdio.h>

main()
{
  struct tm *date_time;
  time_t timer;

  time(&timer);
  date_time=gmtime(&timer);

  printf("%.19s\n",asctime(date_time));
  return (0);
}
```

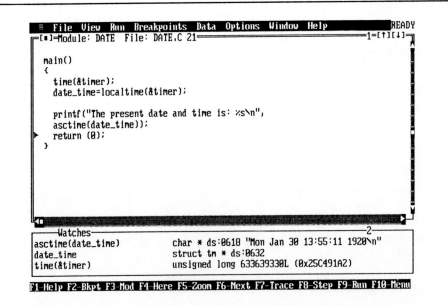

Figure 14-2.   The Debugger's Watch window reports information on several items

The following date and time information was returned by this program:

```
Mon Jan 29 18:16:28
```

Using the strftime Function

The **strftime** function is the most flexible date and time function. The following program illustrates several formatting options:

```
/*
 *    A C program that demonstrates how to call the strftime
 *    function.
 *    Copyright (c) Chris H. Pappas and William H. Murray, 1990
 */

#include <time.h>
#include <stdio.h>

main()
{
  struct tm *date_time;
  time_t timer;
  char str[80];

  time(&timer);
  date_time=localtime(&timer);
  strftime(str,80,"It is %X on %A, %x",
           date_time);
  printf("%s\n",str);
  return (0);
}
```

The sample output for this program is

```
It is 13:16:35 on Monday, 01/29/90
```

The **shrftime** function might not be portable from one system to another, so use it with caution if portability is a consideration.

Using the ctime Function

The following C++ program illustrates how to make a call to the **ctime** function. It shows how easy it is to obtain date and time information from the system.

```
//
//    A C++ program that demonstrates how to call the
//    ctime function.
//    Copyright (c) Chris H. Pappas and William H. Murray, 1990
//

#include <time.h>
#include <iostream.h>

time_t longtime;

main()
{
  time(&longtime);
  cout << "The time is " << ctime(&longtime) << "\n";

  return (0);
}
```

A typical output would appear in the following form:

```
The time is Mon Jan 29 13:16:42 1990
```

PUTTING YOUR KNOWLEDGE TO WORK

1. Explain the relationship between header files and the libraries shipped with your C compiler.

2. What data types are used most often by the functions prototyped in the *ctype, string, math,* and *complex* header files?

3. C uses the **itoa** and **ltoa** functions to convert integer and long types to a string. Could a single routine be developed in C++ to do these conversions? If so, explain.

4. The functions described in the *math* header file accept and return double values. Are there any similar situations in the *ctype* and *string* header files?

5. Examine the prototypes in the C++ *complex* header file. What data types can be passed to the complex functions in the library?

6. How does the **strcmp** function work? You might have to refer to your Borland manuals for the answer.

7. Is there a way of determining how long your computer has been turned on for the current session? If so, write a short program that will accomplish the task.

8. Write a short program that will illustrate the four basic arithmetic operations on complex numbers expressed in rectangular form. Repeat the previous program, but with numbers expressed in polar form. Check your answers with a calculator.

9. Use the **strftime** function to print the number of days passed and the number of days remaining in the current year.

15

SYSTEM RESOURCES
AND GRAPHICS

In this chapter you will learn

- How to use various hardware-dependent function calls
- What the important features of the BIOS, DOS, and graphics functions are
- How to pass function argument parameters
- How to detect video cards and graphics modes
- How to use numerous graphics primitives
- How to plot mathematical and scientific equations
- How to create a presentation quality pie chart

SYSTEM RESOURCES

In the previous chapter, you learned about powerful C and C++ library functions that allow you to work with characters, strings, math functions, and so on. For the most part, these functions meet the ANSI standard and are portable from one C compiler to another and from one system to another. In other words, they are as close to a standard C as you can get.

Most compiler manufacturers also provide functions in their C libraries that are not as standardized. The standardization problem develops because of different operating systems and computer equipment. Borland's C and C++ provide functions that allow you to tap the software and hardware features of the system you are working on. Unfortunately, these system features usually make programs nonportable from one system to another and from one C compiler to another. They are obviously not part of the ANSI standard. However, since many programmers and users work on IBM-compatible computers under DOS with Turbo C, compatibility doesn't become a major problem. Why use functions like this at all? These functions allow you to tap the power of the computer's hardware and provide sound, control of printers, plotters, CD ROM drives, mice, and graphics capabilities.

Without the BIOS and DOS capabilities provided with C and C++, hardware control would be exclusively in the realm of assembly language programmers. With these built-in C and C++ functions, you can now write many programs without assembly language patches. In Chapters 18 and 19, you will see how assembly language can provide many of the same features for controlling system hardware. In Chapter 20, you will learn how to combine C code and assembly code to solve programming problems that you cannot handle with the simple functions described in this chapter.

The *bios.h, dos.h,* and *graphics.h* header files prototype several hundred functions. This section attempts to list each of these functions with a short description and the prototype information. However, it is beyond the scope of this book to illustrate each function; that task alone could fill another book. Instead, this chapter illustrates frequently used functions and functions that will give your programs the professional touch. You should print the three header files just mentioned to view the available definitions, macros, and function prototypes. Keep your library reference handy for a detailed description of each function.

THE BIOS HEADER FILE

The following seven functions allow immediate access to powerful BIOS (basic input and output services) built into IBM-compatible computers.

These functions are very hardware dependent and may not operate on systems that are not 100 percent compatible with IBM equipment.

bioscom	Performs RS-232 serial communications
biosdisk	Issues disk operations through BIOS
biosequip	Checks system hardware
bioskey	Keyboard interface via BIOS
biosmemory	Returns RAM (640K max) size
biosprint	Performs printer I/O with BIOS
biostime	Sets or reads the BIOS timer

With the BIOS functions, disk control, RS-232 communications, memory size, and even timer control are possible. As you saw in the last chapter, other standard C and C++ functions also permit many of these operations. You should use ANSI functions when possible and avoid the problem of incompatibility with systems that don't permit you to use BIOS functions. At other times, the use of BIOS functions will be your only solution to the problem at hand.

BIOS Function Call Syntax

The syntax for each BIOS function is relatively simple, as you can see from the function prototypes included here. Again, for detailed information on the various arguments, consult the C library reference.

```
int bioscom(int cmd,char abyte,int port);
int biosdisk(int cmd,int drive,int head,int track,int sector,
             int nsects,void *buffer);
int biosequip(void);
int bioskey(int cmd);
int biosmemory(void);
int biosprint(int cmd,int abyte,int port);
long biostime(int cmd,long newtime);
```

The seven BIOS functions accept various arguments. The next two examples demonstrate how to use several of these functions. Use the previous listing in conjunction with your reference manual as a quick reference for the BIOS routines.

Checking Base Memory

The following C++ program uses the BIOS functions to check for base memory in a system. The range of memory can be between 0 and 640K. Making the function call is straightforward.

```
//
//    A C++ program that demonstrates how to use the biosmemory
//    function for obtaining the amount of installed RAM memory.
//    This value can vary from 0 to 640K bytes and does not
//    include extended or expanded memory.
//    Copyright (c) Chris H. Pappas and William H. Murray, 1990
//

#include <iostream.h>
#include <bios.h>

main()
{
  int base_memory;

  base_memory=biosmemory();

  cout << "There is " << base_memory
       << "K of base memory installed.";
  return (0);
}
```

The **biosmemory** function is limited to reporting memory in the range 0 to 640K and will not report on extended or expanded memory. Currently, no function in the *runtime* library will allow you to determine this extra memory.

Checking for a Game Adapter

The following program allows a software program to check for the presence of a game adapter card in the system. If a game adapter is present, bit 12 of the value returned by the function will be high or logic 1. Otherwise, the bit is a zero, or logic 0. Binary bit 12, alone, produces the binary number 1000000000000_2. This is equivalent to the hexadecimal value 1000_{16}. An *and* mask is created with this same value. Masks will be described in more detail in Chapters 16 and 17. The purpose of the mask is to isolate that single bit, examine it, and determine if it is 1 or 0.

```
/*
 *    A C++ program that demonstrates how to use the biosequip
 *    function for obtaining current hardware information.
 *    Copyright (c) Chris H. Pappas and William H. Murray, 1990
 */

#include <iostream.h>
#include <bios.h>

#define GAMEADP 0x1000

main()
{
  int online_equip;

  online_equip=biosequip();

  if (online_equip & GAMEADP)
    cout << "There is a game adapter present.\n";
  else
    cout << "There is no game adapter present.\n";
  return (0);
}
```

If the values returned by the BIOS function call and the mask produce a true condition, a game adapter is present. Otherwise, a game adapter is not available. Programs like this can help you determine which hardware items your program can use in a given system.

THE DOS HEADER FILE

The following DOS functions allow immediate access to powerful DOS interrupt capabilities built into IBM and 100 percent compatible computers. These functions are very hardware dependent and may not function properly on noncompatible machines. The DOS functions permit a broader range of operations than the previous BIOS functions, as you can see from this list:

absread	Reads specified disk sectors
abswrite	Writes to specified disk sectors
allocmem	Allocates memory segment
bdos	DOS system call
bdosptr	DOS system call, using pointer argument

ctrlbrk	Handler for CTRL-BREAK
delay	Suspends execution (in milliseconds)
disable	Disables system interrupts
dosexterr	Provides extended DOS error information
dostounix	Converts date/time to UNIX format
emit	Inserts literal values into code
enable	Permits hardware interrupts
freemem	Frees allocated memory segment
getcbrk	Gets CTRL-BREAK setting
getdate	Gets current system date
getdfree	Gets free disk space
getfat	Obtains FAT from given drive
getfatd	Obtains FAT of default drive
getpsp	Gets program segment prefix
gettime	Gets system time
getverify	Gets state of DOS verify flag
harderr	Creates hardware error handler
hardresume	Returns from hardware error handler
hardretn	Returns to program from **harderr**
inport	Reads a word from specified port
inportb	Reads a byte from specified port
int86	General hardware interrupt
int86x	General hardware interrupt with segment
intdos	DOS interrupt
intdosx	DOS interrupt with segment
intr	Alternate software interrupt
keep	Exits and remains resident
nosound	Turns speaker off
outport	Sends a word to given port
outportb	Sends a byte to given port
parsfnm	Parses file name
peek	Returns word from memory location
peekb	Returns byte from memory location
poke	Sends word to memory location
pokeb	Sends byte to memory location
randbrd	Reads a random block from file
randbwr	Writes a random block to file
segread	Reads segment registers
setblock	Modifies size of allocated block
setcbrk	Sets CTRL-BREAK setting

setdate	Sets system date
settime	Sets system time
setvect	Sets interrupt vector entry
setverify	Sets state of DOS verify flag
sleep	Suspends program execution (in milliseconds)
sound	Turns speaker on (frequency is Hertz)
unixtodos	Converts date/time to DOS format
unlink	Deletes the given file

Many of the DOS functions permit operations similar to the BIOS routines. For example, notice that there are several time and date functions, delay functions, disk I/O functions, and so on. DOS functions tend to be more robust. However, you should use the functions included in the ANSI C standard where possible if they achieve the same results for your program.

DOS Function Call Syntax

The syntax for each DOS function is as simple as that for the BIOS function calls. Examine the DOS function prototypes and notice the wide range of services that they provide. For detailed information on the various DOS function arguments, consult the library reference.

```
int absread(int drive,int nsects,int lsect,void *buffer);

int abswrite(int drive,int nsects,int lsect,void *buffer);

int allocmem(unsigned size,unsigned *segp);

int bdos(int dosfun,unsigned dosdx,unsigned dosal);

int bdosptr(int dosfun,void *argument,unsigned dosal);

struct country country(int xcode, struct country *cp);

void ctrlbrk(int (*handler)(void));

void delay(unsigned milliseconds);

void disable(void);

int dosexterr(struct DOSERROR *eblkp);

long dostounix(struct date *d,struct time *t);

void __emit__();

void enable(void);

int freemem(unsigned segx);

int getcbrk(void);
```

```
void getdate(struct date *datep);
void getdfree(unsigned char drive,struct dfree *dtable);
void getfat(unsigned char drive, struct fatinfo *dtable);
void getfatd(struct fatinfo *dtable);
unsigned getpsp(void);
void gettime(struct time *timep);
int getverify(void);
void harderr(int (*handler)());
void hardresume(int axret);
void hardretn(int retn);
int inport(int portid);
unsigned char inportb(int portid);
int int86(int intno,union REGS *inregs,union REGS *outregs);
int int86x(int intno,union REGS *inregs,union REGS *outregs,
           struct SREGS *segregs);
int intdos(union REGS *inregs,union REGS *outregs);
int intdosx(union REGS *inregs,union REGS *outregs,
            struct SREGS *segregs);
void intr(int intno,struct REGPACK *preg);
void keep(unsigned char status,unsigned size);
void nosound(void);
void outport(int portid,int value);
void outportb(int portid,unsigned char value);
char *parsfnm(const char *cmdline,struct fcb *fcb,int opt);
int peek(unsigned segment,unsigned offset);
char peekb(unsigned segment,unsigned offset);
void poke(unsigned segment,unsigned offset,int value);
void pokeb(unsigned segment,unsigned offset,char value);
int randbrd(struct fcb *fcb,int rcnt);
int randbwr(struct fcb *fcb,int rcnt);
void segread(struct SREGS *segp);
int setblock(unsigned segx,unsigned newsize);
int setcbrk(int cbrkvalue);
void setdate(struct date *datep);
void settime(struct time *timep);
void setvect(int interruptno,void interrupt (far *isr) ());
void setverify(int value);
void sleep(unsigned seconds);
void sound(unsigned frequency);
```

```
void unixtodos(long time,struct date *d,struct time *t);
int unlink(const char *path);
```

The following section illustrates several of the DOS functions. When a particular function call is not available, a general DOS interrupt will be used.

Slowing Down Program Output

Usually, you want your programs to execute as quickly as possible. However, sometimes slowing down information makes it easier for the user to view and understand. The **delay** function delays program execution in milliseconds. The following C program includes a one-second delay between each line of output to the screen:

```
/*
 *    A C program that demonstrates how to use the delay
 *    function for slowing program output.
 *    Copyright (c) Chris H. Pappas and William H. Murray, 1990
 */

#include <dos.h>
#include <stdio.h>

main()
{
  int i;

  for (i=0;i<25;i++) {
    delay(1000);
    printf("The count is %d\n",i);
  }
  return (0);
}
```

What other uses might the **delay** function have? Suppose your computer is connected to an external data sensing device, such as a thermocouple or strain gauge. You could use the **delay** function to permit samples every minute, hour, or day.

Examining Free Memory on a Disk

You learned how to read and write to the disk drive in Chapter 11. It is often a good idea to know how much free disk space is available before you make a write attempt. The **getdfree** function provides that information. The following C example reports to the user the available space on drive C:

```
/*
 *    A C program that demonstrates how to use the getdfree
 *    function for obtaining free disk space on drive C.
 *    Copyright (c) Chris H. Pappas and William H. Murray, 1990
 */

#include <dos.h>
#include <stdio.h>

main()
{
  struct dfree df;
  long f_disk;

  getdfree(3,&df);
  f_disk=(long)df.df_avail*(long)df.df_bsec*(long)df.df_sclus;
  printf("Drive C has %ld bytes of memory for use.\n",f_disk);
  return (0);
}
```

Drive C is identified with the number 3 (A is 1 and B is 2). Data concerning memory are returned to the **dfree** structure. This structure holds information on the available clusters, total clusters, bytes per sector, and sectors per cluster. The preceding program combines that information to provide the total free disk space.

Using DOS Interrupt Functions

The DOS and BIOS functions provide a "hook" to many of the interrupts on the computer. When there is not a particular function for your needs, you can call a general interrupt function and supply the necessary parameters. The next C++ example does just that, issuing an interrupt 33h and making the mouse pointer (if a mouse is installed) visible for 1 minute:

```
//
//    A C++ program that demonstrates how to use the int86
//    function to show mouse pointer for 1 minute!
//    (Appendix B lists all possible mouse interrupts).
//    Copyright (c) Chris H. Pappas and William H. Murray, 1990
//

#include <dos.h>

main()
```

```
{
  union REGS regs;

  regs.x.ax=1;
  int86(0x33,&regs,&regs);

  delay(60000);

  regs.x.ax=0;
  int86(0x33,&regs,&regs);

  return (0);
}
```

If you examine the mouse interrupts in Appendix B, you can detect mouse button clicks and coordinate positions using this function. This program simply switched the default pointer on and off. While the pointer is on, you can move the mouse around on the screen.

This program also uses the *REGS* union, described in the *dos.h* header file. Using this union, the user has access to the **ax**, **bx**, **cx**, **dx**, **bp**, **si**, **di**, **ds**, **es**, and **flag** registers of the system. Examine the prototype of this function, shown earlier in the chapter. Notice that register information can be set and passed into the microprocessor registers with *inregs*. Likewise, the function can return the contents of the system registers through the union *outregs*. For 16-bit registers, use *reg.x* and for 8-bit registers use *reg.h*. The syntax is

```
regs.x.ax = (desired value), for 16-bit registers
regs.h.bl = (desired value), for 8-bit registers
```

The Dimension of Sound

Most small computers have poor quality sound reproduction facilities. Nevertheless, sound plays an important role in communicating information to the computer user. Various pitched notes can warn the user of an error or tell them to enter data in a spreadsheet. When you combine sound with graphics, you can get into the realm of computer games.

This simple C++ program demonstrates how to create a simple sound that increases in pitch over a short period of time:

```
//
//    A C++ program that demonstrates how to use the sound
//    function to produce a unique musical sound from the
//    system's speaker.
//    Copyright (c) Chris H. Pappas and William H. Murray, 1990
//
```

```
#include <dos.h>

main()
{
  unsigned frequency=0;
  int i;

  for (i=0;i<2500;i++) {
    sound(frequency);
    delay(5);
    frequency++;
  }

  nosound();
  return (0);
}
```

This program starts with a frequency of 0 hertz and increases to 2500 hertz. A 5-millisecond delay is introduced to slow the overall action just a bit. Can you think of a way to make the tone start at a high frequency and drop to a low frequency? If you are creative, you can have a lot of fun tinkering with the sound function.

THE GRAPHICS HEADER FILE

Borland's C and C++ provide an extensive set of graphics routines. The prototypes for the graphics functions are in *graphics.h*. These graphics functions contain *primitives* for drawing pixels, lines, rectangles, arcs, circles, and ellipses. (They are called primitives because they only draw a basic shape.) More advanced graphics functions include routines for drawing two- and three-dimensional bars and pie slices. Additional graphics functions allow the user to set the graphics mode, select the viewport, size the image, fill objects with colors and patterns, and so on. The *viewport* refers to that portion of the screen that is currently active. By default, the size of the viewport and the screen are identical.

Examine this extensive list of graphics functions:

arc	Draws a circular arc
bar	Draws a two-dimensional bar

bar3d	Draws a three-dimensional bar
circle	Draws a circle
cleardevice	Clears the graphics screen
clearviewport	Clears the current viewport
closegraph	Closes the graphics system
detectgraph	Determines driver and mode from hardware
drawpoly	Draws a polygon outline
ellipse	Draws an elliptical arc
fillellipse	Draws and fills an ellipse
fillpoly	Draws and fills a polygon
floodfill	Flood fills a bound region
getarccoords	Gets coordinates of last call to arc
getaspectratio	Gets aspect ratio for current mode
getbkcolor	Returns current background color
getcolor	Gets the current drawing color
getdefaultpalette	Gets the palette definition structure
getdrivername	Pointer to string with current graphics driver
getfillpattern	Copies user fill pattern to memory
getfillsettings	Gets info on current fill pattern and color
getgraphmode	Returns the current graphics mode
getimage	Saves specified image to memory
getlinesettings	Gets line style, pattern, and thickness
getmaxcolor	Returns max value that can be sent to setcolor
getmaxmode	Returns max value for mode for current driver
getmaxx	Returns max x screen coordinate (in pixels)
getmaxy	Returns max y screen coordinate (in pixels)
getmodename	Returns pointer to string with graphics mode
getmoderange	Returns range of modes for current driver
getpalette	Returns information on current palette
getpalettesize	Gets size of palette color lookup table
getpixel	Gets the color of the specified pixel
gettextsettings	Returns current graphics text font information
getviewsettings	Returns current graphics viewport settings
getx	Gives current x position on screen
gety	Returns current y position on screen
graphdefaults	Resets all graphics to default values
grapherrormsg	Returns pointer to error message string
_graphfreemem	Gives hook to graphics memory deallocation
_graphgetmem	Gives hook to graphics memory allocation
graphresult	Returns error code for last failed operation
imagesize	Returns number of bytes needed to store an image
initgraph	Initializes the graphics system

installuserdriver	Installs a vendor supplied driver
installuserfont	Installs a user supplied font
line	Draws a line
linerel	Draws a line a given distance from a point
lineto	Draws a line from current to specified point
moverel	Moves the current position a given distance
moveto	Moves the current position to a given point
outtext	Displays a string to the viewport
outtextxy	Displays a string to the given position
pieslice	Draws and fills a pie slice
putimage	Outputs a bit image to the screen
putpixel	Plots a pixel at a given point
rectangle	Draws a rectangle
registerbgidriver	Registers a user's driver code to system
registerbgifont	Registers linked stroked font code
restorecrtmode	Returns screen to pregraphics mode
sector	Draws and fills an elliptical pie slice
setactivepage	Sets active page for graphics output
setallpalette	Changes all palette colors as specified
setaspectratio	Changes default aspect ratio
setbkcolor	Changes the background color
setcolor	Changes the default drawing color
setfillpattern	Changes the fill pattern
setfillstyle	Changes the fill style
setgraphbufsize	Changes size of graphics buffer
setgraphmode	Sets the graphics mode and clears screen
setlinestyle	Sets line width and style
setpalette	Changes one palette color
setrgbpalette	Defines colors for IBM 8514 display
settextjustify	Sets text justification for graphics
settextstyle	Sets text characteristics for graphics
setusercharsize	Sets width and height of stroked fonts
setviewport	Sets the viewport size
setvisualpage	Sets the visual page number
setwritemode	Sets writing mode for line drawing
textheight	Returns the height of a string in pixels
textwidth	Returns the width of a string in pixels

With this group of functions, you can obtain professional graphics results. Indeed, you can draw and label presentation quality bar, pie, and line charts.

Graphics Function Call Syntax

The syntax for each graphics function just involves formulating and passing the required arguments. Examine the prototypes for each of the graphics functions; notice that many arguments are self-explanatory. You can find detailed information for others in the library reference.

```
void far arc(int x,int y,int stangle,int endangle,
             int radius);

void far bar(int left,int top,int right,int bottom);

void far bar3d(int left,int top,int right,int bottom,
               int depth, int topflag);

void far circle(int x,int y,int radius);

void far cleardevice(void);

void far clearviewport(void);

void far closegraph(void);

void far detectgraph(int far *graphdriver,int far
                     *graphmode);

void far drawpoly(int numpoints,int far *polypoints);

void far ellipse(int x,int y,int stangle,int endangle,
                 int xradius,int yradius);

void far fillellipse(int x,int y,int xradius,int yradius);

void far fillpoly(int numpoints,int far *polypoints);

void far floodfill(int x,int y,int border);

void far getarccoords(struct arccoordstype far *arccoords);

void far getaspectratio(int far *xasp,int far *yasp);

int far getbkcolor(void);

int far getcolor(void);

char * far getdrivername(void);

struct palettetype *far getdefaultpalette(void);

char *far getdrivername(void);

void far getfillpattern(char far *pattern);
```

```
void far getfillsettings(struct fillsettingstype far
                         *fillinfo);

int far getgraphmode(void);

void far getimage(int left,int top,int right,int bottom,
                  void far *bitmap);

void far getlinesettings(struct linesettingstype far
                         *lineinfo);

int far getmaxcolor(void);

int far getmaxmode(void);

int far getmaxx(void);

int far getmaxy(void);

char * far getmodename(int mode_number);

void far getmoderange(int graphdriver,int far *lomode,
                      int far *himode);

void far getpalette(struct palettetype far *palette);

int far getpalettesize(void);

unsigned far getpixel(int x,int y);

void far gettextsettings(struct textsettingstype far
                         *texttypeinfo);

void far getviewsettings(struct viewporttype far *viewport);

int far getx(void);

int far gety(void);

void far graphdefaults(void);

char * far grapherrormsg(int errorcode);

void far _graphfreemem(void far *ptr,unsigned size);

void far * far _graphgetmem(unsigned size);

int far graphresult(void);

unsigned far imagesize(int left,int top,int right,int
                       bottom);

void far initgraph(int far *graphdriver,
                   int far *graphmode,
                   char far *pathtodriver);
```

```
int far installuserdriver(char far *name,int huge
                      (*detect)(void) );

int far installuserfont(char far *name);

void far line(int x1,int y1,int x2,int y2);

void far linerel(int dx,int dy);

void far lineto(int x,int y);

void far moverel(int dx,int dy);

void far moveto(int x,int y);

void far outtext(char far *textstring);

void far outtextxy(int x,int y,char far *textstring);

void far pieslice(int x,int y,int stangle,int endangle,
                int radius);

void far putimage(int left,int top,void far *bitmap,int
                op);

void far putpixel(int x,int y,int color);

void far rectangle(int left,int top,int right,int bottom);

int registerbgidriver(void(*driver)(void));

int registerbgifont(void (*font)(void));

void far restorecrtmode(void);

void far sector(int X,int Y,int StAngle,int EndAngle,
                int XRadius,int YRadius);

void far setactivepage(int page);

void far setallpalette(struct palettetype far *palette);

void far setaspectratio(int xasp,int yasp);

void far setbkcolor(int color);

void far setcolor(int color);

void far setfillpattern(char far *upattern,int color);

void far setfillstyle(int pattern,int color);

unsigned far setgraphbufsize(unsigned bufsize);

void far setgraphmode(int mode);

void far setlinestyle(int linestyle, unsigned upattern,
                int thickness);
```

```
void far setpalette(int colornum,int color);

void far setrgbpalette(int colornum,
                       int red,int green,int blue);

void far settextjustify(int horiz,int vert);

void far settextstyle(int font,int direction,int charsize);

void far setusercharsize(int multx,int divx,
                         int multy,int divy);

void far setviewport(int left,int top,int right,int
                     bottom,int clip);

void far setvisualpage(int page);

void far setwritemode(int mode);

int far textheight(char far *textstring);

int far textwidth(char far *textstring);
```

Many of these functions will be illustrated in the next sections. You can use an almost intuitive approach when supplying argument values to the various functions, but you should always have your library reference handy. In most cases, you need nothing more than the preceding function prototypes to use your system's graphics capabilities.

Getting Started with Graphics

The graphics environment is very hardware dependent. In fact, most of Turbo C++'s graphics functions will only operate on IBM or compatible computers. Even so, you can use many different video cards and monitors with these systems. If you are writing code for your equipment only, you can write in a more relaxed and less portable manner. However, if your code is to be transported between various video cards and monitors, you must be able to detect what hardware is installed in the system. The first example in this section reports back to you information on the adapter card, video mode, drawing and background colors, and the 16 VGA/EGA drawing colors. The second program was written exclusively for the VGA environment (one with screen dimensions of 640×480 pixels). This program demonstrates many of the graphics primitives with the simplest possible calling sequence. You can easily adapt it to an EGA or CGA screen.

When using graphics, you first need to get the system into graphics mode. This book uses a technique employed by Borland, in many of their examples, for making the switch. While other approaches are possible, this is also the method we prefer and use in the next four examples.

You also need to attach the graphics library to your program code. If you forget, you will be bombarded with error messages stating that the various functions cannot be found. If the graphics library resides in the default directory, you can enter the following command-line statement:

```
tcc program_name.ext graphics.lib
```

Determining Installed Equipment and Modes

The following program uses 18 graphics functions to provide information concerning the graphics environment. These functions include **initgraph, graphresult, grapherrormsg, setbkcolor, setcolor, getmaxx, getmaxy, outtextxy, getaspectratio, getmodename, getbkcolor, getcolor, getpalettesize, setfillstyle, bar, moveto, outtext,** and **closegraph.**

```
/*
 *    A C program that demonstrates how to use several
 *    graphics routines for obtaining information
 *    concerning hardware parameters.
 *    Also draws sample of VGA/EGA default palette.
 *    Copyright (c) Chris H. Pappas and William H. Murray, 1990
 */

#include <graphics.h>
#include <stdio.h>
#include <stdlib.h>
#include <process.h>
#include <conio.h>

main()
{
   char s1[10],s2[10];
   char mcol[5];
   char dcolor[10],bkcolor[10];
   char *drivername;
   char colorlog[16][15]={"Black",
                          "Blue",
                          "Green",
                          "Cyan",
                          "Red",
                          "Magenta",
                          "Brown",
                          "Light Gray",
```

```
                        "Dark Gray",
                        "Light Blue",
                        "Light Green",
                        "Light Cyan",
                        "Light Red",
                        "Light Magenta",
                        "Yellow",
                        "White"};
int gdriver=DETECT,gmode,errorcode;
int xasp,yasp,maxx,maxy,psize,i,deltay,deltax;
double ratio;

initgraph(&gdriver,&gmode,"");

errorcode=graphresult();
if (errorcode != grOk) {
  printf("Graphics Function Error: %s\n",
         grapherrormsg(errorcode));
  printf("Hit key to stop:");
  getch();
  exit(1);
}

setbkcolor(BLACK);
setcolor(WHITE);

maxx=getmaxx();
maxy=getmaxy();
deltay=maxy/24;
deltax=maxx/2;

/* print graphics driver name */
outtextxy(0,deltay,"Graphics Driver:");
outtextxy(deltax,deltay,getdrivername());

/* determine aspect ratio */
getaspectratio(&xasp,&yasp);
itoa(xasp,s1,10);
itoa(yasp,s2,10);
outtextxy(0,deltay*2,"Aspect Ratio (x:y):");
outtextxy(deltax,deltay*2,s1);
outtextxy(deltax+50,deltay*2,s2);

/* get graphics mode */
outtextxy(0,deltay*3,"The video mode is:");
outtextxy(deltax,deltay*3,getmodename(gmode));

/* determine current background color */
outtextxy(0,deltay*4,"The present background color:");
outtextxy(deltax,deltay*4,colorlog[getbkcolor()]);

/* determine current drawing color */
outtextxy(0,deltay*5,"The present drawing color:");
outtextxy(deltax,deltay*5,colorlog[getcolor()]);
```

```
psize=getpalettesize();
itoa(psize,mcol,10);
outtextxy(0,deltay*6,"Max. drawing colors:");
outtextxy(deltax,deltay*6,mcol);
outtextxy(0,deltay*7,"VGA/EGA 16 color palette:");
for (i=0;i<16;i++) {
  setfillstyle(SOLID_FILL,i);
  bar(deltax,deltay*(i+7),deltax+10,deltay*(i+7)+10);
  moveto(deltax+15,deltay*(i+7));
  outtext(colorlog[i]);
}

getch();
closegraph();

return (0);
}
```

The **initgraph** function is passed arguments that will automatically detect the adapter card and set the video mode to the highest mode possible for the hardware. This is done by passing DETECT to the graphics driver argument. This system is automatically placed on the 640 × 480 VGA mode with 16 drawing colors. If this function call fails, an error code can be intercepted and reported to the user with the **graphresult** function. As mentioned, Borland uses this technique in their examples and this chapter does as well.

Now step through the remainder of the program, examining each function call along the way. When you compare the function call with the function prototype given in the earlier graphics section, notice that the argument values are fairly easy to understand without another reference. Enter this program and give it a try. Don't forget to link the graphics library to your program. Tinker with the various function calls and see what you can learn. You will be impressed with the information that you can obtain with simple graphics function calls in this program. A typical screen output is shown in Figure 15-1.

Using Various Graphics Primitives

The following program uses several new graphics functions. These functions include **circle**, **bar3d**, **ellipse**, **pieslice**, **sector**, and **settextstyle**. This program will demonstrate how to use the various graphics primitives in the simplest possible manner. Notice the use of enumerated types for the colors, fill modes, and text styles.

```
Graphics Driver:                       EGAUGA
Aspect Ratio (x:y):                    10000 10000
The video mode is:                     640 x 480 UGA
The present background color:          Black
The present drawing color:             White
Max. drawing colors:                   16
UGA/EGA 16 color palette:                Black
                                       ■ Blue
                                       ≡ Green
                                       ⁒ Cyan
                                       ⁒ Red
                                       ⧅ Magenta
                                       ⧅ Brown
                                       ⊞ Light Gray
                                       ⨯ Dark Gray
                                       ▦ Light Blue
                                       ⁙ Light Green
                                       ⁙ Light Cyan
                                       ⁙ Light Red
                                       ⁙ Light Magenta
                                       ⁙ Yellow
                                       ⁙ White
```

Figure 15-1.   Current system graphics parameters with VGA/EGA 16-color palette

```
/*
*    A C program that demonstrates how to use several
*    graphics primitives on the VGA screen.
*    Copyright (c) Chris H. Pappas and William H. Murray, 1990
*/

#include <graphics.h>
#include <stdio.h>
#include <stdlib.h>
#include <process.h>
#include <conio.h>

main()
{
  int gdriver=DETECT,gmode,errorcode;
  int midx,midy;

  initgraph(&gdriver,&gmode,"");

  errorcode=graphresult();
  if (errorcode != grOk) {
    printf("Graphics Function Error: %s\n",
           grapherrormsg(errorcode));
    printf("Hit key to stop:");
    getch();
    exit(1);
  }
```

```
    setbkcolor(BLACK);

    /* draw a small circle */
    setcolor(BLUE);
    circle(50,50,40);

    /* draw a two-dimensional bar, outline & fill */
    setcolor(GREEN);
    setfillstyle(SOLID_FILL,GREEN);
    bar(100,10,150,90);

    /* draw a three-dimensional bar, outline & fill */
    setcolor(CYAN);
    setfillstyle(LINE_FILL,CYAN);
    bar3d(200,20,250,90,15,1);

    /* draw an ellipse */
    setcolor(RED);
    ellipse(400,50,0,360,70,40);

    /* draw an ellipse, outline & fill */
    setcolor(MAGENTA);
    setfillstyle(SLASH_FILL,MAGENTA);
    fillellipse(50,200,40,70);

    /* draw a pie slice, outline & fill */
    setcolor(BROWN);
    setfillstyle(HATCH_FILL,BROWN);
    pieslice(150,200,0,45,100);

    /* draw an elliptical pie slice, outline & fill */
    setcolor(LIGHTGRAY);
    setfillstyle(WIDE_DOT_FILL,LIGHTGRAY);
    sector(350,200,0,135,75,50);

    /* print some fancy text */
    settextstyle(DEFAULT_FONT,HORIZ_DIR,3);
    outtextxy(50,400,"Now this is fancy!");

    getch();
    closegraph();

    return (0);
}
```

Your library reference contains the full list of color, fill styles, and fonts. The arguments used in this example are entered directly as numeric values. This is usually the easiest way to implement any graphics command, and also the most restrictive. The technique is restrictive because the argument values are set for one video mode only. For example, the function **outtextxy** uses the VGA screen coordinate values (50,400). If used on a CGA or EGA screen, the vertical position exceeds the maximum value for either screen. A

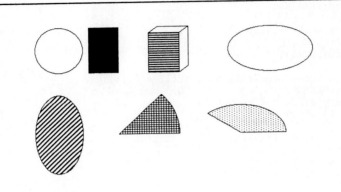

Figure 15-2.   Graphics primitives and fonts coming to life

better approach is to detect the video mode and scale the graphics to that screen. Of course, this approach also requires much more programming, as you will see in the next two examples. This example produces a VGA screen shown in Figure 15-2.

Toward More Advanced Graphics

Graphics are a way of communicating ideas and concepts in a pictorial format. Depending on your area of interest, you may want to express information in the form of bar, pie, or line charts. If you have a scientific or engineering background, you might be more interested in plotting a mathematical, scientific, or engineering equation. The two examples in this section do just that. The first example will plot a damped sine wave. This is a simple mathematical equation that involves the trigonometric sine function multiplied by the natural number (e) raised to a power. The plot of this function is similar to the physical representation of an oscillating spring or auto shock absorber. The second example will show you how to create a presentation quality pie chart. This program will allow a user to enter data on the various pie slices, scale them to size, and plot them correctly on an EGA or VGA screen.

Plotting a Damped Sine Wave

The only new graphics function in this example is **lineto**. This function connects the various points generated by the mathematical equation.

```
/*
 *      A C program that demonstrates how to correctly draw a
 *      damped sine wave on either an EGA or VGA screen.
 *      Copyright (c) Chris H. Pappas and William H. Murray, 1990
 */

#include <graphics.h>
#include <conio.h>
#include <process.h>
#include <math.h>

main()
{
   int gdriver=DETECT,gmode,errorcode;
   int midy,maxx,i,y;

   initgraph(&gdriver,&gmode,"");

   errorcode=graphresult();
   if (errorcode != grOk) {
     printf("Graphics Function Error: %s\n",
            grapherrormsg(errorcode));
     printf("Hit key to stop:");
     getch();
     exit(1);
   }

   setbkcolor(BLUE);
   setcolor(WHITE);

   /* get maximum x & y coordinate values for mode */
   maxx=getmaxx();
   midy=getmaxy()/2;

   /* draw several cycles of a damped sine wave */
   moveto(0,midy);
   for (i=0;i<maxx;i++) {
```

For the example, the total would be 30 + 10 + 20 = 60. Therefore, a 60.0 would be stored in *totalwedge*. Now, each wedge is scaled so that it takes a proportional amount of 360 degrees.

```
for (i=0;i<nwedges;i++)
  wedgeangle[i]=(wedgesize[i]*360.0)/totalwedge;
```

For the first slice of 30, *wedgeangle[0]* will be 180 degrees. For *wedgeangle[1]*, the angle will be 60 degrees and, finally, for *wedgeangle[2]*, the angle will be 120 degrees. Now, 180 + 60 + 120 adds up to the required 360 degrees, or one whole pie. These values will serve as the arc size for each pie slice.

In the complete listing shown earlier, notice that the initialization of the graphics mode is done in the same manner as previous examples. You can use this code as a template for your graphics work. The pie chart is plotted with the following portion of code:

```
startangle=0.0;
endangle=wedgeangle[0];
for (i=0;i<nwedges;i++) {
  setcolor(BLACK);
  setfillstyle(SOLID_FILL,BLUE+i);
  pieslice(midx/2,midy,(int)startangle,(int)endangle,midy/2);
  startangle+=wedgeangle[i];
  endangle+=wedgeangle[i+1];
}
```

The first pie slice is drawn, starting at angle 0 and plotting in the counter-clockwise direction 180 degrees. The starting angle is given by *startangle* and the end of the pie arc by *endangle*. The *endangle* value for the first pie wedge is 180. The pie slices are drawn in black, but filled with an indexed color and solid pattern. The first slice is blue. After the first slice is drawn, the *startangle* value is set to the *endangle* value of the previous slice. The remaining slices are drawn in a similar manner.

The legend and chart titles are drawn last. Examine the complete program and see how these items are placed. Notice in particular that the text for main labels is centered with the **settextjustify** function. Figures 15-4 and 15-5 show two variations on the pie chart that you can produce with this program.

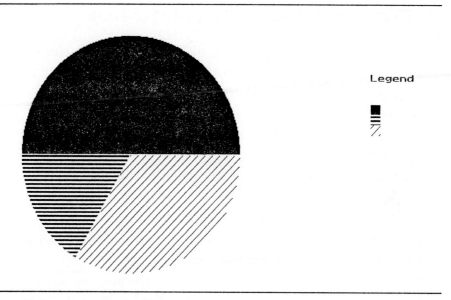

Figure 15-4.   A simple pie chart

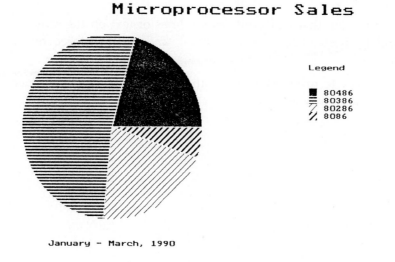

Figure 15-5.   A pie chart with title, legend, labels, and subtitle

PUTTING YOUR KNOWLEDGE TO WORK

1. Explain what the term "hardware dependence" means with respect to the functions described in this chapter.

2. Why aren't the functions described in this chapter part of the ANSI standard?

3. Is there an alternate function call to **bioscom** for setting the serial communications port?

4. Name the ANSI functions that you might use in place of several DOS functions. (Think time and date.)

5. What is a graphics primitive? List several.

6. Use your library reference to determine the various fill styles, line types, and colors available in the graphics environment.

7. Devise a program that will plot a bar chart. The program will allow you to enter up to ten numbers representing the height of individual bars. The program will scale the bars so that the largest bar occupies the full height of the chart. The bar widths, when plotted, will be scaled to fill the full width of the chart. Thus, if two bars are plotted, they will be twice as wide as four bars would be.

8. Write a program that will print several lines of text on the screen. One line will be horizontal, another vertical, and another three times the normal size.

9. Is there a way to print color text to the graphics screen? Experiment to determine your answer.

16

ASSEMBLY LANGUAGE: A SOLID FOUNDATION

In this chapter you will learn

- About the members of the Intel family of microprocessors

- What real and protected modes are

- How to represent numbers in the binary, decimal, and hexadecimal numbering systems

- How to convert from one numbering system to another

- Data types and sizes incorporated by the various microprocessors

- Microprocessor registers and register sizes

- Programming modes available with the Intel family

- The structure and fields of an assembly language program

- Information about assembler directives

Studying assembly language programming is both rewarding and technically challenging. A mastery of assembly language programming provides you with the fundamental constructs that you need to create, design, understand, and modify programs that can have absolute control over the system hardware.

In early programming, all code was machine code. The instructions were written in binary or hexadecimal and were decoded by the hardware to perform their intended operation. As programs grew in size and complexity, it became apparent that a more productive code development method was necessary.

Assembly language programming was the solution. It is easier to understand and will automatically keep track of the many details inherent in machine code. In addition, it does not contain all of the overhead of a high-level language and generates code that executes very quickly.

The next four chapters cover the fundamentals of assembly language programming. In this chapter, you will learn about the Intel family of microprocessors, the difference between real and protected modes, computer arithmetic, data types available in assembly language, microprocessor registers, assembly language addressing techniques, the structure for writing programs, and the various directives frequently encountered in programs. In Chapters 17, 18, and 19, you will learn fundamental programming concepts, how to write powerful macros and procedures, and how to perform basic input/output operations. These chapters include many example programs that tap the system's powerful BIOS and DOS interrupts.

If you haven't studied Chapter 3, you should do so now. Pay particular attention to the editing, assembling, and linking process. The following chapters assume that you have already worked through the chapters pertaining to C or that you already know a high-level language such as BASIC or Pascal.

THE INTEL FAMILY TREE

The following description of the Intel family will help you appreciate all of the features and advantages of 80486/8088 Intel microprocessors. You need this information before you learn to write assembly language programs.

Here is a chronological list of the Intel microprocessors used by IBM and IBM compatibles:

1978	The 8086, 8088 (16- and 8-bit processors)
1984	The 80286 (16-bit processor with protected mode and real mode options)
1987	The 80386 (32-bit processor with protected mode and real mode options)
1989	The 80486 (extended capabilities of 80386)

Intel has delivered microprocessors that are upward compatible with earlier Intel chips. This means, for example, that programs written for the 8088 microprocessor will operate on the 80486 microprocessor. Every previous generation's instruction set becomes a subset of the new generation's instruction set. At the assembly language level, you must understand the hardware you are addressing. For example, 8088 microprocessors can use 16-bit registers directly, but not the extended 32-bit registers of the 80486/80386 microprocessors. Such hardware considerations will be discussed later in this chapter.

REAL VERSUS PROTECTED MODES

The 80486, 80386, and 80286 microprocessors can operate in real and protected modes. Real mode is the current mode used by DOS and is a single-process mode. Real mode is also the default mode used by the whole family of Intel chips. Typically, real mode is limited to 1 MB of directly addressable address space. The 80486/80286 microprocessors can also run in protected mode. Protected mode is a multitasking, multiple-process mode. The protected mode environment allows multiple programs to run safely. It also offers a much greater address range.

Fortunately, there is very little difference between a basic assembly language program written for real mode and one written for protected mode. This book concentrates on real mode programs. For information on protected mode programming, see *Assembly Language Programming Under OS/2* (Murray and Pappas, Osborne/McGraw-Hill, 1989).

NUMBERING SYSTEMS

When learning assembly language programming, you need to understand how a computer stores information. How is data represented internally? The computer only understands voltages—in particular, the presence or absence of two reliable voltage levels. Think of these voltages as either ON or OFF, a 1 or 0. The logical 1 or 0 is called a *bit* and is the smallest data unit. The computer uses these *binary* numbers to represent data. The development of different symbolic code representations was a direct result of this incompatibility between a decimal and a binary numbering scheme.

The ASCII code (American Standard Code for Information Interchange) was invented to represent all of the symbols that you commonly associate with a typewriter keyboard. Other numeric codes were invented to enable the representation of numeric values in a form that the computer can understand. The two's complement allows the computer to represent both positive and negative whole numbers. For assembly language programmers, one of the most important numeric codes is the hexadecimal code, which increases the readability and reliability of information represented in binary form.

Binary Numbers

The decimal numbering system consists of ten (deci) unique symbols (the digits 0 through 9). Binary code, in contrast, has only two (bi) unique symbols (0 and 1).

Consider the decimal number 6231. You can think of the decimal, or base 10, number 6231 in the following manner:

```
6  2  3  1
```

$$1 * 10^0 = 1$$

$$3 * 10^1 = 30$$

$$2 * 10^2 = 200$$

$$6 * 10^3 = 6000$$

_____

6231

The conversion was made by multiplying each value in the number by the base value raised to increasing exponential powers, from the least to the most significant position.

The same principle of conversion will work for any length of binary number. The binary number 1011, when converted to decimal, looks like this:

1 0 1 1

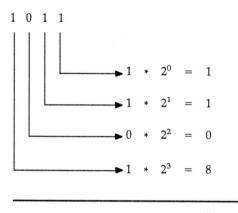

$$1 * 2^0 = 1$$
$$1 * 2^1 = 1$$
$$0 * 2^2 = 0$$
$$1 * 2^3 = 8$$

11

In this case, the diagram uses base 2 and raises the new base to increasing exponential powers, starting with the least significant bit (LSB) and working through to the most significant bit (MSB). To convert from some other base to decimal, use the same procedure, substituting the other base when raising to increasing exponential powers.

You have just seen how easily you can convert a number from binary to decimal. To reverse the process, converting from decimal to binary, you simply subtract the number of exponential powers of 2 that are in the number to be converted. Suppose the number that you want to convert to binary is the decimal number 11. This includes a 2^3, or 8. That leaves a remainder of 3. There is no 2^2, or 4, but there is a 2^1, or 2. Subtracting that leaves you with a 1 and you do have one 2^0, or 1. This gives you a binary conversion of 1011 in binary.

For larger binary numbers, you can also use a method involving a series of repeated divisions. This technique uses the base to which you want the number converted as the divisor, and the number to be converted as the dividend. Here's how you would use this method to convert the decimal number 49 to binary:

Dividend	Divisor	Result	Remainder	
49	2	24	1	Answer = 110001
24	2	12	0	
12	2	6	0	
6	2	3	0	
3	2	1	1	
1	2	0	1	

You can use this method to convert a decimal number to any other base. To change 512 to hexadecimal, simply substitute 512 for the dividend and 16 for the divisor.

Binary Addition and Subtraction

Binary addition and subtraction are similar to decimal addition and subtraction. However, you are generating a carry or borrow in some power of 2 rather than a power of 10. Here are two examples:

$$
\begin{array}{r}
26 \\
+\ 86 \\
\hline
112
\end{array}
$$

In this example, when you add the two 6s you generate a carry into the next significant position, or $1 * 10^1$, thereby adding 10 to the next column. You now add the 8 and the 2 plus the carry, generate another carry to the 10^2 column, and generate a sum of 10.

Here's the example of binary addition:

```
  1011   (11)
+ 0011   (03)
  ────
  1110   (14)
```

In this example, the 1 + 1 in the first column gives a sum of 0 and produces a carry. The next 1 + 1 + carry gives a total of 1 and a carry of 1. The third column adds 0 + 0 + carry, giving a total of 1 with no carry. Finally, the last column adds a 1 + 0, giving a result of 1 without a carry. The answer is 1110, or 14 decimal.

Binary subtraction works on the same principles as decimal subtraction. However, when a borrow is generated from the next significant position, it is the value of 2 raised to some exponential power instead of 10 raised to some power.

For example:

```
  1011
− 0110
  ────
  0101
```

In the LSB, there's no problem subtracting 0 from 1, or subtracting 1 from 1 in the next significant bits. Subtracting 1 from a 0 requires a borrow to the next significant bit, which happens to be $1 * 2^3$, or 8 in decimal. Now subtract the $1 * 2^2$, leaving a difference of $1 * 2^2$. This gives you the 1 in the third column and a final result of 0101.

Binary Multiplication and Division

Binary multiplication and division are really just a repeated series of additions or subtractions. For example:

```
      1011
×      101
    ──────
      1011
     0000
    1011
    ──────
    110111
```

To multiply 1011 by 101, you just need to repeat the multiplicand, holding place position, and add. Don't forget to add in any carries generated.

Performing binary division is just as easy as multiplication, but in this case you repeatedly subtract the divisor:

```
            000111
       ┌─────────
101    │ 100011
        −101
        ─────
          111
        − 101
        ─────
          101
        −  101
        ─────
             0
```

You can apply these principles for binary multiplication and division to numbering systems of other bases.

Bytes

Remember, since all of the programs and data are stored and executed on the computer, the computer architecture will determine the format and range for both the code and the data.

Computers do not randomly store varying length binary numbers or bits. As we know, in the 80486/8088 architectural environments, a hardware memory location is a sequence of 8 consecutive bits known as a *byte*.

The bit positions are numbered from the least significant bit, 0, to the most significant bit, 7. Figure 16-1 shows several consecutive memory locations, each holding one byte's worth of data. This information could be a machine instruction, an address to another memory location, numeric data, or even character data.

Eight bits can generate 256 unique states. This allows one memory location to contain the binary representation for all positive numbers between 0 and 255. This memory location can also hold one ASCII character representation (see Appendix A). A *word* is the technical term for the number of bits stored in a single memory location. Early computer architecture only had 4-bit memory locations, so a word represented 4 bits at that

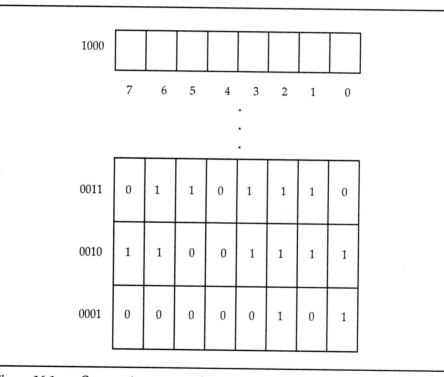

Figure 16-1.   Consecutive memory locations 1 byte (8 bits) in width

Converting from hexadecimal to decimal uses the same underlying principles discussed earlier for converting from binary to decimal. To convert
9AC3 to decimal:

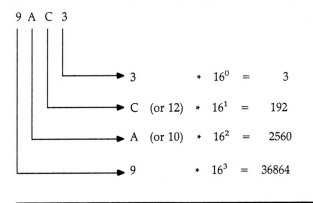

3	$* \ 16^0 \ =$	3
C (or 12)	$* \ 16^1 \ =$	192
A (or 10)	$* \ 16^2 \ =$	2560
9	$* \ 16^3 \ =$	36864

39619

Remember, 9AC3 or 39619 represented in binary would look like

1001101011000011

or

10011010   11000011

if stored in two-byte memory locations. Translated into hexadecimal, the
number is 9A C3.

Signed Numbers

Using the 8-bit byte architecture of the Intel family, take a closer look at
integer data representation. When all 8 bits are used to represent positive
whole numbers, you can represent values from 0 (00000000) to 255
(11111111). Adding 1 to 255 (11111111) brings you full circle back to 0
(00000000).

Representing positive and negative whole numbers then becomes a
compromise because you have to indicate the sign of the number by using
one of the bit positions. This leaves 7 bits to represent the numeric value.

The value 2^7 enables you to represent values from 0 (0000000) to 127 (1111111). Since you are dealing with binary values, reducing by one the number of bits will halve the range of unique states.

The *sign-magnitude data representation* takes the most significant bit to hold the sign of the value. A 0 in the MSB represents a positive number and a 1 in the MSB indicates a negative value.

0000 0101   represents a +5

1000 0101   represents a −5

What about the numeric value 0? Theoretically, you could have

0000 0000   representing a +0
1000 0000   representing a −0

As you might guess, having an 8-bit byte used for this data storage format will require a new set of rules and arithmetic. The first rule specifies that the numeric value 0 will always be represented as positive, 0000 0000.

Because the number of bits used to represent the value of a number has been reduced to 7, you can only specify values between 0, and + or −127.

0000 0000	+0
−0000 0001	+1
1111 1111	−127

Notice that this example did not give you the correct result. In order to perform arithmetic operations on numbers represented in sign-magnitude, you need 1111 1111 to represent a −1. Another example will show the result of subtracting +2 from −2.

1111 1110	− 2
−0000 0010	+2
1111 1100	− 4

If you did a binary conversion of 1111 1100, assuming that the MSB is reserved for the sign of the number, 111 1100 is equivalent to 124. The 1 in the MSB indicates that this is the negative number −124. Then why does the previous example indicate the result is −4?

Two's Complement

For addition and subtraction to work properly on numbers stored in sign-magnitude notation, the numbers must be represented in *two's complement* form. The preceding examples showed the need to represent positive and negative numbers as follows:

0000 0100	+4
0000 0011	+3
0000 0010	+2
0000 0001	+1
0000 0000	0
1111 1111	−1
1111 1110	−2
1111 1101	−3
1111 1100	−4

Note that this format continues to reserve the MSB for the sign of the number. When doing addition and subtraction of two's complement numbers, remember that the result will also be in two's complement form. For example:

```
    0000  0100        +4
 + 1111  1101        − 3
1)  0000  0001        +1     (the carry generated is ignored)
```

To generate the negative two's complement representation of a value, invert each bit and add +1. The next example will show how to change the sign of +5:

```
  0000  0101           +5

  1111  1010           (each bit is complemented)
+ 0000  0001           (a +1 is added)
  ─────────────
  1111  1011           −5
```

Converting in the opposite direction is just as easy. The following example shows how to convert a −4 to its positive counterpart:

```
  1111  1100           −4

  0000  0011           (each bit is complemented)
+ 0000  0001           (a +1 is added)
  ─────────────
  0000  0100           +4
```

Here is one last example:

```
   1111 1001   −7 (two's complement notation)
+  1111 1000   −8 (two's complement notation)
  ───────────
1) 1111 0001   −15 (two's complement notation)
```

Sign Extending

Since the internal data registers on the 80286/8088 processors are 16 bits wide, and one memory location is 1 byte, you may need to add two numbers of different sizes at some point in a program. You might want to add an 8-bit two's complement number represented in sign-magnitude notation to a 16-bit number stored in the same data format.

```
        0000 0101         +5
+  1111 1111 1111 1101     −3
─────────────────────    ─────
```

In this example, you would just append 0000 0000 to the most significant bits of +5. What if you were dealing with an 8-bit negative number?

```
        1111 1111         −1
+  0000 0000 0000 0100     +4
─────────────────────    ─────
```

In this example, since the 8-bit value was negative, you had to append eight 1's: 1111 1111. The general rule in sign extending is to append eight 1's or 0's to the most significant bits, depending upon the sign value of the number. Extending the two preceding negative 8-bit values would give

```
0000 0000 0000 0101     (16-bit representation of +5)
1111 1111 1111 1111     (16-bit representation of −1)
```

The same general rule applies to the 80386 with its 32-bit internal registers. However, you must append 16 rather than eight 1's or 0's.

Binary Operations

The microprocessor does nothing more than a repeated series of bit comparisons when executing even the simplest operations of addition and subtraction. Although various "adder circuits" are included within the CPU, ultimately even these circuits rely on bit-by-bit comparisons.

These bit-by-bit comparisons are a very simple process since there can only be three possible bit-pair combinations. Both of the bits can be a 0. Either one of the two bits may be a 1 or both of the bits may be a 1. Whether the operation being performed is addition, subtraction, multiplication, or division, a simple series of repeated comparisons, based on the previous three bit-pair combinations, is applied.

For addition, the following rules are applied, starting from the least significant bit:

- Adding two 0 bits sets the sum flag to 0.

- If only one of the bits is a 1, the sum flag is a 1.

- If both bits are a 1, the sum flag is set to 0 and the carry flag is set to 1.

This process is repeated on each successive bit, taking into consideration any previous carries or borrows. The CPU keeps track of each individual comparison in an internal storage area, and the result appears to you as binary addition.

Although the CPU is hardwired to perform the operations of addition, subtraction, multiplication, and division, you have access to other bit comparison operations. These operations include the logical AND, OR, EXCLUSIVE OR, SHIFT LEFT, SHIFT RIGHT, ROTATE LEFT, ROTATE RIGHT, and COMPLEMENT. When discussing the logical operations of AND, OR, and COMPLEMENT, it helps to see the bit representations as TRUE or FALSE flags rather than numeric values.

The 80486/80386 microprocessors also have several mnemonics that can manipulate individual bits: **bts**, **btr**, and **btc**.

The Logical AND

Note: If you have read Chapter 6, you may wish to skip sections on AND, OR, and XOR here.

The logical AND operation compares two bits. If both bits are a 1, the result is a 1. Note that this is different from binary addition, where the comparison of two 1 bits would result in a sum flag set to 0 and the carry flag set to 1.

Logical AND

Bit 0	Bit 1	Result
0	0	0
0	1	0
1	0	0
1	1	1

The AND operation is often used to select out, or mask, certain bit positions. For example, you could clear the most significant 4 bits of an unpacked decimal number before performing a decimal multiplication or division. You would accomplish this by ANDing the unpacked decimal number to 0000 1111. For example:

```
      0101 1011 (data)
AND   0000 1111 (mask)
      0000 1011
```

The Logical OR

The logical OR operation compares 2 bits and generates a 1 result if either or both bits are a 1. The OR operation is useful for setting specified bit positions.

Logical OR

Bit 0	Bit 1	Result
0	0	0
0	1	1
1	0	1
1	1	1

For instance, you can set the most significant bit in an 8-bit number by ORing the number with 1000 0000. For example:

```
     0111 1010
OR   1000 0110
     1111 1110
```

The Exclusive OR (XOR)

The exclusive OR operation, XOR, compares two bits and returns a result of 1 when only the two bits are complementary. This logical operation can be very useful when you need to complement specified bit positions, as in the case for computer graphics applications.

Exclusive OR

Bit 0	Bit 1	Result
0	0	0
0	1	1
1	0	1
1	1	0

In the following example, the middle 4 bits of the 8-bit number will be complemented by XORing them with 0011 1100. For example:

```
        1110 0111
XOR     0011 1100
        ─────────
        1101 1011
```

SHIFT LEFT/RIGHT (shl/shr)

The SHIFT LEFT/RIGHT, ROTATE LEFT/RIGHT, and complement operations operate on single operands. The shift instructions provide an excellent method for efficiently doubling or halving a number. This method requires fewer bytes and fewer machine cycles than an actual multiplication or division instruction.

With unsigned numbers, shifting the number one position to the left and filling the LSB with a 0 will double the number's value. For example:

```
shl   0011 0001    (49 decimal)
      ─────────
      0110 0010    (98 decimal)
```

To halve an unsigned number, just shift the bits one position to the right and fill the MSB position with a 0. For example:

```
shr   0010 1010    (42 decimal)
      ─────────
      0001 0101    (21 decimal)
```

Rotate Left/Right (ror/rol)

The rotate instructions enable you to rearrange the bits in a number. As with the shift operations, you can do this in a left or right direction. Unlike the shift operations, which lose the bit position that was shifted out left or right, the rotate operation moves the bit that falls off the one end and rotates it to fill in the vacated position on the other end. For example:

ror   0010 1111   (rotate right)

          1001 0111

rol   0010 1111   (rotate left)

          0101 1110

DATA TYPES

All programming languages have data types. Assembly language is a strongly typed language in that various data sizes cannot be intermixed. Before you can write source code intelligently, you need a good understanding of assembly language data types.

The following sections discuss the data types provided in the 80486/8088 programming environment. You'll learn about the standard data types associated with the Intel family of microprocessors. In addition, you'll learn about two new types that are unique to the 80486/80386, bits and pwords.

Characters

The 8 bits that make up a byte do not always represent numeric values. The 7-bit ASCII code allows the representation of alphabetic and numeric characters. It is an arbitrary assignment of a binary pattern to each letter, digit, and special character originally associated with a standard typewriter keyboard. There are also ASCII representations for special control codes (see the ASCII table in Appendix A).

The 7-bit ASCII code can represent 128 unique symbols and codes. The eighth bit is often used for a data transmission and retrieval error detection code. Some manufacturers of character ROM chips use this eighth bit to access an extended character set. Adding an additional bit doubles the number of uniquely representable symbols to 256. This allows the representation of special foreign language symbols, mathematical symbols, and graphics symbols.

Bit

The bit data type allows a program to access and change directly any selected bit within a bit string. The mnemonic **dbit** allows the definition/initialization of bit data types. To modify and verify the selected bit, assemblers incorporate eight new instructions, **bt**, **btc**, **bts**, **btr**, **bsf**, **bsr**, **ibts**, and **xbts** (more on these instructions later).

Byte

The byte data type was covered in the "Numbering Systems" section of this chapter. Remember, a byte is made up of 8 bits.

Words

Two bytes form a word. A word will allow you to go beyond the unsigned integer byte value of 255 (FF in hexadecimal) to 65535 (or FFFF). The assembler can actually store and manipulate integers as words. Memory locations of string data and integer variables are kept track of by 16-bit address pointers, with values ranging from 0000h to FFFFh.

When an integer word is stored in memory, the 2 bytes are stored in reverse order. The least significant byte is stored first, followed by the most significant byte. The MSB is stored in the next higher address in memory. Remember that the lower order byte is stored at the lower address and the higher order byte at the higher address. For example, storing the value 3456h in memory would look like this:

Memory Address	Value
0000 0000	56h
0000 0001	34h

Under most circumstances, you needn't worry about this addressing/storage scheme. All memory instructions understand the storage format and make all of the necessary transfers. You do need to understand this storage method when tracing through memory—as in a memory dump. The debugging capabilities of assemblers makes this possible. As far as the microprocessor is concerned, it is seeing a 16-bit word, not two 8-bit bytes, as shown in Figure 16-2.

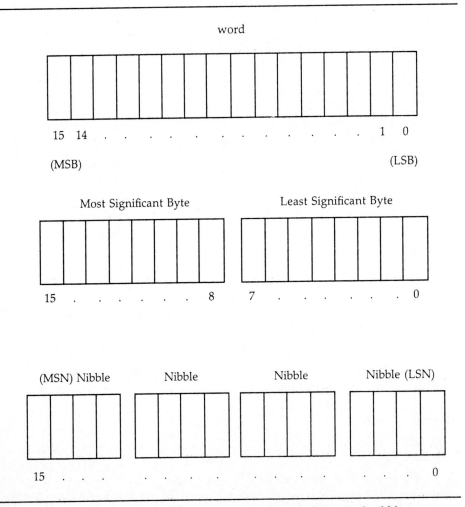

Figure 16-2.   The breakdown of a word data type into bytes and nibbles

Doublewords

A doubleword is made up of two words. Doublewords are 32 bits wide and consist of two consecutively stored adjacent words that evaluate to a number in the range $-2^{32} -1$ to $+2^{32} -1$. The 32-bit doubleword allows arithmetic operations to take advantage of additional precision due to the field width. This allows you to represent very large and small numbers, both in integer and floating-point format.

Doublewords are stored much like words. In this case, the lower order word is stored at the lower address and the higher order word at the next highest memory location. The 32-bit doubleword is stored as a series of 4 bytes, starting with the LSB and ending with the MSB. Figure 16-3 is an illustration of what the number 1234ABCDh would look like stored in memory.

Pword

Between doublewords and quadwords is pword, the second data type directly accessible to the 80486/80386 programmer. A pword is three words, or 48 bits, and can represent values between $-2^{48} -1$ and $+2^{48} -1$. The storage scheme is consistent with all previous examples.

Quadword

A quadword is made up of four words. Numeric quadwords evaluate to a constant in the range $-2^{64} -1$ to $+2^{64} -1$. The storage scheme is consistent with all previous examples. The least significant word is stored at the lowest memory location, up through to the most significant word, which is stored in the highest consecutive memory address. As an example, the number 1234567890ABCDEF stored in memory would look like Figure 16-4.

Tenbytes

The tenbyte data type is an 80-bit value that you can use to store extremely large numbers or character data. This is the largest defined data type for the 80486/8088 microprocessors. Numeric values stored as tenbytes evaluate to a constant in the range $-10^{18} -1$ to $+10^{18} -1$. The storage scheme is identical in structure to doublewords and quadwords. The LSB is stored in the lower memory location, through to the MSB, which is stored in the highest consecutive memory address.

(e)ax   The **(e)ax**, or accumulator, register is most often used for storing temporary data. Many instructions are optimized so that they work slightly faster on data in the accumulator register than on data in other registers.

With division instructions, for instance, the accumulator holds all or part of the dividend before the operation and the quotient afterward. With multiplication instructions, the accumulator holds one of the factors before the operation and all or part of the result afterward. In I/O operations to and from ports, the accumulator holds the data being transferred.

(e)bx   You can use the **(e)bx** register to point to the base address of a data object.

(e)cx   You can use the **(e)cx** register to hold the count for instructions that do looping or other repeated operations. These include the loop instructions, certain jump instructions, repeated string instructions, and shifts and rotates.

(e)dx   The **(e)dx**, or data, register is most often used for storing temporary data. With division instructions operating on word values, **(e)dx** holds the upper word of the dividend before the operation and the remainder afterward. With multiplication instructions operating on word values, **(e)dx** holds the upper word of one of the factors before the operation and the upper word of the result afterward. In I/O operations to and from ports, **(e)dx** holds the number of the port to be accessed.

Index, Pointer, and Base Registers

The physical address of any given element within a selected segment is obtained by the combination of the segment address and the offset. This offset can be contained in any of the pointer, base, or index registers.

Stack operations are facilitated by the stack segment selector **ss** and the (32) 16-bit stack pointer **(e)sp** or base pointer **(e)bp** register pair. Offsets into the data segments **ds** and **es** are obtained from the base register **(e)bx**. You can obtain more complicated data manipulations by using the source index **(e)si** and destination index **(e)di** in conjunction with the currently active data segment.

Segment Registers

The 80286/8088 microprocessors provide four segment address registers: **cs, ds, ss, es.** The 80486/80386 have two additional segment registers: **fs** and **gs.** The segment registers allow the separation of code, data, stack, and other user-definable extra segments. The segmentation scheme permits program modularity and larger programs. The segment registers are shown in Figure 16-6.

The code of the currently executing program, residing in memory, is addressed by the **cs** (code segment) register. The base of the currently active data segment is addressed by the **ds** (data segment) register. Stacks that are typically used for intermediate results and subroutine calls are also given their own segment of memory and the base address of the currently active stack segment is contained in the **ss** (stack segment) register. You

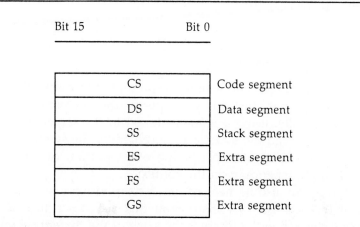

Figure 16-6.   Segment registers

also have access to the currently active data segment, called the extra segment (**es**). The 80486/80386 may have up to three concurrently active data segments addressed by the **es**, **fs**, and **gs** segment registers.

Segment Length

The 80286/8088 can store addresses as 16-bit word values. Therefore, the maximum unsigned value that you can store as an address is 65,535 (0FFFFh). Yet the processors can actually access much larger addresses. The highest possible address is 1 megabyte (0FFFFFh) in real mode.

You specify addresses larger than 65,535 bytes by combining two segmented word addresses: a 16-bit segment and a 16-bit offset within the segment. A common syntax for showing segmented addresses is the segment:offset format. For example, you would represent an address with a segment of 02222h and an offset of 01234h as 2222:1234. In real mode, the address 2222:1234 represents a physical 20-bit address. You can calculate this address by multiplying the segment portion of the address by 16 (10h) and then adding the offset portion, as illustrated here:

```
   22220h    segment times 10h
 + 1234h     offset
 --------
   23454h    physical address
```

Near and Far Addresses

In assembly language, you cannot represent addresses directly in the segment:offset format. Instead, you specify the segment portion of the address symbolically, using a name assigned to the segment in the source code. Then you assign the address represented by the symbol to one of the segment registers. You can specify the offset portion of an address in a number of ways, depending on the context.

An address can also be near or far. A near address is simply the offset portion of the address. Any instruction that accesses a near address will assume that the segment address is the same as the current segment for the type of address being accessed (typically a code segment for code or a data segment for data).

A far address consists of both the segment and offset portions of the address. You can access far addresses from any segment. Both the segment and offset must be provided for instructions that access far addresses. Far addresses are more flexible because you can use them for larger programs and larger data objects. However, near addresses are more efficient, since they produce smaller code and can be accessed more quickly.

Status and Control Registers

The *flags* register is a 16-bit register containing status bits that control various instructions and reflect the current status of the processor. In the 80486/80386, the flags register (called **eflags**) is extended to 32 bits. Some bits are undefined, so there are actually 9 flags for real mode, 11 flags (including a 2-bit flag) for 80286 protected mode, and 13 flags for the 80386.

Flags

Six of the flags, called *status flags,* are changed by, and provide necessary information for, arithmetic and logical control decisions. These are the **cf** (carry flag), **pf** (parity flag), **af** (auxiliary carry flag), **zf** (zero flag), **sf** (sign flag), and **of** (overflow flag), as seen in Figure 16-7.

- The carry flag (**cf**) is set to 1 when a carry or borrow out is generated by an arithmetic operation performed on an 8- or 16-bit operand. Otherwise, it is reset to 0. **cf** is also used in shift and rotate instructions and contains the bit shifted or rotated out of the register.

- The parity flag (**pf**) is used primarily for data communications applications and is set to 1 to generate odd parity or reset to 0 to generate even parity.

- The auxiliary carry flag (**af**) is used in BCD arithmetic and indicates whether there has been a carry out of or borrow into the least significant 4-bit digit of a BCD value.

- The zero flag (**zf**) indicates when a result is 0 by setting itself to 1.

- The sign flag (**sf**) is set to 1 for a negative result and reset to 0 for a positive result.

- The overflow flag (**of**) indicates whether or not an operation has generated a carry into the high-order bit of the result but not a carry out of the high-order bit.

The **eflag** register contains additional flags for the 80486/80386 microprocessors. Four of the thirteen flags—**tf**, **if**, **df**, and **vm**—are used to direct certain 80486/80386 processor operations. The trap flag (**tf**), when set, puts the microprocessor into single-step mode and enables you to debug a program. The interrupt-enable flag (**if**), enables external interrupts when set to 1 and disables external interrupts when reset to 0. The direction of string operations is controlled by the direction flag (**df**). With **df** reset to 0, (**e**)**si** and/or (**e**)**di** are automatically incremented forward. With **df** set to 1, (**e**)**si** and/or (**e**)**di** are automatically decremented. When the virtual mode flag (**vm**) is set, the 80486/80386 will switch from protected mode to virtual 8086 mode. You can set the **vm** flag with the **iret** instruction, or by task switches occurring during protected mode execution.

Instruction Pointer

The instruction pointer (**eip**) for the 80486/80386 contains the offset necessary to address the next instruction to be executed, within the currently active code segment. This generates a full 32-bit pointer for the next sequential program instruction. The 80286/8088 use the 16-bit version of the **eip** register, named **ip**.

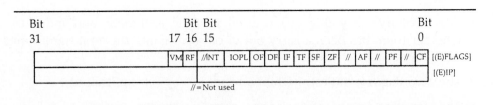

Bit 31		Bit 17	Bit 16	Bit 15													Bit 0	

	VM	RF	//INT	IOPL	OF	DF	IF	TF	SF	ZF	//	AF	//	PF	//	CF	[(E)FLAGS]
																	[(E)IP]

// = Not used

Figure 16-7.   Flag register

Scaling (80486/80386)

Scaling is an 80486/80386 microprocessor feature that you can only use when indirectly addressing 32-bit memory operands. The *scaling* is accomplished by multiplying the value pointed to by the index register, as follows:

*32-bit register * scale factor*

You can multiply the **eax, ebx, ecx, edx, ebp, edi,** and **esi** 32-bit registers either by a constant or by an expression that evaluates to a constant of 1, 2, 4, or 8.

```
mov   eax,[ebx][edx*4]
```

In the preceding example, **ebx** is used as the base index address register and **edx** is used as the index address register scaled by a factor of 4.

When you use only one of the previous registers in indirect addressing mode, by default, the specified register is considered a base register. If the specified register is followed by a scaling factor, it is used as an index register.

Bit Addressing (80486/80386)

The **bt** (test bit), **bts** (set test bit), **brt** (reset test bit), and **btc** (complement test bit) instructions allow manipulation of bit strings. The bit string may be stored in memory or in a general-purpose register. The offset into the bit string must be of an appropriate value for the register/memory operand size addressed. For 32-bit registers, the offset must be within the range 0 to 31; for 16-bit registers, the offset must be within the range 0 to 15, and so on.

When the bit string referenced is a memory address, the offset can range from 0 to 2 gigabits. The addressed bit is numbered (offset MOD 8) within the byte at address

(bit string address + (offset div 8))

div is a signed division rounded towards negative infinity, and MOD returns a positive number. For further explanation of **bt, bts, brt,** and **btc,** see the specific instruction in the Borland reference guide.

ADDRESSING TECHNIQUES

In the last two sections, you learned about data types and microprocessor registers. But how do you get the data to the register? You move data in and out of registers and perform other data manipulations with the various assembly language mnemonics. The style in which the mnemonics are used is called the *addressing mode*.

A microprocessor instruction not only contains information about the particular operation to be performed, but includes the specifications for the type of operands to be manipulated, and the location of these operands. For example:

```
mov        ax,35
```

The **mov** instruction takes a piece of immediate data, 35 decimal, and places it in the **ax** register.

There are eight major modes of addressing:

- Immediate addressing
- Register addressing
- Direct addressing
- Register indirect addressing
- Base addressing
- Direct indexed addressing
- Base indexed addressing
- Special 80486/80386 extensions

Immediate Addressing

The assembler uses the syntax of the operation to decode which addressing mode is being referenced. For example, if the instruction is written as follows,

```
mov   al,00
add   al,04
```

the operand value is contained within the instruction. Here, the **al** register is zeroed out (00) and then a number (04) is added to its contents. The following example moves a 16-bit source operand (a 0 must precede any hexadecimal letter) into the **ax** register

```
mov   ax,0FFFFh
```

while

```
mov eax,09FCD1BD4h
```

moves a 32-bit operand into the 32-bit **eax** register of the 80486 or 80386.

When using the immediate addressing mode, all operand values are sign extended when required. This means that the most significant bit of the operand value is replicated to complete the bit width of the destination operand. For example:

```
mov   ax,12Eh
```

This instruction would take the 10-bit binary equivalent of 12Eh, 100101110, and extend the value to the 16-bit destination operand width by replicating the 0 sign-bit into the most significant bit field of the **ax** register, 0000000100101110. The following instruction

```
mov eax,12Eh
```

would have produced the following 32-bit sign-extended value: 00000000000000000000000100101110.

Sign extending also applies to 8-bit source and destination operands. In the example

```
mov   al,-40
```

the 7-bit representation of −40, 1101000, is extended to 8 bits, 11101000.

Register Addressing

With register addressing, the source operand's value must be stored in one of the internal storage registers. This can be an 8-bit value, a 16-bit value, or, in the case of the 80486/80386, a 32-bit value. The microprocessor interprets the width of the operand by the name of the register. For example,

```
mov edx,ebx
```

moves the 32-bit contents of the **ebx** register into the **edx** internal register. The next example,

```
mov  ds,cx
```

instructs the microprocessor to take the 16-bit contents of the source operand (**cx** register) and move them into the 16-bit **ds** register. You can also employ this mode with 8-bit source and destination registers, as follows:

```
mov  bl,al
```

Of the seven major addressing modes, immediate addressing and register addressing take the least amount of machine cycles to execute. By including the operand data within the instruction itself, or accessing operand data already stored internally, you avoid all time-consuming external memory or external device accessing.

The remaining five addressing modes require more execution time because the microprocessor must calculate the address of the operand based on a segment address, segment offset, and possibly base register or index register contents. This derived operand address is referred to as the operand's effective address, or **ea**.

Direct Addressing

The segment offset of the operand is contained in the instruction as a 16-bit quantity with direct addressing. This offset is added to the shifted contents of the **ds** (data segment) register and returns the 20-bit **ea** or actual physical address. Typically, the direct addressing operand is a variable, as shown in Figure 16-8.

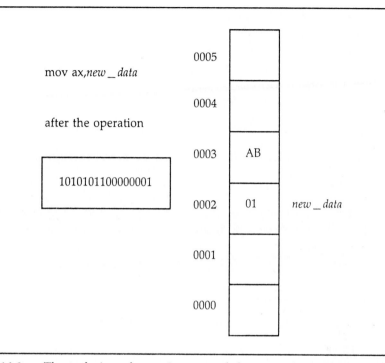

Figure 16-8.   The technique for storing a word data type (*new_data*) in consecutive byte memory locations

This instruction forces the microprocessor to load the **ax** register with the contents of the memory location pointed to by the memory address associated with the variable *new_data*. Again, the microprocessor stores the low-order byte at the lower memory address, and the high-order one at the higher memory address.

Register Indirect Addressing

In register indirect addressing, the operand value is pointed to by an offset address stored in one of the following registers: **si** (source index), **di** (destination index), **bx** (base register), or, under some circumstances, **bp** (base pointer), instead of the source operand's address being referenced by a variable name.

The microprocessor recognizes register indirect addressing by the syntax of the instruction. You should surround the source operand's designator with square brackets.

The example shown in Figure 16-9 only works if the **bx** register is loaded with the offset address of *new_data*. You could accomplish this by using the OFFSET operator as follows:

```
mov  bx,OFFSET new_data
```

You could also use the **lea** (load effective address) instruction:

```
lea  bx,new_data
```

Register indirect addressing is frequently used when referencing data stored in table format. Accessing individual values becomes a more efficient

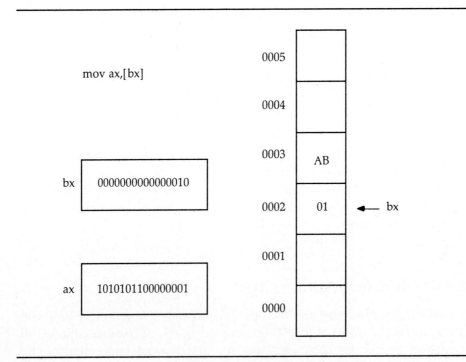

Figure 16-9.   Using the contents of the **bx** register to point to a memory location that contains data

cycle of incrementing the base register and accessing the memory location rather than the more time-consuming cycle of fetching an address from memory and then accessing the source operand.

Base Relative Addressing

You derive the effective address of an operand pointed to with base relative addressing by adding the displacement and contents of a base register (either **bx** or **bp**) relative to the selected segment, as illustrated in Figure 16-10. Base relative mode is often used to access complex data structures, such as records. The base register points to the base of the structure and a particular field is selected by the displacement. Changing the displacement

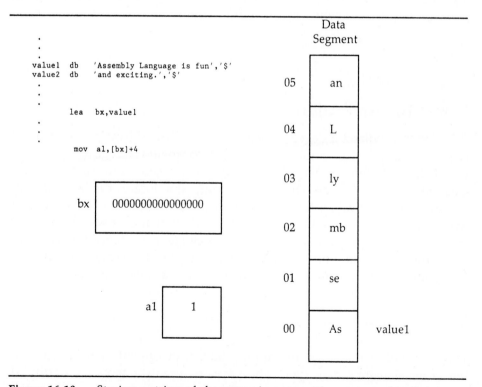

Figure 16-10.   Storing a string of characters in consecutive memory locations

accesses different fields within the record. To access the same field within different records, you just change the contents of the base register.

In the preceding block of code, *value1* contains a character string. The **lea** command loads the offset address into the **bx** register. You reference the fifth element (starting with *As* at an offset of 0) of *value1* by adding the base address (**bx**) of *value1* to the displacement, +4, within the string.

The assembler recognizes the following three methods of indicating base relative addressing:

```
lea   [bx]+4
lea   4[bx]
lea   [bx+4]
```

The first method is the most frequently used, but the displacement may precede the base register or be included within the square brackets.

You move through *value1* by incrementing the displacement and changing message references. You do this by changing the base address (**bx**), possibly with the following instruction:

```
lea   bx,value2
```

Direct Indexed Addressing

When you use direct indexed addressing, the offset address of the operand is calculated by adding the displacement to an index register (**si** or **di**) within the selected segment. You use direct indexed addressing to access elements of a static array. The displacement value locates the beginning of the array, and the value stored in the index register selects a single element within the structure. Unlike records, where individual field widths can vary in size and data type, array elements are homogeneous. Since the elements are of the same data type and size, moving through the array is a matter of systematically incrementing or decrementing the displacement, as shown:

```
mov   si,2
mov   al,an_array[si]
```

You must select with care the appropriate displacement value relative to the array element's data type. The previous example would load the **al** register with the third value of *an_array*.

```
mov ax,an_array[si]
```

The same statement could load the **ax** register with a 16-bit value, depending on the array's data type, as illustrated in Figure 16-11.

Base Indexed Addressing

In base indexed addressing, the operand is located within the selected segment at an offset determined by the sum of the base register's contents, the index register's contents, and, optionally, a displacement value. If a

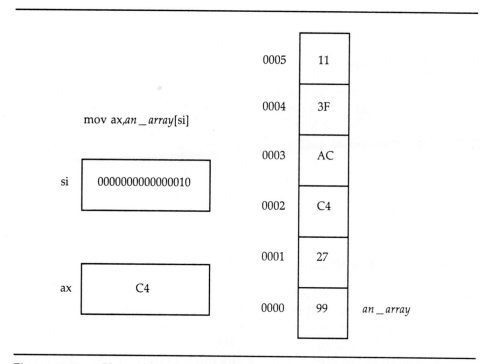

Figure 16-11.   Using the index register (**si**) to point to the location of a data element

displacement is not included, base indexed addressing is most frequently used to access the elements of a dynamic array (an array whose base address can change during the execution of a program). Including a displacement allows the individual element of an array to be accessed—with the array being a field within a structure, such as a record.

In this last case, the base register would point to the base of the record structure, the displacement (stored in **di**) would contain the distance from the beginning of the record to the start of the array field, and the element displacement would be contained in the *element* variable (assuming that *element* contains the offset 02h).

In the example shown in Figure 16-12, the base address for the record structure is 0000 and is stored in the **bx** register. The array field of the third record has a displacement of 0020, stored in **di**. The third element of the array field is accessed by the displacement contained in the initialized offset value of *element*.

80386 Extensions

The 32-bit addressing modes are extended to allow any register to be used as a base register or index register. The 32-bit modes require that the base and index registers, if used, both hold valid 32-bit values. Any 16-bit mode instructions truncate the contents of a 32-bit register and therefore ignore the upper 16 bits.

ASSEMBLY LANGUAGE DIRECTIVES

Unlike assembly language instructions, directives give directions to the assembler itself. Assembly language directives (sometimes called pseudo-ops) define the manner in which the assembler is to generate object code at assembly time. Overall, there are about 100 assembler directives.

This section will discuss several of the more frequently used directives, using an example program. The Borland assembly language reference guide contains additional information on individual directives.

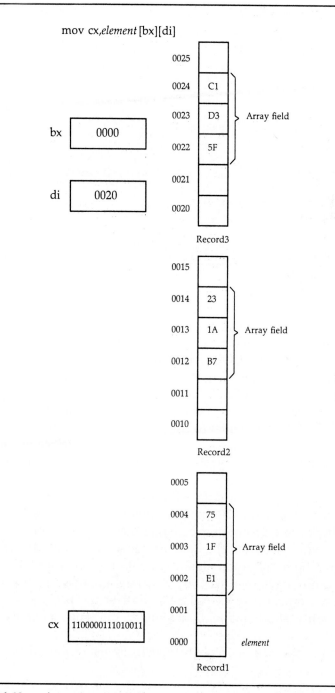

Figure 16-12.   Accessing a record structure using base index addressing

Frequently Used Directives

In the following list,

```
        DOSSEG                  ;use Intel segment-ordering
        .MODEL   small          ;set model size

        .STACK   300h           ;set up 768-byte stack

        .DATA                   ;set up data location


        .CODE
Turbo   PROC     FAR            ;main procedure declaration
            .
            .
            .
            .
Turbo   ENDP                    ;end main procedure
        END                     ;end whole program
```

the first two directives are

```
DOSSEG
.MODEL      small
```

DOSSEG instructs the assembler to order segments according to the Intel segment-order convention (CODE, DGROUP, and STACK). This is very important because, under certain circumstances, segment ordering can affect the proper functioning of a program.

The .MODEL small directive, when used before other segment directives, specifies the memory model to use. The memory model can be small, medium, compact, large, or huge. A memory model specification tells the assembler something about the size of your program's code and data segment requirements.

The small model places all data within a single 64K segment, and all code within a 64K segment. The medium model restricts data to one 64K segment, but the code segment may be larger than 64K. The compact model keeps the code within 64K, but the data may be greater than 64K. The large model can have both code and data segments greater than 64K, but all arrays must be no larger than 64K. Finally, huge models are the same as large models, but arrays may exceed 64K. Most of the programs that you write will be fairly short and will fall under the small memory model category.

You define a stack size of 768 bytes (300h) by using the .STACK directive, as follows:

```
.STACK      300h
```

You may need to adjust this size upwards if the program you are writing incorporates several nested procedures. For most of the examples in this text, a 768-byte stack will be more than sufficient.

Defining the starting location of your data segment is as simple as using the .DATA directive:

```
.DATA
```

Specifically, the DATA directive defines the beginning of a NEAR, initialized, data segment. Program data is placed after the DATA directive and can be as large as the memory model allows.

The code segment is initialized with the following directive:

```
.CODE
```

The .CODE segment directive actually specifies where program code is to begin.

```
Turbo     PROC      FAR
```

The label, Turbo, and directives, PROC FAR, identify a block of source code. Typically, all programs will have at least one PROC with a FAR attribute. Examine the last listing again and notice that all of the lines of code for Turbo are between the Turbo PROC FAR heading and the procedure end statement:

```
Turbo     ENDP
```

The ENDP assembler directive simply indicates the end of a procedure begun with the same label, Turbo.

You let the assembler know that it has reached the end of your program with the END directive:

```
END
```

Additional Assembler Directives

The remaining directives cover a wide range of functions. There are directives, such as ALIGN, that increase an assembly language program's execution speed by forcing the alignment of data on a specified boundary. Values that will not be changed during the execution of a program can be defined by a CONST directive.

Using .ERR, .ERR1, .ERR2, .ERRB, .ERRDEF, .ERRDIF, .ERRE, .ERRIDN, .ERRNB, and .ERRNZ, you can instruct the assembler to perform certain actions based on the presence or absence of specific error conditions.

You can control conditional assembly with the .IF [ELSE], IF1, IF2, IFB, IFDEF, IFDIF, IFE, IFIDN, IFNB, and IFNDEF directives.

You can control the scope of a name with the PUBLIC directive, set the input radix of an expression with .RADIX, start the listing of macro expansion statements that generate code or data with .XALL, and much more.

PROGRAMMING STYLE

You should now understand all of the fundamentals you need to write simple assembly language code. In this section, you will learn how to structure your code in a fairly standard format.

An assembly language program is just a series of executable statements that tell the assembler what operations to perform. This series of statements is often referred to as the *source code*. Like any other language, assembly language source code has a predefined structure syntax.

Each assembly language statement is composed of four fields:

- Name field
- Operation field
- Operand field
- Comment field

However, certain assembler instructions do not use every field. The comment field exists only for internal programming documentation and is optional.

Name Field

The name field, sometimes called the label field, assigns a symbolic name to the actual beginning memory address of an assembler instruction. This allows you to reference an instruction by name and eliminates the need to keep track of instruction addresses. This feature is especially useful when you are generating relocatable code. By using a symbolic reference, you allow the linker to select where in memory the assembly language program will be loaded. All instruction references can then automatically vary with code placement.

Although any instruction can be given a label, this field is usually reserved for instructions that will be referenced in data definitions, constants, segments, loops, jumps, and subroutine calls.

A label must begin with an alphabetic character and may contain up to 31 characters, including

- All letters "A" through "Z"
- Numeric digits 0 through 9
- The special symbols _, $, ., ?, and @

Use caution when selecting a label. You cannot use a label that is the same as an assembler reserved word or directive. If the label is to include a period, the period must be the first character.

Variables

A variable name represents a memory location that is accessible by a program. The contents of this memory location can change during program execution. Variable definitions include information about the memory location's address, data type, and size. Variables can be used as operands in simple, indexed, or structured forms.

Labels

When label names are applied to executable instructions within the applications program, they are said to be code-relative. A name or label has three attributes: a segment address, a segment offset, and a NEAR or FAR accessibility descriptor.

The CPU may address a particular label in one of two ways. If the label being referenced is within the same code segment, the CPU only needs the segment offset to locate the command. In this case, the label type is NEAR. To define a label as NEAR, place a colon immediately after the label or use the NEAR pseudo-op:

```
loop1:
```

This example uses the colon to tell the assembler that this instruction is referenced within the same code segment. Most labels in your programs will be NEAR labels.

```
count   LABEL   NEAR
```

In this example, the label is explicitly defined as NEAR with the LABEL pseudo-op. For more on pseudo-ops, see "Assembly Language Directives" earlier in this chapter.

The second method for addressing a label requires both the segment address and offset address. You need to use this addressing method when the assembler statement to be referenced is not within the same code segment. In this case, the label is defined as being FAR.

```
mycode   LABEL   FAR
```

In the preceding example, the LABEL pseudo-op was used with the FAR attribute. FAR attributes can also be used when labeling equate (EQU), procedure (PROC), and external (EXTRN) statements, as in these two examples:

```
ten     EQU     FAR   10

prntit  PROC    FAR

EXTRN   randm:FAR
```

Constants

You can also give names and labels to memory locations that contain initialized values that do not change during program execution. These initialized values are called constants. Constants can be one of several types.

A binary constant contains a series of 0's and 1's and is followed by the letter "b." For example:

```
eight  EQU  00001000b
```

Decimal constants contain a series of digits, 0 through 9, and are optionally followed by the letter "d." A series of digits is considered to be a decimal number unless the radix or base has been changed. Here is an example decimal constant:

```
forty  EQU  40d
```

Hexadecimal constants contain a series of digits, 0 through 9, and include the letters "A" through "F," followed by the letter "h." The first character must be one of the digits 0 through 9. This tells the compiler that the value is a number and not a label reference or variable name. If the hexadecimal value begins with one of the letters "A" through "F," adding a leading 0 will remove this compiler interpreted ambiguity. A hexadecimal constant declaration would look like this:

```
fifty  EQU  32h
```

```
hexnm  EQU  0FFh
```

The 0 is appended to the MSD to tell the assembler that FFh is a hexadecimal number rather than a label or variable.

A character constant may contain all of the ASCII characters enclosed within single or double quotes. If a constant contains more than two characters, the **db** (define byte) pseudo-op must be used. If the character string contains only one or two characters, the **dd**, **dq**, **dt**, or **dw** pseudo-ops may be used. For example:

```
initl  dd  'V'
name   db  "J. Pepper"
```

You can assign a label in the name field to the value of an operand field expression by using the EQU (equates) pseudo-op, or the equal sign (=). Using the EQU pseudo-op assigns the variable a constant that cannot change during program execution. If you use the equal sign pseudo-op, the value of the constant can be changed during program execution. For example:

```
myadd   EQU [bp+16]
basnum  =   1990
```

In the first example, the name *myadd* can be substituted for the index expression [bp + 16]. Likewise, *basnum* can be substituted for the value 1990. In this last case, *basnum* could be reassigned a new value while the program was executing.

Segment names occur when a segment label is given in the name field of the segment statement, naming the current segment. For example:

```
MYCODE  SEGMENT  PARA  'CODE'
```

Operation Field

The operation field contains a mnemonic for an actual microprocessor instruction. The mnemonic is a two- to six-character English-like abbreviation for you and the assembler. Rather than entering the binary or hexadecimal value for a machine instruction, you can enter the mnemonic. The mnemonic makes it easier to read and understand code and is only one internal conversion table away from the actual binary machine code value. A mnemonic can represent a machine instruction, a macro instruction, or a pseudo-op. For example:

```
initial:  mov    ax,0h
```

initial is the label and **mov** is the operation. Following the operation field is the operand field. Each mnemonic not only tells the assembler which instruction to execute but tells the assembler how many operands of what type are needed.

If the operation contains a reference to a macro, the assembler will process a predefined sequence of code. This causes the assembler to generate source code instructions as if they were in the original part of the program. For example,

```
bios_int  MACRO  branch_id
```

flags the assembler and tells it that the following code is part of the MACRO definition. A *pseudo-operation* (abbreviated to pseudo-op) usually does not produce machine code but instead directs the assembler to perform certain operations on data, code listings, branches, and macros.

Operand Field

The operand field contains the location or locations of the data to be manipulated by the operation instruction. If the instruction requires one or two operands, the operands are separated from the instruction by at least one blank space. If there are two operands, the operands themselves are separated by a comma. However, some mnemonics require no operands.

When an operation requires two operands, the first operand is called the *destination operand* and the second operand is called the *source operand.* Data transfer, register, immediate, and memory storage operations are examples of instructions requiring two operands. For example,

```
mov   ax,8
```

is an example of an immediate operand. Here, the data to be manipulated is included as a source operand and moved into the **ax** register, or destination operand.

Comment Field

The comment field can be one of the most useful fields. You use it to internally document the assembler source code. Comments are ignored by the assembler and are useful only when listing the source code. Comments can actually start in any field position and are initialized with a semicolon (;). You should use comments to describe lines of source code that are not immediately understandable. For example:

```
mov   ah,45h       ;parameter for reading a character
```

In this example, the comment explains why the **ah** register is being loaded with 45h. In this case, the 45h is used to trigger the appropriate action when an interrupt is called.

PUTTING YOUR KNOWLEDGE TO WORK

1. Explain some of the main architectural differences between the various members of Intel family of microprocessors?

2. Discuss real mode and protected mode. Which of the Intel microprocessors can operate in protected mode?

3. A doubleword holds how many bytes? How many words?

4. List the seven assembly language addressing modes. Which mode uses the least number of machine cycles?

5. How many bits are used to hold one hexadecimal digit?

6. Convert the hexadecimal number F1234ABCD to decimal.

7. Convert the decimal number 55667788 to hexadecimal; to binary.

8. Name the four fields that you use when writing assembly language programs.

9. What two microprocessors allow access to **eax**, **ebx**, **ecx**, and **edx** registers?

10. What is the largest data type directly accessible by the 8088 microprocessor? By the 80386 microprocessor?

17

ASSEMBLY LANGUAGE

In this chapter you will learn how to

- Write programs using the immediate, direct, and register indirect programming modes

- Use the Turbo Debugger to single step through programs, watching variables and registers

- Develop assembly language arithmetic procedures for adding, subtracting, multiplying, dividing, raising a number to an integer power, and extracting a square root

- Use loops when code is to be repeated a number of times

- Write programs with byte and word pointers, when data sizes exceed register sizes

- Use BIOS and DOS interrupts to control system hardware

- Write programs that address various I/O ports on the computer

- Write a program that addresses individual pixels on the graphics screen

This chapter concentrates on teaching program syntax by developing numerous programming examples. The examples are simple but complete programs designed to teach individual commands or special techniques. For example, the first part of the chapter focuses on computer arithmetic. All programmers must know how to add, subtract, multiply, and divide. Another section deals with lookup tables. You learn how to create and use a simple lookup table for performing mathematical operations that are not available in the Intel instruction set. The final section teaches you how to tap into the powerful system resources that your computer has built into its BIOS and DOS routines. By using interrupts, you will learn how to control the keyboard, screen, and speaker port. These interrupts are explained in the various IBM technical reference manuals for each computer. If you are using an IBM Model 80 computer, refer to our book by Pappas and Murray, *Inside the Model 80* (Berkeley, Calif.: Osborne/McGraw-Hill, 1988).

The programs in this chapter have been designed to teach you elementary assembly language programming concepts. All of the necessary program overhead has been included with each assembly language example. Every program is complete in itself; if you enter, assemble, and link an example, it will work. Many of the programs in this chapter use the power of the Turbo Debugger. Each program is brief and uncomplicated.

ARITHMETIC PROGRAMS

This section presents several arithmetic assembly language examples. These include the basic arithmetic operators such as addition, subtraction, multiplication, and division. The programs are developed using several different programming modes. One example examines a simple algorithm for determining the square root of a hexadecimal integer. Unless otherwise mentioned, all assembly language arithmetic is done in hexadecimal format. You should buy a calculator that can convert numbers from one base (radix) to another to aid in program debugging.

Hexadecimal Addition with Immediate Addressing

Addition is one of the most basic mathematical operations. The first example illustrates hexadecimal addition using the immediate addressing mode, explained in the previous chapter. The program code is called *straight-line* programming since the program is executed line by line until the whole program is completed. Straight-line programming is simple but not always efficient.

```
;TURBO Assembly Language Programming Application
;Copyright (c) Chris H. Pappas and William H. Murray, 1990

;program to illustrate simple hexadecimal addition with
;immediate addressing

        DOSSEG                          ;use Intel segment-ordering
        .MODEL   small                  ;set model size
        .8086                           ;8086 instructions

        .STACK   300h                   ;set up 768-byte stack

        .CODE
Turbo   PROC     FAR                    ;main procedure declaration

;addition of three numbers using immediate addressing
        mov      ax,01BCh               ;put hex number 1BC into ax
        add      ax,78h                 ;add to ax the number 78h
        add      ax,78                  ;add to ax the number 4Eh

        mov      ah,4Ch                 ;return control to DOS
        int      21h
Turbo   ENDP                            ;end main procedure
        END                             ;end whole program
```

Notice that there are only three lines of actual program code in addition to the program overhead. These three lines are called the *body* of the program. Examine the overall structure of the program. It starts with four lines of comments that briefly describe the program's function. Placing comments at the start of a program not only informs other users of the program's purpose but also reminds you what the program does. Remember, you can place comments in any of the four fields as long as you start the comments with a semicolon. The words DOSSEG, .MODEL small, .8086, .STACK, .CODE, and PROC are pseudo-ops that inform the assembler how to assemble your program code. As you learned in the last chapter, these commands don't appear in the operating version of your program and are only used to communicate with the Turbo Assembler (TASM). Of the four program segments commonly found in assembly language programs, this program uses only a .STACK and .CODE segment directive. This example did not use any separately stored data, so you didn't need to establish a data segment. Every code segment (.CODE) must have at least one procedure. The procedure for this example is called Turbo. The following lines of code make up the heart of the hexadecimal addition program:

```
mov    ax,01BCh        ;put hex number 1BC into ax
add    ax,78h          ;add to ax the number 78h
add    ax,78           ;add to ax the number 4Eh
```

In this example, the hexadecimal number (01BCh) is moved to the **ax** register. Recall that the **ax** register is a 16-bit register. This means that **ax** can hold hexadecimal numbers from 0000h to 0FFFFh. The mov command is one of the most frequently encountered commands in 80486/8088 programming since it enables you to load or save information. The next operand adds the number 78h to the current contents of the **ax** register. The **ax** register will now contain 234h. Another **add** instruction adds a 78, specified in decimal, or 4Eh to **ax**, giving the final sum of 282h. You can observe this process by watching the **ax** register, as you single step through the program with the Turbo Debugger. Figure 17-1 shows the debugger screen, and the final value in the **ax** register.

Recall that during the assembly you must use the command-line argument, -zi, to obtain debugging information. Also, use the /v command-line argument during the link process.

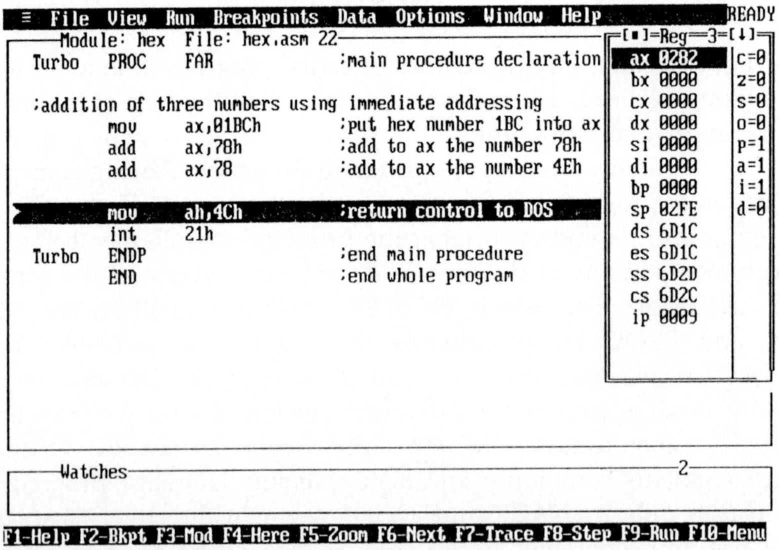

```
≡ File  View  Run  Breakpoints  Data  Options  Window  Help       READY
  ┌─Module: hex  File: hex.asm 22──────────────┌─[■]═Reg═3═[↓]═┐
  Turbo  PROC    FAR              ;main procedure declaration│ ax 0282  │c=0
                                                             │ bx 0000  │z=0
  ;addition of three numbers using immediate addressing      │ cx 0000  │s=0
           mov    ax,01BCh        ;put hex number 1BC into ax│ dx 0000  │o=0
           add    ax,78h          ;add to ax the number 78h  │ si 0000  │p=1
           add    ax,78           ;add to ax the number 4Eh  │ di 0000  │a=1
                                                             │ bp 0000  │i=1
►          mov    ah,4Ch          ;return control to DOS      │ sp 02FE  │d=0
           int    21h                                        │ ds 6D1C  │
  Turbo  ENDP                     ;end main procedure         │ es 6D1C  │
         END                      ;end whole program          │ ss 6D2D  │
                                                             │ cs 6D2C  │
                                                             │ ip 0009  │

  ┌─Watches───────────────────────────────2─
  │
  └─────────────────────────────────────────
  F1-Help F2-Bkpt F3-Mod F4-Here F5-Zoom F6-Next F7-Trace F8-Step F9-Run F10-Menu
```

Figure 17-1.   Illustration of a simple hexadecimal addition program with the Debugger's Register window opened

This program has a number of subtle limitations. First, it does not take into account overflow if the sum in **ax** exceeds 0FFFFh. Second, the program does not allow for the addition of numbers greater than 0FFFFh. Third, what would happen to the program's length if there were 2000 numbers to add? Fourth, if the numbers to be added change, you must return to the code segment and change each program line to accommodate the change. Even with these shortcomings, this program illustrates a very popular technique for adding several numbers. However, good programmers always understand the limitations of their programs.

Hexadecimal Subtraction with Direct Addressing

In assembly language, subtraction is just as easy as addition. In the last example, the immediate addressing mode dictated that the numbers to be added were immediately entered into the individual registers. In the next example, the numbers will first be assigned variable names, in a separate data segment, and then subtracted via direct addressing techniques. This program will also use 16-bit registers. The 16-bit register is the maximum register size in the 80286/8088 chip family. Recall that 80486 and 80386 machines allow 32-bit general registers.

```
;TURBO Assembly Language Programming Application
;Copyright (c) Chris H. Pappas and William H. Murray, 1990

;program to perform hexadecimal subtraction with
;direct addressing

              DOSSEG                 ;use Intel segment-ordering
              .MODEL   small         ;set model size
              .8086                  ;8086 instructions

              .STACK   300h          ;set up 768-byte stack

              .DATA                  ;set up data location
num1          dw       7823          ;1st number, 1E8Fh
num2          dw       45h           ;2nd number, 0045h
num3          dw       0BCh          ;3rd number, 00BCh
ans           dw       ?

              .CODE
Turbo         PROC     FAR           ;main procedure declaration
              mov      ax,DGROUP     ;point ds toward .DATA
              mov      ds,ax
```

```
;actual subtraction using three 16-bit numbers
        mov     ax,num1            ;place num1 in ax register
        sub     ax,num2            ;subtract num2 from ax
        sub     ax,num3            ;subtract num3 from ax
        mov     ans,ax             ;save ax in variable

        mov     ah,4Ch             ;return control to DOS
        int     21h
Turbo   ENDP                       ;end main procedure
        END                        ;end whole program
```

This program introduces a number of new features. For example, this is the first time that a program has used a separate data segment.

```
num1    dw      7823               ;1st number, 1E8Fh
num2    dw      45h                ;2nd number, 0045h
num3    dw      0BCh               ;3rd number, 00BCh
ans     dw      ?
```

This segment declares four variables. The variables *num1, num2,* and *num3* contain three numbers to be used in the subtraction example. Each variable is declared as a defined word (dw). The numbers 7823, 45h, and 0BCh will be padded by the assembler to 16 bits. You can think of these numbers being stored in memory as 1E8Fh, 0045h, and 00BCh. The fourth variable, *ans,* is declared but not initialized to any value, so the entry is a ?. The ? reserves 16 bits of storage for the answer.

The actual code for subtraction is straightforward. The first number is moved into the **ax** register. The next two lines of code subtract *num2* and *num3* from the contents of the **ax** register. Finally, the fourth line of code moves the contents of the **ax** register (1D8Eh) into the variable *ans.*

At this point, you cannot view the actual results of the subtraction except by using either a register or data-segment dump from memory, or the Turbo Debugger. No routine will place the results directly on your screen. Figure 17-2 shows the Turbo Debugger screen, immediately after the program was executed.

This program illustrates hexadecimal subtraction and also shows one technique for overcoming a programming limitation of the previous addition example. Because the program used a data segment, you could change the numbers to be subtracted without having to alter the actual program code. Data segments allow your program code to remain unchanged even when you alter numeric values.

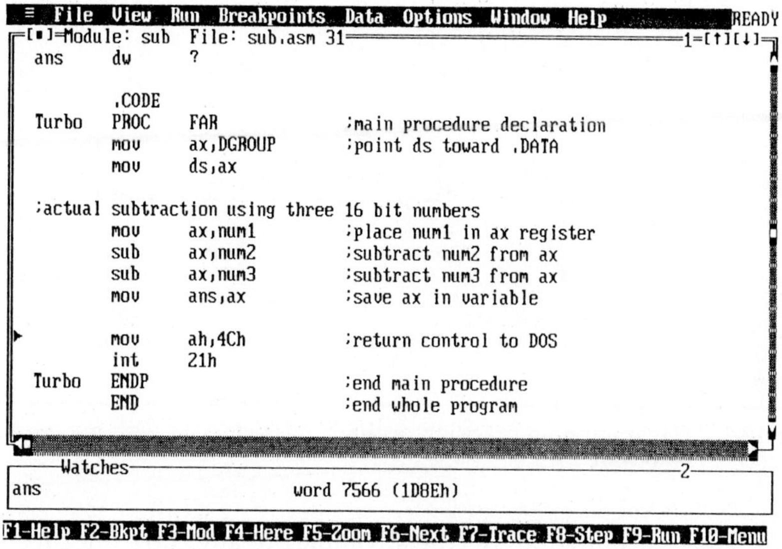

```
 ≡  File  View  Run  Breakpoints  Data  Options  Window  Help        READY
┌[■]=Module: sub   File: sub.asm 31═══════════════════════════════1=[↑][↓]┐
│   ans    dw      ?                                                       ▲
│                                                                         │
│          .CODE                                                          │
│   Turbo  PROC    FAR             ;main procedure declaration            │
│          mov     ax,DGROUP       ;point ds toward .DATA                 │
│          mov     ds,ax                                                  │
│                                                                         │
│   ;actual subtraction using three 16 bit numbers                       │
│          mov     ax,num1         ;place num1 in ax register            █
│          sub     ax,num2         ;subtract num2 from ax                 │
│          sub     ax,num3         ;subtract num3 from ax                 │
│          mov     ans,ax          ;save ax in variable                   │
│                                                                         │
│►         mov     ah,4Ch          ;return control to DOS                 │
│          int     21h                                                    │
│   Turbo  ENDP                    ;end main procedure                    │
│          END                     ;end whole program                    ▼
│◄█▒▒▒▒▒▒▒▒▒▒▒▒▒▒▒▒▒▒▒▒▒▒▒▒▒▒▒▒▒▒▒▒▒▒▒▒▒▒▒▒▒▒▒▒▒▒▒▒▒▒▒▒▒▒▒▒▒▒▒▒█►
├─Watches──────────────────────────────────────────────────2─┐
│ ans                        word 7566 (1D8Eh)                │
└─────────────────────────────────────────────────────────────┘
 F1-Help F2-Bkpt F3-Mod F4-Here F5-Zoom F6-Next F7-Trace F8-Step F9-Run F10-Menu
```

Figure 17-2.   Illustration of hexadecimal subtraction, using the Debugger's Watch window to examine the variable, *ans*

Multiple Precision Addition with Direct Addressing

The general-purpose registers (**ax**, **bx**, **cx**, and **dx**) of the Intel family are limited to 16 bits. If there were not a technique for getting around this limitation, you would be restricted to working with integer numbers from 0000h to 0FFFFh (0 to 65,535 decimal). The next example illustrates a general technique for 32-bit arithmetic. When the range of the arithmetic exceeds the register size, multiple precision arithmetic is used. Thirty-two bit arithmetic will allow numbers as large as 0FFFFFFFFh (4,294,967,295 decimal) on 80286/8088 machines. While the 80386 allows direct 32-bit arithmetic with the use of **eax**, **ebx**, **ecx**, and **edx** registers, you would still need multiple precision programming for numbers greater than 0FFFFFFFFh. Multiple precision arithmetic is possible because all microprocessors can set/clear a carry flag or overflow flag when an arithmetic operation dictates. The first two programs have not used this feature. If a carry or borrow had occurred, it would have gone unnoticed by the program and produced an incorrect answer. The **adc** (add with carry) instruc-

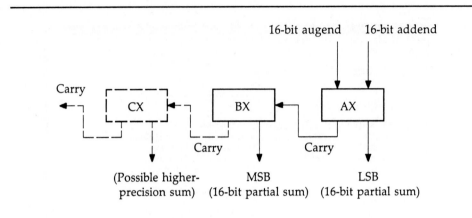

Figure 17-3.   How multiple precision arithmetic is achieved with microprocessor registers

tion will allow this program to take advantage of any carry information and permit multiple precision arithmetic. Figure 17-3 shows how you can carry out multiple precision arithmetic with 16-bit registers.

```
;TURBO Assembly Language Programming Application
;Copyright (c) Chris H. Pappas and William H. Murray, 1990

;program of multiple precision addition using
;direct addressing

        DOSSEG                  ;use Intel segment-ordering
        .MODEL  small           ;set model size
        .8086                   ;8086 instructions

        .STACK  300h            ;set up 768-byte stack

        .DATA                   ;set up data location
num1    dw      OFFABh
num2    dw      4CC0h
num3    dw      0C00Ah
num4    dw      0DD34h
lsbans  dw      0
msbans  dw      0

        .CODE
Turbo   PROC    FAR             ;main procedure declaration
        mov     ax,DGROUP       ;point ds toward .DATA
        mov     ds,ax

;actual code for multiple precision addition
        mov     bx,00h          ;clear bx register
        mov     ax,num1         ;first number moved to ax
```

```
        add     ax,num2         ;add second number
        adc     bx,00h          ;accumulate carry in bx
        add     ax,num3         ;add third number
        adc     bx,00h          ;accumulate carry in bx
        add     ax,num4         ;add fourth number
        adc     bx,00h          ;accumulate carry in bx
        mov     lsbans,ax       ;put ax in lsbans storage
        mov     msbans,bx       ;put bx in msbans storage

        mov     ah,4Ch          ;return control to DOS
        int     21h
Turbo   ENDP                    ;end main procedure
        END                     ;end whole program
```

This program illustrates how easily you can accomplish multiple precision addition. Recall that the carry flag is evaluated (set or cleared) after each **add** or **adc** operation, but only utilized by the **adc** instruction. In general, the program will start with the LSBs (least significant bits) and work toward the MSBs (most significant bits). The addition of two 16-bit numbers may or may not produce a carry. For example, adding 01234h to 11h does not produce a carry, but adding 0FFDEh to 0DC6h does. If the digits being added are LSB numbers, by definition, nothing will be passing a carry to them from a previous addition. For that reason, LSB additions are usually done with the **add** command. If the LSBs produce a carry, the carry flag will be set and utilized by the **adc** instruction when doing the next higher 16-bit addition. In this program, only carry information will be accumulated in the higher 16 bits, since any given number in the data segment is limited to the lower 16 bits. Thus, you must do add with carry operations with a 00h in the immediate addressing mode. The variable *num1* is added to *num2* with the simple **move/add** sequence of the first addition example. Since this addition set the carry flag (FFAB + 4CC0 = (1)4C6B), the next line of code will add the carry to the contents of the **bx** register. The **add/adc** sequence is repeated for each number to be added. The final sum is found in two registers. The **bx** register contains the MSBs and the **ax** register the LSBs of the 32-bit answer. The register contents are moved back to the data segment in two variables, *lsbans* and *msbans*. If these final two numbers are concatenated, the answer can be read as 0002E9A9h. Examine Figure 17-4 and find the answer.

You could extend this programming technique to add or accumulate any number, even something as large as the national debt. Multiple precision arithmetic overcomes the limitations of register size.

```
≡ File  View  Run  Breakpoints  Data  Options  Window  Help          READY
┌[■]═Module: multi1  File: multi1.asm 39══════════════════════════════1═[↑][↓]═┐
│            adc     bx,00h          ;accumulate carry in bx                   ▲
│            add     ax,num3         ;add third number                        █
│            adc     bx,00h          ;accumulate carry in bx                  █
│            add     ax,num4         ;add fourth number                       █
│            adc     bx,00h          ;accumulate carry in bx                  █
│            mov     lsbans,ax       ;put ax in lsbans storage                █
│            mov     msbans,bx       ;put bx in msbans storage                █
│ ▶                                                                           █
│            mov     ah,4Ch          ;return control to DOS                   █
│            int     21h                                                      █
│   Turbo    ENDP                    ;end main procedure                      █
│            END                     ;end whole program                       █
│                                                                             █
│                                                                             █
│                                                                             █
│                                                                             █
│                                                                             ▼
│◄█                                                                          █►│
├──Watches──────────────────────────────────────────────2───────────────────┤
│ msbans                    word 2 (2h)                                        │
│ lsbans                    word 59817 (E9A9h)                                 │
└─────────────────────────────────────────────────────────────────────────────┘
 F1-Help F2-Bkpt F3-Mod F4-Here F5-Zoom F6-Next F7-Trace F8-Step F9-Run F10-Menu
```

Figure 17-4.   An illustration of multiprecision arithmetic with the results shown in *lsbans* and *msbans*

Performing Addition on 80486/80386 Machines

If you are using an 80486 or 80386 computer, you can perform 32-bit additions by using the **eax**, **ebx**, **ecx**, or **edx** registers. The following program performs the same addition as the previous example. However, the numbers to be added are now stored in 32-bit variables.

```
;TURBO Assembly Language Programming Application
;Copyright (c) Chris H. Pappas and William H. Murray, 1990

;program to use the 80486 or 80386 and 32-bit registers
;to add several numbers without the need for
;multiple-precision addition.

        DOSSEG                  ;use Intel segment-ordering
        .MODEL  small           ;set model size
        .386                    ;80386 instructions

        .STACK  300h            ;set up 768-byte stack

        .DATA                   ;set up data location
```

```
num1      dd        0FFABh
num2      dd        4CC0h
num3      dd        0C00Ah
num4      dd        0DD34h
ans       dd        0

          .CODE
Turbo     PROC      FAR                 ;main procedure declaration
          mov       ax,DGROUP           ;point ds toward .DATA
          mov       ds,ax

;actual addition of numbers using 32-bit registers
          mov       eax,num1            ;load num1 in eax
          add       eax,num2            ;add num2 to eax
          add       eax,num3            ;add num3 to eax
          add       eax,num4            ;add num4 to eax
          mov       ans,eax             ;save eax in ans variable

          mov       ah,4Ch              ;return control to DOS
          int       21h
Turbo     ENDP                          ;end main procedure
          END                           ;end whole program
```

In this example, all additions are accomplished with the **add** mnemonic since no carry information will be passed. You can view the results of this operation in Figure 17-5, which shows the Turbo Debugger screen after program execution. Notice that you are viewing the 32-bit results.

There is still one major limitation to these programming techniques, even with the use of 32-bit registers. For each number to be added or subtracted from a register, you need at least one line (sometimes two) of program code. For one or two additions, this is not a problem. However, if the number of additions increases even to 50, the code becomes cumbersome and inefficient.

Multiplication and Division Instructions

The multiply and divide commands are easy to use, but you must use them with caution and with a firm understanding of how they operate. The next example uses the multiply (**mul**) and divide (**div**) instructions to perform a simple algebraic operation. In this example, *num1* is multiplied by *num2* and the resulting product is divided by *num3*. When performing 16-bit arithmetic, the **mul** instruction produces a 32-bit product. The LSBs are stored in the **ax** register and the MSBs in the **dx** register. In a similar manner, the **div** command divides a 32-bit dividend stored in the **ax** and **dx** registers by a

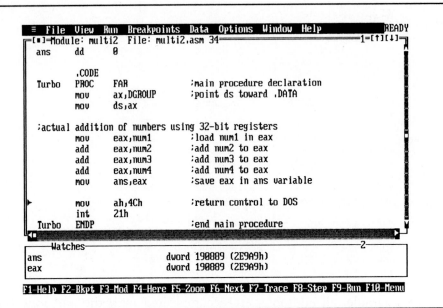

Figure 17-5. An illustration of multiprecision arithmetic with 80386 32-bit registers

16-bit divisor. The resulting quotient is stored in the **ax** register. Any remainder will appear in the **dx** register.

Pay particular attention to the syntax for the multiply and divide commands.

```
;TURBO Assembly Language Programming Application
;Copyright (c) Chris H. Pappas and William H. Murray, 1990

;program to demonstrate the multiply & divide instructions

        DOSSEG                  ;use Intel segment-ordering
        .MODEL  small           ;set model size
        .8086                   ;8086 instructions

        .STACK  300h            ;set up 768-byte stack

        .DATA                   ;set up data location
num1    dw      3E78h
num2    dw      3Ah
num3    dw      3Eh
quo     dw      ?
rem     dw      ?
```

```
        .CODE
Turbo   PROC    FAR                 ;main procedure declaration
        mov     ax,DGROUP           ;point ds toward .DATA
        mov     ds,ax

;code for performing:   (num1 x num2) / num3
        mov     ax,num1             ;place first number in ax
        mul     num2                ;x num2.  answer in dx:ax
        div     num3                ;divides dx:ax by num3
                                    ;quot in ax, remain in dx
        mov     quo,ax              ;save quotient
        mov     rem,dx              ;save remainder

        mov     ah,4Ch              ;return control to DOS
        int     21h
Turbo   ENDP                        ;end main procedure
        END                         ;end whole program
```

This is one of the first examples in which a mnemonic has used a single operand. The **mul** mnemonic expects to find one number (the multiplicand) in the **ax** register. You can specify the other number, the multiplier, with a variable name. Likewise, **div** expects to find the dividend in the **dx:ax** pair of registers; thus, only the divisor is specified with the **div** mnemonic. The actual program is straightforward. The variables *num1* and *num2* are multiplied, producing a product that is located in the **dx:ax** registers. This product is the dividend for the **div** instruction, which divides it by *num3*. The quotient is moved from **ax** to *quo* and the remainder from **dx** to *rem*. In this particular example, the quotient is 3A70h and the remainder is 10h. Can you find this information in Figure 17-6?

Raising a Number to an Integer Power

The basic arithmetic operations available with the Intel family of microprocessors include addition, subtraction, multiplication, and division. If you want additional abilities, you have to develop your own function by writing the program code or developing an algorithm. Raising a number to an integer power is one such useful function. In mathematical or scientific work, you will frequently need to square or cube a number. To square a number, a program can merely multiply the number by itself. You can accomplish cubing in a similar manner. Perhaps there is a way to write a general algorithm for raising a number to an integer power.

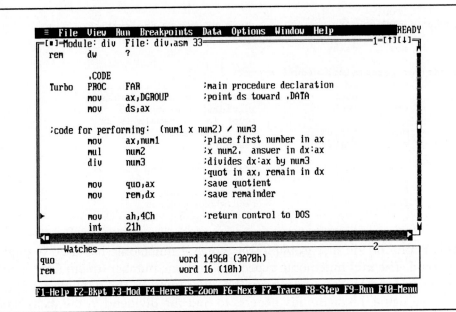

```
≡  File  View  Run  Breakpoints  Data  Options  Window  Help        READY
┌[■]=Module: div  File: div.asm 33══════════════════════════════1=[↑][↓]═┐
│   rem     dw      ?                                                      │
│                                                                         │
│           .CODE                                                         │
│   Turbo   PROC    FAR             ;main procedure declaration           │
│           mov     ax,DGROUP       ;point ds toward .DATA                │
│           mov     ds,ax                                                 │
│                                                                         │
│   ;code for performing: (num1 x num2) / num3                           │
│           mov     ax,num1         ;place first number in ax             │
│           mul     num2            ;x num2,  answer in dx:ax             │
│           div     num3            ;divides dx:ax by num3                │
│                                   ;quot in ax, remain in dx             │
│           mov     quo,ax          ;save quotient                        │
│           mov     rem,dx          ;save remainder                       │
│                                                                         │
│ ►         mov     ah,4Ch          ;return control to DOS                │
│           int     21h                                                   │
│ ◄■══════════════════════════════════════════════════════════►          │
├─Watches──────────────────────────────────────────────────2──────────────┤
│ quo                     word 14960 (3A70h)                               │
│ rem                     word 16 (10h)                                    │
└─────────────────────────────────────────────────────────────────────────┘
 F1-Help F2-Bkpt F3-Mod F4-Here F5-Zoom F6-Next F7-Trace F8-Step F9-Run F10-Menu
```

Figure 17-6.   The Debugger allows us to examine the results of a division program. The Watch window contains the quotient and the remainder with results given in both decimal and hexadecimal

If a program will loop through code, performing one multiplication for each higher power needed, you will have the algorithm.

```
;TURBO Assembly Language Programming Application
;Copyright (c) Chris H. Pappas and William H. Murray, 1990

;program to raise a small number to an integer power

        DOSSEG                  ;use Intel segment-ordering
        .MODEL  small           ;set model size
        .8086                   ;8086 instructions

        .STACK  300h            ;set up 768-byte stack

        .DATA                   ;set up data location
pow     dw      05h             ;raise 4 to the 5th power
num     dw      04h
ans     dw      ?
```

```
          .CODE
Turbo     PROC    FAR                  ;main procedure declaration
          mov     ax,DGROUP            ;point ds toward .DATA
          mov     ds,ax

          mov     ax,num               ;place number in ax register
          mov     cx,pow               ;place power in cx
          dec     cx                   ;decrease by one
more:     mul     num                  ;obtain another power of number
          loop    more                 ;is cx decremented to zero?
          mov     ans,ax               ;save result in ans variable

          mov     ah,4Ch               ;return control to DOS
          int     21h
Turbo     ENDP                         ;end main procedure
          END                          ;end whole program
```

For this example, the number (*num*) 04h is raised to the power (*pow*) 05h. This produces the hexadecimal result (*ans*) of 400h. Since the multiply instruction expects to find the first number in the **ax** register, *num* is loaded into **ax** before entering the loop. The number of multiplies is set in the loop counter, **cx**. Since *num* has already been loaded into **ax**, the program only need multiply it by itself three more times. Thus, **cx** is decremented (**dec**) before actually entering the loop. Each time around the loop, the contents in **ax** are multiplied by *num*, raising it to a successively higher power. When **cx** is decremented to zero, the loop is exited and the results are stored in *ans*. Figure 17-7 shows the Turbo Debugger results for this application.

Determining the Square Root of a Number with a Simple Algorithm

The last example used an algorithm to raise a number to an integer power by repeated multiplication. This example creates another algorithm for extracting the square root of a number.

What follows is an interesting mathematical approach for extracting a square root of a hexadecimal number. The algorithm is as follows: You can approximate the square root of a number by subtracting successively higher odd numbers from the original number until that original number is reduced to zero. The number of subtractions is equal to the approximate

```
 ≡  File  View  Run  Breakpoints  Data  Options  Window  Help            READY
   ┌──Module: exp   File: exp.asm 30────────────────────┌─[■]═Reg═3═[↓]═┐
   │         .CODE                                       │ ax 0400  │c=0│
   │ Turbo   PROC    FAR            ;main procedure declaration│ bx 0002  │z=0│
   │         mov     ax,DGROUP      ;point ds toward .DATA │ cx 0000  │s=0│
   │         mov     ds,ax                               │ dx 0000  │o=0│
   │                                                     │ si 0000  │p=1│
   │         mov     ax,num         ;place number in ax registe│ di 0000  │a=0│
   │         mov     cx,pow         ;place power in cx    │ bp 0000  │i=1│
   │         dec     cx             ;decrease by one      │ sp 030E  │d=0│
   │ more:   mul     num            ;obtain another power of nu│ ds 6DAE  │   │
   │         loop    more           ;is cx decremented to zero?│ es 6D9C  │   │
   │         mov     ans,ax         ;save result in ans variabl│ ss 6DAE  │   │
   │                                                     │ cs 6DAC  │   │
   │►        mov     ah,4Ch         ;return control to DOS │ ip 0016  │   │
   │         int     21h                                 └──────────┘   │
   │ Turbo   ENDP                   ;end main procedure                 │
   │         END                    ;end whole program                 │
   ├──Watches──────────────────────────────────────2──────────────────┤
   │ ans                   word 1024 (400h)                            │
   │ num                   word 4 (4h)                                 │
   │ pow                   word 5 (5h)                                 │
   └───────────────────────────────────────────────────────────────────┘
 F1-Help F2-Bkpt F3-Mod F4-Here F5-Zoom F6-Next F7-Trace F8-Step F9-Run F10-Menu
```

Figure 17-7.   The number 4h is raised to the 5h power

square root of the original number. For example, to find the square root of
110 decimal:

$$110 - 1 = 109$$
$$109 - 3 = 106$$
$$106 - 5 = 101$$
$$101 - 7 = 94$$
$$94 - 9 = 85$$
$$85 - 11 = 74$$
$$74 - 13 = 61$$
$$61 - 15 = 46$$
$$46 - 17 = 29$$
$$29 - 19 = 10 \leftarrow \text{subtraction \#10}$$
$$10 - 21 = -11$$

Thus, the approximate square root of 110 is 10. The same mathematical procedure works in hexadecimal. The following listing is a square root algorithm used with the 32-bit registers of the 80486 or 80386:

```
;TURBO Assembly Language Programming Application
;Copyright (c) Chris H. Pappas and William H. Murray, 1990

;program for finding the square root of a number
;using repeated subtraction technique
;program utilizes 80486 or 80386 32-bit registers

        DOSSEG                          ;use Intel segment-ordering
        .MODEL  small                   ;set model size
        .386                            ;80386 instructions

        .STACK  300h                    ;set up 768-byte stack

        .DATA                           ;set up data location
num     dd      0ACDEA452h
sqrt    dd      ?

        .CODE
Turbo   PROC    FAR                     ;main procedure declaration
        mov     ax,DGROUP               ;point ds toward .DATA
        mov     ds,ax

;program to find the square root of number
        mov     edx,0h                  ;zero temp. storage locat.
        mov     ecx,1h                  ;seed number for subtraction
        mov     eax,num                 ;get original number
cont:   sub     eax,ecx                 ;perform subtraction
        jb      done                    ;if less than zero, done
        inc     edx                     ;increment sq root value
        add     ecx,02h                 ;increase ecx to next odd number
        jmp     cont                    ;continue loop
done:   mov     sqrt,edx                ;save result in sqrt

        mov     ah,4Ch                  ;return control to DOS
        int     21h
Turbo   ENDP                            ;end main procedure
        END                             ;end whole program
```

In this example, **edx** is initially zeroed out since it will form the location for the answer (the square root). The **ecx** register will hold the location of the successively higher odd numbers. It is seeded with the first odd number, one. Upon entering the loop, **ecx** is subtracted from the value contained in the **eax** register. If the result of the subtraction is below zero, the program is ended. If the result of the subtraction is above or equal to zero, **ecx** is incremented to the next odd number and the loop is repeated. After leaving the loop, the square root is stored in *ans*. The square root value obtained in this example is 0D25Eh. Check the answer with the results shown in Figure 17-8.

Using Pointers for Accessing and Storing Data

In most assembly language work, you have to make sure that the variable sizes match the register sizes when loading and storing the contents of registers. Generally, you can only load defined byte (db) variables in 8-bit registers, such as **ah** or **dl**. The same holds true for all of the remaining data types. If you have been writing your own assembly language examples, you have probably encountered the assembler error message "data sizes do not match." This is why the multiple precision examples had to hold answers in two registers and store results in two separate variables. Using pointers eliminates the need for separate variables. Pointers allow you to work with mismatched data and register types, as shown in the next example.

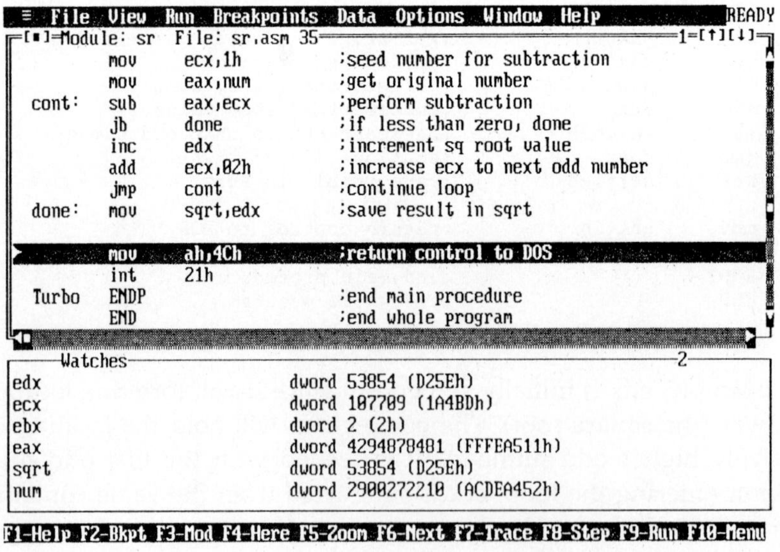

```
 ≡ File  View  Run  Breakpoints  Data  Options  Window  Help          READY
┌[■]═Module: sr   File: sr.asm 35══════════════════════════════1═[↑][↓]═┐
│          mov    ecx,1h          ;seed number for subtraction          │
│          mov    eax,num         ;get original number                  │
│  cont:   sub    eax,ecx         ;perform subtraction                  │
│          jb     done            ;if less than zero, done              │
│          inc    edx             ;increment sq root value              │
│          add    ecx,02h         ;increase ecx to next odd number      │
│          jmp    cont            ;continue loop                        │
│  done:   mov    sqrt,edx        ;save result in sqrt                  │
├──────────────────────────────────────────────────────────────────────┤
│►         mov    ah,4Ch          ;return control to DOS                │
│          int    21h                                                   │
│  Turbo   ENDP                   ;end main procedure                   │
│          END                    ;end whole program                   │
└┤◄├────────────────────────────────────────────────────────────────┤►├┘
┌─────Watches──────────────────────────────────────────────────2────────┐
│edx                    dword 53854 (D25Eh)                             │
│ecx                    dword 107709 (1A4BDh)                           │
│ebx                    dword 2 (2h)                                    │
│eax                    dword 4294070401 (FFFEA511h)                    │
│sqrt                   dword 53854 (D25Eh)                             │
│num                    dword 2900272210 (ACDEA452h)                    │
└────────────────────────────────────────────────────────────────────────┘
 F1-Help F2-Bkpt F3-Mod F4-Here F5-Zoom F6-Next F7-Trace F8-Step F9-Run F10-Menu
```

Figure 17-8.   The Watch window for this 80386 program contains detailed information on 32-bit registers and variables

```
;TURBO Assembly Language Programming Application
;Copyright (c) Chris H. Pappas and William H. Murray, 1990

;program to show the use of pointers when accessing
;and storing various data sizes

        DOSSEG                  ;use Intel segment-ordering
        .MODEL  small           ;set model size
        .8086                   ;8086 instructions

        .STACK  300h            ;set up 768-byte stack

        .DATA                   ;set up data location
num1    dw      1214h
num2    dd      5532AB12h
num3    dq      123456789FEDCBA0h
num4    dw      0021h
num5    dw      0054h
num6    dw      0076h
num7    dw      0022h
num8    dq      ?
num9    dw      4577h
num10   dw      0BA83h
num11   dd      ?


        .CODE
Turbo   PROC    FAR             ;main procedure declaration
        mov     ax,DGROUP       ;point ds toward .DATA
        mov     ds,ax

;moving dw sized number to 8-bit registers
        mov     al,byte ptr num1 ;moves 14h into al
        mov     ah,byte ptr num1+1 ;moves 12h into ah

;moving dd sized number to 16-bit registers
        mov     ax,word ptr num2 ;moves AB12h into ax
        mov     bx,word ptr num2+2 ;moves 5532h into bx

;moving dq sized number to 16-bit registers
        mov     ax,word ptr num3 ;moves CBA0 into ax
        mov     bx,word ptr num3+2 ;moves 9FED into bx
        mov     cx,word ptr num3+4 ;moves 5678 into cx
        mov     dx,word ptr num3+6 ;moves 1234 into dx

;storing 16-bit number in a dq variable
        mov     ax,num4          ;put 0021h into ax
        mov     word ptr num8,ax ;put ax in lsb of num8
        mov     ax,num5          ;put 0054h into ax
        mov     word ptr num8+2,ax ;place in num8
        mov     ax,num6          ;put 0076h into ax
        mov     word ptr num8+4,ax ;place in num8
        mov     ax,num7          ;put 0022h into ax
        mov     word ptr num8+6,ax ;place in msb of num8

;multiplying two dw sized numbers and storing results
;in a dd variable using pointers
        mov     ax,num9          ;place 4577h in ax
        mul     num10            ;multiply by 0BA83h
```

```
        mov     word ptr num11,ax   ;save lsbs in num11
        mov     word ptr num11+2,dx ;save msbs in num11

        mov     ah,4Ch              ;return control to DOS
        int     21h
Turbo   ENDP                        ;end main procedure
        END                         ;end whole program
```

In the first block of code, a *byte ptr* separates a 16-bit number and allows access to either the upper or lower 8 bits. Watch the syntax carefully. In the second block, two *word ptrs* divide a defined double (dd) into two 16-bit numbers. To get to the upper 16 bits, a 2 is added to the displacement in order to skip over two bytes. In the third block, a defined quadword (dq) is divided between four 16-bit registers.

You can save numeric results in the same manner. In the fourth block, information from defined word (dw) variables is packed and placed into a defined quadword (dq). Again, note the syntax.

Finally, the last piece of code multiplies *num9* and *num10*. Recall that the product formed by the **mul** mnemonic (when two words are multiplied together) is stored in the **dx:ax** pair of registers. Rather than storing them in separate variables, this program will pack them into one variable (*num11*), which is a defined double (dd). View the variables in Figure 17-9.

USING A LOOKUP TABLE

A *lookup table*, as the name implies, allows you to look up a value or extract a piece of data from a previously defined table. Lookup tables are often used in high-speed graphics and spelling checker programs. For example, you can enter a whole dictionary into a data segment in the form of a table. If you index the proper amount into the table, you can compare a word with one previously stored in the dictionary. If the word is found, a message such as "correctly spelled" could be printed on the screen. Otherwise, you might see a message such as "the word is not in the dictionary." Depending upon their function, lookup tables can also be called *data tables* or *shape tables*.

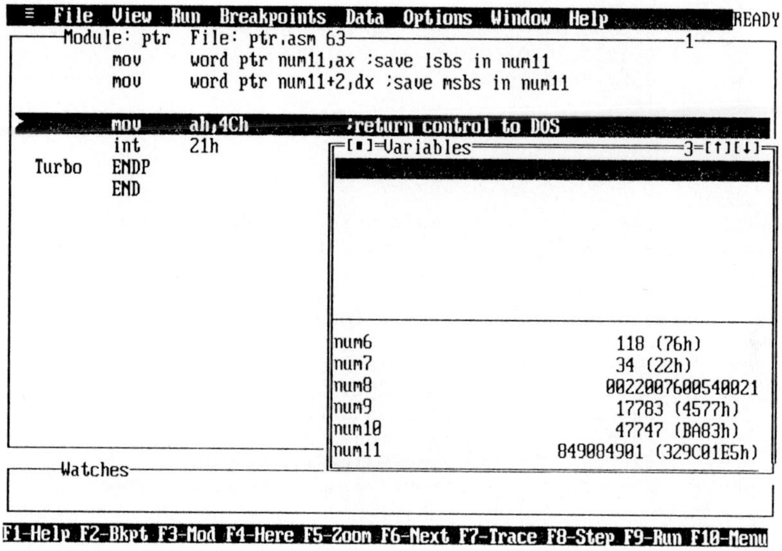

```
≡ File  View  Run  Breakpoints  Data  Options  Window  Help          READY
 ┌─Module: ptr  File: ptr.asm 63────────────────────────────1─┐
 │       mov       word ptr num11,ax  ;save lsbs in num11
 │       mov       word ptr num11+2,dx ;save msbs in num11
 │
 ├──────mov      ah,4Ch            ;return control to DOS───────┤
 │       int       21h       ┌─[■]─Variables════════════3═[↑][↓]═┐
 │ Turbo ENDP                │
 │       END                 │
 │                           │
 │                           │
 │                           │
 │                           │
 │                           │
 │                           │num6                  118 (76h)
 │                           │num7                   34 (22h)
 │                           │num8         0022007600540021
 │                           │num9               17783 (4577h)
 │                           │num10              47747 (BA83h)
 └──Watches─────────────────│num11       849004901 (329C01E5h)
 ┌───────────────────────────────────────────────────────────┐
 │
 └───────────────────────────────────────────────────────────┘
 F1-Help F2-Bkpt F3-Mod F4-Here F5-Zoom F6-Next F7-Trace F8-Step F9-Run F10-Menu
```

Figure 17-9.   A Variable window in which the variables *num6* through *num11* are shown

Creating a Lookup Table to Find Logarithms

You have already seen that special mathematical functions require the implementation of programmer-created algorithms. Algorithms are not only hard to come by, but hard to implement in assembly language. This is the perfect place to illustrate the use of lookup tables to find hard to determine mathematical values. The following program allows you to obtain the sine values for the angles between 0 and 90 degrees, in increments of 10 degrees:

```
;TURBO Assembly Language Programming Application
;Copyright (c) Chris H. Pappas and William H. Murray, 1990

;program shows how to access a lookup table of data

        DOSSEG                  ;use Intel segment-ordering
        .MODEL   small          ;set model size
        .8086                   ;8086 instructions
```

```
        .STACK   300h              ;set up 768-byte stack

        .DATA                      ;set up data location
table   dw       0,1736,3420,5000,6428,7660,8660
        dw       9397,9848,10000
value   dw       70
answer  dw       ?
ten     db       10

        .CODE
Turbo   PROC     FAR               ;main procedure declaration
        mov      ax,DGROUP         ;point ds toward .DATA
        mov      ds,ax

;example of using value given as index into a lookup table
        mov      ax,value          ;number to look up
        div      ten               ;reduce to an index value
        rol      ax,1              ;multiply by 2, for word index
        lea      bx,table          ;find start of table
        add      bx,ax             ;get index+offset
        mov      dx,[bx]           ;get value from table
        mov      answer,dx         ;move value from dx to answer

        mov      ah,4Ch            ;return control to DOS
        int      21h
Turbo   ENDP                       ;end main procedure
        END                        ;end whole program
```

The data segment shows a table (*table*) containing the sine values for the decimal angles 0 through 90, and accurate to three or four places. Each number in the table has an implied decimal point. For example, the number 1736 represents the sine of 10 degrees and is actually 0.1736. Also, notice that these numbers are stored in decimal format so they are easier to read. In a data dump, however, you will see hexadecimal results. To keep the program simple, the sine value to be looked up is contained in the variable *value*. The answer will be returned to a defined word (dw) variable called *answer*. The *value* moved into the **ax** register at the start of the program will serve as the index into the lookup table after some software conditioning.

First, the number in *value* is divided by ten to produce a simple index into the table. Recall that the table contains sine values for each 10 degrees. Because the program deals with a table using defined words (dw), this index must be multiplied by two since a word is made up of 2 bytes. Instead of using the multiply instruction, a simple rotate left command (**rol**) produces faster results. The value in **ax** is added to the starting location of the *table*, given in **bx**, to produce the total offset into *table*. The **mov** instruction returns the digits 9397 (24B5h) to the **dx** register and that value is finally stored in the variable *answer*.

You gain several advantages by using a lookup table. You obtain a relatively easy program, and the possibility of high precision answers in decimal or hexadecimal (or any other) format. The disadvantages might not be as apparent. The results had to be previously stored in the data segment, limiting the program's flexibility. For example, in the preceding case, if you wanted the sine of 45 degrees, you would have to expand the program to include angle increments of 5 instead of 10. Another disadvantage is that the precision and accuracy of the answer is controlled by the programmer, not by a mathematical function. Errors creep into data entry, especially when data tables are many lines long.

Performing Code Conversions Without a Lookup Table

You can also use a lookup table to convert numbers from ASCII to hexadecimal. However, this example performs the conversion with a simple mathematical operation. ASCII codes are used for almost all information read from keyboards and sent to monitor screens or printers. For example, if a 7 is entered at the keyboard, an ASCII 37h might be read into the **al** register. Likewise, if numbers generated from a program are to be displayed on the screen, they must be in ASCII form, not hexadecimal. Observe the relationship between ASCII and hexadecimal numbers in Table 17-1.

For the numerical ASCII digits between 30h and 39h, merely subtract 30h from each number to form the correct hexadecimal result. For the digits from 41h to 46h, subtract 37h. Remember to use hexadecimal arithmetic when making the subtractions. Also, note that there are many possible ASCII values, and that you can only convert numerical digits in this manner. The following example performs no error checking. In other words, it assumes input in the correct range of acceptable values.

```
;TURBO Assembly Language Programming Application
;Copyright (c) Chris H. Pappas and William H. Murray, 1990

;program to convert ascii digits to hexadecimal numbers

        DOSSEG                  ;use Intel segment-ordering
        .MODEL  small           ;set model size
        .8086                   ;8086 instructions

        .STACK  300h            ;set up 768-byte stack

        .DATA                   ;set up data location
```

```
ascii    db        44h            ;ascii "D"
hexdig   db        ?

         .CODE
Turbo    PROC      FAR            ;main procedure declaration
         mov       ax,DGROUP      ;point ds toward .DATA
         mov       ds,ax

;converting an ascii value to a hexadecimal number
;assume ascii input for 0,1,2,3,4,5,6,7,8,9,a,b,c,d,e,f
         mov       al,ascii       ;ascii number to convert in al
         sub       al,30h         ;see if a number 0-9
         cmp       al,9
         jg        isletter       ;if greater than 9, a letter
         jmp       done           ;quit
isletter:
         sub       al,07h         ;sub 7 and finish conversion
done:
         mov       hexdig,al      ;save result in answer

         mov       ah,4Ch         ;return control to DOS
         int       21h
Turbo    ENDP                     ;end main procedure
         END                      ;end whole program
```

Table 17-1.   ASCII and Hexadecimal Equivalents

ASCII	Hexadecimal
30h	0h
31h	1h
32h	2h
33h	3h
34h	4h
35h	5h
36h	6h
37h	7h
38h	8h
39h	9h
41h	0Ah
42h	0Bh
43h	0Ch
44h	0Dh
45h	0Eh
46h	0Fh

Notice that 30h is subtracted from the contents of the variable *ascii*. This is because the input should fall in the range 30h to 46h. Now, if the result of the subtraction is a number between 0h and 9h, the program is over and the conversion is complete. However, if the **cmp** operation finds a number greater than 09h, it must be a hexadecimal "letter." To complete the conversion of a letter, a 07h (a total of 37h, from ASCII) is subtracted to place the data in the correct range of the hexadecimal digits A through F. For this example, a 0Dh will be returned to the variable *hexdig*.

USING THE BIOS/DOS SYSTEM INTERRUPTS AND ADDRESSING PORTS

The BIOS and DOS interrupts are easy to implement and provide access to powerful screen, cursor, character, and graphics routines. These routines are part of your computer's hardware or DOS operating system. They are actually machine code instructions that are either embedded in ROM (read only memory) chips or loaded into RAM (random access memory) when you boot your system. As mentioned, they provide software routines for controlling the computer's hardware. When you tap into these routines, you are harnessing the heart of the machine. Appendix B contains a complete list of the available BIOS and DOS interrupts. In the following examples, you will learn how to use the BIOS and DOS routines and achieve spectacular control over your system with relatively simple programs.

Ports serve as effective input and output channels on your computer. You are undoubtedly familiar with serial and parallel ports. There are other ports, too. For example, the keyboard and speaker ports. Ports have unique identification numbers. The following sections explain how to send and receive information from your computer's ports.

Clearing the Screen with an Interrupt

When you send output to the screen, you will often want the screen cleared first. In many cases, this may just require a simple screen clear operation issued from DOS (the **cls** command). At other times, you may want to clear the screen or change screen colors and attributes from within your program. You can easily achieve screen control with BIOS type 10h interrupts. Examine the various BIOS interrupts in Appendix B. When using BIOS or DOS interrupts, remember that the interrupt call is a hexadecimal number and should be entered in a program as **int 10h**. You will notice that all BIOS interrupts are **int 10h** and that only the parameters, contained in various registers, are changed for the different functions. These parameters are almost always entered as decimal numbers—for example, **mov ah,11**. Also remember that an interrupt call from your program merely points to more code—code written by someone else. When you call an interrupt, you are using code previously stored in ROM or RAM by the computer manufacturer or by DOS.

The first example clears your computer screen:

```
;TURBO Assembly Language Programming Application
;Copyright (c) Chris H. Pappas and William H. Murray, 1990

;program uses bios interrupt to clear the screen

        DOSSEG                  ;use Intel segment-ordering
        .MODEL  small           ;set model size
        .8086                   ;8086 instructions

        .STACK  300h            ;set up 768-byte stack

        .CODE
Turbo   PROC    FAR             ;main procedure declaration

;actual code to clear screen
        mov     cx,0000         ;row,column upper-left corner
        mov     dx,2479h        ;row,column lower-right corner
        mov     bh,07           ;normal char attribute
        mov     ah,06           ;scroll active page up
        mov     al,00           ;scroll entire window
        int     10h             ;call bios interrupt
;end of clear screen routine

        mov     ah,4Ch          ;return control to DOS
        int     21h
Turbo   ENDP                    ;end main procedure
        END                     ;end whole program
```

Before calling an interrupt, the various system registers are initialized to the proper values. In this case, **ah** specifies "scroll active page up" when set to 6. The **al** register will blank the entire window when set to 0. The **bh** register contains the value of the attribute used when printing blank characters to the screen. The normal attribute is 7. The **cx** and **dx** registers control the size of the screen window that will be cleared. The **cx** register is divided so that **ch** and **cl** point to the upper-left corner of the window.

Likewise, the **dx** register is divided so that **dh** and **dl** mark the lower-right corner of the window. In this program, setting **cx** to 0000 sets **ch** and **cl** to 0, or the upper-left corner of the screen. The **dx** register is set to 2479h, which places a 24h in **dh** and a 79h in **dl**. This specifies the lower-right corner of the screen. When the interrupt is finally called, the entire screen is cleared. By altering the values in **cx** and **dx**, you can clear any portion of the screen (called a window). Could you find use for such a program? Why not experiment with different window sizes and see what happens.

Turning Off the NUMLOCK Feature

You may want to control the initial setup of your keyboard. Maybe you like to type in all uppercase, or perhaps you would like to have the SCROLL LOCK turned on automatically. Did you know that the IBM PS/2s automatically set the NUMLOCK to ON when the system is booted? This is a problem for many people. If you use the numeric keypad to move the cursor and forget to turn NUMLOCK off, you will have a string of 4s, 8s, 6s, or 2s across your screen. To fix this, the following program sets NUMLOCK to OFF. If the program is stored and called from the *autoexec.bat* file, the whole process will be automatic and NUMLOCK will be turned off when you boot your machine.

To manipulate the keyboard, you must use a technique called a *segment override*. When using a segment override, you will transmit information to the keyboard port. The information you send affects the keyboard status byte at memory location 417h. This status byte is the same for the PC, XT, AT, and PS/2 series computers. Table 17-2 shows the meaning of each bit in the keyboard status byte. If you want to change another feature, just change the bit that affects that feature.

```
;TURBO Assembly Language Programming Application
;Copyright (c) Chris H. Pappas and William H. Murray, 1990

;program will turn off numlock on the keyboard

        DOSSEG                  ;use Intel segment-ordering
        .MODEL  small           ;set model size
        .8086                   ;8086 instructions

        .STACK  300h            ;set up 768-byte stack

        .CODE
```

```
Turbo   PROC    FAR                     ;main procedure declaration

        mov     ax,0                    ;prepare to set es to zero
        mov     es,ax                   ;move it in
        mov     al,es:[417h]            ;keyboard status byte
        and     al,11011111b            ;prepare to mask numlock
        mov     es:[417h],al            ;return altered information

        mov     ah,4Ch                  ;return control to DOS
        int     21h
Turbo   ENDP                            ;end main procedure
        END                             ;end whole program
```

In this example, the status byte is first read to obtain the current information. That information is then masked so that everything but the NUMLOCK information is retained. The altered information is then returned to the same memory location. Notice that the memory location 417h, the keyboard port, is read into the **es** register. The syntax used here is known as a segment override, with **es** being the extra segment. The information from the read information is stored in the **al** register. This data is then "anded" with the mask 0DFh or 11011111b. The mask allows all information but the NUMLOCK data to be retained. The information is then rewritten to location 417h. You can use the **and** mask technique any time you need to set a particular bit to 0. Similarly, you can use an **or** mask to force a bit to 1.

Table 17-2. Keyboard Bit Information from Port 417h Returned to the **al** Register

Bit	Meaning
0	Right SHIFT key depressed (1)
1	Left SHIFT key depressed (1)
2	CTRL key depressed (1)
3	ALT key depressed (1)
4	SCROLL LOCK active (1)
5	NUMLOCK active (1)
6	CAPS LOCK active (1)
7	INSERT active (1)

If this program were written exclusively for the 80486 or 80386, you could have set or cleared the NUMLOCK bit with

```
btr al,5
```

instead of using a mask.

Sending Information to the Speaker Port

The next example program manipulates information at the speaker port located at 61h. You can turn on the speaker by sending a 0 to port 61h. By alternating an on-off sequence through bit 1 of this port, you can obtain different frequencies. When the program itself turns the speaker on and off, the frequency of the sound will be determined by the execution speed of the software. The actual frequencies produced by this program are dependent upon the speed of your system; you may have to adjust them to obtain the desired effect.

```
;TURBO Assembly Language Programming Application
;Copyright (c) Chris H. Pappas and William H. Murray, 1990

;program will generate a strange sound from the speaker

        DOSSEG                  ;use Intel segment-ordering
        .MODEL  small           ;set model size
        .8086                   ;8086 instructions

        .STACK  300h            ;set up 768-byte stack

        .DATA                   ;set up data location
temp    dw      0               ;storage

        .CODE
Turbo   PROC    FAR             ;main procedure declaration
        mov     ax,DGROUP       ;point ds toward .DATA
        mov     ds,ax

        mov     dx,0            ;initialize dx to zero
        in      al,61h          ;get speaker port info in al
        and     al,0FCh         ;mask all but lower two bits
more:   mov     info,00h        ;place zero in scratch variable
        inc     dx              ;increment dx
        cmp     dx,18           ;repeated sound 18 times?
        je      finish          ;if yes, end program
comp:   xor     al,02h          ;xor lower two bits of al
        mov     cx,info         ;get frequency from storage
        cmp     cx,250h         ;reached 592 hertz?
        je      more            ;if yes, repeat sequence,
```

```
          inc     temp              ;if not, increase frequency
          out     61h,al            ;and output it to speaker
delay1:   loop    delay1            ;the time delay
          jmp     comp              ;complete
finish:

          mov     ah,4Ch            ;return control to DOS
          int     21h
Turbo     ENDP                      ;end main procedure
          END                       ;end whole program
```

Information is retrieved from the port with an **in** operation and written back to the port with an **out** operation. The masking of bit information is done twice, once with an **and** and once with an **xor** mnemonic. From the logic operations of the previous chapter, can you tell what is happening? Three loops are used to determine the number of times the sound is repeated, the frequency of the sound, and the time delay used for each note. In this example, the **dx** register determines how many times the same sound is repeated (18 times). The variable *temp* holds the frequency information during each trip around the frequency loop. Finally, the one-line time delay loop simply decrements the **cx** register to zero. Can you determine where the value of **cx** is being generated? Is **cx** always initialized to the same value?

Printing on the Text Screen

Of all DOS interrupt routines, none is more popular that the DOS interrupt 21h, which allows you to print string information to the screen. When using this interrupt, remember that the string must terminate with a $ symbol.

```
;TURBO Assembly Language Programming Application
;Copyright (c) Chris H. Pappas and William H. Murray, 1990

;this program prints a message to the text screen using a
;standard dos interrupt

          DOSSEG                    ;use Intel segment-ordering
          .MODEL  small             ;set model size
          .8086                     ;8086 instructions

          .STACK  300h              ;set up 768-byte stack

          .DATA                     ;set up data location
text      db          'The TURBO Assembler is great!$'
```

```
            .CODE
Turbo       PROC    FAR                 ;main procedure declaration
            mov     ax,DGROUP           ;point ds toward .DATA
            mov     ds,ax

            lea     dx,text             ;get location of string
            mov     ah,09h              ;set print parameter
            int     21h                 ;call dos print routine

            mov     ah,4Ch              ;return control to DOS
            int     21h
Turbo       ENDP                        ;end main procedure
            END                         ;end whole program
```

The text to be printed is stored in a db variable called *text*. This string terminates with a $ sentinel contained in the string itself. To use this interrupt, the effective address of *text* is loaded into the **dx** register. The interrupt parameter for printing a string (09h) is placed in the **ah** register, and then the interrupt is actually called. Operating at Turbo speeds, the text string will be printed on the screen at the current cursor location.

Try altering this program so that the screen is cleared before the string is printed. (You will need to incorporate the clear screen code from the first example.)

Viewing the Flag Values in the eflag Register of the 80486 or 80386

The following program is for users of 80486 and 80386 computers. However, with just a little effort, you could alter the program to display the **flags** register of the 80286/8088 computers. This example will use several DOS interrupts to print the contents of the **eflag** register, which contains 13 flag fields. Six of these flags, called status flags, are changed by, and provide necessary information for, arithmetic and logical control decisions. These are **cf** (carry flag), **pf** (parity flag), **af** (auxiliary carry flag), **zf** (zero flag), **sf** (sign flag), and **of** (overflow flag).

- The carry flag (**cf**) is set to 1 when a carry or borrow out is generated by an arithmetic operation. Otherwise, it is reset to 0. The carry flag is also used by shift and rotate instructions and can contain the bit shifted or rotated out of the register.

- The parity flag (**pf**) is used for data communication applications and is set to 1 to generate odd parity or reset to 0 to generate even parity.

- The auxiliary carry flag (**af**) is used in Binary Coded Decimal (BCD) arithmetic and indicates whether there has been a carry out of or borrow into the least significant 4-bit digit of a BCD value.

- The zero flag (**zf**) sets itself to 1 to indicate when the result of an operation is zero.

- The sign flag (**sf**) is set to 1 for a negative result and reset to 0 for a positive result.

- The overflow flag (**of**) indicates whether an operation has generated a carry into the high-order bit of the result but not a carry out of the high-order bit.

Four of the thirteen flags—**tf**, **if**, **df**, and **vm**—are used to direct certain processor operations. The trap flag (**tf**), when set, puts the microprocessor into single-step mode and enables the debugging of a program. The interrupt-enable flag (**if**) enables external interrupts when set to 1 and disables external interrupts when reset to 0. The direction of string operations is controlled by the direction flag (**df**). With **df** reset to 0, (e)**si** and/or (e)**di** are automatically incremented forward. With **df** set to 1, (e)**si** and/or (e)**di** are automatically decremented. When the virtual mode flag (**vm**) is set, the 80486/80386 switches from protected mode to virtual 8086 mode. You can set the **vm** flag by using the **iret** instruction, or by using task switches occurring during protected mode execution.

```
;TURBO Assembly Language Programming Application
;Copyright (c) Chris H. Pappas and William H. Murray, 1990

;this program will print out the current 32-bit eflag register
;to the screen

            DOSSEG                  ;use Intel segment-ordering
            .MODEL   small          ;set model size
            .386                    ;80386 instructions

            .STACK   300h           ;set up 768-byte stack

            .DATA                   ;set up data location
tag         db           3 dup (0ah,0dh)
            db           '                reserved        v  r    n'
            db           ' i/o  o  d I t s '
            db           'z    a    p   c',0ah,0dh
            db           '****************************m f 0 t'
            db           '    1 f f f f f '
            db           'f 0 f 0 f 1 f',0ah,0dh
            db           '-----------------------------'
```

```
          db             '--------------------------------'
          db             0ah,0dh,'$'

          .CODE
Turbo     PROC    FAR                    ;main procedure declaration
          mov     ax,DGROUP              ;point ds toward .DATA
          mov     ds,ax

          lea     edx,tag                ;print eflag labels
          mov     ah,09h                 ;dos parameter
          int     21h                    ;dos interrupt

          pushfd                         ;push eflags to stack
          pop     edx                    ;return them in edx register

          mov     cx,32                  ;print 32 bits of eflag
more:     rol     edx,1                  ;rotate to get one bit
          mov     al,dl                  ;prepare to make ascii byte
          and     al,1                   ;mask for lower bit only
          or      al,30h                 ;convert 1 or 0 to 31 or 30
          push    edx                    ;save edx contents on stack
          mov     dl,al                  ;print the ascii byte to screen
          mov     ah,2                   ;dos parameter for char print
          int     21h                    ;dos interrupt
          mov     dl,' '                 ;print space between each digit
          mov     ah,2                   ;dos parameter for char print
          int     21h                    ;dos interrupt
          pop     edx                    ;return contents to edx
          loop    more                   ;repeat until cx is 0

          mov     ah,4Ch                 ;return control to DOS
          int     21h
Turbo     ENDP                           ;end main procedure
          END                            ;end whole program
```

To view the **eflag** register, you need two operations. First, the **pushfd** command places the **eflag**'s register contents on the computer's stack. Next, the stack is popped into the **edx** register (**pop edx**), and the **eflag**'s contents are returned. You can now observe the contents of **eflag** by studying the **edx** register. This program will create a table on the screen and then print the **eflag** information in binary digits. A binary 1 represents a set flag while a 0 represents a reset flag. To print the bits in this manner you need a routine that will print 1 bit at a time, from the **edx** register, to the text screen. To accomplish this, the contents of **edx** are simply rotated, masked, converted to ASCII, and printed to the screen as character data—1 bit at a time. A space is placed between each bit for clarity. This program uses a loop to print each bit, so it will be repeated 32 times. A header is printed to identify each flag before the flag information is actually sent to the screen. Figure 17-10 shows what the screen will look like.

```
C>flag
```

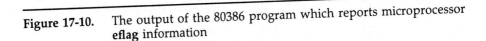

```
                                     u r   n i/o o d I t s z   a   P   c
              reserved              ▓ f 0 t   l f f f f f 0 f 0 f 1 f
         ****************************
         _____
         0 0 0 0 0 0 0 0 0 0 0 0 0 0 0 0 1 1 1 0 0 1 0 0 1 0 0 0 1 1 0
         C>
```

Figure 17-10.   The output of the 80386 program which reports microprocessor **eflag** information

Plotting Dots on the Screen with a System Interrupt

The entire family of IBM personal computers supports at least two graphics modes on color monitors. One is called the medium resolution mode and the other the high resolution mode. The *medium resolution mode* can plot 320 dots horizontally and 200 dots vertically, with four colors present on the screen at any given time. The *high resolution mode* supports 640 dots horizontally and 200 dots vertically, with two colors (usually black and white). Additional modes have been added with the development of EGA and VGA graphics standards. Table 17-3 shows the various graphics modes available for the IBM models 50, 60, 70, and 80, supporting the VGA standard. The following example plots three tiny dots near the center of the 320x200 graphics screen. Each dot is exactly 1 pixel wide—the smallest dot possible in this screen mode. Look carefully; the dots might go unnoticed.

```
;TURBO Assembly Language Programming Application
;Copyright (c) Chris H. Pappas and William H. Murray, 1990

;program to plot dots on medium resolution
;640x200 color graphics screen using a bios interrupt

        DOSSEG                  ;use Intel segment-ordering
        .MODEL  small           ;set model size
        .8086                   ;8086 instructions

        .STACK  300h            ;set up 768-byte stack

        .CODE
Turbo   PROC    FAR             ;main procedure declaration
```

```
;routine for plotting three dots near the center of the screen
        mov     ah,00           ;prepare to set screen mode
        mov     al,04           ;set 320x200 color mode
        int     10h             ;call interrupt

        mov     ah,11           ;set color palette
        mov     bh,00           ;set background color
        mov     bl,01           ;set it to blue
        int     10h             ;call interrupt

        mov     ah,11           ;set color palette
        mov     bh,01           ;select foreground palette
        mov     bl,00           ;green/red/yellow
        int     10h             ;call interrupt

        mov     al,02           ;set dot color to red
        mov     ah,12           ;write dot parameter
        mov     dx,100          ;set for 100 rows down (vert)
        mov     cx,158          ;set for 158 columns (horz)
        int     10h             ;call interrupt
        mov     ah,12           ;write dot parameter
        mov     cx,160          ;plot another
        int     10h             ;call interrupt
        mov     ah,12           ;write dot parameter
        mov     cx,162          ;plot another
        int     10h             ;call interrupt

        mov     ah,4Ch          ;return control to DOS
        int     21h
Turbo   ENDP                    ;end main procedure
        END                     ;end whole program
```

Before any plotting takes place, you need to initialize the medium resolution screen by using the following code:

```
mov     ah,00           ;prepare to set screen mode
mov     al,04           ;set 320x200 color mode
int     10h             ;call interrupt
```

Table 17-4 shows how the values for **ah** and **al** are determined. Next, you need to set the background and foreground colors:

```
mov     ah,11           ;set color palette
mov     bh,00           ;set background color
mov     bl,01           ;set it to blue
int     10h             ;call interrupt
```

With **bh** set to 0, the color selected will form the background color for the screen. Color numbers range from 0 to 15. Table 17-4 shows 16 possible

Table 17-3.   Seventeen Video Modes (all available on VGA, some on CGA and EGA)

Mode (hex)	Type	Colors	Buffer Start	Number Pages	Character Format	Box Size	Graphics Screen
0,1	A/N	16	B8000	8	40x25	8x8	320x200
2,3	A/N	16	B8000	8	80x25	8x8	640x200
0*,1*	A/N	16	B8000	8	40x25	8x14	320x350
2*,3*	A/N	16	B8000	8	80x25	8x14	640x350
0+,1+	A/N	16	B8000	8	40x25	9x16	360x400
2+,3+	A/N	16	B8000	8	80x25	9x16	720x400
4,5	APA	4	B8000	1	40x25	8x8	320x200
6	APA	2	B8000	1	80x25	8X8	640x200
7	A/N	mono	B0000	8	80x25	9x14	720x350
7+	A/N	mono	B0000	8	80x25	9x16	720x400
D	APA	16	A0000	8	40x25	8x8	320x200
E	APA	16	A0000	4	80x25	8x8	640x200
F	APA	mono	A0000	2	80x25	8x14	640x350
10	APA	16	A0000	2	80x25	8x14	640x350
11	APA	2	A0000	1	80x30	8x16	640x480
12	APA	16	A0000	1	80x30	8x16	640x480
13	APA	256	A0000	1	40x25	8x8	320x200

* enhanced modes from EGA adapter
+ enhanced modes

color values that you can use. The background color for this example is blue. You select the foreground palette a bit differently:

```
mov    ah,11          ;set color palette
mov    bh,01          ;select foreground palette
mov    bl,00          ;green/red/yellow
int    10h            ;call interrupt
```

The **bh** register is set to 1 for foreground color selection, while **bl** selects the green/red/yellow palette. You only need to do the three steps for initialization once, unless you want a color change for the whole screen. The remainder of the program uses the "write dot" command three times.

Table 17-4.   Color Choices for the 640x480 Graphics Screen

Number	Color
0	Black
1	Blue
2	Green
3	Cyan
4	Red
5	Magenta
6	Brown
7	White
8	Dark gray
9	Light blue
10	Light green
11	Light cyan
12	Light red
13	Light magenta
14	Yellow
15	Intensified white

When you use "write dot," the **cx** register contains the horizontal displacement while **dx** contains the vertical. For this plot, you can plot the dots in red by setting **al** to 2. The **cx** register is moved twice for the remaining dots. To draw a line using BIOS interrupts, a program would have to plot a series of dots in the desired direction by using a loop. This is usually not a big chore if the line is vertical or horizontal but becomes more taxing if the line is anything else. Very fast algorithms have been developed for plotting lines between two specified screen points.

This program exits in the medium resolution color mode. If you want to switch back to text mode automatically, you need to make two additions. First, you have to write a small piece of code to switch to the text screen. The format would be similar to the code used in the present example for switching to the graphics screen. But you also need a second piece of code to keep your new "set to text mode" routine from returning to text mode before you can view the dots on the screen. Usually, a routine that will wait for a keypress is inserted between the graphics routine and the return to text mode routine.

PUTTING YOUR KNOWLEDGE TO WORK

1. Give several examples of the immediate addressing mode. Use different mnemonics to illustrate your point.

2. Give several examples of the direct addressing mode. Use different mnemonics to illustrate your point. When would direct addressing be more efficient than immediate addressing?

3. Write a program to add the numbers 0BEh, 0ADh, 012h, and 078h. Do you have to worry about a carry here? What is the sum?

4. Write a program to add the numbers 0FEEDh, 01234h, and 078ABh. Is a carry generated? What is the sum?

5. Write a program that will add the following: 1234567890ABCDEFh and 9876543210FDECBAh. Use pointers. Store each number in a *dq* variable. Store the sum in a *dq* variable.

6. Using a lookup table, write a program that will return the cosine values for the angles from 0 to 90 degrees in increments of 5 degrees. Use a calculator to determine the cosine values. Scale the values so that they form a four-digit integer (see lookup table example).

7. Using the keyboard status bits, write a program that will turn the CAPS LOCK on when it is executed. Use an **or** mask.

8. Repeat the preceding program for 80486/80386 computers using the **bts** mnemonic to achieve the same results.

9. Write a program that draws a horizontal line on the 640x480 VGA graphics screen. Use a loop to plot a series of dots.

10. Describe the differences between using ports and interrupts when controlling the computer.

18

PROGRAMMING POWER: MACROS AND PROCEDURES

In this chapter you will learn

- How to define and write simple macros

- How to define and write simple procedures

- How to create and use a macro library

- How to create and use a library of procedures

- How to use the Turbo Librarian, TLIB

- How to create and use an object module library

- How to decide whether a macro or a procedure is the right technique for your program

Macros, procedures, and object module libraries enable assembly language programmers to call and use previously debugged code. Besides making debugging faster, this also frees you from "reinventing the wheel" each time you create a new program. This chapter illustrates why assembly language programmers develop a bias for one particular technique, such as macros or procedures. It deals with macros, procedures, and object module libraries and also explains the advantages and disadvantages of each. The fourth section suggests how to select the best method for your particular application.

MACROS

Macros are a flexible programming option available for Turbo assembly language programmers. The word "macro" is an assembly language directive that instructs the assembler to replace macro calls within the body of the program with a copy of the macro code. Once the operation or code is established in a macro, the assembler inserts the actual macro code into the program in place of the macro name each time a macro is named in a program. Macros are said to execute "in line" since the program flow is uninterrupted. Macros can be created and stored in the actual program or called from a previously established macro library. A *macro library* is an ASCII file of macros that can be called from your program during assembly. Remember, the code in a macro or macro library has not been assembled — it remains in ASCII form. This is one of the ways in which a macro library differs from an object module library that is available at link time. Object module libraries will be explained later in this chapter.

The Framework of a Macro

A macro has three essential parts: a header, a body, and an end (**endm**). The header contains the name of the macro followed by the *macro* directive and any optional arguments that are to be passed to or from the macro. Macros can receive information in the form of arguments or via any global variable or system register. The body of a macro contains the program code — the code that is actually inserted into the program when the macro is called. All macros must end with the **endm** instruction.

   As an example, examine the following listing:

```
;TURBO Assembly Language Programming Application
;Copyright (c) Chris H. Pappas and William H. Murray, 1990

;using a macro for a time delay

        DOSSEG                  ;use Intel segment-ordering
```

```
        .MODEL  small           ;set model size
        .8086                   ;8086 instructions

        .STACK  300h            ;set up 768-byte stack

        .DATA                   ;set up data location
blank   db      2000 dup (' ')

killtime macro  increment
        local   loop1,loop2     ;;loop1 & loop2 are local labels
        push    dx              ;;save dx & cx values
        push    cx
        mov     dx,increment    ;;pass time increment to dx
loop2:  mov     cx,0FF00h       ;;load cx with 00FF00h
loop1:  dec     cx              ;;kill time
        jnz     loop1           ;;if not zero, loop1
        dec     dx              ;;if cx=0, decrement dx
        jnz     loop2           ;;if dx not zero, load cx again
        pop     cx              ;;restore dx & cx values
        pop     dx
        endm                    ;;leave the macro

        .CODE
Turbo   PROC    far             ;main procedure declaration
        mov     ax,DGROUP       ;point ds toward .DATA
        mov     ds,ax
        mov     es,ax

;program will clear the screen by writing 2000 blanks to
;the screen.  By writing these with a different value in bl
;the color of the whole screen can be changed.  The killtime
;macro will hold the color for a specified amount of time.

        mov     cx,9            ;repeat loop 9 times
        mov     bl,0            ;set background color
repeat: lea     bp,blank        ;write string of blanks
        mov     dx,0            ;move cursor to top left corner
        mov     ah,19           ;write string attribute
        mov     al,1            ;print characters and move cursor
        push    cx              ;save loop counter
        mov     cx,2000         ;write 2000 blanks
        int     10h             ;interrupt call
        killtime 10h            ;delay 10 units
        add     bl,16           ;change color of background
        pop     cx              ;restore loop counter
        loop    repeat          ;do it 9 total times

        mov     ah,4Ch          ;return control to DOS
        int     21h
Turbo   ENDP                    ;end main procedure
        END                     ;end whole program
```

The name of the macro in this example is **killtime**. When the assembler
encounters the name **killtime** in a program, it copies the body of the macro
to that location, passing the argument *increment* to the **dx** register. The local

declaration prevents multiple calls to a label by creating a unique label each time **killtime** is requested. These unique labels are substituted for loop1 and loop2 automatically. This macro kills time by decrementing the contents of the **dx** and **cx** registers, creating a time delay when the program executes. The **dx** register serves as the course control for time while the **cx** register can fine-tune the delay. The amount of actual delay depends on the clock speed of your computer.

This program changes the background color of the screen nine times by adding a 16 to the **bl** register each time through the loop. The **killtime** macro will determine how long each differently colored screen remains in view. The value of the **killtime** argument was determined experimentally. Depending on the speed of your computer, you may have to adjust the values up or down.

In the following listing, the *.lst* file for this program shows how the macro was expanded within the program code:

```
Turbo Assembler          1/03/90     20:30:14        Page 1

1
2    ;TURBO Assembly Language Programming Application
3    ;Copyright (c) Chris H. Pappas and William H. Murray, 1990
4
5    ;using a macro for a time delay
6
7                              DOSSEG
8  0000                       .MODEL   small
9                             .8086
10
11 0000                       .STACK   300h
12
13 0000                       .DATA
14 0000   07D0*(20)   blank   db       2000 dup (' ')
15
16                    killtime macro    increment
17                            local    loop1,loop2
18                            push     dx
19                            push     cx
20                            mov      dx,increment
21                    loop2:  mov      cx,0FF00h
22                    loop1:  dec      cx
23                            jnz      loop1
24                            dec      dx
25                            jnz      loop2
26                            pop      cx
27                            pop      dx
28                            endm
29
30 07D0                       .CODE
31 0000              Turbo    PROC     far
32 0000   B8 0000s            mov      ax,DGROUP
33 0003   8E D8               mov      ds,ax
```

```
34 0005  8E C0                    mov     es,ax
35
36
37
38
39
40 0007  B9 0009                  mov     cx,9
41 000A  B3 00                    mov     bl,0
42 000C  8D 2E 0000r repeat: lea  bp,blank
43 0010  BA 0000                  mov     dx,0
44 0013  B4 13                    mov     ah,19
45 0015  B0 01                    mov     al,1
46 0017  51                       push    cx
47 0018  B9 07D0                  mov     cx,2000
48 001B  CD 10                    int     10h
49                                killtime 10h
 1    50 001D  52                 push    dx
 1    51 001E  51                 push    cx
 1    52 001F  BA 000A            mov     dx,10h
 1    53 0022  B9 FF00 ??0001:  mov     cx,0FF00h
 1    54 0025  49      ??0000:  dec     cx
 1    55 0026  75 FD              jnz     ??0000
 1    56 0028  4A                 dec     dx
 1    57 0029  75 F7              jnz     ??0001
 1    58 002B  59                 pop     cx
 1    59 002C  5A                 pop     dx
```

```
Turbo Assembler       1/03/90 20:30:14        Page 2
prog10-2.ASM
```

```
60 002D  80 C3 10                 add     bl,16
61 0030  59                       pop     cx
62 0031  E2 D9                    loop    repeat
63
64 0033  B4 4C                    mov     ah,4Ch
65 0035  CD 21                    int     21h
66 0037              Turbo        ENDP
67                                END
```

```
Turbo Assembler       1/03/90   20:30:14        Page 3
Symbol Table
```

Symbol Name	Type	Value	Cref	defined at #		
??0000	Near	_TEXT:0025	#54	55		
??0001	Near	_TEXT:0022	#53	57		
??DATE	Text	"1/03/90"				
??FILENAME	Text	"prog18-2"				
??TIME	Text	"20:30:13"				
??VERSION	Number	0101				
@CODE	Text	_TEXT	#8	#30		
@CODESIZE	Text	0	#8			
@CPU	Text	0101H	#9			
@CURSEG	Text	_TEXT	#13	#30		
@DATA	Text	DGROUP	#8			
@DATASIZE	Text	0	#8			
@FILENAME	Text	prog18-2				
@WORDSIZE	Text	2	#9	#13	#30	

```
BLANK                        Byte    DGROUP:0000      #14   42
REPEAT                       Near    _TEXT:000C       #42   62
TURBO                        Far     _TEXT:0000       #31

Macro Name                                               Cref
defined at #

Killtime                                         #16    49

Groups & Segments Bit Size Align Combine Class Cref  defined at #

DGROUP                 Group                            #8   8   32
   STACK               16  0300 Para  Stack   STACK     #11
   _DATA               16  07D0 Word  Public  DATA      #8  #13
_TEXT                  16  0037 Word  Public  CODE      #8   8  #30
30
```

Note that the macro is included in the source code but that no machine code is generated to the left. When a macro, or macro library, is used by a program, it will be listed in this manner. However, this code is not yet part of your program's executable code. Notice that the code appears again later in the listing. This is because the line **killtime 10h** called for macro insertion. This time machine code is generated to the left. All comments have been removed from the listing file to save space.

The 1 at the left-hand edge of the screen indicates a macro expansion in the listing file. The number sets this line of code apart from regular program code and should be an aid in debugging. Since **killtime** was only replicated once, the local declaration was not actually required. However, notice that loop1 and loop2 were replaced with strange new labels, ??0000 and ??0001, as a result of the local declaration. If **killtime** had been requested again, those values would be ??0002 and ??0003. To prevent programming accidents, you should make all labels within a macro local labels. Double semicolon (;;) comments are used for macros, and prevent comments from being replicated each time the macro is expanded.

A Macro Library

Macros can be entered and used by a single program or placed in a macro library that you can include with any future programs that you write. Many programmers develop a group of useful macros that they use frequently and place them in a library. They can then save time and avoid debugging headaches by calling the library rather than retyping each macro. What follows is a group of useful macros in a macro library called *tmacro.mac.* Enter this code with your Turbo editor and save it to your disk. Do not attempt to assemble this code—macro libraries remain ASCII files for their entire life.

```
blankscreen macro                       ;;blanks screen
        push    ax                      ;;save registers
        push    bx
        push    cx
        push    dx
        mov     cx,0                    ;;set upper corner of window
        mov     dx,2479h                ;;set lower corner of window
        mov     bh,7                    ;;set normal screen attribute
        mov     ax,0600h                ;;interrupt parameters
        int     10h                     ;;call interrupt
        pop     dx                      ;;restore registers
        pop     cx
        pop     bx
        pop     ax
        endm                            ;;end macro

cursor  macro   spot                    ;;moves cursor to (spot)
        push    ax                      ;;save registers
        push    dx
        mov     ah,15                   ;;get current screen
        int     10h                     ;;call interrupt & set bx values
        mov     dx,spot                 ;;move screen location to dx
        mov     ah,2                    ;;set cursor parameter
        int     10h                     ;;call the interrupt
        pop     dx                      ;;restore the registers
        pop     ax
        endm                            ;;end macro

setscreen macro scrmode
        push    ax                      ;;save registers
        mov     ah,00                   ;;prepare for screen switch
        mov     al,scrmode              ;;desired screen
        int     10h                     ;;bios interrupt
        pop     ax                      ;;restore registers
        endm                            ;;end macro

drawdot macro   shade
        push    ax                      ;;save registers
        push    cx
        push    dx
        mov     ah,12                   ;;write dot parameter
        mov     al,shade                ;;color of dot
        int     10h                     ;;bios interrupt
        pop     dx
        pop     cx
        pop     ax
        endm

numout  macro   value
        local   loopl,printit           ;;prints ascii number to screen
        push    ax                      ;;save registers
        push    bx
        push    cx
        push    dx
        push    di                      ;;save di for future use
        mov     dx,value                ;;number to convert to ascii
        mov     cx,0                    ;;zero out cx
```

```
          lea     di,mybuffer      ;;address of temp buffer
loop1:    push    cx               ;;save value of cx
          mov     ax,dx            ;;copy dx into ax, then
          mov     dx,0             ;;zero out dx
          mov     cx,10            ;;convert hex value to this base
          div     cx               ;;perform division: ax/cx
          xchg    ax,dx            ;;remainder goes in ax
          add     al,30h           ;;convert byte digit to ascii
          mov     [di],al          ;;save at di mybuffer location
          inc     di               ;;indicate next storage location
          pop     cx               ;;get orig cx
          inc     cx               ;;increment
          cmp     dx,0             ;;check dx for zero
          jnz     loop2            ;;if no, go around again
printit:  dec     di               ;;if yes, print digits
          mov     al,[di]          ;;get a character from mybuffer
          push    dx               ;;save dx
          mov     dl,al            ;;prepare to print
          mov     ah,2             ;;dos print char parameter
          int     21h              ;;do it
          pop     dx               ;;restore dx
          loop    printit          ;;next character to print
          pop     di               ;;restore di
          pop     dx               ;;restore registers
          pop     cx
          pop     bx
          pop     ax
          endm                     ;;end macro
```

A technique for clearing the screen was shown in the last chapter as an entire program. Now, you can call an equivalent routine contained in the **blankscreen** macro as often as you like, without having to enter the code repeatedly. The **cursor** macro uses the value in the argument, *spot,* to obtain the vertical **dh** and horizontal **dl** locations for the cursor on the 80×25 text screen. The **setscreen** macro will allow you to switch screens with the use of a BIOS 10H interrupt. The screen value is passed through the argument *scrmode*. If you want to do graphics, the **drawdot** macro accepts the color of the dot in the argument *shade*. The screen coordinates are passed in **cx** (horizontal) and **dx** (vertical). **numout** will be used to place a single ASCII number on the screen. The value to be printed is passed to the macro through the argument *value*. Remember, a number must be converted to an ASCII value before it can be placed on the screen. **numout** requires that a variable, *mybuffer*, be declared in the data segment. It should reserve 4 bytes:

```
4 dup (' ')
```

The following example shows how a macro library can speed up the program development process and shorten the amount of code that you must write:

```
;TURBO Assembly Language Programming Application
;Copyright (c) Chris H. Pappas and William H. Murray, 1990

;program to display a count sequence on the screen

INCLUDE TMACRO.MAC                      ;get Turbo macro library

        DOSSEG                          ;use Intel segment-ordering
        .MODEL  small                   ;set model size
        .8086                           ;8086 instructions

        .STACK  300h                    ;set up 768-byte stack

        .DATA                           ;set up data location
text    db      'Incrementing a count on the screen $'
mybuffer db     4 dup (' ')

killtime  macro   increment
        local   loop2,loop1             ;;loop2 & loop1 are local
        push    dx                      ;;save dx & cx values
        push    cx
        mov     dx,increment            ;;pass increment value to dx
loop2:  mov     cx,0FF00h               ;;load cx with 00FF00h
loop1:  dec     cx                      ;;kill time
        jnz     loop1                   ;;if not zero, continue
        dec     dx                      ;;if cx=0, decrement dx
        jnz     loop2                   ;;if dx not zero, load cx again
        pop     cx                      ;;restore cx & dx
        pop     dx
        endm                            ;;leave the macro

        .CODE
Turbo   PROC    far                     ;main procedure declaration
        mov     ax,DGROUP               ;point ds toward .DATA
        mov     ds,ax

        blankscreen                     ;call blankscreen macro
        cursor  0018h                   ;center message to screen
        lea     dx,text                 ;print the message
        mov     ah,9                    ;print parameter
        int     21h                     ;call interrupt

        mov     ax,00                   ;initialize count to zero
repeat: cursor  0C28h                   ;move to center screen
        numout  ax                      ;print number on screen
        killtime 10h                    ;wait 10 units of delay
        add     ax,1                    ;add a 1 to ax
        cmp     ax,100                  ;counted to 100?
        je      done
        jmp     repeat                  ;do it again?
done:   blankscreen                     ;blank screen again

        mov     ah,4Ch                  ;return control to DOS
        int     21h
Turbo   ENDP                            ;end main procedure
        END                             ;end whole program
```

This program will use several macros; some are contained in the *tmacro.mac* library. The program will clear the screen, print the message "Incrementing a count on the screen" at the top, and then continuously display a count

Table 18-1.   Color Choices for Dot Colors

0 - Black	4 - Red	8 - Dark Gray	12 - Light Red
1 - Blue	5 - Magenta	9 - Light Blue	13 - Light Magenta
2 - Green	6 - Brown	10 - Light Green	14 - Yellow
3 - Cyan	7 - White	11 - Light Cyan	15 - Intense White

from 0 to 99 at the center of the screen. The program will terminate operation after reaching 99. To include the macro library in the program, the *INCLUDE* directive is used. Use the *INCLUDE* directive to specify the drive and the complete path to the macro library.

The **blankscreen** macro clears the monitor screen. The **cursor** macro moves the cursor to the first row and then over to column 18h (24 spaces) to center the message. The **numout** macro places the numbers on the screen. When **numout** is called, the digits in the **ax** register are converted to ASCII characters and printed to the screen. Decimal numbers are generated by the **numout** macro, in a complicated process that converts the hexadecimal digits to decimal. Before you leave the program, the screen is once again cleared. If you have the time, assemble the file and examine the *.lst* file. You will be surprised how many lines of code were saved by macros.

The following final example uses the macro library to perform a simple graphics line draw routine. Table 18-1 lists the various color choices that you can use for the dots.

```
;TURBO Assembly Language Programming Application
;Copyright (c) Chris H. Pappas and William H. Murray, 1990

;program to draw a line on the VGA screen

INCLUDE TMACRO.MAC              ;get Turbo macro library

        DOSSEG                  ;use Intel segment-ordering
        .MODEL   small          ;set model size
        .8086                   ;8086 instructions

        .STACK   300h           ;set up 768-byte stack

        .CODE
Turbo   PROC     far            ;main procedure declaration

        blankscreen             ;call blankscreen macro
        setscreen 12h           ;set to 640 x 480 screen
        mov      dx,0           ;start in upper-left corner
```

```
          mov      cx,0
repeat:
          drawdot 12                    ;plot a light red line
          inc      dx                   ;move down and to the right
          inc      cx
          cmp      dx,479               ;at bottom of screen yet?
          je       finish               ;if yes, leave loop
          jmp      repeat               ;if no, do loop again
finish:
          mov      ah,07                ;wait for a key press
          int      21h

          setscreen  3                  ;now return to text screen

          mov      ah,4Ch               ;return control to DOS
          int      21h
Turbo     ENDP                          ;end main procedure
          END                           ;end whole program
```

The **setscreen** macro is used to switch to the 640x480 VGA graphics screen. (Refer to Appendix B for the various screen parameters.) If you are using an EGA or CGA monitor, select the appropriate screen mode and adjust the value in **dx** to the correct length. The **drawdot** macro is placed in a loop for this program. Recall that you can only plot a single dot with this routine. To draw a line, a series of dots are plotted with repeated calls to **drawdot**. To allow you to observe the line before returning to the text screen, a simple DOS interrupt is used to make the program wait for a keypress. Try writing a few macros that allow you to draw a box or filled rectangle. A box is made up of four lines. You can draw a filled rectangle by plotting a series of horizontal lines.

PROCEDURES

All assembly language programs must have at least one procedure. Assembly language programs can contain many procedures, just as C programs can contain many functions. Assembly language procedures can be considered as *near* (intrasegment) or *far* (intersegment). Debugged routines, such as the ones in the previous macro library, can be placed in procedures within the program; the procedure behaves more like a subroutine. You can call these procedures from the main procedure by using the **call** instruction. The following section illustrates both intrasegment and intersegment procedures.

The Framework of a Procedure

In most assembly programs, the placement of the .STACK, .DATA, and .CODE declarations is about the same. In the example programs, the main procedure, called **Turbo**, always has a far attribute when it is declared. Every additional procedure added to your program code will be structured in a similar manner with either a near or far attribute.

The near or far attribute for a procedure helps determine the type of call instruction generated when that procedure is requested. A path must also be established for the return from the procedure. This path of instructions will differ depending upon the near or far attribute. If the procedure has a near attribute, the **ip** (instruction pointer) will be saved to the stack. If the procedure has a far attribute, both the **cs** (code segment) and the **ip** (instruction pointer) are saved to the stack.

The next example demonstrates the similarity of code used in macros and procedures. The **killtime** macro of the first example is converted into a near procedure, which is also named **killtime**.

```
;TURBO Assembly Language Programming Application
;Copyright (c) Chris H. Pappas and William H. Murray, 1990

;program to blank screen

        DOSSEG                      ;use Intel segment-ordering
        .MODEL  small               ;set model size
        .8086                       ;8086 instructions

        .STACK  300h                ;set up 768-byte stack

        .DATA                       ;set up data location
blank   db      2000 dup (' ')

        .CODE
Turbo   PROC    far                 ;main procedure declaration
        mov     ax,DGROUP           ;point ds toward .DATA
        mov     ds,ax
        mov     es,ax

;program will clear the screen by writing 2000 blanks.
;If these are written with a different value in bl,
;the color of the whole screen will be changed.  The killtime
;procedure will hold the color for a specified amount of time.
        mov     cx,9                ;repeat loop 9 times
        mov     bl,0                ;set background color
repeat: lea     bp,blank            ;write a string of blanks
        mov     dx,0                ;set cursor to top left corner
        mov     ah,19               ;write string attribute
        mov     al,1                ;print characters and move
```

```
cursor
        push    cx              ;save loop counter
        mov     cx,2000         ;write 2000 blanks
        int     10h             ;interrupt call
        call    killtime        ;call the near delay procedure
        add     bl,16           ;change background color
        pop     cx              ;restore original loop counter
        loop    repeat          ;do it 9 total times

        mov     ah,4Ch          ;return control to dos
        int     21h
Turbo   endp                    ;end main procedure

killtime proc   near
        push    dx              ;save original dx & cx values
        push    cx
        mov     dx,10h          ;amount of time increment
loop2:  mov     cx,0FF00h       ;load cx with 00FF00h
loop1:  dec     cx              ;kill time
        jnz     loop1           ;if not zero, continue
        dec     dx              ;if cx=0, decrement dx
        jnz     loop2           ;if dx not zero, load cx again
        pop     cx              ;restore dx & cx
        pop     dx
        ret                     ;determine path back
killtime endp                   ;end near procedure

        end                     ;end whole program
```

Notice that the **killtime** procedure is listed after the main procedure, unlike the macro that was placed before the main procedure. You should include all additional procedures in this manner. Notice also that the call to the **killtime** routine has been changed from **killtime 10** to **call killtime**. You invoke macros by just using their name; you invoke procedures with the **call** instruction.

A subtle change is the removal of the 10 during the call to the procedure. Arguments cannot be passed to procedures as they were to macros. To get the 10 hexadecimal units of time delay, the 10 is loaded directly in the **killtime** procedure. The **killtime** procedure itself looks like a miniature program.

At this point, there seems to be little difference between a macro and a near procedure. Actually, the differences are tremendous. The next listing is the *.lst* file for this program (all comments have been deleted to fit the listing on the page).

```
Turbo Assembler        1/03/90    20:35:02      Page 1
prog18-3.ASM

1
2   ;TURBO Assembly Language Programming Application
```

```
 3    ;Copyright (c) Chris H. Pappas and William H. Murray, 1990
 4
 5
 6
 7                                    DOSSEG
 8    0000                            .MODEL   small
 9                                    .8086
10
11    0000                            .STACK   300h
12
13    0000                            .DATA
14    0000    07D0*(20)      blank    db       2000 dup (' ')
15
16    07D0                            .CODE
17    0000                   Turbo    PROC     far
18    0000    B8 0000s                mov      ax,DGROUP
19    0003    8E D8                   mov      ds,ax
20    0005    8E C0                   mov      es,ax
21
22
23
24
25
26    0007    B9 0009                 mov      cx,9
27    000A    B3 00                   mov      bl,0
28    000C    8D 2E 0000r    repeat:  lea      bp,blank
29    0010    BA 0000                 mov      dx,0
30    0013    B4 13                   mov      ah,19
31    0015    B0 01                   mov      al,1
32    0017    51                      push     cx
33    0018    B9 07D0                 mov      cx,2000
34    001B    CD 10                   int      10h
35    001D    E8 000A                 call     killtime
36    0020    80 C3 10                add      bl,16
37    0023    59                      pop      cx
38    0024    E2 E6                   loop     repeat
39
40    0026    B4 4C                   mov      ah,4Ch
41    0028    CD 21                   int      21h
42    002A                   Turbo    endp
43
44    002A                   killtime proc     near
45    002A    52                      push     dx
46    002B    51                      push     cx
47    002C    BA 0010                 mov      dx,10h
48    002F    B9 FF00       loop2:    mov      cx,0FF00h
49    0032    49            loop1:    dec      cx
50    0033    75 FD                   jnz      loop1
51    0035    4A                      dec      dx
52    0036    75 F7                   jnz      loop2
53    0038    59                      pop      cx
54    0039    5A                      pop      dx
55    003A    C3                      ret
56    003B                   killtime endp
57
58                                    end
```

```
Symbol Table

Symbol Name              Type    Value              Cref   defined at #

??DATE                   Text    "1/03/90"
??FILENAME               Text    "prog18-3    "
??TIME                   Text    "20:35:01"
??VERSION                Number  0101
@CODE                    Text    _TEXT                      #8   #16
@CODESIZE                Text    0                          #8
@CPU                     Text    0101H                      #9
@CURSEG                  Text    _TEXT                      #13  #16
@DATA                    Text    DGROUP                     #8
@DATASIZE                Text    0                          #8
@FILENAME                Text    prog18-3
@WORDSIZE                Text    2                          #9   #13
#16
BLANK                    Byte    DGROUP:0000                #14  28
KILLTIME                 Near    _TEXT:002A                 35   #44
LOOP1                    Near    _TEXT:0032                 #49  50
LOOP2                    Near    _TEXT:002F                 #48  52
REPEAT                   Near    _TEXT:000C                 #28  38
TURBO                    Far     _TEXT:0000                 #17
```

Groups & Segments Bit Size Align Combine Class Cref defined at #

Groups & Segments	Bit	Size	Align	Combine	Class	Cref	defined at #		
DGROUP	Group					#8	8	18	
STACK	16	0300	Para	Stack	STACK	#11			
_DATA	16	07D0	Word	Public	DATA	#8	#13		
_TEXT	16	003B	Word	Public	CODE	#8	8	#16	16

Unlike the previous .lst listing, this listing contains no 1's along the left edge of the printout. This is because no macros were expanded in the code. When the **killtime** procedure was called, it was coded just like any other program code. You can call a procedure such as **killtime** frequently by just typing **call killtime**. The actual code for **killtime** only appears once, regardless of the number of calls to the procedure in your program.

Programs written with procedures are often more compact, since procedures, unlike macros, are not expanded with each use. There is a price to be paid for compactness, however. Programs that use procedures instead of macros do not execute in line. Jumping from the main procedure to a subprocedure takes additional time. If this call is made frequently, say within the body of a loop, the difference in time can become quite noticeable.

A Procedure Library

A group of procedures can be assembled into a *procedure library*. This collection of *.obj* routines will be coupled to the user's program at link time. A procedure library must be handled a little differently than a macro library or procedures contained within the program itself. First, these procedures will have a far attribute since they are external to the current code segment. Second, notice that *mybuffer, shade,* and *scrmode* are declared public in the data segment. Third, an **extern** declaration is required for all procedures that are external to this listing. This declaration is required to avoid assembly and link conflicts. These variables are to be shared with the external procedure library. The next example, which demonstrates how to use a procedure library, is similar to an earlier program that used a macro library:

```
;TURBO Assembly Language Programming Application
;Copyright (c) Chris H. Pappas and William H. Murray, 1990

;program to increment a count to the screen

            DOSSEG                      ;use Intel segment-ordering
            .MODEL  small               ;set model size
            .8086                       ;8086 instructions

            extrn   blankscreen:far,cursor:far
            extrn   setscreen:far,drawdot:far,numout:far

            .STACK  300h                ;set up 768-byte stack

            .DATA                       ;set up data location
            public  mybuffer,shade,scrmode
text        db      'Incrementing a count on the screen $'
mybuffer db 4 dup (' ')
shade    db     0
scrmode  db     0

            .CODE
Turbo   PROC    far                 ;main procedure declaration
            mov     ax,DGROUP           ;point ds toward .DATA
            mov     ds,ax

            call    blankscreen         ;call blankscreen macro
            mov     dx,0019h            ;set location for cursor
            call    cursor              ;center message
            lea     dx,text             ;point to text for printing
            mov     ah,09               ;interrupt parameter
            int     21h

            mov     ax,0                ;initialize to zero
repeat: mov     dx,0C28h            ;set cursor location
            call    cursor              ;move to center screen
            call    numout              ;print number on screen
            mov     dx,10h              ;put in 10h delay units
            call    killtime            ;call killtime
            add     ax,01               ;increment ax
            cmp     al,100              ;have we reached 100?
            je      done
            jmp     repeat              ;do it again?
```

```
done:   call    blankscreen      ;blank screen again

        mov     ah,4Ch           ;return control to DOS
        int     21h
Turbo   ENDP                     ;end main procedure

killtime proc   near
        push    dx               ;save original dx & cx values
        push    cx
        mov     dx,10h           ;time increment value
loop2:  mov     cx,0FF00h        ;load cx with 00FF00h
loop1:  dec     cx               ;kill time
        jnz     loop1            ;if not zero, continue
        dec     dx               ;if cx=0, decrement dx
        jnz     loop2            ;if dx not zero, load cx again
        pop     cx               ;restore dx & cx
        pop     dx
        ret                      ;determine path back
killtime endp                    ;end near procedure
        end                      ;end whole program
```

Notice that the **extern** directive lists the names of each procedure and
attaches a far call attribute.

```
extrn   blankscreen:far,cursor:far,
extrn   setscreen:far,drawdot:far,numout:far
```

Compare this first section of main code with that of the macro example.
Note that the cursor position is placed in **dx** before the **cursor** procedure is
called. This technique solves the problem of passing parameters by passing
them in registers that are global in scope. Look at the procedure library.
The file name that these procedures are stored under is only required when
linking this code with the main program. Here, it is called *tproc.asm*.

```
        dosseg
        .model  small
        .8086

        .code
        public blankscreen,cursor,setscreen,drawdot,numout
        extrn   mybuffer:byte,scrmode:byte,shade:byte
start:
blankscreen proc far             ;clears screen
        push    ax               ;save registers
        push    bx
        push    cx
        push    dx
        mov     cx,0             ;set upper corner of window
        mov     dx,2479h         ;set lower corner of window
        mov     bh,7             ;set normal screen attribute
```

```
          mov      ax,0600h          ;interrupt parameters
          int      10h               ;call interrupt
          pop      dx                ;restore registers
          pop      cx
          pop      bx
          pop      ax
          ret
blankscreen endp

cursor    proc     far               ;moves cursor to (spot)
          push     ax                ;save register
          mov      ah,15             ;get current screen
          int      10h               ;call interrupt, set bx values
          mov      ah,2              ;set the cursor parameter
          int      10h               ;call the interrupt
          pop      ax                ;restore the register
          ret
cursor    endp

setscreen proc     far               ;sets screen mode
          push     ax                ;save register
          mov      ah,0              ;prepare for screen switch
          mov      al,scrmode        ;desired screen
          int      10h               ;bios interrupt
          pop      ax                ;restore register
          ret
setscreen endp

drawdot   proc     far
          push     ax                ;save registers
          push     cx
          push     dx
          mov      ah,12             ;draw dot parameter
          mov      al,shade          ;color value
          int      10h               ;bios interrupt
          pop      dx
          pop      cx
          pop      ax
          ret
drawdot   endp

numout    proc     far               ;prints number at cursor location
          push     ax                ;save registers
          push     bx
          push     cx
          push     dx
          push     di                ;save di, again, for future use
          mov      dx,ax             ;number to convert to ascii
          mov      cx,0              ;zero out cx
          lea      di,mybuffer       ;address of temp buffer
loop1:    push     cx                ;hold cx, each time through
          mov      ax,dx             ;copy dx into ax, then
          mov      dx,0              ;zero out dx
          mov      cx,10             ;convert hex value to this base
          div      cx                ;perform division: ax/cx
          xchg     ax,dx             ;remainder in ax
          add      al,30h            ;convert byte digit to ascii
```

```
              mov      [di],al            ;save in mybuffer location
              inc      di                 ;point to next storage location
              pop      cx                 ;get cx before conversion
              inc      cx                 ;increment
              cmp      dx,0               ;is dx reached zero yet?
              jnz      loop1              ;if no, go around again
      printit: dec     di                 ;if yes, let's print digits
              mov      al,[di]            ;get a char from mybuffer
              push     dx                 ;save dx
              mov      dl,al              ;prepare to print
              mov      ah,2               ;dos print char parameter
              int      21h                ;do it
              pop      dx                 ;restore dx
              loop     printit            ;get next character to print
              pop      di                 ;restore di
              pop      dx                 ;restore registers
              pop      cx
              pop      bx
              pop      ax
              ret
      numout endp

              end      start
```

The program overhead for external procedures is minimal:

```
public blankscreen,cursor,setscreen,drawdot,numout
```

In this case, each procedure in the library is declared public so that it can be shared with other programs. The variables that are being shared are declared as **extrn**, because they will be defined in the host program. Notice that their size **db** is also registered. This will permit the intersegment exchange of information. The remainder of the overhead is standard fare.

The procedure's name is followed by the directive **proc** and a far attribute. Additionally, all procedures end with the **ret** instruction followed by the name of the procedure and the **endp** directive. The body of each procedure has only been modified slightly from its macro counterpart.

At this point, there are two separate programs. You can consider one the host program and the other a procedure library. Each of these must be assembled separately with TASM. Once this is done, the *.obj* files for each can be combined by the Turbo Linker. The Borland TASM manuals describe how to do this and how to take advantage of various linker options. The following example is one possible method for linking these files. This method assumes that the linker and the files to be linked are on the C drive.

```
c:tlink mainfile + tproc
```

Recall that a macro library is a collection of unassembled routines that reside in a source code file, whereas a procedure library is a collection of assembled routines that reside in an object file. Macros are brought in at the time of assembly (TASM), while the procedure library is brought in at the time of linking (TLINK).

OBJECT MODULE LIBRARIES

An *object module library* doesn't differ greatly from a macro library or a procedure library. All three can store debugged code, which can be called by other programs at a future date. Object module libraries are most closely associated with the Turbo Linker. Recall that when you link a program, the following menu arguments are possible:

```
TLINK  objfiles, exefile, mapfile, libfiles
```

You have learned how to specify the first three TLINK options. What are those *libfiles*? The *libfiles* option used by TLINK is closest to the procedure library that was used in the last section. Libraries that are called at link time are actually collections of assembled procedures, much like the procedure library. The Turbo Assembler package also includes a library manager, TLIB, that you use to help build, edit, and manage library object modules. When you need a particular library, enter its name as a link argument at the *libfiles* parameter. Like macro and procedure libraries, object module libraries can greatly reduce program development time because frequently called procedures have already been written and debugged.

The Turbo Librarian, TLIB, supports the following operations:

- Add object files (+)
- Delete object files (−)
- Extract an object module (*)
- Replace an object module (−+ or +−)
- Extract and remove an object module (_* or *_).

The following example shows how to create an object module library with the Turbo Librarian. Basically, you will convert the previous procedure library to an object module library. The conversion and management of the procedure library is the job of the Turbo Librarian. To find out the options provided with the librarian, just type

```
c>tlib
```

The following list should appear on the screen:

```
Syntax: TLIB libname [/C] [/E] commands, listfile
    libname     library file pathname
    commands    sequence of operations to be performed (optional)
    listfile    file name for listing file (optional)

A command is of the form: <symbol>modulename, where <symbol> is:
    +               add modulename to the library
    -               remove modulename from the library
    *               extract modulename without removing it
    -+ or +-        replace modulename in library
    -* or *-        extract modulename and remove it

    /C              case-sensitive library
    /E              create extended dictionary

Use @filepath to continue from file "filepath".
Use '&' at end of a line to continue onto the next line.
```

For this example, your collection of procedures from the previous example, called **tproc**, will be converted to a library named *turbolib.lib*:

```
c:tlib  turbolib +tproc, turbolib
```

The library name immediately follows the call to TLIB. Next is any module of procedures to be added or deleted from the library. In this case, **tproc**, is to be added. Finally, a listing file can optionally be specified. Libraries default to a *.lib* file extension and listing files default to *.lst*. Once the library has been created, you can add more procedures and routines at any time with the Turbo Librarian. To incorporate this library at link time, simply type **turbolib** as the fourth argument in the TLINK specifications.

At first, the object module library doesn't seem very different from a procedure library. It is, however. First, remember that a procedure library is coupled with other object modules at link time, at the *.obj* option. Second, with the Turbo Librarian, you can add or subtract new procedures from the library at any time. You cannot do this with a procedure library without going back to the source code. This makes a link library more dynamic than either of the previous methods. Plus, it enables you to add new procedures to an already established library without revealing the contents of the whole library.

If you want to view the contents of *turbolib*, just request the listing file:

```
c>turbolib.lst
```

The library listing file will return a list of all public procedures used in the library:

```
Publics by module

MYPROC      size = 116
      BLANKSCREEN                    CURSOR
      DRAWDOT                        NUMOUT
      SETSCREEN
```

CONTRASTING MACROS, PROCEDURES, AND LIBRARIES

Macros, procedures, and libraries perform many of the same functions. They give you the flexibility to write and debug code once. You can then use that code in any program you like. This makes programming more efficient and more modular. Each type has its own advantages and disadvantages. The proper selection of a macro, procedure, or library can make the difference between small code size and large, or a fast and a slow program.

The Advantages of Macros

- Macros produce fast code since they execute "in line" within a program.
- Macros can pass and receive arguments that affect how they operate.
- You can save macros in a source code library that you can easily edit.
- The programming overhead for macros is simple.

- You can bring macro libraries into your program with a simple *INCLUDE* directive.

The Disadvantages of Macros

- Macros make the source code longer since they are expanded each time they are called.
- A macro library reveals your code to any user of the library.

The Advantages of Procedure Libraries

- Procedures allow source code to remain short, since procedures are not expanded within a program's code.

The Disadvantages of Procedure Libraries

- Procedures tend to slow program execution. This is because each call to a procedure must leave the "main" code and jump to another location within the program.
- The overhead for procedure use is more involved. Procedures must be declared as near or far, and any library files must be marked as external.
- You cannot send parameters to a procedure to alter how it executes.

The Advantages of Object Module Libraries

- Same advantages as for procedure libraries.
- With a Turbo Librarian, you can easily add or delete routines from a library.
- Library source code is known only to you.

The Disadvantages of Object Module Libraries

- Same disadvantages as for procedure libraries.

Which method is the best for you? When should you chose a macro over a procedure? When is an object module library better than a procedure library? Here are some recommendations:

- For short pieces of code, use a macro. Their operations are faster, with little increase in code length.

- For infrequently called routines within a program, choose a macro. If routines are not called frequently, code expansion will not seriously affect the program.

- If you are just starting the program creation process, use a macro. Macros tend to be easier to write, edit, and manage.

- For long routines, choose a procedure. Procedures tend to make the source code shorter.

- For frequently called routines within a program, choose a procedure. Procedures do not expand program code each time they are called.

- If the same routines are used frequently in your programs, put them in an object module library for easy access.

- If you are developing a package of routines for commercial use, choose an object module library. You will only need to ship the .obj file, thus offering a degree of protection to your source code.

PUTTING YOUR KNOWLEDGE TO WORK

1. Indicate whether or not procedures execute "in line."

2. Describe the framework of a macro.

3. Name two methods for passing information to a macro.

4. What is the purpose of double semicolons within a macro?

5. Is there a functional difference between the **ret** in a near and a far procedure?

6. Can you edit a macro library with the Turbo C++ editor?

7. When are libraries of procedures brought into a program? (Hint: At assembly time (TASM) or link time (TLINK)?)

8. Does the Borland Library Manager Program allow you to create, add, delete, and update libraries of procedures that are in *.obj* form?

9. For a long routine that is used frequently, should you use a macro or a procedure?

10. From the hardware stack's viewpoint, is a near or a far procedure faster to access? Why?

19

CHARACTERS, STRINGS, AND FILES IN ASSEMBLY LANGUAGE

In this chapter you will learn

- How to intercept and process character information in a program
- How to read the keyboard for character and string input
- How to create strings from groups of characters
- How to manipulate string information
- How to use very fast string commands
- How to create a file
- How to write to a file
- How to read information from a file

You have already discovered that almost every program must move data in and out of the computer. Like many high-level languages, C makes it relatively easy to format and control the flow of input and output information. C's ability to process command-line information makes it unique even among high-level languages. Unfortunately, input and output tasks are a bit more of a challenge in assembly language.

Regardless of the language, you need to understand what takes place when you send or receive information. Information being fed in to or out of the computer is usually in ASCII format. For example, if you want to print a 1 on the screen, you must send the ASCII value 31h to the screen's memory location. Information fed into a small system through a keyboard, joystick, light pen, mouse, analog-to-digital converter, scanner, disk drive, modem, or CD-ROM player is usually in ASCII format. Likewise, information sent to the monitor, printer, plotter, digital-to-analog converter, device controller, and so on is in ASCII format.

This chapter explains various techniques for obtaining information from the keyboard and sending information to the monitor. The example programs will first deal with character information. You will learn how to intercept characters from the keyboard, how to form strings from individual characters, and how to print string information. The programs will then concentrate on string manipulations. For example, you will learn how to find a certain character in a string or compare two strings. Finally, you will learn how to send string information to external files. While most of these routines are built in to various C and C++ libraries, you will have to develop your own techniques in assembly language.

WORKING WITH CHARACTERS

Table 19-1 repeats several of the more important DOS commands used to intercept and send information. Appendix B contains a complete list of DOS interrupts. You can also use BIOS interrupts in some situations, but this chapter develops character and string example programs around the more robust DOS interrupts.

Many of the commands in the table are directed toward character input and output. Handling character information is important for two reasons: First, a character is the smallest data element that most devices can send or receive directly. Second, you can use collections of characters to form strings or even numbers. Thus, if you can manipulate character data, you should have full control over all I/O operations.

Intercepting a Single Character

A DOS interrupt for intercepting a single character and echoing it to the screen is available when you set the **ah** register equal to 1. If you use this

Table 19-1.   Important DOS 21h Character and String Functions

AH value	Function	Action
1h	Wait and echo print keyboard character with CTRL-BREAK check	al returns character
2h	Display character to output device	dl character to display
3h	Asynchronous character input	al returns character received
4h	Asynchronous character output	dl character to send
5h	Character to write	dl character to write
6h	Keyboard character input	dl = 0FFH al character entered
7h	Keyboard character wait. No display	al character entered
8h	Keyboard character wait. No display CTRL-BREAK check	al character entered
9h	Display string	ds:dx = address of string string must end with $
Ah	Keyboard string to buffer	ds:dx = address of buffer 1 byte = max size 2 bytes = actual number
Bh	Keyboard status input	al = 0FFh (if character) = 0 (no character)
Ch	Clear keyboard buffer and call function	al = 1h,6h,7h,8h,0Ah (function to call)

interrupt in a program, the program will halt at the interrupt call until you press a key on the keyboard. The character value, in ASCII, is returned in the **al** register. This interrupt also checks for a CTRL-BREAK action. Examine the following application:

```
;TURBO Assembly Language Programming Application
;Copyright (c) Chris H. Pappas and William H. Murray, 1990

;Prepare to intercept a single character from the keyboard.
;Return it to the al register and echo print it to screen.

          DOSSEG                  ;use Intel segment-ordering
          .MODEL  small           ;set model size
          .8086                   ;8086 instructions

          .STACK  300h            ;set up 768-byte stack

          .CODE
Turbo     PROC    FAR             ;main procedure declaration

          mov     ah,01h          ;intercept keyboard character
          int     21h             ;return character to al

          mov     ah,4Ch          ;return control to DOS
          int     21h
Turbo     ENDP                    ;end main procedure
          END                     ;end whole program
```

Notice that the value in **al** was not even saved. It could have been, but the program currently just halts all computer action until a key is pressed. Can you think of an application where this piece of code might be useful? Other DOS interrupts perform similar character manipulations. For example, if **ah** is set to 8h, everything will be the same but the character will not be echoed to the screen.

Intercepting a Series of Characters

The last example did nothing with the character received from the keyboard except echo it to the screen. The intercepted character was returned in the **al** register in ASCII format, however. Thus, if you type **C** on the keyboard, a 43h would be returned to the **al** register. If you type **2**, a 32h would be returned.

In the following example, a loop will continually sample keyboard information, one character at a time. The only way to terminate the loop is to type $. While this might seem like an odd choice for termination, it is the character chosen to terminate string printing operations with another DOS interrupt, as you will see later in this chapter. Of course, if you plan to incorporate this code in your own program, you may wish to use an E for end or Q for quit.

```
;TURBO Assembly Language Programming Application
;Copyright (c) Chris H. Pappas and William H. Murray, 1990

;Intercept a series of characters from the keyboard.
;Also echo print to the screen.

            DOSSEG                      ;use Intel segment-ordering
            .MODEL   small              ;set model size
            .8086                       ;8086 instructions

            .STACK   300h               ;set up 768-byte stack

            .CODE
Turbo       PROC     FAR                ;main procedure declaration
            mov      ax,DGROUP          ;point ds toward .DATA
            mov      ds,ax

repeat:
            mov      ah,01h             ;intercept character
            int      21h                ;from the keyboard
            cmp      al,'$'             ;if $, then stop input
            jne      repeat             ;otherwise, continue

            mov      ah,4Ch             ;return control to DOS
            int      21h
Turbo       ENDP                        ;end main procedure
            END                         ;end whole program
```

Notice that although character information is continuously entered from the keyboard, only a $ character has any effect. This means that every time around the loop, a new value replaces the previous value in the **al** register—not a very useful program. The character information is echoed to the screen, but you need additional code to save the string for other work.

Intercepting and Sending a Series of Characters

In the previous examples, character information was echoed to the screen when it was intercepted with a DOS interrupt where the **ah** register is set to 1. In this example, character information will again be intercepted, but this time with **ah** set to 7. When **ah** is 7, character information is not echoed.

This example will introduce you to an additional interrupt. When **ah** is 2, a character in the **dl** register will be printed to the screen at the current cursor position. If this code immediately follows character interception, it will appear to operate like the previous example.

```
;TURBO Assembly Language Programming Application
;Copyright (c) Chris H. Pappas and William H. Murray, 1990

;Intercept a series of characters from the keyboard.
;Printing will be done with interrupt, not echo printing.

        DOSSEG                  ;use Intel segment-ordering
        .MODEL  small           ;set model size
        .8086                   ;8086 instructions

        .STACK  300h            ;set up 768-byte stack

        .CODE
Turbo   PROC    FAR             ;main procedure declaration
        mov     ax,DGROUP       ;point ds toward .DATA
        mov     ds,ax

repeat:
        mov     ah,07h          ;intercept character
        int     21h             ;from keyboard
        cmp     al,'$'          ;if $, then done
        je      done            ;otherwise, repeat
        mov     ah,02h          ;call interrupt
        mov     dl,al           ;to write character
        int     21h             ;call interrupt
        jmp     repeat          ;get another?
done:

        mov     ah,4Ch          ;return control to DOS
        int     21h
Turbo   ENDP                    ;end main procedure
        END                     ;end whole program
```

While this program operates just like the last example, there is a very important difference. Since additional code is inserted between the interception and printing of the character, you can manipulate the character data. This would be useful if, for example, you wanted to convert string information to uppercase, as does the function **toupper**.

Using Characters to Create a String

The last examples worked with individual character information. While the printed characters appeared as a string on the screen, you never really had more than one character at a time. In the strictest sense, the information was not a string at all, but individual characters intercepted and printed one at a time. To build more complicated routines, you must be able to collect and manipulate strings of character information.

The next example creates a string from individual characters. The characters will be intercepted one-by-one and saved to a table called *chstr*. This table is actually a one-dimensional array, similar in concept to those used in earlier programs. This program will also print the entire string to the screen by using a DOS string printing routine.

```
;TURBO Assembly Language Programming Application
;Copyright (c) Chris H. Pappas and William H. Murray, 1990

;Intercept a series of characters from the keyboard,
;print when intercepted and also save as a string.
;Print string with an interrupt routine.

                DOSSEG                      ;use Intel segment-ordering
                .MODEL   small              ;set model size
                .8086                       ;8086 instructions

                .STACK   300h               ;set up 768-byte stack

                .DATA                       ;set up data location
chstr   db      80 dup (' '),'$' ;storage for string
nline   db      0Ah,0Dh,'$'       ;line feed + carriage return

                .CODE
Turbo   PROC    FAR                         ;main procedure declaration
                mov      ax,DGROUP          ;point ds toward .DATA
                mov      ds,ax

;Read a group of characters and save in "chstr".
                mov      cx,0               ;set init. count to zero
                mov      si,0               ;set init. index to zero
repeat:
                mov      ah,01h             ;intercept character
                int      21h                ;from keyboard
                cmp      al,0Dh             ;carriage return? typestr!
                je       typestr            ;otherwise, repeat
                mov      chstr[si],al       ;send char to chstr[si]
                cmp      cx,79              ;do you have all characters?
                je       typestr            ;if yes, then typestr
                inc      si                 ;if not, inc. index
                inc      cx                 ;inc. count
                jmp      repeat             ;get another char.

typestr:
                lea      dx,nline           ;get new line
                mov      ah,09              ;only stop for '$'
                int      21h                ;print interrupt
                lea      dx,chstr           ;print out all characters
                mov      ah,09              ;only stop for '$'
                int      21h                ;print interrupt

                mov      ah,4Ch             ;return control to DOS
                int      21h
```

```
Turbo    ENDP                    ;end main procedure
         END                     ;end whole program
```

The variable *chstr* is declared as a **db** table and initialized with 80 blanks and a $ sentinel character. The size, 80, is the number of characters on a line in normal screen mode. The $ sentinel character is attached to *chstr* for the DOS printing routine. Notice another variable, *nline,* which is used for a linefeed and carriage return. These are ASCII values that can be embedded in normal text to force the printer to perform the given action. Examine the small section of program code that follows:

```
        mov     cx,0            ;set init. count to zero
        mov     si,0            ;set init. index to zero
repeat:
        mov     ah,01h          ;intercept character
        int     21h             ;from keyboard
        cmp     al,0Dh          ;carriage return? typestr!
        je      typestr         ;otherwise, repeat
        mov     chstr[si],al    ;send char to chstr[si]
        cmp     cx,79           ;do you have all characters?
        je      typestr         ;if yes, then typestr
        inc     si              ;if not, inc. index
        inc     cx              ;inc. count
        jmp     repeat          ;get another char.
```

Within the loop is the DOS intercept and echo interrupt when **ah** is set to 1. The loop will continue until either the loop counter, **cx**, has reached 79 or a carriage return, 0Dh, has been entered. In this program, each character entered from the keyboard is also stored in the *chstr* table, indexed by the **si** register. Thus, each trip around the loop increments the loop counter and the index register, building a string of characters in *chstr*.

When either a full line of characters is entered or a carriage return is typed, the program jumps to the typestr label.

```
typestr:
        lea     dx,nline        ;get new line
        mov     ah,09           ;only stop for '$'
        int     21h             ;print interrupt
        lea     dx,chstr        ;print out all characters
        mov     ah,09           ;only stop for '$'
        int     21h             ;print interrupt
```

If the string is to be printed to the screen, you need a new line since the original characters were echoed when they were intercepted. You can send a new line, which consists of a linefeed and carriage return, to the printer by using a DOS interrupt. In fact, the DOS interrupt called by setting **ah** to

9 is a popular print routine. The string location must be loaded in the **ds:dx** register pair. If the string is located in the **ds** segment, you can use **lea** to load the effective address of the string into the **dx** register. When you use the interrupt service, the string must end with the $ character. In the previous listing, notice that the interrupt is actually called twice. The first string to be printed is *nline*. The second string is the table *chstr*, which contains the information entered from the keyboard. The print routine will produce a line of text identical to the one that was entered character by character; however, the second line was really printed as a string.

What do you think would be necessary to enter several lines of characters? Was there a size limitation to character arrays in C or C++?

Reading Strings Directly

As sparse as these assembly language routines already are, they can be more so. There is a DOS interrupt service for directly reading string information from the keyboard. In other words, you can eliminate the loop from the previous program. Eliminating loops always makes assembly code faster. DOS's more efficient technique for string handling involves setting **ah** to 0Ah. Here is the complete program:

```
;TURBO Assembly Language Programming Application
;Copyright (c) Chris H. Pappas and William H. Murray, 1990

;Intercept characters from the keyboard as a character
;string via the keyboard buffer.  Print the string
;"chstr" with another interrupt.

            DOSSEG                      ;use Intel segment-ordering
            .MODEL   small              ;set model size
            .8086                       ;8086 instructions

            .STACK   300h               ;set up 768-byte stack

            .DATA                       ;set up data location
infostruc label  byte
maxlen  db       81                     ;max length of string
actlen  db       ?                      ;actual length
chstr   db       79 dup (' ')           ;storage for chstr
nline   db       0Ah,0Dh,'$'            ;new line

            .CODE
Turbo   PROC     FAR                    ;main procedure declaration
        mov      ax,DGROUP              ;point ds toward .DATA
        mov      ds,ax

        lea      dx,infostruc           ;get address of structure
        mov      ah,0Ah                 ;in ds:dx
        int      21h                    ;call interrupt
```

```
          lea     dx,nline        ;do a line feed
          mov     ah,09           ;stop on '$' char.
          int     21h             ;call interrupt

          mov     si,0            ;init. index to zero
repeat:
          mov     dl,chstr[si]    ;get character in dl
          mov     ah,02           ;print it to screen
          int     21h             ;call interrupt
          inc     si              ;point to next char.
          mov     al,actlen       ;printed them all?
          cbw                     ;convert byte to word
          cmp     si,ax           ;compare with index
          jge     done            ;greater or equal? Done.
          jmp     repeat          ;else, get next char.
done:

          mov     ah,4Ch          ;return control to DOS
          int     21h
Turbo     ENDP                    ;end main procedure
          END                     ;end whole program
```

The first new thing that you will notice is *infostruc,* a label declaration. Label declarations are in some respects similar to the structure declarations in C. They enable you to reference a group of instructions by the label name or by the individual elements defined therein. However, they are not really structures. If you access values by pointing to the *infostruc* address, the *maxlen, actlen, chstr,* and *nline* variables are ordered or structured in that label definition. You can also access these variables by using their name directly or referring to them as label members. The ordering of this information is critical for the proper use of the following DOS routine:

```
infostruc label  byte
maxlen  db      81              ;max length of string
actlen  db      ?               ;actual length
chstr   db      79 dup (' ')    ;storage for chstr
nline   db      0Ah,0Dh,'$'     ;new line
```

When the DOS interrupt is actually called, string information is intercepted from the keyboard until either 79 characters are entered or a carriage return is typed. Notice the setup in the following code:

```
lea     dx,infostruc    ;get address of structure
mov     ah,0Ah          ;in ds:dx
int     21h             ;call interrupt
```

It is the address of the *infostruc* label that is actually passed to the interrupt. The interrupt is, in turn, looking for three storage locations. The first value received will represent the maximum length of the string. The second value will represent the actual number of characters entered at the keyboard when the interrupt is called, and the third location specifies where the character information is to be stored. The *maxlen* variable must contain two more bytes than the maximum length of the string, since *maxlen* also contains the total length of the label directive. In this case, that's a byte for *maxlen*, a byte for *actlen*, and 79 bytes for *chstr*. When this routine is called, it will intercept characters from the keyboard until either 79 have been entered or a carriage return is typed. In both cases, the actual count of characters is returned to *actlen*. As you can now see, the label directive allows you to get to the two length values, *maxlen* and *actlen*, without pointers or indexing.

The string that was just intercepted could now be printed to the screen with the DOS string printing function if a $ were the last character in the string. You could easily concatenate the $ character to the string—however, there is another way to print this information.

Although the DOS print string interrupt will not allow you to print the $ character, the following new technique will allow you to print the $ character:

```
        mov     si,0            ;init. index to zero
repeat:
        mov     dl,chstr[si]    ;get character in dl
        mov     ah,02           ;print it to screen
        int     21h             ;call interrupt
        inc     si              ;point to next char.
        mov     al,actlen       ;printed them all?
        cbw                     ;convert byte to word
        cmp     si,ax           ;compare with index
        jge     done            ;greater or equal? Done.
        jmp     repeat          ;else, get next char.
done:
```

The character printing routine is created with the print character interrupt used in an earlier example. When **ah** is 2, the character in the **dl** register is printed to the screen at the current cursor location. By putting this interrupt in a loop and feeding the interrupt one character at a time from the *chstr* table, you can print the whole string.

The number of trips around the loop is determined by the number of characters that need to be printed. The **si** register is used to point to the next character, while the *actlen* variable contains the actual number of characters to print. There is a little flurry of activity in the program code because the value in *actlen* is a byte while that in **si** is a word. These two values are to be compared, so the value from *actlen* is converted to a word with **cbw** via the **al** register. When the **si** register equals the actual length of the string, the loop is terminated and the printing stopped. With this routine, you can print any ASCII character to the screen.

ADVANCED STRING OPERATIONS

Now that you know how to enter character and string information into your program, you need to learn some additional microprocessor commands. Intel's family of microprocessors has a set of fast and powerful string operations. The examples that follow demonstrate how to use these routines to produce a variety of actions with strings.

A group of microprocessor instructions, shown in Table 19-2, is associated with string manipulations. To use these instructions, you need to know a few details. First, the direction of the string operation is noted by either **cld** or **std**. The **cld** instruction signals the microprocessor for a left to right scanning of the string, which is done by setting the direction flag to zero. This is also the default scan mode. The **std** instruction sets the direction flag to one and the scan direction from right to left. Next, the source string's address must be placed in the **ds:si** (or **esi** for the 80486/80386) register pair. If there is a destination string, the destination string's address must be placed in the **es:di** (or **edi** for the 80486/80386) register pair. If the string information is short and will not exceed the 64K segment limit, the **ds** and **es** registers can point to the same portion of data as here:

```
mov     ax,DGROUP        ;point ds & es toward .DATA
mov     ds,ax
mov     es,ax
```

Finally, the string operations, such as scan and compare, are used with the correctly chosen repeat operation. The **cx** register is used to set the number of possible repeat operations. For example:

```
mov     cx,39        ;characters to scan
mov     al,'c'       ;look for a "c"
```

```
repne   scasb                    ;scan byte by byte
        jnz     nochar           ;if zf<>0, no match
```

This line of code requests a string scan, byte by byte, to be repeated as long as the results are not equal. During each compare, the **cx** register is decremented and the index register is incremented. The operation will terminate if **cx** is decremented to zero or earlier if a comparison is equal; that is, if a character in the string matching the specified character in the **al** register is found.

Table 19-2.   String Operations Available for 80486/8088 Microprocessors

Mnemonic	Action
cld	Clear direction flag (left to right)
std	Set direction flag (right to left)
rep	Repeat instruction
repe	Repeat instruction if equal
repz	Repeat instruction if zero
repne	Repeat instruction if not equal
repnz	Repeat instruction if not zero
cmps	Compare string
cmpsb	Compare string, a byte at a time
cmpsw	Compare string, a word at a time
cmpsd	Compare string, a double word at a time (80486 and 80386 only)
scas	Scan string
scasb	Scan string, a byte at a time
scasw	Scan string, a word at a time
scasd	Scan string, a double word at a time (80486 and 80386 only)

Looking for a Character in a String

This section develops the first piece of foundational code for finding a specified character within a string of characters using the new string instructions. Examine the following code and see if you can determine the actions taking place:

```
;TURBO Assembly Language Programming Application
;Copyright (c) Chris H. Pappas and William H. Murray, 1990

;Scanning a string for the occurrence of a character.

        DOSSEG                      ;use Intel segment-ordering
        .MODEL  small               ;set model size
        .8086                       ;8086 instructions

        .STACK  300h                ;set up 768-byte stack

printit macro   buffer              ;;macro to print string
        push    ax                  ;;save registers
        push    dx
        lea     dx,buffer           ;;get address of string
        mov     ah,09               ;;call interrupt
        int     21h
        pop     dx                  ;;restore registers
        pop     ax
        endm

        .DATA                       ;set up data location
searchstr db    'Do not wear yourself out to get rich...'
messg1  db      'Found the character in the string.$'
messg2  db      'Did not find the character in the string.$'

        .CODE
Turbo   PROC    FAR                 ;main procedure declaration
        mov     ax,DGROUP           ;point ds & es toward .DATA
        mov     ds,ax
        mov     es,ax

        cld                         ;set for left to right scan
        lea     di,searchstr        ;address of string to scan
        mov     cx,39               ;characters to scan
        mov     al,'c'              ;look for a "c"
repne   scasb                       ;scan byte by byte
        jnz     nochar              ;if zf<>0, no match
        printit messg1              ;if zf=0, match!
        jmp     done                ;done
nochar:
        printit messg2              ;no character found
done:

        mov     ah,4Ch              ;return control to DOS
        int     21h
Turbo   ENDP                        ;end main procedure
        END                         ;end whole program
```

Notice that a macro has been created for calling the DOS print string interrupt. The macro, named **printit**, accepts an argument, named *buffer*, that passes the address of the string to be printed. The **printit** macro will be used to print one of two messages to the screen — one reporting that the character was found and the other reporting that it was not found in the string. You might want to place the **printit** macro in your macro library, *tmacro.mac*.

The real action starts with the **cld** instruction:

```
        cld                      ;set for left to right scan
        lea     di,searchstr     ;address of string to scan
        mov     cx,39            ;characters to scan
        mov     al,'c'           ;look for a "c"
repne   scasb                    ;scan byte by byte
        jnz     nochar           ;if zf<>0, no match
```

The **cld** instruction sets the scan flag to zero, for a left to right scan of the string. The address of *searchstr* is loaded into the **di** (destination index) register. The **cx** register contains the number of elements in the string. The scan count is set to the string length. The character that is to be searched for is contained in the **al** register. In this case, the search is for the letter "c." The **repne scasb** operation is used since you are looking for the first occurrence of the letter "c" and want the scan to run as long as one hasn't been found or until you reach the end of the string. If a "c" is found, the program will break out of this line and print the "character found" message. If a "c" is not found, the scan will continue, character by character, until **cx** is decremented to zero. Naturally, you can change the character to any ASCII value you choose.

Remember that if the program breaks out of the repeat line, either **cx** was decremented to zero or a match for the character was found. By using the test **jnz**, you will acknowledge that the character has or has not been found.

Determining the Occurrences of a Given Character

The last example searched for the occurrence of a character in a string. When the first occurrence of the character occurred or the scan terminated, the program was over. But what if you wanted to find out how many occurrences of a given character were in any particular string? This might be useful, for example, if you wanted to determine how many words occurred in a string. Since words are separated by a space, you could devise a program to count the number of spaces in a string. Add one to the total, and you would have the word count for the string. (You need to add a one since the first word of the string usually won't have a space in front of it.)

```
;TURBO Assembly Language Programming Application
;Copyright (c) Chris H. Pappas and William H. Murray, 1990

;Scan string for how many spaces occur in the string.

INCLUDE c:tmacro.mac                 ;include our turbo macros

        DOSSEG                       ;use Intel segment-ordering
        .MODEL  small                ;set model size
        .8086                        ;8086 instructions

        .STACK  300h                 ;set up 768-byte stack

        .DATA                        ;set up data location
searchstr  db      'Listen to advice and accept instruction,
           db      'and in the end you will be wise.'
mybuffer   db      4 dup (' ')
result     dw      0

        .CODE
Turbo   PROC    FAR                  ;main procedure declaration
        mov     ax,DGROUP            ;point ds & es toward .DATA
        mov     ds,ax
        mov     es,ax

        cld                          ;left to right scan
        lea     di,searchstr         ;location of string
        mov     cx,73                ;string length
        mov     al,' '               ;the "blank" char.
repeat:
repne   scasb                        ;scan string, byte by byte
        jne     noinc                ;end of string?
        inc     result               ;if no, increment
        jmp     repeat               ;continue scan
noinc:
        numout  result               ;print number to screen

        mov     ah,4Ch               ;return control to DOS
        int     21h
Turbo   ENDP                         ;end main procedure
        END                          ;end whole program
```

Note that the core of this program is the code developed in the previous example. In this example, instead of searching the string for a "c," you search the string for a blank. You also need to add a loop.

```
repeat:
repne   scasb                        ;scan string, byte by byte
```

```
          jne      noinc              ;end of string?
          inc      result             ;if no, increment
          jmp      repeat             ;continue scan
noinc:
          numout   result             ;print number to screen
```

The loop is necessary because when the character is located the program will drop out of the repeat line. With the loop, the program can be forced back to the repeat line to continue scanning. Each time a character is found and the repeat line is left, the program will have to increment a counter. The ability to jump back into the repeat line is allowed because the values in the **cx** and **di** registers are still intact.

Each time a space is encountered in the string, the variable *result* is incremented. When the whole string has been scanned — that is, **cx** is 0 — the macro **numout** is called to print the value. The macro is contained in the *tmacro.mac* library developed in the last chapter.

Figure 19-1 shows a Debugger window. Examine the values in the Watch window. What can you conclude?

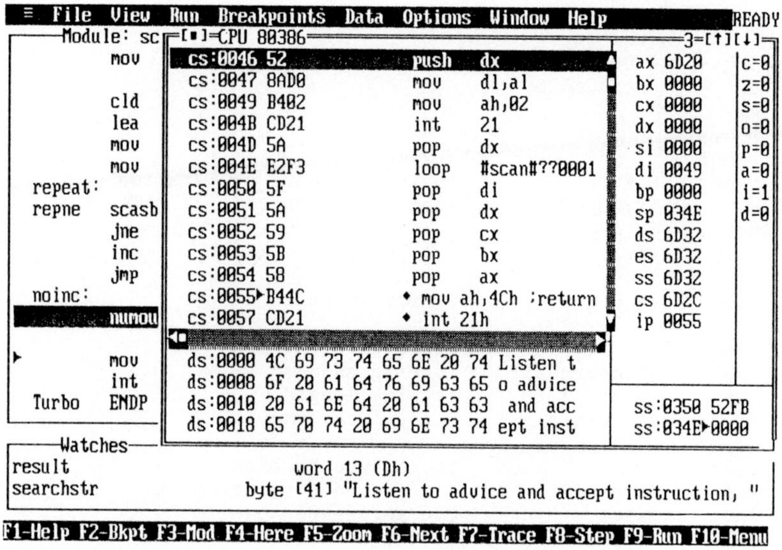

Figure 19-1.   The Debugger window

Looking for Vowels

The last example scanned for the multiple occurrence of a single character. It is relatively easy to make that program scan for the multiple occurrence of several characters. To find several characters in a string, you have to change the letter in the **al** register and restart the scan. Scanning for multiple characters is useful if you want to find the total number of vowels, consonants, or numeric digits in a string.

```
;TURBO Assembly Language Programming Application
;Copyright (c) Chris H. Pappas and William H. Murray, 1990

;Counting the number of vowels in a string

INCLUDE c:tmacro.mac              ;include our turbo macros

        DOSSEG                    ;use Intel segment-ordering
        .MODEL  small             ;set model size
        .8086                     ;8086 instructions

        .STACK  300h              ;set up 768-byte stack

        .DATA                     ;set up data location
searchstr db    'It is not good to have zeal without '
        db      'knowledge, nor to be hasty and miss '
        db      'the way.'
mybuffer db     4 DUP (' ')
vowels  db      'aeiouAEIOU'
value   dw      ?

        .CODE
Turbo   PROC    FAR               ;main procedure declaration
        mov     ax,DGROUP         ;point ds & es toward .DATA
        mov     ds,ax
        mov     es,ax

        mov     si,0              ;init. index to 0
another:
        cld                       ;left to right scan
        lea     di,searchstr      ;string address
        mov     cx,80             ;string length
        mov     al,vowels[si]     ;individual vowel
repeat:
repne   scasb                     ;scan byte by byte
        jne     novowel           ;if yes, don't increment
        inc     value             ;if no, found vowel
        jmp     repeat            ;continue the scan
novowel:
        inc     si                ;point to next vowel
        cmp     si,10             ;done all vowels?
        jl      another           ;if no, do another
        numout  value             ;print the value
```

```
             mov      ah,4Ch              ;return control to DOS
             int      21h
    Turbo    ENDP                         ;end main procedure
             END                          ;end whole program
```

To facilitate switching the character that is being scanned, the group of characters is placed in a string. The variable *vowels* contains 'aeiouAEIOU'. Both upper- and lowercase characters are needed since they are different. This program will gather a character from *vowels* and scan the string for all occurrences of that character. A total of occurrences will be kept in the variable *value*. The process is repeated for each subsequent character, with the total count in *value* being the total number of vowels in the string.

```
             mov      si,0                ;init. index to 0
    another:
             cld                          ;left to right scan
             lea      di,searchstr        ;string address
             mov      cx,80               ;string length
             mov      al,vowels[si]       ;individual vowel
                        .
                        .
                        .
                        .
             inc      si                  ;point to next vowel
             cmp      si,10               ;done all vowels?
             jl       another             ;if no, do another
             numout   value               ;print the value
```

The **si** register is used as the index into the string of vowel characters. A character pointed to by **si** is moved into the **al** register before the string is scanned. After one pass through the entire string, the **si** register is incremented. Now **si** is pointing to the next character in the *vowels* string. To ensure that the string of vowels has not been exhausted, a check is made to see if all ten (ten since you have upper- and lowercase) vowels have been used. When all of the vowels have been used, the **numout** macro prints to the screen the number of vowels found in the string.

What additional code would you need to obtain a total for each individual vowel?

String Comparisons

As you know from C, the ability to compare strings is a very important programming tool. String comparisons are often used to create spelling checkers for word processors. The concept is rather simple. The string or word being checked is compared with a dictionary of strings or words. This dictionary can be nothing more than a table of strings. If there is an exact match between the entered string and a string in the dictionary, the word is spelled correctly. If an exact match is not found, the word is either spelled incorrectly or it is not in the dictionary.

The next example is a simple programming application that compares two strings. It prints a message to the screen announcing the results of the comparison. Notice the subtle difference between the two strings.

```
;TURBO Assembly Language Programming Application
;Copyright (c) Chris H. Pappas and William H. Murray, 1990

;A program to compare two strings.  Are they identical?

          DOSSEG                    ;use Intel segment-ordering
          .MODEL  small             ;set model size
          .8086                     ;8086 instructions

          .STACK  300h              ;set up 768-byte stack

printit macro   buffer             ;;macro to print string
          push    ax                ;;save registers
          push    dx
          lea     dx,buffer         ;;get address of string
          mov     ah,09             ;;call interrupt
          int     21h
          pop     dx                ;;restore registers
          pop     ax
          endm

          .DATA                     ;set up data location
string1 db      'He who answers before listening -  '
        db      'that is his folly and his shame.'
string2 db      'He who answers before listening -  '
        db      'that is his folly and his slame.'
messg1  db      'The two strings are identical.$'
messg2  db      'The two strings are not identical.$'

          .CODE
Turbo   PROC    FAR               ;main procedure declaration
          mov     ax,DGROUP        ;point ds & es toward .DATA
          mov     ds,ax
          mov     es,ax

          cld                      ;left to right scan
          mov     cx,67            ;length of strings
          lea     si,string1       ;address of string1
          lea     di,string2       ;address of string2
repe    cmpsb                     ;scan char by char
          jne     nomatch          ;if zf<>0, then no match
```

```
            printit messg1              ;display success message
            jmp     done                ;done program
nomatch:
            printit messg2              ;display no success message
      done:

            mov     ah,4Ch              ;return control to DOS
            int     21h
Turbo ENDP                              ;end main procedure
      END                               ;end whole program
```

This is the first string application where both a source and a destination string are present. Source string addresses are placed in the **si** register, often called the source index in applications such as this. The destination string address is placed in the **di** register, called the destination index. Notice that a **repe** and **cmpsb** instruction pair is used during the comparisons.

```
            lea     si,string1          ;address of string1
            lea     di,string2          ;address of string2
repe  cmpsb                             ;scan char by char
            jne     nomatch             ;if zf<>0, then no match
            printit messg1              ;display success message
            jmp     done                ;done program
nomatch:
            printit messg2              ;display no success message
```

String1 serves as the source string while *string2* is defined as the destination string. The two strings will be compared byte by byte, from left to right. The comparisons will continue as long as each character in each string matches. If there is a mismatch, the program will break out of the operation. If a mismatch occurs before the end of the string, the zero flag **zf** will not be zero, and the "no match" message will be printed. On the other hand, if the string is exhausted and the zero flag equals zero, the strings match and a "success" message will be printed.

A Search and Replace Mission

In an earlier program, you learned how to obtain a word count in a string by searching for spaces. The following example will use that technique to search for the beginning of each new word in a string. The first character of the new word will be checked to see if it is lower- or uppercase. If it is lowercase, the program will convert it to uppercase.

```
;TURBO Assembly Language Programming Application
;Copyright (c) Chris H. Pappas and William H. Murray, 1990

;Change first letter of each new word to uppercase.

        DOSSEG                          ;use Intel segment-ordering
        .MODEL  small                   ;set model size
        .8086                           ;8086 instructions

        .STACK  300h                    ;set up 768-byte stack

printit macro   buffer                  ;;macro to print string
        push    ax                      ;;save registers
        push    dx
        lea     dx,buffer               ;;get address of string
        mov     ah,09                   ;;call interrupt
        int     21h
        pop     dx                      ;;restore registers
        pop     ax
        endm

        .DATA                           ;set up data location
scanstr db      'A man of many companions may come to ruin, '
        db      'but there is a friend who sticks closer '
        db      'than a brother.$'

        .CODE
Turbo   PROC    FAR                     ;main procedure declaration
        mov     ax,DGROUP               ;point ds & es toward .DATA
        mov     ds,ax
        mov     es,ax

        cld                             ;set for left to right scan
        lea     di,scanstr              ;get location of string
        mov     cx,98                   ;string length
        mov     al,' '                  ;put blank in al register
repeat:
repne   scasb                           ;check string, byte by byte
        jne     strend                  ;at end of string?
        mov     ah,byte ptr[di]         ;take a look at letter
        cmp     ah,61h                  ;is it lowercase?
        jl      repeat                  ;if not lowercase, don't convert
        sub     byte ptr[di],20h        ;if lowercase, make uppercase
        jmp     repeat                  ;continue scan
strend:
        printit scanstr                 ;print the string to the screen

        mov     ah,4Ch                  ;return control to DOS
        int     21h
Turbo   ENDP                            ;end main procedure
        END                             ;end whole program
```

The string search progresses from left to right. The scanning is for the space
character contained in the **al** register. If a blank is found and the end of the
string has not been encountered, a switch will be made. Examine the
following code:

```
repne   scasb                       ;check string, byte by byte
        jne     strend              ;at end of string?
        mov     ah,byte ptr[di]     ;take a look at letter
        cmp     ah,61h              ;is it lowercase?
        jl      repeat              ;if not lowercase, don't convert
        sub     byte ptr[di],20h    ;if lowercase, make uppercase
        jmp     repeat              ;continue scan
strend:
        printit scanstr             ;print the string to the screen
```

In this example, a repeat-not-equal is used for the string compare operation. If a space is found in the string, the **di** register is used to point to the first character of the word that follows. Since the **di** register is incremented when leaving the string compare line, it is not pointing to the location of the blank character. Thus, **di** can be used as a pointer into the data segment. If the character being pointed to is lowercase, a 20h is subtracted from its ASCII value. This effectively converts it to uppercase. Appendix A lists the ASCII values for characters. If the character is already uppercase, the conversion is not performed.

Figure 19-2 shows a Debugger trace of this action. Notice the partially uppercase string and the values in the Watch window.

USING THE DOS FILE SERVICES

DOS provides a number of services for file creation, reading, and writing. Examine the various interrupts shown in Appendix B. Several of the more important file interrupts are repeated in Table 19-3 for your convenience.

Many of the commands in Table 19-3 will be used in the next three programming examples. The first example will allow you to create a file by specifying the drive, path name, and file name from the keyboard. The second example allows you to open, write to, and close a file. The final program prints the contents of the file to the screen. All work is done with text or ASCII files.

If you understand the basic file manipulations shown in these three programs, you can go on to larger projects. For example, you may want to create a spelling checker. If so, the dictionary can now reside in a separate file that you can call during a spelling check.

```
≡  File  View  Run  Breakpoints  Data  Options  Window  Help          READY
┌[■]=Module: cap  File: cap.asm 32═══════════════════════════════1=[↑][↓]┐
│          .DATA                     ;set up data location
│  scanstr db     'A man of many companions may come to ruin, '
│          db     'but there is a friend who sticks closer '
│          db     'than a brother.$'
│
│          .CODE
│  Turbo   PROC   FAR                ;main procedure declaration
│          mov    ax,DGROUP          ;point ds & es toward .DATA
│          mov    ds,ax
│          mov    es,ax
│
│          cld                       ;set for left to right scan
│          lea    di,scanstr         ;get location of string
│          mov    cx,98              ;string length
│          mov    al,' '             ;put blank in al register
│  repeat:
│► repne   scasb                     ;check string, byte by byte
└◄■═══════════════════════════════════════════════════════════════►┘
┌─Watches─────────────────────────────────────────────────2─────────┐
│di                         word 15 (Fh)
│scanstr                    byte [43] "A Man Of Many Companions may come to ruin, "
└───────────────────────────────────────────────────────────────────┘
F1-Help F2-Bkpt F3-Mod F4-Here F5-Zoom F6-Next F7-Trace F8-Step F9-Run F10-Menu
```

Figure 19-2.   A Turbo Debugger trace

Table 19-3.   DOS File Services (int 21h)

File Services

Make Directory (ah = 39h)
Remove Directory (ah = 3Ah)
Change Directory (ah = 3Bh)
Create File (ah = 3Ch)
Open File (ah = 3Dh)
File Handle (ah = 3Eh)
File (or device) Read (ah = 3Fh)
File (or device) Write (ah = 40h)
File Delete (ah = 41h)
Move File Pointer (ah = 42h)
File Attribute (ah = 43h)
Duplicate File Handle (ah = 45h)
Force Duplicate File Handle (ah = 46h)
Get Current Directory (ah = 47h)

Creating a New File

Before using a file for the first time, you must create the file by using the DOS interrupt and setting the **ah** register to 3Ch. If the file already exists, the original file will be destroyed. If there is no check for the file's existence, as in this program, you will want to use this code cautiously. The following listing contains the **printit** macro, which displays a prompt on the screen:

```
;TURBO Assembly Language Programming Application
;Copyright (c) Chris H. Pappas and William H. Murray, 1990

;Program will create a file with user selected drive,
;name and extension.

            DOSSEG                       ;use Intel segment-ordering
            .MODEL   small               ;set model size
            .8086                        ;8086 instructions

            .STACK   300h                ;set up 768-byte stack

printit macro    buffer                  ;;macro to print string
            push     ax                  ;;save registers
            push     dx
            lea      dx,buffer           ;;get address of string
            mov      ah,09               ;;call interrupt
            int      21h
            pop      dx                  ;;restore registers
            pop      ax
            endm

createfile MACRO                         ;;create a file
            mov      ah,3Ch              ;;use DOS interrupt
            mov      cx,00h              ;;normal attribute
            lea      dx,filename         ;;name.ext of file
            int      21h
            endm

            .DATA                        ;set up data location
information db   'To create a file, specify:  drive, file '
            db       'name and extension.',0Dh,0Ah,'$'
filestruct label byte
maxlen   db       40
actlen   db       ?
filename db       40 dup (' '),0

            .CODE
Turbo    PROC     FAR                    ;main procedure declaration
            mov      ax,DGROUP           ;point ds toward .DATA
            mov      ds,ax

            printit information          ;print information message
```

```
        lea     dx,filestruct    ;get a file name
        mov     ah,0Ah           ;from keyboard input
        int     21h              ;call interrupt

        mov     bh,0             ;string length in bx
        mov     bl,actlen
        mov     filename[bx],' ' ;remove carriage return

        createfile               ;call macro to create

        mov     ah,4Ch           ;return control to DOS
        int     21h
Turbo   ENDP                     ;end main procedure
        END                      ;end whole program
```

The **createfile** macro does the real work in this program. This macro
supplies the DOS create file parameters along with the *filename* contained in
the data segment.

```
createfile MACRO                 ;;create a file
        mov     ah,3Ch           ;;use DOS interrupt
        mov     cx,00h           ;;normal attribute
        lea     dx,filename      ;;name.ext of file
        int     21h
        endm
```

The value in the **cx** register sets the file's attribute:

0h	Normal file attribute
1h	Read-only file attribute
2h	Hidden file attribute
4h	System file attribute
20h	Archive file attribute
8h	Volume label
10h	Subdirectory

The *filename* variable points to an ASCIIZ string. These strings terminate
with a null character. This information is contained in *filestruct,* along with
the *maxlen* and *actlen* of the string. The *filename* can contain the drive letter,
path name, file name, and file extension (up to 40 characters). The file name
ends with a null character, as you can see.

The **createfile** macro will open and/or create a file. When it does, the
length of the file is set to zero. This is why you should only use **createfile**

once, to create a new file or erase an existing file. The macro also obtains the file's ID, called the file handle, but that information is not needed at this point.

This program will allow you to create an endless number of new, empty files. Create a few files and examine the directory listing. They are all empty—waiting for your input.

Sending Information to a File

The last example merely created a file. The next example will show you how to write information to that file. This program will open the previously created file, write information to it, and then close the file before ending the program. The program will use several macros to open (**openfile**), index to the end of file (**fileindex**), write (**sendfile**), and close (**closefile**) the file. Study this listing carefully:

```
;TURBO Assembly Language Programming Application
;Copyright (c) Chris H. Pappas and William H. Murray, 1990

;Program will open a previously created file and
;write information to it.

INCLUDE c:tmacro.mac              ;include our turbo macro

        DOSSEG                    ;use Intel segment-ordering
        .MODEL  small             ;set model size
        .8086                     ;8086 instructions

        .STACK  300h              ;set up 768-byte stack

printit macro   buffer            ;;macro to print string
        push    ax                ;;save registers
        push    dx
        lea     dx,buffer         ;;get address of string
        mov     ah,09             ;;call interrupt
        int     21h
        pop     dx                ;;restore registers
        pop     ax
        endm

openfile macro                    ;;Open previously created file
        mov     al,02h            ;;make the file - write only
        mov     ah,3Dh            ;;DOS open file parameter
        lea     dx,filename       ;;filename and extension
        int     21h               ;;call the interrupt
        mov     filehand,ax       ;;save the returned file handle
        endm
```

```
fileindex macro                  ;;macro to determine EOF
        mov     al,02h           ;;DOS parameters
        mov     ah,42h
        mov     bx,filehand      ;;file handle
        mov     cx,0h            ;;move to EOF
        mov     dx,0h
        int     21h              ;;call interrupt, get index
        endm

sendfile macro                   ;;macro to write info to file
        mov     ah,40h           ;;DOS parameter
        mov     bx,filehand      ;;file handle
        mov     cx,81            ;;write 80 bytes
        lea     dx,infodata      ;;characters to be written
        int     21h              ;;call the interrupt
        endm

closefile macro                  ;;macro to close file
        mov     ah,3Eh           ;;DOS parameters
        mov     bx,filehand      ;;file handle
        int     21h              ;;call the interrupt
        endm

        .DATA                    ;set up data location
screen1 db      'Supply: drive, path, filename and '
        db      'extension information.',0Dh,0Ah,'$'
screen2 db      '    Enter text to place in file: $'
filestruct label byte
maxlen  db      40               ;max length of file spec.
actlen  db      ?                ;actual length
filename db     40 dup (' ')     ;file info placed here
infostruc label byte
mlength db      80               ;maximum length of info
infoline db     ?                ;actual length of info
infodata db     80 DUP(' '),0Dh  ;info to send to disk
filehand dw     ?                ;file handle

        .CODE
Turbo   PROC    FAR              ;main procedure declaration
        mov     ax,DGROUP        ;point ds & es toward .DATA
        mov     ds,ax
        mov     es,ax

        printit screen1          ;print information to user

        lea     dx,filestruct    ;get file name
        mov     ah,0Ah           ;from keyboard input
        int     21h              ;call interrupt

        mov     bh,0             ;place string length
        mov     bl,actlen        ;in bx register
        mov     filename[bx],' ' ;remove carriage return

        blankscreen              ;blank the screen
        openfile                 ;open file
        fileindex                ;set index to EOF
```

```
repeat:
        call    write_to_file    ;call write_to_file proc.
        cmp     infoline,0       ;if yes, end program
        jne     repeat           ;if no, repeat
        closefile                ;close file
        mov     ax,4C00h         ;return control to DOS
        int     21h
Turbo   ENDP                     ;end main procedure

write_to_file PROC NEAR
        cursor  0000H            ;set cursor to top
        printit screen2          ;print information
        cursor  0100h            ;set cursor down a row
        lea     dx,infostruc
        mov     ah,0Ah           ;put string in file name
        int     21h              ;call interrupt
        blankscreen              ;blank screen
        cmp     infoline,0       ;finished?
        je      done             ;if yes, end
        mov     bh,0             ;if no, length of info
        mov     bl,infoline      ;goes in bx
        mov     infodata[bx],' ' ;then blank out cr
        sendfile                 ;write data to disk

        cld                      ;set string scan direction
        lea     di,infodata      ;blank name field
        mov     cx,40            ;write 40x2 blanks
        mov     ax,2020h         ;character to write
        rep     stosw            ;repeat byte by byte
done:
        ret
write_to_file ENDP

        END                      ;end whole program
```

Macro Power

A file must be opened before information can be sent to or read from it. To open a previously created file, **ah** is set to 3Dh before the DOS interrupt is called. The address of *filename* must be in the **dx** register. When the file is successfully opened, the file handle will be returned in *filehand*. A 2 in the **al** register states that the operation to be performed is a write-only operation. The file handle is required for subsequent read, write, and close operations.

```
openfile macro                   ;;Open previously created file
        mov     al,02h           ;;make the file - write only
        mov     ah,3Dh           ;;DOS open file parameter
        lea     dx,filename      ;;filename and extension
        int     21h              ;;call the interrupt
        mov     filehand,ax      ;;save the returned file handle
        endm
```

Since this might not be the first time that this file has been used, you need to obtain the location of the end of file, EOF, to keep from overwriting previously stored information. A macro named **fileindex** will obtain this information for the program.

```
fileindex macro                 ;;macro to determine EOF
        mov     al,02h          ;;DOS parameters
        mov     ah,42h
        mov     bx,filehand     ;;file handle
        mov     cx,0h           ;;move to EOF
        mov     dx,0h
        int     21h             ;;call interrupt, get index
        endm
```

DOS allows you to determine information about the file pointer by setting **ah** to 42h before calling the interrupt. The **bx** register is loaded with the file handle *filehand*. The **al** register contains the file pointer's starting location. If **al** is set to 0, the file's offset is measured from the starting point of the file. If **al** is a 1, the file's offset is measured from the current file pointer location. Finally, if **al** is a 2, the offset is measured from the end of file. The offset value is placed in the **cx:dx** register pair. In this example, you need to find the EOF, so **al** is set to 2. However, no offset will be required since new information will be written starting with the EOF position.

The **sendfile** macro will provide the necessary DOS parameters to allow writing to the file. In order to send information to a file, the **ah** register is set to 40h.

```
sendfile macro                  ;;macro to write info to file
        mov     ah,40h          ;;DOS parameter
        mov     bx,filehand     ;;file handle
        mov     cx,81           ;;write 80 bytes
        lea     dx,infodata     ;;characters to be written
        int     21h             ;;call the interrupt
        endm
```

Notice that the macro doesn't care what the file name is, as long as the file handle is loaded into the **bx** register. This is because the file handle is unique to the associated file name. The **cx** register contains the total number of bytes that will be written to the file each time the macro is called. In this program, **cx** is 81. The address of the string information is held in the **ds:dx** pair. Recall that if the information is in the data segment, the address of *infodata* can be loaded into **dx** directly. In this example, *infodata* has been initialized with 80 blanks and a carriage return.

When all writing has been accomplished and you wish to exit the program, you need to close the file. The final macro, **closefile**, performs this task. The **ah** register is set to 3Eh and the file handle is placed in the **bx** register. That is the only information required by DOS to close the file and free the file handle.

```
closefile macro                 ;;macro to close file
        mov     ah,3Eh          ;;DOS parameters
        mov     bx,filehand     ;;file handle
        int     21h             ;;call the interrupt
        endm
```

In applications that open several files, make sure that the correct file handle is being used at any given time.

The Main Program

When this application is started, the user will be presented with the contents of *screen1* requesting drive, path, file name, and extension information. The screen will then be cleared before the file is opened and the index set to EOF. The file is now ready to have additional information sent to or read from it. A near procedure, named **write_to_file**, is used to process information being sent to the file. A call to this procedure is contained in a loop that will continuously cycle, requesting new information from the user.

```
repeat:
        call    write_to_file   ;call write_to_file proc.
        cmp     infoline,0       ;if yes, end program
        jne     repeat           ;if no, repeat
        closefile                ;close file
```

The information to be sent to the file is entered from the keyboard and saved in the variable *infodata*. A label directive is used that also associates the maximum length of the information, *mlength,* and the actual length, *infoline,* with *infodata.* If the current string of information just contains a carriage return, the program will end by first calling the **closefile** macro.

The write_to_file Procedure

Most of the action in the program takes place in the **near** procedure. The **write_to_file** procedure accomplishes quite a bit. The cursor is moved to the upper-left corner of the screen with the **cursor** macro from the *tmacro.mac* macro library. The **printit** macro, included at the top of the program, then prints the second user prompt, *screen2*, at the top of the screen. This prompt asks the user to enter a line of characters. The cursor is then moved to the beginning of the next line in order to accept and echo keyboard information. This information can actually be any combination of ASCII characters, even printer control characters. When 80 characters are entered or a carriage return is detected, input is terminated. The information typed, as well as its actual length, is saved in *infostruc*. Once this information is saved, the screen is cleared for further data entry. Note that the actual string length is moved to the **bx** register and the carriage return is overwritten with a blank. The **sendfile** macro transfers the text information to the disk and the file pointer is indexed to the new EOF.

If the user is entering multiple lines of text, the buffer (*infodata*) that holds the text information must be *blanked out*, or cleared. This is necessary since the second line of text might be shorter than the first. If the buffer were not cleared, part of the first line of text would still be in the buffer when the second line was written to the file.

```
cld                      ;set string scan direction
lea     di,infodata      ;blank name field
mov     cx,40            ;write 40x2 blanks
mov     ax,2020h         ;character to write
rep     stosw            ;repeat byte by byte
```

The address for *infodata* is placed in the **di** register. The **cx** register is loaded with 40, and **ax** with 2020h. Now a single 20h is the ASCII equivalent for a blank. In this case, two blanks will be written at a time. Thus $2 \times 40 = 80$ character positions in *infodata*. The **stosw** is used here to write the word information.

The **write_to_file** loop is called repeatedly until a carriage return is entered without text. When this occurs, the program ends and the file is closed. You can view this file by just printing it to the screen:

```
c>type [drive/path/filename/extension]
```

Reading a File

The last program enabled you to send information to a file. This information is in ASCII format and hence the file can be printed directly to the screen. The next example develops a program that will open the file, read information from it, and close it:

```
;TURBO Assembly Language Programming Application
;Copyright (c) Chris H. Pappas and William H. Murray, 1990

;Program will open a previously created file and
;read information from it.

INCLUDE c:tmacro.mac              ;include our turbo macro

        DOSSEG                    ;use Intel segment-ordering
        .MODEL   small            ;set model size
        .8086                     ;8086 instructions

        .STACK   300h             ;set up 768-byte stack

printit macro    buffer           ;;macro to print string
        push     ax               ;;save registers
        push     dx
        lea      dx,buffer        ;;get address of string
        mov      ah,09            ;;call interrupt
        int      21h
        pop      dx               ;;restore registers
        pop      ax
        endm

openfile macro                    ;;open previously created file
        mov      al,02h           ;;make the file - write only
        mov      ah,3Dh           ;;DOS open file parameter
        lea      dx,filename      ;;filename and extension
        int      21h              ;;call the interrupt
        mov      filehand,ax      ;;save the file handle
        endm

readfile macro                    ;;write info to file
        mov      ah,3Fh           ;;DOS parameter
        mov      bx,filehand      ;;file handle
        mov      cx,81            ;;read 80 bytes
        lea      dx,infodata      ;;write here
        int      21h              ;;call the interrupt
        endm

closefile macro                   ;;macro to close file
        mov      ah,3Eh           ;;DOS parameters
        mov      bx,filehand      ;;file handle
        int      21h              ;;call the interrupt
        endm

        .DATA                     ;set up data location
screen1 db       'Supply: drive, path, filename and '
        db       'extension information.',0Dh,0Ah,'$'
screen2 db       '   Enter text to place in file: $'
filestruct label byte
maxlen  db       40               ;max length of file spec.
actlen  db       ?                ;actual length
```

```
filename db       40 dup (' ')      ;file info placed here
infostruc label byte
mlength db        80                ;max length of info
infoline db       ?                 ;actual length of info
infodata db       81 DUP(' '),'$'   ;info to send to disk
filehand dw       ?                 ;file handle
cr       db       0Dh,'$'           ;carriage return


         .CODE
Turbo    PROC     FAR               ;main procedure declaration
         mov      ax,DGROUP         ;point ds & es toward .DATA
         mov      ds,ax
         mov      es,ax

         printit screen1            ;print information to user

         lea      dx,filestruct     ;get file name
         mov      ah,0Ah            ;from keyboard input
         int      21h               ;call interrupt

         mov      bh,0              ;place string length
         mov      bl,actlen         ;in bx register
         mov      filename[bx],' '  ;remove carriage return

         blankscreen                ;blank the screen
         openfile                   ;open file

repeat:
         call     read_the_file     ;call near procedure
         cmp      infoline,00       ;if no info, end the program
         jne      repeat            ;else, continue to input
         closefile                  ;close file
norepeat:

         mov      ax,4C00h          ;return control to DOS
         int      21h
Turbo    ENDP                       ;end main procedure

read_the_file PROC NEAR
         cursor   0000h             ;cursor to top of page
         printit screen2            ;print information
         cursor   0100h             ;cursor down a line
additional:
         readfile                   ;read file
         mov      infoline,al       ;get something?
         cmp      infoline,0        ;if no, done
         je       norepeat          ;end the program
         printit infodata           ;else, string len. to bx
         printit cr                 ;carriage return
         jmp      additional        ;additional file info.
         ret
read_the_file ENDP

         END                        ;end whole program
```

Notice the four macros at the top of the listing. Now go to the end of the listing and observe the *near* procedure. The first macro is **printit**. The other macros are **openfile** (open the file), **readfile** (read the file), and **closefile** (close the file). The open and close file macros are the same as the macros in the last example. When macros are used frequently by more than one program, they are good candidates for the *tmacro.mac* macro library. Why not move them over to the macro library now?

More Macro Power

This section will concentrate on the new **readfile** macro. DOS provides file reading capabilities when **ah** is set to 3Fh.

```
readfile macro                         ;;write info to file
        mov     ah,3Fh                 ;;DOS parameter
        mov     bx,filehand            ;;file handle
        mov     cx,81                  ;;read 80 bytes
        lea     dx,infodata            ;;write here
        int     21h                    ;;call the interrupt
        endm
```

Again, only the file handle, *filehandle,* is required to identify the file in question. Recall that the handle value is returned when the **openfile** macro is called. The **cx** register gives the number of bytes to be read. The address of *infodata* is placed in the **ds:dx** register pair. This, again, assumes that the **ds** register contains the address of the data segment. When the DOS interrupt is issued, the **ax** register will contain the actual number of bytes read from the file. If **ax** contains a zero, the end of file (EOF) occurred.

The Main Program

Since this program was kept as similar as possible to the last example, it should come as no surprise that the data segment is almost identical in both examples. The information to be read from the file will be in the same format that it was entered in originally.

As in the last example, the main procedure is short and straightforward. The program prompts the user to enter the file information by displaying *screen1*. Once this information is entered, the screen is cleared and the **openfile** macro is called. If successful, a call to the **read_the_file** procedure will return information to the program. If **read_the_file** returns nothing from the file, the variable *infoline* will equal zero, and the program will end and the file will be closed. The **read_the_file** procedure uses the **cursor** macro from the *tmacro.mac* library. This macro sets the cursor to the upper-left portion of the text screen. The **printit** macro prints the *screen2* message at the top of the screen. The **readfile** macro then places the information in *infostruc* on the screen. The routine looks for an end of file, EOF, to determine whether or not to continue.

PUTTING YOUR KNOWLEDGE TO WORK

1. What is the ASCII code? Give examples of where it is used.

2. Outline the assembly language steps necessary for intercepting and echoing a character from the keyboard.

3. What technique is used to intercept a string from the keyboard? What terminates input in this routine?

4. Write a program that counts the number of characters in a string; exclude spaces and punctuation.

5. Write a program that counts all uppercase letters in a string. (Uppercase letters don't need to be at the start of a word.)

6. Write a program that substitutes a carriage return for the space between words in a string.

7. Write a program that creates two files and prints the file handles to the screen. What values are assigned to the file handles?

8. Move each of the macros from the last two examples to your *tmacro.mac* macro library. Alter the program code to call this library.

9. Examine each example in this chapter. Where possible, write the name of the C or C++ function that performs an equivalent action.

10. What exactly is an EOF?

20

BINDING C AND ASSEMBLY LANGUAGE CODE

In this chapter you will learn

- How to write inline assembly language routines

- How C programs call assembly language routines

- The conventional C syntax for passing arguments

- The mechanics of combining C and assembly language code

- How to control hardware features of your system

- How to use the *make* utility when compiling and assembling program code

The Borland C++ package may at first seem to offer several separate and complete products. The C++ compiler is certainly the reason you purchased the software. You also received a Linker, Assembler, Debugger, and Profiler. The preceding chapters have shown how to write code in two distinct ways. First, you learned how to use the Compiler, Linker, Debugger, and Profiler to develop C and C++ code. Second, you learned how to write assembly language programs with the Assembler, Linker, and Debugger.

In this chapter, you will learn how to combine C and C++ and assembly language object code into one working program. You will soon be able to combine your knowledge of C and assembly language to produce programs that are faster and can control hardware features that you can't control with built-in C and C++ functions.

The discussion will focus on calling assembly language code from C. The C code will appear as the main routine and the assembly language code as an external function. However, it is also possible, although not as common, to call C programs from assembly language source code.

USING INLINE ASSEMBLY LANGUAGE

Instead of splicing C and assembly language code together, you can actually write assembly language code in your C source file. This is called *inline code*. Your C++ compiler allows you to insert assembly language code directly into the C or C++ source code. This technique is ideal for simple assembly language routines, such as DOS and BIOS interrupt calls. To use this technique, include the following pragma at the start of your C code to notify the compiler that your program contains assembly language code:

```
#pragma  inline
```

The actual inline assembly language code is included between two braces and starts with the *asm* keyword. For example:

```
asm {
    push    dx                      /*save general registers*/
    push    cx
    push    bx
    push    ax
    mov     cx,0                    /*upper corner of window*/
    mov     dx,2479H                /*lower corner of window*/
    mov     bh,7                    /*normal screen attribute*/
    mov     ax,0600H                /*BIOS interrupt value*/
    int     10H                     /*call interrupt*/
    pop     ax
    pop     bx
    pop     cx
    pop     dx                      /*restore general registers*/
}
```

Notice that comments are inserted as though they were C comments, even though they are associated with the inline assembly language code. This assembly language routine will clear the text screen with a call to the BIOS interrupt function. This is an adaptation of an assembly language program illustrated in Chapter 18. Additional BIOS and DOS interrupt values are listed in Appendix B.

Your C++ compiler must also know the path to the subdirectories in which your assembler is located. You can do this by setting the path command for your system.

The Parallel Port Connection

The next example will demonstrate how to send information to the computer's parallel port with inline assembly language instructions. First, however, you need to know some details concerning the parallel port.

The parallel port on most IBM compatible computers is a general-purpose 8-bit communications port used to drive a wide range of printers, plotters, and other external devices. The data lines of the parallel port interface respond to one I/O class of assembly code instructions: **out**. You can use data from these lines to control hardware circuits of your own choosing. (The IBM family of PS/2 computers has parallel ports that can be programmed to read 8 bits of data and respond to the assembly language instruction **in**.) If you want more information on parallel and serial ports or require a more technical treatment of ports, see *Inside the Model 80* (Pappas and Murray, Osborne/McGraw-Hill, 1988).

The parallel port is an 8-bit data port, which means that 8 bits of data can be sent to the port. The 8-bit assembly language data type is **byte**, while the corresponding C data type is **char**. Data is written to the output pins when a write (**out**) instruction occurs. The output signals from the parallel port have sink currents of 20 mA. and can source 0.55 mA. The high-level output voltage is 5.0 Vdc while the low-level output voltage is 0.5 Vdc. Data is present at pins 2 through 9 and represents the data lines D0 to D7.

Figure 20-1 shows the parallel port D shell connector. Table 20-1 describes the pin assignment for this connector.

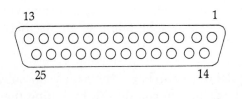

Figure 20-1.   The parallel port D shell connector

Don't be put off by the technical information on ports; the programming is fairly straightforward.

Table 20-1.   Pin Assignment for the Parallel Connector

Pin	Description
1	−STROBE
2	Data bit 0
3	Data bit 1
4	Data bit 2
5	Data bit 3
6	Data bit 4
7	Data bit 5
8	Data bit 6
9	Data bit 7
10	−ACK
11	BUSY
12	PE
13	SLCT
14	−AUTO FEED XT
15	−ERROR
16	−INIT
17	−SLCT IN
18 to 25	Ground

The L.E.D. Lights

The example in this section is a complete program that makes two calls to inline assembly language routines. The first routine clears the screen and the second sends an 8-bit value to the parallel port.

The previous section described the parallel port's output as having sink currents of 20 mA. and source currents of 0.55 mA. Since the output voltage from the port is TTL compatible (logic 1 is 5.0 Vdc while logic 0 is 0.5 Vdc), the parallel port can directly drive small LED lights.

If you want to wire eight LED lights to your parallel port, you need only a cable that will connect the parallel port to a prototyping board, some hookup wire, and eight LED lights. This example used a 25-pin D shell connector to connect to the parallel port with a ribbon cable terminating in a 24-pin male dip header. It also discarded pin #13 from the D shell connector. The prototyping board was the type that allows DIP chips to be inserted and removed easily. You can find these parts at electronic supply stores throughout the United States. If you purchase connectors that clamp over the ribbon cable, no soldering will be necessary.

The voltages present at the parallel port are lower than that of a car battery and don't present a shock hazard. It is also nearly impossible to damage the computer even if you make wrong connections. You must remember, however, that you are making "live" connections to the computer. Be very careful not to connect the parallel port to any external device or outlet where unsafe voltages are present. Figure 20-2 illustrates the circuit used for this example.

The following C code contains the screen clearing routine, shown earlier in this chapter, and a routine for accessing the parallel port:

```
/*
 *    A C program that demonstrates how to use inline
 *    assembly language to clear the screen and access
 *    the parallel port.  This program will sequentially
 *    light 8 LED lamps connected to data lines D0 - D7
 *    of port 956 (LPT1).
 *    Copyright (c) Chris H. Pappas and William H. Murray, 1990
 */

#pragma  inline

#include <dos.h>
#include <stdio.h>
#include <math.h>

main()
{
```

```
int i,temp;
int port=956;

/*clear the text screen*/
asm {
    mov     cx,0            /*upper corner of window*/
    mov     dx,2479H        /*lower corner of window*/
    mov     bh,7            /*normal screen attribute*/
    mov     ax,0600H        /*BIOS interrupt value*/
    int     10H             /*call interrupt*/
}

for (i=0;i<9;i++) {
    temp=(int) pow(2.0,(double) i);

    /*gain access to the parallel port*/
    asm {
        mov     dx,port     /*place the parallel port number*/
        mov     ax,temp     /*value to be sent to port*/
        out     dx,al       /*send only lower 8 bits*/
    }

    printf("%d\n",temp);
    delay(1000);
}

return (0);
}
```

Details of how the separate C and assembly language routines work have been covered in earlier chapters, so further detail on that code will not be included here. However, this program does something far more interesting than just printing numbers to the screen: It sequences the 8-bit values at the parallel port.

With the correct timing sequence, you can create a set of miniature chaser lights. Since each data bit at the parallel port corresponds to an integer power of 2, the numbers 1, 2, 4, 8, 16, 32, 64, and 128 are generated with the **pow** function and sent to the parallel port. (Actually, 256 is also generated and has the effect of turning the sequence off at the completion of the program.)

Why not wire this circuit and experiment with what you can achieve? Writing inline assembly language code makes an efficient use of your professional tools. Try altering the program so that successive pairs of LED lights are sequenced.

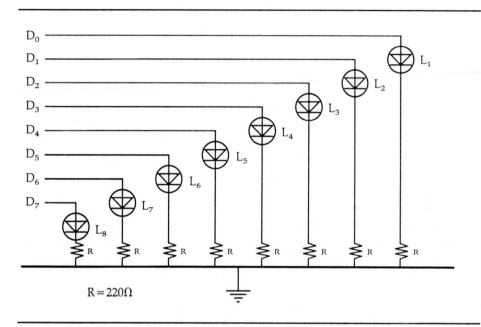

Figure 20-2.   Wiring eight LED lamps to the parallel port

WRITING SEPARATE C AND ASSEMBLY LANGUAGE MODULES

Inline assembly language code becomes unmanageable and hard to understand as your program size grows. When you need more complicated assembly language routines, a separate assembly language procedure is often the best solution.

When you use separate assembly language modules, they are treated as an external function and called from the C host program. The assembly language routine must, therefore, be prototyped as a function in the C or C++ host program, along with a list of arguments that are to be passed. The technique for performing this operation will be described in the next sections.

When combining C and assembly language code, you must learn how arguments are passed from the C host program to the assembly language routine.

The New Method of Passing Arguments

There are two methods for passing arguments in C: an older, more complicated method, and a new streamlined method. The old method demands a
comprehensive understanding of the computer's stack frame and an assembly language skill for receiving and dealing with the values from the C
calling program. The new method puts much less demand on the programmer to understand the computer's architecture. Your compiler uses the new
method, but will also permit you to use the older technique. The strongest
argument for learning the old technique is that some people are still
writing code in that form. If this becomes a problem for you, see Borland's
Programmer's Guide for information on using the stack frame for passing
arguments. The following examples will use the new method of passing
arguments with the traditional C calling convention.

An external assembly language function, prototyped in the C host program, might look something like this:

```
int adder(int num1,int num2,int num3);
```

This prototype seems similar to those used for C functions within the host
program. The assembly language program can intercept these arguments
with the following line of code:

```
adder   PROC   C NEAR  n1,n2,n3:WORD
```

The capital *C*, a keyword here, tells the program to expect the arguments to
be passed from right to left via the stack. The alternate form is to use
PASCAL instead of *C*. If you use *PASCAL*, the arguments are passed from
left to right. The *C* form of passing arguments is the preferred technique
and the one used in all of the examples. The *PASCAL* form is an alternate
form employed by Microsoft for calling Windows and OS/2 functions. The
procedure is *NEAR* when using the small memory model. If you are using
the medium, large, or huge memory model, the procedure would be declared *FAR*. Again, for additional information on these techniques, consult
your Borland manuals. The other new feature is listing the arguments and
their assembly language data type. Recall that the popular data types in
assembly language include **byte**, **word**, and **dword** because you can place
them directly in system registers.

A First Look at Argument Passing

This first example uses three separate files. The first is a *make* file named *first*, the second the program named *first.c*, and the third the assembly language module named *task.asm*. You should use *make* files whenever you are linking more than one module. (The *make* utility was explained in Chapter 3.)

This example passes an 8-bit char, a 16-bit integer, and a 32-bit long value to the assembly language program. The assembly language program performs several operations on these values and returns a 16-bit integer to the C calling program via the **ax** register. In other words, the contents of the **ax** register at the end of the assembly language routine are returned automatically. This value can also be a 16-bit pointer.

The following listing contains all three files, which must be entered separately in your editor before compiling:

```
THE MAKE FILE (first):

first.exe: first.obj task.obj
  tlink c0s first task,first, ,cs

task.obj: task.asm
  tasm task.asm

first.obj: first.c stdio.h
  tcc -c first.c


THE C PROGRAM (first.c):

/*
 *    A C program that demonstrates how to pass several
 *    data types to an external assembly language routine.
 *    The program uses the new argument passing technique.
 *    Copyright (c) Chris H. Pappas and William H. Murray, 1990
 */

#include <stdio.h>

int task(char,int,long);

main()
{
  char num1=15;
  int  num2=1234;
  long num3=12345678;
  int answer;

  answer=task(num1,num2,num3);
```

```
    printf("%d\n",answer);

    return (0);
}
```

THE TASK ASSEMBLY MODULE (task.asm):

```
;TURBO Assembly Language Programming Application
;Copyright (c) Chris H. Pappas and William H. Murray, 1990

;Program accepts several arguments from a C calling program
;and performs mathematical & logical operations with them.
;This is an 80386 program.

        DOSSEG                  ;use Intel segment-ordering
        .MODEL  small           ;set model size
        .386                    ;80386 instructions

        .DATA
little  db      3

        .CODE
        PUBLIC  C task
task    PROC    C NEAR num1:BYTE,num2:WORD,num3:DWORD
        mov     ax,DGROUP
        mov     ds,ax

        mov     edx,0
        mov     eax,num3        ;get 32-bit (long) in eax
        div     WORD PTR num2   ;divide & discard remainder
        and     eax,DWORD PTR num1 ;mask and keep 16 bits
        add     al,little       ;add a small number

        ret                     ;return to calling program
task    ENDP                    ;end main procedure
        END
```

Of particular interest here is the *make* file. The following section of the *make* file is responsible for compiling the C code:

```
first.obj: first.c stdio.h
  tcc -c first.c
```

The statement says to compile but not link the C code. The C code is combined with the named header file to produce an object file.

The next section of code assembles the assembly language module to an object file:

```
task.obj: task.asm
  tasm task.asm
```

This is just a simple call to the assembler to assemble the file.

The final statement controls the linker. Here, the object modules of the C and assembly language code are linked.

```
first.exe: first.obj task.obj
  tlink c0s first task,first, ,cs
```

Notice in the linker expression a call to the small library. If you wanted the medium library, for example, you would have used *c0m* and *cm,* respectively. Also note that the *c0s* and *cs* files are in the current directory. If your files are in the library subdirectory, use *lib\c0s* and *lib\cs* in the *make* file.

The program code is straightforward and is used primarily to illustrate how values are passed. Incidentally, the answer printed to the screen is 7. Can you figure out why?

A SIMPLE C AND ASSEMBLY LANGUAGE CONNECTION

Earlier in this chapter, you learned how to use inline assembly language code to clear the screen and send information to the parallel port. The next example is a program that functions like that earlier program, but is built with separate assembly language modules. This program uses one external routine to clear the screen and another to send information to the parallel port.

More L.E.D. Lights

Four files are needed to compile the next example. The first is a *make* file named *second.* The next is the C program named *second.c.* The last two files are assembly language routines named *clsscr.asm* and *outport.asm.*

The following listing contains all four files, which must be entered separately in your editor before compiling:

```
THE MAKE FILE (second):

second.exe: second.obj clsscr.obj outport.obj
  tlink c0s second clsscr outport,second, ,maths fp87 cs
```

```
clsscr.obj: clsscr.asm
  tasm clsscr.asm

outport.obj: outport.asm
  tasm outport.asm

second.obj: second.c dos.h stdio.h math.h
  tcc -c second.c
```

THE C PROGRAM (second.c):

```
/*
 *    A C program that demonstrates how to call an external
 *    assembly language program to access the parallel port.
 *    Program will sequentially light 8 LED lamps connected
 *    to data lines D0 - D7 of port 956 (LPT1).
 *    Copyright (c) Chris H. Pappas and William H. Murray, 1990
 */

#include <dos.h>
#include <stdio.h>
#include <math.h>

void clsscr(void);
void outport(int,int);

main()
{
  int i,temp;
  int port=956;

  clsscr();

  for (i=0;i<9;i++) {
    temp=(int) pow(2.0,(double) i);

  outport(temp,port);

  printf("%d\n",temp);
  delay(1000);
  }

  return (0);
}
```

THE CLSSCR ASSEMBLY MODULE (clsscr.asm):

```
;TURBO Assembly Language Programming Application
;Copyright (c) Chris H. Pappas and William H. Murray, 1990

;program will clear the screen by calling a BIOS interrupt.
```

```
        DOSSEG                      ;use Intel segment-ordering
        .MODEL   small              ;set model size
        .8086                       ;.8086 instructions

        .CODE
        PUBLIC   C clsscr
clsscr  PROC     C NEAR

        mov      cx,0               ;upper corner of window
        mov      dx,2479H           ;lower corner of window
        mov      bh,7               ;normal screen attribute
        mov      ax,0600H           ;BIOS interrupt value
        int      10H                ;call interrupt

        ret                         ;return to calling program
clsscr  ENDP                        ;end main procedure
        END
```

THE OUTPORT ASSEMBLY MODULE (outport.asm):

```
;TURBO Assembly Language Programming Application
;Copyright (c) Chris H. Pappas and William H. Murray, 1990

;program accepts two arguments from C calling program and
;makes access to the specified port.

        DOSSEG                      ;use Intel segment-ordering
        .MODEL   small              ;set model size
        .8086                       ;8086 instructions

        .CODE
        PUBLIC   C outport
Outport PROC     C NEAR temp,port:WORD

        mov      dx,port            ;port id in dx register
        mov      ax,temp            ;value to be sent
        out      dx,al              ;send lower 8 bits to port

        ret                         ;return to calling program
outport ENDP                        ;end main procedure
        END
```

Notice that the *make* file for this example contains additional libraries in the link command line. The host program looks like the earlier inline example, except for the addition of the function prototypes and actual calls. As you examine the two assembly language modules, notice that the code itself is also identical to the inline assembly language code of the earlier example. Pay particular attention to the function prototypes in the code, and how the arguments are intercepted in the assembly language modules.

A HARDWARE INTERFACE USING C++ AND ASSEMBLY LANGUAGE

The next example again uses the *clsscr.asm* and *outport.asm* files developed in the previous examples. However, this time the interface will be made with C++ in an example that simulates the roll of a die. The C++ program will generate pseudorandom numbers between 1 and 6 and send the numbers to the parallel port's data lines D0 to D2. The binary representation of the decimal numbers is 001, 010, 011, 100, 101, and 110. A die will be created by arranging 7 LED lights in the pattern shown in Figure 20-3. You also need a decoding scheme to convert the binary numbers to the correct LED lighting sequence. The decoding could be done with software or hardware. The example uses the hardware solution. Figure 20-4 shows the logic circuit required to decode the binary information.

If you interface this circuit with your computer's parallel port, you will need a cable to connect the parallel port to a prototyping board, hookup wire, seven LED lights, a 5 volt power supply, a 7408 (AND gates) chip, and a 7432 (OR gates) chip. This example used a 25-pin D shell connector to connect to the parallel port with a ribbon cable terminating in a 24-pin male dip header. Pin #13 was discarded from the D shell connector. The proto-

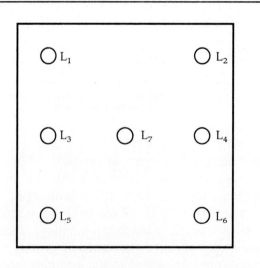

Figure 20-3.   LED layout for an electronic die

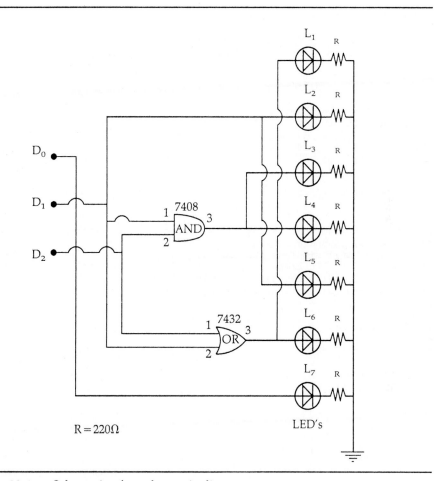

Figure 20-4.   Schematic of an electronic die

typing board is the type that allows TTL DIP chips to be easily inserted and removed. All of these parts can be found at electronic supply stores.

Simulating the Roll of a Die

Notice that the following listing contains four files that must be entered and saved separately. The first file is the *make* file *third*. The next file is the C++ program *third.cpp*. The last two files are the familiar assembly language routines *clsscr.asm* and *outport.asm*.

THE MAKE FILE (third):

```
third.exe: third.obj clsscr.obj outport.obj
  tlink c0s third clsscr outport,third, ,cs

clsscr.obj: clsscr.asm
  tasm clsscr.asm

outport.obj: outport.asm
  tasm outport.asm

third.obj: third.cpp dos.h stream.h stdlib.h
  tcc -c third.cpp
```

THE C++ PROGRAM (third.cpp):

```cpp
//
//    A C++ program that demonstrates how to call an external
//    assembly language program to access the parallel port.
//    Program will simulate the roll of a die and light the
//    appropriate LED lamps connected to the parallel port.
//    Port 956 (LPT1) and data lines D0 - D2 are used.
//    Copyright (c) Chris H. Pappas and William H. Murray, 1990
//

#include <dos.h>
#include <iostream.h>
#include <stdlib.h>

void clsscr(void);
void outport(int,int);

main()
{
  char ch;
  int i,temp;
  int port=956;

  clsscr();

  for (;;) {
    cout << "(Q) for quit, (Enter) for roll of die: ";
    cin.get(ch);
    if (ch =='Q' || ch=='q') break;

    for (i=0;i<50;i++) {
      temp=1 + (rand()/3 % 6);
      outport(temp,port);
      delay(20);
      }

    cout << temp << "\n";
  }
  return (0);
}
```

THE CLSSCR ASSEMBLY MODULE (clsscr.asm):

```
;TURBO Assembly Language Programming Application
;Copyright (c) Chris H. Pappas and William H. Murray, 1990

;program will clear the screen by calling a BIOS interrupt.

        DOSSEG                  ;use Intel segment-ordering
        .MODEL  small           ;set model size
        .8086                   ;8086 instructions

        .CODE
        PUBLIC  C clsscr
clsscr  PROC    C NEAR

        mov     cx,0            ;upper corner of window
        mov     dx,2479H        ;lower corner of window
        mov     bh,7            ;normal screen attribute
        mov     ax,0600H        ;BIOS interrupt value
        int     10H             ;call interrupt

        ret                     ;return to calling program
clsscr  ENDP                    ;end main procedure
        END
```

THE OUTPORT ASSEMBLY MODULE (outport.asm):

```
;TURBO Assembly Language Programming Application
;Copyright (c) Chris H. Pappas and William H. Murray, 1990

;program accepts two arguments from C calling program and
;makes access to the specified port.

        DOSSEG                  ;use Intel segment-ordering
        .MODEL  small           ;set model size
        .8086                   ;8086 instructions

        .CODE
        PUBLIC  C outport
outport PROC    C NEAR temp,port:WORD

        mov     dx,port         ;port id in dx register
        mov     ax,temp         ;value to be sent
        out     dx,al           ;send lower 8 bits to port

        ret                     ;return to calling program
outport ENDP                    ;end main procedure
        END
```

You have already learned how the function arguments are passed from the source code to the assembly language routines. This program generates pseudorandom numbers by calling the C++ **rand** function.

```
temp=1 + (rand()/3 % 6);
```

The random number generator returns values in the range 0 to RAND_MAX. RAND_MAX is defined in *tdlib.h* and is approximately 32,768. The random number generator can also be initialized, or *seeded*, with a call to the **srand** function. True random number generators are difficult to create, and a pseudorandom generator is just a close approximation of the real thing. For a detailed discussion of random number generators, see *Advanced Turbo C* (Herbert Schildt, Osborne/McGraw-Hill, 1989).

Numbers in the range 1 to 6 are generated with the modulo operator. Actually, the random numbers after the modulo operation are in the range 0 to 5. A 1 is added as an offset to these values.

If you have a little technical experience, a whole world of hardware interfacing has been opened to you. Instead of LED lamps, you can wire the parallel port's data lines to speech synthesizers or digital-to-analog converters. These circuits will allow you to control a wide range of electronic devices.

PASSING ARRAYS FROM C TO ASSEMBLY LANGUAGE

The last example in this chapter will show how to pass two arrays (call by reference) to an assembly language routine. The assembly language routine will add each element of each array and produce a final sum that will be returned to the host program. As you examine the following listing, which includes three separate files, notice that the *make* file included specifications that will allow the final program to be examined in the Debugger. The three files include the *make* file *myarray*, the C program *myarray.c*, and the assembly language module *myasm*. You must create each of these files separately with your editor.

```
THE MAKE FILE (myarray):

myarray.exe: myarray.obj myasm.obj
    tlink /v /m /s /l c0s myarray myasm,myarray, ,cs

myasm.obj: myasm.asm
  tasm /zi myasm.asm
```

```
myarray.obj: myarray.c stdio.h
  tcc -c -v myarray.c
```

THE C PROGRAM (myarray.c):

```
/*
 *    A C program that demonstrates how to pass two arrays
 *    to an external assembly language program.
 *    The assembly language program will add the elements of
 *    both arrays together and return the sum to the C program.
 *    Copyright (c) Chris H. Pappas and William H. Murray, 1990
 */

#include <stdio.h>

int myasm(int array1[],int array2[]);

main()
{
  int array1[10]={2,4,6,8,10,12,14,16,18,20};
  int array2[10]={1,2,3,4,5,6,7,8,9,10};
  int temp;

  temp=myasm(array1,array2);

  printf("%d\n",temp);

  return (0);
}
```

THE ASSEMBLY LANGUAGE MODULE (myasm.asm):

```
;TURBO Assembly Language Programming Application
;Copyright (c) Chris H. Pappas and William H. Murray, 1990

;The program will accept array information from a C host
;program.  Arrays are passed by reference.  The assembly
;language routine will add the elements of both arrays
;together and return the sum.

        DOSSEG                          ;use Intel segment-ordering
        .MODEL  small                   ;set model size
        .8086                           ;8086 instructions

        .CODE
        PUBLIC  C myasm
myasm   PROC    C NEAR   array1,array2:WORD

        mov     ax,0                    ;initialize ax to 0
        mov     cx,10                   ;array size
        mov     bx,array1               ;address of array1
        mov     bp,array2               ;address of array2
more:   add     ax,[bx]                 ;value at array1 address
        add     ax,[bp]                 ;value at array2 address
        add     bx,2                    ;point to next array1 number
```

```
         add      bp,2           ;point to next array2 number
         loop     more           ;till all elements summed

         ret                     ;return to calling program
myasm    ENDP                    ;end main procedure
         END
```

In the previous examples, arguments were passed by value. When array information is passed, it is passed by reference. Thus, the intercepted values are the addresses of the arrays. In assembly language, the addresses can be placed in the **bx** and **bp** registers. You can use indirect register addressing to obtain the array elements. Recall that indirect register addressing places square brackets around the register containing the address. This, in turn, returns the value stored at that address.

This program sums the individual elements of each array. Notice how the Debugger can be useful in tracing the action of a program such as this. Figures 20-5 to 20-8 show various stages of program execution.

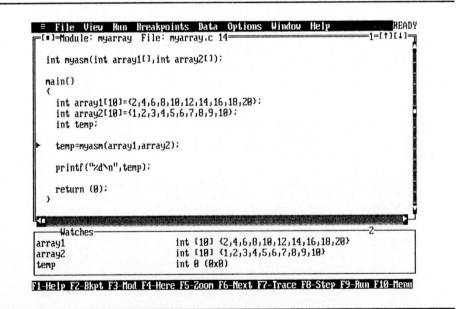

Figure 20-5.   Original MYARRAY.C source code with three variables in the Watch window

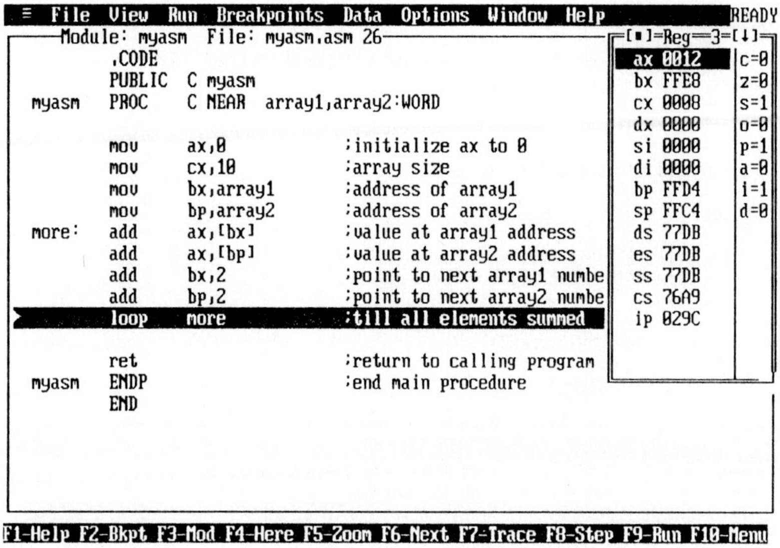

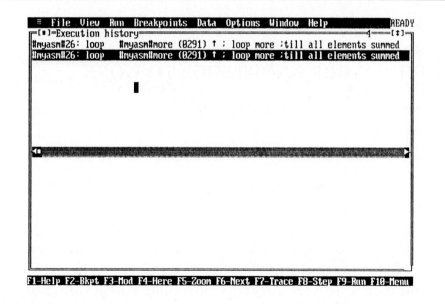

Figure 20-6.   Switching to the MYASM.ASM source code module and observing register values after three passes through the loop

Figure 20-7.   Viewing the execution history of the assembly language module

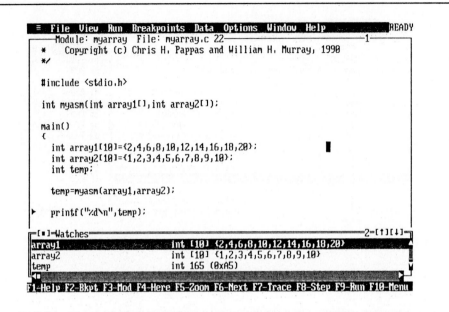

Figure 20-8.   The original source code after the execution of the program

PUTTING YOUR KNOWLEDGE TO WORK

1. What considerations must be taken into account in deciding to use inline assembly language in a C or C++ program?

2. What is unique about inline assembly language comments?

3. What C and assembly language data types can be sent to the parallel port?

4. Write a program, using inline assembly language code, that will count off the binary numbers 00000000 to 11111111. Hint: A simple modification of the inline example in this chapter is all that you need.

5. Name the C data types that correspond to the assembly language data types **byte**, **word**, and **dword**.

6. Describe the function of a *make* file. Why are they so important as project size and the number of files increase?

7. Wire an LED lamp to the first seven data lines of the parallel port. With software, write a program that will simulate the roll of a die. (This program will do the decoding in software instead of hardware; otherwise, it is similar to the C++ example in this chapter.)

8. Show, with two separate examples, the difference in assembly language code when passing arguments by value and by reference.

21

INTRODUCTION TO OBJECT-ORIENTED PROGRAMMING

In this chapter you will learn

- The basics of object-oriented programming
- The differences between procedural and object-oriented programming
- The definitions for C++ and object-oriented terms, including objects, encapsulation, hierarchy, inheritance, and polymorphism
- The components of an object-oriented linked-list program

PROCEDURAL VERSUS OBJECT-ORIENTED PROGRAMMING

This book has introduced you to C and C++ concepts in a traditional *procedural* programming environment. In a procedural environment, there is typically a main function and many additional functions (subroutines) that are called from the main one. In this top-down approach, the main function is usually short, farming the work out to the remaining functions. Program execution generally flows from the top of the main function and terminates at the bottom of the same function. This technique is common among all structured languages, including C, C++, FORTRAN, PASCAL, and PL/I. The procedural approach suffers from several disadvantages, the chief of which is program maintenance. When you have to make additions or deletions to the program, you must often rework the entire program to include the new routines.

Object-oriented programming (OOP), on the other hand, is different from the traditional procedural approach. If you have written program code for Microsoft's Windows or the OS/2 Presentation Manager, you have gotten a taste of object-oriented programming techniques. In object-oriented programming, your program consists of a group of often related *objects*. C++ classes form the foundation of object-oriented programming, since classes provide a set of values and the operations that act on those values. Objects are manipulated with *messages*. It is the message-based system that is common to Windows and the Presentation Manager. Object-oriented programs offer many advantages over procedural ones, the chief of which is less program maintenance. You can often make additions and deletions to object-oriented programs by simply adding or deleting objects.

Earlier chapters explained that many C programs can be converted to C++ programs by simple program alterations. This is because the conversion was from and to a procedural programming structure. However, you can work with object-oriented programs only in C++, as C does not provide the class structure.

C++ AND OBJECT-ORIENTED PROGRAMMING

Classes are what make C++ suitable for developing object-oriented programs. The class structure meets the requirements for creating objects. However, object-oriented programming is also supported by C++'s strong typing, operator overloading, and less reliance on the preprocessor.

You already learned a good deal about classes in Chapters 13 and 14. The next section formulates object-oriented programming terms more clearly, and shows how C++ classes fit in with this new programming style.

OBJECT-ORIENTED PROGRAMMING DEFINITIONS AND TERMINOLOGY

Object-oriented programming allows you to view concepts as a variety of objects. You can represent the interaction, the tasks that are to be performed, and any given conditions that must be observed among the stated objects. The C++ class can contain closely related objects that share attributes, and is thus the prototype for objects in C++. In a more formal definition, a class defines the properties and attributes that depict the actions of an object that is an instance of that class.

Encapsulation

Encapsulation refers to how each object is defined. Typically, this definition is part of a C++ class and includes a description of the object's internal structure, a description of how the object relates to other objects, and some form of protection that isolates the functional details of the object outside of the class. The C++ class structure does all of this.

Recall from Chapter 13 that a class can have private, public, and/or protected sections. In object-oriented programming, the public section is used for the interface information that makes the class reusable across applications. The private section is used to define the data structure for the data type. Thus, the class meets the object-oriented requirements for encapsulation.

Class Hierarchy

In C++, classes actually serve as a pattern for creating objects. The objects created are *instances* of the class. You can develop a *class hierarchy* where there is a *root* or *parent* class and several *subclasses* or *child classes*. In C++, the basis for class hierarchies is *derived classes*. Parent classes represent more generalized tasks while derived child classes are given specific tasks.

Inheritance

Inheritance refers to deriving a new class from an existing parent class. The parent class serves as a pattern for the derived class and can be altered in several ways. For example, you can overload member functions, add new members, and change access privileges. Inheritance is an important concept since it allows you to reuse a class definition, for simple changes, without requiring major code changes.

Polymorphism

Common messages can be sent to the root class objects and all derived subclass objects. In formal terms, this is called *polymorphism*. Polymorphism allows each subclass object to respond to the message format in a manner appropriate to its definition. Imagine a class hierarchy for gathering data. The root class might be responsible for gathering the name, social security number, occupation, and number of years of employment for an individual. Subclasses could then be used to decide what additional information would be added based on occupation. In one case, a supervisory position might include yearly salary while in another case a sales position might include an hourly rate and commission information. Thus, the root class gathers general information common to all subclasses while the subclasses gather additional information relating to specific job descriptions. Polymorphism allows a common data gathering message to be sent to each class. Both the root and subclasses respond in an appropriate manner to the message.

Virtual Functions

Virtual functions, first introduced in Chapter 13, are closely associated with the concept of polymorphism. Virtual functions are defined in the root class when subsequent derived classes will overload the function by redefining its implementation. When you use virtual functions, messages are passed to a pointer that points to the object instead of being passed directly to the object itself.

As you follow the example program for this chapter, many of these definitions will become more clear and will fit in with what you have already learned.

DEVELOPING AN OBJECT-ORIENTED LINKED-LIST PROGRAM

Chapter 12 included a linked-list program that was developed in C++ using the traditional procedural programming approach. This program created a linked list for the P and M used car inventory. With the traditional procedural approach, this linked-list program is difficult to alter or maintain. This chapter develops a linked-list C++ program using objects that let you establish a list of employee information and then add and delete items from that list. To limit the size of the program, the user interface for gathering data has not been included in this program. Input information for the linked list has been "hard wired" in the **main** function. If you want to continue developing this program, both Chapters 12 and 13 show how to gather input information in an interactive way.

The Root or Parent Class

The parent class that will be used for this linked-list example is **P_and_M_auto_dealership**. The linked-list program will keep pertinent information on a variety of company employees. The job of the parent class, **P_and_M_auto_dealership**, is to gather information that is common to all subsequent derived subclasses. In this case, that information includes an employee's last name, first name, occupation title, social security number, and years employed at the dealership. The protected section of this class indicates the structure for gathering the data common to each derived class. The public section shows how that information will be intercepted from the function **main**.

```
// ROOT OR PARENT CLASS
class P_and_M_auto_dealership {

friend class employee_list;

protected:
  char lastname[20];
  char firstname[20];
  char occupation[20];
  char social_security[12];
  int years_employed;
  static P_and_M_auto_dealership *pointer;
  P_and_M_auto_dealership *next_link;
```

```
public:
  P_and_M_auto_dealership(char *lname,char *fname,char *ssnum,
                          char *occup,int c_years_employed)
  {
    strcpy(lastname,lname);
    strcpy(firstname,fname);
    strcpy(social_security,ssnum);
    strcpy(occupation,occup);
    years_employed=c_years_employed;
    next_link=0;
  }
            .
            .
            .
            .
```

Notice that this class and all subsequently derived subclasses will use a friend class named **employee_list**. Also note that *pointer* is of type specifier **static**. As you examine the complete listing later in this chapter, note that all derived classes share this common value.

A Sample Derived Subclass

The following sample program uses four child classes derived from the parent class in the last section. This section looks at one representative example, the **salespersons** class. A portion of this derived class is shown next. The C++ derived class satisfies the concept of inheritance.

```
//SUB OR CHILD DERIVED CLASS
class salespersons:public P_and_M_auto_dealership {

friend class employee_list;

private:
  float unit_sales_average;
  int comm_rate;

public:
  salespersons(char *lname,char *fname,char *ssnum,
               char *occup,int c_years_employed,
               float w_avg,int c_rate):
               P_and_M_auto_dealership(lname,fname,ssnum,
               occup,c_years_employed)
  {
    unit_sales_average=w_avg;
    comm_rate=c_rate;
  }
          .
          .
          .
```

In this case, the **salespersons** child class gathers information and adds it to the information gathered by the parent class. This then forms a structure of last name, first name, social security number, years employed, weekly average of total monthly sales, and appropriate commission rate.

Here is the remainder of the child class description:

```
void fill_average(float w_avg)
{
  unit_sales_average=w_avg;
}

void fill_comm_rate(int c_rate)
{
  comm_rate=c_rate;
}

void add_data()
{
  pointer=new salespersons(lastname,
                           firstname,
                           social_security,
                           occupation,
                           years_employed,
                           unit_sales_average,
                           comm_rate);
}

void send_info()
{
  P_and_M_auto_dealership: :send_info();
  cout << "\n Weekly Sales Average (units): "
       << unit_sales_average;
  cout << "\n Commission Rate: "
       << comm_rate << "%";
}

};
```

Add_data sets aside memory for an additional linked-list node with the use of the **new** free store operator. Remember that this node is being assigned a pointer to a variable, *pointer,* that in turn points to a **P_and_M_auto_dealership** node.

When you examine the full program listing, note that the **delete** free store operator is used in the **employee_list** class for deleting items from the linked list.

Of particular interest here is the technique for printing the salesperson's information. Notice that **salespersons'** *send_info* makes a call to the root class's **send_info** function. This function prints the information common to all derived classes. Then **salespersons'** *send_info* prints the information unique to the child class. That information includes the weekly sales average and the commission rate.

By altering the objects, you could have printed all of the information about the salesperson from this subclass. However, this example illustrated another advantage of using C++ in object-oriented programming: the successful use of virtual functions.

The Friend Class

The friend class, **employee_list**, is how the linked list is printed, and how items are inserted and deleted from the list. This class is divided to make the explanation more clear.

```
//FRIEND CLASS
class employee_list {

private:
  P_and_M_auto_dealership *location;

public:
  employee_list()
  {
    location=0;
  }

  void print_employee_list();

  void insert_employee(P_and_M_auto_dealership *node);

  void remove_employee_id(char *social_security);

};
     .
     .
     .
     .
```

Messages which are sent to **print_employee_list**, **insert_employee**, and **remove_employee_id** form the functional part of the linked-list program.

Consider the function **print_employee_list**, which begins by assigning the pointer (to the list) to the pointer variable *present*. As long as the pointer, *present*, is not 0, it will continue to point to items in the linked list, send them to **send_info,** and update the pointer until all items have been printed. Observe how this is achieved here:

```
        .
        .
        .
void employee_list: :print_employee_list()
{
  P_and_M_auto_dealership *present=location;

  while(present!=0) {
    present->send_info();
    present=present->next_link;
  }
}
        .
        .
        .
        .
```

Remember that *pointer* contains the memory address of nodes inserted via **add_data.** This value is used by **insert_employee** to form the link with the linked list. Since the technique inserts alphabetically by an employee's last name, the linked list is always ordered alphabetically by the last name.

Correct insertion is achieved by comparing the last name with those already in the list. When it finds a name (*node—>lastname*) already in the list that is greater than the *current_node—>lastname,* the first *while* loop terminates. This standard linked-list insert procedure leaves the pointer variable *previous_node* pointing to the node behind where the new node is to be inserted and leaves *current_node* pointing to the node that will follow the insertion point for the new node.

When the insertion point is determined, a new link or node is created by a calling *node—>add_data.* The *current_node* is linked to the new node's *next_link.* The last decision to make is whether the new node is to be placed as the front node in the list or between existing nodes. The program accomplishes this by examining the contents of the pointer variable *previous_node.* If the pointer variable is 0, it cannot be pointing to a valid previous node so *location* is updated to the address of the new node. If *previous_node* contains a nonzero value, it is assumed to be pointing to a valid previous node. In this case, *previous_node—>next_link* is assigned the address of the new node's address or *node—>pointer.*

```
        .
        .
        .
    void employee_list: :insert_employee(P_and_M_auto_dealership
                           *node)
    {
      P_and_M_auto_dealership *current_node=location;
      P_and_M_auto_dealership *previous_node=0;

      while (current_node != 0 &&
             strcmp(current_node->lastname,node->lastname) < 0) {

        previous_node=current_node;
        current_node=current_node->next_link;
      }
      node->add_data();
      node->pointer->next_link=current_node;
      if (previous_node==0)
        location=node->pointer;
      else
        previous_node->next_link=node->pointer;
    }
        .
        .
        .
        .
```

You can only remove items from the linked list if you know the employee's social security number. This adds a small level of protection against accidental deletion of an employee. As you examine *remove_employee_id,* shown in the next listing, note that the structure for examining the nodes in the linked list is almost identical to that of *insert_employee.* However, the first *while* loop leaves the *current_node* pointing to the node to be deleted, not the node after the one to be deleted.

The first compound *if* statement deletes a node in the front of the list. It accomplishes this by examining the contents of *previous_node* to see if it contains a 0. If so, the front of the list, *location,* needs to be updated to the node following the one to be deleted or *current_node—>next_link.* The second *if* statement deletes a node between two existing nodes. This requires the node behind to be assigned the address of the node after the one being deleted, or *previous_node—>next_link=current_node—>next_link.*

```
        .
        .
        .
    void employee_list: :remove_employee_id(char *social_security)
    {
```

```
  P_and_M_auto_dealership *current_node=location;
  P_and_M_auto_dealership *previous_node=0;

  while(current_node != 0 &&
     strcmp(current_node->social_security,
     social_security) != 0) {
    previous_node=current_node;
    current_node=current_node->next_link;
  }

  if(current_node != 0 && previous_node == 0) {
    location=current_node->next_link;
    delete current_node;
  }
  else if(current_node != 0 && previous_node != 0) {
    previous_node->next_link=current_node->next_link;
    delete current_node;
  }
}
```

The Whole Linked List

The next listing is a completely operational C++ object-oriented program. Again, the only thing it lacks is an interactive user interface. When executed, this program will add eight employees, with different occupations, to the linked list and then print the list. The program will next delete several employees from the list by giving their social security numbers. Finally, the altered list will be printed.

```
//
//       C++ program illustrates object-oriented programming
//       with a linked list.  This program keeps track of
//       employee data at the P & M automobile dealership.
//       Copyright (c) Chris H. Pappas and William H. Murray, 1990
//

#include <iostream.h>
#include <string.h>

// ROOT OR PARENT CLASS
class P_and_M_auto_dealership {

friend class employee_list;

protected:
  char lastname[20];
```

```
  char firstname[20];
  char occupation[20];
  char social_security[12];
  int years_employed;
  static P_and_M_auto_dealership *pointer;
  P_and_M_auto_dealership *next_link;

public:
  P_and_M_auto_dealership(char *lname,char *fname,char *ssnum,
                          char *occup,int c_years_employed)
  {
    strcpy(lastname,lname);
    strcpy(firstname,fname);
    strcpy(social_security,ssnum);
    strcpy(occupation,occup);
    years_employed=c_years_employed;
    next_link=0;
  }

  P_and_M_auto_dealership()
  {
    lastname[0]=NULL;
    firstname[0]=NULL;
    social_security[0]=NULL;
    occupation[0]=NULL;
    years_employed=0;
    next_link=0;
  }

  void fill_lastname(char *l_name)
  {
    strcpy(lastname,l_name);
  }

  void fill_firstname(char *f_name)
  {
    strcpy(firstname,f_name);
  }

  void fill_social_security(char *soc_sec)
  {
    strcpy(social_security,soc_sec);
  }

  void fill_occupation(char *o_name)
  {
    strcpy(occupation,o_name);
  }

  void fill_years_employed(int c_years_employed)
  {
    years_employed=c_years_employed;
  }

  virtual void add_data() {
  }
```

```
  virtual void send_info()
  {
    cout << "\n\n" << lastname << ", " << firstname
         << "\n Social Security: #" << social_security;
    cout << "\n Job Title: " << occupation;
    cout << "\n Years With Company: " << years_employed;
  }

};

//SUB OR CHILD DERIVED CLASS
class deal_closer:public P_and_M_auto_dealership {

friend class employee_list;

private:
  float yearly_salary;

public:
  deal_closer(char *lname,char *fname,char *ssnum,
              char *occup,int c_years_employed,
              float y_salary):
              P_and_M_auto_dealership(lname,fname,ssnum,
              occup,c_years_employed)
  {
    yearly_salary=y_salary;
  }

  deal_closer():P_and_M_auto_dealership()
  {
    yearly_salary=0.0;
  }

  void fill_yearly_salary(float salary)
  {
    yearly_salary=salary;
  }

  void add_data()
  {
    pointer=new deal_closer(lastname,
                            firstname,
                            social_security,
                            occupation,
                            years_employed,
                            yearly_salary);
   }

  void send_info()
  {
    P_and_M_auto_dealership: :send_info();
    cout << "\n Yearly Salary: $" << yearly_salary;
  }

};

//SUB OR CHILD DERIVED CLASS
```

```
class salespersons:public P_and_M_auto_dealership {

friend class employee_list;

private:
  float unit_sales_average;
  int comm_rate;

public:
  salespersons(char *lname,char *fname,char *ssnum,
               char *occup,int c_years_employed,
               float w_avg,int c_rate):
               P_and_M_auto_dealership(lname,fname,ssnum,
               occup,c_years_employed)
  {
    unit_sales_average=w_avg;
    comm_rate=c_rate;
  }

  salespersons():P_and_M_auto_dealership()
  {
    unit_sales_average=0.0;
    comm_rate=0;
  }

  void fill_average(float w_avg)
  {
    unit_sales_average=w_avg;
  }

  void fill_comm_rate(int c_rate)
  {
    comm_rate=c_rate;
  }

  void add_data()
  {
    pointer=new salespersons(lastname,
                             firstname,
                             social_security,
                             occupation,
                             years_employed,
                             unit_sales_average,
                             comm_rate);
  }

  void send_info()
  {
    P_and_M_auto_dealership: :send_info();
    cout << "\n Weekly Sales Average (units): "
         << unit_sales_average;
    cout << "\n Commission Rate: "
         << comm_rate << "%";
  }

};
```

```
//SUB OR CHILD DERIVED CLASS
class mechanics:public P_and_M_auto_dealership {

friend class employee_list;

private:
  float hourly_salary;

public:
  mechanics(char *lname,char *fname,char *ssnum,char *occup,
            int c_years_employed,float h_salary):
            P_and_M_auto_dealership(lname,fname,ssnum,
            occup,c_years_employed)
  {
    hourly_salary=h_salary;
  }

  mechanics():P_and_M_auto_dealership()
  {
    hourly_salary=0.0;
  }

  void fill_hourly_salary(float h_salary)
  {
    hourly_salary=h_salary;
  }

  void add_data()
  {
    pointer=new mechanics(lastname,
                          firstname,
                          social_security,
                          occupation,
                          years_employed,
                          hourly_salary);
  }

  void send_info()
  {
    P_and_M_auto_dealership: :send_info();
    cout << "\n Hourly Salary: $" << hourly_salary;
  }

};

//SUB OR CHILD DERIVED CLASS
class parts:public P_and_M_auto_dealership {

friend class employee_list;

private:
  float hourly_salary;

public:
  parts(char *lname,char *fname,char *ssnum,char *occup,
        int c_years_employed,float h_salary):
        P_and_M_auto_dealership(lname,fname,ssnum,
```

```
         occup,c_years_employed)
 {
   hourly_salary=h_salary;
 }

 parts():P_and_M_auto_dealership()
 {
   hourly_salary=0.0;
 }

 void fill_hourly_salary(float h_salary)
 {
   hourly_salary=h_salary;
 }

 void add_data()
 {
   pointer=new parts(lastname,
                     firstname,
                     social_security,
                     occupation,
                     years_employed,
                     hourly_salary);
 }

 void send_info()
 {
   P_and_M_auto_dealership: :send_info();
   cout << "\n Hourly Salary: $" << hourly_salary;
 }

};

//FRIEND CLASS
class employee_list {

private:
  P_and_M_auto_dealership *location;

public:
  employee_list()
  {
    location=0;
  }

  void print_employee_list();

  void insert_employee(P_and_M_auto_dealership *node);

  void remove_employee_id(char *social_security);

};

void employee_list: :print_employee_list()
{
  P_and_M_auto_dealership *present=location;
```

```
    while(present!=0) {
      present->send_info();
      present=present->next_link;
    }
  }

  void employee_list: :insert_employee(P_and_M_auto_dealership
                              *node)
  {
    P_and_M_auto_dealership *current_node=location;
    P_and_M_auto_dealership *previous_node=0;

    while (current_node != 0 &&
          strcmp(current_node->lastname,node->lastname) < 0) {
      previous_node=current_node;
      current_node=current_node->next_link;
    }
    node->add_data();
    node->pointer->next_link=current_node;
    if (previous_node==0)
      location=node->pointer;
    else
      previous_node->next_link=node->pointer;
  }

  void employee_list: :remove_employee_id(char *social_security)
  {
    P_and_M_auto_dealership *current_node=location;
    P_and_M_auto_dealership *previous_node=0;

    while(current_node != 0 &&
        strcmp(current_node->social_security,
        social_security) != 0) {
      previous_node=current_node;
      current_node=current_node->next_link;
    }

    if(current_node != 0 && previous_node == 0) {
      location=current_node->next_link;
      delete current_node;
    }
    else if(current_node != 0 && previous_node != 0) {
      previous_node->next_link=current_node->next_link;
      delete current_node;
    }
  }

  main()
  {
    employee_list workers;

    cout.setf(ios: :fixed);
    cout.precision(d2);

    // static data to add to linked list
    salespersons salesperson1("Friendly","Fran","212-98-7654",
                              "Salesperson",1,7.5,4.50);
```

```
salespersons salesperson2("Pest","Perry","567-45-3412",
                          "Salesperson",2,2.0,2.20);
salespersons salesperson3("Yourfriend","Yancy","213-44-9873",
                          "Salesperson",1,10.6,5.70);
mechanics mechanicperson1("Hardwork","Harriet","076-45-3121",
                          "Mechanic",7,10.34);
mechanics mechanicperson2("Lugwrench","Larry","886-43-1518",
                          "Mechanic",1,8.98);
deal_closer closerperson("Slick","Sally","111-22-4444",
                          "Closer",10,40000.00);
parts partperson1("Muffler","Mike","555-66-7891",
                  "Parts",4,7.34);
parts partperson2("Horn","Hazel","345-77-7654",
                  "Parts",5,9.52);

// add the eight workers to the linked list
workers.insert_employee(&mechanicperson1);
workers.insert_employee(&closerperson);
workers.insert_employee(&salesperson1);
workers.insert_employee(&partperson1);
workers.insert_employee(&partperson2);
workers.insert_employee(&salesperson2);
workers.insert_employee(&mechanicperson2);
workers.insert_employee(&salesperson3);

// print the linked list
workers.print_employee_list();

// remove three workers from the linked list
workers.remove_employee_id("555-66-7891");
workers.remove_employee_id("111-22-4444");
workers.remove_employee_id("213-44-3412");

cout << "\n\n*********************************";

// print the revised linked list
workers.print_employee_list();
}
```

Study this listing and see if you understand how workers are inserted into and deleted from the list.

A Sample Output

The next listing is a composite listing that shows the output of the linked-list example. The first part of the listing contains the eight names that were originally used to create the list. The remaining part of the listing shows the list after an attempt to remove three workers.

```
Friendly, Fran
 Social Security: #212-98-7654
 Job Title: Salesperson
 Years With Company: 1
 Weekly Sales Average (units): 7.50
 Commission Rate: 4%

Hardwork, Harriet
 Social Security: #076-45-3121
 Job Title: Mechanic
 Years With Company: 7
 Hourly Salary: $10.34

Horn, Hazel
 Social Security: #345-77-7654
 Job Title: Parts
 Years With Company: 5
 Hourly Salary: $9.50

Lugwrench, Larry
 Social Security: #886-43-1518
 Job Title: Mechanic
 Years With Company: 1
 Hourly Salary: $8.98

Muffler, Mike
 Social Security: #555-66-7891
 Job Title: Parts
 Years With Company: 4
 Hourly Salary: $7.34

Pest, Perry
 Social Security: #567-45-3412
 Job Title: Salesperson
 Years With Company: 2
 Weekly Sales Average (units): 2.00
 Commission Rate: 2%

Slick, Sally
 Social Security: #111-22-4444
 Job Title: Closer
 Years With Company: 10
 Yearly Salary: $40000.00

Yourfriend, Yancy
 Social Security: #213-44-9873
 Job Title: Salesperson
 Years With Company: 1
 Weekly Sales Average (units): 10.60
 Commission Rate: 5%


**********************************
```

```
Friendly, Fran
 Social Security: #212-98-7654
 Job Title: Salesperson
 Years With Company: 1
 Weekly Sales Average (units): 7.50
 Commission Rate: 4%

Hardwork, Harriet
 Social Security: #076-45-3121
 Job Title: Mechanic
 Years With Company: 7
 Hourly Salary: $10.34

Horn, Hazel
 Social Security: #345-77-7654
 Job Title: Parts
 Years With Company: 5
 Hourly Salary: $9.50

Lugwrench, Larry
 Social Security: #886-43-1518
 Job Title: Mechanic
 Years With Company: 1
 Hourly Salary: $8.98

Pest, Perry
 Social Security: #567-45-3412
 Job Title: Salesperson
 Years With Company: 2
 Weekly Sales Average (units): 2.00
 Commission Rate: 2%

Yourfriend, Yancy
 Social Security: #213-44-9873
 Job Title: Salesperson
 Years With Company: 1
 Weekly Sales Average (units): 10.60
 Commission Rate: 5%
```

Notice that only two workers have been removed from the original list. What happened? The social security number for the third worker did not match anyone on the list!

Debugger Information

The Debugger will allow you to view this program's class hierarchy. Enter the debugger after compiling and linking the linked-list program and select the View menu. One of the menu options is "Hierarchy." Select this option to open the Class Hierarchy window, shown in Figure 21-1.

Profiler Information

The profiler can also yield some interesting results for overall program performance. Figure 21-2 shows a snapshot of the execution profile for the linked-list program.

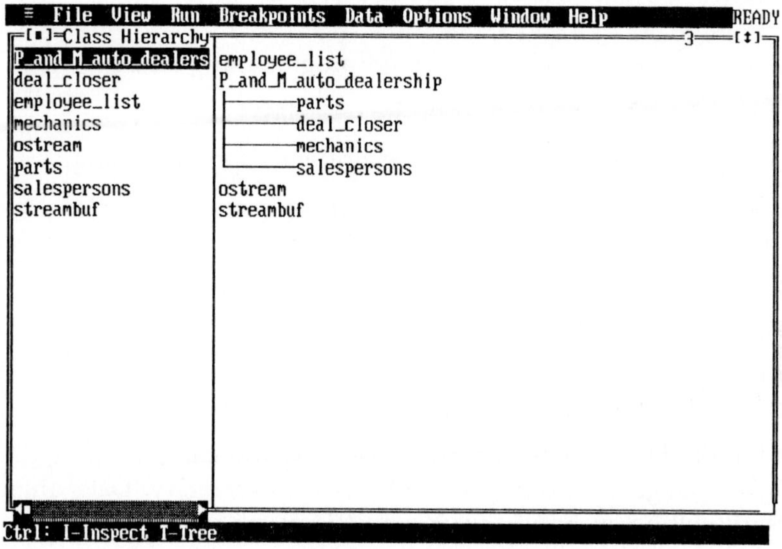

Figure 21-1. "Debugger Hierarchy" menu option

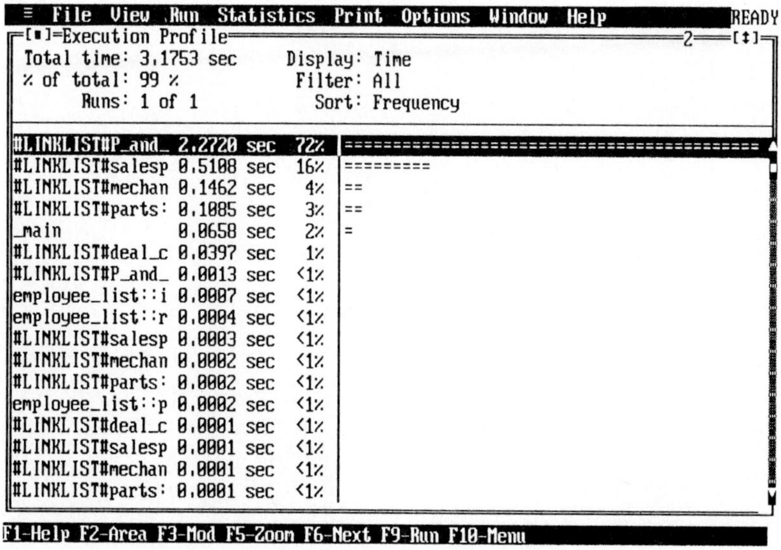

Figure 21-2. Execution profile for the linked-list program

PUTTING YOUR KNOWLEDGE TO WORK

1. What advantages does object-oriented programming offer?

2. How is encapsulation achieved in the C++ class?

3. Why is inheritance important to object-oriented programming?

4. What role do virtual classes play in the linked-list example developed in this chapter?

5. Define, in your own words, the concept of polymorphism. Can you give a nonprogramming example?

6. Alter the original linked-list program so that you can obtain a telephone number for each employee. Do this in the root class.

7. Alter the original linked-list program so that you can add an additional employee category. The new category is class **secretary**. Data unique to **secretary** will be an hourly wage and the number of sick days used in the current month.

8. Alter the original linked-list program so that you can also delete employees by giving their last names or social security numbers.

A

EXTENDED ASCII TABLE

Decimal	Hexadecimal	Symbol	Decimal	Hexadecimal	Symbol
0	0		20	14	¶
1	1	☺	21	15	§
2	2	☻	22	16	▬
3	3	♥	23	17	↨
4	4	♦	24	18	↑
5	5	♣	25	19	↓
6	6	♠	26	1A	→
7	7	•	27	1B	←
8	8	◘	28	1C	∟
9	9	○	29	1D	↔
10	A	◙	30	1E	▲
11	B	♂	31	1F	▼
12	C	♀	32	20	
13	D	♪	33	21	!
14	E	♫	34	22	"
15	F	☼	35	23	#
16	10	►	36	24	$
17	11	◄	37	25	%
18	12	↕	38	26	&
19	13	‼	39	27	'

Decimal	Hexadecimal	Symbol	Decimal	Hexadecimal	Symbol
40	28	(	76	4C	L
41	29	)	77	4D	M
42	2A	*	78	4E	N
43	2B	+	79	4F	O
44	2C	,	80	50	P
45	2D	-	81	51	Q
46	2E	.	82	52	R
47	2F	/	83	53	S
48	30	0	84	54	T
49	31	1	85	55	U
50	32	2	86	56	V
51	33	3	87	57	W
52	34	4	88	58	X
53	35	5	89	59	Y
54	36	6	90	5A	Z
55	37	7	91	5B	[
56	38	8	92	5C	\
57	39	9	93	5D	]
58	3A	:	94	5E	^
59	3B	;	95	5F	_
60	3C	<	96	60	`
61	3D	=	97	61	a
62	3E	>	98	62	b
63	3F	?	99	63	c
64	40	@	100	64	d
65	41	A	101	65	e
66	42	B	102	66	f
67	43	C	103	67	g
68	44	D	104	68	h
69	45	E	105	69	i
70	46	F	106	6A	j
71	47	G	107	6B	k
72	48	H	108	6C	l
73	49	I	109	6D	m
74	4A	J	110	6E	n
75	4B	K	111	6F	o

Decimal	Hexadecimal	Symbol	Decimal	Hexadecimal	Symbol
112	70	p	148	94	ö
113	71	q	149	95	ò
114	72	r	150	96	û
115	73	s	151	97	ù
116	74	t	152	98	ÿ
117	75	u	153	99	Ö
118	76	v	154	9A	Ü
119	77	w	155	9B	¢
120	78	x	156	9C	£
121	79	y	157	9D	¥
122	7A	z	158	9E	Pt
123	7B	{	159	9F	ƒ
124	7C	|	160	A0	á
125	7D	}	161	A1	í
126	7E	~	162	A2	ó
127	7F		163	A3	ú
128	80	Ç	164	A4	ñ
129	81	ü	165	A5	Ñ
130	82	é	166	A6	ª
131	83	â	167	A7	º
132	84	ä	168	A8	¿
133	85	à	169	A9	⌐
134	86	å	170	AA	¬
135	87	ç	171	AB	½
136	88	ê	172	AC	¼
137	89	ë	173	AD	¡
138	8A	è	174	AE	«
139	8B	ï	175	AF	»
140	8C	î	176	B0	░
141	8D	ì	177	B1	▒
142	8E	Ä	178	B2	▓
143	8F	Å	179	B3	│
144	90	É	180	B4	┤
145	91	æ	181	B5	╡
146	92	Æ	182	B6	╢
147	93	ô	183	B7	╖

Decimal	Hexadecimal	Symbol	Decimal	Hexadecimal	Symbol
184	B8	╕	220	DC	▄
185	B9	╣	221	DD	▌
186	BA	║	222	DE	▐
187	BB	╗	223	DF	▀
188	BC	╝	224	E0	α
189	BD	╜	225	E1	β
190	BE	╛	226	E2	Γ
191	BF	┐	227	E3	π
192	C0	└	228	E4	Σ
193	C1	┴	229	E5	σ
194	C2	┬	230	E6	μ
195	C3	├	231	E7	τ
196	C4	─	232	E8	ϕ
197	C5	┼	233	E9	Θ
198	C6	╞	234	EA	Ω
199	C7	╟	235	EB	δ
200	C8	╚	236	EC	∞
201	C9	╔	237	ED	$\emptyset$
202	CA	╩	238	EE	ϵ
203	CB	╦	239	EF	$\cap$
204	CC	╠	240	F0	$\equiv$
205	CD	═	241	F1	$\pm$
206	CE	╬	242	F2	$\geq$
207	CF	╧	243	F3	$\leq$
208	D0	╨	244	F4	$\lceil$
209	D1	╤	245	F5	$\rfloor$
210	D2	╥	246	F6	$\div$
211	D3	╙	247	F7	$\approx$
212	D4	╘	248	F8	$\circ$
213	D5	╒	249	F9	$\bullet$
214	D6	╓	250	FA	$\cdot$
215	D7	╫	251	FB	$\sqrt{}$
216	D8	╪	252	FC	^{n}
217	D9	┘	253	FD	^{2}
218	DA	┌	254	FE	■
219	DB	█	255	FF	(blank)

B

OS/2 10H, 21H, AND 33H
INTERRUPT PARAMETERS
FOR REAL MODE

This appendix contains the most popular DOS, BIOS, and MOUSE interrupts and parameters.

SCREEN CONTROL WITH BIOS-TYPE 10H INTERRUPTS

Syntax: INT 10H (when the following parameters are set to the required values)

INTERFACE CONTROL OF THE CRT

AH Value	Function	Input	Output
AH = 0	Set the mode of display	AL = 0	40 × 25 color text
		AL = 1	40 × 25 color text
		AL = 2	80 × 25 color text
		AL = 3	80 × 25 color text
		AL = 4	320 × 200 4-color graphics
		AL = 5	320 × 200 4-color graphics
		AL = 6	640 × 200 2-color graphics
		AL = 7	80 × 25 monochrome text
		AL = 13	320 × 200 16-color graphics
		AL = 14	640 × 200 16-color graphics
		AL = 15	640 × 350 monochrome graphics
		AL = 16	640 × 350 16-color graphics
		AL = 17	640 × 480 2-color graphics
		AL = 18	640 × 480 16-color graphics
		AL = 19	320 × 200 256-color graphics
AH = 1	Set cursor type	CH =	Bits 4-0 start of line for cursor
		CL =	Bits 4-0 end of line for cursor
AH = 2	Set cursor position	DH =	Row
		DL =	Column
		BH =	Page number of display (zero for graphics)
AH = 3	Read cursor position		DH = row
			DL = column
			CH = cursor mode
			CL = cursor mode
			BH = page number of display
AH = 4	Get light pen position		AH = 0, switch not down/ triggered
			AH = 1, valid answers as follows:
			DH = row
			DL = column
			CH = graph line (0-199)
			BX = graph column (0-319/639)

AH Value	Function	Input	Output
AH = 5	Set active display page	AL =	New page value (0-7) modes 0 and 1 (0-3) modes 2 and 3
AH = 6	Scroll active page up	AL =	Number of lines, 0 for entire screen
		CH =	Row, upper-left corner
		CL =	Column, upper-left corner
		DH =	Row, lower-right corner
		DL =	Column, lower-right corner
		BH =	Attribute to be used
AH = 7	Scroll active page down	AL =	Number of lines, 0 for entire screen
		CH =	Row, upper-left corner
		CL =	Column, upper-left corner
		DH =	Row, lower-right corner
		DL =	Column, lower-right corner
		BH =	Attribute to be used

HANDLING CHARACTERS

AH Value	Function	Input	Output
AH = 8	Read attribute/ character at cursor position	BH = AL = AH =	Display page Character read Attribute of character
AH = 9	Write attribute/ character at cursor position	BH = CX = AL = BL =	Display page Count of characters to write Character to write Attribute of character
AH = 10	Write character at cursor position	BH = CX = AL =	Display page Count of characters to write Character to write

GRAPHICS INTERFACE

AH Value	Function	Input	Output

AH = 11	Select color palette	BH =
		 BL =
			Palette ID (0-127)
			 Color for above ID
			 0—background (0-15)
			 1—palette
			     0—green(1), red(2), yellow(3)
			     1—cyan(1), magenta(2),
			        white (3)

AH = 12	Draw dot on screen	DX = CX = AL =	Row (0-199) Column (0-319/639) Color of dot
AH = 13	Read dot information	DX = CX = AL =	Row (0-199) Column (0-319/639) Value of dot

ASCII TELETYPE OUTPUT

AH Value	Function	Input	Output
AH = 14	Write to active page	AL = BL =	Character to write Foreground color
AH = 15	Get video state	AL = AH = BH =	Current mode Number of screen columns Current display page
AH = 16	(Reserved)		
AH = 17	(Reserved)		
AH = 18	(Reserved)		
AH = 19	Write string	ES:BP = CX = DX = BH = AL = 0	Point to string Length of string Cursor position for start Page number BL = attribute (char,char,char . . .char) cursor not moved

AH Value	Function	Input	Output
		AL = 1	BL = attribute (char,char, char...char) cursor is moved
		AL = 2	(char,attr,char,attr...) cursor not moved
		AL = 3	(char,attr,char,attr...) cursor is moved
AH = 1A	R/W display combination code		
AH = 1B	Return functionality state information		
AH = 1C	Save/restore video state		

SPECIFICATIONS AND REQUIREMENTS FOR THE DOS 21H INTERRUPT

Syntax: INT 21H (when the following parameters are set to the required values)

AH Value	Function	Input	Output
AH = 0	End of program		(similar to INT 20H)
AH = 1	Wait and display keyboard character with CTRL-BREAK check		AL = character entered
AH = 2	Display character with CTRL-BREAK check	DL =	Character to display
AH = 3	Asynchronous character input		AL = character entered
AH = 4	Asynchronous character output	DL =	Character to send
AH = 5	Character to write	DL =	Character to write
AH = 6	Input keyboard character	DL =	0FFH if character entered, 0 if none
AH = 7	Wait for keyboard character (no display)		AL = character entered

AH Value	Function	Input	Output
AH = 8	Wait for keyboard character (no display— CTRL-BREAK check)		AL = character entered
AH = 9	String display	DS:DX =	Address of string; must end with $ sentinel
AH = A	Keyboard string to buffer	DS:DX =	Address of buffer. First byte = size, second = number of characters read
AH = B	Input keyboard status		AL—no character = 0FFH character = 0
AH = C	Clear keyboard buffer and call function	AL =	1,6,7,8,0A (function #)
AH = D	Reset default disk drive	None	None
AH = E	Select default disk drive		AL = number of drives DL—0 = A drive 1 = B drive, and so forth
AH = F	Open file with unopened FCB	DS:DX =	Location AL = 0FFH if not found AL = 0H if found
AH = 10	Close file with FCB	DS:DX =	Location (same as AH = 0FH)
AH = 11	Search directory for match of unopened FCB. DTA contains directory entry	DS:DX =	AL = 0FFH if not found AL = 0H if found Location
AH = 12	Search (after AH = 11) for other files that match wildcard specifications		(same as AH = 11H)
AH = 13	Delete file named by FCB	DS:DX =	Location (same as AH = 11H)
AH = 14	Sequential read of open file. Number of bytes in FCB (record size)	DS:DX =	Location AL = 0 transfer OK AL = 1 end of file AL = 2 overrun DTA segment AL = 3 EOF/partial read

AH Value	Function	Input	Output
AH = 15	Sequential write of open file. Transfer from DTA to file, with FCB update of current record	DS:DX =	Location AL = 0 transfer OK AL = 1 disk full/ROF AL = 2 overrun DTA segment
AH = 16	Create file (length set to zero)	DS:DX =	Location (same as AH = 11H)
AH = 17	Rename file	DS:DX =	Location AL = 0 rename OK AL = 0FFH no match found
AH = 18	(DOS internal use)		
AH = 19	Drive code (default)		AL − 0 = A drive 1 = B drive, and so forth
AH = 1A	Set Data Transfer Add	DS:DX =	Points to location
AH = 1B	File Allocation Table	DS:DX =	Address of FAT DX = number of units AL = record/alloc. unit CX = sector size (same as AH = 1B)
AH = 1C	Disk drive FAT information	DL =	Drive number: 0 = default 1 = A 2 = B
AH = 1D	(DOS internal use)		
AH = 1E	(DOS internal use)		
AH = 1F	(DOS internal use)		
AH = 20	(DOS internal use)		
AH = 21	Random read file	DS:DX =	Location of FCB (same as AH = 14H)
AH = 22	Random write file	DS:DX =	(same as AH = 21H)
AH = 23	Set file size	DS:DX =	Location of FCB AL = 0 if set AL = 0FFH if not set
AH = 24	Random record size	DS:DX =	Location of FCB
AH = 25	Set interrupt vector (change address)	DS:DX = AL =	Address of vector table Interrupt number
AH = 26	Create program segment	DX =	Segment number

AH Value	Function	Input	Output

AH = 27	Random block read	DS:DX =	Address of FCB
			AL−0 read OK
			    1 EOF
			    2 wrap around
			    3 partial record

AH = 28	Random block write	DS:DX =	Address of FCB AL−0 write OK 1 lack of space
AH = 29	Parse file name	DS:SI = DS:DI =	Point to command line Memory location for FCB AL = bits to set options
AH = 2A	Read date		CX = year (80 to 99) DH = month (1 to 12) DL = day (1 to 31)
AH = 2B	Set date		CX & DX (same as above) AL−0 if valid 0FF if not valid
AH = 2C	Read time		CH = hours (0-23) CL = minutes (0-59)
AH = 2D	Set time		CX & DX (same as above) AL−0 if valid 0FF if not valid
AH = 2E	Set verify state	DL = AL =	0 0 = verify off 1 = verify on
AH = 2F	Get DTA	ES:BX =	Get DTA into ES
AH = 30	Get DOS version		AL = version number AH = sub number
AH = 31	Terminate and remain resident		AL = exit code DX = memory size in paragraphs
AH = 32	(DOS internal use)		
AH = 33	CTRL-BREAK check	AL = AL =	0, request state 1, set the state DL = 0 for off DL = 1 for on

AH Value	Function	Input	Output
AH = 34	(DOS internal use)		
AH = 35	Read interrupt address	AL =	Interrupt number ES:BX point to vector address
AH = 36	Disk space available	DL =	Drive (0 = default, 1 = A, 2 = B, and so forth) AX = sectors/cluster (FFFF if invalid) BX = number of free clusters CX = bytes per sector DX = total number of clusters
AH = 37	(DOS internal use)		
AH = 38	Country dependent information (32-byte block)	DS:DX	Location of memory Date/time Currency symbol Thousands separator Decimal separator
AH = 39	Make directory	DS:DX =	Address of string for directory
AH = 3A	Remove directory	DS:DX =	Address of string for directory
AH = 3B	Change directory	DS:DX =	Address of string for new directory
AH = 3C	Create a file	DS:DX = CX =	Address of string for file AX = file handle File attribute
AH = 3D	Open a file	DS:DX = AL =	Address of string for file 0 = open for reading 1 = open for writing 2 = open for both AX returns file handle
AH = 3E	Close a file handle	BX =	File handle
AH = 3F	Read a file or device	BX = CX = DS:DX =	File handle Number of bytes to read Address of buffer AX = number of bytes read
AH = 40	Write a file or device	BX = CX =	File handle Number of bytes to write

AH Value	Function	Input	Output
		DS:DX =	Address of buffer
			AX = number of bytes written
AH = 41	Delete a file	DS:DX =	Address of file string
AH = 42	Move file pointer	BX =	File handle
		AL =	Pointer's starting location
		CX:DX	Number of bytes
		DX:AX	Current file pointer
AH = 43	Set file attribute	AL = 1	
		CX =	Attribute
		DS:DX =	Address of file string
AH = 45	Duplicate file handle	BX	File handle
			AX = returned file handle
AH = 46	Force duplicate file handle	BX	File handle
			CX = second file handle
AH = 47	Current directory	DL =	Drive number (0 = default, 1 = A drive, 2 = B drive)
		DS:SI =	Buffer address
			DS:SI returns address of string
AH = 48	Allocate memory	BX	Number of paragraphs
			AX = allocated block
AH = 49	Free allocated memory	ES	Segment of returned block
AH = 4A	Set block	ES	Segment block
		BX	New block size
AH = 4B	Load/execute program	DS:DX	Location of ASCIIZ string (drive/path/file-name)
			AL—0 =load and execute
			3 = load/no execute
AH = 4C	Terminate (exit)	AL	Binary return code (all files closed)

AH Value	Function	Input	Output
AH = 4D	Retrieve return code		AX returns exit code of another program
AH = 4E	Find first matching file	DS:DX	Location of ASCIIZ string (drive/path/file-name) CX = search attribute DTA completed
AH = 4F	Next matching file		(AH = 4EH called first)
AH = 50	(DOS internal use)		
AH = 51	(DOS internal use)		
AH = 52	(DOS internal use)		
AH = 53	(DOS internal use)		
AH = 54	Verify state	none	AL − 0 if verify off 1 if verify on
AH = 55	(DOS internal use)		
AH = 56	Rename file	DS:DX =	Address of string for old information
		ES:DI =	Address of string for new information
AH = 57	Get/set file date/time	AL	00 (return) 01 (set)
		BX	File handle
		DX and CX	Date and time information
AH = 59	Extended error code	BX =	DOS version (3.0 = 0) AX = error code BH = class of error BL = suggested action CH = where error occurred
AH = 5A	Create temporary file		CX = file attribute CF = Set on error AX = error code
		DS:DX =	Points to string
AH = 5B	Create a new file		(same as above)

Note: For DOS versions above 2.0, use AH = 36H + for file management.

MOUSE CONTROL FUNCTIONS ACCESSED THROUGH INTERRUPT 33H

Syntax: INT 33H (when the following parameters are set to the required values)

AH Value	Function	Input	Output
AX = 0	Install flag and reset	BX = CX = DX =	If AX = 0 and BX = −1 Mouse support not available AX = −1, then BX = number of supported mouse buttons
AX = 1	Show pointer	BX = CX = DX =	Does nothing if already visible, otherwise increments the pointer-draw flag by 1 Shows pointer image when pointer-draw flag = 0
AX = 2	Hide pointer	BX = CX = DX =	Does nothing if already hidden, otherwise decrements the pointer-draw flag. Value of −1 hides image
AX = 3	Get position and button status	BX = CX = DX =	For 2- or 3-button mice, BX returns which button pressed: 0 leftmost, 1 rightmost, 2 center button. Buttons 3-15 reserved. CX = x coordinate; DX = y coordinate of pointer in pixels
AX = 4	Set pointer position	CX = DX =	New horizontal position in pixels New vertical position in pixels For values that exceed screen boundaries, screen maximum and minimum are used
AX = 5	Get button press information	BX =	Button status requested, where 0 = leftmost, 1 = rightmost, 2 = center button.

AH Value	Function	Input	Output
			AX—bit 0 (leftmost) = 0 or 1 bit 1 (rightmost) = 0 or 1 bit 2 (center) = 0 or 1 If 0 button up, and if 1 button down. BX = number of times button pressed since last call CX = horizontal coordinate of mouse DX = vertical coordinate of mouse
AX = 6	Get button release information	BX =	Button status requested, same format as for AX = 5 above. AX, BX, CX, and DX as above. If 0 button up, if 1 button down
AX = 7	Set minimum and maximum horizontal position	CX = DX =	Minimum virtual-screen horizontal coordinate in pixels Maximum virtual-screen horizontal coordinate in pixels
AX = 8	Set minimum and maximum vertical position	CX = DX =	Minimum virtual-screen vertical coordinate in pixels Maximum virtual-screen vertical coordinate in pixels
AH = 9	Set graphics pointer block	BX = CX = DX = ES =	Pointer hot-spot horizontal coordinate in pixels Pointer hot-spot vertical coordinate in pixels Address of screen/pointer masks Segment of screen/pointer masks
AX = 10	Set text pointer	BX = CX = DX =	Pointer select value Screen mask value/hardware cursor start scan line Pointer mask value/hardware cursor stop scan line

AH Value	Function	Input	Output
			BX = 0 select software text pointer
			BX = 1 select hardware cursor
			CX and DX bits map to:
			0-7 character
			8-10 foreground color
			11 intensity
			12-14 background color
			15 blinking
AX = 11	Read mouse motion counters	BX = CX = DX =	CX = horizontal count DX = vertical count Range −32,768 to +32,768 read in mickeys
AX = 12	Set user-defined subroutine	CX = DX = ES =	Call mask Offset of subroutine Segment of subroutine CX word bit map: 0 pointer position changed 1 leftmost button pressed 2 leftmost button released 3 rightmost button pressed 4 rightmost button released 5 center button pressed 6 center button released 7-15 reserved = 0 Following values loaded when subroutine is called: AX = condition of mask BX = button status CX = pointer horizontal coordinate DX = pointer vertical coordinate SI = last vertical mickey count read DI = last horizontal mickey count read
AX = 13	Light pen emulation on	BX = CX =	Instructs mouse driver to emulate a light pen

AH Value	Function	Input	Output
		DX =	Vertical mickey/pixel ratio Ratios specify number of mickeys per 8 pixels
AX = 14	Light pen emulation off	BX = CX = DX =	Disables mouse driver light pen emulation (same as AX = 13)
AX = 15	Set mickey/pixel ratio	CX = DX =	Horizontal mickey/pixel ratio (Same as AX = 13)
AX = 16	Conditional off	CX =	Left column coordinate in pixels
		DX =	Upper row coordinate in pixels
		SI =	Right column coordinate in pixels
		DI =	Lower row coordinate in pixels Defines an area of the screen for updating
AX = 19	Set double speed threshold	BX = DX =	Doubles pointer motion Threshold speed in mickeys /second
AX = 20	Swap user-defined sub-routine	CX = DX = ES =	Call mask Offset of subroutine Segment of subroutine Sets hardware interrupts for call mask and subroutine ad- dress, returns previous values CX word call mask: 0 pointer position changed 1 leftmost button pressed 2 leftmost button released 3 rightmost button pressed 4 rightmost button released 5 center button pressed 6 center button released 7-12 reserved = 0 Following values loaded when subroutine is called: AX = condition of mask BX = button status CX = pointer horizontal coordinate

AH Value	Function	Input	Output
			DX = pointer vertical coordinate
			SI = last vertical mickey count read
			DI = last horizontal mickey count read
AX = 21	Get mouse state storage requirements	BX = CX = DX =	Gets size of buffer in bytes needed to store state of the mouse driver
			BX = size of buffer in bytes
AX = 22	Save mouse driver state	BX = CX =	Saves the mouse driver state
		DX =	Offset of buffer
		ES =	Segment of buffer
AX = 23	Restore mouse driver state	BX = CX =	Restores the mouse driver state from a user buffer
		DX =	Offset of buffer
		ES =	Segment of buffer

TRADEMARKS

Apple®	Apple Computer, Inc.
DEC® PDP-7® and PDP-11®	Digital Equipment Corporation
IBM®	International Business Machines Corporation
IBM PC XT/AT®	International Business Machines Corporation
IBM PS/2®	International Business Machines Corporation
Intel®	Intel Corporation
Microsoft®	Microsoft Corporation
Microsoft Windows™	Microsoft Corporation
MS-DOS®	Microsoft Corporation
OS/2® Presentation Manager™	International Business Machines Corporation
PL/I™	Digital Research
Sprint®	Borland International
Turbo Assembler®	Borland International
Turbo C®	Borland International
Turbo C++® Professional	Borland International
Turbo Cross-Reference™	Borland International
Turbo Debugger®	Borland International
Turbo Librarian™	Borland International
Turbo Linker™	Borland International
Turbo Profiler™	Borland International
UNIX®	AT&T
VAX® C™	Digital Equipment Corporation

PL/I™	Digital Research
RS-232	
Simula67	
Sprint	Borland International
Turbo Assembler	Borland International
Turbo C	Borland International
Turbo C++ Professional	Borland International
Turbo Cross-Reference	Borland International
Turbo Debugger	Borland International
Turbo Librarian	Borland International
Turbo Linker	Borland International
Turbo Profiler	Borland International
UNIX	AT&T
VAX C	Digital Equipment Corporation

INDEX

M

T

The manuscript for this book was prepared and submitted to
Osborne/McGraw-Hill in electronic form.
The acquisitions editor for this project was Jeffrey Pepper,
the technical reviewer was Eric Geyer,
and the project editor was Janis Paris.

Text design by Stefany Otis and Mary Abbas
using Zapf for both text body and display.

Cover art by Graphic Eye, Inc. Color separation by Phoenix
Color Corp. Screens produced with InSet
from Inset Systems, Inc. Book printed and bound by
R.R. Donnelley & Sons Company, Crawfordsville, Indiana.